"Few textbook writers have a long and distinguished record of first-rank scholarship, but this one does. Even fewer have been able to write successfully for disciplinary specialists, interested intellectuals, and first-time inquirers, but this one has. Almost none of these can offer the fruit of a lifetime's reflection on philosophy from an informed and discerning Christian viewpoint, but this one can. Steve Evans's new survey is a rare gift, as he himself is, and I trust this book will gain the wide reading it deserves."

John G. Stackhouse Jr., Samuel J. Mikolaski Professor of Religious Studies, Crandall University, Moncton, Canada

"We have here an overview of western philosophy from the pre-Socratic philosophers of ancient Greece to the twentieth century. It offers a summary of the basic teachings of the major thinkers we have come to call philosophers that is comprehensive, succinct, lucid, and evenhanded. In addition there are occasional reflections on the significance of the material for Christian thought. Combined with the appropriate primary source readings, this volume will be a very useful textbook for a variety of college level courses."

Merold Westphal, distinguished professor of philosophy emeritus, Fordham University

"When a world-class Christian philosopher writes on the history of Western philosophy, one can expect a first-rate work that illuminates and enriches—and that is just what we find here. Evans's book effectively distills key philosophical figures and their ideas, considering both their historical context and their lasting influence. What we have in this volume is a marvelous resource that engages key thinkers and philosophical concepts judiciously, insightfully, and Christianly."

Paul Copan, the Pledger Family Chair of Philosophy and Ethics, Palm Beach Atlantic University, author of *A Little Book for New Philosophers*

"Evans's *A History of Western Philosophy* is a superb instance of its kind, skillfully combining breadth of coverage with insightful philosophical analysis of the ideas and arguments covered. It is accessible enough to be helpful to those who are new to philosophy, yet comprehensive and accurate enough to offer something to graduate students and professors. This book would be especially suitable as the sole secondary text assigned in an introductory philosophy course or in more advanced undergraduate courses in the history of philosophy. It would also be a great resource for clergy and laypeople who are interested in philosophical thought."

Michael Rota, associate professor of philosophy, University of St. Thomas

"C. Stephen Evans has performed a tremendous service for Christian philosophers, especially those new to the field. *A History of Western Philosophy* is an excellent single-volume history of the progress of western philosophical thought. Dr. Evans hits all the major players, concentrating on the essentials of each philosopher's contribution to the ongoing discussion. His style is clear, lucid, and accessible for the novice while also presenting insightful evaluations for those who are advanced. It is a superb work that should be on the shelf of every thoughtful Christian."

Mark W. Foreman, professor of philosophy and religion, Liberty University

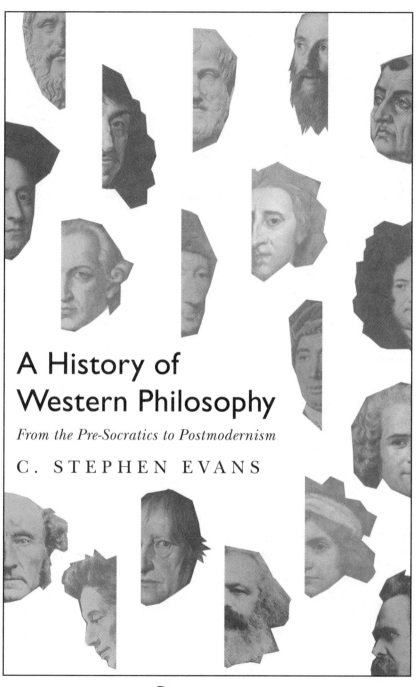

A History of
Western Philosophy

From the Pre-Socratics to Postmodernism

C. STEPHEN EVANS

IVP Academic

An imprint of InterVarsity Press
Downers Grove, Illinois

InterVarsity Press
P.O. Box 1400, Downers Grove, IL 60515-1426
ivpress.com
email@ivpress.com

InterVarsity Press® is the book-publishing division of InterVarsity Christian Fellowship/USA®, a movement of students and faculty active on campus at hundreds of universities, colleges, and schools of nursing in the United States of America, and a member movement of the International Fellowship of Evangelical Students. For information about local and regional activities, visit intervarsity.org.

All Scripture quotations, unless otherwise indicated, are taken from The Holy Bible, New International Version®, NIV®. Copyright © 1973, 1978, 1984, 2011 by Biblica, Inc.™ Used by permission of Zondervan. All rights reserved worldwide. www.zondervan.com. The "NIV" and "New International Version" are trademarks registered in the United States Patent and Trademark Office by Biblica, Inc.™

Photo of Arthur Holmes: Courtesy of Special Collections, Buswell Library, Wheaton College (IL).

Cover design: David Fassett

Interior design: Jeanna Wiggins
Images: Augustine: Portrait of Saint Augustine by Philippe de Champaigne at the Los Angeles County Museum of Art / Wikimedia Commons; Hegel: Hegel portrait by Jakob Schlesinger/ Wikimedia Commons; Marx: A portrait of Karl Marx by John Jabez Mayal / International Institute of Social History in Amsterdam, Netherlands / Wikimedia Commons; Kierkegaard: Kierkegaard portrait by Luplau Janssen; John Stuart Mill: Hulton Archive / Wikimedia Commons; John Locke: Portrait of John Locke by Sir Godfrey Kneller, National Portrait Gallery / Wikimedia Commons; Leibniz: Portrait of Gottfried Leibniz by Christoph Bernhard Francke at Herzog Anton Ulrich Museum / Wikimedia Commons; Immanuel Kant: Wikimedia Commons; Altar von San Domenico in Ascoli: Deutsch: Altar von San Domenico in Ascoli, Polyptychon, linke äußere Aufsatztafel: HI. Thomas von Aquin / The National Gallery, London / Wikimedia Commons; Aristotle: Bust Portrait of Aristotle by after Lysippos at Museo nazionale romano di palazzo Altemps, Rome, Italy / photo by Jastrow (2006) / Wikimedia Commons; Plato: Plato. Luni marble, copy of the portrait made by Silanion ca. 370BC for the Academia in Athens. From the sacred area in Largo Argentina / photograph by Marie-Lan Nguyen / Wikimedia Commons; Berkeley: Portrait of Bishop George Berkeley by John Smybert at The National Portrait Gallery, London / Wikimedia Commons; Hume: Portrait of David Hume by Allan Ramsay at Scottish National Portrait Gallery / Wikimedia Commons; Reid: Portrait of Thomas Reid by Sir Henry Raeburn / National Trust for Scotland, Fyvie Castle, Aberdeenshire, UK / Wikimedia Commons; Rousseau: Portrait of Jean-Jacques Rousseau by Maurice Quentin de La Tour at musèe Antoine-Lècuyer / Wikimedia Commons; Wollstonecraft: Portrait of Mary Wollstonecraft by John Opie, ca. 1790–1791 / Wikimedia Commons; Descartes: Portrait of René Descartes by Frans Hals at The Louvre Museum, France / photograph by Andrè Hatala Wikimedia Commons; Pythagoras: Galilea / Wikimedia Commons; Socrates: Eric Gaba/Sting / Wikimedia Commons; Epicurus: ChrisO and Interstate29Srevisited / Wikimedia Commons; Anselm of Canterbury: unknown, late 16th century / Wikimedia Commons; Bonaventure: unknown, 1650–1660 / Claude François / Wikimedia Commons; Pascal: unknown, circa 1690 / Wikimedia Commons

ISBN 978-0-8308-5222-2 (print)
ISBN 978-0-8308-7369-2 (digital)

Printed in the United States of America ∞

InterVarsity Press is committed to ecological stewardship and to the conservation of natural resources in all our operations. This book was printed using sustainably sourced paper.

Library of Congress Cataloging-in-Publication Data
Names: Evans, C. Stephen, author.
Title: A history of western philosophy : from the pre-Socratics to
*   postmodernism / C. Stephen Evans.*
Description: Downers Grove : InterVarsity Press, 2018. | Includes index. |
*   Identifiers: LCCN 2018022298 (print) | LCCN 2018025100 (ebook) | ISBN*
*   9780830873692 (eBook) | ISBN 9780830852222 (hardcover : alk. paper)*
Subjects: LCSH: Philosophy—History.
Classification: LCC B72 (ebook) | LCC B72 .E925 2018 (print) | DDC 190—dc23
LC record available at https://lccn.loc.gov/2018022298

| **P** | 25 | 24 | 23 | 22 | 21 | 20 | 19 | 18 | 17 | 16 | 15 | 14 | 13 | 12 | 11 | 10 | 9 | 8 | 7 | 6 | 5 | 4 | 3 | 2 | 1 |
| **Y** | 39 | 38 | 37 | 36 | 35 | 34 | 33 | 32 | 31 | 30 | 29 | 28 | 27 | 26 | 25 | 24 | 23 | 22 | 21 | 20 | 19 | 18 |

To Arthur Holmes,

who taught me the history of

Western philosophy and is dearly missed,

and to Alice Holmes,

his wonderful wife, who continues to

be a good and faithful friend.

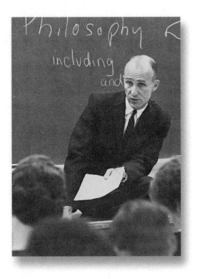

Contents

Acknowledgments

I AM GRATEFUL TO INTERVARSITY PRESS and especially to Andy Le Peau for the invitation to write a one-volume history of Western philosophy. I initially declined the offer, since I already had many other commitments. However, shortly after I had received the offer, my mentor and dear friend, Arthur Holmes, had a stroke. Arthur Holmes taught me the history of Western philosophy. He also showed the value of philosophy, particularly its value for a Christian. My life was changed by him and his courses in the history of philosophy, as were the lives of so many other students at Wheaton College. After learning of Arthur's illness I changed my mind and decided to write this book as a tribute to him. Shortly before his passing, I was able to visit him and tell him about this project. It is a book I know he wanted me to do. I hope it is a worthy memorial to him, and I am dedicating it to him and to another good friend, his wonderful wife, Alice Holmes.

The book took much longer than I imagined when I agreed to do it, but I have enjoyed the seven years I have worked on it very much. I have learned an enormous amount in the course of the work. I owe a great debt to the students to whom I have taught the history of Western philosophy over a period that now exceeds forty years. I particularly must thank four Baylor students, one undergraduate and three graduate assistants, Abigail Adams, Robert Elisher, Burke Rea, and David Skowronski. Each gave me an enormous amount of help, running down bibliographical references, filling in footnote references, checking quotations, and proofreading for mistakes. Each also gave me good advice on substantive issues. I also need to thank several friends and colleagues who read various chapters and made good suggestions: George Marsden, Douglas Henry, Merold Westphal, David Jeffrey, Brandon Dahm, Tom Ward, and Todd Buras. Thanks are also due to Derek McAllister for creating the index. I apologize to anyone I have forgotten; seven years is a long time, and my memory is not what it used to be. Finally, I must thank my wife, Jan Evans, the love of my life, without whom I could never have written this book. Her patience, support, and encouragement cannot be measured.

1

Introduction to the Project

THIS BOOK IS A HISTORY OF WESTERN PHILOSOPHY. Before launching into the subject properly, it seems fitting to reflect on the key terms that define the project. What is philosophy? What is history, and what kind of history is required for a history of philosophy? Finally, what does it mean to be "Western"? These are all daunting questions that could easily require book-length treatments, so all I can do in the space available is sketch the perspectives on them that will be assumed in this work.

WHAT IS "WESTERN" PHILOSOPHY?

Let me begin with the last of these questions. I shall not try to say in general what it means to be "Western" or what constitutes "the West" in human history. Sometimes the best way of defining something is to "point" at it, to give what philosophers call an "ostensive" definition. I shall try to give such a description of *Western philosophy* as a particular intellectual movement that began in Ionia (particularly in Miletus) in the sixth century BC among Greek-speaking inhabitants of what is today Turkey. This movement flourished in the centuries that followed, particularly in Athens in the thought of Socrates, Plato, and Aristotle. In the "Hellenistic" world the movement spread throughout the Middle East and later helped shape the Roman Empire, particularly in places such as Alexandria and Rome itself. This movement continued among Islamic, Christian, and Jewish thinkers during the medieval period in Europe and the Middle East, and developed further in Europe in the "modern period" under the influence of such thinkers as René Descartes, Thomas Hobbes, John Locke, and Benedict Spinoza. The eighteenth century saw in Europe the triumph of "the Enlightenment" in the work of such thinkers as David Hume and Immanuel Kant. In the nineteenth century, Western philosophy was shaped by such movements as idealism and positivism, and in the twentieth century split into two strands: "analytic" philosophy (dominant in the English-speaking world, including North America, Australia, and New Zealand) and "continental" philosophy, with strong roots in France and Germany.

In speaking of *Western philosophy* I simply want to refer to the particular tradition described in the last paragraph. It is important to recognize that other regions of the world, such as China and India, have ancient and profound philosophical traditions of their own, and hence Western philosophy is far from the whole of philosophy. Despite this fact, what is called Western philosophy today is a global phenomenon, in that the thinkers and questions that constitute this intellectual tradition are solidly represented in universities throughout the world. This means that the era of Western philosophy as an identifiable, more or less self-contained intellectual movement may be over or at least nearing an end, since all the world's great philosophical traditions are now in conversation with each other.

To say this is to look forward, however, and as one of the great Western philosophers (Søren Kierkegaard) memorably said, life is lived forward but must be understood backward. Since this work is history and not prophecy, it will take this backward view and focus on Western philosophy as a discrete intellectual tradition. Throughout the long history of Western philosophy, geographical isolation meant that most of the great Western philosophers knew little about the traditions of India and China, or other regions of the world. Although Western philosophy is only one of the world's great philosophical traditions, it clearly has enormous historical importance in the development of what is today called "the West" and "modernity" and is thus well worth historical study in its own right. Most of the time, when I speak of "philosophy" in this book I shall mean "Western philosophy." I shall not always use the qualifier *Western* for the sake of conciseness, but the adjective should always be understood as implied, except in contexts where philosophy in a more global sense is being discussed.

WHAT IS PHILOSOPHY?

Even if we are content with identifying Western philosophy as a particular historical tradition, one would like to be able to say something about the nature of philosophy itself. What does it mean to do philosophy or to be a philosopher? These are also very difficult questions. In fact, there is no agreed-on view of what counts as philosophy. Different philosophers have decidedly different views of philosophy, and thus the question "What is philosophy?" is itself one of the philosophical questions philosophers argue about. Some philosophers believe that philosophy is a quest for timeless truths that are universally valid. Marxist philosophers believe that philosophy reflects the class conflicts that are grounded in various economic systems of production. Some "materialist" or "naturalist" philosophers see philosophy as something that must be based on the progress of science. Many more such views could be described.

Even if we limit ourselves to philosophy as it has been understood in the West, it seems pretty clear that the meaning of the term has undergone some significant changes during the course of its long history. Philosophy is today considered to be a separate subject of study, distinguished from mathematics, the natural and social sciences, theology, and from such subjects as literary criticism. Among the early Greek practitioners of philosophy, however, it included all these subjects and much more besides. Philosophy is, etymologically speaking, the love of wisdom, and the early Greek philosophers seemed to have thought that the search for wisdom encompassed a quest for all kinds of knowledge.

This early view of philosophy is dimly preserved in the contemporary university, which still awards the degree "doctor of philosophy" as the highest achievement of many fields, including the sciences. This older view of philosophy can also be understood if we recognize that although philosophy is now a separate "discipline" or "subject," philosophical questions are not the exclusive property of professional philosophers. When scholars or researchers in various fields ask basic or foundational questions about those fields, they continue to do philosophy. The literature professor who asks how it is that a text can mean something is really doing philosophy, as is the physicist who asks whether the models he or she uses to make sense of mathematical equations that describe the physical world are in some sense "real."

The early Greek philosophers began by asking questions about the natural world that we today would describe as the beginnings of natural science. They can therefore be described as early scientists as well as philosophers. However, they were not just concerned with seeking theoretical knowledge. They were also intensely concerned with practical questions that bear on the meaning of human life and how it should be lived. Most of the early philosophers were concerned above all with questions about the good life: What is happiness? What does it mean to live well? They did not see wisdom merely as what we today would call scientific knowledge of nature; rather wisdom encompasses an understanding of human life and how it should be lived. Although the early Greek thinkers were doubtless driven in part by sheer intellectual curiosity, even their speculations about the cosmos were partly connected to a desire to understand human existence. Human persons are obviously part of the natural world, and some account of their place in it is necessary to have a view of how human life should be lived. Whatever else wisdom may be, it surely encompasses an understanding of human life and how it should be lived.

However, when one looks at contemporary philosophy, it is easy to doubt that philosophy continues to be a search for wisdom in this sense.

Professional philosophers as a group seem no wiser than other folks, and it is far from clear that people who study philosophy academically necessarily become wiser by doing so (although I believe that the study of philosophy still makes such growth in wisdom possible). Those points may not undermine the claim that philosophy is a quest for wisdom, since to say that one is looking for something is by no means an assurance that one will find it. However, the problem is not just that contemporary philosophy has failed to find wisdom. Rather, it appears that a great deal of contemporary philosophy has little interest in the subject. To be sure, ethics remains a branch of philosophy, and there are philosophers who continue to debate questions about the good life. But much of philosophy today seems focused on technical questions that have, at best, a remote link to the kind of wisdom that would help a person to live well. To say this is by no means to imply that the study of contemporary philosophy is without value, but it does raise questions about whether that academic subject called "philosophy" has much in common with what the Greeks called philosophy.

Despite these differences, and the worries they raise, I believe that one can see in contemporary philosophy the descendant of something that started with the Greeks, and that has wisdom as its chief end. However, in order to grasp what they have in common, I believe one must begin with the earlier, Greek conception, and use that conception as a guide for understanding the later history of what we call "philosophy." Philosophy is a quest for wisdom, and wisdom is, at least in part, practical. A wise person would be a person who understands what it is to be a human being and how human life should be lived. That in turn requires an understanding of the world in which humans live. The person who is looking for the right things can see these concerns as present in the whole history of Western philosophy, but it is easier to do that if one's conception of philosophy is shaped by the early Greeks, in whom the quest for wisdom as including an understanding of the good life stands out so vividly.

That what we call "philosophy" has changed over time in the West is
not surprising if we think of philosophy, as I think we should, as a
human cultural creation and not a "natural kind." To say this is not to
say philosophy could be just anything. We would not make ditch-
digging philosophy just by calling it "philosophy." There are, as we shall
see, a set of enduring questions, as well as strategies for finding answers
to those questions, that characterize Western philosophy, despite the
significant changes in our understanding of philosophy that have occurred. These questions define what are usually regarded as the core
areas of philosophy: metaphysics, ethics, and epistemology.

Metaphysics comprises the questions philosophers ask about the
nature of reality. Philosophy began when some of the ancient Greeks
began to speculate about the true nature of the world: What is the basic
"stuff" of which the natural world is composed? Is reality one interconnected whole, or is it composed of many discrete entities? Is material
reality composed of indivisible particles (atoms) or is it continuously
divisible? Contemporary philosophers still ask recognizable versions of
these questions as well as many more that ancient philosophers asked:
Do humans have souls? What happens to humans after death? Are there
divine beings? What are the gods like, and how are they related to
humans and the natural world?

Ethical questions were, as I have already said, clearly urgent for the
early Greek philosophers as well. They were well aware of the differences in ethical beliefs and customs between various Greek city-states
as well as the differences between Greeks and Persians. In light of those
differences they asked whether ethical ideals are simply a human cultural construction or whether some ethical norms were rooted in nature
or perhaps in some transcendent reality and thus have a kind of objectivity. What does it mean to live well, and what should the goals of
human life be, both for the individual and for the community?

As divergent answers quickly appeared to these metaphysical and
ethical questions, epistemological issues naturally came to the fore as

well, for enduring disagreement naturally leads to questions about one's convictions. Epistemology is the part of philosophy that asks questions about truth, knowledge, and beliefs. What is truth? Can truth be known, and if so, how is knowledge possible? When are humans justified in their beliefs? What counts as a justification for a belief? Quite early some philosophers were led to skepticism about human knowledge, and this in turn led to renewed attempts to develop various accounts of how knowledge could be attained.

In pursuing all these questions, philosophers from the beginning have relied on reasoning, or intellectual reflection, to gain answers. Even those philosophers, termed empiricists, who believe that all knowledge ultimately comes from sense experience have given rational arguments for this view. Obviously, different philosophers have different views of human reason and its limits, but all have done philosophy by reasoning. It is not surprising then that most philosophers have regarded logic, understood as an account of what constitutes good reasoning, to be a central tool for answering the questions of philosophy.

William James famously defined philosophy simply as "an unusually obstinate effort to think clearly." This definition may not quite work as it stands, since we need to say something more about the kinds of questions philosophers think about, but if we specify that the questions philosophers think about are the basic or foundational questions that arise for all humans or that are posed by the fundamental assumptions made by the special disciplines, James's definition is probably as good a definition as one can find.

WHAT IS THE HISTORY OF PHILOSOPHY?

The last thing I want to do in this introduction is to say something about what I view as a history of philosophy. The English term *history* is famously ambiguous, in that we use it to refer to the series of events that really occurred in the past (as in "that event was history and not fiction; it really happened"), but also to the narratives that humans construct to represent those historical events. What is the goal of these narratives? In the nineteenth century, some historians claimed that history should see itself as a kind of objective science, which tries to describe historical reality "as it really happened."[1] Others saw this as an impossible goal. Historians cannot replicate the past, since historical narratives are always selective and written from a particular point of view. The second group stresses that all historians have biases, personal and political and religious concerns that may motivate and shape the stories about the past that they tell.

I believe that the consensus among historians today is that there is something right about both of these perspectives. Good historians strive for honesty; they want to know and describe what really happened, and they seek to base their conclusions on the best evidence and reasoning they can. However, it is equally true that no historian occupies what philosopher Thomas Nagel has called "the view from nowhere." Everyone who writes a history sees the world, including that part of the world he or she wants to write a history about, from a particular perspective. A Marxist historian will understand the French Revolution very differently than a libertarian conservative. An atheist historian who thinks that religious beliefs are rooted in ignorance and superstition is likely to understand the decline of religious belief among intellectuals in Europe after the Enlightenment as due to an increase in reasoning ability and scientific knowledge, while a religious thinker such as Kierkegaard will see the same development as explained by a decline in the emotional and imaginative capacities of European intellectuals.

How should we respond to this "situated" character of historians? We should not, I think, despair of truth. It is true that all humans are historically situated individuals, and that it is impossible to shed all of one's particularities. However, the various perspectives we bring to the issues are not always distorting lenses; sometimes they may be just what is

---

[1] This phrase is associated with the famous nineteenth-century German historian Leopold von Ranke, often credited as the founder of modern history.

needed to bring the truth into clearer focus. It is also the case that historical truth is often complex; historians who seem to be disagreeing may be emphasizing different aspects of a fuller story. We should not respond to our situatedness by pretending to be completely "neutral" or "objective." Rather, those who tell a historical story should honestly recognize and make clear the perspectives they bring to the issues, making it easier, both for themselves and for their audiences, to decide what might be distortion and what might be insight.

A recognition that no one occupies the view from nowhere does not mean that one cannot care about truth, or seek evidence that will be convincing, even to people who approach the questions from very different personal perspectives. However, even though a commitment to honesty and fairness in this sense is important, it does not eliminate the importance of a particular point of view. All historians recognize the importance of honestly considering evidence, but points of view may shape how evidence is interpreted and weighed; they certainly have a lot to do with what a historian considers important and therefore chooses to select or omit.

There are two facts about me that are relevant to understanding the perspective I shall bring to the history of Western philosophy. The first is that I am a philosopher, and I think of the history of philosophy not simply as the history of ideas, but as a part of philosophy itself. Part of the motivation for studying the history of philosophy is to make progress in philosophy. I do not simply want to describe what various philosophers claimed, but to evaluate their ideas as well, and I see such evaluations as providing part of the explanation for the way the story has gone. Part of the explanation for the development of new views in philosophy is intellectual dissatisfaction with other ideas. One cannot tell the story of philosophy properly without paying attention to the arguments and criticisms philosophers make of each other, and this cannot be done in a completely impartial way. Sometimes the best explanation for why a philosophical view is rejected is that it is a bad theory, based on inadequate reasoning. If I were simply doing what I would call the history of ideas, I might focus predominantly on the social and economic causes of various philosophical theories, but such concerns would not necessarily help us gain insight into the validity of those theories. (Although a recognition of such causes can give us insight into why philosophers accepted views that now seem obviously false and even repugnant; it is instructive here to look at what some of the great philosophers have said about women, race, and slavery and see how their views may have been shaped by their own social situations.)

The second important fact about me is that I am a Christian believer. Part of my interest in philosophy stems from a conviction that philosophy is a valuable tool for a Christian who wants a deeper understanding of his or her faith, and who wants a deeper understanding of the Western world that has been partly shaped by philosophy. The history of Western philosophy is particularly interesting for a Christian because that history often intersects with the history of theology and the history of various religions, especially the three Abrahamic faiths: Christianity, Judaism, and Islam. Although I want to tell the history of philosophy, that history cannot be sharply separated from the history of religion, just as it cannot be sharply separated from the history of science or the history of art. In my account of philosophy, I shall therefore pay special attention to the links between philosophy and religious faith. For people of biblical faith, "the fear of the LORD is the beginning of wisdom" (Ps 111:10; Prov 9:10), and so it is plausible to think that such faith may have something important to contribute to philosophy as well. Philosophy has something valuable to offer people of faith, but faith may in turn provide something that philosophy badly needs.

Some may think that this perspective will limit the value of the work, on the grounds that philosophy and religion ought to be clearly distinguished. I agree that philosophy and religion must be distinguished, but I will argue that a history of Western philosophy will be a better and truer history if it takes full account of the relations between philosophical thought and religious belief. Some contemporary philosophers may have little interest in religion, but virtually all the great thinkers of the ancient, medieval, and even modern European worlds were intensely interested in questions about God and spiritual realities. A history of philosophy that neglects this fact will be a poorer history, just as a history of philosophy that neglected the connections between philosophy and scientific developments would be a poorer history.

The Beginnings of Western Philosophy

The Pre-Socratics

AS NOTED ALREADY, WESTERN PHILOSOPHY began in Ionia, in the city of Miletus, during the sixth century BC. Miletus was a Greek city on the coast of what is now Turkey. Why did philosophy begin among the Greeks? And why in Ionia?

Many possible explanations have been offered, though it is doubtful that any definitive answers can be given. Some attribute the origins of philosophy simply to the special characteristics of the Greek temperament or Greek mind. The Greeks were simply a people of genius. There is little doubt that if one looks at Greek art and literature, as well as philosophy, Greek civilization made some impressive achievements. Artists still marvel over Greek sculpture and architecture, just as lovers of literature never tire of the *Iliad*. The questions and problems that Plato and Aristotle discuss often seem amazingly contemporary. However, to point out the greatness of Greek civilization is not to offer an explanation, but rather to highlight what needs to be explained. Why were the Greeks capable of such astounding intellectual and artistic achievements?

A more helpful answer may lie in the character of Greek society. Many of the Greek city-states were very prosperous economically, and this prosperity made possible a leisured class who had time to devote to such cultural activities as philosophical reflection. Unlike some societies in the ancient Middle East, Greek city-states were not typically dominated by a single absolute ruler, but had a reasonably large class of aristocrats with shared interests in intellectual issues as well as the arts. Nor were Greek city-states controlled by a caste of priests with an entrenched set of theological beliefs. There were of course religious cults and social roles for priests, but there was no dominant caste of priests who enforced an orthodox view. There was thus both a larger community available for such pursuits and more "space" for alternative points of view.

Miletus shared these economic and social characteristics, and had some special features of its own. Besides being prosperous, it was a trading center and had contacts with Persian, Babylonian, and Egyptian cultures, and it makes sense that the clash of ideas inevitable when cultures mix would stimulate creative reflection. Egyptian and Babylonian culture had made impressive achievements in both mathematics and astronomy, and it is likely that educated people in Miletus would have known about this work. There was a stock story about many of the earliest philosophers, such as Thales, that they had traveled to Egypt. Whether this is true or not, it certainly points to Egyptian influence.

To say that the early Greeks learned from others is not to underestimate their originality. Egyptian mathematics, for example, seems highly practical in nature, motivated by the need to do accounting, surveying, and other such tasks accurately. The Greeks learned from the Egyptians, but Greek mathematics included a desire for generalized theorems and rational proofs, and thus it is to Greeks that we owe the birth of mathematics as a genuine science. Babylonian astronomers were gifted and careful observers of the stars and planets, and this allowed them to make very accurate predictions about the heavenly bodies. However, their interest in astronomy was tightly bound up with astrological and religious interests, and it is again the Greeks who seemed to be interested in the study of the heavenly bodies as natural phenomena. It is thus justifiable for Plato to claim that though the Greeks have borrowed much from foreigners, they have brought what they borrowed to a higher level of perfection.[2]

Another factor that may partially explain the rise of philosophy among the Greeks may lie in the special characteristics of Greek religion and mythology. In Greek culture, just as in India and China, religion and poetry existed long before philosophy as a recognizable activity. Educated Greeks absorbed religion not only through cultic worship but also through the Homeric epic poems and later in the tragedies of such playwrights as Aeschylus and Sophocles. Greek religion as presented in these poetic forms embodies many tensions and sometimes seems to present outright contradictions. The gods are presented as immortal and noble, to be revered and honored, but they are also described as engaging in behavior that seems far from honorable. To a thoughtful person, Greek religion left many questions about the nature of the gods and their relation to the world unanswered, and this perhaps contributed to the growth of philosophical reflection as well. Certainly from the earliest period, we see Greek philosophers questioning and correcting the religious traditions handed down to them.

THALES AND THE MILESIANS

No whole works survive from the earliest philosophers; indeed, some of them may only have transmitted their ideas orally. We only know what we know about them through statements attributed to them in later, surviving works. Since many of these works are critical, we cannot be sure that their views are always represented fairly. However, though the evidence is scanty, ancient witnesses agree that the origins of philosophy lie in Miletus, and that the story begins with Thales, who lived approximately from 624 to 546 BC. We know little about Thales, but a number of stories about him were circulated in antiquity, some of which

---

[2]Plato, *Epinomis* 987d-e, in *Plato: Complete Works*, ed. John M. Cooper and D. S. Hutchinson (Indianapolis: Hackett, 1997), 1629.

seem more likely than others. Among the more likely anecdotes is the claim that Thales successfully predicted an eclipse of the sun in 585 BC. Other plausible stories hold that he determined a way to measure the height of the Egyptian pyramids while traveling in Egypt, and that he hit on an engineering solution that allowed the Lydian army successfully to bridge and cross the Halys River. More inventive stories include Plato's account of a "joke" made by a Thracian maid, who claimed that Thales was so intent on observing the heavens that he fell into a well while gazing up into the sky.[3] Aristotle repeats a story that Thales, tired of being reproached for his poverty as a philosopher, used his knowledge of the weather to make a small fortune by securing a monopoly on olive presses in a year when he knew there would be a record crop of olives. These latter stories seem less plausible because, as Plato himself says, they trade on what were already stereotypes of philosophers, and thus seem to be the kinds of tales one would expect to be invented about the founder of philosophy.

What is really important about Thales is his attempt to give a comprehensive theoretical account of the natural world by affirming that water is the "basic stuff" out of which the whole of reality is composed. At first glance, this claim seems simplistic as well as implausible, but Aristotle speculates that Thales had reasons for making the claim.[4] Evaporation shows that water can become air, and of course it is obvious that water can achieve a solid form when it freezes. Aristotle points out that it is natural to think that moisture is associated with the origins of life, a point that is still understood by scientists who look for evidence of water in looking for signs of life on other planets.

What Thales is trying to do is more significant than his actual theory. In viewing all of reality as water, Thales is attempting to explain the whole of the natural world in terms of one basic principle, one *archē*, to use a Greek word with a variety of meanings, including "beginning,"

---

[3]Plato, *Theaetetus* 174a, in Cooper and Hutchinson, *Complete Works*, 193.
[4]See Aristotle, *Metaphysics* 983b20-27, in *The Basic Works of Aristotle*, ed. Richard McKeon (New York: Random House, 1968), 694.

"first cause," or "first principle." The achievement of Thales was to dare
to assume that the incredible variety and complexity of the natural
world nonetheless could be explained by a relatively simple principle.
The *archē* he sought was something like an "ultimate underlying substance," the basic stuff out of which everything else was composed. As
we shall see, Thales's successors did not accept his theory, and proposed
a good number of alternative views of the *archē*. They did, however,
accept and carry on his project of explaining the natural world.

Thales and his successors made several key assumptions: (1) The
natural universe is rational and intelligible. (2) The natural universe is
a unity, in that all of it can be explained by one or more simple principles. The challenge such a view faces lies in explaining the apparent
diversity of the natural world as well as the changes it undergoes.
(3) There is a distinction between reality and appearance; the natural
world is not simply as it appears but must be understood in terms of a
true nature that differs from that appearance. These assumptions not
only have been determinative of the history of Western philosophy, but
continue to shape the natural sciences even today.

ANAXIMANDER

The next important Milesian figure is Anaximander, reported to have
been an "associate" or perhaps a student of Thales. Anaximander's dates
are somewhat uncertain, but there is a report that he died in 547 BC at
the age of sixty-four. Anaximander believed that the incredible complexity and diversity of the natural world could not all be accounted for
in terms of water, and so proposed that the *archē* was something he
called the "boundless" or the "indefinite." The Greek term he used was
the *apeiron*, a term that later comes to mean the infinite but for Anaximander more likely meant simply that which is indeterminate.

This "unbounded" stuff was for Anaximander something like the
ground of all reality, but is itself in some ways indescribable, beyond
language. The *apeiron*, while far from being a personal God, has some

of the transcendence of a divine reality. Things in the world come and go, but the *apeiron* is eternal. Things do not come and go randomly, however. According to Anaximander, things that have come into being perish because they must "pay penalty and retribution for their injustice."[5] The idea seems to be that there is a cosmic order, with necessary laws that govern what comes into being and what passes out of being. The processes of motion and change are eternal because they are grounded in what is eternal.

Anaximander is also credited with some interesting cosmological and scientific speculations. Thales was reputed to have taught that the earth was a flat disk floating on a sea of water. Anaximander, however, held that the earth is "aloft" and not supported by anything. It stays in place because it is "equidistant." It is not completely clear what the earth is equidistant from, but the idea seems to be that the earth is simply the center of the universe and has no reason to move in any direction. Anaximander also offers an early speculation that humans may have evolved from other animals.[6]

ANAXIMENES

Anaximenes, the last of the important Milesians, who lived roughly from 585 to 528 BC, was a student or associate of Anaximander. Anaximenes agrees with his predecessors that there must be some *archē* for the natural world. However, he finds Anaximander's idea of the *apeiron* to be too vague to be useful. A principle that lies beyond language is a principle we cannot really understand, and that we cannot really employ to explain anything. The *archē* is indeed infinite, but it must not be completely indeterminate.

---

[5]DK12A9, in *Readings in Ancient Greek Philosophy from Thales to Aristotle*, ed. S. Marc Cohen, Patricia Curd, and C. D. C. Reeve, 5th ed. (Indianapolis: Hackett, 2016), 9. Otherwise unidentified page numbers in this chapter are all to this volume. I follow common practice in giving the "DK" citation for the references to the pre-Socratics. "DK" refers to the standard text collection for the pre-Socratics edited by Hermann Diels and Walther Kranz (1951). DK assigns an identifying number to each pre-Socratic passage (thus, e.g., Anaximander is 12 and Heraclitus is 22), followed by either "A" or "B" and finally a number. "A" indicates testimony from an ancient source, while "B" indicates direct quotations of the figure. Thus 12A9 refers to Anaximander's testimony number 9.
[6]DK12A10, p. 9.

Rather than return to Thales's theory of water as the basic stuff, Anaximenes proposes that the *archē* is best understood as air. Of course, he did not possess the contemporary scientific concept of the air as a mixture of gases. Rather, Anaximenes thought of air as something like a fine, invisible mist. The standard "four elements" as most Greeks conceived of them were air, fire, water, and earth. Anaximenes believed that the basic stuff was air, and that air could become any of the other elements through processes of condensation and rarefaction. As air becomes rarefied it is transformed into fire; as it becomes more dense it first become water and, if the process continues, is transformed into earth.

One can see in Anaximenes's account an attempt to combine the strengths and avoid the problems of his predecessors. Air seems more ethereal and indefinite than Thales's water, and thus Anaximenes tries to meet the concern of Anaximander. Indeed, it seems that the air for Anaximenes has the same religious quality as the unbounded did for Anaximander. The air is seen as infinite and even divine. However, air clearly has more content than the indefinite or the unbounded of Anaximander, and thus is less vulnerable to the charge of being contentless and unthinkable.

In his cosmology, Anaximenes views the earth, sun, and moon as all "riding upon the air." Again, this seems an attempt to synthesize the views of his predecessors. Seeing the earth, air, and sun as "riding in the air" seems a bit like the view of Anaximander that the earth is simply suspended in space, but the air nevertheless is something and not nothing, and thus the view tries to meet Thales's desire to give an explanation for what holds the earth in place.

In 499 Miletus was involved in a revolt against the Persian Empire, resulting in the destruction of Miletus by the Persians in 494. This brought an end to the Milesian school, but their ideas survived to be adopted, modified, and rejected by later Greek thinkers. Philosophy as a cultural enterprise was on its way. The Milesians are often described as "naturalists" because their major concern was for an understanding of the natural world. However, they should not be understood as "naturalists" in the contemporary sense. Indeed, the very distinction between nature and what is "divine" or supernatural would have been foreign to them.

XENOPHANES OF COLOPHON

Though not a Milesian, Xenophanes (570–478 BC) was from Colophon, a town in Ionia not far from Miletus, and deserves some discussion before moving on to other pre-Socratic philosophers, since he over-lapped with the Milesians chronologically and probably knew of their ideas. Xenophanes is important chiefly for his critique of traditional religious beliefs. He subjects traditional Homeric stories about the gods and Greek Olympic religion in general to rational criticism. The Greek gods do not measure up to this rational standard, either morally or metaphysically: "Homer and Hesiod have ascribed to the gods all deeds which among men are a reproach and a disgrace; thieving, adultery, and deceiving one another."[7] Metaphysically, Xenophanes implicitly criti-cizes the anthropomorphic conception of the Greek gods as having bodies like that of the Greeks themselves, noting that "Ethiopians say that their gods are flat-nosed and dark, Thracians that theirs are blue-eyed and red-haired." Adding ridicule to such criticism, he asserts that "if oxen and horses and lions had hands and were able to draw with their hands and do the same things as men, horses would draw the shapes of god to look like horses and oxen to look like oxen, and each would make the gods' bodies have the same shape as they themselves had."[8]

Here Xenophanes seems to anticipate Feuerbach's argument in the nineteenth century that humans are not created in God's image, but rather create gods in their own image.[9] However, Xenophanes was no atheist, but the first known Greek thinker clearly to assert something that can justly be called monotheism: "God is one, greatest among gods

---

[7]DK21B11, p. 17.
[8]DK21B15, p. 17.
[9]Feuerbach's view is briefly discussed in chap. 20, 470-71.

and men, not at all like mortals in body or thought."[10] Nor is God remote or unconnected to the universe; God has direct control over everything: "But without effort he shakes all things by the thought of his mind."[11] Xenophanes even anticipates some of what will later be known as the classical theistic attributes. For example, God seems immutable in respect to motion: "He always remains in the same place, moving not at all."[12] And, though it is unlikely that Xenophanes grasped the later concept of God as absolutely simple, God is seen as a unity who does not act by virtue of parts: "All of him sees, all of him thinks, all of him hears."[13]

Xenophanes, like his Milesian contemporaries, also engages in some cosmological speculations, but these are of lesser interest. What is more important is that his rejection of traditional religious ideas led him to more general skepticism about what humans know and how they know: "No man has seen nor will anyone know the truth about the gods and all the things I speak of."[14] Xenophanes distinguishes between truth and belief, affirming that only what is true can be known, but that true belief by itself does not necessarily count as knowledge. Xenophanes therefore has been said to be the "father of epistemology" in philosophy.[15]

PYTHAGOREANISM

Pythagoras (ca. 570–497 BC) was born in Samos, a small island in the Aegean Sea, not too far from Miletus. However, he was dissatisfied with conditions in Ionia, and emigrated to a Greek colony in southern Italy. Pythagoras was clearly a charismatic figure, the kind of person who attracts devoted followers and about whom many legends accumulate. He founded a kind of religious community in Italy that endured until about 400 BC. Since, as is usually the case with the pre-Socratics, we

[10]DK21B23, p. 17.
[11]DK21B25, p. 17.
[12]DK21B26, p. 17.
[13]DK21B24, p. 17.
[14]DK21B34, p. 18.
[15]Richard D. McKirahan, *Philosophy Before Socrates*, 2nd ed. (Indianapolis: Hackett, 2010), 66.

have no writings from Pythagoras, it is often difficult to say what ideas come from Pythagoras himself and which come from the community he founded, and I shall speak sometimes of Pythagoras and sometimes of the community, the members of which came to be known as Pythagoreans. Some of the rules of the community seem odd, and we can do little more than speculate about their point or justification:

> Do not stir the fire with a knife.
> Rub out the mark of a pot in the ashes.
> Do not wear a ring.
> Do not have swallows in the house.
> Spit on your nail parings and hair trimmings.
> Roll up your bedclothes on rising and smooth out the imprint of
>   the body.
> Do not urinate facing the sun.

The Pythagoreans were also forbidden to eat beans; perhaps the flatulence associated with beans was thought to be spiritually disturbing.

More comprehensible is the commitment of the Pythagoreans to vegetarianism, since a hallmark of Pythagoras's teaching was the view that the soul after death is reincarnated in some new life form. In such a case, if one eats meat there is a real danger one might be eating one's own grandmother! This view that the soul is immortal and is reincarnated after death was attributed by the Greeks to the Egyptians; today such views are linked to religions that originated in India, such as Hinduism and Buddhism. As we shall see later in discussing Plato, these kinds of views about the soul, linked to what is sometimes term "Orphic" Greek religion, will be very influential throughout ancient philosophy.

The Pythagoreans were also noted for their work in mathematics. Even today, students in geometry learn the "Pythagorean theorem," which asserts that the square of the hypotenuse of any right triangle is equal to the sum of the squares of the other two sides. It is likely that the Pythagoreans did not study mathematics out of pure intellectual curiosity, but saw the rigors of mathematical thought as an activity that purified the soul. In any case, mathematics had for them deep philosophical significance; Aristotle affirms that the Pythagoreans "supposed the elements of numbers to be the elements of all things."[16] They are also credited with holding that numbers constitute "the whole heaven" and are "the substance of all things."[17]

It seems that, unlike the Milesians, who affirmed that the *archē* was either water, or the unbounded, or air, Pythagoras held that the universe was *mathematical* in character. What could this mean, and why did he hold such an apparently strange view? Part of the motivation for the view was the exciting discovery that musical intervals correspond to mathematical ratios. A harp string of course gives a specific note if plucked. If one doubles the length of the string, the note will be exactly one octave lower; halve the string and the note is one octave higher. Perhaps this discovery led the Pythagoreans to believe that the "deep structure" of the string was something mathematical, a ratio that was expressed both in the harmony of the sound and the physical character of the string.

The Pythagoreans then developed a view that the natural world is not merely "physical stuff" but that the natural world is an appearance of a reality that could be described as hidden and spiritual. This is an anticipation of what comes to be called "metaphysical idealism." Once more, the impact of this view is particularly visible in Plato. It is in fact sometimes hard to determine what elements in Plato are simply taken over from Pythagoreanism and what elements are his own original development of ideas inspired by the Pythagoreans. In any case, the Pythagorean view that reality consists of numbers seems less bizarre if one thinks of contemporary physics. Contemporary physical theory increasingly consists of mathematical equations that give precise descriptions of the physical world. The "models" and pictures employed to make sense of those equations may not be truly understandable by anyone who does not grasp the underlying mathematics.

---

[16]DK58B4, Aristotle, *Metaphysics* 986a1-2, in McKeon, *Basic Works*, 698.

[17]DK58B5, Aristotle, *Metaphysics* 986a15-21, in McKeon, *Basic Works*, 698. *Metaphysics* 987a13-19, in McKeon, *Basic Works*, 700.

HERACLITUS

Heraclitus, a native of Ephesus, who was probably born around 540 and died in 484 BC, is one of the most significant of the pre-Socratic philosophers. His views are difficult to interpret; even in antiquity he was known as "Heraclitus the Obscure." He would likely have been a difficult person to like, since he clearly believed himself to be superior to others and shows contempt both for the citizens of his native city and his philosophical predecessors: "Every grown man of the Ephesians should hang himself and leave the city to the boys; for they banished Hermodorus, the best man among them."[18] "Much learning does not teach insight. Otherwise it would have taught Hesiod and Pythagoras and moreover Xenophanes and Hecataeus."[19] For Heraclitus, human opinions were simply children's playthings.[20]

At first glance Heraclitus seems to be similar to the Milesians, searching for the *archē*, or basic stuff of the universe, by claiming that everything is fire: "All things are an exchange for fire and fire for all things."[21] However, it is not clear whether Heraclitus thought of fire as literal fire, or whether he sees fire as a metaphor for the constant flux that he believes to lie at the heart of the natural world. For Heraclitus puts great emphasis on the natural world as constantly changing. Perhaps the most famous saying attributed to Heraclitus is the claim that "it is not possible to step twice into the same river."[22] Some contemporary philosophers see Heraclitus as an inspiring model of a thinker who is willing to embrace change and affirm the impermanence of all things.[23]

However, Heraclitus does not simply affirm the transience of all things. Rather, he affirms that the constant change we observe is governed by

---

[18]DK22B121, p. 25.

[19]DK22B40, p. 20.

[20]DK22B52, p. 25.

[21]DK22B90, p. 22.

[22]DK22B91, p. 22. Although Heraclitus is famous for this claim, there is actually some doubt about its authenticity, for reasons that will become clear.

[23]For an example, see John Caputo, *Radical Hermeneutics: Repetition, Deconstruction, and the Hermeneutic Project* (Bloomington: Indiana University Press, 1987), chap. 1.

some kind of natural necessity. Nature is governed by what he calls the *Logos*, a Greek word with multiple meanings, including "reason," "word," and "explanation." Significantly, a few hundred years later the writer of the Fourth Gospel chooses this word to describe the exalted status of Jesus the Christ: "In the beginning was the *Logos*." It is difficult to know exactly what Heraclitus meant by his claim that there is a *Logos* that governs all the changes in the physical universe. (Again, it is not for nothing he is called "Heraclitus the Obscure.") But it seems most likely that he believed that the constant change in nature nevertheless is the expression of an underlying order. This leads Heraclitus to assert that it is precisely constant change that gives things their identity, a view that he loves to express in paradoxes, reveling in the idea that apparent opposites are really identical: "The road up and the road down are one and the same."[24] Opposite qualities occur successively, but they do not disturb an underlying identity: "The same thing is both living and dead, and the waking and the sleeping, and young and old, for these things transformed are those, and those transformed back again are these."[25]

Heraclitus sees these constant processes of change as necessary. Perhaps for that reason, and because they are the expression of *Logos*, he affirms that our human relative evaluations of what is good and bad are unreliable: "To god all things are beautiful and good and just, but humans have supposed some unjust and others just."[26] Heraclitus thus initiates a venerable series of philosophers who are willing to affirm that if we could only see the world as God sees it, *sub specie aeternitatis* (under the aspect of eternity), to use the phrase Spinoza will later champion, then we would see that all is perfect, and that the apparent evils in the world reflect our partial view. Many will have difficulty accepting the perfection of a world that is shaped by violence and strife, but not Heraclitus: "War is the father of all and king of all."[27]

---

[24]DK22B60, p. 23.
[25]DK22B88, p. 24.
[26]DK22B102, p. 24.
[27]DK22B53, p. 23.

Many of Heraclitus's views have a strong influence on the later philosophy of Stoicism, as we shall see. The points of affinity include the view that the universe is born out of fire, the view that there is a divine order (*Logos*) that permeates and governs the natural world, and the view that the world, for all its apparent imperfections, nonetheless can be loved and embraced as perfect if we see it from the right perspective.

THE ELEATICS: PARMENIDES AND ZENO

Heraclitus was famous in the ancient world for his affirmation of change; his antipode was the philosopher Parmenides (515–450 BC), who rejected the reality of change altogether. Parmenides, along with his disciple Zeno, was from Elea, a Greek colony in southwest Italy, and the views of the two, along with those of their followers, are commonly described as the Eleatic philosophy. Although Parmenides's philosophy is startling in its rejection of what seems to be common sense, he was revered in Elea, and is reported to have written a very wise set of laws. A good portion of Parmenides's most famous work, written in poetry as a kind of revelation from a goddess, has survived.

The goddess begins by describing two distinct "routes" or "paths" that can be followed, a path of persuasion that is linked to truth, and another path, less clearly described but that seems to be the path of "appearances" that most people's opinions reflect.[28] Parmenides poses a stark logical disjunction: what has reality either is or is not.[29] But the choice between these options is clear, since what is not does not exist, and what does not exist has no being at all. Since that which is not does not exist it cannot be known, or named or thought.[30] From this seemingly unassailable foundation, Parmenides proceeds to draw a series of increasingly hard-to-accept conclusions.

Since only what has being can exist, it is impossible for nonbeing to exist. However, it is not possible to make sense of any kind of change

---

[28]DK28B2, p. 27.
[29]DK28B2, p. 27.
[30]DK28B6, p. 28.

without positing the reality of nonbeing. Take, for example, the kind of change involved in coming into existence. Parmenides argues that for something to come into existence it would have to undergo a change from nonbeing to being, but there is no such thing as nonbeing. All change must involve some state of affairs that either did not exist in the past or will no longer exist after the change. The whole idea of "becoming" is a self-contradictory idea, and so change must be an illusion. Just as shocking, Parmenides holds that plurality is also just appearance. In order for there to be plurality, there would have to be something that divides the parts of being, but this could only be nonbeing, whose possibility has already been denied.[31] Reality then is just one undifferentiated absolute unity, with no change or parts. Only "the One" then exists.

This kind of philosophical view is usually termed "absolute monism," and it certainly goes against ordinary experience. Parmenides himself may have been a materialist who thought that the one absolute reality was an all-embracing sphere, spatially as well as temporally uniform.[32] However, there are elements in his thought that fit poorly with materialism. Many monists are also metaphysical idealists, in that they claim that true reality is not the physical world that we experience with our senses, but a spiritual reality knowable by thought. Parmenides at least anticipates a major element in idealism by claiming that "the same thing is for thinking and for being."[33] He also leans toward philosophical rationalism (the view that gives priority to reason over experience) in his epistemology, since he asserts that true reality is that which can be grasped by reason, and sense experience is an unreliable guide to true reality. It gives us only how things appear rather than how they are.

Before dismissing such a view too quickly, it is worth noting that a similar view is prominent in a major strand of Hindu thought called Advaita Vedanta. Like Parmenides, Advaita Vedanta makes a strong

---

[31]See DK28B8, pp. 28-29, for arguments for all these claims.
[32]DK28B8.42-49, p. 29.
[33]DK28B3, p. 27.

distinction between reality and appearances. The world appears to be composed of many changing entities, but the Vedantist holds that in reality everything, even the human soul, is identical to Brahman, the divine reality that is an absolute unity. This way of thinking may be far from that of the typical modern Westerner, but it has a venerable pedigree, and often appeals to mystics. We cannot know for sure, but the religious character of absolute monism may have been part of its appeal for Parmenides as well.

ZENO

At the age of sixty-five, Parmenides is reported to have visited Athens, accompanied by his then forty-year-old student Zeno, where both of them encountered the young Socrates. Parmenides's philosophy, which denies the reality of differences as well as the possibility of change, just seems absurd to many people. Zeno tries hard to show that if one accepts the reality of plurality and change, equally absurd consequences follow.

Zeno is most famous for his development of a set of puzzles and paradoxes that are inherent in the acceptance of plurality and change, but I will only discuss a few of the more famous ones. The first I will explain is called "the racecourse." In order for a runner to go from the beginning of a race to the finish line, he must first travel half of the distance to the finish line. After reaching this halfway point, before he can reach the finish line, he must then travel half of the remaining distance. Similarly, when he reaches that point, he must travel half of the remaining distance, and so on indefinitely. Although each segment he travels gets progressively smaller, each one has a finite length and so will take some time to complete. However, the number of units he must traverse to reach the finish line is infinite, and it is impossible for him to complete an infinite number of segments of the racecourse in a finite time. So it is not possible to run a race and reach the finish line. The affirmation of motion leads to absurd consequences.

A second paradox is called "Achilles and the tortoise." Imagine that Achilles, a legendarily fast runner, is racing a tortoise, and gives the tortoise a head start. At the time when Achilles begins to run, the tortoise will be at a particular point. However, by the time Achilles reaches that point, the tortoise will have traveled further to a new point. By the time Achilles reaches that new point the tortoise will have gone yet further ahead, and so on to infinity. Hence Achilles can never catch the tortoise.

The third paradox I want to describe is called "the arrow." When an archer shoots an arrow we believe the arrow travels from one position to another until it reaches its target. However, at any given moment the arrow will always be in a particular place with definite boundaries corresponding to the length of the arrow. But for an object to be in a particular place with definite boundaries that correspond to the size of the object is just for that object to be at rest. If the arrow is at rest at every moment, when does it move? If there is no point at which it is in motion, it is never in motion.

Zeno also argues that taking physical objects as having spatial parts leads to absurdity. If we think that something has some particular size and thickness, then each part of the object will also have a particular size and thickness, and the number of such parts will be unlimited. But it is impossible for something with an infinite number of parts, each of which has some definite size and thickness, to be itself finite.[34]

While Zeno's paradoxes have not convinced many people of the unreality of motion and change, they have provided enduring challenges to philosophers who want to defend motion and plurality, both in the ancient world and even today. At the very least Zeno shows that our ordinary concepts of space, time, and change may not be fully coherent as they stand. The Eleatic denial of the reality of change left an indelible mark on Plato, and through Plato, has continued to haunt Western philosophy. Many thinkers who do not go all the way to absolute monism

[34]DK29B1, p. 32.

nevertheless agree, as Plato affirms, that what is ultimately real must be changeless. Whatever changes does not have reality in the fullest sense. This conviction has not only shaped much of Western philosophy but has also had a profoundly influential impact on Western theology, since it implies that a God who is absolutely real must be absolutely immutable as well.

EMPEDOCLES AND ANAXAGORAS

The conflict between the Eleatics and Heraclitus, particularly the arguments of Parmenides and Zeno against the possibility of change, sets the agenda for all later Greek philosophers, but is especially important for Empedocles and Anaxagoras, two of their immediate successors. Both of these thinkers struggle hard to give an account of change while essentially accepting Parmenides's view that what has being can neither be created nor destroyed.

Empedocles (ca. 490–430 BC) was from Sicily, not far from Elea, and he clearly shows the influence of Parmenides. He affirms that it is impossible that what is real can come into existence or perish, and thus Parmenides is right about the basic reality that makes up the world.[35] However, Empedocles thinks that change is nonetheless real. The objects we see are constantly changing, because those objects are in some sense not the things that really exist; ordinary objects are composed of more basic elements. The objects change as the "mixtures" that compose them change. The elements themselves then do not change, but there is a Heraclitean flux in the way the elements are mixed together to form objects. According to Empedocles, the basic constituents of the natural universe are the "four elements": earth, air, fire, and water. These elements can neither be created nor destroyed, but their proportions in everyday objects change constantly. Empedocles also gives a speculative (though somewhat unclear) account of what generates the changes: some objects have an affinity for others, and objects come

---

[35]DK31B8, p. 38.

together and fall apart due to the influence of two great principles: love and strife.[36]

Anaxagoras (500–428 BC) was from Clazomenae, a town near Ionia, but he spent the greater part of his life in Athens. He was close to Pericles, and late in his life he was put on trial for impiety (like Socrates later) by Pericles's enemies and condemned to die, but was rescued from prison (unlike Socrates) and escaped from Athens. Like Empedocles, Anaxagoras agrees that change is a process in which more basic unchanging realities are being combined and separated.[37] However, he disagrees with Empedocles, both about the nature of the underlying, unchanging reality and about the principles that govern the processes of mixing and dissolving.

For Anaxagoras there are not just four elements, but an innumerable variety of basic elements, which he calls "seeds." Objects are not composed of simply a single kind of seed, but are always a mixture containing the whole variety of seeds, though the seeds that predominate give objects their observable character. The "hidden" seeds, however, are present, and explain how objects can change their characteristics as the mixture changes and different kinds of seeds that were only latent before become predominant. This view must be distinguished from that of the atomists (to be discussed in the next section), since Anaxagoras does not believe that there is a "smallest part" of an object.

What causes the mixing and unmixing of the seeds? Anaxagoras sees no value in "love and strife," the quasi-mythical principles of Empedocles. Instead, he gives an account that is partly physical and mechanical, but not wholly so. The mixing and unmixing is caused by a great vortex that operates continually, and the swirling gives off, separates, and mixes the seeds of things. However, the ultimate cause of the vortex itself is Mind (*Nous* in Greek). Anaxagoras thus clearly distinguishes the material world and Mind, and makes the latter to be the ultimate or final

[36]DK31B22, p. 42.
[37]DK31B17.16-17, p. 39.

explanation of the behavior of the former. (He does not see Mind as *creating* the material world, since the basic elements of reality can neither be created nor destroyed.) Still he affirms that Mind "has control over all things," both animate objects and the cosmos as a whole.[38]

Anaxagoras's view of *Nous* is clearly a move in the direction of monotheism, and has a marked effect on his successors. Aristotle, for example, says that Anaxagoras "seemed like a sober man in comparison with his predecessors," and Plato has Socrates recall his high hopes when he hears that Anaxagoras affirmed Mind as the ultimate cause of the universe.[39] However, both of these philosophers also express disappointment that Anaxagoras does not make full use of Mind as an explanation. Aristotle says that when Anaxagoras "is at a loss to tell from what cause something necessarily is, then he drags reason in, but in all other cases ascribes events to anything rather than to reason."[40] Similarly, Plato has Socrates express his disappointment that "the man made no use of Mind, nor gave it any responsibility for the management of things, but mentioned as causes air and ether and water and many other strange things."[41] Both agree that Anaxagoras made a major step forward by positing Mind as the ultimate cause of the natural universe, but charge that he failed to see and develop the real implications of this move.

DEMOCRITUS AND THE ATOMISTS

The last group of pre-Socratic philosophers I shall discuss are among the most interesting. The atomists proposed a metaphysical view that is both bold and strikingly anticipates some of the main ideas of modern physics. The basic ideas of atomism were first formulated by Leucippus, reputed to be a native of Miletus who was a contemporary of Empedocles. Unfortunately, however, we know little or nothing about

---

[38]DK59B12, pp. 49.

[39]For Aristotle's comment, see *Metaphysics* 984b15-22, in McKeon, *Basic Works*, 695-96. For Plato, see *Phaedo* 97b-98c, in Cooper and Hutchinson, *Complete Works*, 84-85.

[40]Aristotle, *Metaphysics* 985a19-22, in McKeon, *Basic Works*, 697.

[41]Plato, *Phaedo* 98b-c, in Cooper and Hutchinson, *Complete Works*, 85.

Leucippus, and any writings of his have been lost. Most of what we know about atomism comes from Democritus, who developed and defended the main idea of Leucippus: that reality consists of tiny, indivisible particles (atoms) that move about in the void. We know that Democritus was born in Abdera in Thrace (an area north of Greece) and he was reported to have lived one hundred years, from 460 to 360 BC. Democritus is therefore not really "pre-Socratic," but a contemporary of Socrates, who also overlapped with Plato. However, the ideas Democritus elaborates come from the pre-Socratic period, and so it seems right to treat atomism as a view that was "on the scene" already at the time of Plato and Aristotle.

It seems clear that the inspiration behind atomism was to respond to the arguments of Parmenides and Zeno that the view that there is a plurality of physical objects is incoherent. Parmenides had argued that in order for two objects to be distinct they would have to be separated by something. However, what separates the two would appear to be nothing at all, and Parmenides claims that one cannot coherently affirm the existence of nonbeing. What does not exist cannot exist.

The atomists challenged the argument by holding that what separates physical objects is not really nothing, but *the void*. The void is not just nonbeing, but a kind of something, a place or container in which matter moves. Many of the arguments of Zeno depended on the idea that matter is infinitely divisible. The atomists rejected this by holding that atoms, indivisible particles that are too small to see, are what is real. An element of Parmenides's view is still preserved, in that Democritus holds that atoms can neither be created nor destroyed. One might say that each individual atom is like Parmenides's One, eternal and fully real. However, Democritus sees no problem in affirming that these atoms exist in space, a kind of container that can be empty or full.

Democritus believed there was an indefinitely large number of atoms, but that there are nonetheless different types of atoms. Types of atoms differ from each other, however, only with regard to such characteristics as size, shape, and location. Atoms are in constant motion, but Democritus sees no need to explain their motion. Atoms have always been in motion and continue to move in a particular direction until they collide with other atoms. When such collisions take place, atoms sometimes interlock with other atoms, particularly when their shapes allow this. The resulting combinations produce what we call physical objects, which persist until they are struck by other atoms in ways that cause them to separate.

Atoms have no color; qualities like color and sound and smell are the result of the atoms impinging on human sensory organs. The observed characteristics of ordinary physical objects are all to be explained by the underlying characteristics of the atoms that compose them, and all the explanations given are mechanistic in character. For example, lead is said to be heavier than iron, because the atoms in lead are more densely packed together.[42] There is no room for mind or purpose in Democritus's universe. Human persons, like everything else in the universe, are composed of atoms in the void, and what we call thinking must be a process that is explained by atoms.

To explain our perceptions of the physical world, the atomists adopted the theory that physical objects are constantly giving off or shedding "effluences," thin films of atoms that impinge on our sensory organs, and in some way produce an image of the object in the perceiver. Since atoms are not visible in ordinary perception, in his epistemology Democritus argues for the priority of rational thought over perception as the source of knowledge.

Democritus does give some attention to ethical implications of his metaphysic. Surprisingly, perhaps, he does not opt for simple hedonism by viewing pleasure as the chief good. Rather, he thinks the good life for a human person consists in what he calls "cheerfulness," a state of contentedness in which the soul is "disturbed by no fear or superstition or any

---

[42]DK68A135, p. 56.

other emotion."[43] Pleasure is to be sought only when it is beneficial by contributing to this end. In practice Democritus thinks that a life of moderation, in which people limit their desires to what is achievable, best leads to this cheerfulness.[44] People who drink or eat to excess, or focus their lives on sex, gain more pain than pleasure in the long run.

Democritus does not deny the existence of the gods; he was no atheist. However, on his materialistic view, the gods must be long-lasting combinations of atoms, like everything else. While he does not deny the existence of the gods, they play little role in his thought. The gods have little concern for humans, and when we recognize this we free ourselves from superstitious fears. As we will see, when atomism is revived in the Roman world by Lucretius, this element of atomism is particularly significant.

As already noted, modern science revived atomism, and classical chemistry was founded on the idea that the basic elements were composed of atoms of distinct types. It might appear that contemporary science has rejected atomism, since it is now common to speak of nuclear reactors that "split atoms." From the perspective of the Greek atomists, this is an oxymoron, since an atom for them was simply defined as that which cannot be divided, and thus an atom that can be split is not a true atom. This apparent contradiction reveals a shift in the meaning of the term. The small particles identified by nineteenth-century scientists as atoms were believed to be indivisible, but turned out not to be. However, in one sense contemporary science continues in the spirit of Greek atomism. The particles called atoms have turned out to be composed of other particles: electrons, protons, and neutrons, all of which are in turn composed of yet smaller entities. Still, contemporary scientists are still seeking to break reality down into its smallest components and thereby explain the qualities of the observable world. They thereby are the intellectual descendants of the Greek atomists.

---

[43]DK68A1, p. 59.

[44]See DK68B191, p. 59 and 68B235, p. 93 (68B235 can be found in the 4th ed. of Cohen, Curd, and Reeve, *Readings in Ancient Greek Philosophy*).

Socrates and the Sophists

THE FIGURE OF SOCRATES, an Athenian who lived from 470 to 399 BC, looms almost as large over the history of Western philosophy as does the figure of Jesus over the history of Christianity. Socrates's significance is shown by the fact that all the philosophers we have discussed so far, covering a period of nearly two hundred years, are known collectively as the "pre-Socratics." However, before discussing Socrates in depth, I shall set out some of the context for his life by describing the Sophists, a group of Socrates's contemporaries with whom he had strong disagreements, but with whom he was often grouped by the broader public of Athens, a confusion that contributed to Socrates's death.

THE SOPHISTS AS TEACHERS OF RHETORIC

Under the leadership of Pericles in the fifth century BC, Athens had become a democracy. This opened up the possibility of political power to a broader share of the public, though women and slaves were of course still excluded from participation in public affairs. In this new context, public speaking became an important skill, since a person could only get a new law enacted or win a lawsuit by convincing his fellow citizens that his views were correct. The sons of wealthy families who wished to wield influence particularly wanted to gain such persuasive skills, and such families had the means to pay someone who could offer this kind of training. A group of men, collectively called "Sophists," who professed to be able to offer such an education, soon arose to meet the need. The term *Sophist* had already been in use, and had formerly meant simply "wise person" or even "philosopher." In the fifth century the term now refers to a specific group of thinkers and, as we shall see, eventually takes on negative connotations.

The Sophists tended to be outsiders rather than Athenian natives. Protagoras, Gorgias, and Thrasymachus (all to be discussed below) came, respectively, from Thrace, Sicily, and Chalcedon. Their outsider status gave them a sensitivity to the strong differences in ethical and political outlooks found in different societies. Most of the pre-Socratic philosophers had sought to find a basis for ethics in nature, or what the Greeks called *physis.* The Sophists were skeptical about the possibility of grounding ethics in nature, and tended to see ethical principles as rooted in custom, or *nomos.* If ethical principles are conventional in this way, it follows that they are changeable. There are no objective, absolute principles; a relativistic view seems to follow inevitably.

Although the Sophists' strong suit was rhetoric, they claimed to offer a more general education as well. Hippias, for example, offered instruction in a huge range of areas. According to Plato, he taught mathematics, astronomy, painting, sculpture, and history, and even such crafts as metalworking, jewelry, shoemaking, and weaving.[1] As noted above, initially there was a demand for the Sophists' educational services. However, in time the relativistic thrust of Sophist teaching created a backlash among the wealthy aristocrats who paid for their services. Rich aristocrats tend to be conservatives who value tradition, but a relativistic view of traditions undermines respect for the old ways. The Sophists sold themselves as people who could teach their students how to win arguments; even if the case was weak, their rhetorical skills allowed "the weaker argument [to] defeat the stronger."[2] However, what

---

[1] Plato, *Lesser Hippias* 368b-e, in *Plato: Complete Works*, ed. John M. Cooper and D. S. Hutchinson (Indianapolis: Hackett, 1997), 928 (unless otherwise indicated, all page numbers in citations of Plato throughout this chapter are from this volume).

[2] See Plato, *Apology* 18c, in *Plato: The Last Days of Socrates*, trans. Hugh Tredennick (New York: Penguin, 1979) 47; Aristotle, *Rhetoric* 1402a23-25, in *The Basic Works of Aristotle*, ed. Richard McKeon (New York, Random House, 1968), 1431 (all page numbers in citations of Aristotle throughout this chapter are from this volume).

is sauce for the goose is sauce for the gander, and such rhetorical skills could be employed on behalf of all kinds of causes. The Sophists began to be viewed as "hired guns," willing to work for any view, but with no real commitments of their own except a commitment to their own financial advancement. Perhaps they appeared to the Athenians in something like the way people view unscrupulous lawyers today, the kind of lawyers who would use any argument so long as it allows them to "win." The legacy of the Sophists can be seen even in contemporary English, in which the adjective *sophistical* is still used to describe an argument that convinces through some kind of logical fallacy or verbal trickery.

There is clearly a fit between this kind of opportunism and the Sophists' tendency to be skeptical about objective truths, particularly in ethics. If ethical principles are conventional and relative, then there are no absolute obligations that govern human actions. If one is skeptical about the possibility of objective truth, then it seems plausible to think that the purpose of rational argument is to convince others to do what one wishes; reason is a tool for power and influence rather than an organ intended to help us gain truth. In advancing such views the Sophists gave philosophy a bad name. Socrates, along with his student Plato, tried hard to show the difference between their own use of reason and the arguments of the Sophists, but the distinction was not always clear to the Athenians of their day. Before giving a fuller account of Socrates, I shall briefly describe the views of three of the most important Sophists.

Protagoras of Abdera. Protagoras (ca. 490–420 BC) was one of the earliest and most successful (financially) of the Sophists. He is most famous for his relativistic aphorism: "Man is the measure of all things: of the things which are, that they are, and of the things which are not, that they are not."[3] There is some dispute about whether by "man" Protagoras meant to refer to individual human persons or to human beings collectively, but most believe that he meant to refer to individuals. In effect

---

[3]Quoted in Plato, *Theaetetus* 152a, p. 169.

Protagoras is claiming that truth is a human creation; we human beings decide what is true and what is false. Protagoras thus is the first "anti-realist" in Western philosophy, rejecting the claim that truth is something objective that humans discover for the claim that truth is something humans make for their own purposes.[4] Remarkably enough, then, a view that is often associated with "postmodernism" in recent Western thought is already anticipated in one of the earliest Greek philosophers.

Protagoras is also known for his skepticism about religious matters, affirming that "concerning the gods I am unable to know either that they are or that they are not."[5] This view eventually got Protagoras into trouble, as he was banned from Athens and his books burned. Protagoras is also credited with the view that equally good arguments could be constructed on both sides of every issue, a claim that likely led to the accusation that the Sophists were people who made "the worse argument seem the better," which became a stock charge against them.[6]

Gorgias. Gorgias was another late fifth-century thinker, who came to Athens as an ambassador from a city in Sicily in 427 BC. He is best known for a book, *On What Is Not, or On Nature,* a work whose title and arguments seem to parody those of the Eleatics. Though the book has not survived, summaries of it have been passed down. There is some controversy over whether the claims and arguments in the work were meant seriously or simply as a parody to show the futility of philosophical arguments.

In the work, Gorgias argues for three increasingly nihilistic claims: (1) Nothing exists. (2) If anything exists, it could not be known. (3) If anything could be known it could not be communicated.[7] A summary of the argument offered for the first thesis could go something like this: If something existed, either it must be what is or what is not. But what is

[4]See the discussion of postmodernism and antirealism in chap. 24.
[5]DK80B4, in *Readings in Ancient Greek Philosophy from Thales to Aristotle,* ed. S. Marc Cohen, Patricia Curd, and C. D. C. Reeve, 5th ed. (Indianapolis: Hackett, 2016), 64 (see n5 in chap. 2 above for an explanation of this notation; all page numbers correlated to these citations are from this volume).
[6]See, e.g., Aristotle on Protagoras's method in *Rhetoric* 1402a24-26, p. 1431.
[7]DK82B66, 77, and 83, pp. 67-69.

not cannot be anything. However, nothing that is can exist either. For to exist, it would either have to be eternal or else have had a beginning. But both are impossible, according to Gorgias. If it did not have a beginning, then it would be infinite, but if infinite it would be unlimited and indefinite, and this means it would exist nowhere. But what exists nowhere does not exist at all. The other alternative is equally impossible, since for something to have a beginning it must come into existence, but it could not come from nothing but only from something that already exists.

As mentioned, there is controversy as to whether Gorgias meant these arguments as sober philosophy or just as parodies of philosophical arguments. Given the character of the claims, it is safe to say that either way philosophy as the quest for truth goes nowhere, and so it is not surprising that Gorgias became simply a teacher of rhetoric.

Thrasymachus. Our knowledge of Thrasymachus is based chiefly on a portrayal of him in Plato's *Republic*, which I shall discuss in the next chapter. In the *Republic* Plato, through the character of his teacher Socrates, defends the value of justice, both in the individual and in the state. Thrasymachus angrily breaks in on the discussion in book one and claims that justice is simply "the advantage of the stronger."[8] Thrasymachus regards justice merely as a set of rules imposed on others by those who have the power to do so. Such a definition of justice actually undermines belief in the value of justice, since it boils down to the claim that "might makes right." Those who have the power to do so make the rules; it is rational to obey those rules only to the degree that it is expedient to do so. Thrasymachus thus anticipates Nietzsche's later account of morality as simply an expression of the "will to power."[9] Morality in general and justice in particular is simply a tool to control others and get what one wants. Obviously someone who accepts such a view will not believe in the objective validity of morality and will conform to morality only to the degree that it is expedient to do so. There is little

---

[8]Plato, *Republic* 338c, p. 983.
[9]See the discussion of Nietzsche in chap. 23.

wonder that conservative Athenians found the Sophists' views to be disturbing and unsettling, and blamed them for some of the disasters that befell Athens during the war with Sparta. The ferment created by the Sophists is the backdrop against which we must understand the life and teachings of Socrates.

SOCRATES: SOURCES FOR OUR KNOWLEDGE

Socrates wrote nothing. His legacy comes down to us solely through the accounts given by others of his philosophical activity, and the influence he left on his disciples and associates, most notably Plato. There are three main sources of information about Socrates. The first is the comic poet Aristophanes, who wrote a play called *The Clouds*, in which Socrates is portrayed as a pompous and vain person, making an entrance in a basket in the sky and claiming to contemplate the sun and travel through the air. In the play the stock charge against the Sophists is made against Socrates: that he "makes the weaker argument defeat the stronger." Since Aristophanes's play is intended as satire, it cannot be regarded as close to the historical truth. However, it may well give us some insight as to how Socrates and other philosophers were viewed by the general public.

A more valuable portrait can be found in Xenophon's *Memorabilia*. Xenophon was an aristocrat who remembers Socrates as a courageous and stalwart fellow soldier. He portrays Socrates's philosophical activity as almost exclusively directed toward ethical questions; Socrates simply wanted to make his Athenians better people. Most scholars have regarded Xenophon's portrait as accurate as far as it goes, but there is a suspicion that because Xenophon himself was not a first-rate philosopher, he may well have failed fully to appreciate Socrates's philosophical work.

This brings us to the portraits of Socrates provided in Plato's writings, which consist almost exclusively of dialogues, in which Socrates is generally though not always the leading character. The problem posed by the Platonic dialogues can be simply put: Does Plato in these dialogues give us accurate information about the historical Socrates, or is "Socrates" simply a character Plato invents as a vehicle for presenting Plato's own ideas? On the one hand, Socrates was a very public figure, and presumably his views would have been well known by those who heard him philosophize. Therefore, some scholars argue that Plato would not have invented views and put them into the mouth of Socrates unless there was some historical basis for those views in what Socrates said. On the other hand, it was not uncommon in the ancient world for the disciples of a famous master to credit the master for their own work, so perhaps Plato is simply showing reverence for his teacher in putting into Socrates's mouth views that were Plato's own original contribution. The main issue at stake is whether the elaborate metaphysical views of Plato (to be discussed in the next chapter), especially the "theory of Forms," were first developed by Socrates, or whether they were Platonic views. There are respected scholars who hold both positions.[10]

I shall here follow the views of the majority of scholars, however, who rely on a comment of Aristotle, who affirmed that Socrates sought universal definitions, but did not view the "Forms" or "essences" of things as existing separately.[11] The idea that objects have such a Form was a view invented by Plato. Since Aristotle was a member of Plato's school (the Academy) for many years, it seems reasonable to think that he would have had reliable knowledge about this issue. Those who follow this view typically take some of Plato's dialogues, such as the *Apology*, *Euthyphro*, and *Crito*, to be early ones, which present an accurate picture of Socrates's philosophical activity and do not credit him with speculative metaphysical views. Other Platonic dialogues are regarded as later ones in which Socrates as a character puts forward the ideas we now associate with Platonism.

---

[10]For the arguments that the picture of Socrates in the Platonic dialogues is historically authentic, see J. Burnet, *Greek Philosophy: Thales to Plato* (London: Macmillan, 1914) and A. E. Taylor, *Plato: The Man and His Works* (Mineola, NY: Dover, 1937).

[11]"Socrates did not make the universals or the definitions exist apart; *they* [his successors], however, gave them separate existence, and this was the kind of thing they called Ideas." Aristotle, *Metaphysics* 1078b30-32, p. 894.

This view is not without its problems. For example, some of the most important discussions of the theory of Forms occur in the *Phaedo*, a dialogue about the death of Socrates generally regarded as early and as presenting a reliable picture of how Socrates died. Perhaps the best way to go forward is to accept the view that the theory of Forms is a Platonic view, but that Plato himself regarded the theory as developing the logical consequences of views that Socrates had. Perhaps from our perspective Plato seems to be inventing original theories, but he himself thought of them as elaborations and developments of views that Socrates undoubtedly held. One's judgment on how much of Plato comes from Socrates may then depend in part on what one sees as the logical implications of Socrates's views.

PLATO'S *APOLOGY* AND *EUTHYPHRO*

Of all Plato's dialogues, it is the *Apology* that is generally regarded as the most important source about Socrates's life. In 399 Socrates was accused of "not believing in the gods in whom the city believes, but in other new spiritual things," and also "corrupting the young."[12] He was convicted of the charges and eventually executed. Plato's *Apology* purports to be a presentation of the long speech Socrates made in his own defense at the trial. Since the trial was a public event attended by hundreds of people, and Plato's purpose in writing the dialogue was to vindicate his beloved teacher Socrates by showing that the verdict and sentence were unjust, it is highly unlikely that Plato would give an inaccurate account of what Socrates said at the trial. It is not, of course, a word-for-word transcript, since there were no video recorders or court stenographers in ancient Greece. However, if Plato had substantially falsified Socrates's defense, this would have been easily recognized by the eyewitnesses, and his attempted defense of Socrates would have been undermined.

---

[12]Plato, *Apology* 18c, 24b-c; pp. 19, 23. The charges were brought by Meletus, instigated by a prominent politician, Anytus. In ancient Athens, criminal charges could be filed by one citizen against another. There was no need for a public prosecutor.

In the *Apology* Socrates defends himself in part by giving an extended account of his life as a philosopher. Socrates had made a career of sorts out of critically examining the views of many prominent Athenians, politicians, Sophists, and poets included. A typical example of this activity is given in another Platonic dialogue, the *Euthyphro*, which is set shortly before Socrates's trial. Awaiting the trial, Socrates meets Euthyphro, who is in court to accuse his father of manslaughter, because the father had allowed a servant who was a murderer to die. Most Greeks would have thought that Euthyphro's actions here were highly dubious; for a son to prosecute his own father, especially with respect to such ambiguous circumstances, would have been scandalous. Euthyphro, who sees himself as a religious expert, is convinced he is doing the right thing. True religious piety demands he prosecute his father.

Socrates responds, with irony that seems completely lost on Euthyphro, by claiming that this is a great stroke of luck for him. Since Euthyphro is such an expert on piety, he will be able to educate Socrates about this subject, and thus enable Socrates to defend himself at his trial. When Euthyphro is asked to explain piety, he initially responds by simply telling Socrates that piety is doing what Euthyphro is doing: prosecuting his own father (or anyone else) when it is right to do so. Socrates responds that this is only an example of piety; what he wants from Euthyphro is a general account of piety. What is it that all pious actions have in common, which makes them pious? (On the view of Plato's relation to Socrates I am taking, Socrates is asking for what Plato would later describe as a description of the Form of piety, the Ideal of piety that all piety must resemble.)

Euthyphro responds to this request for a general definition by saying that piety is simply what the gods love or approve of. Socrates first objects by pointing out that, on Euthyphro's polytheistic conception of the gods, the gods might disagree with each other, and thus the same act might be both pious and impious. However, even if one assumes the gods all agree (or even if one were a monotheist), there is a more fundamental problem with Euthyphro's view: Why do the gods love what they love? Would just any act be pious if the gods loved it? If so, they do not love the act because it is pious. Rather, the act is pious because they love it. If, however, we say that the gods love pious acts because they are pious, then those acts must have some quality, distinct from being loved by the gods, that makes them pious and is the ground of the gods' approval.[13] In the dialogue, Euthyphro appears to see the problem with his view, but in the end returns to the view with which he began. Like many of the Socratic dialogues, no positive result is achieved.

Many of the characteristics of Socrates's philosophical activity can be seen in the *Euthyphro*. One of the most significant is Socrates's practice of interrogating his fellow citizens who claim to understand some important concept, and exposing the fact that they lack the wisdom they claim to possess. Socrates does not normally give lectures or offer sweeping opinions, but proceeds by asking questions of others, but this "Socratic method" is painful for those on whom it is practiced. It is not surprising that prominent politicians, poets, playwrights, and other leading figures who claim to be wise do not enjoy being shown up in the way Euthyphro's pretensions are exposed in this dialogue.

In the *Apology* Socrates acknowledges that his practice of examining people has made him unpopular, but he argues that his activity has been a kind of religious duty. He began to examine others as a response to a message from the oracle of Apollo at Delphi. Socrates's friend Chaerophon had gone and asked the oracle whether there was anyone wiser than Socrates, and the oracle had responded that there was no

---

[13]The *Euthyphro* has often been regarded as relevant not only to piety but also to morality. Philosophers have argued that an argument similar to Socrates's in this dialogue can be made against the view that moral obligations are constituted by God's commands. If God could make anything right just by commanding it, then his commands seem arbitrary. However, if God commands acts because they are morally right, then moral rightness must be independent of his commands. This objection can be met, however. An act is morally obligatory or forbidden because God commands it or forbids it. God's commands are not arbitrary, however; God commands what he commands because he is good and loving and aims at the good. For more on this "Euthyphro objection" to seeing God as the basis of moral duty, see C. Stephen Evans, *God and Moral Obligation* (New York: Oxford University Press, 2013).

one wiser than Socrates. When this was reported to Socrates, he says he was initially puzzled, since he did not claim to be wise or indeed to have any knowledge about anything important at all. So he began to examine those who seemed to be wise so as to see if the oracle's claim was correct. The sad result of this activity was always the same: the people who claimed to understand virtue, or friendship, or courage, or other important moral qualities were revealed to be ignorant and confused. Socrates is wiser than these others in this respect: they believe they understand what they do not understand, but Socrates at least knows what he does not know. Socrates finally concludes that the oracle was right:

> What is probable, gentlemen, is that in fact the god is wise and that his oracular response meant that human wisdom is worth little or nothing, and that when he says this man, Socrates, he is using my name as an example, as if he said: "This man among you, mortals, is wisest who, like Socrates, understands that his wisdom is worthless."[14]

A second notable characteristic, one associated with Socrates throughout the centuries, is Socrates's use of irony. Socrates begins his discussion with Euthyphro by apparently taking Euthyphro's grandiose claims to have expert knowledge about the gods at face value. But it is hard not to see this attitude as ironic, given the repeated failures of the people Socrates examines to measure up to the claims they make.

Over two thousand years later the Danish philosopher Søren Kierkegaard, who wrote his doctoral dissertation on Socrates's use of irony, took Socratic irony as a model for how to critique the complacent Christianity of nineteenth-century Denmark. In Denmark, everyone was a Christian by virtue of being born a Dane (except for the Jews), yet Kierkegaard believed that genuine New Testament Christianity had virtually become extinct. His strategy in "reintroducing Christianity into Christendom" was to imitate Socrates, and take his contemporaries'

---

[14]Plato, *Apology* 23a-b, p. 22.

claims to be Christian at face value, ironically confessing that he himself was the only one in Denmark who found it really hard to be a Christian.

A third element of the *Euthyphro* that seems characteristic of Socrates's philosophical activity is the quest for clarity through a universal definition. In this dialogue Socrates attempts to clarify the nature of piety. In other Platonic dialogues, Socrates seeks to define such concepts as justice, friendship, and virtue in general as well as specific virtues such as courage, knowledge, and many more important concepts. Socrates seems to have assumed that the qualities described by such universal terms have a kind of objectivity; one can be right or wrong in one's understanding of them. It is this assumption of Socrates that probably led Plato to his view that in addition to particular instances of justice there is such a thing as justice. To seek an understanding of these universal concepts is to seek to know what Plato called the "Forms" or "Ideas" that particular things participate in or imitate.

A fourth aspect of the *Euthyphro* that seems characteristic of Socrates is its inconclusive character. Although progress is made in the dialogue, by sweeping aside mistaken accounts of piety, in the end no positive conclusion is reached. The dialogue ends with puzzlement, though there are hints of a way forward if Euthyphro had been wise enough to follow them. This willingness honestly to acknowledge uncertainty and lack of knowledge is then characteristic of Socrates's wisdom, always emphasizing that true wisdom does not claim to know what it does not know.

The final aspect of Socrates's philosophical activity I want to emphasize is its practical character. Although Socrates admits that as a young man he was interested in the physical theories of the earlier Greek philosophers, he soon gave up the quest to understand the natural world and turned his attention to what it means to live well as a human person. His concerns are focused on key questions as to what it means to live rightly and honorably: What is virtue? Can it be taught? How can it be acquired? Why should we care about virtue? One might think that

this aspect is in tension with Socrates's concern with universal definitions, since these may seem abstract and removed from practical questions. However, this is not the way Socrates saw things. To live well is to
live reflectively; we cannot seek for virtue or wisdom or courage without
understanding them. In the *Apology* Socrates goes so far as to claim that
"the unexamined life is not worth living."[15]

From my own point of view Socrates here goes too far. Generations
of philosophy teachers have repeated this slogan, yet it may well be the
most unexamined claim in the history of Western philosophy. Human
life is surely valuable and worth living, even if it is lived unreflectively
and without critical examination. Nevertheless, even one who rejects
this Socratic claim can certainly agree that a life that includes such reflective examination may be far richer than one in which a person never
asks what life is all about or how it should be lived.

SOCRATES AS A RELIGIOUS THINKER

When we look at Socrates's speech in the *Apology* it is clear that
Socrates's claim to be wiser than others only because he knows what he
does not know must be something of an exaggeration. For Socrates
does claim to know some things, and he makes these claims with great
conviction. Many of the claims he makes have a strongly religious character. In fact, it is a sad irony that Socrates was convicted on a charge of
being irreligious, since he was clearly a person of deep religious faith,
even having some of the characteristics that might get him dismissed
today for being a "religious fanatic." His life has been inspiring even to
Christian thinkers over the years. Kierkegaard, for example, expresses
the idea that what contemporary Christendom needs is a new Socrates,
and does not hesitate to give Socrates a retrospective baptism of sorts:
"True, [Socrates] was no Christian, that I know, although I also definitely remain convinced that he has become one."[16]

---

[15]Plato, *Apology* 38a, p. 33.
[16]Søren Kierkegaard, *The Point of View*, trans. Howard Hong and Edna Hong (Princeton, NJ: Princeton University Press, 1998), 54.

First, it is a striking fact that though Socrates often talks about "the gods" as supernatural beings when he is engaging his accusers or talking about the beliefs of the Athenians who served as the jury, when he speaks about his own life he frequently switches to the singular and speaks only about "the God."[17] Thus, he says that he will not stop his philosophical activity even if the court orders him to, because "god ordered me . . . to live the life of a philosopher, to examine myself and others."[18] Since this is so, he must continue, even at the risk of death, and he tells the officials of Athens he will not obey an order to cease: "I will obey the god rather than you."[19] Socrates thus claims to have a personal calling or vocation from God to do philosophy, and he clearly believes that God has the authority to give such commands.

Socrates, however, did not merely have an abstract belief about God, but claimed to have special experiences in which he received instruction as to how to live his life. From early on in his life, he has repeatedly heard what he calls a "prophetic voice," which he relies on for guidance. At the trial, Socrates infers from the fact that this "prophetic voice," or *daimōn*, never once stopped him or opposed him, as he was making his defense, that he has been following the right path, even though it will lead to his death. In fact, he takes this as evidence that death is not, contrary to the views of most people, really an evil at all, but "a blessing."[20] Socrates relies on his "divine sign" to know God's will, and he is confident that if he is following God's will, good things will happen to him. "It is impossible that my familiar sign did not oppose me if I was not about to do what was right."[21]

---

[17]Many scholars claim that when Socrates uses this phrase he is not committed to monotheism, but is just referring to one of the many Greek gods, probably Apollo. This is possible, but by no means obviously correct. Its plausibility depends on the assumption that Socrates could not have been a monotheist. However, the example of Aristotle (see chap. 5) shows that belief in one God was certainly possible in ancient Greece.

[18]Plato, *Apology* 28e, p. 27.

[19]Plato, *Apology* 29d, p. 27. Socrates's words here strikingly anticipate the words of the apostles in Acts 5:29. After being ordered to cease to teach in the name of Jesus, Peter and the other apostles refuse, saying, "We must obey God rather than human beings."

[20]Plato, *Apology* 40b-c, p. 35.

[21]Plato, *Apology* 40c, p. 35.

What does happen to us at death? In the *Apology* Socrates, though confident that death is a good thing, seems unsure about whether the human soul survives death. In this dialogue he affirms that death is one of two things: "Either the dead are nothing . . . or it is, as we are told, a change and a relocating for the soul from here to another place," a world in which people are immortal, and are judged in accordance with true justice.[22] In the *Phaedo*, a dialogue that purports to recount Socrates's last conversation before his execution by drinking hemlock, Socrates is more unambiguous in affirming a belief that humans have immortal souls that survive the death of their bodies. Those who achieve true goodness will eventually escape reincarnation and live in a world of perfection.[23] This view articulated in the *Phaedo* actually fits better with what Socrates says about human life and its purpose in the *Apology* as well.

Perhaps Socrates's most radical conviction is this: God has given humans the task of "soul-making." Socrates's own life is compared to the life of a soldier who has been assigned to a "post," and humans should be concerned above all with becoming good and righteous people. Socrates implores the people of Athens to recognize this task and take it seriously; he even begs them to help his sons to recognize this truth: "When my sons grow up, avenge yourselves by causing them the same kind of grief that I caused you, if you think they care for money or anything else more than they care for virtue."[24]

Since the achievement of goodness is the human task, it makes sense that Socrates claims that the worst thing that can happen to a person is not to be treated badly or unjustly, or even to suffer a disease, but to do something that is evil. For it is only the latter that can damage a person's soul. Thus he begs the Athenians not to convict him and execute him, not because death is an evil to him, but because by doing so they will be staining their own souls by unjustly executing an innocent person. The person who follows the path of goodness may walk without fear:

---

[22]Plato, *Apology* 40d-41c, pp. 35-36.
[23]Plato, *Phaedo*, 114c., p. 97.
[24]Plato, *Apology* 41e, p. 36.

"Keep this one truth in mind, that a good man cannot be harmed either in life or in death, and that his affairs are not neglected by the gods."[25] This is why Socrates can claim that his accusers cannot really harm him: he does "not think that it is permitted that a better man be harmed by a worse."[26]

THE DEATH OF SOCRATES

Normally, Socrates's sentence would have been executed immediately after the trial. However, just before the trial, a ship had been sent on a sacred mission, and the law did not allow any executions to take place during this period. The mission was delayed, and so Socrates was in prison for a substantial period. While he waited, his friends developed a plan to bribe the jailors and spirit Socrates away into exile, saving his life. In Plato's *Crito* we have an account of why Socrates refused to go along with the plan.

Crito, who is a well-to-do friend of Socrates, visits him in prison, tells him about the plan, and urges him to allow his friends to arrange the escape. Crito's arguments in favor of escaping focus mainly on the consequences of the two courses of action. If Socrates is executed, his friends will miss him, his sons will not have a father to guide them, and people will think his friends were unwilling to spend the money to bribe the jailers and get him out. Socrates does not find these reasons compelling. He does not care what most people will think of him; only views of the good and the wise based on good reasons should be considered.[27] In his customary way, he questions Crito and thereby constructs an argument for staying in prison.

The argument starts from the premise that it is not mere life that is important, but "the good life."[28] Crito agrees with Socrates that "the

[25]Plato, *Apology* 41d, p. 36.
[26]Plato, *Apology* 30d, p. 28.
[27]Plato, *Crito* 46c-47d, p. 41.
[28]Plato, *Crito*, 48b, p. 42.

good life, the beautiful life, and the just life are the same."[29] This means, according to Socrates, that there are some acts that are always wrong, and should be avoided; what is right does not always depend on circumstances.[30] If an act is wrong, it must never be done, regardless of the consequences. But if it is always wrong to do what is wrong, it cannot be right to do wrong to another, even if that other person has wronged you. Injuring another person is certainly wrong, and hence Socrates claims it is wrong to retaliate by injuring another person who has injured you. Here Socrates seems to agree with Jesus' teaching in the New Testament, that a person should not return evil for evil, but should do good toward all: "You have heard that it was said, 'Love your neighbor and hate your enemy.' But I tell you, love your enemies and pray for those who persecute you" (Mt 5:43-44).

How does all this bear on Socrates's decision about escaping from prison? Socrates makes the application by first securing agreement on another principle: that it is right to keep one's agreements or promises, and failing to do so is a way of injuring another.[31] By accepting an education and choosing to live in Athens, Socrates has implicitly promised to obey the laws of the state, since it is understood that those who live in a country and benefit from its laws are thereby agreeing to abide by those laws.[32] If this is so, then if Socrates were to break the law by escaping from prison without official permission, he would be injuring the state, and thereby doing wrong. Though Crito can hardly bear the thought that he will lose his friend, he cannot find any defect in Socrates's reasoning, and agrees that staying in prison is the right thing to do.

The death of Socrates is movingly described in Plato's *Phaedo*, which recounts how he bravely, even cheerfully, drank a hemlock poison after a full day of conversation with his friends. In the dialogue, Socrates

---

[29]Plato, *Crito*, 48b, p. 42.
[30]Plato, *Crito* 49a, p. 43.
[31]Plato, *Crito* 49e, p. 44.
[32]Plato, *Crito* 50a-52d, pp. 44-46.

presents a number of arguments that the human soul is immortal and will survive death, and thus bolsters the conviction of the *Apology* that death is not really an evil for the good person. I shall postpone a discussion of those arguments until the next chapter, since many scholars believe that at least some of this dialogue represents Plato's own philosophy more than Socrates. However, it is worth noting that this confidence in life after death fits the profoundly religious worldview Socrates evidently holds. For him, the world is one in which humans are here to achieve goodness, and it is shaped by a moral order and providence that ultimately guarantees that virtue will be rewarded.

Plato

PLATO WAS BORN OF A DISTINGUISHED Athenian family around 428 BC. Although a person with his family background would naturally have gone into public service, Plato was disillusioned by the failure of Athenian democracy to produce good leadership in the Peloponnesian war with Sparta, and no doubt even more by the execution of his friend and teacher Socrates. So, except for some trips to Sicily, where Plato tried to attend to the education of a ruler (and things turned out poorly in this case), he devoted his life to philosophy rather than seeking political or military office. Around 387 BC Plato gathered a group of colleagues and students, and founded the Academy, the institution in Western history that is often termed the first university, though it is probably better described as a forerunner or anticipation of the university in the modern sense. Plato and his colleagues not only offered instruction but also conducted original research in a number of fields, making particularly important contributions to mathematics. The Academy offered much more to its members than purely academic instruction. Rather, we might think of it as a kind of committed community with shared visions of the good and moral and spiritual practices that formed the members.[1] Plato remained active as the leader of the Academy until his death in 348/347 BC at the age of eighty.

It would be hard to overestimate the influence of Plato on Western culture. The twentieth-century philosopher, logician, and mathematician

---

[1] I wish at this point to acknowledge the help that Douglas Henry has given me with respect to this chapter at many points. Obviously, infelicities that remain are my responsibility.

Alfred North Whitehead memorably said that "the safest general characterization of the European philosophical tradition is that it consists of a series of footnotes to Plato."[2] Personally, after forty years of teaching the history of Western philosophy, I find Whitehead's statement not hyperbole, but close to the sober truth. However, Plato's influence is seen not only in philosophy but also in theology, political theory, and even the visual arts. Sometimes that influence is seen in strongly critical reactions, but even those who find Plato's thought repugnant can scarcely escape his towering shadow. It is important not to read back all the ideas of Plato's followers into his own thinking; one should not assume that Plato is responsible for everything that has been called "Platonism." Nevertheless, most of the ideas associated with Platonism can at least be traced to elements in Plato's corpus.

Although Plato lectured in the Academy, no copies of his lecture notes, if he used any, have been preserved, though some of the reactions of his listeners, notably Aristotle, are available. A historian of philosophy would like to have copies of these lectures, because some scholars believe that in them Plato developed some technical and sophisticated ideas that he did not think suitable for a public audience. Most of Plato's dialogues do seem intended for a broad audience, and fortunately it appears that all of them have been preserved.

In most of Plato's dialogues Socrates is the main protagonist, and this raises the problem, discussed in the last chapter, as to what in the dialogues is derived from Socrates and what ideas are distinctively Plato's. Although there can be no certainty about this matter, and many excellent scholars diverge from the most popular view, I shall follow the majority view, which divides Plato's dialogues into three groups: (1) Early dialogues, presumed to be mainly Socratic, and focusing chiefly on ethical concepts and questions. This group includes the *Apology, Euthyphro, Crito, Protagoras*, and *Gorgias*. (2) The middle dialogues, in which elements of Socrates's personality can still be seen at

---

[2]Alfred North Whitehead, *Process and Reality* (New York: Harper and Row, 1929), 63.

times, but that focus not only on ethical concepts but also on metaphysical and epistemological questions. Some of the major ideas here are presumed to be Plato's own, though questions can be raised about whether they are logical extensions of Socratic views. Most scholars include the *Meno, Phaedo, Symposium, Phaedrus,* and the *Republic* as the most important ones in this group. (3) Later dialogues often include more technical discussions, and some show a greater interest in religious questions as well. The more important later dialogues include the *Parmenides, Sophist, Statesman, Timaeus,* and the *Laws.*

PLATO'S METAPHYSICAL AND EPISTEMOLOGICAL VISION

It is true of most philosophers that their metaphysical and epistemological views are tightly connected, and this is especially so in the case of Plato. It therefore makes sense to try to explain his views on reality and knowledge together. Of course Plato wrote dialogues and not systematic treatises, so any reconstruction of his thought into a systematic form will fail to do full justice to the character of his writings. Nevertheless, some kind of summary provides a good entry point to his thinking. A good place to begin is with what Francis Cornford called the "twin pillars of Platonism": the theory of Forms and the immortality of the soul. At the heart of Platonism lies a conviction that the visible, physical universe is not the highest reality. What is truly real are the Forms: invisible, spiritual realities that do not exist in space and time and are completely unchangeable. Particular objects in the physical world are said to imitate or "participate" in the Forms, and the Forms in some way explain or make possible the characteristics of the objects visible to the senses. Human persons have a link to this higher, spiritual reality, in that the human soul is itself an invisible spiritual reality that has a capacity to know the Forms. Virtually all forms of Platonism share some version of these twin "pillars," by holding that there is an invisible reality that is higher than the physical world, and that human beings understood at the deepest level are also spiritual beings who have a natural affinity to that higher reality. I shall begin by discussing Plato's theory of Forms, leaving a discussion of the soul and immortality until after I have examined Plato's account of knowledge.

What are the Forms, and why should Plato believe in their reality? A natural starting place is with the Socratic quest for definitions. In many of Plato's dialogues, Socrates begins by asking a "What is it?" question about such things as beauty, piety, courage, or virtue. Merely asking such questions seems to assume that they can be answered, and that the answers can be right or wrong. This in turn seems to presuppose that courage and virtue and beauty and other such qualities are objective realities; it is possible to understand them correctly or incorrectly.

But what kind of reality can they have? Let us consider as an example a particular person, call him Sampson, who possesses courage. Sampson may be courageous and he may do many courageous acts, but neither Sampson nor his actions are identical to courage itself. Sampson may become more or less courageous or even lose the virtue altogether and become cowardly, but courage itself always remains courage. Obviously Sampson is not the only thing that possesses courage; there are other courageous people who do courageous acts. Plato believes that all particular examples of courage must share something in common; they all share or participate in Courage, which can be seen as a kind of ideal or standard that particular things can approximate to in different degrees. Courage is then a Form, an unchanging reality that must be distinguished from the particular objects in the world that have courage (and other qualities) to various degrees and are constantly changing.

The Forms themselves are neither in time nor space. Courage itself has no particular size or shape and is not located in some discrete region of space. It is timeless because it never changes. Plato speaks of the relation between Forms and particulars in a variety of ways. Particular things can be said to manifest a Form or "participate" in a Form. The latter metaphor is difficult to unpack, but it must mean at the very least that there is an ontological relationship between particulars and Forms. The particular gets some of its reality from the Form. The particular is thus enhanced though the Form is not diminished.

Often the Forms are described as providing a kind of ideal standard that particulars imitate but never perfectly realize. The Forms are also reflexive in the sense that they are said to manifest or exemplify their own qualities. If there is a Form of the Good that particular good things approximate, then that Form must itself be perfectly good. (I shall discuss the Form of the Good in more detail below.)

What Forms are there for Plato? The answer is not completely clear. Plato seems most confident that there are Forms for ethical qualities (and other normative qualities, such as beauty), and for mathematical qualities. (The latter kind of Form almost certainly reflects the influence of Pythagoreanism, which Plato may have encountered in Sicily.) Therefore, there certainly are Forms for such qualities as courage, beauty, and justice. Plato is equally confident that there must be such things as Equality and Circularity. No two drawn circles are ever perfectly circular, so circularity itself must be a kind of timeless ideal that drawn circles approximate. Plato often speaks of Forms for such qualities as colors (Whiteness, for example) and relational qualities such as Largeness, though these seem less central to his thinking. He denies there are Forms of negative qualities; what is bad or evil is simply a lack of Form. And in the *Parmenides* Plato has Socrates appear perplexed about whether there are Forms for insignificant qualities, and says there are "not at all" Forms for such things as mud and dirt.[3]

Plato's metaphysical views can be seen as a kind of synthesis of some of the thinking of his predecessors. In his account of the ordinary world that we experience through perception, Plato sides with Heraclitus, who, it will be recalled, claimed that the world is one of constant flux, in which it is "not possible to step into the same river twice." Such a world

---

[3]Plato, *Parmenides* 130d3-5, in *Plato: Complete Works*, ed. John M. Cooper and D. S. Hutchinson (Indianapolis: Hackett, 1997), 364 (all page numbers in citations of Plato throughout this chapter are from this volume).

of becoming is too evanescent to be the object of knowledge. Parmenides was right that genuine knowledge must be knowledge of Being, and what has Being must be constant and unchangeable. As we will see, Plato's views here have had an abiding influence on Western thought, especially its theology, which has tended to see God as supremely real and therefore as completely incapable of any kind of change.

THE DIVIDED LINE AND THE CAVE

This metaphysical vision, along with its epistemological implications, is powerfully illustrated in two memorable sections of Plato's *Republic*. The first is called the "divided line," and it usefully pictures both Plato's view of reality and his account of human knowledge and belief. Plato has Socrates imagine a line divided into two unequal lengths. Some prefer to think of the line as drawn horizontal, but I prefer to think of it as a vertical line, with the top part being the larger part. We are further asked to think of each section of the divided line as again divided in two unequal lengths proportional to the original division.[4] The bottom section of the line represents the world of becoming, reality as it is perceived by the senses, while the top half of the line represents what Plato calls the "intelligible world," the world of Being that is known through pure thought. The lower half of the lower half is the realm of appearances, shadows, and images, when physical things appear in a misleading or confused way to us; while the top half of the bottom section is the world of actual ordinary objects, including such things as plants and animals. (An illustration of the line is found in figure 1.)

Corresponding to these metaphysical distinctions are a set of epistemological divisions. When we apprehend shadows and images, we grasp only the imaginary, and if we believe these objects are real we have error. When we rightly grasp that an animal or plant exists, we have what Plato calls true belief or right opinion. This true belief, however valuable it may be for ordinary practical life, does not count as knowledge

---

[4]Plato, *Republic* 509d, p. 1130.

because knowledge must be directed toward what is universal and unchanging. Genuine knowledge requires certainty, but the world we grasp through sense perception is a world of flux that can never be known with certainty.

The top section of the line, which represents the intelligible world, is the world of genuine knowledge. However, this section of the line, like the lower half, is divided into two sections. The lower half represents the realm of Forms when they are grasped with the help of images, as when a geometer uses a drawn circle to help grasp some features of the circle.

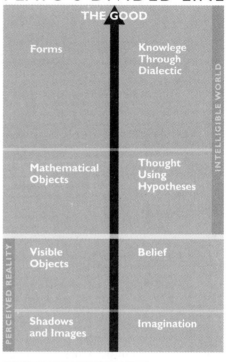

Figure 1. Plato's divided line

This kind of intellectual activity, as Plato sees it, employs "hypotheses" that are assumed but not really clearly and definitively known. The top half of the upper section of the line represents the intellectual sphere in which these features are transcended; the mind employs "dialectic," a kind of pure conceptual thinking, and eventually is able to have the purest kind of knowledge, which for Plato is an intellectual "seeing" of the Forms themselves. In this sphere the "hypotheses" are not simply taken-for-granted assumptions, but literally beginning points, springboards from which reason eventually arrives at a pure vision of the truth.[5]

---

[5]Plato, *Republic* 511b, p. 1132.

The divided line analogy is further clarified by Plato's famous "cave allegory," also found in the *Republic*. Plato has Socrates describe a long, deep cave in which prisoners have been bound for their entire lives in the dark regions at the back of the cave. There is a fire at the very back of the cave, behind the prisoners, and a screen-like wall in front of them. The prisoners are bound so that they cannot turn their heads and can only see what is in front of them. Behind them is a kind of wall with a ledge or pathway behind the wall. Men walk along this ledge and hold up little puppets or toys that resemble objects in the normal visible world, such as humans, animals, and tools (see figure 2). The result is that the prisoners see on the screen shadows cast by these figures, and when the men behind them make sounds they hear the echoes of the sounds off the wall-screen. Plato asks us to imagine that the prisoners have a kind of competition in which they try to describe and name the "objects" they are seeing. (Of course in reality they are only seeing the shadows cast by the puppets.)

Plato then imagines that one of the prisoners is liberated from his bonds. If such an individual were to turn around and look at the puppets, the brightness of the light behind the puppets would no doubt confuse him, and he would be unable to see the objects clearly. If he looked directly at the fire his vision would be even worse, as the brightness would blind him until his eyes could adjust. Doubtless such a person would prefer to go back to his old way of "seeing." Imagine that the person is dragged by force up through the entrance to the cave and brought out into the sunlight. Again, he would initially be unable to see anything, especially if he gazed directly at the sun itself. In time such a person would recognize that what he used to call reality consisted of shadows and images, and even the objects that were behind him in the cave were just copies of the real objects he has finally learned to recognize. This person would realize that he has found true wisdom and pity his fellow prisoners who are still bound.

However, Plato warns, if this person were to come back into the cave and try to help those prisoners, he would appear ridiculous to them.

PLATO'S ALLEGORY OF THE CAVE

Figure 2. Allegory of the cave

Since his eyes have become accustomed to the light of the actual world, he would no longer be able to see in the darkness of the cave and thus could not play well in the game in which the shadows are recognized. The prisoners would think his eyesight had been ruined, and would resist any attempt on his part to help them. In a clear allusion to Socrates's fate, Plato says that the prisoners might even try to kill the man who had come back to free them.[6]

The cave analogy is a vivid picture of Plato's account of the mind's ascent to true knowledge. The puppets held behind the prisoners symbolize the ordinary objects of the physical world, which are copies of the Forms. The prisoners who describe the shadows cast by the puppets see only imitations of imitations and even lack true beliefs about ordinary objects. The prisoner who turns around and looks at those objects has what corresponds to true belief or correct opinion in the divided line. The liberated prisoner who has been dragged out of the cave and sees real physical objects corresponds to the person who has true knowledge of the Forms. The sun itself corresponds to what Plato calls the Form of the Good, a topic I shall discuss later in this chapter.

KNOWLEDGE AS RECOLLECTION AND THE IMMORTALITY OF THE SOUL

For Plato genuine knowledge is knowledge of the Forms, but how is such knowledge possible? Clearly, we cannot know the Forms through sense perception, since we only come to know the changing world of spatiotemporal objects through the senses, and the Forms are eternal realities, not located in space and time. In the *Meno* Plato has Socrates describe what he calls a "trick argument," which affirms that it is not possible to seek to learn anything. The argument affirms that learning is impossible, because a person must either know or not know what he is seeking to learn. If he already knows it, he does not

---

[6]Plato, *Republic* 517a, p. 1134.

need to discover it, but if he does not know it, he will not recognize it even if he finds it.[7]

Plato suggests a solution to this dilemma can be had if we think of human knowledge as made possible by "recollection." There is a sense in which humans already do know what they learn. Human beings have an innate knowledge of the Forms, though it is a knowledge that has been "forgotten" at birth. The human soul is itself immortal and non-physical, like the Forms themselves, and at some point prior to birth had a perfect knowledge of the Forms. At birth this knowledge is lost, but the capacity to understand the Forms remains and can be actualized through reason. The details of this description may be the kind of thing that Plato describes as a "myth," a story that conveys some important truth though without insisting that the story gets things exactly right. Regardless of how seriously Plato may take the idea of the soul's pre-existence, he certainly takes seriously the idea that the soul is immortal and has a capacity to grasp timeless truths.

In a way the doctrine of recollection is present everywhere in the Platonic dialogues, in that Socrates characteristically seeks to help others acquire wisdom by questioning them. The assumption that underlies this is that each person has a capacity to grasp the truth for himself. Socrates compares himself to a midwife, who does not give birth directly but helps others give birth to the truth that is already within them.[8]

In the *Meno* Plato goes on to illustrate the doctrine of recollection by depicting a memorable encounter with an uneducated slave. Socrates, without ever directly telling the slave anything, but simply asking a series of questions, helps the slave to understand an important geo-metrical truth: how to construct a square that will be double the size of a given square. The slave first believes that all he has to do is double the size of the sides of the existing square; through questioning Socrates gets him to see that this will result in a square four times the size of the

---

[7]Plato, *Meno* 80e, p. 880.
[8]Plato, *Theaetetus*, 150b-c, p. 167.

original, rather than double. The correct answer is found by drawing a new square using the diagonals of the existing square, an answer that implicitly shows the slave boy has a grasp of the Pythagorean theorem, since the diagonals will create right triangles.[9] Though the slave has received no formal education, he has the capacity to recognize mathematical truths when questioned and thus must have some knowledge of those truths.

For Plato, this result is not merely one of importance to epistemology. Rather, the capacity to recollect the Forms is evidence of the human soul's true character. If humans have a knowledge they could not have obtained in this life, then they must be beings who have a more than temporal existence: "Then if the truth about reality is always in our soul, the soul would be immortal so that you should always confidently try to seek out and recollect what you do not know at present—that is, what you do not recollect."[10] The link between immortality and recollection is even clearer in the *Phaedo*, in which Socrates, facing death at the end of the day, passionately defends his belief in immortality. The emphasis is not so much on recollection as a process as on the soul's capacity to grasp eternal truth, a capacity that tells us something important about the nature of the soul. The vocation of the philosopher is there described as preparation for death. True philosophy requires an ascetic discipline in which the distractions of physical desires are disciplined, as the philosopher seeks to purify himself and prepare for life after death as a pure soul freed from earthly passions, a life in which the Forms will be clearly known.

Plato's view of the human person is thus a strong form of dualism, in which a nonphysical soul resides in a physical body. The body is simply a part of the world of flux, and therefore constantly changes and eventually perishes. The soul, however, is essentially eternal, and exists even before birth. After death the soul may be reincarnated in yet another

---

[9]The Pythagorean theorem of course is that in a right triangle the sum of the square of the hypotenuse is equal to the sum of the squares of the other two sides.
[10]Plato, *Meno* 86b, p. 886.

body, but the person who achieves wisdom and virtue will eventually achieve a spiritual existence in the realm of the Forms.

BEAUTY AND THE FORM OF THE GOOD

If one read only the *Phaedo*, one would think that Plato had a very negative view of the body, and indeed, a low view of physical reality is often associated with Platonism. However, in the *Symposium* and in the *Phaedrus* Plato gives a somewhat different picture. In the *Symposium* Socrates describes erotic, physical love as something that can be a springboard to wisdom. To be sure, physical love is only the beginning of a process, and in the end physical desire is transcended. Nevertheless, in the *Symposium* Socrates recounts a speech he supposedly heard from Diotima, a prophetess, that shows how physical love can be the beginning of true wisdom. A lover begins by loving and desiring someone who has a beautiful body. However, as the person matures, this love becomes a love of beauty itself, first as found in other bodies, and eventually as found in beautiful actions. At last the lover is able to appreciate the beauty of knowledge, and in the end grasps the Form of Beauty itself.

The Form of Beauty here is not merely one Form among the others, but seems to be something like a supreme Form that unifies all the Forms. A similar role is played in the *Republic* by what is described as the "Form of the Good." The Form of the Good is not merely one Form among others, but the source of the reality of all the Forms, and even that which makes possible knowledge of the Forms: "Not only do the objects of knowledge owe their being known to the good, but their being is also due to it, although the good is not being, but superior to it in rank and power."[11] Sometimes Plato speaks of the supreme Form as "the One" rather than as the Form of Beauty or the Good, but most scholars agree that these are different descriptions of the same reality in Plato's thought.

---

[11]Plato, *Republic* 509b, p. 1130.

The idea that there is one supreme Form that is the source of the reality of all the Forms is an important contribution to answering one of the questions that Plato's doctrine of Forms raises: How are the Forms related to each other? The postulation of the Form of the Good answers this question by insisting that the Forms are unified; there is ultimately one transcendent reality that gives rise to all of the Forms. However, it is not completely clear what this means. Perhaps it is meant to be unclear, since Plato himself insists that the Form of the Good is so transcendent that it resists clear description in human language.

The other important question raised by the doctrine of Forms is this: What is the relation between the Forms and the ordinary objects in our ordinary world? The answer Plato provides to this question relies heavily on various metaphors: ordinary objects are imitations or copies of the Forms, or they are said to "participate" in the Forms. The Forms are in some way the source of the world of becoming. Ordinary objects have a degree of reality, derived from the Forms, even if they are not the highest kind of reality.

The relation of the Forms to ordinary objects is further explored in Plato's *Timaeus*, which provides a kind of creation story. The physical world we experience through the senses is the work of a divine craftsman, often called the "Demiurge," who uses the Forms as patterns and fashions physical objects out of a formless, preexistent matter. Later Christian theologians were deeply influenced by the *Timaeus*, although the Christian understanding of creation differs significantly from Plato's. The Christian God creates *ex nihilo* (out of nothing), not out of a preexistent matter. The Christian God is not merely a craftsman who uses preexistent stuff but, like Plato's Form of the Good, is the source of the reality of everything but himself. The Forms that Plato's Demiurge uses as his models for creation seem external to himself. Christian Platonists, as we shall see later in looking at such philosophers as Augustine, think of the Forms as God's Ideas, not realities external to God that God simply recognizes.

In general we can say that Plato has many elements of the Christian concept of God, but from a Christian perspective does not have those elements arranged in the right way. The Form of the Good is the transcendent source of all being and knowledge, but Plato does not seem to see the Good as a personal agent. The Demiurge is a personal agent, but does not have the status of a transcendent Creator. Later Christian Platonists will take these elements and unify them; God is both a personal agent and the source of all reality, truth, and value.

PLATO'S ETHICAL AND POLITICAL PHILOSOPHY

I have examined some of the metaphysical and epistemological doctrines that Plato develops in his *Republic*, but the book is actually primarily directed to ethical and political questions. The book begins with a discussion about justice, in which some standard views of justice (such as "justice is giving to each person what is owed" and "justice is helping friends and harming enemies") are criticized by Socrates. A man named Thrasymachus, clearly impatient with Socrates, jumps into the conversation and puts forward the radical view that "justice is what is in the interest of the stronger." Thrasymachus holds that "might makes right" in the sense that what society calls "just" and "unjust" are those rules or policies that are intended to safeguard the position of the rich and powerful. Morality is purely conventional, and there is no reason for the person who is powerful to abide by moral principles when it is in the interest of that person to flout morality. Socrates takes up this challenge and mounts a defense of the claim that justice is inherently good and worthwhile, not just a necessary evil that a person must accept because of expediency.

At this point Glaucon and Adeimantus jump into the argument. Although they want to believe that Socrates's view is correct, they challenge him to provide a stronger argument. Glaucon tells the story of Gyges, a man who obtains a magic ring that can make him invisible, and uses the ring to murder the king and marry the queen.[12] Would not

---

[12]Actually, it is not clear whether the story is about Gyges or an ancestor of Gyges. It is his ancestor in book 2 and Gyges himself in book 5. But most readers describe the ring as the ring of Gyges.

anyone who had such a ring act as Gyges did? Is it really worthwhile to *be* a just person, or is it simply the case that people want to be *thought* to be just? To convincingly argue that justice itself is worth having, and not simply a reputation for justice, Socrates is challenged to compare a person who is perfectly just but is thought to be unjust (and so is unpopular and subject to punishment and hardships) with a person who is in fact unjust but is regarded by others as just (and so is popular and is given honors and rewards). This latter person in fact resembles the "Prince" that will later be described by Machiavelli: a ruler who unscrupulously does what he must to hold on to power, while cleverly cultivating a reputation as moral and beneficent.[13]

Plato has Socrates respond to this challenge by giving a full account of justice, both in the individual and in society. Since a city is so much larger than a person, perhaps we can come to see the nature of justice more clearly by first describing a just city. After gaining a clearer picture of justice in the city, we may able to understand what a just individual person is like, and in both cases come to see why justice is valuable. Both the ethical and political philosophy presented center on the possession of key virtues, or admirable qualities.

Plato's ideal city has three classes of people. The majority of people are workers, producers of goods and services, who specialize in what they do best and exchange their goods and services with others. The second category of people are the guardians, people who defend the city against external threats as well as citizens who break the laws. From the second category, a third group is formed. Some of the guardians who seem especially talented and intelligent, as well as being people of good character, are given a special education, including physical education and mathematics, culminating in philosophy. The role of the arts in their education is to be strictly regulated. Literature that contains false ideas about the gods should be censored, and the future rulers should listen to music that is not seductive or sensuous but helps to

---

[13]See chap. 11 for a discussion of Machiavelli.

instill discipline and order. Eventually, after some years of practical experience gained through public service, a few of these people become the rulers of the city. Plato is convinced that the democracy he experienced in Athens was a disaster, and that a healthy commonwealth requires rulers who are chosen not for popularity but because of their wisdom. A good city requires "philosopher-kings," who combine wisdom with power.

Some of what Plato proposes for the philosopher-kings seems radical and even astonishing. In a society in which women were regarded as inferior and incapable of participating in civic affairs, Plato asserts that women who are intelligent and wise should be included among the leaders. Also, to ensure that the rulers will not use their power for selfish ends, they are not to be allowed to have any private property but hold their goods in common. Even the wives of the men will be shared! The idea clearly is that these people will use their power only for the good of all and not to advance their own private interests. Plato seems to believe that people who are properly educated will not behave in the way humans generally behave. Legitimate questions certainly arise at this point about whether Plato's ideal city is "utopian" in the sense that it is unrealistic to expect such changes in human nature. Plato himself seems none too optimistic that his ideal city could actually be achieved, perhaps because of his negative experiences with politics both in Athens and in attempting to educate a ruler in Syracuse.

An ideal city requires that the various classes of people found there learn to do well what they are best suited to do. Similarly, Plato thinks that a human person has distinctive parts, and for a person to flourish, the various parts of the self must "do their job," so to speak. The human soul (which is the true self) has three distinct parts: reason, spirit, and appetite. In the *Phaedrus* the self is compared to a chariot with a driver and two horses. One of the horses is unruly and wild, something that can barely be controlled even by a whip, while the other horse responds to admonitions and commands readily. Reason is of course supposed

to be the charioteer, while the unruly horse corresponds to the appetites that have their source in the body. The disciplined horse is the
"spirited" part of the soul. The three parts correspond to the three most
important virtues: temperance requires control of the appetites, courage
lies in the ability to seek steadfastly what is right, and wisdom is the
ability to discern the true good that the person should seek. In a similar
way, the three parts of the city correspond to these three virtues: temperance is especially important for the workers, the guardians must
have courage, and the rulers have to provide wisdom. Interestingly,
Plato does say that temperance as a virtue must be present in all of the
people, and so even if it has a special significance for the workers, it is a
virtue that all must have.

If reason gives true guidance, then, with the help of the spirited part,
a person can live harmoniously and be at peace with oneself, making
progress toward the goals recognized by reason. Similarly, in the state
where the wise give guidance, peace will prevail. Each element of the
city must do their own proper work, not usurping the roles of the other
parts. When the rational part rules the appetites, receiving help from
the spirited part's desire for honor and aversion to shame, justice obtains. Injustice, by contrast, arises when, for example, the appetites rule
or when the spirited element honors something other than wisdom.
Humans should want to be genuinely just, and not just appear just, because it is only the just person who can truly flourish. Those who gain
riches or power by being unjust in the end harm themselves by dam-
aging their souls. Power and riches are of little value if a person does not
know for what purposes these are to be used, but it is only the just and
wise person who has such knowledge.

CONCLUSION

It is easy to see why Plato's thought has had so much enduring influence,
both within Christianity and as a philosophical tradition in its own
right. In Plato's dialogues, the figure of Socrates, who can truly be

regarded as a philosophical saint and martyr, comes to life. In the later dialogues, Plato develops and extends Socrates's ideas, sometimes in ways that Socrates himself might not have done. The final result is a memorable vision of human persons as beings with a spiritual and eternal vocation, coming to know a reality that includes both a visible, changing world and a higher, invisible reality that is unchanging.

Aristotle

ARISTOTLE WAS BORN IN 384 IN STAGIRA, on the seacoast of Thrace, near Macedonia. His father at some point became the physician of the king of Macedonia, and Aristotle's life remained connected with Macedonia, most notably from around 343 to 340 BC, when Aristotle served as tutor to the young prince who would become famous as Alexander the Great. Prior to this period, Aristotle had come to Athens as a teenager, and spent twenty years as a student and later as an associate of Plato in the Academy. When Plato died, around 348 BC, his nephew Speusippus became the leader of the Academy, and Aristotle left Athens, first going to Assos, before going to the court of Macedon. Some have speculated that Aristotle thought he should have been Plato's successor, but we do not really know. We do know that under Speusippus the Academy turned in the direction of mathematics, a subject Aristotle had no great interest in. (As we shall see, Aristotle's own interests lay in more empirical subjects, such as biology and political science.)

After Alexander ascended to the throne, Aristotle eventually returned to Athens and founded his own school, the Lyceum. The story developed that Aristotle and his students liked to talk philosophy while walking in the Peripatos, a columned walkway. Since the Greek word for "walking around" (*peripatētikos*) is very similar to "Peripatos," Aristotle and his followers became known as the "Peripatetics." It is hard to know whether Aristotle really did his philosophizing while walking around, but it is a nice story and the label has stuck.

Aristotle was the head of the Lyceum for roughly twelve years, and gathered a group of outstanding researchers who helped him with his work in many areas. However, after the death of Alexander the Great in 323 BC, Athens became decidedly unfriendly to Macedonians, and Aristotle was charged with "impiety." With Socrates's fate clearly weighing on his mind, Aristotle chose to leave Athens, "lest the city sin twice against philosophy." He died shortly afterward.

Just as was the case with Plato, it is almost impossible to overestimate the importance of Aristotle for Western philosophy. Often called the "master of those who know," Aristotle invented logic and wrote foundational works, still hugely influential, in aesthetics and political theory, as well as the core areas of philosophy: ethics, metaphysics, and epistemology. His scientific work (in the modern sense) in physics and biology dominated Western thought for well over a millennium; even today questions about the role of teleology in nature remain important, though the modern scientific revolution has taken the natural sciences down a road that seems anti-Aristotelian on first glance.

LOGIC AND EPISTEMOLOGY

Aristotle saw logic not simply as providing us with an account of correct and incorrect reasoning, but as a tool to gain scientific knowledge. His logical work is not found in one single book, but is developed in such books as the *Categories*, the *Analytics*, and *Topics*. Aristotle was a "realist" in the sense that he did not sharply separate questions about being from questions about human thought and language. For example, in the *Categories* Aristotle develops a list of the kinds of predicates we may apply to a subject, but he sees these categories not just as categories of thought or human language but as a list of possible types of qualities that can inhere in a substance. The possible ways of conceiving of an object correspond to the possible ways an object can be. So logic is not just an account of human reasoning, but a tool that gives us metaphysical insight.

When we validly reason from premises that are known with certainty, the conclusion of the argument achieves the status of something that has been demonstrated, and this is the highest form of scientific knowledge. Of course not all logically valid arguments count as scientific demonstrations. It hardly needs to be said that the premises of an argument must be true for the argument to give us knowledge, but truth alone is not enough for science. A scientific demonstration requires that the premises be better known than the conclusion and that in some way they provide real insight into the conclusion; a scientific demonstration gives a kind of explanation. Some logical arguments begin with premises that are widely accepted though not known with certainty, and Aristotle calls such reasoning "dialectical." Though not science in the highest sense, such reasoning can be very valuable, as it allows us to "explain the appearances," one of the goals of philosophy. Still other arguments may have premises that are downright dubious and contentious.

Aristotle's logic is a logic of the syllogism; that is, it looks at reasoning in which a conclusion can be seen as following necessarily from particular premises, as in the following (famous) example:

All humans are mortal
Socrates is a human.
Therefore, Socrates is mortal.

The first premise, which states some universal principle, is called the major premise, while the second or minor premise states a truth about some particular reality. This type of syllogism, called *modus ponens*, is probably the most famous, but there are other valid forms of the syllogism as well. *Modus tollens*, for example, has the following form (using *p* and *q* to stand for propositions): "If p then q. Not q. Therefore not p." Disjunctive syllogisms are also important, as in the following case: "Either p or q. Not p. Therefore q." As late as the nineteenth century, Aristotle's logic was regarded as more or less definitive of the field, but modern symbolic logic has developed new tools, such as a "predicate calculus" that uses "quantifiers" and "variables" in propositions, which allows the logician to formally express relations between propositions that take account of the internal structure of the propositions. Despite these more recent developments, every logician acknowledges a debt to Aristotle as the inventor of the field.

Aristotle clearly saw that not all knowledge could be the result of logical demonstrations, since such a demonstration always requires premises that are already known. Of course it is possible we might come to know the premises for some particular argument through further demonstrations that have those premises as their conclusions, and the premises for those demonstrations might also be known because they have been demonstrated logically to be true. However, it does not seem possible for all premises to be known in this way, since that would require either an infinite number of demonstrations, something clearly beyond the capacity of a human knower, or else a circular chain of arguments.

Aristotle recognizes this and thus holds that the "first principles" of a science do not have to be demonstrated. They are truths that are "recognized" or "seen" to be true after a person has had a significant amount of experience. (Here is one place Aristotle diverges from Plato; basic truths are not "recollected" through reason, but known through a process that involves experience.) Aristotle's account of knowledge is thus often described as "foundationalist," since it holds that some of our knowledge must be basic or foundational in character, not derived though any kind of logical inference. Foundationalist epistemology continues to be an important option today; it has many contemporary defenders, though there is much disagreement about what is required for our foundational knowledge.

Exactly how the basic principles of knowledge are known is a matter of some controversy among interpreters of Aristotle. Since he rejects the Platonic view that knowledge is "recollection," in some broad sense Aristotle is an "empiricist"; that is, he holds that our basic knowledge is not innate but derived from experience. However, Aristotle is clearly not an empiricist in the sense this term takes on in the modern period;

his views diverge sharply from such philosophers as John Locke, George Berkeley, and David Hume. First principles for Aristotle are not simply inductive generalizations. Rather, a basic principle is something that a person who has the requisite experience can come to recognize, because that person has come to grasp the universal *form* that is present in the particulars experienced. (I shall discuss Aristotle's view of form and its relation to matter below.) Aristotle thinks that in some way a knowledge of universals is already implicit in a knowledge of particulars; this knowledge just has to be made explicit, a process that is often assisted by dialectical reflection. It is this kind of knowledge of universals that provides us with the basic principles from which a demonstration can come.

Aristotle's account of a "first principle" is not always consistent. He sometimes clearly means something like a universal definition that can serve as the premise of a syllogism (the kind of knowledge gained through experience that is discussed in the previous paragraph), but at other times he means a basic principle that is presupposed by a science. For example, the logical principle of noncontradiction ("a proposition and its negation cannot both be true") is presupposed by all logical reasoning, though it is not usually a premise from which one reasons. The justification for first principles in this second sense is again that on reflection their truth is simply evident. For example, the principle of noncontradiction must be assumed by anyone who wants to make a meaningful assertion, even by someone who wishes to assert that the principle of noncontradiction is false.

Although Aristotle was clearly a foundationalist in his epistemology, it would be a mistake to read back into his views the kind of foundationalism found in early modern philosophers such as Descartes and Locke, who insisted that our foundational knowledge had to be absolutely certain and impervious to doubt. For Aristotle, although the scientific ideal was a logical demonstration that would provide certainty, he recognized that there are degrees and kinds of certainty, and affirmed that a reasonable person aimed only at the degree of certainty that a particular subject allowed. For example, he famously says in his *Nichomachean Ethics* that "precision is not to be sought for alike in all discussions," and thus that his discussion of ethics will be adequate if "it has as much clearness as the subject-matter admits of."[1]

Aristotle's general procedure in doing philosophy is to seek to set out the appearances of things and work through the puzzles that arise.[2] In working through these "difficulties" Aristotle gives special attention to the "most authoritative" opinions of the wise, his philosophical predecessors, and he ultimately seeks an account that preserves as much as is possible of the "common opinions" about such matters, and provides answers to the objections those received views have given rise to. An account that can do this will "have proved the case sufficiently," even though it is obvious that such an account is not so certain that no one could doubt it.[3] Thus we can see that Aristotle does not always demand the kind of certainty that the early modern philosophers sought. One might say that he lacks the anxiety about knowledge that these later philosophers felt, and thus it is fitting that Aristotle says, in a passage that echoes one from Plato's *Theaetetus*, that philosophy begins with wonder, not with doubt as in the case of Descartes.[4]

METAPHYSICS

Aristotle's metaphysics is discussed not merely in the work we have by that name, but also in the *Physics* and a number of other works. What we call "metaphysics" Aristotle himself called "first philosophy." The title of *Metaphysics* was given to that work by Andronicus, a follower of Aristotle who edited a full edition of the more scholarly, "esoteric" works of Aristotle. (A number of more popular "exoteric" works have

---

[1]Aristotle, *Nicomachean Ethics* 1094b12-26, in *The Basic Works of Aristotle*, ed. Richard McKeon (New York, Random House, 1968), 936. All page numbers in citations of Aristotle in this chapter are from this volume.
[2]Aristotle, *Nicomachean Ethics* 1145b2-5, p. 1037.
[3]Aristotle, *Nicomachean Ethics* 1145b6-7, p. 1037.
[4]Aristotle, *Metaphysics* 982b12, p. 692.

been lost.) Aristotle's treatise on "first philosophy" deals with the nature of "being as being." Andronicus placed this treatise immediately following the *Physics*, and our term *metaphysics* comes from the Greek *ta meta ta physica* (that which comes after physics). The name stuck because metaphysics does indeed deal in part with questions that arise when the questions of physics (natural science in the modern sense) have been answered.

For Aristotle, all sciences deal with being or reality, and the various special sciences, such as physics and ethics, deal with different regions of being. It is the special task of metaphysics to inquire as to what all forms of being have in common. Metaphysics thus asks, What does it mean to say of anything that it has being? What does it mean "to be"? It is worth noting that in contemporary philosophy the term *metaphysics* has taken on broader connotations than it had for earlier philosophers, throughout the ancient period and going all the way up to early modern times. In contemporary philosophy, many questions about the nature of specific forms of reality are treated under the title "metaphysics," including such questions as whether humans have immaterial souls and free will. The term *ontology* has thus come into common use to describe the narrower study of "being as being." (However, the term *ontology* sometimes is simply used in a wider way as well, as a synonym for *metaphysics*.) In this section I will treat Aristotle's metaphysics in both the wider (contemporary) sense and in the narrower sense, giving an account of "being in general," but also discussing his views on God, the natural world, and human beings.

Form and matter. Aristotle agrees with Plato that scientific knowledge must be knowledge of what is universal; he thus affirms the reality of universal forms. However, Aristotle is well-known for his attack on the Platonic doctrine that Forms exist independently of the space-time world of particulars. Instead, Aristotle affirms a view often called "hylomorphism" (from the Greek words for matter and form), which is the view that all natural objects are a composite of form and matter. While form and matter can be conceptually distinguished, there are no forms that are not embedded in material realities; there is no matter that is not structured by form. The one possible exception to this principle is God, who will be discussed later.

Aristotle has a number of distinct reasons for rejecting Forms in the Platonic sense. (I will capitalize *Forms* when speaking of Platonic Forms.) First, he thinks that the postulation of Platonic Forms is scientifically useless, both to explain the qualities of things and to explain our knowledge. The Forms are supposed to provide an account of the nature of things, but Aristotle claims that the Forms have no explanatory value. Of course Plato had said that particulars "imitate" or "participate in" the Forms, but Aristotle claims that such phrases are just "poetical metaphors" that do not provide any actual explanations.[5] Plato had of course postulated the "Demiurge" in the *Timaeus*, as a kind of creative agent who uses the Forms as a guide in fashioning the natural world. Aristotle, who thinks, as we shall see, that the natural world had no beginning, apparently did not take this view of Plato's seriously, and fails to discuss it.

Aristotle also criticizes the Platonic Forms because, being timeless and unchangeable entities, they are incapable of accounting for the changes in the natural world. This criticism seems particularly important to Aristotle for at least two reasons. First, unlike Plato, who regarded the changing world of particulars as unknowable, Aristotle had a deep interest in natural objects and wanted to understand them. Second, Aristotle criticizes a particular version of the doctrine of Forms, one that identifies them with "numbers," or mathematical entities. (It seems likely that this was a view, no doubt influenced by Pythagoreanism, that was held for a period in the later Academy, though there are only hints of such a view in Plato's writings.) One can easily see why Aristotle would argue that timeless entities such as mathematical entities could not be the cause of natural processes. How can an entity that

---

[5]Aristotle, *Metaphysics* 1079b25-27, p. 896.

is itself timeless and unchanging be the cause of changes that occur at some specific time?

The final Aristotelian criticism I shall discuss is his famous "third man" argument. This criticism depends on the view, found in some Platonic discussions of the Forms, that the Forms are self-exemplifying; for example, the Form of Whiteness must itself be white. The "third man" criticism goes like this: Suppose that one posits a Form "Man" to account for what actual, particular men have in common. We could say that it is the fact that all men participate in the form "Man" that explains why they resemble each other. However, if we say that the Form Man is itself an ideal man and thus that particular men must resemble this Form, it seems that we have to posit an additional Form to explain the resemblance between the Form Man and actual men, just as we needed to posit a Form to explain the resemblance between ordinary humans. If that new Form in turn resembles the Form of Man, then we will need yet an additional Form to explain that resemblance, and so on to infinity.

Substances and qualities, essences and accidents. For Aristotle, what exists or has being must be something that can have various properties or qualities. Aristotle's term for a thing that can be a bearer of qualities in this sense is *substance*. We have seen that all natural existents for Aristotle are a union of form and matter. It follows that for Aristotle, actual substances are enduring particular objects, such as Socrates or the desk on which I am writing. Such particular composites of form and matter constitute "primary substances." Of course the properties of subjects have a kind of reality, but they cannot exist all by themselves. They must be properties *of* a substance. Socrates is (or was) an existing subject, a human being. "Being snub-nosed" or "being somewhat ugly" are properties often attributed to the substance that is the human being Socrates.

There is an important difference in the kinds of properties a substance can possess, however. Those properties an object has by virtue of its form are those properties that determine what *kind* of substance the object is. For Aristotle these properties are part of the essence of a subject, and such properties are essential properties, in that a substance cannot lose them without ceasing to be the thing that it is. Suppose it is true (as Aristotle thought) that human beings are essentially rational animals. It follows that a human being who permanently lost the capacity to reason or ceased to be an animal (perhaps by being transformed into a god) would cease to be a human being.

Lots of the properties possessed by an object are not essential properties, however, and Aristotle calls these accidental or contingent properties, since a substance can gain or lose them without ceasing to be the kind of thing it is. Perhaps Socrates had the property of "being a fast runner" as a young man, but lost this property as he aged. Such a change does not affect whether he is a human being, since "being a fast runner" is not an essential human property. Substances cannot exist without having some accidental properties; what is accidental is which such properties they possess.

Although in the primary sense only individual existents are substances, Aristotle sometimes speaks of the forms of objects as describing substance in a secondary sense. The reason for this is that it is the forms, the essences, that make things the kind of beings that they are, and such terms can be used to describe the class of things that possess this form. There is a sense in which "humans" continue to exist as a species even while individual humans pass in and out of existence.

The four causes. As already noted, Aristotle is very interested in the changes that the natural world undergoes, and sees it as part of the task of science to explain these changes. We have seen that much of the work of Aristotle's predecessors was devoted to explaining the changes in the natural world, and Aristotle attempts to draw on their work in giving a comprehensive account of the kinds of changes the natural world undergoes and the kinds of explanations possible for such changes. In many translations of Aristotle, the Greek word for "change" is translated as "motion," and this can be confusing for readers. It is well to keep in mind that when Aristotle speaks of change or "motion" he has in mind such things as coming into existence and passing out of existence, growth and decay, as well as motion in a more contemporary sense, in which an object changes its place.

For Aristotle there are four different ways change can be explained. We can speak then of four types of causes: formal, material, efficient, and final. Sometimes a change in an object can be explained by the kind of thing it is. For example, a young tomato plant, when it has adequate nourishment and moisture, grows into a mature tomato plant because it is part of the nature of a plant to grow. Such an account explains by describing the form of the plant.

Second, changes can be explained by virtue of the material "stuff" of which a substance is composed. A tomato plant that lacks moisture may for that reason fail to grow properly; it may wither and even die. Its matter is deficient in a crucial way that inhibits the potential of the plant to grow into a mature tomato plant.

The efficient cause of some change is the *source* of the change. A tomato plant may be where it is because it has been planted by a farmer. The efficient cause of a statue is the sculptor who brought the statue into being. There is some ambiguity here in that Aristotle sometimes speaks of the efficient cause as the art or practice that makes some change possible; in this sense it is the knowledge of the sculptor (or the farmer) that is the efficient cause.

The fourth type of cause is the final cause, which for Aristotle is the purpose or goal of the process. Thus, the final cause of the tomato plant may be to produce delicious tomatoes for eating; the final cause of the statue may simply be the existence of the statue as a beautiful object the sculptor intends to create.

Aristotle does not believe that all four types of cause are found for every change. For example, he says that there is no final cause for an eclipse. Furthermore, the four causes are not always distinct. In the natural world, for example, the final cause usually coincides with the formal cause, because the end or goal of a process is the actualization of the form that is inherent in some substance. Aristotle distinguishes an explanation of what is typical or normal from what is unique or idiosyncratic, and generally typical properties are explained by formal causes, while more individual properties by matter, which is for Aristotle what individuates. All humans possess the form of humanness, but individual humans differ from each other because they are composed of different matter. Thus the form explains what all members of a species have in common; more individual properties are explained by particular material factors.

The notion of a final cause seems clearest in the case where there is a personal agent with an intention, such as an artist who paints a picture or carves a sculpture. However, Aristotle is clear that final causality is present in nature generally, and not just in cases of human agency. In some sense nature is "teleological"; there are regular processes that result in features that are good for the existence or flourishing of creatures. We might say that the final cause of some natural organ, such as the heart, is its function; the function of a heart is to pump blood and make it possible for a creature to be alive and flourish. Not only is final causality present in nature; for Aristotle, final and formal causes are in some ways primary. Aristotle does not, however, think of these functions in nature as consciously intended by some agent, though later theistic Aristotelians (Jewish or Muslim or Christian) would naturally think of these natural functions as rooted in God's creative intentions. Aristotle does not think of the natural world as something created in time, and as we shall shortly see, he does not think of God as creating the world either in time or timelessly.

The most general account of change is given in terms of potentiality and actuality. Natural objects, just by being the kinds of things they are, have various kinds of potentiality, and change occurs when those potentialities are realized or actualized. An acorn has the potential to become an oak tree, and will do so if conditions are right. A rock held in the air has the potential to fall to the earth and will do so if the person holding the rock releases it from their grip. Matter is linked to potentiality, while form is a kind of actuality. A seed has the potential to become a plant; to become that plant is to actualize the form or structure it has the potential to become. If we ask which comes first, potentiality or actuality, Aristotle answers that from an explanatory point of view, actuality is primary. Something that has the potential to become hot can only become hot through something that already is hot. The fertilized egg that can become a human being must be the result of actual human beings.

Psychology. Although Aristotle does not offer a psychology in the contemporary sense, he does give an account of what human persons are like, one that focuses on the relation between the soul (or mind) and the body. Aristotle's hylomorphism requires him to modify the strongly dualistic view of Plato, for whom the soul preexists the body and will survive the death of the body. Aristotle sees the human soul as the form of the body, and thus the emphasis is on the human person as a psychosomatic unity. Since humans are animals, the human soul contains the powers found in lower forms of life. Even plants as living things have a "vegetative soul," a form that allows them to take in nutrition and grow. Animals have in addition a "sensitive soul," that allows them to experience their world. Human souls have these functions but also are "rational souls." Humans have the power to understand the relationships between things and obtain scientific knowledge. Reason is also practical; it includes the power to deliberate and will a course of action in a rational manner.

In some ways Aristotle sees the higher rational functions of the human soul as having some independence from the body, but it is not at all clear that this implies any kind of personal immortality. Humans in some way manifest "active intellect," which has a kind of immortality, but this does not necessarily mean that humans survive death as individuals. As "pure actuality" the active intellect may indeed be immortal, but such an intellect seems godlike and not human, and cannot be identified with any particular human being. It is thus fitting to turn to Aristotle's view of God.

God. Although Aristotle focuses, as we have seen, on the natural world, he is far from being a "naturalist" in the contemporary sense who thinks the physical universe is all there is. On the contrary, he maintains that there must be a God, and that God is the ultimate cause of all natural changes. As we saw above, Aristotle holds that the ultimate cause of change must be something actual; pure potentiality by itself can cause nothing without something actual. The world of change as we know it is a world of things that are more or less actual, with potentialities that are more or less realized. The ultimate cause of all this change must be something that is "pure actuality," something with no unrealized potentiality at all. Such a reality would be the "Unmoved Mover," that reality that explains all change without changing itself in any way. This reality is God.

Such a God is not a creator who brought the world into being, because Aristotle does not believe the universe had a beginning in time. God is the cause of the natural world in the sense that he is the final cause of all change. Aristotle compares God to a beloved who moves the lover by being the object of love. All of the natural world in some way desires actuality, and such a yearning is a desire for God, who is perfect actuality.

If we ask what kind of activity God carries on, Aristotle says that we must think of God as thinking, since this is the most perfect kind of activity imaginable. If we ask what God thinks about, the answer must be that God thinks about himself, since it would be unworthy of this most perfect being to think about anything less than perfect.

Centuries later, Aristotle's reflections on God will be employed by Thomas Aquinas to prove God's existence. However, it is important to see the differences between Aristotle's God and the kind of God Christians believe in. Although many Christians do believe that God is perfect and unchangeable, they do not think of God as thinking only of himself, but as involved in his creation. The Christian God is not just an object of love and desire, but a Creator who brings the universe into existence and is responsible for its continued existence and providential care. Of course Christians believe that God exists in three persons and that one of these persons ultimately became incarnate as Jesus of Nazareth. Such views are not only absent from Aristotle, but it is likely he would have found them inconceivable had he known about them.

ETHICS

Aristotle's ethics, found in his *Eudemian Ethics* and the even more famous *Nichomachean Ethics*, remains enormously influential. His account is best understood as a "teleological" view in that he emphasizes the "ends" at which any activity aims. Every human activity, whether an art or practice or even an individual action, is purposive in character. Everything we do is done for an end, but Aristotle recognizes a distinction between ends that are instrumental in character, and ends that are in some way "final." I might, for example, brush my teeth because I want healthy teeth. Brushing is not an activity I value for its own sake. Not every goal can be instrumental, however. I may desire some things for the sake of others, but ultimately some things must be desired for their own sakes if our activities are not to be pointless. Aristotle argues that the ultimate goal for humans, the good at which human life aims, is happiness. The Greek term he uses is *eudaimonia*, which could also be translated as "flourishing." The claim that happiness is the end of human life is not controversial, on his view, but closer to a platitude. However, this is not the end of the inquiry but just the beginning. The real question concerns the nature of happiness, and here is where the disagreements start.

Many contemporary people identify happiness with pleasure or some other subjective sensation. On that view if I feel happy, then I am happy. Aristotle considers such a view, since clearly many people do seek enjoyment as a primary good, but rejects it for several reasons.

It is true that pleasure is a good and that it is one we desire for its own sake, and Aristotle admits that pleasure is a component in a happy life. However, happiness must be something that is complete; the happy person must not be lacking in anything required for a flourishing existence. However, a person who had lots of pleasure but no friends or excellent achievements would be lacking a great deal. Another problem with identifying happiness with pleasure is that not all pleasures are good. Imagine, for example, a sadist who takes pleasure in torturing a dog.

Aristotle also considers the view that happiness is to be identified with honor, but rejects it as well. One reason is that honor seems something that depends on other people; it is a function of how others view a person. Happiness, however, ought to be something that is the person's own possession, and not dependent on the views of others. Besides that, Aristotle argues that people want to be honored for being good, so there must be some more fundamental good than honor.

Aristotle thinks that to understand happiness we must understand human nature and what purposes or functions that nature serves. We have already seen that Aristotle's view of the whole natural world is teleological, in that substances are what they are because of their forms. For an acorn to grow into an oak tree is simply for its form to be actualized. The form embodies what an oak tree can and should be, and a "good" oak tree will be one that fully actualizes its potentiality. Substances, as well as the parts of substances, characteristically have a function. To understand what a good carpenter should be like, we must understand the nature of carpentry, including its goal. We determine what is good and bad by understanding the nature of things, and those natures include purposes or functions.

Aristotle applies this same teleological view to humans, since we are also part of nature: "Have the carpenter, then, and the tanner certain functions or activities, and has man none? Is he born without a function? Or as eye, hand, foot, and in general each of the parts evidently has a function, may one lay it down that man similarly has a function apart from all these?"[6] We already know that what is distinctive about the human soul is rationality, and Aristotle sees this as the key to understanding our purpose in the natural order. Humans are rational animals, and Aristotle concludes that the best life for humans will be a life in which we actualize our potential to act rationally. Happiness is neither pleasure nor honor, but rather is to be found in activity of a certain kind. Happiness is a life lived in accordance with reason.

Reason can be exercised both theoretically and practically. The highest form of happiness would be a life devoted to theoretical contemplation. Few people can live in such a manner, however, and no one (except God) can live purely as a theoretical being, since even the scientist must eat and drink, and even scientists have families and friends. Humans are social beings, and hence Aristotle spends most of his time focusing on what it means to live rationally in a practical way. What does it mean to live rationally, or, as Aristotle frequently says, to act "in accordance with right reason"? The person who characteristically acts in this way is the person who possesses "the virtues" or excellences that a human life ought to possess. Aristotle's ethic, like Plato's, ultimately centers on the virtues. We might say that it is an ethic that focuses on character more than on specific duties. The specific virtues that a good human will have are perfections of his human capacities. (Here the male pronoun is appropriate since Aristotle does not think women are fully rational; the highest human virtues are achievable by free males.) Just as was the case for Plato, the most important virtues turn out to be wisdom, justice, courage, and temperance.

Humans of course have desires and urges; they have loves and hates, and are not purely rational. The person who has practical wisdom is the person who regulates these by reason. Such a person is also temperate; he characteristically does not even want to do what is against reason. He is not a glutton who lives for food, but also not an ascetic who takes no

---

[6]Aristotle, *Nicomachean Ethics*, 1097b29-33, p. 942.

enjoyment in eating. He is also courageous in the sense that he is not dissuaded by danger from doing what is right and honorable.

In general Aristotle says that the virtuous person looks for the "mean" or middle ground between extremes. The courageous person does not have excessive fear that prevents him from acting, but he also is not a foolhardy person who takes unnecessary risks. We might say he fears the right things and to the appropriate degree. In a similar way the temperate person desires the right things in the right amount. There is no one mean for everyone; what is appropriate requires good judgment based on the particular circumstances. An athlete in training needs to eat more than a scholar who sits all day long. The virtuous person has a character that gives him a disposition to act in accord with the mean, as determined by reason. The standard is not absolute, but it is far from being totally relative. We come to recognize the standard by recognizing exemplars. The virtuous person imitates the person who already possesses practical wisdom. Aristotle does not think his doctrine of the mean covers the whole of moral activity. Some acts are just dishonorable and wrong intrinsically; there is no mean for adultery, no proper amount of cheating on a spouse.

How does one acquire the virtues? A good upbringing is helpful. Aristotle goes so far as to say that a person of bad character who has had a poor upbringing is unlikely to gain much understanding of what is good and bad.[7] However, upbringing is not everything; virtues have to be developed. No one acquires the virtues simply by nature, but they are also not something that is contrary to nature. The virtues are acquired by practice. We imitate others who have the virtues and thereby acquire the habits that characterize the virtuous person.

Aristotle's account of happiness is complex. Socrates had argued that ultimately happiness is virtue. A person cannot be harmed by what others do but only by doing evil, which corrupts the soul. This conviction fits well the Socratic/Platonic view of life after death, in which

---

[7]See Aristotle, *Nicomachean Ethics* 1095b4-10, pp. 937-38.

there will be moral judgment based on the kind of life one has lived. The more this-worldly Aristotle cannot accept this view. He would like to maintain that happiness is something totally within our control, since we are responsible to cultivate virtue. However, he ultimately admits that happiness is not totally under our control. It seems counterintuitive to him to think that a person who is suffering injustice or great pain could be happy. Since it is clearly possible for a person of great virtue to be in such a situation, it follows that genuine happiness is not something we can guarantee. It requires good fortune as well.

Socrates and Plato had also argued that all wrongdoing is the result of ignorance. Aristotle is attracted to this view as well, but he recognizes that sometimes people know what is right but do not act accordingly. The intemperate person is in this state because the person has not developed a virtuous character and cannot control his desires. However, even virtuous people sometimes act "out of character." It is possible for a person to have "weakness of will," and be unable to do what he believes to be right. Aristotle struggles to explain this phenomenon, and finally concludes that the person who exhibits weakness of will knows what is right in one sense but not in another. He may know, for example, that injustice is wrong, but fail to realize that the act he is about to perform is unjust.

Aristotle recognizes that the term *justice* is somewhat ambiguous. Sometimes we use the term to refer simply to a person who is completely virtuous, who has all the virtues and avoids the corresponding vices. The just person in this sense is never lawless, greedy, or unfair to others. However, we also use the term *justice* to refer to a particular virtue, that virtue that is concerned with relating fairly to others, particularly with respect to how goods are distributed and exchanged.

Since human beings are social or "political" creatures, our relations to others are very important to our happiness. No human person is completely self-sufficient as an individual. The relation of friendship is particularly important, since in such relations the distinction between egoism and altruism breaks down, and there is a sense in which there is no need to think about issues of justice any longer. The true friend is the "other-self" or "other-I." I so identify with my friends that their happiness is partly my own happiness. Aristotle distinguishes the highest form of friendship from relations formed for utilitarian reasons. True friendship requires a degree of similarity in virtue and ethical outlook, and true friends enjoy spending time together and sharing activities. This kind of intimacy means that the number of true friends a person can have is relatively small.

POLITICAL THEORY

Aristotle and his associates in the Lyceum had collected and studied the constitutions of the various Greek city-states, and he was well aware of the different kinds of states that are possible. Unlike Plato, who put forward an ideal blueprint for society in the *Republic*, Aristotle thinks there are healthy and unhealthy versions of three different kinds of states. A healthy state ruled by one person is a monarchy; when that one ruler does not advance the common welfare but uses his power simply for his own good, then we have a tyranny. Similarly, a state ruled by a few people of excellence is an aristocracy, but when those rulers do not make the good of the community their primary goal, then Aristotle calls such a state an oligarchy. When the people as a whole rule, we have a polity, but again when they do not seek their own good, we have democracy. Aristotle's own preference is for aristocracy; he doubts that the masses have the capacity for good governance. However, he recognizes the importance of history and tradition, and does not claim that one type of government will work for every society.

PHILOSOPHY OF ART

Aristotle believes that the arts have great importance. It is not only the case that people enjoy the arts, though they do and that is significant. Plato had viewed artists as providing "imitations of imitations," since the artist typically paints or describes particulars that are themselves imitations of the Forms. Since Aristotle thought that forms were present in material particulars, he is open to the idea that art can actually teach us about reality.

Poetry is particularly important in this respect, since the poet does not limit himself to describing particular actions, as does the historian, but focuses on universal possibilities. Aristotle distinguished epic, tragic, and comic poetry, and saw tragic poetry as having particular value. The tragic poet who depicts sorrow and death evokes emotions of fear and pity in the audience; experiencing a tragic play allows the audience to "purge" themselves of these emotions or have a "catharsis." (It is not completely clear whether Aristotle means that these emotions can be safely vented or whether we can actually transcend them.) In some ways tragedies allow us to come to terms with those difficult aspects of human existence that we cannot fix.

CONCLUSION

It is clear that Aristotle's influence looms large over many areas of Western philosophy, even without mentioning the way he shaped physics and biology for so many hundreds of years. In the immediate aftermath of Aristotle's death, his philosophy was not as influential as one might have expected. Nevertheless, his influence can be seen in every major school of philosophy in the period to follow. In the Christian West, following the breakup of the Roman Empire, most of Aristotle's writings were lost for many years. However, a knowledge of Aristotle was preserved in the East, both among Byzantine Christians and in Islam. During the period of the Muslim dominance of Spain, Christian scholars again became familiar with the whole of Aristotle's writings as we know them today, and the resulting revival of Aristotle left an indelible mark on the high medieval period, particularly in such philosophers as Thomas Aquinas and Duns Scotus. In the story of Western philosophy, Aristotle, like Plato, appears again and again.

Philosophy in the Hellenistic and Roman Periods

Epicureanism, Stoicism, Skepticism, and Neoplatonism

IN THE PERIOD AFTER PLATO AND ARISTOTLE, the Greek city-states, including Athens, declined in importance. Greece was first absorbed into Macedonia, as Alexander the Great's empire was divided up by Alexander's generals. In 197 BC Macedonia was defeated by Rome; initially it appeared that this freed Greece from Macedonian control, but soon Rome absorbed Greece into its own empire. Although the Greek city-states had little political or military power, the influence of Greek culture on Rome was pervasive; one might say that the conqueror became culturally the conquered. The dominance of the Roman Empire throughout the Mediterranean world went hand in hand with the spread of Greek language and culture, a process that had already begun with Alexander. This period of Western history stretching from the death of Alexander in 323 BC to the end of the Roman Republic in 31 BC is often called the Hellenistic period. However, the dominant philosophies that developed in this age continued, sometimes with little changes though at other times with significant developments, through the period of the Roman Empire. I shall therefore treat the Hellenistic period and the period of the Roman Empire together as one philosophical era, and refer to this time collectively as the Hellenistic period because of the continuities in the dominant philosophical traditions. The ending dates for this era, like its beginning, are somewhat arbitrary, but it is reasonable to think of it as extending until sometime in the fifth century AD, since Rome was sacked in 410 and the last Roman emperor was deposed in 476.

Hellenistic philosophy is dominated by four important and enduring "schools" of philosophical thought: Epicureanism, Stoicism, Skepticism, and Neoplatonism. Each of these schools, as we shall see, has a predominantly practical orientation. All were concerned fundamentally with questions about what constituted "the good life," and how such a life could be achieved. Such a focus seems natural for people living in a vast empire. For the citizens of Socrates's Athens, life was largely taken up with civic and political affairs, and the meaning of life was linked closely to the traditions and customs of relatively small communities. Especially in democratic Athens, citizens had a sense that they could shape their world through their common life. In the Roman Empire, most individuals had no such sense of control or participation in civic life, and it seems natural that the focus of attention should change to how the lives of individual and their families should be carried on.

However, to say that the interests of these philosophers were primarily ethical and practical does not mean that they ignored metaphysical and epistemological questions. The Hellenistic philosophers, like almost all ancient philosophers, thought that the good life for humans was one that fit human nature, as well as the nature of the world in which humans found themselves. So they continued to address metaphysical questions. Furthermore, the existence of the rival philosophical schools gave them good reason to reflect on epistemological issues, as they defended their claims against competing philosophies.

I shall discuss each of these four philosophical traditions, treating the history of each individual school chronologically. Thus, this chapter as a whole will not follow a strict chronological line. I will, for example, tell the story of Stoicism from its early beginnings in the period just after Plato to the later Stoics, who wrote during the later Roman Empire. It should be obvious, however, that the thinkers of the various schools were aware of their contemporaries from other traditions, and not simply their own philosophical ancestors.

EPICUREANISM

Epicurus was born around 342 BC, a few years after Plato's death, when Aristotle would have been in his early forties. Born in Samos, an island in the Aegean Sea, Epicurus lived for a time in Asia Minor (modern-day Turkey), before moving to Athens and establishing his own school with a group of friends. The fact that Epicureanism is named after him is not surprising, since he was evidently a person of such noble character that he left an indelible mark on his followers. It is in fact somewhat ironic that Epicureans, though in many ways adherents of the most "secular" and least religious philosophy of the period, tended to treat Epicurus himself as an almost godlike being, a saintly figure who inspired all his followers. The philosophy Epicurus developed maintained its popularity throughout the Roman period, particularly as the result of the great poem *De Rerum Natura (On the Nature of Things)*, written by Lucretius sometime in the late first century AD. Because of the continuity of Epicurean thought, a good deal of what I shall attribute to Epicurus actually comes from Lucretius and could be regarded as Lucretian. It was actually the rediscovery of Lucretius's poem in early modern Europe that led to a revival of Epicureanism in modern Europe. In any case, it is remarkable that Epicureanism retained its popularity for nearly five centuries, with very little change or development during that period. The actual surviving writings of Epicurus are scant, and so it is common to interpret his teachings partly by reference to what his later followers maintained.

The starting point for Epicurus's thought is the human fear of death and what comes after death. He actually maintains that there would be no need to study "natural science" except for the "misgiving that death somehow affects us." His goal is to "banish fear on matters of the highest importance" by gaining a knowledge of the "nature of the whole universe." People who lack such knowledge "lived in dread of what the legend tells us."[1] Epicurus thinks that this fear of death not only poisons our happiness but also leads directly to the vices that make human life miserable.

The fear of death that Epicurus has in mind is not a fear of nonexistence. To the contrary, as we shall see, an understanding of death as simply a state of nonbeing is for him not the problem but part of the solution. To see Epicurus's point we have to recognize that for many people in the ancient world, religion was not a source of comfort and hope, but fear. Since we live in a post-Freudian world where the view that religious belief is fueled by wish-fulfillment is widespread, it is hard to grasp how frightening were ancient stories about the gods and the afterlife. A great illustration of this fear is found in a speech attributed to a man named Cephalus in Plato's *Republic*: "When someone thinks his end is near, he becomes frightened and concerned about things he didn't fear before. It's then that the stories we're told about Hades, about how people who've been unjust here must pay the penalty there—stories he used to make fun of—twist his soul this way and that for fear that they're true."[2] What Epicurus wants to do is banish such fears by helping humans see that these "tales" are false. Death is the end of a person's existence, and nothing can harm someone who does not exist. Rather than fearing that death will end a person's existence, Epicurus thinks a rational person will be glad that this is the case.

Epicurean metaphysics. To banish the fear of what might happen after death, Epicurus thinks we must have the right view of reality, and he finds that view in the atomism of Democritus, discussed in chapter two. On this view, everything that exists is made up of atoms, tiny bits of matter that have always existed and are indestructible. When we say that an object has come into existence or perished, what has really

---

[1]Epicurus, *Principal Doctrines* 11 and 12, in *Greek and Roman Philosophy After Aristotle*, ed. Jason Saunders (New York: Free Press, 1966), 54. Otherwise unidentified page numbers following ancient sources in this chapter are from this volume.

[2]Plato, *Republic* 330d-e, in *Plato: Complete Works*, ed. John M. Cooper and D. S. Hutchinson (Indianapolis: Hackett, 1997), 975 (all page numbers in citations of Plato throughout this chapter are from this volume).

happened is that a group of atoms has combined in a particular way into a cluster or that such a cluster has been dissolved. Ordinary objects—tables and chairs, human beings and animals—come and go, but the atoms remain. The atoms interact in a basically mechanical way, colliding as they fall through space, forming the clusters we call ordinary things by virtue of the shapes of the atoms, which allow them to link together in various ways.

The perceived qualities of ordinary objects are all explained by the properties of the underlying atoms. Experience itself is a causal process, in which the objects we are experiencing constantly shed a thin film of atoms; what we call a sensation is simply a causal encounter with that film. The atoms themselves do not have properties such as color and taste, those properties modern philosophers will call "secondary properties." Rather, those secondary properties are explained by the properties that the atoms do have. For example, such qualities as "tasting sweet" or "tasting bitter" are the product of the shapes of atoms. Objects composed of smooth atoms are agreeable (sweet), while objects composed of rough and angular atoms taste harsh and bitter.

One should not think that Epicurus (or Democritus, whom he is following) was an atheist. He does not deny the existence of a god or gods; if there are such beings they too will be material in nature. What he does maintain is that the natural world is not controlled by gods; it is the product of mindless, mechanical causes. It was not created by the gods, and the gods have no interest in what happens on earth and no power to control events. There is no grand purpose or teleology in nature. Humans can live in peace without concern for pleasing the gods or fear of displeasing them.

Interestingly, Epicurus does not quite embrace a fully mechanistic picture of everything. In his account of the atoms' interaction, he posits a certain element of randomness. The atoms occasionally "swerve" as they plunge through space rather than follow a strictly straight path. Lucretius and other followers of Epicurus exploit these "swerves" to maintain that human beings, though composed of atoms, are not strictly determined to act as they do, but have some freedom of action. It is important to Epicurus that people are responsible agents who can make wise decisions, since he wants to urge them to live ethically. What is not clear, however, is how a random "swerve" can explain a free choice. An action that comes about through chance seems no more something a human can be responsible for than one that happens through necessity.

It is easy to see why Epicurus should hold that death is the end of a human person's existence. He holds that a human being, including the human soul, is just a collection of atoms, like everything else. Even mental states, according to Epicurus, are composed of very light, fine, and quickly moving atoms. When the atoms that make up a person are no longer connected in the right way, the person ceases to be, and the atoms eventually disperse. For Epicurus this means we should not fear death. Death is nothing to us, for nothing can harm us when we do not exist. It is as unreasonable to fear what will happen after death as it would be to fear what happened to one before birth.

Epicurus's account of knowledge. Democritus had defended atomism on the basis of reason, even though he recognized that it went contrary to our experience of the natural world. Aristotle had in turn criticized atomism because it did not make sense of our experience. Epicurus tries to defend atomism, but he wants to do so on empirical grounds. One might say that he wants to arrive at conclusions similar to Democritus, but base those conclusions on an epistemology more like Aristotle's.

Defending any kind of metaphysical view had become more problematic, because of the growth of Skepticism, a philosophy I will discuss later in this chapter. The Skeptics argued that there was no principled way to tell when our experience gave us truth. Or, to put the same point in another way, they argued that we could know appearances but could not know when appearances corresponded to reality. The Skeptics asked any "dogmatist," who defended some metaphysical view, to explain by what "criterion" one could tell which experiences gave us truth and which did not.

As we shall see later in this chapter, the Stoics tried to supply such a criterion. However, Epicurus tries to solve the problem by denying any such criterion is necessary. He claims that we must begin by trusting our senses, since if we do not we will wind up as complete skeptics, and, unlike the Skeptics themselves, he does not see such a position as one that offers peace and tranquility. Epicurus does not think Skepticism can be coherently argued for, since we have to know some things in order to have premises for arguments.

When asked by the Skeptics which of our sense experiences are trust-worthy, Epicurus claims that they all are. The obvious problem with this is that our experiences sometimes seem to conflict with each other. The stick on the beach appears straight, but when we place it in the water it appears bent. So is the stick bent or straight? Epicurus argues that it is both. For Epicurus perception is simply the reception of "films" of atoms that are continually shed by objects. The film shed by the atoms of the stick in the water are bent by the water, and thus our perception of the stick in the water is truthful, just as our perception of the stick on the beach is truthful. The difficulty with this reply is that it does not appear to give us knowledge of objects themselves but only how they appear to us. We have accurate knowledge of the "films" shed by objects, but not about the objects themselves.

Epicurean ethics. The goal of philosophy for Epicurus is to help us live "the good life," or to obtain what Aristotle called happiness. For Epicurus the good life is characterized by what the Greeks called *ataraxia*, a life of tranquility and peace, with as little pain and trouble as is possible.

Since Epicurus thinks that all knowledge comes from experience, our understanding of the good and the bad must do so as well. He claims that we immediately know from our experience that pleasure is good and pain is bad. His theory of value, then, is a form of "hedonism," from *hēdonē*, the Greek word for pleasure. Aristotle had admitted that pleasure plays an important role in a happy life, but Epicurus simply identifies the goal of human life as obtaining pleasure and avoiding pain. As a result of this hedonism, the adjective *epicurean* in contemporary English refers to a person who is dedicated to sensual pleasure, particularly the pleasures of fine food and drink. However, this linguistic fact gives a misleading picture of Epicurus's own thought. His own account of a life devoted to obtaining pleasure and avoiding pain turns out to be surprisingly moderate. One could even call Epicurus's advice on living an endorsement of an ascetic lifestyle.

Epicurus thinks that the wisest way of obtaining pleasure and limiting pain is to live a life of moderation, especially with regard to sensuous pleasures associated with the body. When we eat rich foods or drink large amounts of alcohol, we may gain pleasure in the short run, but in the long run such practices cost more than they are worth. It is not that the pleasures derived from such actions are bad, for all pleasure as such is good. Rather, the problem is that a person who is devoted to sensual indulgences finds that it is difficult or even impossible continually to satisfy such desires, and thus the person who commits to such a lifestyle is doomed to frustration. The person who is always seeking more money, more fame, more expensive food and wine, or anything else will always be dissatisfied. The wise person learns to be content with simple food and drink, and takes satisfaction in simple pleasures, such as those linked to friendship. A person who wants only simple food and drink is much more likely to be able to be satisfied, and avoid the pains of unsatisfied longing. Paradoxically, Epicurus was no "epicurean" in the modern English sense of the word.

Epicurus recommended that his followers avoid entanglements with other people except for friends, but he realizes that this is not completely possible. The state plays an important role in protecting individuals from others who might want to inflict pain. The origin of justice is just the desire for happiness that people have, the desire to gain pleasure and avoid pain. There is no natural or metaphysical basis for justice. Rather, the origin of justice can be found in the agreements people make with each other to avoid hurting others in exchange for freedom from being hurt by those others. There is no absolute justice, since the agreements made by different groups of people in different times and places are different.

STOICISM

As a philosophical movement, Stoicism was founded by Zeno of Citium (334–262 BC). Zeno was reputed to philosophize on "the porch" (*stoa* in Greek), and thus his followers were called Stoics, and the philosophy eventually became known as Stoicism. Stoicism was developed by thinkers in Athens such as Cleanthes (303–233 BC) and Aristo of Chios, whose dates are somewhat vague but was also a third-century philosopher. Cleanthes may be best known today for his *Hymn to Zeus*, which St. Paul quotes from in his speech in Athens recorded in Acts 17. Aristo (spelled sometimes Ariston) is a somewhat atypical Stoic who eschewed metaphysical speculation and blended Stoic ideas with those of the Cynics, who flouted social conventions. Stoicism flourished throughout the Roman Empire, though it was never a mass movement and had its greatest following among the elite, perhaps reaching its high points in the writings of Cicero (106–43 BC), Seneca (4 BC–AD 65), Epictetus (AD 60–117), and the Roman emperor Marcus Aurelius (AD 121–180).

Like so much of ancient philosophy after Socrates, the Stoics were inspired by Plato's teacher, particularly by the way Socrates faced his death with serenity. Like the Epicureans (and just about everyone in the Hellenistic period) the Stoics wanted to find "the good life." However, they rejected the idea that happiness could be equated with pleasure, and instead sought to follow the Socratic idea that true happiness is found through wisdom, which leads to virtue. The person who has wisdom and lives in accordance with reason will be virtuous. Such a person is able to govern his emotions, and it is through control of the emotions that happiness is to be had.

Stoic metaphysics. The metaphysical picture of the world accepted by the Stoics seems paradoxical today and is somewhat difficult for contemporary people to grasp. We tend to think of materialism as an antireligious view, and that a religious person will believe in a higher, nonphysical reality. The Stoics were materialists of a sort and rejected the idea of nonphysical entities. At the same time, however, Stoicism is a profoundly religious view of the world that sees God as present throughout all of reality. To understand how the Stoics combined these two ideas we must grasp their complex view of matter as well as their view of God.

The Stoics did not deny the meaningfulness of the incorporeal altogether. There are aspects of reality that are important that are not physical things, such as "meaning, void, place, and time."[3] What they deny is that these "incorporeals" are objects that have causal powers. Real entities or objects are material things that do have causal powers. This materialism is not a form of reductionism, since they reject the doctrine of atomism. Matter is continuously divisible, and the ordinary objects we interact with are realities, not just collections of atoms. Although all objects are indeed material, their nature is determined not just by the stuff of which they are composed, but by the form or structure they possess. (Here the influence of Aristotle's "hylomorphism" is obvious.) Matter has both a passive and active character, and it is the form that provides the active character.

The active, ordering character of matter is in turn identified with God. God is conceived as the principle of order and rationality that pervades and governs all of reality. Although the Stoics do not say that God is completely impersonal, they do think of God as present throughout the natural world. The Stoics often describe God as Reason (*logos* in Greek), and thus see all of reality as shaped by Reason. The Stoics describe the

---

[3]See Saunders, *Greek and Roman Philosophy*, 82.

orderly patterns that the natural world displays as "natural law," and see the natural law as the result of God's presence throughout the world. All that happens in the world is in accord with natural law, and all is thus shaped by Reason. For the Stoics, this means that all that happens is to be attributed to Providence. What happens is both necessary and ultimately for the best.

Drawing on the views of Heraclitus about the primal stuff of the universe, the Stoics often speak of God as Fire. Fire seems to be the finest and most active form of matter, and thus it is appropriate to see it as divine. It is possible that some Stoic thinkers did not think of the ultimate principle to be literal fire, but perhaps used the concept more metaphorically. However, no less a thinker than Augustine affirmed that the Stoics "thought that fire, i.e., one of the four material elements of which this visible world is composed, was both animate and intelligent, the maker of the world and all things contained in it, that it was in fact God."[4] The Stoics thought not only that fire gave birth to the universe but also that the world will end with a fiery, purifying conflagration, giving rise to a new world in an endless cycle.

Although the Stoics see God as immanent within the natural order, they are not simply pantheists. God in some way transcends the natural order that he pervades. Clear evidence for this is given by the fact that the Stoics made a distinction between the world and the universe. The latter consists of the world plus God and the void.

The Stoic view of human persons is similar to their view of God and the world. God can be seen as the "soul" of the world and the world as God's body. Human persons, like the natural world in general, are material beings, but they have a soul, a fiery substance that permeates the body. The soul is a material substance, one that is transmitted from parents to children in a physical way. However, it is composed of the higher and purer form of matter that we call spirit (Greek *pneuma*, literally "breath"), and it gives the human person the power to move and

---

[4]Saunders, *Greek and Roman Philosophy*, 85.

to perceive the world through the senses. Above all, the soul is the seat of Reason. As such the soul partakes of God's own nature, and the Stoics were fond of saying that every human has a spark of the divine within.

Stoic ethics. With one exception (to be discussed shortly) Stoic metaphysics emphasized that everything that happens does so by necessity. God's providential will rules all things inexorably. It is pointless to regret what cannot be otherwise and could not have been different. The key to human happiness, which the Stoics saw as the proper goal of human life, is then to recognize and accept what is inevitable. The proper state of mind of a person who accepts that what happens is both necessary and rational is a kind of resignation or acceptance that the Stoics called *apatheia*. *Apatheia* is not really identical with apathy in the modern sense, but is closer to what we might call serenity or peace. Humans cannot ultimately control what happens to them, so they must accept the role they have been given.

The late Stoic Epictetus uses the image of a play here powerfully to express the Stoic view of how to live. "Remember that you are an actor in a play, and the Playwright chooses the manner of it: if he wants it short, it is short; if long, it is long. If he wants you to act a poor man you must act the part with all your powers; and so if your part be a cripple or a magistrate or a plain man."[5] God is in control and decides all such matters; the task of the human is to accept the role he or she has been given and play the part well.

The heart of this Stoic ethic is a conviction that unhappiness is something we can control. We cannot control what happens to us, but we can control our attitude toward what happens to us. Epictetus summarizes this clearly and succinctly: "Ask not that events should happen as you will, but let your will be that events should happen as they do, and you shall have peace."[6] Many things happen to a person that are commonly thought to be bad, but nothing can be bad to you if you do not believe that it is bad. This

---

[5]*Manual of Epictetus*, no. 17, p. 137.
[6]*Manual of Epictetus*, no. 8, p. 135.

Stoic view that happiness is not found in external circumstances but solely in your reactions to those circumstances is beautifully symbolized by the fact that the two most famous late Stoic thinkers were Epictetus and Marcus Aurelius. Epictetus was born a slave, while Marcus Aurelius was a Roman emperor (perhaps the last really effective and conscientious emperor). If a person accepts his or her role then that person can be happy, whether the role be that of a slave or the emperor of the Mediterranean world.

This general perspective was common to all Stoics, but there were some differences at least in emphasis in how this should be understood. Marcus Aurelius emphasized resignation as the heart of the Stoic attitude toward the world. Epictetus often strikes a more positive tone, emphasizing gratitude as the proper response of the person to the divine providence that shapes all that happens.

There is one grave problem linked to the Stoic doctrine that everything happens in accordance with divine Reason. If all that happens does so in accordance with necessity, how is it possible for a person to control his or her response to events? If I am part of the world, and the world is governed by necessity, then how can I freely choose my attitude toward what happens to me? I am not free to choose the "part" I play in life, but why should we not think that my "part" includes my attitude toward life? The Stoics fiercely maintained that humans do have the freedom to control their own attitudes, but it was difficult for them to explain *how* it is possible for humans to have this freedom. The problem is twofold really: (1) How is it possible for humans to have any freedom at all in a world governed by natural law? (2) If humans do have freedom, why is that freedom limited to control over their own beliefs and attitudes?

Perhaps the second question can be answered by affirming that people do have free will with respect to their choices as well as their inner attitudes, but that what they cannot consistently control is the outcome of those choices. The really difficult question is the first one. Given the metaphysical picture of a world ruled by necessity, where does the "island of freedom" that is found in human choices arise?

A second difficulty that is internal to Stoic ethics is that their indifference to what happens externally is hard to reconcile with the love a person naturally has for family and friends. If one has a friend or family member one loves, and that person dies or suffers some grave misfortune, it is difficult not to be upset. Even worse, one might think that a failure to be upset would itself express lack of love. Can I really love a person and not grieve when the person is taken from me by death? Don't we think that grief is actually a good thing in such circumstances? The Stoics tried to answer this problem by affirming that one can "kiss your child or your wife" (and thus have genuine affection for them), but still be undisturbed if death takes them.[7] In a similar way, it is permissible to have preferences for what might happen, and thus desire one outcome rather than another, but these preferences must always be tempered by and accompanied by a stronger desire: "to keep my will in harmony with nature."[8]

The Stoics affirmed that Socrates was right in affirming that happiness is to be found in virtue, and that virtue is in turn wisdom, a life in accordance with reason. They made an energetic effort to see how the claim Socrates made in his *Apology* could be true: "A good man cannot be harmed either in life or in death, and his affairs are not neglected by the gods."[9]

Stoic views of justice. In earlier Greek philosophy, it is difficult to find a clear doctrine that our ethical duties extend beyond our friends, family, and city to all humans universally. Probably the closest approximation to such a view is found in Socrates, who affirms that it is never right to harm anyone, even a person who is your enemy. However, for Aristotle, our ethical duties stem from our place in a social network, and naturally vary depending on whether a person is a friend, family member, or stranger. Stoicism, however, with its doctrine that all human persons have a spark of divinity within, because all possess reason, clearly

---

[7]*Manual of Epictetus*, no. 3, p. 134.
[8]*Manual of Epictetus*, no. 4, p. 134.
[9]Plato, *Apology* 41 c-d, p. 36.

developed the idea that all humans have moral duties, and that we have moral duties that extend to all humans. This idea also has profound implications for how humans should relate to other humans.

Justice on this view is not simply a product of a particular society or state; nor is it the result of a social contract or agreement. Rather, justice is grounded in the natural law, and the natural law is something that all humans can grasp by virtue of the presence of the Logos within them. Although the Stoics did not reject the idea of loyalty to one's own city or community, they embraced a "cosmopolitan" view that implies that all humans are part of one grand community, the human community. Stoic views about justice and natural law had tremendous influence on later thought in the West, particularly among medieval Christian thinkers.

Stoic epistemology. It is obvious that Stoic views of the good life depend on the truth of their metaphysical vision. The truth of that vision, however, was anything but obvious to non-Stoics of the period. Stoic philosophers therefore did not neglect epistemology, since they needed to defend their claims about nature and God from rival views, such as those of the Epicureans, not to mention the Skeptics, whom I will shortly discuss. Some of the early Stoics in fact made important contributions to logic. The Stoics in fact used the term *logic* broadly to encompass what we would today term logic, but also epistemology generally.

The Stoics generally held that there were three types of intellectual states concerned with truth: knowledge, comprehension, and opinion. Opinion is a "weak and false assent," while knowledge is "sure, certain, and unchangeable by argument."[10] The idea of comprehension is less clear, but it is regarded as something intermediate between knowledge and opinion. Perhaps we should say that comprehension involves an awareness of truth but one that has not yet attained to certainty and stability, a kind of fallible state that can become knowledge when it has become secure.

---

[10]See Saunders, *Greek and Roman Philosophy*, 69.

The challenge faced by the Stoics is the "problem of the criterion." The Stoics admit that some of our experiences are unreliable and deceptive. How can we recognize the ones that are reliable, that can give us comprehension, and (eventually) even knowledge? The Stoics say that some of our experiences are "irresistible." They involve a "grasping" or "apprehending" of an object as it really is; we can recognize these experiences because they bring with them a kind of conviction that compels our assent.

Obviously, this does not seem very persuasive as it stands, since people often feel compelled to believe that things are a certain way when they are not. The Stoic responds to this difficulty by saying that you cannot assume that just anyone is capable of recognizing irresistible experiences. Rather, one must pay attention to the judgments of the "wise man," the sage, who is the expert on such matters. The sage is the person who is experienced, reflective, and has a comprehensive view that allows that person reliably to recognize experiences that give us truth. Undoubtedly the Stoics think of the sage here simply as best exemplified by the Stoic philosopher himself.

Skeptics (and others) may object that this account is circular. We must trust the sage to tell us what experiences are truthful. But how can we recognize the sage? One might think that it is by seeing that the sage can recognize which experiences are truthful. But that seems to require that we can recognize truthful experiences independently of the sage. For otherwise how could we tell the true sage from someone who just claims to be a sage? Surely we cannot say that Stoicism is true simply because it is claimed to be true by Stoic philosophers.

There may be ways for the Stoic to avoid this type of criticism. Perhaps there is some way of recognizing the sage that is independent of the sage's ability to decide which experiences are truth-conducive. We might, for example, recognize the sage by the moral character or serenity the sage possesses.

Another response that seems implicit in Stoic thinking is an appeal to what contemporary philosophers call "holism." It is true that some of our experiences are unreliable. However, it could not be the case that all of our experiences are unreliable, for we only recognize some as unreliable because they conflict with others that we judge reliable. Perhaps the sage is a person who has a "comprehensive" knowledge of experience, and uses that comprehensive perspective to judge which experiences are reliable. The idea is perhaps similar to Aristotle's epistemology in some ways, in that raw experience must be complemented by critical reflection on that experience in order to arrive at knowledge. The Stoics seem to embrace a mixed view in which reason and sense experience work together to give us knowledge.

SKEPTICISM

Skepticism in the ancient world was not just a stance of individual thinkers but, like Stoicism and Epicureanism, a philosophical "school" or tradition. (I will spell *Skepticism* with an initial capital letter when I mean to refer to this school, and speak of the Skeptic when I wish to refer to members of this school. Thus I will distinguish skepticism as a set of doctrines from Skepticism.) Skepticism as a set of views in the ancient world was viewed by its proponents quite differently from the way skepticism has often been viewed in the modern period. First of all, it is important to see that the Greek word *skeptikoi*, from which the name of the movement is taken, does not mean "skeptic" in the modern sense, but "seeker" or "inquirer," and this is how the Skeptics perceived themselves. They were seekers, unhappy with the "dogmatism" that they thought characterized other philosophies.

Many modern philosophers have seen skepticism as a problem; one of the great tasks of philosophy is to refute the skeptic. For the ancient Skeptics, however, skepticism is not a problem to be overcome but a solution. Skepticism, like Stoicism and Epicureanism, is an answer to the problem of how life should be lived. The Skeptics taught that their philosophy was a way of attaining happiness, which they defined, in a way similar to the Epicureans, as centered on *ataraxia*, or peace of mind.

As the Skeptics saw things, the contradictions between the teachings of the various philosophies led not only to uncertainty but also to anxiety as people fruitlessly attempted to decide what is true. The solution is to recognize and accept the limits of human reason, and thereby attain calmness and mental peace.

Ancient Skepticism is generally regarded as stemming from the thought of Pyrrho of Elis (ca. 365–270 BC), and skepticism in general is sometimes called "Pyrrhonism" in his honor. We actually do not have a great amount of reliable information about Pyrrho's views. Nothing written by him has survived, and indeed it is possible he wrote nothing. Nevertheless, Pyrrho attracted followers, at least locally, and his views, or views that were attributed to him, were defended by later thinkers.

A distinct tradition of Skepticism arose somewhat later in Plato's Academy, at the time when the Academy was led by Arcesilaus (ca. 316–241 BC). It may seem strange that the institution Plato founded would be associated with skepticism, but later members of the Academy tended to reject Plato's distinctive metaphysical doctrines and return to the inconclusive dialectical thinking of Socrates. A later prominent thinker from the Academy who is often regarded as a Skeptic is Carneades (215–129 BC), who differs from most Skeptics in that he developed a sophisticated account of probability, which he recognized as important in shaping beliefs even if we lack knowledge. As a result of its presence in the Academy, ancient Skepticism is also sometimes called the Academic philosophy.

Most of what we know about Skepticism is derived from Sextus Empiricus, who wrote the *Outlines of Pyrrhonism* around AD 200. Although Sextus obviously wrote several centuries after the origins of Skepticism, his work is generally thought to be a reliable summation of the main ideas of the Skeptics, and it provides a clear portrait of the motivation for being a Skeptic.

There is a difficulty faced by any Skeptic who wishes to formulate Skepticism as a positive doctrine. The Skeptic wants to deny that humans can gain knowledge. However, if Skepticism is true, then how can we know it is true? How can we know that it is not possible to gain knowledge? If the Skeptic says that we know that it is impossible to know anything, it appears he has contradicted himself. It looks as if dogmatic assertion of Skepticism would undermine Skepticism.

The ancient Skeptics were very aware of this problem and used ingenious strategies to avoid it. The primary one is that rather than simply advancing Skepticism as a positive doctrine to be believed, they sought to achieve a suspension of judgment, a state of mind the Greeks called *epochē*. This was not easy to do. Unlike some modern philosophers, who sometimes see skepticism as the "default" mode and thus work hard to motivate belief, the Skeptics thought that belief was the natural and easy state of mind. To achieve this condition of *epochē* one had to work hard. The primary technique was to practice what the Skeptics called equipollence, which basically meant constructing or considering equally powerful arguments for and against any view one was tempted to form a belief about. When one considered the arguments for the opposing views, the temptation to believe one proposition rather than its negation was lessened or removed.

The Skeptics also appealed to a standard set of considerations that they thought would tend to produce uncertainty and undermine the various sources of what others claimed to be knowledge. These set arguments were called the "modes" or "tropes" by Skeptics, and Sextus himself says there are ten of them. Many of these are intended to induce doubt about the reliability of the senses as giving us true information about the world. The first, for example, calls attention to the differences between the senses of various animals.[11] Presumably, frogs, beetles, grasshoppers, cows, dogs, and humans all have ways of sensing the world, but it seems clear that the world must appear very differently to a frog than it would to a human being. Why should one think that the way the world appears to one species corresponds to the way the world really is?

---

[11]Sextus, chap. 14, p. 160.

Other tropes cited by Sextus appeal to the differences in perception between different human beings, as well as the differences between the different senses possessed by one human. Appealing to a stock example, Sextus argues that perception also differs based on distance and location. A tower may appear round from a distance but quadrangular when seen up close. The reliability of perception is also cast into question by dreams and hallucinations. When one is having a dream, the objects perceived in the dream often seem quite real, and yet later are judged to be phantoms.

As part of the argument Sextus cites the "problem of the criterion" mentioned earlier in discussions of Stoicism and Epicureanism. The Skeptics thought that no one accepts all sensory impressions as giving true information; rather, we pass judgment on them, affirming some as veridical and some as illusory. It appears, however, that such judgments require a criterion by which the veridical impressions are recognized. But how can we know that the criterion itself is valid? Either the criterion will be dogmatically asserted without proof, or else it would seem yet another criterion will be needed, a criterion that enables us to judge which criterion is valid. However, if we provide a criterion for the valid criterion, the same problem recurs; either the criterion is put forward dogmatically or else it will require yet another criterion, and so on to infinity. As we have seen, the Epicureans responded to this argument by claiming that all impressions are reliable, while the Stoics said that we must trust the judgment of the wise sage.

It is important to recognize that Skepticism is not completely skeptical. In particular, the Skeptics did not deny that we have experiences in which the world appears to us in some particular way, and they do not deny that we have knowledge of how things appear. Their skepticism is not about appearances but about whether the way things appear corresponds to the way things really are. Sextus is very clear about this: "Our doubt does not concern the appearance itself but the account given of that appearance."[12]

---

[12]Sextus, chap. 10, p. 156.

One might think that Skepticism would be a paralyzing philosophy, for it would seem that our actions are always premised on our beliefs about the world. However, the Skeptics claimed that this is not the case. It is possible to act in the world while avoiding dogmatic beliefs by "going with the appearances." Even though we do not know that the way things appear is the way they are, we are still justified in acting on the basis of appearances, if we do so in a nondogmatic way. The Skeptics knew that life requires action, though they recommended a quiet life by and large. When people must act, they should be guided by four things: (1) The guidance of nature, since sensations and thoughts happen whether we wish them to or not. (2) The "constraint of the passions," which is the way in which some natural desires (such as hunger) more or less drive us to certain actions. (3) Accepted laws and customs; the Skeptics urged people simply to conform to the practices of those around them, particularly with respect to such issues as religious piety. In other words, we don't know the truth about the gods so we might as well go along with local practices rather than causing offense and trouble for ourselves. (4) Instruction of the arts; we can rely on practical experience to help us decide what is useful with respect to those practices we engage in.

The fact that the Skeptics believed that peace of mind and serenity could be found in Skepticism is impressive testimony to the anxiety and distress caused by an inability to know the truth about important matters. Ultimately, however, we can rightly wonder whether it is possible simply to give up the quest for this kind of knowledge. Even the Skeptics acknowledged that this was very difficult. An even more troubling question is whether a person with no convictions about important issues in fact would obtain serenity and peace. Skepticism seems to be a philosophy that encourages conformism and "going with the flow." Perhaps if I never know for sure, I should just "do as the Romans do" when I am in Rome. However, it is hard to see how Skepticism could provide a basis for questioning gross injustice in one's society or even attempting to remediate widespread ignorance. If we ultimately cannot know, why should we even try?

NEOPLATONISM

The philosophy that we call Neoplatonism stems from Plotinus (ca. AD 204–270), who was born and educated in Alexandria, then one of the great centers of learning and culture in the ancient world, but moved to Rome when he was around forty years old and established his own school of philosophy. Plotinus did not call his philosophy "Neoplatonism," but saw himself as restating Plato's great ideas and thus simply as a follower of Plato. However, scholars today are nearly unanimous in judging that Plotinus's development and rearrangement of Platonic ideas represents an original and novel philosophical view. Plotinus wrote fifty-four works, which were arranged and published after his death by his student Porphyry. Porphyry arranged the fifty-four pieces in six groups of nine, and they became known as the *Enneads*, the Greek word for the number nine.

Neoplatonism presents us with one of the great speculative metaphysical visions from the history of philosophy. Nevertheless, it would be a mistake to think of Plotinus simply as putting forward a set of philosophical doctrines. We have seen that philosophy throughout the Hellenistic period has an intensely practical character; all the important philosophers attempt to tell humans what the good life is and how to achieve it. This is even more true for Plotinus, whose philosophy takes on a decidedly religious character. For him rational, philosophical thought is not an end in itself, but a pathway toward mystical union with God. That experience of union with God goes beyond what language can describe or even what can be thought.

Although Plotinus drew ideas from Aristotle, the Pythagoreans, and the Stoics, he is most clearly indebted to Plato. In various dialogues, as we saw in chapter four, Plato develops a number of different metaphysical ideas. The idea that there are "Forms" that are immaterial but nevertheless more real than the physical world is present in many dialogues. In the *Timaeus* he describes the craftsman or "Demiurge" who fashioned the natural world, using the Forms as patterns. In the *Republic* Plato describes the "Form of the Good," which he describes as the source of both reality and knowledge of reality. In the *Parmenides* Plato speaks of a supreme Form that is there called "the One," while in the *Symposium* the supreme reality is called the Form of Beauty. Plato also teaches a soul-body dualism in which the soul preexists its time in the body and earnestly longs to be reunited with its spiritual home. We will see all of these ideas in Plotinus's thought, though usually put together in new and original ways.

Plotinus's metaphysical vision: *The divine beings and emanation.* Plotinus presents us with a metaphysical vision that is hierarchical in nature. At the top of the hierarchy are a series of divine beings. The supreme reality is God, which Plotinus usually calls the One. For Plotinus, the One is completely and utterly transcendent, unlike anything we experience in the changing physical world. We cannot really say what God is like, but only what he is not like. The idea that God can only be described negatively later becomes hugely important in Christian theology, especially in the Eastern Orthodox churches, and is today usually called "apophatic theology." The One cannot change, is not in space or time, and is indeed beyond being described by any positive predicate. In fact one really cannot even think of the One as "a being" at all.[13] "That First is no being but precedent to all Being."[14] Although Plotinus endeavors to describe the One, and argues for its reality, since all the things that exist must stem from one source, in the end all our language will be recognized as inadequate by the person who succeeds in gaining a mystical awareness of God.

Although the One is the source of all reality, Plotinus does not think of the One as a personal being who chooses to create the world. To

---

[13]Plotinus, *Enneads* 5.1.10, p. 259.
[14]Plotinus, *Enneads* 6.9.3, p. 264.

think of God as a person would be to think of God as a particular entity, and we have already seen that God is too transcendent to be a being. Besides that worry, personal action would be a kind of change that is impossible for the One. Therefore, for Plotinus, the One does not really do anything to produce a world. Rather, God simply is what God is. The relation between God and other reality is described through the metaphor of *emanation*. Just as rays of light come streaming from the sun, Plotinus thinks that reality in some way radiates or emanates from the One, an inexhaustible source of Being that is never emptied or even diminished by the process.

The One does not directly give rise to the physical world; one might say that it is too exalted to have contact with that world. Instead the One gives rise to a Divine Being that Plotinus calls (in Greek) *Nous*, variously translated as Mind or Intellect or the Intellectual Principle. I shall call this reality the Divine Mind. This Mind is described as "the Image of the One," in language curiously similar to that of the New Testament, which describes Christ several times as the "image of God" (see, e.g., 1 Cor 11:7; 2 Cor 4:4; Col 1:15). Plotinus himself makes no reference to Christianity in his writings, so there is no direct evidence that he was borrowing from Christian thinking. Clearly, the Pauline epistles in which this language occurs antedate Plotinus, so there is no influence in the other direction either. Still, the parallel is striking enough to make one wonder if these Platonic ideas were in some way circulating in the intellectual world that early Christianity inhabited, or perhaps had come into that Platonic world from Christian sources.

The Divine Mind solves one problem that Plato had bequeathed his followers: Where and how do the Forms exist? Plotinus thinks of the Forms as Ideas in the Divine Mind. Like Aristotle's God, the Divine Mind is pure thought contemplating itself. Like the One, the Divine Mind is timeless, as it must be if it encompasses the timeless Forms. However, the process of emanation continues. Just as the Divine Mind emanates from the One, so the Divine Mind in turn gives rise to a

Cosmic Soul or World Soul, who has many of the characteristics of Plato's Demiurge. The World Soul fashions the physical universe, using its knowledge of the Forms gained from its vision of the Divine Mind, and it governs the physical universe. Unlike the Divine Mind, the World Soul is in time and is capable of consecutive reasoning and action.

So Plotinus posits three divine beings, a kind of trinity: the One, the Divine Mind, and the World Soul. Again, one might wonder whether at this point some knowledge of Christian ideas may have somehow come into Plotinus's purview, perhaps indirectly, but there is no evidence for this. It is certain that many of Plotinus's ideas about God were known by Christian thinkers from the fourth and fifth centuries on and influenced the development of Christian theology. However, Plotinus's trinity differs from the Christian Trinity in several important respects. The most important difference is the hierarchical nature of the three divine beings for Plotinus. Although orthodox Christian formulations of the Trinity also speak of Christ as coming from the Father in an eternal process ("begotten not made"), and also of the Spirit as coming from the Father (and the Son, in the Western church), the three persons of the Christian Trinity are nevertheless equal in power and worth. There is no metaphysical difference in status between the persons of the Trinity, as there is for Plotinus, for whom the World Soul is temporal, but the other two divine realities are timeless. There is also an asymmetry between the One and the Divine Mind, in that the latter is a Being, albeit a timeless and transcendent reality, while the One is absolutely beyond any description.

The soul and the world. In Plotinus's hierarchy of being, the physical world, including human beings, falls below the One, the Divine Mind, and the World Soul. Nevertheless, the human persons who inhabit that physical world have a nonphysical soul that emanates from the World Soul, and because of this, human beings participate in the World Soul. One might say that a human person, because of the soul, has one foot in the divine world and one in the physical. Humans have a kind of middle status between the divine world, which is the world of Being, and the natural physical world, which is a world of Becoming.

It is in its view of human persons that Neoplatonism most strongly breaks with Stoicism and Epicureanism. Both of these two philosophies adopt forms of materialism, but Plotinus sees materialism as a grave error, and does not think progress can be made in philosophy or on the road to union with God until one recognizes that there are immaterial realities that in fact are more perfect and real than physical things. A person cannot begin to understand the universe until that person recognizes that within each of us is a spiritual soul that has the capacity to relate to the higher immaterial world.

The physical world itself is a further emanation from the world of Being. It exhibits traces of the divine, found in the beauty of nature as well as the natural order that shows that the world is governed by Reason. (Here Stoic influence may be seen.) However, with each emanation, we go further away from what is truly real and what is truly good. Matter is, we might say, the final stage of emanation, where Being begins to shade over into Nonbeing, the realm of shadows and darkness.

The process of emanation thus functions to explain evil for Plotinus. In some sense evil must be necessary, since it stems from emanation, itself a necessary process. As things stream away from their ultimate source in the One, and as they seek individuality, there is a necessary loss of fullness. For Neoplatonism, it is an axiom that being and value (as well as beauty) are ultimately one. To have less being is to be less good and less beautiful, but as things emanate away from the One they necessarily lose being.

Plotinus's account of what we might call the "fall" of the human soul is somewhat paradoxical. On the one hand, the whole process is, as we have seen, necessary, a part of the emanation by which the One gives rise to things that are inevitably less than itself. Particularly when discussing the Divine Mind and the World Soul, there is no hint of evil. However, when the human soul becomes attached to matter by acquiring a body, Plotinus speaks of guilt, though he also describes the process as necessary, "a voluntary descent which is also involuntary."[15] He says that all degeneration is involuntary, but something like sin occurs when the soul "submits" to its inferior status.[16]

The degrading character of matter leaves its stamp on the human soul. Although the soul retains a capacity to reascend to the One, its besetting problem is that it is dragged down by its attachment to the body and bodily desires. Here the influence of Plato's *Phaedo*, in which the true philosopher is described as always preparing for death by ascetic practices that free the soul from bodily yearnings, is apparent.

The soul's reascent to the One. Corresponding to the emanation of all things from the One, there is a natural desire to reunite with the source of all things. This natural longing in a human soul can be rekindled by an encounter with physical beauty. (Here the influence of Plato's *Symposium* as well as the *Phaedrus* is evident. In both of these dialogues erotic love and physical beauty can be the spark that reminds the soul of its true home.) Physical beauty, both in the natural world and in art, shows symmetry, unity, and harmony. It is a reflection of the "ideal form" that the material world is patterned after, and when we love the beauty we see in the world, our souls sense our own affinity with the source of beauty.[17]

Our recognition and love of beauty ought to move us toward contemplating Beauty itself, the Form that is not itself a material thing. This prepares us to recognize higher types of beauty, which are nonphysical, the beauty of the virtues, for example. Only the soul that is properly formed can recognize the beauty of Justice and of Moral Wisdom, which are "beautiful beyond the beauty of Evening and of Dawn."[18] For Plotinus, the moral virtues are valuable not just in themselves, but even more so because they advance us on our journey back to the One. The soul that loves these beauties is a soul that is purified and thus prepared

---

[15]Plotinus, *Enneads* 4.8.5, p. 245.
[16]Plotinus, *Enneads* 4.8.5, p. 245.
[17]Plotinus, *Enneads* 1.6.3, pp. 232-33.
[18]Plotinus, *Enneads* 1.6.4, pp. 234.

for the higher delights that are made possible when we turn away from the degrading desires and lusts of the body. "If a man has been immersed in filth or daubed with mud, his native comeliness disappears and all that is seen is the foul stuff besmearing him; his ugly condition is due to alien matter that has encrusted him, and if he is to win back his grace it must be his business to scour and purify himself and make himself what he was."[19] This physical picture is an allegory of how the soul must purify itself morally by acquiring the virtues, all of which involve the soul acquiring independence of bodily desires, as Plotinus sees things.[20]

The soul that is thus purified "is all Idea and Reason," and can thus contemplate the Divine Mind.[21] The virtues themselves are penultimate, however. We want to become good and beautiful because this brings us closer to God: for the soul "becoming a good and beautiful thing is its becoming like to God, for from the Divine comes all the Beauty and all the Good in beings."[22] The human soul longs for and moves toward true Beauty and the Good by means of the World Soul and the Divine Mind. "We must ascend again towards the Good, the desired of every Soul."[23] Even the desire for the Good is a good, more precious than any finite good.[24]

This path to the One is not the only way for the soul to reascend to God, according to Plotinus. There are actually three distinct paths, corresponding to different types of personal temperaments: the path of the musician, the path of the lover, and the path of the metaphysician.[25] The

---

[19]Plotinus, *Enneads* 1.6.5, p. 235.

[20]Plotinus, *Enneads* 1.6.6, p. 236.

[21]Plotinus, *Enneads* 1.6.6, p. 236.

[22]Plotinus, *Enneads* 1.6.6, p. 236.

[23]Plotinus, *Enneads* 1.6.7, p. 236.

[24]Some readers here may well be reminded of C. S. Lewis's *Surprised by Joy.* Lewis describes the experience of Joy as one in which he had a desire for something that could never be really experienced fully, something that gives him intimations of a good beyond the finite goods of this life. Although he could never possess this good, he says that the desire for it was itself sweeter than any other good. Thus he longed for the experience of Joy, even though the experiences left him with a deep and unfulfilled yearning.

[25]Plotinus, *Enneads* 1.3.1-1.3.3, pp. 271-72.

musically inclined person must enjoy the "tone, rhythm, and design in things of sense," and be led by these to the invisible Harmony that underlies this musical beauty.[26] The "born lover" must learn, through mental discipline, the "One Principle" underlying earthly beauty, a Principle that is not itself physical. The "metaphysician," who already lives in the realm of thought, has less need of disengagement from the lower types of desires; such an individual "needs only a guide."[27] Plotinus here makes a distinction between "natural virtues," which seem similar to Aristotle's virtues made possible by practical reason, and the higher virtues that require philosophical wisdom, which calls to mind the happiness Aristotle says can be achieved by theoretical contemplation.[28]

Nevertheless, the highest goal for Plotinus is not even philosophical wisdom or understanding. An awareness of the One "takes us beyond knowing; there may be no wandering from unity; knowing and knowable must all be left aside; every object of thought, even the highest, we must pass by."[29] The highest joy of human life is an experience of the One that is ineffable, "not to be told, not to be written."[30] Since this experience cannot be described, Plotinus does not really describe it; it is something we can, as it were, "point to" and direct people toward. He merely claims that those who enjoy it are supremely blissful. It is our true destiny.

Plotinus accepts the Platonic doctrine that the human soul preexists its fall into the body and can, after death, be reborn in a new body. However, the emphasis is not on the doctrine of transmigration of souls, but on the soul's ultimate destiny. The experience of union with the One that can be enjoyed in this life is merely a foretaste of the immortal bliss that is possible when the soul finally escapes from the body altogether. The good life for Plotinus is life with God.

---

[26]Plotinus, *Enneads* 1.3.1, p. 272.
[27]Plotinus, *Enneads* 1.3.3, p. 272.
[28]Plotinus, *Enneads* 1.3.6, pp. 274-75.
[29]Plotinus, *Enneads* 6.9.4, p. 265.
[30]Plotinus, *Enneads* 6.9.4, p. 265.

Early Christian Thought Through Augustine

Since the philosophers of the ancient world consistently maintained a focus on the good life and how it should be lived, often basing their accounts on their views about the gods and the world and developing explicit ethical stances based on those views, it is not surprising that early Christians would encounter philosophy and have to deal with it. The views of the philosophers often were perceived as providing competitors to Christian views of life and how it should be lived, and thus some kind of response was needed. However, as we shall see, some of the early Christians quickly saw possibilities for using philosophy in positive ways, not only to do apologetics but also to develop their theology and solve theological problems. This use of philosophy was almost never completely uncritical, but it certainly meant that the encounter between Greek philosophy and Christianity would be one that was not merely combative.

PHILO OF ALEXANDRIA AND JEWISH
ENCOUNTERS WITH GREEK THOUGHT

Actually, the earliest encounter between biblical faith and Greek philosophy preceded Christianity. Philo of Alexandria was born around 20 BC and died around AD 50. He was thus roughly a contemporary of Jesus, and it is possible (though by no means certain) that his writings were known to St. Paul and to the author of the Fourth Gospel. Though some earlier Jewish thinkers had attempted to relate Jewish teachings to Greek philosophy, Philo is the first figure to do so in an extensive way. Philo's writings were actually more influential for Christianity than for Judaism, which at the time had a very practical orientation with little use for metaphysical speculation. Hence it is not too surprising that many of Philo's writings were preserved by Christians. There is actually a tradition that Philo met with St. Peter when Philo led a delegation to Rome to meet with the emperor, though most contemporary historians are skeptical about this claim.

Philo attempted a synthesis of Jewish thought as found in the Hebrew Bible and Greek philosophy. The major philosophical influence was Plato, though Stoic influence can also be clearly seen. There are many similarities to Plotinus, though Plotinus was a later figure and thus cannot have influenced Philo. Philo claimed that biblical thought embodied the highest wisdom, a wisdom that the philosophers sought and approximated. Philo went so far as to claim that the Greek philosophers were inspired by Moses, a view that historians find doubtful. However, despite this veneration of the Bible, his interpretation of biblical passages was clearly often powerfully shaped by Greek philosophy. He tended to deal with apparent inconsistencies by reading biblical passages as myths that express metaphysical truths in figurative language, and he often gives allegorical interpretations of the Bible that allow him to fit biblical teachings to philosophical views.

A good example of this is provided by Philo's treatment of creation. He attempts to reconcile the story of Genesis with the kind of account given by Plato in the *Timaeus*. However, for Philo creation does not mean the world had an actual beginning; God's creation is an "eternal creation" that happens continuously. The biblical account of the fall is understood as a myth that symbolically expresses the truth about human evil, since sin is understood as linked to embodiment in a way clearly reminiscent of Plotinus.

Philo's most important contribution lies in the use he made of the Greek concept of the *Logos*. This Greek term can mean "reason," "word," and "principle," and it was, as we saw in the last chapter, an important element in Stoic theology. Philo probably took the concept from the Stoics, who thought of the Logos as a divine principle of rationality immanent in the world, but he adds features inspired by Plato that resemble the later ideas of Plotinus, who postulated a "Divine Mind" as the rational principle that emanates from the One. Just as Plotinus sees the One as completely transcendent, beyond all meaningful human language, so Philo sees God as utterly transcendent. The Logos is the creative expression of God and it is the Logos who is actually responsible for the creation of the world. Just as is the case for Plotinus's Divine Mind, the Logos produces the Eternal Forms, which in turn are responsible for the existence of the natural world. It is not clear, however, that Philo's Logos is a fully personal being. The Logos seems more like a Stoic principle of order and rationality.

PHILOSOPHY IN THE NEW TESTAMENT

Before treating some early Christian thinkers who grapple with philosophy, I shall briefly discuss some passages from the New Testament that already seem to embody an awareness of philosophy. It is hard not to hear echoes of Philo (and the Stoic/Platonic background of Philo's thought) when the Fourth Gospel tells us that "in the beginning was the Logos [the Word]" (Jn 1:1) and goes on to identify the Logos with the agent of creation: "Through him all things were made; without him nothing was made that has been made" (Jn 1:3). What is most unlike Philo, however, is the way this Divine Logos is identified with the human Jesus of Nazareth. "The Word became flesh and made his dwelling among us" (Jn 1:14).

Probably the most dramatic New Testament reference to philosophy is found in Acts 17, a narrative that situates St. Paul in Athens itself. Several hundred years after Socrates, Athens was still full of people who loved philosophy; the author of Acts (traditionally Luke) wryly comments that "all the Athenians and the foreigners who lived there spent their time doing nothing but talking about and listening to the latest ideas" (Acts 17:21). While waiting for some of his companions to arrive, Paul meets some of the Epicurean and Stoic philosophers in the city, who invite him to the Areopagus to explain his own teachings. Paul begins with a critique of pagan views of the gods, a critique he doubtless knew would be received sympathetically both by the Epicureans and Stoics: "The God who made the world and everything in it is the Lord of heaven and earth and does not live in temples built by human hands. And he is not served by human hands, as if he needed anything" (Acts 17:24-25). Paul continues by striking a cosmopolitan theme, dear to the hearts of Stoics who liked to see themselves as "citizens of the world": "From one man he made all the nations, that they should inhabit the whole earth" (Acts 17:26). It is clear that Paul is making a strong effort to establish common ground with his audience, as he next displays considerable knowledge of pagan culture by two quotations. The source of the first ("In him we live and move and have our being") is not completely certain, but it is often thought to be from Epimenides of Crete, a shadowy figure from around 600 BC. Paul describes the author of the second quotation ("We are his offspring") as "one of your own poets" (Acts 17:28 LB). Most scholars believe this quotation is taken from Aratus, a Stoic philosopher who dates from around 300 BC, though it could also be read as a loose paraphrase of a line from Cleanthes's famous *Hymn to Zeus.*

So far Paul probably had his audience on his side, but the situation changed when he went on to affirm that God would "judge the world with justice by the man he has appointed," and that God had given assurance of this by raising this man from the dead (Acts 17:31). The resurrection of the dead seemed preposterous to rational Greek ears, so it is not surprising that Paul's claim led to mockery from some in the audience. Nevertheless, Luke adds that others wanted to hear more about these things, and even that "some of the people became followers of Paul and believed" (Acts 17:34).

Paul also touches on philosophical themes in several places in his letter to the Colossians. In Colossians 1:15 he describes Christ as the "image of the invisible God, the firstborn over all creation," language that is strikingly like that used by Platonists (and later by Plotinus) to characterize the Divine Mind that is produced by the One. Christ is given a striking metaphysical role. Christ is the one by whom "all things were created" (Col 1:16). The phrase "all things" here includes not only the natural, visible world but also the invisible "thrones or powers or rulers or authorities" that are not part of the physical world. Christ not only created the world, but also continues to preserve it: "In him all things hold together" (Col 1:17).

Paul also famously warns the Colossians against "hollow and deceptive philosophy" in Colossians 2:8. Some have taken this to be a command to steer clear of philosophy in general, but in context it does not appear that Paul is issuing a general warning about philosophy, but only about the kind of philosophy that "depends on human tradition and the elemental spiritual forces of this world" rather than on Christ. In this passage Paul is clearly urging the Colossians to avoid a legalistic philosophy that focuses on placating "powers and authorities" (Col 2:15) of the world rather than on Christ. Paul's concluding admonition is "Do not let anyone judge you by what you eat or drink, or with regard to a religious festival, a New Moon celebration or a Sabbath day" (Col 2:16). All these things are "shadows," but the reality is Christ, in whom "all the fullness of the Deity lives in bodily form" (Col 2:9). The "powers and authorities" have been disarmed by Christ and do not have to be feared. What Paul is really arguing, then, is not that philosophy per se is to be avoided, but rather that Christians should be wary of the kind of philosophy that ignores Christ, "in whom are hidden all the treasures of wisdom and knowledge" (Col 2:3). Paul seems to be issuing a manifesto for a Christ-centered philosophy, since it is through Christ that one can obtain "the full riches of complete understanding" (Col 2:2).

Paul develops a similar theme in 1 Corinthians 1:18-30. Here he emphasizes that God's wisdom appears to the unbelieving world to be foolishness. God has "made foolish the wisdom of the world" (1 Cor 1:20), and the message of the cross carries with it the possibility of offense: "Jews demand signs and Greeks look for wisdom, but we preach Christ crucified: a stumbling block to Jews and foolishness to Gentiles" (1 Cor 1:22-23). Nevertheless, Paul is not conceding that the gospel is in reality foolish. On the contrary, Christ is the "power of God and the wisdom of God" (1 Cor 1:24). Since Jesus is in fact for us "wisdom from God" (1 Cor 1:30), Paul is really saying that the wisdom that the philosopher seeks is to be found in Christ.

TERTULLIAN

These passages from St. Paul express what might be called a "perspectival" view of human reason. There is no "neutral" or "objective" account of wisdom, but rather what is accepted as true wisdom depends on one's perspective. The pagan world had sought wisdom in human reason, but Paul insists that true wisdom is found in God's revelation in Christ, which turns natural human thinking upside down. These themes from Paul provide the inspiration for the thinking of the first important Christian thinker to write in Latin, Tertullian (ca. 160–220), who lived in Carthage in North Africa, and had been well-educated in rhetoric, literature, and law. Tertullian wrote several uncompromising defenses of Christianity against pagan attacks, insisting that there is little of value for Christians to be found in philosophical thought. Tertullian asked rhetorically,

> What indeed has Athens to do with Jerusalem? What concord is there between the Academy and the Church? What between heretics and Christians? Our instruction comes from "the porch of Solomon," who had himself taught that "the Lord should be sought in simplicity of heart." Away with all attempts to produce a mottled Christianity of Stoic, Platonic, and dialectic composition! We want no curious disputation

after possessing Christ Jesus, no inquisition after enjoying the gospel! With our faith, we desire no further belief.[1]

Tertullian is often interpreted as an irrational fideist who rejected reason altogether, and is frequently regarded as the source of the phrase *Credo quia absurdum* ("I believe what is absurd," sometimes altered to "I believe because it is absurd"). However, this quotation is actually not to be found in Tertullian's extant writings. The quotation is, however, in the spirit of Tertullian, who often glories in paradoxical overstatement. For example, he says that the resurrection of Christ is "certain because it is impossible." However, when one looks at such passages in context it is clear that Tertullian is not rejecting reason altogether, but emphasizing the ways in which human thinking that is not shaped by revelation goes awry. In fact, he emphasizes the rationality of God throughout his writings. Human thinking is distorted by human sinfulness, and thus if we are to gain true wisdom we must receive it from God, who thus makes it possible for ordinary, uneducated people to gain an understanding of salvation.

Tertullian is also important for his development of what is called a "traducian" view of the human soul as something that comes into being through physical procreation. (The rival and more common Christian view is "creationism," which maintains that God himself creates each new human soul.) One of the strengths of traducianism for those who believe in original sin is that it gives a plausible explanation for how sin is transmitted, since it hard to see why God would create new souls tainted with Adam's fall. Despite his professed rejection of philosophy, Tertullian was probably influenced in his development of traducianism by Stoic metaphysical materialistic views, which viewed even the human soul as physical in character. Some recent Christian theologians, impressed by the dependence of the human mind on the brain, have

---

[1]Tertullian, *On the Prescription of Heretics* 7, in *The Ante-Nicene Fathers*, ed. Alexander Roberts and James Donaldson (1885–1887; repr., Grand Rapids: Eerdmans, 1986), 3:246. Otherwise unidentified volume and page numbers following ancient sources in this chapter are from *The Ante-Nicene Fathers*.

moved in a traducian direction by viewing the human soul as something that is either identical to the brain or as something that emerges from the brain.[2]

Tertullian was a fiery and combative person who always showed a tendency to extremism. For example, he rejected the idea that widows and widowers could remarry, and seems to have thought that some sins could not be forgiven. In the end, his rigorism and extremism led him into a sect called Montanism, which combined this kind of legalism with an acceptance of contemporary prophecies not sanctioned by the church. His late writings then contain polemics against the mainstream Catholic Church itself, from which he had very likely been excommunicated.

JUSTIN MARTYR AND CLEMENT OF ALEXANDRIA

Early Christian thinkers found themselves dealing with Greek philosophy for two main reasons. The first, already mentioned, is that Christians found it necessary and valuable to mount defenses of Christian beliefs against the attacks of pagans, and they needed to understand Greek philosophical views in order to show the advantages of Christian faith over pagan rivals.

However, in the second and third centuries a movement generally called Gnosticism arose within the ranks of Christians. Gnosticism drew on biblical and Christian sources to arrive at views that eventually would be judged heterodox by the church, but it was not always clear to everyone involved in the controversies at the time what views were orthodox. The term *gnostic* comes from the Greek word *gnōsis*, the common term for knowledge. The Gnostics claimed to have a higher, "spiritual" kind of knowledge that was only available to the elite, and they often posited a hierarchy of higher spiritual beings, some of which had to be placated through various rituals and legalistic practices. Some

---

[2]See Nancey Murphy, "Non-reductive Physicalism: Philosophical Issues," in *Whatever Happened to the Soul? Scientific and Theological Portraits of Human Nature*, ed. Warren S. Brown, Nancey C. Murphy, and H. Newton Malony (Minneapolis: Fortress Press, 1997), 1-30, and William Hasker, *The Emergent Self* (Ithaca, NY: Cornell University Press, 1999).

early Christian thinkers would find philosophical concepts and arguments helpful in showing the differences between Gnostic views and those convictions that were rooted in the "deposit of faith" that had been bequeathed to the church by the apostles and other early Christians. Thus, at least for apologetic purposes, responding to attacks both by pagan critics and Gnostics, some Christian thinkers took a much more positive view of philosophy than Tertullian.

The earliest to do so was Justin Martyr, who was martyred around 165. In two apologetic works addressed to the emperor, Justin argued that Christianity provides a clear, accessible, and perfected form of the truth that had been dimly glimpsed by Plato and other Greek philosophers. Justin makes good use of the Logos principle, and connects the biblical theme of God as "unsayable" to Platonic views about the transcendence of the ultimate source of Being.

This type of approach was developed much more extensively by Clement of Alexandria (ca. 150–215). Alexandria at the time was a city of more than a million people that surpassed Athens as a center of culture and learning. It was also a city full of Gnostic teaching, home to Valentinus and Basilides, two leading Gnostic thinkers. Clement was born to pagan parents, perhaps in Athens, but moved to Alexandria after seeking wisdom from a number of teachers in Greece and Italy. As a learned and cultured man, the converted Clement was called on to teach catechism at a school of the church in Alexandria. Clement was not a highly systematic thinker; his most important work, the *Stromata* (*Miscellanies*), contains a vigorous defense of the value of philosophy, but he draws on various philosophical positions in an eclectic way. Clement argues that even if philosophy were useless and harmful, Christians would still need to know about it in order to refute it.[3] However, philosophy is far from useless. In fact, philosophy was part of God's plan in preparing the Greek world for the gospel.[4] It was a way

---

[3]Clement of Alexandria, *The Stromata* 1.2, 2:303.
[4]Clement of Alexandria, *The Stromata* 1.5, 2:305.

of preparing the Greeks for the coming of Christ, just as the Old Testament prepared the Jews for Christ's coming.

To be sure, one cannot be saved by philosophy alone; one needs Christ to be saved.[5] (Although Clement at times seems to imply that ultimately everyone will be saved by Christ's redemptive work.) True knowledge of God does require faith, because God is partially hidden to human reason.[6] Human philosophies can reach partial truths, but these philosophies must be assisted by faith. Faith is necessary not only because human finitude means God cannot be fully grasped through human reason but also because true knowledge of God requires moral purification. Faith is not mere opinion, but a trusting acceptance of God's own self-revelation that transforms the character of the individual. Such faith can lead to deeper understanding, and thus Christianity is the true philosophy.[7] Christians should not fear Greek philosophy, because it contains some truth and all truth comes from God.[8]

Clement had to flee Alexandria as the result of persecution and ended his life in Asia Minor (modern-day Turkey). However, before leaving he had taught Origen (though this is disputed by some), who eventually succeeded him in Alexandria and became perhaps the greatest of the early church thinkers prior to Augustine.

ORIGEN

Origen, who eventually succeeded Clement at the catechetical school in Alexandria, lived from about 185 to 254. His thinking is marked by boldness and originality, sometimes exploring views that later Christians have tended to reject. Origen, unlike Clement, was born to Christian parents. His father, who was a prominent and well-educated Roman citizen, was arrested and eventually executed for his Christian beliefs. The young Origen, full of passion, wanted to share his father's

---

[5]Clement of Alexandria, *The Stromata* 1.7, 2:308.
[6]Clement of Alexandria, *The Stromata* 2.2, 2:348.
[7]Clement of Alexandria, *The Stromata* 2.2, 2:348-49.
[8]Clement of Alexandria, *The Stromata* 6.10, 2:498.

fate, but was prevented from doing so when his mother hid his clothes, so that to join his father he would have had to appear naked in public! Persecutions of Christians were frequent in Origen's lifetime, and he himself barely survived many times, and spent much time encouraging and supporting those who were martyred. At the end of his life, after having been forced to leave Alexandria, Origen was himself tortured, but bravely refused to recant his faith.

Eusebius, an historian of the early church, and an admirer of Origen, tells us that Origen actually castrated himself, perhaps following the passage from Matthew 19:12, where Jesus speaks of some who have become eunuchs for the sake of the kingdom of heaven. Such an act would also have prevented any hint of scandal when Origen privately instructed female students. Eusebius is our only source for Origen's castration, and some have doubted this really happened, especially because Origen himself explicitly criticizes the practice of castration in his writings and rejects the idea that it is justified by Matthew 19:12.

Origen's fame as a theologian and defender of Christianity led to his making several trips at the invitation of notables in various places, including Rome, Palestine, and Arabia (actually modern-day Jordan). These trips caused trouble for Origen on his return to Alexandria. On one trip he was invited to preach by the local bishop, although Origen was merely a layperson, and the bishop of Alexandria found this outrageous. On a later trip a local bishop actually ordained Origen to be a priest. This also incensed the Alexandrian bishop, who considered this act to be a violation of his privileges and authority. As a result, for the last period of his life Origen had to leave Alexandria and open a new school in Caesarea in Palestine. As noted above, during a great time of persecution, he was arrested and tortured, but apparently not killed.

Origen's two greatest works are *Against Celsus*, an apologetic response to the most influential and powerful pagan critique of Christianity, and *On First Principles*, a more systematic work of theology that clearly draws on philosophical concepts and arguments. Like Clement (and Philo before him), Origen draws on Platonic themes in his work. There are, however, many original and speculative elements to his thought, some of which led some later Christians to question his orthodoxy.

In his account of creation, Origen affirms that the Genesis account teaches that the world did have a beginning in time, but he treats many elements of the narrative as "things that are to be spiritually understood," since it "comprehends matters of profounder significance than the mere historical narrative appears to indicate."[9] In general, Origen frequently gives allegorical interpretations of Scripture. Origen also gives a philosophical argument for the claim that the world had a beginning in time, claiming that God comprehends the world, but that it is not possible, even for God, to comprehend that which is infinite. "That which is altogether without any beginning cannot be at all comprehended."[10]

Plotinus had of course seen creation as an eternal process. Support for this view and an argument against the claim that the world had a beginning in time can be made on the grounds that creation in time would leave God nothing to do prior to creation, and that one cannot conceive of God as inactive, or goodness that does no good. Origen replies to this objection by speculatively proposing that our world is not the only world God has created. He thus supports a kind of "multiverse theory," similar in some ways to some contemporary theorists who hold that the Big Bang that began our universe will end in a "Big Crunch" that will give rise to yet another universe, and so on indefinitely. (The Stoics, it will be recalled, held a similar view.) Origen does not hold that these other universes exist simultaneously, but that "there were ages before our own, and there will be others after it."[11]

Almost alone among Christian thinkers, Origen also developed an account of the fall that included a doctrine of the preexistence of souls. This obviously reflects Platonic influence, though Origen attempted to defend the idea on biblical grounds. The root of his idea

[9]Origen, *On First Principles* 3.5.1, 4:341.
[10]Origen, *On First Principles* 3.5.2, 4:341.
[11]Origen, *On First Principles* 3.5.3, 4:342.

is that God originally created human souls as pure spirits, and that the original fall was a spiritual rebellion. This allows Origen to posit a kind of "karma" type view, in which the earthly conditions of humans as embodied are the result of their own free choices, and not simply the result of luck or fate.[12]

Origen also shows a tendency to universalism. Drawing on the scriptural teaching that, as a result of Christ's work, "all things shall be subjected to Him [the Father]," and thus that in the end "God may be all in all," Origen proposes that God's final victory will be complete.[13] The victory will not be won by force, however, but "by word, reason, and doctrine; by a call to a better course of things, by the best systems of training."[14] Origen insists that this must be possible for God, "for nothing is impossible to the Omnipotent, nor is anything incapable of restoration to its Creator."[15]

Origen also makes a distinction with respect to God's creation of humans between the "image of God" and the "likeness of God." Most Hebrew scholars regard this distinction as exegetically dubious today, but Origen exploited the idea to propose that, although humans were originally made in the image of God, and thus had from the beginning a special dignity, the "likeness of God" is something that is reserved for those who have learned to imitate God, and thus something that will be given to the elect at the end of time.[16] Though humans were created as good, they were still created incomplete, with possibilities to be realized. Salvation is not simply a restoration of what was present in the beginning, but the realization of a process that God had in mind all along, a process that that will take some time. This idea that God made humans less than fully perfect so as to allow them to embark on a process of "soul-making" has been influential on many contemporary theologians,

---

[12]Origen, *On First Principles* 3.5.5, 4:343.
[13]Origen, *On First Principles* 3.5.6, 4:343.
[14]Origen, *On First Principles* 3.5.8, 4:344.
[15]Origen, *On First Principles* 3.6.5, 4:346.
[16]Origen, *On First Principles* 3.6.1, 4:344.

especially for those who accept Darwinian accounts of human origin, since it seems obvious that on such accounts the first humans were far from perfect.

As an orthodox Christian thinker, Origen of course affirms the doctrine of the resurrection of the body, a view that fits poorly with Platonism. He does, however, emphasize the apostle Paul's teaching that the resurrected body will be a transformed "spiritual body," and that the matter of the world to come will generally be transformed from the materiality we currently know.[17] Quite properly, he affirms that our understanding of this kind of material body is quite limited, but he affirms the ability of God to create a kind of matter that will be fully responsive to spiritual governance and not subject to any kind of corruption.

THE CAPPADOCIAN FATHERS

Space does not permit a full treatment, but before going on to treat the towering figure of Augustine, some mention should be made of three important thinkers from Cappadocia, a region of what was then called Asia Minor, part of modern Turkey. Three important thinkers from this region shaped the theology and approach to philosophy of the Eastern (Orthodox) churches for many centuries. Basil of Caesarea (ca. 330–380), Gregory of Nazianzus (ca. 330–390), and Gregory of Nyssa (ca. 335–395) all contributed significantly to the development of Christian thought, especially with respect to the christological and trinitarian controversies, and the eventual victory of the Nicene Creed. The Cappadocians are today influential as providing inspiration for what is called "social trinitarianism," which takes seriously the claim that the persons of the Trinity, though one in essence, are distinct persons. Basil, in addition to being a theologian, was a remarkable practical pastor who organized monastic life and helped the church take on the tasks of helping the poor and treating the sick. His friend Gregory of Nazianzus was an accomplished poet as well as a thinker.

---

[17]Origen, *On First Principles* 3.6.5-9, 4:346-48.

Gregory of Nyssa combined an Aristotelian account of knowledge with a Neoplatonic metaphysic. Our natural knowledge is based on sense experience. However, since God cannot be known through the senses, God's essence cannot be grasped by humans through the intellect. We can know that God exists, and we can know something about the divine actions and powers. However, for humans God is not known through speculative thought but through mystical contemplation and devotion. No positive words are adequate to describe God, and the *via negativa*, or way of negation, becomes the key to philosophical theology. Our task is to become one with God, and this of course can only be accomplished through an act of grace on God's part.

AUGUSTINE

Aurelius Augustinus (354–430) was born to a pagan father and Christian mother in Tagaste in North Africa. His mother, Monica, was a huge influence on Augustine, and she took an active role in his life (she has even been called a busybody) until her death at the age of fifty-six in 387. Monica died happy that she had lived to see both her son and husband converted to Christian faith. Augustine's education began in Carthage in North Africa, and he became devoted to philosophy after reading Cicero. His initial commitments were not to Christianity, however, but to Manichaeism, a dualistic offspring of Gnosticism, which posited two divine beings, one evil and one good. Manichaeism appealed to Augustine because it seemed to explain the evil in the world, and because the sect claimed to base its teachings solely on reason with no appeal to faith. After nine years, however, Augustine began to see the shortcomings of Manichaeism, which had an intellectual explanation of evil but no real solution to the moral struggles Augustine himself faced. After his disillusionment with Manichaeism, Augustine was for a time attracted to Skepticism, or "the Academic philosophy."

As a young adult Augustine lived a life of sexual immorality, actually fathering a child by a mistress. In fact, the life of chastity demanded by

Christianity was a huge barrier to faith for Augustine. Even after he became intellectually convinced that Christianity was true, he was unable to commit himself to the church. In his autobiographical *Confessions*, a book that has had a profound influence on the whole of Western culture, Augustine recounts that he had prayed as a young man for deliverance from lust, but with a divided heart: "Give me chastity and continence, but not yet!"[18] After a period in Rome, Augustine secured a professorship in Milan, where the sermons of Bishop Ambrose made a striking impression on him. Two things about Ambrose were particularly impressive: the way in which he combined Neoplatonism with Christian faith, and the allegorical readings Ambrose gave to certain Old Testament passages, which had caused Augustine difficulty. Augustine began to see that Christianity had plausible answers to the problems raised by the Manichees.

Augustine's journey back to his mother's faith was facilitated by his own reading of "the Platonists" (very likely Plotinus and Porphyry), though it is not clear that Augustine ever read Plato's own writings. It is probably not right to say that Augustine became a Neoplatonist and then a Christian. Rather, it is closer to the truth that he was attracted to a Platonized Christianity partly because he was attracted to Neoplatonism. In any case the Platonic influences in Augustine's work are clear and evident, and he has been the inspiration for many Christian Platonists through the centuries, including such twentieth-century figures as C. S. Lewis. Although the influence of Platonism never disappeared in Augustine's thought, it is true that the Platonic strands seem much more prominent in his early writings.

Augustine's actual conversion is memorably recounted in the *Confessions*. In 386 he heard the voice of a child chanting *tolle lege, tolle lege* (take and read, take and read). Augustine interpreted the voice as a command of God to pick up the Scriptures and read. Picking up Paul's

---

[18]Augustine, *Confessions* 8.7, in Augustine, *Confessions*, trans. John Kenneth Ryan (Garden City, NY: Image, 1960), 194.

epistle to the Romans, he opened the book to Romans 13, and read Romans 13:13-14: "Not in carousing and drunkenness, not in sexual immorality and debauchery, not in dissension and jealousy. Rather, clothe yourselves with the Lord Jesus Christ, and do not think about how to gratify the desires of the flesh." Immediately, Augustine was suffused with a sense of conviction and certainty, not only that Christianity was true but also that he could live in the way Christian faith required.

Back in Africa, Augustine was ordained a priest and eventually became bishop of Hippo. Despite the labors of being a pastor and administrator, Augustine found time to write prolifically until his death in 430, with over one hundred works surviving. Beside the *Confessions*, his longer and more influential writings include the *City of God* and *On the Trinity*. However, many of Augustine's shorter writings are profoundly significant as well, and several will be discussed in the following sections.

Augustine's epistemology and response to the Skeptics. Many of Augustine's writings are not systematic in nature, but are occasioned by controversies or needs of the church at the time. Augustine makes no clear distinction between philosophy and theology, for example, and certainly does not organize his work by using standard philosophical categories. Nevertheless, it will be useful for a contemporary student of philosophy to think about Augustine's insights for all of the major areas of philosophy. I will therefore say something about Augustine's epistemology, metaphysics, and ethics, though I shall try to show how his work relates to problems and issues of his own day.

Augustine's views about knowledge and belief are highlighted in two of his works that embody a response to the Skeptics: *De beata vita* (On the good life) and *Contra academicos* (Against the Skeptics). It is good here to remember that the ancient Skeptics did not see "skepticism" as a problem in the manner of modern philosophers, but were drawn to Skepticism as a philosophy that could lead to a good life. The Skeptics saw their philosophy as one that made possible *ataraxia* (peace of mind).

It is fitting, then, that Augustine first engages the Skeptics on the basis of the value of knowing. The very word *skeptic* comes from the Greek word for "seeker." However, Augustine argues that someone who seeks must desire to find what he or she seeks. Valuing knowledge is necessary if one is to gain knowledge. A person who claims to seek knowledge but does not really wish to know is in a state of bad faith. We can see here the seeds of Augustine's view of faith and knowledge, memorably expressed in the phrase that one must "believe in order to understand." Faith is not believing without good reasons; it is the willingness to seek and receive the truth. Thus "faith is understanding's step, understanding is faith's reward."

Carneades, one of the leading Skeptical philosophers of the Academy, had argued that although knowledge was impossible, humans could achieve probability in their beliefs. Augustine argues, however, that if we possess probability we must possess knowledge as well. We cannot know that A is more probable than B unless we know something about both A and B. Even the Skeptic knows basic truths of logic, such as that some proposition p is either true or not true. Simply knowing that one is in doubt or that one might be mistaken is already to know something. I must at least know that I exist if I am doubting. (The idea that if I doubt I know that I exist anticipates Descartes's later "I think therefore I exist.")

How is this knowledge possible? Like a good Platonist, Augustine says it is made possible by our awareness of Universals, what Plato had called the Forms. All humans have a capacity to grasp basic truths of logic and ethics. In place of the Platonic theory of recollection and the myth of preexisting souls, Augustine posits a theory of divine illumination. The Universals that humans can grasp mirror the Divine Ideas in the mind of God. Since humans are made in God's image, they are given the capacity by the divine Logos to grasp something about these eternal truths. The Logos is the true light that "enlightens everyone who comes into the world."[19]

---

[19]See Jn 1:9. Some modern translations say that the true light that gives light to men was "coming into the world."

Augustine's views on knowledge thus give priority to the knowledge of what is universal and eternal, as is usual in Platonic thinking. However, Augustine does give a theory of sense perception that is less skeptical than that of Plato himself. Human sense perception is not a drag on the quest for knowledge, but a gift of God, adequate for human practical needs. The structure of the physical world reflects the Eternal Ideas, and thus our knowledge of the latter gives us some insight into the former as well. Something like this is already implicit in Plato's view that particular natural objects copy the Forms or participate in the Forms, but Augustine develops the idea by talking about the *rationes seminales* (rational seeds) that God has implanted in nature.

Augustine's metaphysic. Augustine's metaphysical thought, as well as further strands in his epistemological thought, are clearly displayed in Augustine's polemics against the Manichaeism that he himself had been an adherent of. The Manichees combined elements of a Gnostic doctrine of "emanations" (similar to Plotinus) with a dualistic metaphysic that resembled Persian Zoroastrianism. The Manichees believed that there are two divine eternal beings, one good and one evil, and that the universe (including human nature) was a battleground between these two principles. Like many of the Hellenistic philosophies (such as Stoicism), the Manichees combined all this with a basically materialistic view of the universe.

Manichaeism, like earlier Gnostic views, prided itself on having knowledge (*gnōsis*), and they denigrated Christians for relying on faith, which was understood by them as unjustified opinion, which is equivalent merely to hoping that something is true. Augustine rejects the view that faith is simply "hoping that" something is the case, and he also refuses to accept the idea that faith is merely an inferior form of cognition. Rather, as we saw in Augustine's response to the Skeptics, faith and reason work together harmoniously so as to help humans toward truth. Faith already shows some understanding, since it is a response to God's grace. This response of faith transforms the individual and makes possible a deeper understanding. Thus faith is indeed "understanding's step," and understanding is "faith's reward."

In some ways Augustine's whole philosophy is an expression of this view of faith and reason. In *Of True Religion*, the last work Augustine finished before becoming a priest, he further develops the kind of view of the relation between philosophy and Christian faith found in Clement and Origen. Just as the Old Testament was God's preparation of the Jewish people for the coming of Christ, so Greek philosophy was part of the providential preparation of the Greeks for the gospel. One could say that the major theme of the essay is that "Christ fulfilled Plato's hopes," in that Augustine argues that Christianity provides exactly what the great philosophers of Greece had been seeking. Philosophy by itself cannot achieve salvation, and the philosophers at best saw only dimly and partially some of God's truth. Nevertheless, Augustine was confident that if Plato were alive during his time, he would be a Christian, and the evidence for this is that many contemporary Platonists were converting. In his later years Augustine's dependence on Platonic thought receded and the Bible became more central to his thought, but it is nonetheless true that it was Neoplatonism that made it possible for Augustine to see how Christianity could be true.

First and foremost, Neoplatonism freed Augustine from the "commonsense materialism" he had absorbed as a Manichee, and gave him a conviction that the true and higher reality was nonphysical. Augustine's full response to Manichaeism focuses centrally on his understanding of God and creation. The Manichaean doctrine of two gods is philosophically untenable. Only one God is needed to account for the universe, and two beings with infinite power cannot possibly exist, as each would limit the other. God is the source of all being, and all being is fundamentally good. Evil is understood not as an opposite and equal principle to God, but simply as privation or loss of being. As we will see, Augustine has a healthy understanding of the way in which evil in humans stems from the will, but he nonetheless maintains that evil is not a positive substance, but a defect in what exists. This understanding of evil enabled Augustine to move decisively away from Manichaean dualism.

In Augustine's thought creation takes the place of Plotinian emanation. God's creation is not a necessary effusion of his being, but a free and sovereign act. Besides being free, God's creation is *ex nihilo*, out of nothing, rather than, as in Plato's *Timaeus*, a reworking of a preexistent material reality. Since matter is itself God's creation, Augustine maintains that matter itself is not bad or evil. It is true that it is bad to place more value on the material and visible than on the nonphysical and invisible. God is more important than God's creation. However, that creation is material is not in itself a bad thing. Thus Augustine moves away from the Platonic view that evil is the result of the immaterial soul's being embodied.

Creation for Augustine is also *ad extra*; that is, God creates the world not from his own nature but as something distinct from himself. (This is a view that is increasingly challenged by some contemporary theologians who have adopted "panentheism.") God is immanent in creation in the sense that it reflects his nature. He is present in all of the world in the sense that he is aware of it all and can act at any time and any place, but the creation must be clearly distinguished from the Creator.

Although Augustine clearly believes that creation involves the universe having a beginning, he does not limit God's creative activity to that beginning. God's creation activity continues, both in the sense that he maintains and conserves the world in existence, and in the sense that God's creative activity includes bringing into existence processes that continue over time.

God himself is eternal, not in the sense that he is an everlasting temporal being, but in the stronger sense that in God there is no change at all. Time is the "measure of change," but eternity is an unchanging realm with no movement. Many of the scriptural descriptions of God are thus accommodations to the limitations of the human mind, and do not describe

God as God understands himself. God's act is fundamentally one eternal decree, but the outcome of that decree is a sequential, temporal process, and so it is natural for us to think of God's actions as sequential.

Augustine's ethics. It is pointless and anachronistic to try to describe Augustine's ethics using the categories of modern ethics. He has much to say about right and wrong actions and also about God's law, but that does not make him a "deontologist" or "divine command theorist" in the modern sense. He has much to say about the virtues, but that does not make him a "virtue theorist." He has much to say about the consequences of our actions and the ends to which our lives should be directed, but that does not make him any kind of "consequentialist." Rather, it seems likely that Augustine saw all of these kinds of considerations as important.

We can begin with what is often called Augustine's "eudaimonism," from the Greek term for "happiness." As we have seen, Hellenistic thought in all its forms, from Epicureans to Neoplatonists, was intensely practical, concerned above all with the question as to how humans could achieve happiness and live the good life. Augustine shares a conviction with the Neoplatonists that humans are intended for happiness, and that their true happiness requires a relation to a higher spiritual reality, which of course for him is God. As he memorably says to God in the *Confessions,* "You have made us for yourself, and our heart is restless until it finds rest in you."[20] True happiness lies in knowing God. Though God can be known in this life, and thus blessedness is possible, a direct awareness of God (what is often called the "beatific vision") is only possible in eternity when humans have transcended their temporal condition.

The question of happiness for Augustine thus resolves into the question as to how God can be known. The answer to that question, of course, is that God is known when one commits to Christ in faith and in the hope of the resurrection. (This is of course for Augustine made possible by God's revelation and the church, which provides the sacraments,

---

[20]Augustine, *Confessions* 8.7, in Ryan, 43.

which are means of grace.) Knowing God cannot be divorced from the transformation of the person into someone who is godly, and thus is capable of knowing God. The key quality for Augustine turns out to be love, since God is himself love. It is love that makes it possible for us to live as God wills to fulfill God's law, a view Augustine memorably expresses in the epigram "Love and do what you will."

As we saw already, for Augustine, everything that exists is in some way good, since all being stems from God, and thus in some sense everything that exists is worthy of love. The problem for humans is that our love is disordered. Ontologically, there is a hierarchy of being, and a corresponding hierarchy of value. What is lower in the scale is not intrinsically bad, since everything is good that retains its structure and form and manifests the glory of God. However, it is bad to prefer what is lower to what is higher, and that is what humans do when they love sensual goods more than God. There is no fundamental conflict between spirit and the body, but there is a conflict when a person loves self more than God, and thus prefers to gratify bodily desires rather than submit to God's law. A human's loves can be ordered properly only when God is loved absolutely, as in the "first and greatest" biblical commandment: "Love the Lord your God with all your heart and with all your soul and with all your mind" (Mt 22:37). However, this requires the complete transformation of the person, something that can only be achieved by God's grace.

The Pelagian controversy. For roughly the last twenty years of his life, Augustine was involved in a dispute over the nature of original sin. Pelagius, a British monk, had argued that humans can only be responsible and blameworthy for sin if it is possible for them not to sin. He therefore argued that humans retain the ability to choose God freely, and thus cooperate with God's grace. Augustine argues decisively that this is a fundamental mistake. Human beings after Adam are sinners by nature and thus can do nothing to please God without divine assistance. The sin of Adam has been transmitted to all of his posterity, and without

God's grace humans will perish in their sins. The strength of Augustine's view is his uncompromising claim that salvation is solely due to God, and that human merit has no role in the story. The difficulty is that Augustine wants to insist that a human's sin is justly punished by God, and that later humans cannot rightly blame Adam for their sin and the deserved punishment that sin brings with it.

Augustine's critique of Pelagius leads him to a strong doctrine of predestination. All humans have sinned and deserve eternal punishment. However, to manifest God's grace and goodness God elects a group of people to receive his grace and thereby, through faith, to become holy and righteous. Interestingly, some of Augustine's opponents in this battle used Augustine's own early writings, in which he argued that a rational being can only be corrupted if the person's will consents to the corruption, as ammunition against him. Augustine holds strongly to divine predestination, but also wants to maintain human responsibility for sin. How the two are to be reconciled is a problem Augustine bequeaths to the later church.

Interestingly, Augustine's strong doctrine of original sin makes it difficult for him to formulate a clear view of the human soul. The traducian view of Tertullian, which makes the soul something transmitted through biological reproduction, would fit best with the Augustinian view that Adam's sin is transmitted to later humans. However, Augustine's Platonic leanings prevent him from viewing the soul as a material object. If one sees each human soul as something created by God, it is hard to see why God would endow each soul with the taint of sinfulness supposed to be inherited from Adam.

Augustine on politics and history. Although the Roman Empire had been in decline ever since the third century, many historians date the fall of Rome to AD 410, when the city was sacked by Visigoths. Although the last Roman emperor in the West was not deposed until 476, it was clear during Augustine's lifetime that Rome was no longer the ruler of the Mediterranean world. Not surprisingly, some pagan thinkers blamed the fall of Rome on the decline of pagan religions and the growth of Christianity. The emperor Constantine had officially designated Christianity a religion to be tolerated in 312, and Christianity became the official religion of the empire under Theodosius through a series of edicts between 381 and 392. Christianity was still far from being a majority religion, especially in the West, and it is easy to understand how pagans might have thought the demise of the empire to be connected to the undermining of the historic Roman ways of worship.

One of Augustine's major works, the *City of God*, is in part a response to such criticism. In this work Augustine develops what we would today call a "metanarrative," a description of the major outlines of human history and its meaning. Augustine's narrative is given structure by theological categories. History begins with creation and continues with the fall, but most of history consists of the outworking of God's redemptive plan, beginning with Israel and culminating in Christ and the church. History will culminate with God's final victory, when God will be "all in all."

In between the fall and that final redemption, history must be understood as the history of two distinct realms, the earthly City of Man and the heavenly City of God, one city rooted in love of self and the other grounded in love of God. The distinction between the two cities actually predates human history, and begins with the rebellion of some of the angels, who used their freedom to declare their independence from God. Throughout human history, the contrast between the two cities can be seen. Augustine argues that the earthly city, even when it opposes God, ultimately carries out God's will. God's final plan and victory cannot be thwarted, since God, through his omnipotence, can bring good out of evil, just as he brought salvation out of Christ's death.

The Christian church is the visible expression of the City of God at the present time, as in earlier times it had been expressed through the people of Israel. However, being a member of the church does not guarantee that a person is in fact a citizen of the City of God. The City of

God is at present an invisible reality, and only God knows finally who is part of his kingdom. The City of God will finally be fully established and last eternally; the City of Man will end.

Although the earthly city is founded on love of self and even enmity for God, God nonetheless uses it for his ends. Even earthly authorities hold their power by virtue of God's providential ordering. The purpose of the human state is the achievement of justice and peace. Of course human states do this very imperfectly, but because this is their rightful end, those who are part of the City of God can still be good citizens of earthly states, and can help those states to achieve their divine purposes.

Augustine goes so far as to argue that Christians can legitimately support war in some situations. Most early Christians seem to have thought that Christianity demanded a pacifistic commitment to non-violence, but Augustine believes that those entrusted by God with the authority to govern must seek justice and peace, even though this sometimes requires force. Though he does not develop a complete "just war theory," as did his medieval successors, Augustine lays down all the elements of such an account. For a war to be just, it must be fought for a just cause, such as to protect the innocent against aggression. A war is not just if it is fought merely to expand territory or gain riches. A just war must be fought with the right intentions, and declared by proper authorities. Conduct during the war is also subject to moral censure. No suffering in excess of that which is necessary to achieve the just ends of war is permitted, and a clear distinction should be made between combatants who can be killed and innocent noncombatants, who ought to be protected.

Augustine's account of history is noteworthy simply for the attention paid to history. Aristotle had argued that "poetry is more philosophical than history," in that philosophy is concerned with the universal and not the particular. Neoplatonism had even less use for the particulars of history. Many ancients, such as the Stoics, held a view of history as cyclical. In contrast August sees human history as having a beginning, an end, and a direction. The particular events that make up that history are not meaningless because they are the means whereby God accomplishes his great plan of salvation.

Augustine's significance. Augustine can be seen both as the last philosopher of the ancient world and also as providing the beginnings of medieval philosophy. It is difficult to overestimate the significance of his thought. He is revered as a saint and doctor of the church by both Catholic and Orthodox branches of Christianity. His influence on the Western church during medieval times was profound and extensive. Even thinkers such as Thomas Aquinas, who are more influenced by Aristotle than by Plato, constantly quote and defer to Augustine. However, Augustine is also a seminal figure in the Protestant Reformation, appealed to again and again by both Luther and Calvin. Even today Augustine's thinking about sin, love, politics, and many other issues are hugely influential, even on secular thinkers such as Hannah Arendt. Even his thinking about particular moral issues, such as lying, remain relevant.[21] His synthesis of Christianity and Platonism remains an attractive perspective for many.

---

[21]See, for example, Paul Griffiths's treatment of lying in *Lying: An Augustinian Theology of Duplicity* (2004; repr., Eugene, OR: Wipf and Stock, 2010).

Early Medieval Philosophy

THE FIVE CENTURIES AFTER the death of Augustine in 430 did not constitute a period in which philosophy flourished in the West. At Constantinople, the Byzantine Empire persisted until the Ottoman Turks conquered the city in 1453, and thus classical learning was preserved there. However, after the fall of Rome, there was a decline of learning in the West, due to barbarian invasions and political unrest. Monasteries and cathedral schools were places where learning was preserved, but it was a time of preservation rather than increase of knowledge. There was a renaissance of sorts at the time of Charlemagne, who became king of the Franks in 768 and was later crowned emperor by the pope, ruling a united Europe until his death in 814. Charlemagne established more schools and encouraged translations of Greek works into Latin. However, another period of cultural decline followed what has come to be called the "Carolingian Renaissance." Philosophical work began to flourish, however, during the eleventh and twelfth centuries, and by the thirteenth century, great universities began to appear in Western Europe. I shall try to tell the story of medieval philosophy up to about 1200 in this chapter, leaving the developments of the High Middle Ages to the next chapter.

It is characteristic of this period that no clear distinction is made between theology and philosophy. Of course this was not new, since the same could be said of Augustine, Origen, and other early Christian thinkers. For that matter, virtually all the classical Greek philosophers had something to say about God or the gods. During the early medieval period, a distinction was made between views that were defended simply by rational arguments and those that were defended as taught by an authoritative revelation. However, this distinction does not coincide neatly with one between theology and philosophy, since philosophical issues are addressed in Scripture and were sometimes settled primarily by appeal to authority, while theological issues were often addressed by appeal to rational arguments. In some ways this practice mirrors the situation found in contemporary Christian philosophy, in which hard-and-fast distinctions between philosophy and theology are also not present. Christian philosophers often debate and develop distinctively Christian doctrines and themes, such as the incarnation and the atonement, appealing to rational arguments and not simply to Scripture, but also feeling free to appeal to biblical teachings in attempting to develop philosophical accounts of such items as human nature.

PSEUDO-DIONYSIUS AND BOETHIUS

Two thinkers' works from the period shortly after Augustine had a profound influence on later Western thought. The first is a writer who identified himself as "Dionysius the Areopagite." This writer was believed during the Middle Ages to be a disciple of St. Paul dating from the famous speech in Athens recorded in Acts 17. It seems likely that medieval Christians gave these works great authority based on this attribution. Scholars today are virtually unanimous in holding that the writings do not date from the time of Paul but are likely from the late 400s, because of the clear reliance on and knowledge of Neoplatonism that "Dionysius" shows. The books are therefore generally described today as the work of "Pseudo-Dionysius," since the real author is unknown.

Pseudo-Dionysius was much read and commented on throughout the Middle Ages, and a translation of his works from Greek to Latin was done by John Scottus Eriugena, finished by 827. Eriugena, who will be discussed later in this chapter, also wrote a commentary on the works, and many medieval thinkers did likewise. Pseudo-Dionysius emphasizes the oneness of God and the transcendence of God. His book *Mystical Theology* emphasizes "negative theology," the "way of negation" or *via negativa*, in which God is described by denying that some term applies to him. This negative theology is indebted to Gregory of Nyssa and to the Neoplatonism that influenced Gregory in turn. We describe God best by "denying or removing all things that are." For example, God is not in time and does not have a body. In the end we know God best when we recognize that we do not know him, that he exceeds every human idea of him, and thus God is grasped in the "darkness of unknowing."

To be sure, Pseudo-Dionysius also affirms, in his book *The Divine Names*, that there are positive affirmations to be made about God. We can ascribe to God such general terms as *goodness* and *being* because God is the source of all goodness and being. However, when we ascribe these terms to God they must be qualified. God is not just Beauty or Goodness as we know them, but is rather superessential Beauty or Goodness, a kind of Goodness or Beauty that exceeds our comprehension. He is the source of goodness and being, but his goodness and being is not like anything we know. The way of negation thus gains a kind of priority.

Equally important during the early Middle Ages are the writings of Boethius, who lived from roughly 480 to 524. Boethius studied in Athens and later held a high position under Theodoric, the king of the Ostrogoths, though he was eventually executed by Theodoric for high treason. Besides writing several original works of philosophy, Boethius translated some of Aristotle's works into Latin, and thus transmitted some knowledge of at least Aristotle's logic to the West. However, he is best known for his work *The Consolations of Philosophy*, written while he was in prison awaiting execution.

Boethius gives definitions of some key terms that become standard in the Middle Ages. One is his account of a person as "an individual substance of a rational nature." Another is his famous definition of eternity as "the complete, simultaneous and perfect possession of everlasting life." With this definition Boethius implied that the concept of God as a personal, living being could be combined with the Platonic idea of eternity as an unchanging state, a view already developed in Augustine's *Confessions*.

Boethius uses this concept of eternity to try to resolve one of the most famous problems in the philosophy of religion, reconciling God's foreknowledge of human actions with human free will. In *The Consolations of Philosophy* Boethius first poses the problem. Human freedom, in the sense required for moral responsibility, seems to require that humans have alternative possibilities, since people are not held responsible for doing what they could not help doing. However, if God knows beforehand what a person will do, and if God is necessarily omniscient and cannot be mistaken, it is hard to see how a person can do anything else than what God foresees. Boethius first argues that merely knowing what a person will do does not causally necessitate the person to do a particular action, since we can observe a person who is acting freely without negating the freedom. He then argues that since God as eternal has no temporal before and after, it is false to say that God foreknows any human action. God simply knows—in his timeless, eternal mode of being—what a person will do, but for God this is not foreknowledge. Every moment of time is for God "present."

Boethius had a student named Cassiodorus (ca. 477–ca. 568), who also worked for Theodoric for a time. Cassiodorus is most important for his categorization of the seven "liberal arts." These were subdivided into the "trivium," which is composed of grammar, logic (or dialectic), and rhetoric, and the "quadrivium," which is composed of arithmetic, geometry, music, and astronomy. This way of organizing knowledge became important in the medieval university.

JOHN SCOTTUS ERIUGENA

The most noteworthy philosopher in the West between the time of Boethius and Anselm (who will be discussed shortly) is John Scottus

Eriugena (ca. 800–ca. 877). John signed one of his manuscripts "Eriugena," which means "son of Erin" or "native of Ireland," and the term "Scottus" (sometimes spelled "Scotus") in this period referred primarily to Ireland. I will henceforth refer to him as "Eriugena" to avoid confusion with the later medieval philosopher Duns Scotus. Eriugena was an Irish scholar who may or may not have been a monk, but clearly benefited from the learning that had been preserved in Irish monasteries. Indeed, it appears that a thorough knowledge of Greek was largely confined to the Irish in this period. In any case Eriugena had a remarkable knowledge of Greek and, after coming to the court of Charles the Bald, who was king of the area that is now France, translated the writings of Pseudo-Dionysius into Latin, as well as the writings of several other important Eastern thinkers, including Gregory of Nyssa. In addition to his knowledge of Greek, Eriugena was known for his original, bold speculations, and use of rational argument. (His opponents criticized him for relying too much on dialectic rather than appeals to Scripture.)

Building on the work of Pseudo-Dionysius and Gregory, Eriugena developed an original synthesis of Neoplatonism and Christianity. There is no doubt that Eriugena considered himself an orthodox Christian and did not intend to develop any heretical views. However, suspicion that his views implied some form of pantheism was widespread in the Middle Ages, and his doctrines were explicitly condemned by councils of the church in 855, 859, and 1050. Given Eriugena's belief that Pseudo-Dionysius was a disciple of St. Paul, it is likely that he assumed that these writings were more orthodox than is actually the case, and he gave them more authority than was warranted.

The charge of pantheism stems from Eriugena's view of creation. Under the influence of the Neoplatonism of Pseudo-Dionysius, Eriugena saw creation in terms of an eternal emanation, somewhat similar to Plotinus himself. The problem this poses is that it seems to imply that the created order originates out of God's very being rather than being created *ad extra*, as something outside of God, as Augustine had maintained. Like Plotinus, Eriugena also sees emanation as culminating in a correlative process in which everything returns to God. He links this process theologically with the concept of *theosis* or "divinization," an important part of the way the Eastern church understood salvation as involving a real union with God.

In his work *The Division of Nature*, Eriugena developed a fourfold categorization of reality. The term *nature* does not refer just to the created order, as it usually does today, but to the whole of reality, including God. Nature is divided into "nature that creates and is uncreated," "nature that is created and creates," "nature that is created and does not create," and "nature that neither creates nor is created." By the first Eriugena clearly means God. Nature that is created and creates refers to the Forms, which are the primordial causes of everything in the natural world we live in and experience, but also angels and other created beings that are incorporeal. Nature that "neither creates nor is created" refers, as one might think, to nonbeing, but for Eriugena, nonbeing still has a kind of reality, since God transcends being and is in a sense to be identified with nonbeing, understood as the alluring final cause to which everything ultimately returns.

As one might expect from a thinker influenced by Neoplatonism, Eriugena, like Gregory of Nyssa and other Eastern thinkers, emphasizes negative theology, as God transcends any positive concepts we can form of him. Eriugena goes so far as to say that God's infinity is such that God is incomprehensible even to himself! Though God in himself is beyond predication, the process that Eriugena calls "creation" (but is perhaps better described as emanation) involves the articulation or expression of God in "the Word," identical with the second person of the Trinity, which became incarnate in Jesus. The Word creates by first creating the Ideas or Forms, which are the causes of the objects in the created world.

Human beings occupy a kind of midpoint in this Neoplatonic hierarchy of being. They have a rational, nonmaterial soul, but they are connected in a mysterious way with the body, which allows them to be part of and relate to the natural world. For Eriugena, Christ's incarnation is part of the process by which everything will return to God. By taking on flesh, God can redeem even the natural world and bring all things back to himself. Here Eriugena seems to reflect the influence of Origen's universalism.

Given the suspicions of unorthodoxy, Eriugena's impact on medieval philosophy was not pervasive. However, a knowledge of his writings was preserved, and he had a significant influence on later mystical writers such as Meister Eckhart (1260–1327) and Nicholas of Cusa (1401–1464). In the nineteenth century, G. W. F. Hegel and his followers took particular interest in Eriugena, because they interpreted him as one of the fathers of monistic idealism. One element in his thought they found particularly congenial was Eriugena's use of dialectical assertions, particularly (though not exclusively) with respect to God. Eriugena taught that a true understanding of something may require predications that are apparently contradictory, though not actually so once the context or "mode" of speech was clarified. Hence, in one sense it may be true to say that God is "nothing" (in that God transcends the categories of being), but in another sense God is the highest reality. All this sounds somewhat like the "dialectical logic" that Hegel developed, which will be discussed in chapter nineteen.

ANSELM OF CANTERBURY

Saint Anselm (1033–1109) was born in what is now northern Italy, and educated in a Benedictine abbey in Normandy in present-day France. He was made archbishop of Canterbury, the head of the church in England, in 1093, but had contentious relations with both King William Rufus and his successor, Henry I, both Norman kings who wanted to exercise control over the English church themselves and were unwilling to allow popes or archbishops to stand in their way.

Anselm is traditionally and rightly seen as a philosopher in the tradition of Augustine. Like Augustine, he does not pretend to start from a neutral perspective but rather from a perspective of faith: "For I do not seek to understand in order to believe; I believe in order to understand. For I also believe that 'Unless I believe, I shall not understand.'"[1] Thus Anselm's motto could well be described as "faith seeking understanding." This should not be understood as if faith were some kind of inferior cognitive state that gets upgraded to or replaced by understanding. Faith is not mere belief, but a state in which one trusts and loves God, and Anselm sees this affective stance as one that makes a deeper understanding possible. Nor is the understanding that faith makes possible something that replaces faith; it is rather a state that faith continually nourishes and renews. However, to say that Anselm's philosophy is one that sees philosophical thinking as rooted in faith is not to say that such thinking has no value or relevance to the unbeliever. As we shall see, Anselm explicitly addresses some of his arguments to unbelievers.

Arguments for God's existence. In his *Monologion*, and also in his *Proslogion*, Anselm develops arguments for the existence of God. He opens the *Monologion* by claiming that most of the things we believe about God are things a person could become convinced of through reason alone.[2] The argument in the *Monologion* is long and complex, while the argument in the *Proslogion* is relatively short and, at least on the surface, easy to follow. I shall only discuss what I regard as the main argument in each book, although Anselm certainly gives multiple arguments for God in the *Monologion*, and has sometimes been read as providing more than one argument or at least the materials for more than one argument in the *Proslogion* as well. Despite the relative simplicity and brevity of the *Proslogion*, it is this work that has been most influential. Just about every subsequent Western philosopher has discussed Anselm's argument, either to endorse it as profound and sound, or to

---

[1] Anselm, *Proslogion* 1, in *Anselm: Basic Writings*, ed. and trans. Thomas Williams (Indianapolis: Hackett, 2007), p. 81 (all page numbers in citations of Anselm throughout this chapter are from this volume).
[2] Anselm, *Monologion* 1, p. 7.

reject it as logically unsound or even denounce it as a verbal trick. This argument from the *Proslogion* is now standardly described as the onto-logical argument (a name that Kant gave it), but in medieval times it was simply called Anselm's argument.

***The argument of the* Monologion.** The argument of the *Monologion* is clearly inspired by Platonic ways of thinking. Whenever we say that various things have some quality in various degrees, we are committed to saying that it is the quality itself that they have. Thus, if two cities are just to different degrees it is because they participate in justice, and hence there must be such a thing as justice, not merely things that are just. Similarly, things that are good must be good because of goodness. Goodness itself, since it is the source of all goodness, must be supremely good. What is supremely good must be good in itself, not just good because of something else.

Anselm thus argues that if there are degrees of goodness or excel-lence, then there must be some supreme standard of goodness that provides the measure, and this standard is itself real. Must the reality that provides the standard be just one thing? Anselm argues that it must. Suppose that there are several things that are supremely good. If they are all supremely good, they must be equal in goodness. But what makes them equal? Whatever it is, it must either be identical with the things that are supremely good or else different from them. If it is iden-tical with those things, then they must be identical with each other and therefore are not really different things at all. However, if what makes them good is something distinct from these things, then it is that thing that is responsible for their goodness, and that thing is itself the highest and greatest reality. So there must ultimately be just one highest reality, which Anselm identifies with God. Anselm then goes on to argue that this highest reality must possess many of the attributes traditionally ascribed to God.

***The ontological argument from the* Proslogion.** As noted before, the argument given in the *Proslogion* (in chapter 2) is much briefer and apparently simpler. Anselm begins by quoting the psalmist: "The fool has said in his heart, 'There is no God.'"[3] Even to deny the existence of God, the fool must have an understanding of the concept of God. God at least must exist as an idea in the mind of the fool. What is this idea? Anselm says that God is the greatest possible being, "a being than which none greater can be conceived."[4]

However, Anselm claims that if I conceive of God as the greatest possible being, I should not believe that he merely exists in my own mind. Obviously a being who existed in reality as well as in my mind would be greater than a being who exists only in my mind. Hence to say that God exists only in my mind is to say that the greatest possible being is not the greatest possible being. God must exist in reality, and the fool is a fool because the very idea of God that the fool must possess to deny God's existence shows that God must exist.

Even in his own day Anselm's argument was controversial. A contemporary monk called Gaunilo wrote a response, *On Behalf of the Fool*. Gaunilo tried to show that something must be wrong with Anselm's argument by developing a parody of it. He claimed that he had an idea of a perfect island, "an island than which none greater can be conceived."[5] If this island existed only in his mind, it would not be the greatest possible island, since an island that exists both in Gaunilo's mind and in reality is greater than one that exists only in someone's mind. Therefore, Gaunilo concluded, this perfect island must exist. However, we know that this is absurd, and since the reasoning for the island parallels Anselm's reasoning for God, something must be wrong with Anselm's argument as well.

Anselm responded by claiming that the idea of a perfect island is incoherent. Only a necessary being could be such that its nonexistence

---

[3]Anselm, *Proslogion* 2, pp. 81-82.
[4]Anselm, *Proslogion* 2, p. 81. Williams translates this as "something than which nothing greater can be thought," but I prefer "a being than which none greater can be conceived."
[5]Gaunilo's *Reply on Behalf of the Fool*, 102. Williams translates this as an island "more excellent than all others," but "an island than which none greater can be conceived" fits better with n4.

is impossible, and only a necessary being could be "a being than which none greater can be conceived." In effect, Anselm argues that God is not like Gaunilo's island, since islands, like all natural entities, are contingent beings, capable of existing and not existing. God as a necessary being is unique.

A common criticism of Anselm's argument is that it is fallacious because it treats existence as if it were a property a thing could have or fail to have, since it sees a being that has the property of "existing in reality" as greater or more perfect than a being that only has the property of "existing in the mind." The critic argues this is wrong because existence is not a property something can have or fail to have. Something that does not exist can have no properties at all. This criticism stems from Kant, and will be discussed more extensively in chapter eighteen. However, contemporary defenders of the argument, such as Alvin Plantinga, have denied that the argument requires treating existence as a property. On their reading, the crucial "great-making property" that God must possess is "necessary existence," and this may be a property even if mere existence is not.[6]

As might be expected, this reply hardly settles the issue. Many philosophers, such as Kant and empiricists such as Hume and his contemporary followers, deny that any being can exist necessarily. For the empiricists at least, necessity is only a function of language and not reality. However, many great philosophers, including Descartes, Spinoza, and Leibniz, have defended the view that something can exist necessarily. In addition to Plantinga, such contemporary philosophers as Norman Malcolm and Charles Hartshorne have also championed the argument.

Anselm's argument is not simply an argument for the existence of God, but a fertile source for speculation about God's nature. If one thinks that God must be the greatest possible being, and if one has views about what counts as a perfection, then one can develop plausible

---

[6]For an excellent articulation and defense of Anselm's historical argument, see Thomas Williams and Sandra Visser, *Anselm*, Great Medieval Thinkers (Oxford: Oxford University Press, 2009).

views of God's attributes. Anselm himself employs this strategy. For example, if we believe (as Anselm does) that knowledge is a perfection, then God must be omniscient, since if he did not possess the greatest possible amount of knowledge a more perfect being could be imagined. For similar reasons God must be omnipotent.

Anselm himself, relying on Platonic views about perfection, uses such arguments to defend the view that God is "impassible" (cannot be affected by anything outside of himself), changeless, timeless, and utterly simple. Reflection on God's attributes using the method of what has come to be called "perfect being theology" is still very much alive. However, some contemporary philosophers, while still employing perfect being theology, have questioned some of Anselm's Platonic ideas about what counts as a perfection. For example, is it really a perfection not to be able to be affected by what else happens? Might it be that a God who is capable of interacting with and responding to his creatures is actually more perfect than a God who is incapable of change? It seems particularly important to think about how a God who chose to become incarnate as a human being might change and interact with his creatures.

Anselm not only develops an account of God's attributes but also argues that these attributes are coherent with each other. To take one obvious example, on the surface, there are problems with how a being can be both unable to sin and omnipotent. We think an omnipotent being can do anything that is logically conceivable, but clearly sinful action is logically possible for some beings. Anselm argues that to be able to sin is a defect that is grounded in weakness. An omnipotent being would not be subject to any weakness, and so the inability of such a being to sin is not due to any lack of power.

Anselm's account of the atonement. Besides his arguments for God's existence, Anselm is best known for his account of Christ's atonement in his book *Cur Deus Homo* (*Why God Became Man*). It is interesting that the Christian doctrine that Christ atoned for human sin through his death and resurrection did not, unlike such doctrines as the incarnation and the Trinity, become the subject of controversy in the early church, and therefore never was explained or spelled out in the early, ecumenical creeds. The New Testament itself, in describing Christ's atonement, employs a number of different images or metaphors. Christ's death is variously described as a sacrifice, a punishment that Christ bore on behalf of humans, and as a "ransom for many."[7] Early Christian thinkers mainly relied on the last of these images, seeing Christ's death as a ransom paid by God that liberated humans from the power of sin, death, and Satan.

The idea that Christ's death was a ransom is still defended, but Anselm found it problematic in ways that many still do. If Christ's death is a ransom, to whom is the ransom paid? One might think that the answer is God, but why should God require such a ransom, and if he does, how can he pay it to himself? Many of the patristic thinkers thought that the ransom was paid to Satan. God gave his son to Satan as a ransom for humans who were in Satan's power, but Satan did not realize that Christ would rise from death and be victorious over sin. In trying to include Jesus within his domain, Satan overreached and lost his power over humans. This idea, though beautifully presented in literary form in C. S. Lewis's *The Lion, the Witch, and the Wardrobe*, also seems problematic to many. Does Satan really have some kind of rightful claim on sinful humans? Some versions of the ransom theory seem to interpret God as tricking or deceiving Satan; it is as if Jesus were bait offered to Satan, which Satan swallowed without realizing that he thereby would be "hooked." However, it seems wrong to think of God as deceiving or tricking anyone, even Satan.

Anselm avoids such problems by understanding Christ's atonement in terms of satisfaction. God is the Creator and owner of the universe,

---

[7]See Mk 10:45 and 1 Tim 2:5-6 for examples of the ransom image. For the idea that Christ offered himself up as a sacrifice, see Heb 7:27 and Rom 3:25. For representative passages that are often interpreted as supporting a view that Christ bears the punishment of humans as a substitute, see Gal 3:10-13; 1 Pet 2:24; 2 Cor 5:21.

and as such is owed due honor and gratitude by his creatures. Humans have, however, failed to honor God as they should have, and therefore are in debt to God. However, this is a debt that humans cannot repay, since humans owe their Creator unlimited honor. Even if they whole-heartedly honor God from now on, they will only be giving God what is owed to God, and will never be able to repay the debt from the past. The debt is one that is owed by humans, but God is the only one who has the resources to pay it, since the debt is infinite. By becoming human himself, God can pay the debt as a human on our behalf. Because Jesus lived a sinless, perfect life, he did not need to die, but in offering to die on behalf of sinners, Christ gives honor and glory to God that can satisfy the debt humans owe.

Anselm's treatment was hugely influential, and many of his successors incorporated aspects of this view, or developed alternatives to it. At the time of the Reformation, Protestant thinkers accepted some of the basic ideas of Anselm, but incorporated them into a different conceptual framework. Anselm thought chiefly in terms of the feudal concept of honor. Theologians such as Calvin developed an account of the atonement that leaned more heavily on juridical metaphors, in which God is seen as a just ruler. On this account, Jesus does not so much satisfy God's honor by paying a debt, but rather suffers the punishment that God's justice demands and that humans deserve. On Anselm's view, Christ pays a debt that humans owe; on Calvin's view Christ suffers a punishment that humans would otherwise be subject to.

Anselm on sin and freedom. Anselm thinks of freedom not primarily as "freedom from" restrictions or limitations but rather in term of "freedom to" or "freedom for" some positive goal. In his work *On Freedom of Choice* he defines freedom as the power to do what is right for its own sake. Right action is in turn understood in a teleological way. In general for Anselm something is "right" or "true" when it does what it was designed to do.[8] For example, statements are true when they

---

[8]See Anselm, *On Truth* 12, pp. 135-41.

represent reality because that is what statements are *for*. The human will was designed to allow humans to will what is "just." Here "justice" does not mean what it means in political philosophy, but is a general term for willing what is right because it is right. It is not enough to do what is right because of fear of punishment or the inducement of some external reward. The right must be willed for its own sake.

Human beings (and the angels when originally created) were given wills in which they have a natural desire for both happiness and justice. Sin consists in rebelling against God by willing one's own happiness ahead of justice, and this is just what humans and the angels who fell did. One might ask why God would give humans and angels such divided wills. Anselm's answer is that it is only by giving a creature such a will that God grants creatures the dignity of being the ultimate source of their own actions. If God had given creatures only the capacity to will happiness or only the capacity to will what is just, then it would be God who determined their will.

ABELARD AND THE MEDIEVAL CONTROVERSY OVER UNIVERSALS

A major issue throughout the medieval period was the status of universals. This was of course a major theme in Plato and a major point of division between Plato and Aristotle. Plato had taught that besides particular things that were just or white or beautiful there were the Forms of Justice, Whiteness, and Beauty. Aristotle, while accepting the reality of general or universal qualities, argued that such universals do not exist separately or independently but only as part of particular things, which must be understood "hylomorphically" as a synthesis of form and matter.

In the Middle Ages, this issue was continually debated, and broadly speaking, the positions taken can be grouped into three categories. Realists (both Platonists and Aristotelians) affirmed the reality of universals. (Aristotelian versions of realism become prominent in the thirteenth century and will be discussed in the next chapter.) Most of the early medieval thinkers tended towards a strong form of Platonic realism, a view often called (at least by its critics) "exaggerated realism" or "extreme realism." One factor that motivated this view was its ability to explain original sin. If there is only one human substance that all humans share, then we can understand why Adam's sin affects all his descendants.

The opposite view to realism is called nominalism, because its proponents denied that there are real universals at all. Instead, they argued that universal terms are just "names" that refer to a group of particulars that humans, for various reasons, find it useful to lump together. The most famous defender of nominalism is William of Ockham, who will be discussed in chapter ten. However, an important early proponent of this view was Roscellinus (or Roscelin), who probably lived from about 1050 to 1125. Not much is known about Roscellinus, and his writings have not survived. However, he was a teacher of Abelard (to be discussed below), and a prominent defender of nominalism. His denial of universals led him to a view of the Trinity that for a time got him in hot water. He argued that the Father, Son, and Holy Spirit cannot be the same substance, for if they were one substance no distinctions between them could be made. The Father and the Spirit would have become incarnate, for example, not just the Son. Roscellinus was accused of tritheism, but it is likely he was developing what would today be described as a social theory of the Trinity.[9]

Roscellinus's student Peter Abelard (1079–1142) is one of the most important thinkers of the twelfth century. While Abelard's philosophical contributions are substantial, he may be most famous for his torrid love affair with a young woman who had been his student, Heloise. Abelard and Heloise had a secret affair, which led to her pregnancy. After the pregnancy, the two were secretly married, but Heloise's

---

[9]For a contemporary account of a social theory of the Trinity, see Cornelius Plantinga Jr., "Social Trinity and Tritheism," in *Trinity, Incarnation, and Atonement: Philosophical and Theological Essays*, ed. Ronald J. Feenstra and Cornelius Plantinga Jr. (Notre Dame, IN: University of Notre Dame Press, 1989).

powerful uncle, Canon Fulbert of Paris, took a terrible revenge, hiring a group of thugs to break into Abelard's room and castrate him. After this, both Abelard and Heloise entered religious orders, Heloise doing so at Abelard's own request. The two saw each other only once after this, but remained in contact through a remarkable set of letters, some of which were only discovered late in the twentieth century.

Philosophically, Abelard is best known for his defense of a mediating position between realism and nominalism, often called "conceptualism," though this is not Abelard's own term. According to this view, universals are not just names, but concepts that humans develop that have some basis in the reality they are used to describe. Conceptualism agrees with nominalism that universals do not exist extramentally. In fact, Abelard does affirm that universals are "mere names," and thus some categorize him as a nominalist. However, although universal qualities do not exist extramentally, common names do convey what we might call semantic or informational content. One might say that for the conceptualist, nominalism is right about what universal terms refer to; common nouns refer to a group of particulars. However, it is no accident that we group particulars in the way we do. There are real resemblances that form the basis of the grouping, and provide the foundation for the concept that gives the name sense or meaning.

Theologically, Abelard is also important for his development of what is often called the "moral influence" or "moral example" theory of the atonement. Rejecting Anselm's satisfaction theory, which saw Christ's death as an offering made to God to repay humans' debt to God, Abelard focused on Jesus' death as a powerful example that demonstrates God's love for humans. This love shown in Christ is such that it transforms human hearts and melts our resistance and rebellion to God. An obvious problem with Abelard's view here is that it seems to undermine the claim that Jesus' death is necessary for human forgiveness. It would appear that there have been many examples of God-inspired selfless love that could serve as moral examples or influence.

Abelard was important as a teacher, and had a major influence on later medieval thinkers due to his book *Sic et non* (Yes and no). In this work, Abelard arranged quotations from patristic authors on contradictory sides of a large number of questions. In the work he makes no attempt to reconcile or resolve the contradictions, though he does give advice about how to do so. This work became a key source for later thinkers who took these apparent contradictions as dialectical challenges. This work, along with the *Sentences* by Peter Lombard (ca. 1095–1160), a collection of biblical passages combined with sections of commentary on those passages from various recognized thinkers, became standard textbooks for theological and philosophical education for generations to come.

MUSLIM AND JEWISH PHILOSOPHY IN THE MIDDLE AGES

For much of the early Middle Ages, there was little contact between Western Europe and the East. After the Muslim conquest of what had been the Christian heartland in the Middle East and North Africa beginning in the middle part of the seventh century, contact was reduced still further. However, after the Muslim conquest of Spain in the early eighth century, Spain gradually became an area where some interaction between Muslim and Christian (and Jewish) thinkers occurred. There is no doubt that contact with Muslim philosophers, who had retained a knowledge of Aristotle's writings that had largely been lost in the West, stimulated a new knowledge of Aristotle and his philosophy, which became increasingly important in the late Middle Ages. A number of outstanding Muslim and Jewish thinkers worked in this period, and a comprehensive treatment of the history of philosophy would give due attention to them for their own intrinsic importance. However, since in this work I am concentrating only on the history of philosophy in the West, I shall mainly look at these philosophers with respect to their influence on the West.

Avicenna. Avicenna, sometimes known as Ibn Sina, is generally regarded as the greatest and most influential Muslim philosopher of the Middle Ages. Born in 980 in Bukhara in what is now Uzbekistan, he flourished in Persia and died in 1037 in present-day Iran. Avicenna was a polymath who wrote hundreds of works on everything from physics and mathematics to geography and medicine, of which 240 are still extant. His writings on medicine remained influential in Western Europe into early modern times. Avicenna was a controversial figure during his lifetime, partly because of an active sex life that did not conform to Muslim standards.

Philosophically, his work is a synthesis of Aristotle and Neoplatonism. Because of the latter, creation is understood as a process of emanation that includes a hierarchy of beings. God creates an Intelligence, a spiritual being, which in turn creates another Intelligence. There are ten levels of such beings, with the top nine constituting the "celestial spheres" governing the heavens, but the tenth and final such being is what Avicenna called the "Agent Intellect" or "Active Intellect" responsible for the creation of the physical world.

Christian philosophers were understandably suspicious of this cosmology, since it seems to make God a being very remote from the created order. The implications of Avicenna's views for psychology or anthropology led to still more opposition. Avicenna taught that human minds, though they inherently possessed the possibility of knowing, could not actually gain rational knowledge without the work of the Active Intellect, which was the same for all people. To many Christian thinkers this view appeared to threaten human individuality, and even the possibility of individual life after death. The universal Active Intellect was nonphysical and immortal, and at death the Active Intellect present in an individual returns to this Universal Intellect. Avicenna himself may have intended to maintain some kind of personal immortality, but it was feared that the implications of his view made this impossible.

Since many of the writings of Aristotle were first transmitted to the West through Muslim thinkers, it is not surprising that initially Aristotle was viewed with some suspicion in Western Europe. There were in fact a number of "condemnations" in which lists of Aristotelian views, often as interpreted by Muslim commentators, were prohibited. (The most famous of these was by the bishop of Paris in 1277.) Despite such opposition, however, Aristotle's natural philosophy eventually became accepted by most scholars, and ways of interpreting his work so that it conformed to Christian orthodoxy were developed.

Averroës. Averroës was born in 1126 in Cordova (today Cordoba) in Muslim Spain, an important center of culture and learning in which there were some periods that allowed Muslim, Jewish, and Christian scholars to exchange ideas. Muslim Spain was not always a tolerant place, however, and Averroës himself had to leave Spain and spent the last part of his life in North Africa.

Averroës is most important for his commentaries on Aristotle. Even Christian thinkers such as Aquinas, who makes a point of refuting what he takes to be Averroës's errors, clearly learned much from these commentaries, and always treated Averroës with respect. Interestingly, in Dante's *Inferno*, both Averroës and Avicenna are placed by Dante in Limbo, along with virtuous pagans, even though Muhammad himself is placed in hell.

Averroës's views make personal immortality even more problematic than was the case for Avicenna. Avicenna had at least held that the "passive intellect" (that which had the potential for knowledge) was individual, but Averroës taught that even the passive intellect was something universal. He therefore held that personal immortality was something that philosophically could not be defended, though he affirmed it as a revealed, religious truth.

This leads to an even more controversial aspect of Averroës's thought: the doctrine of the "twofold truth." The claim was that a proposition could be affirmed as philosophically false while it might legitimately be held as theologically true. This seems to be a direct denial of the logical principle of noncontradiction, and Averroës was sometimes accused by his opponents of doing just this. However, it seems more likely that his primary aim was the defense of philosophy as an autonomous discipline, based on reason. It seems unlikely that Averroës actually meant that the same proposition, understood in the same way, could be both true and false. When he affirmed that a proposition could be philosophically false while theologically true, he probably meant that it could be theologically true if interpreted in a symbolic or allegorical way. Nevertheless, the practical import of his view still seems to be that philosophy has a certain superiority to religion. He interprets religion as providing a kind of pictorial version of truths that is suitable for the masses of ordinary people not capable of following the subtleties of philosophical reasoning. This doctrine of "twofold truth" came to be called "Averroism," and it also contributed significantly to the suspicion attached both to Aristotle and to philosophical speculation in medieval Europe, at least initially.

Maimonides. Moses Maimonides (sometimes known as Moses ben Maimon) was born either in 1135 or 1138 (sources disagree) in Cordova, Spain, and so was a contemporary of Averroës. Maimonides's most famous philosophical work, *A Guide for the Perplexed*, was widely read and exercised great influence on Christian thinkers such as Thomas Aquinas and Duns Scotus. When Maimonides was a child, the Jewish community in Cordova enjoyed relative tolerance, but in 1148 a more extreme form of Islam conquered the area, and required non-Muslims to convert, or be exiled or executed. For a period, Maimonides's family was able to practice Judaism secretly at home while behaving publicly as Muslims, but eventually they had to leave Spain, going first to Morocco, and eventually to Cairo in Egypt. There Maimonides became a court physician and also wrote a number of important works that systematized the tenets of Judaism and showed how a monotheistic religion could be synthesized with the science of the day.

Maimonides argued that the heart of Judaism is an uncompromising monotheism that not only affirms the existence of God but also sees God as one, immaterial, completely unchanging, and timelessly eternal. To worship God with false beliefs about God (such as believing that God is material) is in fact to be an idolater. For him all the commandments in the Torah (of which there are 613) have as their purpose helping God's people to believe in and worship God properly. Maimonides thought that this austere monotheism had been revealed to Adam and Eve, but the knowledge was later lost, and had to be given to Abraham again. During the captivity of the Jewish people in Egypt the knowledge was lost once again, requiring the Mosaic revelation. Moses did not merely give the Israelites this philosophical knowledge, but provided them with a basis for a social order that would allow this knowledge to be preserved.

The knowledge that God provided for the Israelites through the patriarchs and Moses was made possible for the Greeks by Plato and Aristotle. There is no fundamental divergence between Jerusalem and Athens, according to Maimonides. He does not believe that the truths of Judaism are uniquely Jewish, and he is willing to recognize the claim that the truth about God can be found in different cultures and different religious traditions, even though he argues for the truth of his own Jewish faith, properly understood and interpreted.

That interpretation requires that many passages not be taken literally. The Torah accommodates itself to human weakness, using anthropomorphic descriptions of God. When the Scriptures speak of those who had visions of God or saw God, Maimonides argues that the "seeing" is an intellectual vision, rather than one provided to the senses. In general if interpreting the Bible in a literal way produces a reading in which the Bible affirms what is known to be false on philosophical or scientific grounds, then that reading must be a mistaken interpretation.

Maimonides provides arguments for God's existence that are inspired by Aristotle, particularly an argument that the motion of the heavenly bodies requires a "first mover," which must be incorporeal and infinite in power. Although we can prove by reason that God exists, we cannot come to know what God is in a positive sense. Maimonides thus defends the *via negativa*, the way of negative theology. We know that God does not have a body, does not change, does not have parts. Positive statements about God are dubious, however. Even to say that God is more powerful than humans, or wiser, or has more knowledge than humans, is to mistakenly assume that God can be compared with humans using some common scale. God is so transcendent, however, that we have no knowledge of his essence at all. Even our negative affirmations are questionable, since God is so far above our human language and capacities. The highest praise we can offer to God is actually silence.

In reality, human religion needs more than silence, and God has commanded us to pray. Even though we cannot describe God as God is, we can say something about God's effects. The Torah contains speech about God that is, one might say, "authorized," and therefore permissible. However, even when we use this language we must remember that it is inadequate to capture what God is really like.

In discussing creation, Maimonides seriously considers three views. The first view, which is attributed to Moses, is that God created the world out of nothing and that it had a beginning. The second view, attributed to Plato, is that God created the world out of a preexistent matter. The third view is Aristotle's, which affirms that God is the "first cause" of an eternally existing universe. On this view God is responsible for the existence of the world but there was no moment at which the world failed to exist.

Although some have speculated that Maimonides had sympathies for Aristotle's view, since he so revered Aristotle, his expressed preferred view is creation from nothing, though he admits the Platonic view has merits as well. No scientific or philosophical proof can be given for creation out of nothing. (Here Maimonides rejects the *kalam* argument given by Muslims that the world must have had a beginning in time, and that it requires a "first cause" in a temporal sense.) However, there is some evidence in favor of creation out of nothing. The main line of argument is that an eternal world would have to be a world governed by necessity. What is eternally so must necessarily be as it is, and no change is conceivable. However, Maimonides argues that there is some evidence for contingency even in the heavenly bodies, and this means that God could have chosen to create a different world than he in fact did. He also believed that it was important to hold to divine freedom since God has issued commandments, and it certainly seems possible that some of the commandments could have been different.

There is no doubt that Maimonides and the Muslim philosophers of the era were powerful thinkers who exercised a strong influence on medieval Christian thinkers. They are a main channel for the rediscovery of many of Aristotle's works and widespread dissemination of Aristotle's philosophy and science. In the next chapter, I will examine the challenges Western Christians faced in coming to terms with Aristotelian thought.

9

The High Middle Ages (I)

Thomas Aquinas

THE THIRTEENTH CENTURY WAS A PERIOD of great intellectual activity in Europe, contrary to the popular stereotype of the medieval period as the "Dark Ages." By the year 1300 at least thirty-three universities had been founded in Europe. These typically grew out of "cathedral schools" primarily designed to train clergy. The earliest universities date from the ninth century in Italy, probably in Salerno and Bologna. Oxford University was founded around 1115, with Cambridge following around 1209. It is not always clear when a school became a university, but sometimes the date can be fixed by a charter or edict from the pope or a monarch that gave an institution the right to award higher degrees. By the early 1200s the University of Paris, which grew out of several earlier schools, had become renowned all over the Continent as the place to study theology and law, as well as the arts and sciences. Two of the most important philosophers of the medieval period were both associated with the University of Paris: Bonaventure and Thomas Aquinas. I shall devote this chapter solely to Aquinas, since his thought has had greater historical importance and continues to exercise great influence on contemporary philosophers, treating Bonaventure separately in the next chapter.[1]

---

[1]I wish to thank Brandon Dahm for several good suggestions for changes to this chapter, as well as for some excellent bibliographical suggestions.

AQUINAS'S LIFE

Aquinas was born near Naples, the youngest son of an important Italian family, most likely within a year or two of 1225.[2] He was initially educated at the Benedictine abbey at Monte Cassino and then at the University of Naples. There he came to admire the Dominicans, a recently founded order of preachers and teachers, and decided to join the order himself. His family was greatly opposed to this decision, going so far as to forcibly kidnap him and hold him captive for a considerable period of time to prevent his going to Paris as a Dominican for further study. Eventually the family relented, and in 1245 Aquinas was allowed to go to Paris to study.

There he encountered Albert the Great, an expert on the newly rediscovered works of Aristotle. Albert became Aquinas's teacher, and Aquinas followed Albert to the University of Cologne in 1248, later returning to Paris. Aquinas's family still hoped he would return to Italy, and prevailed on the pope to offer Aquinas the position of abbot of Monte Cassino, even though Aquinas was a Dominican and the abbey was a Benedictine institution. However, Aquinas turned down this generous offer so that he could stay on the course of scholarship and teaching, which he clearly viewed as his vocation.

Aquinas was famously large as a person, and also very modest and quiet, thus acquiring the unflattering nickname of "the dumb ox." Nevertheless, his intellectual gifts quickly became apparent. After finishing his master of theology degree (the medieval equivalent of the modern PhD) he was appointed regent master in theology at Paris in 1256. After teaching in Paris for a number of years, the Dominicans ordered Aquinas back to Italy, where he taught at Naples, Orvieto, and in Rome. Aquinas was ordered back to Paris in 1268, partly to deal with controversies concerning the ideas of Aristotle that will be discussed below.

---

[2]For a detailed account of Aquinas's life, see Jean Pierre Torrell, *St. Thomas Aquinas*, vol. 1, *His Life and Work*, trans. Robert Royal, rev. ed. (Washington, DC: Catholic University of America Press, 2005).

In 1272 all lectures at the university were canceled because of a dispute with the bishop of Paris, and so Aquinas returned once more to Italy. After returning to Naples, Aquinas had some kind of mystical experience, after which he ceased all writing and dictation. He himself said that everything he has previously written seemed to him "like straw" in comparison with what he saw in this experience. Shortly after this, in 1274, he died while en route to the Council of Lyons, which he had been ordered to attend.

AQUINAS'S WRITINGS

Although he died when he was just forty-nine (approximately), Aquinas wrote prodigiously and his corpus is massive. He is best known for two encyclopedic works, the *Summa theologiae* and the *Summa contra Gentiles*. The former, though massive, was left incomplete at Aquinas's death. It is intended as a comprehensive summary of Christian theology, though it includes much material that would today be considered philosophy. The *Summa theologiae* is written in the distinctive "dialectical" style of medieval philosophy. A question is proposed, followed by a number of arguments (termed "objections") defending an answer to the question that Aquinas considers to be at least partially mistaken. After these "objections" are explained, Aquinas says "on the other hand" and gives a brief defense of the correct answer, normally consisting of an appeal to some authority. This is followed by "I answer that . . .," which gives Aquinas's own view of the matter along with arguments for his position. Finally, Aquinas adds a list of replies to the objections to his position previously discussed.

The *Summa contra Gentiles* is written in a more straightforward prose style, however. Some scholars have thought that this book was written by Aquinas as a manual for missionaries in Spain, where there were vigorous arguments between Christian, Islamic, and Jewish thinkers. This seems somewhat doubtful, however, since most of the book consists of rational arguments for monotheistic views, which would have been accepted without question by Muslims and Jewish thinkers. Only part 4 of the *Summa contra Gentiles* deals with distinctively Christian doctrines.

Besides these two massive works, Aquinas wrote many commentaries. Many are on biblical books, but Aquinas also wrote two commentaries on Boethius's work, as well as thirteen commentaries on works of Aristotle. These latter commentaries are often line-by-line accounts of Aristotle, and are still regarded as important and valuable by contemporary Aristotle scholars. Aquinas also wrote many books on "disputed questions," the consideration of which was a normal part of the duty of a medieval theology professor. He also wrote quite a few independent, shorter works, such as *On Being and Essence*, and two works dealing with aspects of Aristotle's thought that had occasioned controversy, the nature of the human soul and the eternality of the world.

Today Aquinas is widely regarded as the preeminent Catholic philosopher, but it is important to recognize that he was in his own day a somewhat controversial figure, with many of his important claims placed on a list of heretical theses by the bishop of Paris. As we shall see, he steered a middle road between Franciscans such as Bonaventure, who were cautious in their use of Aristotle, and the more radical "Averroist" Aristotelians, who developed Aristotle in ways that made it difficult to square Aristotle with Christian orthodoxy.

AQUINAS, ARISTOTLE (AND AVERROËS), AND AUGUSTINE

It is easy to see the influence of Aristotle on Aquinas, particularly when philosophical questions are at issue. Since most of Aristotle had only recently been translated into Latin and made available in Europe, it is not surprising that much of what Aquinas defends philosophically was opposed by some of his colleagues at the University of Paris. Aquinas not only defends many recognizably Aristotelian views, but often cites Aristotle himself. He also discusses commentaries on Aristotle by others, including Muslim and Jewish writers, from whom Aquinas clearly learned much.

Aquinas sometimes displays a negative attitude toward views that are identified with Platonism. This is especially true in his arguments against the claim that universals, or "Forms," exist separately or independently from objects. Despite these anti-Platonic arguments, Aquinas does hold, with Augustine, that universals exist in God's mind, and he also incorporates a Platonic-sounding view that finite objects "participate" in a higher reality, so the break with Plato is less decisive than may appear. Although Aquinas clearly regards Aristotle as a great philosopher, he by no means sees himself as rejecting the work of Augustine. Indeed, he frequently cites Augustine in positive ways.

Nonetheless much of what is new in Aquinas stems from his creative reading of Aristotle. The tilt toward Aristotle is clear in Aquinas's epistemology, in which the concept of recollection plays little role. Instead, Aquinas maintains that knowledge begins with sense experience that enables us to "abstract" the Forms or universal properties that are present in objects. Aquinas himself, like other medieval writers, had almost no firsthand knowledge of Plato, except for the *Timaeus*. Despite this, he absorbed a good deal of what we would today call Platonism through his reading of Augustine, Boethius, and Pseudo-Dionysius.

There were two particular aspects of Aristotle that created controversy in medieval Europe. One concerned the personal immortality of humans. Aristotle for the most part seems to think of the human soul as forming an intimate unity with the body, not as something capable of existing separately and independently, as in Plato. However, in one crucial passage in his book *De Anima* (*On the Soul*), Aristotle distinguishes between two aspects of the human soul or mind, the active mind or intellect and the passive mind or intellect. The former, Aristotle says, is capable of existing apart from the body, because it is not the form of any bodily entity, but is characterized by its own purely intellectual activities.

This passage in Aristotle, which is notoriously condensed and unclear, has been the subject of controversy from early medieval times right up until the present day. The early Islamic philosopher Avicenna, who was deeply influenced by Neoplatonism as well as by Aristotle, had maintained that the human soul was separable and immortal, and thus interpreted Aristotle as speaking about an individual soul that can exist apart from the body. However, Averroës, in his commentary on Aristotle, taught that when Aristotle referred to the active intellect he was referring to something universal. There is ultimately only one active intellect or mind, which individual humans in some sense share or participate in. This Mind is indeed immortal, but this does not mean that individual humans survive. Rather, at death the active intellect that is in each of us continues to exist as part of the universal reason, but we cease to exist as individuals.

Aquinas vigorously opposed this interpretation of Aristotle. He argued instead that each individual human has an active mind or intellect, and because of this the human soul can indeed exist separately from the body, though a human's final destiny is not to exist in Platonic fashion as a disembodied soul, but to be resurrected, body and soul. The soul of a human being is immaterial, since it can conceive of immaterial substances, and it can exist separately, even though it cannot carry out some of its functions without a body. Not only is its existence after death possible, but it does continue to exist in a disembodied state between the time of death and the resurrection.

The second major aspect of Aristotle that created controversy was Aristotle's view that the natural universe had no beginning but exists eternally. Averroës appears to accept this view, not just as the correct interpretation of Aristotle, but also as the sober truth of the matter. Perhaps he thought of the biblical story of creation as a kind of mythical picture of the underlying metaphysical truth that the universe depends on God, a picture suitable for the masses incapable of philosophy.

On this issue Aquinas could hardly argue that Averroës had got Aristotle wrong. Aquinas accepted the traditional Christian view that the world had a beginning and was created by God out of nothing. However, he argued that this is a truth that is only knowable through divine revelation. From a scientific or philosophical perspective, we cannot demonstrate whether the world had a beginning in time. There are probable arguments on both sides, but no decisive proof either way. Thus, in one sense, Aristotle, not having the benefit of the biblical revelation, was not mistaken in his reasoning, even though his view was wrong. Aquinas may well have been influenced by Maimonides here, who also argued that there are several different views of creation that are rationally defensible.

Some interpreted Averroës as affirming a doctrine of "twofold truth": that a proposition could be true in theology but philosophically false and vice versa. It is unlikely that Averroës actually held that the same proposition could be both true and false, since this would violate the law of noncontradiction. What he most likely believed was that two propositions, one in philosophy and one in theology, could both be true even though they appear to contradict each other. However, this appearance is due to the fact that theology often uses highly metaphorical and pictorial language, so that when properly understood the two propositions do not contradict each other. (As we shall see in chap. 19, Hegel would later affirm something like this view.)

Regardless of what Averroës himself taught, the doctrine of the twofold truth came to be known as Averroism, and seems to have had some support among philosophers, including some at the University of Paris. The appeal of the doctrine is that it allowed philosophy to go its own way, free from theological constraints. The problem of course is that it undermined the notion of theological truth. It is not clear what it means to say that it is true that God created the world and that the world had a beginning, if it is false as a matter of science or philosophy that the world had a beginning. It is not surprising then that in 1277 the archbishop of Paris condemned 219 theses, a number of which were regarded as "Averroist" doctrines.

In his work at Paris, Aquinas then found himself confronted with opposition on two fronts in his work to develop a synthesis of Christian thought and Aristotelian philosophy. On the one hand, he was opposed by conservative and traditional thinkers, such as Bonaventure, who saw Aristotle as dangerous and unnecessary, even if he had valuable insights that could be appropriated. Such thinkers were not necessarily reactionaries opposed to new ideas, but they continued to believe in the value of Augustinian and Neoplatonic thought. These thinkers were understandably alarmed by the uses to which Aristotle was being put. On the other hand, Aquinas also had to defend himself (and the value of Aristotle) over against the radical, Averroist Aristotelians.

AQUINAS'S METAPHYSICS

Primary substances. To explain Aquinas's metaphysics is to explain his view of substances.[3] The term *substantia* (substance) is a technical term in Aquinas, and it is not equivalent to the ordinary English term *thing*. We might well think of the material parts of a tree, such as its branches and leaves and trunk, as things, and Aquinas would agree that they are in some sense real objects, but they do not qualify as substances, at least when they are part of a living tree. In this section I shall only discuss what Aquinas calls primary substances. Following Aristotle, Aquinas holds that there is also a "secondary" sense of substance, in which a substance refers to a *kind* of thing, and thus all the things that fall under that kind. A primary substance is a particular thing that has a certain character.

For Aquinas there are two kinds of substances: nonmaterial substances, such as angels and demons, and material substances, such as plants and animals. Nonmaterial substances, like material substances, have a "form" or structure, but they have no matter that is joined with that form and is structured by it. I shall say a little more about

---

[3]For a detailed account of Aquinas's metaphysics, see John F. Wippel, *The Metaphysical Thought of Thomas Aquinas: From Finite Being to Uncreated Being* (Washington, DC: Catholic University of America Press, 2000).

nonmaterial substances later, but want to focus now on material substances. Aquinas follows Aristotle in claiming that all material substances have both form and matter, the view usually called hylomorphism. It is not easy to say what Aquinas means by "form." On the one hand, form is often described as the principle of actuality, while matter represents potentiality. The difficulty is that Aquinas seems to think of the form of some substance as a configuration of that thing, what we might call its structure, along with the properties and causal powers that a thing has by virtue of that structure. However, perhaps because of these causal powers, the form of a substance can also be thought of as that which is *responsible* for the configuration. It is both the configurer and the configuration.

Actually existing matter always must have some form. Matter without form would be what Aquinas calls prime matter, but prime matter is (for him) only a conceptual possibility. It is simply the result of conceiving matter without any form, but in reality no such thing exists. We can see why Aquinas identifies form with actuality, since nothing can be actual without form. (This holds true for immaterial substances as well.) The substantial form of a substance is what makes that substance the *kind* of thing it is. It determines what something is essentially. A substance that loses this form ceases to exist as the kind of thing it is.

Besides substantial forms, Aquinas follows Aristotle in holding that there are also accidental forms, forms that characterize a substance but that can be altered or lost without that substance's ceasing to be. In contemporary philosophy, such forms are usually described as accidental properties. "Having two arms" is an accidental property of most humans, since if a human loses an arm that person does not necessarily cease to exist.

Interestingly, Aquinas holds that a primary substance can have only one substantial form. This has several important implications, some of which may seem implausible. Human flesh that is detached from a human person is a substance and thus has a substantial form. However, when existing as part of a human person, the flesh of the person does not have a form of its own, since there can only be one form in a human person. It might appear that the flesh in the two cases is quite similar, and thus must have the same form, but Aquinas holds that this is not the case. In a living person, the flesh carries out functions it does not when it is detached, and so its character is different than when it is separate. One might say the flesh in a living person has the character it does because of the form of the person, which provides the structure of the whole. Thus, if a human person dies and the body of the person is chopped into pieces, it is possible for several substances (arms, legs, bones, etc.) to come into existence, each with its own form, in the place of the one person (and form) that existed previously. Also, if two substances are combined in some way, the rule of "one substance with one form" still holds. When this happens, either the two substances continue to exist, and their union is an accidental property of both, or else, if the two things do merge so as to become a new substance, the two previous substances cease to exist.[4] The former kind of case is what often happens in the case of artifacts, where two or more previously existing substances are combined, as when a wooden handle is combined with a piece of steel to form a shovel, but in this case the artifact has no substantial form of its own. Artifacts then are usually not genuine substances, but composites of substances.

How are substances individuated from each other? Since all the substances of a particular kind have the same essential form, the differences between one substance and another cannot be due to their forms. Each thing of a particular kind has a nature common to that kind. Aquinas's answer is that particular substances are individuated by their matter. Each substance comes into existence at a particular place and time, and is the particular thing it is by virtue of this origin and the history it undergoes as a material thing. Obviously this cannot work for nonmaterial

---

[4]See Eleonore Stump's clear discussion of this kind of case (and others) in *Aquinas*, Arguments of the Philosophers (New York: Routledge, 2003), 39-44.

substances such as angels. Aquinas holds that individual angels must then have unique forms, and each angel is different from other angels by virtue of the unique form that characterizes that angel.

One of the important respects in which Aquinas's metaphysics goes beyond Aristotle has to do with the distinction between essence and existence.[5] For everything except God there is a difference between what something essentially is (essence) and actual existence. Although substantial forms are, in relation to matter, actual, Aquinas holds that forms themselves are potential (or "in potency") relative to something else: existence or the act of being. God, who is pure being, is responsible for the existence or being of everything other than God, and thus in relation to God essences are potentially actual. Here Aquinas's theistic metaphysic differs strongly from Aristotle. Aristotle believed in a God, but the Aristotelian God was not a creator and was not responsible for the existence of the world. For Aquinas, God is not only the Creator but also the sustainer of the universe. God himself, as we shall see, cannot be understood merely as one being among other beings. Aquinas draws on the biblical name of God as "I am" and says that God is not merely *a* being, but is "pure being" or the "act of being." As such God is responsible for the being of everything other than himself.

Arguments for God's existence. Thus, besides immaterial substances such as angels, and material composite substances such as humans, Aquinas also affirms the reality of God. In fact, this way of putting things is misleading, since it might lead us to think that in speaking of God, we have simply introduced one more substance into our ontology. However, for Aquinas God cannot be just one more existing thing added to the list of beings. God's being is absolutely unique. Every other entity is a composite of form and existence. We can always distinguish the question of what something is, the question about its essence, from the question of whether that something exists. Even though

---

[5]For an influential treatment of this issue in Aquinas, see Etienne Gilson, *Being and Some Philosophers* (Toronto: Pontifical Institute of Medieval Studies, 2001).

angels have no matter, we can distinguish their essence or form from the fact of their existence. In God, however, there is no such distinction: God is Being itself, and his essence is identical to his existence. God is not just another entity, but the source of all reality.

This means that God, unlike all other creatures, exists necessarily. It is his nature to exist, and thus his existence requires no cause or explanation beyond God himself. One might think that this would mean that Aquinas would endorse Anselm's ontological argument for God's existence, and in one sense he does. It is God's nature to exist, and if we understood God's essence, then the existence of God would be self-evident to us. However, Aquinas affirms that God's nature, being identical to his existence, is mysterious to us, at least in this life. Hence, God's existence is not self-evident to us, though it must be to God himself, who perfectly understands his own essence. Aquinas therefore provides rational arguments for God's existence, although he does not say that one's belief in God must be based on such arguments. It is perfectly reasonable to believe in God on the basis of faith in God's revelation of himself through the Scriptures and the church.

In his *Summa theologiae* Aquinas presents five arguments for God's existence, the "Five Ways" often included in philosophy of religion textbooks.[6] Most of these arguments are difficult to understand today, because they are couched in the language of Aristotelian physics. The first three arguments are often described as versions of a "cosmological" argument, because they all begin from very general and obvious features of the world. All of them argue that this feature requires a cause or explanation, defend the claim that the chain of causation or explanation cannot be infinite, and conclude that there must therefore be a "first" or "ultimate" cause of explanation, which is identified with God.

The first is an argument from "motion" that concludes God must exist as the "First Mover" of the things in the world that are in motion. This

---

[6]The "Five Ways" can be found in Aquinas, *Summa theologiae* Ia.2.3, in *Aquinas: Basic Works*, ed. Jeffrey Hause and Robert Pasnau, trans. Eleonore Stump and Stephen Chanderbhan (Indianapolis: Hackett, 2014).

argument is particularly difficult to grasp, as Aquinas does not mean that God is the first cause of motion in a temporal sense. First of all, by "motion" Aquinas does not mean simply a change in spatial location, but almost any kind of physical change or alteration. We must also recall that Aquinas does not think it is possible from a philosophical or scientific point of view to determine whether the world had a beginning. Hence, when Aquinas says that there is chain of causes which must have a "first" cause, he does not mean a cause that is temporally the first. Rather, the series of causes he is referring to are causes that are operating simultaneously. We might illustrate the idea by thinking of a person who picks up a stick. The stick is moving because of the hand of the person. That hand is in turn moving because of the willing of the person, and all of those causes can be operating at the same time.

Aquinas's argument makes perfect sense in the context of Aristotelian physics, since Aristotle postulated that the "motion" or change taking place in the natural world was due ultimately to celestial "movers" who are in turn moved by God, the "Unmoved Mover" who is the cause of all change by being the object of love or desire. It is difficult to make sense of the argument, however, without these Aristotelian scientific presuppositions. The same is true of Aquinas's second argument, which argues that God must exist as the first "efficient cause" of the existence of objects in nature. The argument again assumes an Aristotelian understanding of efficient causality, which does not easily line up with contemporary physics.

The "Third Way," however, seems more promising, and arguments recognizably similar to this one have been defended by such philosophers as Samuel Clarke and Leibniz, and continue to have defenders. In this argument, Aquinas begins with the claim that there are some things that exist in the natural world that do not have to exist. It is possible for such objects both "to be and not to be." Contemporary philosophers would say that such objects exist contingently. Aquinas argues that if an object exists, but could possibly have not existed, an explanation or cause of its existence is required. That explanation or cause could be some other contingent object, but then that object in turn will require a cause. Aquinas argues that the chain of causes cannot be infinite, and so there must be a first cause, which does not exist contingently but necessarily, and which therefore requires no cause or explanation for its existence.[7] A necessary being that is the cause of the existence of all contingent beings can only be God.

We might ask why Aquinas believes that the chain of causes must be finite, which is an assumption that all of the first three arguments make. I believe the reasoning behind this is that an infinite chain of causes would necessarily be an incomplete and unfinished series. But such an incomplete series would essentially be an incomplete explanation. If you ask me why some fact is true, and I begin to give an explanation but never finish, I have not really given an explanation. But the arguments begin with some fact that demands explanation. This shows, I think, that all of these arguments, like other forms of the cosmological argument, depend on what is sometimes called the "principle of sufficient reason."[8] There are various ways of stating this principle, but one common way is that there must be a sufficient explanation for any positive fact about the world.

The "Fourth Way" is an argument from value. Aquinas says that in the world we recognize some things as good or noble, and also that some of these things are better or more noble than others. This means, Aquinas says, that we are measuring them by some absolute standard of value. So far the argument seems plausible. However, many contemporary philosophers would claim that such a standard does not have to

---

[7]The actual argument Aquinas gives is more complicated than this, because he assumes the possibility of beings who exist necessarily but still owe their existence to something other than themselves. We might think of this as a kind of "relative necessity." Such causes could be part of the chain, but eventually what is required is a being who is absolutely necessary to terminate the causal chain. I think the idea of such a relatively necessary being would be this: the being exists eternally but is caused to exist (necessarily) by some other being. The argument is simpler and clearer if this wrinkle is left out of the story.

[8]For a good discussion and defense of the principle of sufficient reason, see Alexander Pruss, *The Principle of Sufficient Reason: A Reassessment* (Cambridge: Cambridge University Press, 2006).

exist, but can simply be an imagined ideal. Aquinas does not see this as a viable alternative, however. This is one place where the Platonic assumptions in his thought (which may be present in Aristotle as well) surface. He argues that this absolute standard must exist, because it is the ultimate cause of the value finite things possess. This is similar to the Platonic assumption that all good things possess what goodness they have by participating in the Form of the Good. Of course Aquinas identifies the ultimate standard of perfect goodness that is the source of all goodness as God.

The last of Aquinas's Five Ways is a version of the argument often termed the "argument from design." The starting point is the claim that that there are things in the natural world that lack intelligence or mind, but that nevertheless "always or most often act in the same way so as to attain what is best."[9] In effect Aquinas is saying that there are parts of nature that exhibit two features. The first is regularity; they "always or most often act in the same way." The second feature is that this regularity makes possible the achievement of value. The regularity makes possible a good result. We might take any number of natural processes as illustrative of this. For example, consider the activity of the lungs in exchanging carbon dioxide for oxygen or the activity of the heart in pumping blood throughout the body. When we have this kind of regularity in the service of value, Aquinas says that this cannot be "fortuitous." It cannot be merely the result of chance, because regularity in the service of value is the mark of intelligence. Since these things lack intelligence themselves, they must be directed to their ends by some intelligence, and the intelligence that is the source of the regularity and order of nature could only be God, understood as the cause of the natural order.

In effect Aquinas is saying that there are many obvious examples of design in nature, and that design requires a designer. Critics today often dismiss this argument as one that has been undermined by the theory of evolution. They argue that the design in nature is only apparent

---

[9]Aquinas, *Summa theologiae* Ia.2.3, p. 54.

design, and not genuine design, and that it can be explained as the result of survival of the fittest and random genetic mutations, which result in features of nature that appear to be designed.

However, it is far from clear that evolution undermines Aquinas's argument. After all, the regularity and value that Aquinas affirms as the basis of the argument are really present and are not illusions. If the theory of evolution is true, then this observable order, which we might call "surface order," is the result of a deeper order, described by the scientific laws that make the evolutionary process occur. However, it is hard to see how the fact that the surface order depends on a deeper order invalidates Aquinas's argument. If his principle that order that results in value is the result of intelligence is plausible, then the argument still has force. In any case if God wished to give humans evidence of his reality by displaying signs of purposive intelligence in nature, those signs would have to be readily discernible. One should not have to know either the truth or falsity of a complicated scientific theory to recognize such signs. And that is precisely what we find in the purposive order observable in nature.

God's nature. Many of God's characteristics can only be known with the help of God's self-revelation, according to Aquinas. These include such "mysteries" as the Trinity and the incarnation. Such truths about God are "above" the capacity of the natural reason, but not against reason. If someone objects to these doctrines as irrational, reason can properly respond, but the positive case for them must come from faith in God's revelation.

However, there are many truths about God that can be philosophically discerned. Before discussing some of these, I must first examine the question as to whether Aquinas believes that humans can know anything positive about God in this life. There are some passages in which Aquinas seems to say that God's nature is so far above the capacities of human reason that we can know nothing about what God is like. Aquinas certainly does hold that "only do we know God truly when we believe Him to be above everything that it is possible for man to think about Him."[10] Certainly, this means that our understanding of God will always be inadequate in important ways. However, does this mean that we can know nothing about God at all?

Some commentators have affirmed that Aquinas has this kind of agnostic view about God. We can know that God exists, but cannot really know what God is like; we can only know what he is not. This is the *via negativa*, or the path of negative theology. On this view we can say that God does not have a body, does not have parts, and many other such claims, but can make no positive assertions. However, it does not seem coherent to affirm that we can know that God exists if we literally know nothing about what God is like.

Eleonore Stump has argued convincingly that Aquinas does not hold this extreme form of agnosticism.[11] One important piece of evidence is that Aquinas criticizes the views of Maimonides, who seems to hold exactly this view. What makes it possible for Aquinas to say that we can speak positively about God as well as negatively is his doctrine of analogy. Even though we do not in this life comprehend God's essence, we can say some things about God by virtue of the relation between God and the created order. God is the cause of the existence of all of nature, and Aquinas thought that there are real affinities between a cause and its effect. Thus, when we say God is good, we are not merely saying that God is the cause of goodness in the natural world, but, because he is the cause of goodness, "what we call goodness in creatures pre-exists in God and in a higher mode."[12]

It is true that we do not fully understand God's goodness, because it is "in a higher mode" than the goodness we experience. But we nevertheless can say that God's goodness in some way resembles the goodness

---

[10]Aquinas, *Summa contra Gentiles* 1.5.3, in Thomas Aquinas, *Contra Gentiles*, trans. Anton C. Pegis (New York: Hanover House, 1955–1957), online edition updated by John Kenny, OP, http://dhspriory.org/thomas/english/ContraGentiles.htm.

[11]See Stump, *Aquinas*, 93-96.

[12]Quoted in Stump, *Aquinas*, 95. This is Stump's translation of *Summa theologiae* Ia.13.2.

we know. We therefore apply the predicate to God analogously. This is not univocal predication, but it is not equivocal either.[13]

So what predicates can we attribute to God? One of the most important is the claim that God is perfectly "simple," meaning he has no parts. Fundamentally this is a negative claim. However, it is grounded in the claim that God is "pure act," and that God's existence or being is not something different from his essence. As we saw above, every being other than God has an essence that is distinct from that being's existence. However, God's very nature or essence is to be; he is not a being like other beings, but his essence is "To Be." To support this Aquinas draws on the biblical passage in which Yahweh tells Moses that his name is "I AM" (Ex 3:14). However, the doctrine of divine simplicity is also defended by philosophical considerations. For Aquinas, God's simplicity follows from his absolute perfection and from the fact that he is "pure actuality" and has no potentiality, as well as the fact that he exists necessarily as the cause of all other beings. It follows from the doctrine of divine simplicity that although we humans can conceptually distinguish God's will from his intellect, in God himself there is no such distinction.

Besides simplicity, Aquinas defends the full package of what we might call "classical theism."[14] God is "impassible," unable to be acted on or affected by anything other than himself. God is eternal, not in the sense of being a temporal being who exists without beginning or end, but in the stronger sense of a being who is completely timeless. Obviously, a timeless being must also be completely immutable, since change requires a difference between what a thing was before and what it was after. The effects of God's creative action obviously are temporal, with one event following another in time, but everything God himself wills he wills in one timeless act.

---

[13]Interestingly, Richard Swinburne argues that Aquinas misunderstands univocal predication, and in fact is committed to the claim that we can speak univocally about God. See Richard Swinburne, "The Words of Theology: Medieval and Modern Accounts," chap. 5 of *The Coherence of Theism*, 2nd ed. (Oxford: Oxford University Press, 2016).

[14]For a detailed, in-depth treatment of Aquinas's view of God, see Rudi Te Velde, *Aquinas on God: The "Divine Science" of the "Summa Theologiae"* (Aldershot: Ashgate, 2006).

In addition to these properties, Aquinas affirms that God is perfectly good. For Aquinas, being and goodness are actually equivalent, and hence if God is Being itself it follows that God must also be Goodness itself. God is also omniscient or all-knowing. The highest form of reality is intellect, but an intellect that was ignorant would not have the required perfection. Aquinas holds that God knows what we humans call the past and future, but since God is timelessly eternal, the whole of time is in some way present to God. Thus God does not "foreknow" what we will do before we do it, but knows our future actions as we know the actions of a contemporary whom we are observing. There are obvious differences between our knowledge and God's knowledge, however. One is that since God is simple, there is for God no difference between his act in creating something and his knowledge of that something. There is thus a sense in which God's knowledge of X is the cause of X.

God is also omnipotent, which means for Aquinas that God can do anything that is logically possible. God cannot create a square circle, but that is not a limit on God's power. Since a square circle is not a coherent possibility, it is not a "thing" at all, and thus God's inability to create one is not a real limitation. Although human minds necessarily must think of these divine attributes as distinct, we should keep in mind that the doctrine of divine simplicity implies that in God himself all of his attributes are really identical.

AQUINAS'S EPISTEMOLOGY AND PSYCHOLOGY

Aquinas, like Aristotle, does not offer an epistemology that could be seen as a refutation of skepticism. Rather, he takes it for granted that knowledge is possible; the job of the philosopher is not to prove that we have knowledge but to explain how knowledge is possible. Aquinas also follows Aristotle in holding that the origins of knowledge lie in sense perception. However, also like Aristotle, he agrees with Plato that the objects of knowledge must be universal and necessary; knowledge must be directed to what is permanent or enduring, and that means knowledge, at least what we might call scientific knowledge, is knowledge of universals.[15]

There is no innate knowledge of the Forms, as in Plato, and there are no innate ideas, except in the sense that we have an innate capacity to develop certain ideas when we confront the world. Aquinas thus affirms that "whatever is in our intellect must have previously been in the senses."[16] Nevertheless, though knowledge has its origins in sense perception, scientific knowledge aims at an understanding of the necessary, enduring features of the world.

Though the Forms exist independently only as the objects of the Divine Intellect (a Platonic echo of Augustine), they exist in the created world as the "essences" of particular things. They also can exist in the human mind after the human has perceived those particular things, and the active intellect has performed an act of "abstraction" that grasps such essences. Aquinas (again like Aristotle) is not completely clear as to how this act of abstraction takes place. It is clearly the work of the active intellect, and thus perception is not simply a passive reception of something. A "phantasm" from the object perceived is received, and from this the active intellect abstracts the form. The active intellect somehow abstracts from the particular qualities of what is perceived and grasps what is universal or essential in the particular. Thus, if one sees a particular triangle, the intellect abstracts from the particular qualities of the triangle perceived, and grasps what is universal and thus must be true of all triangles. Thus perception seems to be a process that involves a causal relationship to the object, from which a representation of the object is grasped, and from this the active intellect in turn is able to gain a grasp of what is universal and essential in what is perceived.

---

[15]Aquinas uses the Latin term *scientia* to refer to scientific knowledge. Since this term is often just translated as "knowledge" his views are sometimes misunderstood, since there are forms of cognition that we would call "knowledge" in English that are not *scientia*.

[16]Aquinas, *De veritate*, q. 2 a. 3 arg. 19, trans. Robert Mulligan, SJ (Chicago: Henry Regnery, 1952). online edition updated by Joseph Kenny, OP, http://dhspriory.org/thomas/english/QDdeVer2.htm.

Is Aquinas a soul-body dualist? Although the human person is a "hylomorphic" composite of body and soul, the active intellect is not itself a physical entity. As we saw above, this allows Aquinas to reject the Averroistic view of the human self, which seemed to leave no room for individual immortality. Since the activity of the active intellect is to grasp the forms of objects, it is itself essentially immaterial, since its activity, unlike sense perception itself, does not require any assistance from the body. At death the soul separates from the body, and continues to exist between death and the resurrection.

There is some controversy over whether this view of Aquinas should be considered a form of mind-body (or soul-body) dualism. On the one hand, Aquinas says that the human person is a soul-body composite and thus that the person does not exist during the period between death and the resurrection. Because of this, some have argued that Aquinas is a monist who rejects soul-body dualism. However, Aquinas says that the *soul* of the person does exist during this interim period, and can even engage in such activities such as repenting of and being purged of sins in purgatory, for those souls who are in purgatory. If I am conscious of my sins and can improve in my character during this period, it is hard to see how it could be true that *I* do not exist.

I think the answer to this puzzle lies in seeing that Aquinas holds to the Aristotelian view of a human substance as a soul-body composite that does not exist without the body. However, the term *substance* is here being used in a technical Aristotelian sense. There must be a sense in which I exist if my soul exists. Perhaps I do not exist as fully human without a body, but *something* still exists that can be the bearer of personal identity. Between my death and my resurrection I continue to exist, but I do not exist in a fully human way. To exist in that fully human way I require a body, and thus the resurrection is required for me completely to become what God intends me to be. My own view is that some Aquinas commentators do not want to describe him as a dualist because they equate dualism with a Cartesian view of the soul and body.[17] However, Cartesian dualism is only one kind of dualism, and Aquinas may be a dualist of sorts without being a Cartesian.

Aquinas on the capacities of the human soul. Since humans are bodily beings, human souls have a variety of capacities. We share with plants and lower animals the "vegetative capacities," capacities to gain nourishment, growth, and renewal of the body. We share with the higher animals the sensory and locomotive capacities, capacities to sense the outside world and move around in it. However, the distinctly human capacities of the soul are the higher, rational faculties, preeminently intellect and will. Our rational capacities have a kind of universal sphere of action. Through the senses we can apprehend physical objects, but the intellect can conceive of anything that has being, including immaterial beings.

The rational capacities are recognizable as higher because of the role they play in directing the other capacities. A tiger may simply recognize another animal as food through the senses and instinctively pounce on it. A human being, however, may recognize a delicious piece of chocolate cake, but still reflect on whether the cake should be eaten.

The intellect is our capacity to seek and find truth, to find out what the world is actually like. However, simply knowing the truth about things does not in itself move us to action. What does move us to action is will understood as "rational appetite," a desire for what is good understood *as* good. When we will an action, we do not merely follow a blind instinct, but desire something because we understand it as good in some way. The intellect and the will work together, though Aquinas's view is often described as "intellectualistic," in that the will is dependent in its operations on the judgments of the intellect. We can only rationally will what we believe to be good in some way, and thus for a possible course of action to be embraced by the will it must be presented to the will by the intellect as being good. I will say more about this apparent intellectualism and the problems it creates for Aquinas below.

---

[17]See the discussion of Descartes's view in chap. 12.

The operation of both the intellect and the will can be affected by the "passions," which involve such emotions as love, joy, and hatred. The passions can augment or distort the work of the intellect, depending on the degree to which they are themselves reasonable. Someone who has an unreasonable fear of heights may fail to appreciate the beauty and therefore the goodness of a mountain vista. Conversely, someone who has a proper fear of doing what is evil will be sensitive to the human tendency to rationalize a selfish act, and more prone to make accurate judgments about such actions.

It is not hard to see that Aquinas's view that humans can only choose what they perceive as good creates problems in understanding how humans do bad things. It seems undeniable that humans do bad things and sometimes desire what is bad, both for themselves and others. Aquinas's explanation of this begins by noting that things can be good in many different ways, and that there are different degrees of goodness. An action that is overall bad can still be good in some respects, and it can thus be willed as good when considered in those respects. A bad action can be seen as one in which a lesser good is preferred to a higher good. (This is similar to Augustine's view that evil involves a "disordered" form of love, in which some good that is lesser than God is loved more than God.) Thus a person who commits adultery seeks a good, namely, the good of sexual pleasure, but the act is wrong because this pleasure is gained at the expense of the greater good of marital fidelity.

This move does not fully solve the problem, however. Why does the human person prefer the lesser good to the greater good? The intellectualism Aquinas embraces seems to commit him to the view that one can only will what the intellect judges to be good, and so it would seem that when one wills a lesser good in preference to a higher good, it must be that the intellect has made a mistaken judgment about the relative goodness of the two possible courses of action. Does this mean that an evil action is simply an intellectual mistake?

Aquinas does hold that some sins are intellectual in origin, namely, those that involve negligence and those that involve what he calls "willful ignorance." However, for such intellectual errors to count as sins, it would seem that the will would still have to play a key role. If I am willfully ignorant of what I ought to do, then I must in some way have wanted to be ignorant. I carefully avoided asking certain questions, perhaps because I did not want to know the answers. If I did not know what was right, it seems that this is due in part to willing not to know. But in that case the will is not merely the servant of the intellect, but is sometimes causing the intellect to look at issues one way rather than another. Aquinas does indeed say that the will has the power to will that the intellect refuse to consider certain questions, and even the power to make its own activity its object, by willing to will something or willing not to will something. But in that case it looks like the will is not simply dependent on the intellect, as the intellectualist view of the will would imply. It is not the case simply that the will errs because it is presented by the intellect with a mistaken view about what is good. Rather, sometimes it looks as if we have a mistaken view about what is good because we will to have such a view.

Aquinas is aware of this problem, I believe, and to deal with it he develops a more dynamic view of the will and its relation to the intellect. Instead of a simple dependence of the will on the intellect, he says that the will and the intellect have a kind of mutual influence on each other.[18] The intellect affects the will as a final cause, and the will can move the intellect as an efficient cause. We can and do will to reflect more about a decision, for example, or to end reflection about it. If, however, the will in doing this simply reflects mistaken intellectual judgments about the value of reflecting more or closing the process of reflection, then it

---

[18]There is an excellent discussion of the apparent tension in Aquinas's views here in Rebecca Konyn-dyk DeYoung, Colleen McCluskey, and Christina Van Dyke, *Aquinas's Ethics: Metaphysical Foundations, Moral Theory and Theological Context* (Notre Dame, IN: University of Notre Dame Press, 2009), 115-23. These authors argue that it is possible to interpret Aquinas in such a way that his views are seen as consistent. See also Eleonore Stump's complicated discussion of these issues in her *Aquinas*, 277-306.

looks like all the real work is being done by the intellect. If we are to be culpable for willing what is a lesser good in preference to a higher good, then it would seem that this must not be purely an intellectual mistake, but one that reflects the influence of the will as well, perhaps distorted by the passions.

Aquinas's account is clearly very complicated, and perhaps if one explores its full depth a consistent account can be developed that will relieve the apparent tension in his view. Put most simply, the tension arises between the claim that the will is dependent on the intellect, and the view that the will and the intellect interact in complicated ways that allow the will to influence the intellect as well. I shall say no more about this issue at this point, but the problem of the relation between the will and the intellect in human actions is one that Aquinas bequeaths to his successors, and it will continue to be a point of contention among both later medieval and modern thinkers.

AQUINAS'S ETHICS

Aquinas's ethics, like his theory of action, are complex and can be correctly described in different ways.[19] Although there are obvious similarities to Aristotle that reflect the influence the great Greek philosopher had on Aquinas, there are also clear differences. In its general form, however, Aquinas's ethic does seem to be much like Aristotle's. First, it is *eudaimonistic*; that is, it is a teleological or end-driven ethic that focuses on happiness as the highest good for humans. (The Greek word *eudaimonia* means happiness, and thus ethical accounts that focus on happiness are forms of eudaimonism.) Second, it is a virtues ethic. Although Aquinas certainly believes that certain types of actions are intrinsically bad and must not be done, his focus is not on rules for behavior, but on acquiring a certain kind of character, one that includes certain virtues and excludes certain vices. Finally, it is a natural law ethic.

---

[19]For a reasonably concise general account of Aquinas's ethic, see Stephen J. Pope, "Overview of the Ethics of Thomas Aquinas," in *The Ethics of Thomas Aquinas* (Washington, DC: Georgetown University Press, 2002), 30-56.

I will give a fuller explanation of this term later, but I will initially describe such an ethic as one that claims that normative principles are somehow rooted in the natures of things.

Eudaimonism. Aquinas follows Aristotle in holding that human life is one in which we seek to realize certain ends, and he also follows Aristotle in distinguishing between ends we seek as a means to other ends, and ends that we seek for their own sake. Unless there are some ends of the latter sort, then human actions would be pointless. Aquinas holds that there must be some ultimate or final or complete end of human life and that this end is described as happiness. The term *happiness* here should not be taken "hedonistically," that is, as referring simply to a life full of pleasure. Rather, a happy life is one in which a person flourishes; it is a life of fulfillment. Aristotle had of course held that happiness consisted in activity of a sort, a life in which a person manifests the virtues, which in turn can be acquired by living in accordance with reason, since humans are rational animals and our happiness must in some way be a fulfillment of our nature.[20]

In saying that happiness is the final end or goal of human life, Aquinas is describing that end abstractly or formally. In some sense, the claim that happiness is the goal of life seems to him almost a platitude, one that everyone recognizes to be true. However, in saying this, he does not mean that there are no disagreements about the end of life, for he realizes that there are huge differences in how people conceive of happiness as well as differences about how it is to be sought. Everyone is seeking happiness, but this does not mean everyone has a clear understanding of what he or she is seeking.

One large difference between Aristotle and Aquinas concerns the nature of true happiness. For Aquinas the final end that humans seek that constitutes their true and perfect happiness is union with God, a view that is of course not found in Aristotle. Nevertheless, he does not simply reject Aristotle's view of happiness. Aquinas accepts the

---

[20]See chap. 5 for a discussion on Aristotle's eudaimonism.

Aristotelian view that happiness is a life of virtue in accordance with reason as an "imperfect" or preliminary account of human happiness. He sees Aristotle as giving a picture of human happiness that is correct as far as it goes. One might say that although not everyone living a life of virtue understands this, such a life is in fact directed toward the knowledge of God because it is directed toward the good. The "cardinal virtues" (wisdom, prudence, courage, and temperance, which will be discussed in the next section) are directed toward the good, even though people seeking these virtues do not necessarily have a full understanding of the good that they are seeking.

Aquinas thinks (as we saw earlier in this chapter) that humans can by reason gain a knowledge that God exists. However, the knowledge of God that humans must have to experience union with God and obtain true happiness exceeds our human natural capacities. Thus complete or perfect happiness depends on divine assistance; it is achievable only through grace. It is through divine grace that humans receive the "supernatural virtues" of faith, hope, and love, also to be discussed below. Even with divine assistance, the union with God that is our true and perfect happiness cannot be fully realized in this life. Final happiness will consist in the "beatific vision" of God after death, in which we will know God truly and also be joined to God in love, as both our intellect and will are perfected.

The virtues. Although Aquinas discusses many specific virtues, such as gratitude and patience, his account of the virtues follows what had become a tradition by focusing on seven primary virtues. The four cardinal or natural virtues are prudence, justice, courage, and temperance, while the three supernatural virtues are faith, hope, and love. The latter are in one sense "natural" as well, in that they are ultimately ways of perfecting human nature; they make it possible for us to be what we were meant to be. However, they are described as supernatural for several reasons. One is that they have God directly as their objects. As I just noted in the last section, the natural virtues also are directed to

God, but they do so indirectly by aiming at other goods. A second reason is that the supernatural virtues cannot be achieved through human effort. A person can only acquire them when God directly "infuses" them into a person.

The infused virtues created by God's direct action are therefore distinguished from the kind of "acquired virtues" that Aristotle saw humans as achieving through habitual practices. However, it would be a mistake to read Aquinas as simply giving us a "two-stage" account of moral development, in which we acquire the natural virtues ourselves, and then add to them the supernatural virtues when God infuses them. Such a picture leaves out something important. Aquinas does not think that the natural virtues are completely in order as they are, leaving only the addition of the supernatural virtues to make us complete. Rather, when God infuses the supernatural virtues, this change has a transformative effect on the natural virtues as well. Those natural virtues thus also require God's grace in order to be perfect, and thus it is proper to speak of infused versions of the natural virtues as well. For example, Aquinas holds that the unity of the virtues is made possible partly by prudence, which is connected to all other virtues, but even more so by charity, participation in the love of God. Charity stands as the root of all the virtues, and all of them require charity to be made perfect.

All the virtues are orientations toward the good. Thus prudence, or practical wisdom, is an intellectual virtue directed toward good actions and provides judgments about which actions are really good. Justice directs our will toward those goods that reason can apprehend, such as friendship, keeping one's obligations, and seeking the good of others. Temperance orders those goods perceived by the senses so that external goods do not overpower such higher goods as the goods of the soul, and ultimately God. Courage allows us to seek the good in the proper way in the face of fears that might hamper us, and also unreasonable recklessness that would incline us to take unnecessary risks.

Faith, hope, and the special kind of love usually translated as "charity" take God as an object in a more direct way. Through faith we can come in this life to know God and love him. However, since the union with God possible in this life cannot be perfect, the virtue of hope is required if our relation with God is to endure. Ultimately, as said above, our relation to God must be characterized by love or charity. As we love God properly, we will love in proper ways the goods of God's creation as well.

One might wonder how Aquinas can take infused virtues to be virtues at all. Aristotle had defined virtues as states we acquire through habitual practice, but the infused virtues are put directly into us by God, and we can do nothing to achieve them except to consent to God's activity. Aquinas of course realizes that such infused virtues will be different from acquired virtues, but he argues they are still "perfections of human capacities" that lead to good activities, and thus are properly described as virtues. The infused virtues are not merely virtues; they can properly be said to be really in the people who possess them, because the people who receive them from God can and must use these capacities and in so doing they develop them further.

Law. The Christian character of Aquinas's ethic is also shown by the role in it played by the concept of law. Aristotle of course had a concept of law, but for Aristotle laws are the creation of the *polis*, the city-state. Aquinas's ethic is an ethic of law in a deeper sense. Christianity of course has its roots in Judaism, in which the notion of law, or torah, is central. Humans do not relate merely to human rulers or lawgivers, but must relate to God, who is the rightful ruler of the universe. The notion of law in Aquinas also reflects the influence of Stoic philosophers, who had taught that everything in nature was governed by the divine Logos.

Law is best thought of as an ordering of things for the sake of the good. God as the providential creator and ruler ultimately orders all things in the universe to the good, so God's law cannot be separated from his providential direction of the universe. God's eternal law is a name for God's timeless will for the universe. Since God is himself timelessly eternal, his will for the creation must also be eternal, even if that will manifests itself through a temporal process. Physical things and animals without reason obey God's law, but humans, as conscious subjects of God, can consciously grasp (partially) God's providential ordering and thereby "participate" in God's rule. Aquinas calls this participation in the eternal law on the part of humans the natural law. Neither eternal law nor natural law should be seen as arbitrary in any way. Just as the human will is guided by the intellect's understanding of the good, so God's law is grounded in God's understanding of the good.

The most fundamental principle of the natural law is that "we should do and seek good, and shun evil."[21] Aquinas thinks that this principle is self-evidently true, and is presupposed by all our practical reasoning. Beyond this fundamental principle, our actions must be guided by our understanding of the goods in the natural order, which in turn are determined by their nature. Aquinas realizes that because of human sinfulness, we do not automatically follow the natural law. Such laws then do not function merely descriptively but normatively as well. They describe how we ought to act, whether we do so or not.

Some of the precepts of the natural law that Aquinas affirms will be surprising to some. For example, Aquinas holds, as we might expect, that theft is a sin, and in fact a mortal sin. However, he claims that, when a person in great need takes from someone who has more than he needs, it is not a case of theft:

> In cases of need, all things are common. And so it does not seem to be a sin [of any kind] if one person [in great need] takes a thing belonging to [the abundance of] another, for it has been made common as a result of his need.[22]

Our sinfulness also impairs our ability to recognize the natural law, and thus we need the "divine law," which is that portion of the eternal law that God chooses to reveal to humans through special revelation.

---

[21] Aquinas, *Summa theologiae* Ia-IIae.94.2, trans. Richard J. Regan, in Hause and Pasnau, *Basic Works,* 647.
[22] Quoted by Stump, *Aquinas,* 322. This is her translation of *Summa theologiae* IIaIIae.66.7 s.c.

The divine law reveals God's will directly and includes absolute prohibitions, thus adding a "deontological" element to Aquinas's ethic. (A deontological ethic is one that focuses on duty.) The divine law not only corrects for the imperfections of the natural law but also gives us an understanding of the supernatural good and end that we must seek to achieve perfect happiness. God's law is given in Scripture as a whole, but the "new law" is given in Christ and in the New Testament; and it is a law that we can obey by the inner help of the Holy Spirit. Law and grace thus function together to help humans achieve the end God has set for them. The gifts and fruits of the Holy Spirit also play an important role in the Christian moral life.

Although the emphasis in Aquinas's ethic certainly seems to be on the virtues as excellences that help us realize the happiness that is our intended end, the concept of law in his ethic provides a dimension that is lacking in Aristotle. The law is law because behind the law lies the authority of God. The person who does what is bad does not merely fail to become virtuous and achieve happiness, but also offends God.

THOMISM

When one looks at the amazing length of the writings Aquinas produced in a relatively short life, it is obvious that there is much more to be said about his philosophical contributions in all the areas discussed, not to mention areas I have not treated, such as political philosophy and aesthetics. A history of the whole of Western philosophy such as this one cannot do justice to such a corpus, and the reader who wants to know Aquinas should look at the primary source writings as well as the many scholarly treatments of Aquinas available.

However, before concluding this chapter I wish to make some comments on the history of the reception of Aquinas's thought. Aquinas remains a living figure in philosophy. Contemporary philosophy includes not only historical scholars who study Plato, Aristotle, and Aquinas; it also includes Platonists, Aristotelians, and "Thomists" who see themselves as carrying on and defending a living tradition.

In the immediate period after Aquinas's death, his philosophy was controversial. Some of the suspicion that fell on the Averroist readings of Aristotle fell on his work as well, and the result was that some of Aquinas's
views were officially condemned by the bishop of Paris in 1277. These
condemnations were officially revoked in 1325, shortly after Aquinas was
canonized. However, controversy continued to swirl around his thought,
partly because of partisan debates between Dominicans, who naturally
tended to defend Aquinas as a great Dominican scholar, and Franciscans,
who tended to criticize Aquinas's putative departures from the Christian
tradition rooted in Augustine. Some of this opposition was inspired by the
great Franciscan philosopher Bonaventure, whom I will discuss in the
next chapter. Some was inspired by the other great medieval thinkers
Duns Scotus and William Ockham, to be discussed in the next chapter.

The study of Aquinas was continually maintained, especially in Dominican monasteries and other institutions. However, Aquinas's
thought received new stature in Catholic circles as a result of the efforts
of Pope Leo in the late nineteenth century. Leo founded the Pontifical
Academy of St. Thomas in Rome, and in 1879 issued a famous encyc-
lical, *Aeterni Patris*, which called for the reinvigoration of Catholic
learning and singled out the philosophy of Aquinas as especially important for the church. This was one factor among others that eventually led to a fresh view of Aquinas's thought in twentieth-century
philosophy through the work of such Thomists as Jacques Maritain and
Etienne Gilson. This movement is sometimes called "Neo-Thomism."

Today the situation has changed once again. The idea (never really accurate) that Aquinas was somehow the unofficial "philosopher of the
Catholic Church" seems to have faded. Paradoxically, however, this has
made Aquinas a more important figure in contemporary philosophy,
someone not merely of interest to Catholics, but also to Protestants and
even secular thinkers. Contemporary "analytic philosophers" such as Eleonore Stump and John Haldane have succeeded in bringing Aquinas into
conversation with contemporary philosophy in new and exciting ways.

The High Middle Ages (II)

Bonaventure, Scotus, Ockham

A LARGE NUMBER OF INTERESTING and important philosophers lived and wrote during the medieval period.[1] However, a one-volume history of Western philosophy that aspires to moderate length cannot do justice to this profusion of riches. In this chapter, I shall try to discuss three of the more important of these thinkers: the thirteenth-century contemporary of Aquinas, Bonaventure, and two important later philosophers, Duns Scotus and William of Ockham.

BONAVENTURE

The philosopher we call Bonaventure was born Giovanni Fidanza in Tuscany in 1221. As a child Bonaventure was healed of an illness, and the healing was attributed to prayers directed to Francis of Assisi. Thus it was natural for Bonaventure eventually to join the Franciscan order. After his talents were recognized, he became the minister general of the Franciscans, and was made a bishop and cardinal late in his life. As a leader of the church, Bonaventure was renowned for his personal piety and integrity, and in his work for the Franciscans, he is regarded as the "second founder" of the order, because he reformed and reorganized a community that was in disarray. Near the end of his life he played a key role in attempting to develop rapprochement with the

---

[1]For discussion of many of these thinkers, see John Marenbon, *Medieval Philosophy: An Historical and Philosophical Introduction* (New York: Routledge, 2007), and Jorge Gracia and Tim Noone, eds., *A Companion to Philosophy in the Middle Ages* (Malden, MA: Blackwell, 2003).

Eastern Orthodox churches, dying in the middle of a conference seeking this goal in 1274.

Bonaventure was educated at Paris and, after his education, taught there until called to perform his arduous duties as administrator of his order and as a bishop. While at Paris he certainly became familiar with the newly rediscovered Aristotelian philosophy, and in his writings he freely draws on Aristotelian concepts and categories, such as the principles of actuality and potentiality and the Aristotelian view of the four kinds of causes. However, in comparison to Aquinas, Bonaventure is more selective in his use of the new learning and its value for Christian thought. Rather, Bonaventure followed the Franciscan tradition (and the example of his teacher Alexander of Hales) in continuing to rely mainly on the intellectual paths pioneered by Augustine. What we find in his work is an original synthesis that draws on Neoplatonic ideas as well as Aristotle, all shaped by Bonaventure's commitment to Christian revelation.

As was true of Augustine, Bonaventure made no sharp distinction between theology and philosophy, and freely drew on biblical sources in his work. For this reason, those who think philosophy must be autonomous and independent of theology have sometimes questioned whether Bonaventure is really a philosopher at all. However, to deny him this title would be to assume one side of a disputed philosophical question: whether philosophy can and should draw from sources such as religion and science. The lack of a clear distinction between philosophy and theology is actually characteristic of many medieval thinkers, and for that matter even many philosophers of the ancient world, who frequently answer questions about God or the gods, as is evident from earlier chapters of this book. Bonaventure certainly arrives at philosophical conclusions: views about the nature of reality, how truth can be known, and how happiness can be achieved. Since he often defends his conclusions with arguments, and does not simply appeal to authority, I believe it is proper to consider his work in a history of Western philosophy, as has traditionally been the case.

It is true that Bonaventure believed that a philosopher who is not guided by the Christian revelation will inevitably fall into error. It is also true that Bonaventure did not value philosophical truth primarily for its own sake, but for its ability to contribute to the knowledge of God that is necessary for union with God. It is that union that is our highest good and final end. However, those claims are themselves philosophical, and to claim dogmatically that they are inconsistent with critical reflection would itself be unphilosophical. Once more there is a parallel with many ancient philosophers, who often saw philosophy as intensely practical, aimed primarily at enabling a person to live a good and happy life.

Bonaventure on the existence of God. Bonaventure, like Thomas Aquinas, holds that the existence of God can be known with certainty by reasoning that makes no appeal to revelation. Aquinas's arguments, as we saw in the last chapter, mostly take Aristotelian physics as their starting point, beginning with evident features of the physical world and reasoning to God's existence as the first cause of those features. Bonaventure also believes that a person can start with the existence of the natural world and reason to God, though his preferred arguments rely less on Aristotelian principles and more on innovative reflections from the realm of natural philosophy such as the light metaphysics of Adam of Exeter and Robert Grosseteste.[2] However, Bonaventure also emphasizes other routes to the knowledge of God. He develops an argument inspired by Augustine that argues for God's existence as the source of the illumination provided to the mind that makes certain knowledge possible. He also develops a version of the "ontological argument" developed by Anselm. (Although the label "ontological argument" is neither Anselm's nor Bonaventure's but comes much later, from Immanuel Kant.)

---

[2]For more on the idea of the "metaphysics of light," see John Flood, James R. Gunther, and Joseph W. Goering, eds., *Robert Grosseteste and His Intellectual Milieu* (Toronto: Pontifical Institute of Medieval Studies, 2013). See especially the essay by Celia Panti, 167-76. I thank David Jeffrey for help on this chapter, including providing this reference.

Bonaventure, like Aquinas, adopts Aristotle's "hylomorphic" view of natural entities, according to which all natural objects are a union of form and matter. The form provides the essence or being of a thing, but that essence must be actualized materially for an object to exist as a particular entity. Indeed, Bonaventure goes even further than Aquinas, who had held that angels have no matter, and thus are individuated by form, each angel having a unique essence. Bonaventure holds that every created entity has both matter and form, even angels. Like Aquinas he holds that creatures who have both matter and form, thus both potentiality and actuality (understanding form and matter as Aristotle did), must be derived from a cause that has no such compositional character, but exists as pure form and thus as pure actuality. All material beings thus are in some sense "signs" that point to God as their Creator.

At this point Bonaventure displays a major difference with Aquinas. Bonaventure argues that one can show philosophically that the world had a beginning in time. Aquinas, respectful of Aristotle's view that the world was eternal, had argued that one can only know the world had a beginning through revelation. Bonaventure, however, argues that the view that the world is infinitely old and thus contains an actually infinite number of finite events leads to absurdities.

Bonaventure's preferred way of arguing for God's reality, however, does not start from external material objects in the natural world but from the mind itself. He follows Augustine in holding that the best way to find God is to "turn within,"[3] for the intellect is not merely caused to exist by God, as are nonintellectual material objects, but is itself an entity that images God. The human mind is even seen as having a triadic structure that mirrors the trinitarian character of God. Tim Noone and R. E. House interpret Bonaventure as employing three different kinds of arguments, which have the human intellect as their starting point.[4]

---

[3]See Augustine, *Confessions* 7.10, in Augustine, *Confessions*, trans. F. J. Sheed (1942; repr., Indianapolis: Hackett, 1993), 117-18.

[4]What follows leans heavily on Tim Noone and R. E. Houser, "Bonaventure," in *The Stanford Encyclopedia of Philosophy*, winter 2014 ed., ed. Edward N. Zalta, http://plato.stanford.edu/entries/bonaventure/.

Each of these arguments begins, not with particular entities, but with the "transcendentals" that the mind grasps: being, unity, truth, and goodness. These transcendentals are not mere "properties" possessed by some things and not others but universal features of reality.

The first kind of argument, clearly inspired by Augustine, focuses on illumination. The human mind has a capacity to grasp truth, but our ability to grasp truth presupposes a "Truth" that is ultimate and certain. God is not the sole cause of our knowledge; our created faculties also play a role. However, the human mind's ability to generalize and abstract universals from particulars requires a "light" that makes it possible for humans to grasp such things with certainty.

In a loose sense the argument from illumination seems causal, but Bonaventure also develops an argument from the human intellect that is more clearly causal in nature. Bonaventure thinks of truth not merely in epistemic terms, as something possessed by propositions or statements. Rather, truth, since it is one of the transcendentals, is ontological as well. Everything that exists is "true" to the degree that it realizes or actualizes what it was meant to be. Bonaventure holds that such truth owes its being to an eternal Truth in which it participates. God may be seen as a kind of "formal cause" not only of epistemic truth but also of this ontological truth.

The third argument, like Anselm's famous ontological argument, begins from the idea of God. Once we see that all natural objects, as hylomorphic, must derive their reality from a cause that is pure actuality, we clearly have a grasp of a being whose very nature must be pure actuality and thus must exist. Those who fail to grasp this do so only because they have not properly understood God's nature. When we properly understand God's nature as pure actuality, we can see that God cannot fail to exist, and also cannot exist merely as one creature among other creatures. In the face of "parody objections" such as Gaunilo's "greatest possible island" objection to Anselm (see chap. 8), Bonaventure argues that only God, who—unlike islands and other finite creatures—has no matter and no potentiality, has an essence that implies his existence. Bonaventure is the last great philosopher to defend the ontological argument until it is revived in the modern period by Descartes, Spinoza, and Leibniz.

Bonaventure on creation as a process. Bonaventure also follows Augustine in holding that God's creative activity is not complete at the beginning, even though it is true that the world had a beginning. Augustine had held that God had placed structures into the natural order that he calls *rationes seminales* (literally, "seminal ideas"), which have the potential to develop in particular ways. Because of these "seminal ideas" it is possible for new and higher forms of animal life to develop. Some have viewed this idea as a precursor of modern theories of evolution. There are, however, obvious major differences with Darwinian theory. Bonaventure has nothing like the Darwinian view that species emerge through competition with other species. Most importantly, Bonaventure held that human souls have to be directly created by God, and thus could not have emerged simply through a natural process.

Like other medieval thinkers, Bonaventure also had interesting things to say about physics, biology, how knowledge is attained, and a host of other questions, though many of his writings focus on issues of scriptural interpretation. As of yet, some of his most important writings have yet to be translated, and hence much of his work is currently available only to specialists.

JOHN DUNS SCOTUS

The term *Scotus* simply means "the Scot" and thus really is a kind of nickname. The family name was actually Duns. Scotus was born in a small village just north of the English border, probably in late 1265 or early 1266, and was ordained as a Franciscan in 1291. Scotus studied at Oxford between 1288 and 1301. He then taught at Paris, with a brief interruption when he was expelled (along with a large number of other friars) for taking the pope's side in a dispute with the king. In 1304

Scotus was appointed regent master for the Franciscans in Paris, and in 1307 he was transferred to a Franciscan institution in Cologne, where he died in 1308. During this relatively short life, Scotus wrote a large number of works characterized by great originality and complex arguments. He quickly acquired the descriptive title "Subtle Doctor." As one might expect, complex arguments do not lend themselves well to brief summary, but I shall try to sketch some of Scotus's most important ideas in several areas.

Natural theology. Much of what Scotus says about our natural knowledge of God is consistent with the views of Aquinas. Scotus agrees with Aquinas that all of our knowledge stems from our experience of finite things. Despite this limitation, he agrees with Aquinas that we can prove God's existence through an argument that starts with the existence of natural objects and reasons to God as the ultimate cause of the natural world. He also agrees with Aquinas that during this life we humans cannot know God's essence.

Despite these points of agreement, there is one major point of disagreement between the two thinkers. Aquinas had argued that the positive concepts we apply to God can only be applied analogously. Thus, when we say God is good or loving or powerful, these concepts are only analogous to those we use when we say that a creature is good or loving or powerful. Scotus argues that this view is false. We can attribute positive qualities to God, and when we do so we use the same concepts we use when we talk about creatures. The concepts we correctly apply to God are thus "univocal" and not analogical.

Scotus argues for this univocal predication in several ways. One argument is that, if all our concepts are derived from our experience of finite objects, there is no viable source for any concepts that are distinct from our ordinary ones. Hence if we could not apply those concepts to God we could not speak of God at all. Scotus takes it as certain that we can speak of God, so we must be able to apply our concepts to God.

A second argument for univocal predication is inspired by Anselm. Anselm had memorably described God as a "being than which none greater can be conceived." When we consider our concepts, Scotus claims that some of them designate "perfections." There are some perfections, such as having strong muscles, that imply limitation, since one cannot have strong muscles without having a body, and a body brings with it limitations. However, there are some perfections that are "pure perfections" that do not imply such limitations. These concepts can be applied univocally to God.

Of course Scotus recognized that when we apply human concepts to God, we do not mean to say that God is just like the finite objects we experience that are the source of the concept. When finite objects possess a perfection, they always possess a finite form of that perfection. God, however, is infinite, and thus has all the pure perfections to an infinite degree. So even though we cannot grasp God's essence in this life we nonetheless can know some of God's attributes.

Scotus's main argument for God's existence is best thought of as a form of the cosmological argument, an argument that God must exist as the first or ultimate cause of the universe. The argument he develops is enormously complex, and a full exploration of it would probably require a book-length treatment.[5] However, some of the major elements can be explained. One is a distinction Scotus makes between two kinds of causal series: an "accidentally ordered series" and an "essentially ordered series." In an accidentally ordered series, A gives rise to B, and B to C, but A's existence is not essential to C's existence, even if B's existence is, since B might come into existence through some agent other than A. Thus it is possible that B might exist and cause C even if A does not exist. However, in an essentially ordered series, every element in the series depends on every preceding element, all of which are necessary for the occurrence of the later elements. One might think of such a

---

[5]For an extended treatment of the argument, see the article on Scotus by Thomas Williams, on which I rely heavily for much of my interpretation of Scotus, "John Duns Scotus," *The Stanford Encyclopedia of Philosophy*, spring 2016 ed., ed. Edward N. Zalta, http://plato.stanford.edu/entries/duns-scotus/.

series as one in which all the causes operate simultaneously, as when I kick a football, which is caused by moving my leg, which is in turn caused by my volition to kick the ball.

With this distinction in place, Scotus proceeds to argue that God must exist as the first agent or cause of the natural world. Nothing can be the cause of itself, and nothing comes from nothing, so a cause of the natural world is necessary. The cause cannot be an infinite chain, since such an infinite regress is impossible, and a circular chain of causes is also impossible. Hence the cause must be something beyond the natural world itself. If the causal series that produces the effects in the natural world is an essentially ordered series, then that cause must exist.

The complexities of the argument chiefly stem from subarguments Scotus gives for the premises of the main argument. For example, he argues that the existence of an accidentally ordered series implies the existence of an essentially ordered series, and since there are acciden-tally ordered series in nature, there must be at least one essentially or-dered series. He also offers arguments that the "first agent" that is proved must be God: a being that is not only the ultimate cause of everything other than God but also a being that is the ultimate goal of the activities of finite things and a being that is maximally excellent. Scotus was attempting to make his cosmological argument a true dem-onstration, not relying on contingent facts (such as that something has been produced) but on necessary facts about the nature of being (such as that something is producible).[6]

For Scotus, the key to understanding God lies in the concept of in-finity. When we conceive of God we must think of him as "infinite being." This does not mean God simply has a greater amount of some quality that we possess. The relevant concept of infinity is a qualitative concept; infinite being cannot be grasped simply as a "potential infinite," as when one conceives of a series of numbers to which additions can

---

[6]Thanks to Thomas Ward for this insight. For a nice explication of Scotus's natural theology, see Richard Cross, *Scotus on God* (Farnham, UK: Ashgate, 2005).

always be made. Such a potential infinite is necessarily conceived quantitatively, but infinite being is an intrinsic, qualitative feature of whatever has it. Scotus holds that the other perfections of God that we can understand are all implicit in this concept of infinite being.

Metaphysics. Scotus holds that metaphysics is the "science of being," but he understands this in a broader way than Aristotle. For one thing, in accord with Bonaventure (and many other medievals) he puts great stress on the "transcendentals." These include being, unity, truth, and goodness, all of which are characteristics of everything that exists, finite or infinite. Metaphysics also studies the "categories," basically as Aristotle had developed the list, including substance, quantity, quality, relation, action, passion, place, time, position, and state.[7]

Following Aristotle, and in basic agreement with Aquinas, Scotus views individual substances as a union of form and matter. Form provides the essence of a thing, and matter is responsible for the accidental properties of a thing. However, Scotus diverges from Aquinas in several important ways. First, he claims that matter can exist even when it has no form at all. Aquinas (following Aristotle) had called such matter "prime matter," but Aquinas held that prime matter was only a theoretical possibility, since form provides actuality and nothing can exist that is purely potential. (Scholars disagree as to whether Aristotle held this same view.) Scotus believed that matter can persist through substantial changes, and thus it must have some kind of actuality in itself. He also believed that purely immaterial beings could have potentiality, unlike Bonaventure, who had taught that angels must be material since they have potentiality. Hence for Scotus the equation of form with actuality and matter with potentiality is not complete. An immaterial being with just form (such as an angel) can have some potentiality, while matter as such has some actuality.

Scotus also denies the Thomistic doctrine that each substance can possess only one substantial form. One problem with this Thomistic

---

[7]This list is taken from Williams, "John Duns Scotus."

view is that it seems to imply that the body of a dead person becomes a different substance at death. During life the person's soul is the form of the body, but the death of the person means that the soul departs from the body. Strictly speaking, then, after death the person's body becomes a different substance, since it no longer has the same form. However, it certainly appears that the body of someone who has died is the same body that previously was ensouled. Scotus solves this problem by holding that, besides the soul, the body has a kind of form of its own, which allows the body of the deceased person to persist, at least until the body decomposes.

One of the most interesting and important elements of Scotus's metaphysical theory is his account of individuation. On Aquinas's view, the form of human nature is a universal, and what individuates that form is the matter in which it is embodied. Thus one person differs from another due to the different matter that the common form each has is embodied in, and the separate histories that each material thing enjoys. (It is for this reason that Aquinas holds that each angel must have a distinct form in order to be individuated, since angels have no matter.) The Scotistic doctrine that a substance can possess more than one form allows for a different view of individuation. Scotus holds that in addition to the universal form of human nature that each person possesses, human beings also possess individual forms. A universal form gives a thing its universal nature, its "whatness." Scotus adds that substances also possess a "thisness" (*haecceity* in Latin). Thus Socrates has not only the form of human nature but also a unique individual form that we might call "Socrateity" (meaning a form possessed only by the unique individual who was Plato's teacher, not a property anyone named "Socrates" would have). In effect, when God creates human persons, he conceives of them as possessing not only a common human nature but also a unique individual character. As we shall see later, in the discussion of the thought of Søren Kierkegaard, this idea that God creates particular individuals and wills these individuals to have unique characteristics will reverberate through modern Western thought, strengthening a kind of "individualism" that is already implicit in the Christian idea that human persons are individually responsible before God.

Since Scotus views the human soul as distinct from the body, his view obviously allows for the possibility that the soul survives death, and as a Christian thinker, he affirms this possibility, as well as the eventual reuniting of body and soul at the resurrection. However, Scotus does not think that a philosophical proof can be given of the soul's immortality. The soul's ability to survive death is thus more a function of God's will than of the soul's intrinsic characteristics.

Epistemology. Scotus accepts the Aristotelian picture, already developed by Aquinas, that humans have not only a sensory or "passive" intellect, dependent on the bodily sense organs, as is the case with other animals, but also an "active" intellect that is immaterial and thus does not depend on the body for its operation. Like Aquinas, Scotus holds that when a human comes to know a form, the person must receive a "phantasm" through the senses, from which the active intellect can "abstract" the universal. In this life, our ability to grasp concepts and even our ability to employ those concepts thus depends on the body.

Scotus believes that after death this will no longer be the case. However, at times he seems to suggest that even in this life we can have the power to develop "intellectual intuitions." In general, intuitive knowing is a kind of direct awareness of an object. When I perceive a dog, it is through abstraction that I become aware of "doghood," but it is through sensory intuition that I actually come to know there is a particular dog that is present to me. However, besides sensory intuitions, Scotus (at least at times) believes we have the power to become aware of the existence of immaterial things, such as our own intellect and its activity, without the use of any sensory phantasms.

Scotus provides a spirited defense of our natural human cognitive powers, both against forms of skepticism and against theories that posit a need for a special divine illumination that makes knowledge possible. If our natural intellectual powers are not reliable, then we cannot avoid skepticism by an appeal to divine illumination, for in that case we could not really know God or know that God helps make our knowledge possible. For Scotus, certain knowledge is possible, at least with respect to "first principles," as well as anything that can be logically derived from these principles, and even for some causal judgments based on experience.

Moral psychology and ethics. We saw in the last chapter that Aquinas adopts an "intellectualist" account of the relation between the will and the intellect, which maintains that the operation of the will is dependent on the activity of the intellect in presenting to the will an end that is understood to be good. Scotus believes this psychological picture to be inadequate to give us an understanding of our lives as moral beings. He holds that morally responsible action must be free, since we cannot be responsible for what we cannot help doing. To be free, the choice of a moral agent cannot then be determined simply by the intellect's understanding. When I am presented with a morally significant choice, it must be possible for me to act in more than one way, even if we take into account how I understand the ends I am considering. Thus Scotus develops a more "voluntarist" view of the human will. One should not understand this as meaning that the will acts arbitrarily, in a way that is unrelated to its understanding of what is good. When an agent acts, the agent does act for reasons. However, we often possess reasons for performing more than one action, and thus our reasons do not always determine us to do just one thing. In contemporary philosophical language, Scotus has a "libertarian" view of human freedom, and clearly rejects the view that human actions are causally determined.

Scotus holds, borrowing a distinction from Anselm, that humans have two great "affections" or inclinations, which we might describe as two importantly different kinds of reasons for action. On the one hand there is an inclination to "advantage," in which we want to satisfy our desires and obtain happiness. However, we also have an inclination to "justice," or to do what is morally right. Sometimes we find these two affections are at cross-purposes. If we simply follow our desires, we will do what is wrong. To do what is right we must not simply follow our desires. Scotus therefore rejects the "eudaimonistic" conception of ethics that Aquinas takes from Aristotle, in which the end of human life that guides moral decisions is simply happiness.

Though Scotus rejects what we might call a simple eudaimonism, this does not mean he thinks that happiness is unimportant to human life. In fact, he agrees with Aquinas that our ultimate end is a blissful eternal life with God. However, the achievement of that end requires us to become the kinds of persons who will rightly prioritize justice over our desires for happiness in this life. Paradoxically, the route to ultimate happiness requires me to value something more than my own happiness, at least when happiness is understood in temporal, this-worldly ways.

What exactly are the requirements of morality or justice? Here Scotus develops a "divine-command" account of moral obligation, in which the moral law is determined by God's edicts. A divine-command account of moral obligations is often caricatured in ethics textbooks as a view that God could make anything moral by a command; on such a view God's commands appear to be completely arbitrary.

The view Scotus holds is far from this extreme view. We can see this by looking at what Scotus says about the Ten Commandments, or the Decalogue, an important statement of God's commands in Scripture. Scotus holds that the Decalogue can be divided into two parts or "tables." The first table of the law, which includes such commands as that humans should worship God and only God, consists of commands that God necessarily makes. God cannot command us to worship anything other than God, because any such command would be fundamentally opposed to the good. However, God is essentially good and thus cannot command what is against the good.

The second table of the law, however, contains commands that are not necessary. The actions commanded do aim at the good, and thus they are "fitting" or "appropriate" for God to command. However, there are other possible commands God could have given that are equally aimed at the good. For example, instead of commanding us not to steal and thereby to respect private property, perhaps God could have commanded us to share everything with others, as did the apostles and other early Christians in Acts 2:44, thus abolishing private property. Such commands are neither necessary nor completely arbitrary. They are contingently true and made true by God's commands, just as it is contingently true that there are elephants but no unicorns by virtue of God's creative decree.[8] However, the fact that they are fitting or appropriate means to the good shows that God's commands are not arbitrary.

Scotus then is far from holding that morality is completely the result of arbitrary divine decrees. He holds that some moral truths are necessary truths and thus not even God can alter them. Other truths about moral obligations are made true by divine commands, but even here God's commands are fitting or appropriate in relation to the good. There is clearly a difference between such a view and the "natural law" view we saw in Aquinas, but the differences are not absolute. Aquinas also holds that the principles of the natural law are part of God's law, a "participation" in the eternal decree of God. The major difference is perhaps that Scotus thinks that God has more discretion over what he commands than does Aquinas, who sees God's commands to us as fixed by God's understanding of what is good and good for us, given the natures he has given us. As we will see in the next section, the kind of radical voluntarism sometimes attributed to Scotus is actually closer to the view of William of Ockham.

---

[8]For a fuller discussion of Scotus as a divine command theorist, see John E. Hare, *God and Morality: A Philosophical History* (Oxford: Blackwell, 2007), 75-115.

WILLIAM OF OCKHAM

William of Ockham (also spelled "Occam") is thought to have been raised in a small village (called Ockham naturally) southwest of London. Not much reliable information is available on his early life, but he was ordained as a Franciscan in 1306, and thus was probably born sometime around 1285. (Estimates vary from 1280 to 1288.) He studied theology at the Franciscan House in London for a period before beginning studies at Oxford around 1318. Ockham never actually finished his degree at Oxford, and thus is sometimes called the "Venerable Inceptor," an inceptor being a person who has not yet finished his degree. In 1323 he was summoned to the papal court in Avignon, France, to answer charges of heresy. (The papacy had during this period been moved from Rome to Avignon.) He stayed at Avignon for four years while his case was investigated. (Some think he was under a loose form of house arrest during this time.) While there he became embroiled in a bitter dispute with the pope, along with some other Franciscans, over the meaning of the voluntary poverty that was central to the Franciscan rule. Eventually Ockham decided that the pope was not only mistaken but also corrupt, and he and some other Franciscans escaped on stolen horses and found refuge with Louis of Bavaria, a nobleman who was also an opponent of the pope.

Ockham was never actually found guilty of heresy. However, after the escape, he and the other Franciscans who fled were excommunicated. Efforts were made to capture them, but Ockham lived out his final years with Louis and avoided any punishment. Those years were spent mostly writing nonauthorized treatises on issues dealing with the relation between the church and the state. Ockham is one of the earliest advocates of the separation of church and state, and in the course of making his case he also argued for a form of freedom of speech and toleration for those who hold unorthodox views.

Ockham's razor. Ockham is most famous for the principle called "Ockham's razor." This principle is often stated in the following form:

"Entities should not be multiplied beyond what is necessary." In reality nothing like this formula can be found in Ockham's writing, and he never described his own "principle of parsimony" as a "razor." Ockham did indeed argue that simplicity was a great virtue in theorizing, but he applied his principle to hypotheses rather than entities. In fact, though Ockham's name is tightly linked to the principle, he was far from the first to employ such a principle, which can be traced to Aristotle at least. Something like this principle was accepted by almost all medieval philosophers, although Ockham perhaps was more vigorous in using the principle than others. Although contemporary philosophers (and even contemporary scientists) frequently invoke this principle in debates, it is often unclear what counts as a simpler hypothesis or explanation. A scientific theory, for example, can be simpler in terms of the kinds of entities it posits, or in terms of the number of laws required, and sometimes a theory that is simpler in one respect is more complicated in another respect. Simplicity can also be a feature of the laws themselves, and there is also vigorous disagreement on when it is necessary to introduce a new hypothesis or entity to explain some datum.

Nominalism. A major issue in medieval philosophy concerned the status of "universals," including properties such as "whiteness" as well as the "substantial forms" such as "human nature" that provide the essence for a substance. Early medieval thinkers, heavily influenced by Augustine, had mostly leaned toward a Platonic view of universals that saw them as real entities, existing however not in a Platonic heaven, but as ideas in God's mind. (This view is often called "extreme realism" by its opponents, especially Thomists.) Aquinas and Scotus had defended a more Aristotelian view of universals, which accepts their reality but emphasizes that they exist immanently in the natural world, not as separate entities. (Proponents often call this view "moderate realism.") Ockham is well known for challenging this realist view of universals. His ontology is one in which only concrete individuals exist, and this view is usually described as "nominalism." (The term comes from the

Latin word for "names," since we have names for universals but those names do not derive their meaning by referring to real entities.)

One might think that Ockham derived his nominalism from an application of his principle of simplicity or parsimony, with the thought being that the postulation of universals as realities is an unnecessary extravagance. However, Ockham's reasons for rejecting realism about universals are stronger than this; he actually argues that postulating universals is incoherent and thus we can know the falsity of such a view. He claims that if universals were real and provided a common essence for things that are part of the same species, then God could not annihilate one individual without annihilating the whole species. If God were to destroy the one individual, he would have to destroy the universal, but in that case he would be destroying all the things given their identity by possessing that universal. Ockham thought it was obvious that God, being omnipotent, could destroy one individual without doing anything to others, so he concluded that universals do not exist. Proponents of universals reject this argument by claiming that what God would destroy in such a case is not the universal but just a particular instantiation of that universal. The intuition that lies behind Ockham's view is that whatever exists must be in some way a unity, but what is shared by multiple individuals cannot be such a unity.

Textbooks discussing the problem of universals sometimes claim that there is a middle position between realism and nominalism that is called "conceptualism." Conceptualism is supposed to be the view that we have real concepts of universals, but those concepts are human constructions and do not refer to real entities. However, this view is arguably just Ockham's position, and thus is a form of nominalism. Ockham does not deny that we have human concepts of universals. When we perceive individual objects, our minds sort them into groups or categories based on the ways they resemble each other, and we do develop concepts of such groups or categories. Realist critics of such a view respond by arguing that when individuals resemble each other, they do so by sharing a common property, such as whiteness, and thus that conceptualism does not make sense unless there are real universal properties. So the viability of nominalism depends on our being able to recognize similarities and differences between individuals without recognizing the possession or lack of possession of common properties.

The problem of universals assumed huge importance in the medieval world because of the role it played in theology in explaining the transformation of the wine and bread during the Mass. The doctrine of transubstantiation, as articulated by Aquinas, for example, held that during Communion the substance of the bread and wine was miraculously transformed into the body and blood of Christ, even though the bread and wine appeared outwardly the same. This appearance was the result of the fact that the "accidental properties" of the bread and the wine were preserved, even though the substance was changed. An opponent of universals, such as Ockham, was thus faced with the problem of giving an alternative explanation of the Mass, and suspicions about the adequacy of his view could and did lead to suspicions about his orthodoxy.

Logic and epistemology. Ockham made important contributions to logic, but much of his work in this area is technical and requires some expertise in logic (as well as the history of logic) to understand. Some of his important contributions concern how logical "connectors" and "operators" work; that is, he gives interesting accounts of how such terms as *and* and *or* as well as *not* work in logic. Ockham also developed what would today be called a "causal theory of reference," which holds that many of our terms gain their meaning by referring to objects, and that their ability to refer in this way is grounded in a causal connection to the objects referred to.

This account is linked as well to a theory that underneath our actual spoken and written languages (such as English and Latin) is a "language of thought." Thoughts are the ultimate bearers of meaning, and thoughts get their meaning (at least partly) by virtue of their causal links to objects in the world. Thus, when I say or write *water*, the word gets its meaning by virtue of my thought of water, and that thought refers to water because it in some way is caused by my experience of water.

Ockham is, like Aquinas and Scotus, a kind of empiricist who wants to claim that all our concepts are derived from sense experience. However, unlike most other medieval thinkers, Ockham is a "direct realist" in his account of sense experience. Most medieval thinkers had been "representational realists," holding that what we are directly aware of in sense experience is some mental reality, such as a "phantasm," that is caused to occur in us by objects in the external world through the senses, and which then represent those objects to us and allow us to gain knowledge of them. Ockham, like the later philosopher George Berkeley, who will be considered in chapter fourteen, thinks that if we have no direct contact with the external world, then our knowledge of that world is threatened. Unlike Berkeley, who rejects the existence of material objects in favor of a world of ideas, Ockham argues, in a way that anticipates another later philosopher, Thomas Reid, that our experience is experience of real objects and not representations of those objects.

Ethics and divine-command theory. Traditionally, Ockham has been interpreted as a divine-command theorist about moral obligations in a more radical sense than Scotus. On this interpretation, Ockham held that moral obligations are grounded in a "positive law" that must be the result of the commands of an authoritative ruler, and God is the one who must provide such laws if there are to be moral obligations. However, Ockham goes much further than Scotus by holding that all of God's laws are the result of his free choice, and none are therefore necessary. Scotus had held, it will be recalled, that though moral obligations are the result of God's commands, some of God's commands are necessary, and all of them are constrained by God's nature, in such a way that they are fitting or appropriate in furthering the good.

On Ockham's more radical voluntarism, God's laws are not constrained in this way. God could have commanded humans to rape and murder each other, and if he had done so, then those actions would have been morally right and even obligatory. The main motivation for this extreme voluntarism seems to have been a concern to safeguard divine sovereignty. If God's commands were limited by some objective standard of goodness, then God's freedom would be limited. He would in some way be subject to a standard of goodness alien to him. (Those who reject radical voluntarism normally reject this claim by arguing that the standard of goodness derives from God's nature and thus is not external to him.)

Recently, the traditional reading of Ockham as a radical voluntarist has been challenged by scholars who claim that Ockham is more of an Aristotelian than has been thought.[9] They emphasize that in addition to the positive law that is grounded in divine commands, Ockham also recognizes that our human nature and our desire for happiness give us reasons to act in accordance with God's commands, thus making his views more similar to Aquinas and Scotus than has traditionally been thought. It is true that Ockham does believe that pagans who lack access to God's commands in Scripture can through "right reason" come to recognize and live by much of the content of morality. Thus a person can live morally simply by following reason, and this seems very similar to the natural law theories of Aquinas and Scotus.

These are important points, and I agree that Ockham does recognize the role reason can play in coming to live morally, especially in the case of pagans who do not have access to special revelation. However, in my judgment the traditional view of Ockham as a radical voluntarist still seems correct.[10] As it stands, God has commanded us to live in ways such that what is morally obligatory overlaps considerably with what reason tells us to do. However, Ockham claims that God was under no compulsion to give the commands he did. Thus it still seems right to say

---

[9]See, for example, Marilyn McCord Adams, "Ockham on Will, Nature, and Morality," in *The Cambridge Companion to Ockham*, ed. Paul Vincent Spade (Cambridge: Cambridge University Press, 1999), 245-72.
[10]For a reply to Marilyn Adams defending the view I take here, see Thomas Osborne, "Ockham as a Divine-Command Theorist," *Religious Studies* 41, no. 1 (March 2005): 1-22.

that if God had given radically different commands, then what is morally right would have been radically different from what actually is the case. That "right reason" and "morality" coincide is thus a contingent fact. The voluntaristic character of actual moral obligations remains.

Rejection of natural theology. Probably the sharpest disagreement between Ockham and his great predecessors concerns his rejection of natural theology. As a Christian, Ockham of course believed in God and thought such belief was rational. However, he rejected the view that God's existence could be demonstrated. His empiricist account of language and knowledge led to a critique of both the ontological and cosmological arguments.

On his view the ontological argument is an attempt to prove that there must be a greatest possible being. Ockham grants that there must be a greatest being. If there were no God or angels, then humans would be the greatest beings. However, he does not believe it can be proved that the greatest being is God. For one thing, the greatest being might not be one being at all. Proponents of the argument will respond that the argument does not rest on the idea of a greatest actual being but a greatest possible being. At this point Ockham's empiricism leads him to be skeptical that we can know the existence of such a being simply by a priori thought.

Ockham considers two forms of the cosmological argument and rejects both. One form of the argument claims that God must exist as the first efficient cause of the universe, because an infinite series of such causes is impossible. Ockham denies that this is so, because, like Aristotle, he claims that from a scientific or philosophical view the world might not have had a beginning, and in that case there would be an infinite series of causes. Such a series is not impossible, because not all of the causes have to exist simultaneously. The other form of the argument claims that there must be a conserving cause of the existence of the world, and in the case of a conserving cause all of the causes must operate simultaneously. In that case Ockham agrees that an infinite series would be impossible, but he denies that we can know that the world needs a conserving cause. From a rational point of view, the world might just be what today would be termed a brute fact.

Belief in God for Ockham is thus not grounded in philosophical or scientific theorizing, but in faith. Because of the prominence of faith in his account, Ockham is often called a fideist. But if we understand fideism as a rejection of reason or rationality, Ockham is certainly not a fideist. He does not think of the belief that is a component of faith as irrational or nonrational, but as a reasonable response to God's self-revelation. Like many later Protestants, he wants to argue that our primary means of coming to know God is through God's special revelation.

CONCLUSION

The disagreements between Aquinas, Bonaventure, Scotus, and Ockham show the great diversity of thought in the Middle Ages, contrary to the stereotype of this period as one of intellectual conformity. Those committed to the "Thomism" of Aquinas often portray later medieval philosophy as a kind of decline, in which the rational basis for Christian faith was undermined. It is probably true that in some ways the disagreements of the late Middle Ages prefigure later disagreements among Christian thinkers, including those that will occur at the time of the Reformation. Ockham's appeal to the Scriptures to criticize the pope is a good illustration of this. However, it ought to be remembered that all of these thinkers were trying to be faithful both to the demands of reason as well as the Bible and Christian tradition. They all accepted the essentials of Christian faith as summarized in the ancient creeds. Perhaps they show that even Christian philosophy is inevitably pluralistic in a fallen world in which philosophy is being done by finite and fallible thinkers.

Philosophy Between the
Medieval and Modern Periods

To UNDERSTAND HUMAN HISTORY, human beings find it nec-
essary to slice that history into periods or eras; we are unable to understand the whole story at once. Of course the divisions we draw between
periods are always somewhat arbitrary; there is no definite date at which
we can say the medieval period ended and the modern period began. In
this chapter I shall discuss a number of intellectual developments and
important thinkers who helped European thought make its way from
what is recognized as the High Middle Ages to what we might properly
call the modern period, which is generally agreed to begin philosophically with the work of the French thinker René Descartes. We might describe this intervening period in different ways and be equally accurate:
as the waning of the Middle Ages, or as the dawning of the modern
period. In addition to looking at notable figures, to understand this
period we must discuss three influential developments: the Renaissance,
the Protestant Reformation, and the development of modern science.

MEISTER ECKHART: A LATE MEDIEVAL THINKER
WITH INFLUENCE ON LATER THOUGHT

Before proceeding to look at those developments, I shall first pause to
take a brief look at Meister Eckhart, a medieval thinker, whose life
(1260–1328) actually overlapped with those of Scotus and Ockham
from a strictly chronological point of view, but whose influence was

mainly felt much later. Eckhart was a German priest, ordained as a Dominican, and he became recognized not only as a theologian/ philosopher but also as the successful administrator of a number of monastic establishments. Eckhart was also renowned as a preacher, and in fact, until the nineteenth century, the only writings of his that survived were a selection of his sermons (although oral transmission of some of his teachings had continued). During the nineteenth century, however, a number of writings that had been thought to have been lost were found, and there has been a revival of interest in his thought. Late in his life, Eckhart found himself accused of heresy, and in fact the pope issued a bull condemning many of his statements.

Unlike his contemporaries, mostly influenced by Aristotle, Eckhart was more influenced by a different strand of ancient writings also becoming more widely known in the West: Neoplatonism as propounded in the writing of Proclus the disciple of Plotinus. Eckhart also drew on the writings of Pseudo-Dionysius, a major influence on many earlier medieval thinkers. The writer we call Pseudo-Dionysius was also deeply influenced by Neoplatonism.[1] The result of this for Eckhart was a philosophical view that emphasized mystical union with God over rational insight, drawing on the strong current of "negative theology" present in many medieval thinkers.

What created trouble for Eckhart were passages in his works that seemed to undermine the distinctions between God and the created world as well as the distinction between God and the human soul. He seems to suggest at times that there is a portion of the human self that always retains an identity with God, and that the world itself was in some way part of God or at least stems from God. Such a view is today often termed "panentheism," and there is little doubt that Eckhart's views were influential on some of the "German Idealists" who followed Kant, notably including Hegel, who taught a monistic view that all of reality was one interconnected whole.

---

[1]See chap. 6 for an account of Neoplatonism.

Eckhart's writings were unsystematic and often seem contradictory, so interpretation of his work is controversial. Many Catholic Christians still defend his orthodoxy, while some contemporary post-Christian mystics celebrate his unorthodoxy as a fine example of the "freethinking" that would characterize so much of modern and contemporary philosophy.

THE RENAISSANCE AND PICO DELLA MIRANDOLA

The Renaissance (meaning "rebirth") was mainly an artistic movement, inspired by the rediscovery of and renewed appreciation for the art of antiquity. Medieval art, particularly in the early periods, evoked deep spiritual meaning and tended to focus on biblical scenes and themes. Art in the great cathedrals was not intended to be "high art" to be observed as in a museum; it was supposed to inspire, to educate (most people were illiterate), and to be a focus for devotion and spiritual contemplation. It is not surprising then that the art was not "realistic" or "naturalistic," but stylized and shaped by symbolism. In the late Middle Ages, artists began to display human anatomy and landscape scenes more realistically, and to use artistic techniques that evoked a three-dimensional experience. This trend came to fruition in the Renaissance through such artists as Leonardo de Vinci (1452–1519) and of course Michelangelo, with his stunning statue *David* in Florence, and the powerful ceiling of the Sistine Chapel in the Vatican.

In time the Renaissance inspired a renewed and deeper engagement, not just with the art of the ancient world, but with its philosophy as well. Ancient schools such as Skepticism and Stoicism began to be studied again. All of this, combined with other developments of the time, combined to give people the sense that they were indeed living in a "new" or "modern" age that was quite different from that which the medievals had inhabited.

Perhaps the figure who most perfectly captures this Renaissance understanding of a new beginning is the Italian thinker Pico della Mirandola (1463–1494), who is most famous for his *Oration on Human Dignity*. The idea that humans have a special value and dignity was not of course new. Medievals had taught that humans, made in the image of God, had an exalted role in the "great chain of being," the hierarchical cosmos God had created that contained everything from angels to shadows. Pico, in his *Oration*, understands human dignity in a new way. Our dignity comes not simply from the place God has assigned to us in the hierarchy of being. Rather, what is special about humans is that we are given the privilege of deciding who we are, of choosing our place in the great chain. Of course humans have a nature, but they also have the freedom to define their nature and in one sense become their own creators, or at least co-creators with God. Pico's view obviously resonates with the views of many later thinkers in the West, such as the existentialists who insist that we humans have the power to define our own "essence." Pico himself does not go that far, but the impetus of his position pushes toward such a view. Pico is rightly renowned as one of the champions of "Renaissance humanism," which focused more on this-worldly, human life than God and eternity.

NICCOLÒ MACHIAVELLI

Another influential Italian thinker from the period who definitely focused on "this-worldly" issues was Machiavelli, the renowned author of *The Prince*. Although Machiavelli wrote a series of discourses in which he extolled the virtue of republican self-governance, *The Prince* continues to be his best-known work, a classic in political philosophy. In some ways *The Prince* echoes the arguments given by Thrasymachus and Glaucon in Plato's *Republic*.[2] There Thrasymachus challenges Socrates by claiming that justice is simply "the advantage of the stronger." Thrasymachus believes that those with power make the rules and that those rules are designed to benefit the rulers. Doing what is right or just is not really in the best interests of ordinary people, but the punishments and sanctions attached to the rules of morality give them no

---

[2]See chap. 4 for the discussion of the arguments of Thrasymachus and Glaucon, along with the reply given by Socrates.

choice but to follow morality. After Socrates refutes Thrasymachus, Glaucon jumps in and pushes the argument further. Although Glaucon wants to believe Socrates is right, he worries that what people really value is not being just or morally upright, but rather a reputation for being just or morally upright. Socrates is challenged to show that justice is valuable for its own sake, not just for the goodwill and benefits that come when other people believe that a person is just.

In *The Prince* Machiavelli tries to show that Glaucon's challenge contains truth, at least for the rulers. The skillful prince will certainly laud the principles of moral rightness, and attempt to educate his people to follow such principles. Furthermore, the prince will, as much as possible, seek to have a reputation among the people as a good and just person. However, the bottom line for the prince is to maintain power and order in his realm. When push comes to shove, the wise prince will not allow moral principles to stand in the way of doing what must be done to maintain control. Machiavelli puts his point bluntly: "A prince who wants to keep his post must know how not to be good, and use that knowledge, or refrain from using it, as necessity requires."[3] Thus the "good" prince keeps promises selectively, making sure only that he can rationalize and excuse his behavior when he fails to keep his word.[4]

Is it better for the prince to be loved or feared? Obviously, most princes would probably prefer to be both loved and feared. However, Machiavelli unhesitatingly affirms that when a choice must be made, the prince must always choose to be feared, and must do what is necessary to ensure that this is the case. A good prince will try to ensure that he is not hated by being careful not to take too much of the goods of his people, but he will be happy if those subjects fear him nonetheless. No one can control whether another loves him, and so the shrewd prince will seek to maintain what he can control and ensure

---

[3]Niccolò Machiavelli, *The Prince* 13, in Niccolò Machiavelli, *The Prince*, trans. and ed. Robert M. Adams, Norton Critical Editions (New York: W. W. Norton, 1977), 44.
[4]Machiavelli, *The Prince* 18, Adams, 49-51.

that he is feared.[5] It is easy to understand why those who flout morality for the sake of expediency are often described as "Machiavellian."

THE PROTESTANT REFORMATION

The transformational movement we call the Protestant Reformation began on October 31, 1517, when Martin Luther, an Augustinian monk, according to legend nailed a document that came to be known as the Ninety-Five Theses to the door of the castle church in Wittenberg, Germany. At the time Luther had no intention of breaking with the church or starting a new church. Rather, he was protesting some of the corrupt practices of the Catholic Church of the time, particularly the sale of "indulgences," which allowed a person to lessen time in purgatory after death. Luther's protest was quickly printed in both Latin and German, and distributed throughout Germany. The protests against corruption broadened into arguments about larger issues. Luther propounded a Christian gospel in which salvation was solely due to God's grace, and he argued for the principle of *sola Scriptura*: the church's teachings should be based solely on the teachings of the Bible rather than tradition.

Luther was summoned to the Diet of Worms in 1521 to account for his views. He refused to recant his views or withdraw his works, unless he was shown to be in error by Scripture. The result was excommunication from the Catholic Church, and he became an outlaw in the Holy Roman Empire of the Germany of his day. Luther's views were, however, supported by a number of the princes of Germany, who had long chafed at the corruption of the papacy. The "protests" of these princes against an imperial edict trying to enforce uniformity gave the new movement a name: the protesters and their supporters became known as Protestants. One of these princes, Frederick of Saxony, sheltered Luther in his castle at Wartburg, and while there Luther translated much of the Bible into German. Luther made very good use of the newly invented printing

---

[5]Machiavelli, *The Prince* 17, Adams, 47-49.

press, and his views quickly spread through Germany and much of the rest of Europe.

In Switzerland the Reformation began with the preaching and writings of Ulrich Zwingli in 1519. In 1541 the French theologian John Calvin settled in Geneva, Switzerland, having written his *Institutes of the Christian Religion*. Geneva became a refuge for Protestants from all over Europe and in time the "Reformed" Christianity linked to Calvin became dominant in the Netherlands and in Scotland.

In England the Reformation began with a political maneuver. King Henry VIII wanted to annul his marriage to Catherine of Aragon to ensure an heir. The pope refused to annul the marriage, and Henry declared himself the head of the Church in England. Succeeding monarchs veered first toward Calvinist Protestantism and then back toward Catholicism, until Queen Elizabeth I established a "middle way" between Catholicism and Calvinism, with the worship of the Church of England rooted in the Book of Common Prayer written by the archbishop of Canterbury Thomas Cranmer.

The Reformation had far-reaching consequences for Europe. The division of Christendom into Catholic and Protestant regions, with the Protestants themselves split in many ways, led quickly to bloody wars and strife that lasted well into the seventeenth century. However, it is important to recognize that the wars were not simply due to theological disagreements, as the kings and princes that went to war often used religion as a pretext to seek to expand their power and rule. It is hard to overestimate the shock to European minds that resulted from the fundamental and seemingly intractable disagreements that broke out over matters of such importance. Such disagreements led to anxiety and a longing to show what can be known with certainty. This anxiety clearly put epistemology at the center of modern philosophy, as we shall see. In the long run the disagreements led to greater religious tolerance, a view particularly defended by such Protestants as John Locke and John Milton. The Protestant Reformation also led to the Catholic

Counter-Reformation, in which the Catholic Church renewed its intellectual and doctrinal vigor, with new orders such as the Jesuits carrying the banner of a renewed and reformed Catholicism.

THE REVIVAL OF SKEPTICISM: MONTAIGNE AND PASCAL

As noted above, during the Renaissance there was a revival of many of the schools of philosophy present in the ancient world, and among the most influential was Skepticism, associated with Pyrrho and systematized by Sextus Empiricus.[6] Many of the great philosophers of the modern period, beginning with Descartes, can be seen as responding to the challenge of skepticism. However, some thinkers, some of whom were religious and some of whom had a more secular cast of mind, also positively embraced skepticism. Preeminent among the former is the brilliant French writer Blaise Pascal (1623–1662), while Michel de Montaigne (1533–1592) represents a kind of cool-headed perspective that shies away from deep commitments of any kind.[7]

Montaigne is best known for his work *Essays.* As the title indicates, he provides nothing like a "system" of philosophy, but rather adopts skepticism, in something like the way the ancient Skeptics did, as a way of life. Montaigne did not see skepticism as a state of mind in which one believed nothing. Rather, skepticism for him was closer to an attitude in which one maintained a willingness constantly to revise one's beliefs and commitments in light of new inquiry and developments. He wanted to avoid the kind of dogmatism that he believed led to violence and created anxiety, conditions that often accompanied the religious wars following the Protestant Reformation, of which Montaigne was a contemporary. The genuine skeptic simply lives in accordance with the customs and beliefs that prevail in a person's society, without giving these undue weight or presuming any kind of ultimate truth. Montaigne

---

[6]See chap. 6 for a discussion of Greek Skepticism.

[7]For a clear discussion of the ways skepticism was developed by both religiously inspired thinkers as well as those who kept their distance from such commitments, see Terence Penelhum, *God and Skepticism: A Study in Skepticism and Fideism* (Boston: D. Reidel, 1983).

believed that human beings should focus their attention on the art of living well, giving attention to their own experience but modestly refraining from universal judgments that would require others to live in the same way.

Blaise Pascal, like Montaigne, had a keen sense of the limits of human reason. Pascal was a brilliant mathematician and physicist who made important contributions to conic geometry and did important work on hydraulics, atmospheric pressure, and the vacuum. Among his other achievements, Pascal invented the syringe and also the first mechanical calculating machine, a predecessor of today's computer. Pascal suffered from ill health for his entire life, and was a lifelong defender of Catholic Christianity. His faith deepened after 1846, when his family became involved with the Jansenist monks of the Abbey of Port-Royal. The Jansenists were Catholics who took seriously the Augustinian doctrine that humans were saved solely by God's grace. For them this divine grace required a life of strict devotion and ascetic practices, and under their influence Pascal's Christian faith became far more important in his life.

An even more crucial event in Pascal's life took place on November 23, 1654, when he experienced a "night of fire," a religious experience that produced a "total submission to Jesus Christ." Pascal wrote down a kind of record of this event, and sewed it into the lining of his jacket, where it was discovered after his death. The document includes this memorable passage: "God of Abraham, God of Isaac, God of Jacob, not of the philosophers and scholars. Certitude, certitude, feeling, joy, peace. God of Jesus Christ. My God and your God. Thy God will be my God."[8] After this experience Pascal announced he was abandoning his scientific and mathematical studies, though he continued occasional work on some problems and even published some important results under pseudonyms.

Pascal is best known for two works composed during this last period of his life. The *Provincial Letters* was a series of essay-like "public letters"

---

[8]This is only part of what Pascal had sewn into his coat, a short document usually called Pascal's "Memorial." A good account can be found in David Simpson, "Blaise Pascal (1623–1662)," *Internet Encyclopedia of Philosophy*, http://www.iep.utm.edu/pascal-b/.

(also written under a pseudonym) defending Jansenism and attacking the lax Catholicism that often prevailed in France. The Jesuits were the particular object of his polemics. These letters, read throughout the country, were written in a witty, clear, and articulate style, and are often regarded as having revolutionized modern French prose.

During this period Pascal worked strenuously on a work of apologetics defending Christian belief, which was not finished during his lifetime. At his death, this fragmentary work was published under the title of *Pensées*, a work that has deeply influenced both scholars and ordinary people who are moved by the depth of Pascal's spirituality. The work consists of aphorisms, short essays, short sermons, and fragmentary notes. The brilliance of the literary style and the originality of the thinking comes through powerfully in many memorable and often-quoted passages, and the book became a classic despite its unfinished character.

In the work Pascal does not lean on the traditional arguments for God's existence. Rather, his primary defense is a combination of what would today be called an "existential" argument, and appeals to Scripture. Much of the work is devoted to highlighting the human dilemma, seeing human beings without God as both wicked and wretched. Much of human existence consists in half-successful attempts to hide this truth from ourselves, as we humans seek "diversions," ranging from innocent amusements to debauchery, so as not to face our true condition. In his plan for the work Pascal hoped to awaken his contemporaries to this wretchedness and to help them see that the remedy prescribed by Christian faith provides the precise cure that the human condition demands.

Pascal provides arguments and appeals to miracles to show the plausibility of the Christian revelation. However, in the end he recognizes that, although evidence is necessary for faith, faith is never the product solely of evidence, for humans will in the end believe what they find most attractive: "There is enough light for those who desire only to see, and enough darkness for those of a contrary disposition."[9] Rational

---

[9]Blaise Pascal, *Pensées*, trans. William Finlayson Trotter (New York: Dutton, 1958), 118.

evidence is important, but "the heart" is equally important, for "the heart has its reasons that reason does not know."[10] For Pascal, the limits of human reason should not push us toward total skepticism, but should make us open to God's self-revelation, in which God shows us who we really are and invites us to become the people we can become through the grace manifested in Christ.

THE DEVELOPMENT OF MODERN SCIENCE

The final movement I shall discuss that had a huge influence on modern philosophy is the development of modern science. Natural science had by no means died during the Middle Ages, and new ideas and theories were developed during that period. It is, for example, not true that during the Middle Ages all people believed that the world was flat; educated people were well aware that the earth was round. However, it is true that what we would today call the "paradigms" that dominated medieval science came from the ancient world: the physics of Aristotle and the astronomy of Ptolemy, which provided a geocentric model of the Earth, sun, and other planets. The general attitude of the medievals toward ancient texts is that they had transmitted knowledge and wisdom. Where problems arose, either apparent contradictions in the tradition, or tensions with observations, those problems called for thought and were addressed creatively. However, these thinkers had a general confidence that the problems could be solved and thus that the tradition was sound.

Beginning in the 1500s, however, new discoveries and new ideas began to percolate throughout Europe, and the idea gradually took hold that natural science needed to strike out in fundamental new ways. Microscopes and telescopes were invented, thereby making new kinds of observations possible. Exciting new discoveries in both chemistry and biology were made by such thinkers as Robert Boyle and William Harvey. However, it is probably the transformation of

---

[10]Pascal, *Pensées*, 78.

astronomy and physics that had the greatest impact on the thinking of the time. The realization that the Earth was not the center of the universe, but a medium-sized planet among other planets orbiting the sun, shook up the complacent assumption that the Earth was the primary focus of God's attention.

Nicholas Copernicus (1473–1543), a Polish astronomer, first proposed that the sun was the center of the universe and that the apparent daily revolution of the sun around the Earth was due to the earth's rotation on its axis. Copernicus was followed by Tycho Brahe (1546–1601), who made important observations that confirmed the new theory, which in turn made possible the work of Johannes Kepler (1571–1630), who formulated mathematical models of planetary motion that fit these observations. The picture was further developed by Galileo Galilei (1564–1642), who discovered new laws of acceleration and dynamics, defending his theories with experiments and observations made possible by the telescope. Galileo discovered, for example, the moons of Jupiter. Galileo's work in turn laid the foundation for Isaac Newton's laws of motion, which showed that physics could explain the movement of bodies in the heavens and the Earth with the same laws.

All of these discoveries led to new reflection on the methods of science itself. Two different aspects of the new science were apparent, and each had a great influence on modern philosophy. One aspect was the recognition of the importance of empirical observation and inductive evidence in the development of science. The deductive reasoning of Aristotelian logic had to be supplemented by a logic of induction, famously defended by the English thinker Francis Bacon (1561–1626). Bacon criticized reliance on tradition, and he developed a series of inductive tests for supporting a scientific claim. Bacon's emphasis on empirical observation and induction had a lasting influence on philosophy in the British Isles, where "empiricism" dominated the intellectual world for centuries.

Bacon said that "knowledge is power," and he believed that scientific knowledge of how the natural world worked would lead to new power over nature. He criticized traditional knowledge as merely verbal and "useless." Bacon's account of science is, however, notably deficient in one way when judged by modern standards. He seems to have thought that scientific knowledge simply grows naturally through inductive observations, but failed to see the importance of *theory* in shaping how one sees the world, formulates hypotheses, and even sets up experiments.

The other fundamental aspect that comes through in modern science has to do precisely with theory. Modern scientists increasingly relied on mathematics and mathematical models in understanding nature. Ptolemaic astronomy had reconciled theory with observation by postulating a series of "epicycles." As the sun and the other planets revolved around the Earth, according to this theory, each heavenly body completed smaller circles while making the larger circle around the earth. To accommodate all the data, epicycles had to be added to the epicycles. Strictly speaking, the theory thus developed could be made consistent with all the empirical observations. Part of the appeal of Kepler's planetary laws was that he showed that a small set of relatively simple equations, corresponding with geometrical figures, could explain all the data. The rival Copernican and Ptolemaic theories were empirically equivalent. The elegance and simplicity of Kepler's mathematical model were what made the view compelling to younger scientists willing to break with traditional views. Scientific breakthroughs depended not simply on observations but on elegant theories that could be expressed in mathematical models.

This use of mathematics was further developed by Isaac Newton, who invented calculus to help him develop his scientific theories. (The calculus was also invented independently by Leibniz, whose thought will be discussed in chap. 13.) The prestige of mathematics, particularly geometry, had a great impact on the "rationalist" strand of modern philosophy, as we shall see when we examine the work of such thinkers as Descartes, Spinoza, and Leibniz.

A final aspect of modern science is the revival of "materialist" accounts of the physical world, including atomistic accounts. The atomists of the ancient world had argued that the "primary qualities" of the atomic constituents of matter, such as weight, shape, and velocity, could explain the "secondary properties" (such as color and sound) of perceived objects. The secondary properties were "subjective," simply the result of how bodies with primary qualities affected human sense organs. The emerging picture of the world that modern scientists presented seemed "mechanistic" and "materialistic." To be sure, all of these scientists were themselves religious believers. (Newton actually wrote more about theology than he did about science.) However, God played little or no role in the work they did as scientists. And the world that they described seemed to be a world devoid of color, sound, and value. Much of modern philosophy is either a development of or reaction to this kind of "mechanism."

THE MATERIALISM OF THOMAS HOBBES

Thomas Hobbes (1588–1679) was actually a contemporary of Descartes, who will be discussed in the next chapter, and thus could easily be classed as a "modern" philosopher. Hobbes was slightly older than Descartes, but he lived to the ripe age of ninety-one, and thus outlived Descartes, who died relatively young, by many years. However, I shall follow the tradition of ascribing to Descartes the title of "father of modern philosophy," and thus (somewhat arbitrarily) will discuss Hobbes in the conclusion of this chapter.

Hobbes's long life encompassed much of the bloodiest history of England, including the English Civil War, won by Cromwell and the defenders of Parliament. Hobbes had aristocratic connections, serving as a tutor to the Earl of Cavendish, and had to leave the country for a time. However, he was eventually allowed back by Cromwell, and had very good relations with Charles II after the restoration of the monarchy. There is little doubt that this bloody history shaped Hobbes's view of human nature.

Although Hobbes is best known as a political philosopher, and I shall examine his political thought below, his most-read work, *Leviathan*, also contains a comprehensive account of reality and knowledge. That account is thoroughly materialistic, reflecting the emerging scientific view that the world can be understood mechanistically, as "matter in motion."

Hobbes's epistemology reflects this metaphysical commitment to materialism. To be sure, Hobbes was an empiricist who taught that there are "no concepts in a man's mind, not begotten upon the organs of sense."[11] However, those sense organs are physical entities, and Hobbes regards the experiences to be literally movements in the brain. The concepts we gain through those experiences are similarly physical; memory and imagination are simply "decaying movements" of the original experiences. Once the brain has been disturbed by incoming sensations, traces of the original movements remain and they compose our mental life. What we call knowledge and reasoning is made possible by language, the conventional sounds and marks by which we designate those internal movements.

This materialism doubtless seems crude by contemporary standards, and it is hard to believe that all of our thinking consists simply of particles moving around inside the brain. However, despite the crudity, Hobbes's view of the mind is essentially that of many contemporary secular philosophers who, like Hobbes, are convinced that our mental states must somehow be reducible to material processes. Those contemporary thinkers have the advantage of much more knowledge of the brain and how it works than Hobbes enjoyed. However, despite this difference, those contemporary thinkers still have difficulty explaining what Hobbes so obviously failed to explain: how our conscious sensations and thoughts can be simply identical to physical states and processes, even if those mental events obviously depend on the brain. Identity is not the same thing as causal dependence.

---

[11] Thomas Hobbes, *Leviathan* 1.1.2, in Thomas Hobbes, *Leviathan: With Selected Variants from the Latin Edition of 1668*, ed. Edward Curley (Indianapolis: Hackett, 1994), 6. Page numbers following references to *Leviathan* are to this edition.

Contemporary philosophers who are materialists are invariably atheists as well, but Hobbes did not deny God's reality. God exists, but since Hobbes cannot imagine any nonphysical reality, he says that God must also be understood as physical. Hobbes certainly knew that this went against orthodox views of God, so he adds that if God is not material, then his nature must simply be incomprehensible to humans. Hobbes moves toward what we might call a "naturalistic" explanation of the origin of religions, postulating that religion stems from fear of the unknown and curiosity about origins. Hobbes seems suspicious of "natural religion," since for him it is connected to superstition.

Hobbes's ethic is grounded in subjective emotions. What is "good" is simply what we desire and are drawn to, and what is "bad" is what we hate and have an aversion to. Good and bad thus do not represent objective qualities, and if people love and hate different things, then what is good and bad for them will be different as well. To be fair, Hobbes probably believed that there was a common human nature so that there is a degree of uniformity about what humans love and hate. Still, this represents a strong break with the Aristotelian tradition that dominated much of later medieval philosophy, since for Aristotle the good is what leads to human flourishing, not simply what humans desire. It is, I believe, this subjectivist account of ethics that leads to a drastically truncated account of the "natural law" we find in Hobbes's political philosophy.

Hobbes's political philosophy begins with a memorable description of human beings who live in a "state of nature," in which there is no recognized, effective government. There is a kind of natural equality in such a state. Hobbes admits that humans differ in strength and knowledge, but he sees these differences as unimportant, since a person who is weaker or less intelligent can still kill another person, either by use of a weapon or by getting help from others. Hobbes believes that in such an environment there would be a "state of war," a war in which every individual is at war with every other individual. There are three causes of this war. First, there is the fact that some people are greedy and there is competition for goods. Second, there is fear, since a person never knows when someone will try to take what he or she has. Finally, there is the desire for "glory," or reputation, which induces people to war over "trifles" such as a lack of respect or acknowledgment.

Hobbes says that in the state of nature we have a right to self-preservation, in that we have a fundamental right to do whatever we must to preserve our lives. However, without a "power" to protect this right, life is insecure. I have a right to do what I can to protect myself, but my neighbor may nonetheless try to take that life. My "right to life" then does not imply a corresponding duty for others to protect that life.

In the state of nature there are no private-property rights. There is in fact no such thing as justice or injustice, but "every man has a 'right' to everything, 'even to another's body.'"[12] At least each person has a right to anything they can acquire and control. In such a situation, no one would be secure, and violence would be a frequent occurrence. The result would be a society that is bad for everyone, since in it

> there is no place for industry, because the fruit thereof is uncertain, and consequently no culture of the earth, no navigation nor use of the commodities that may be imported by sea, no commodious building, no instruments of moving and removing such things as require much force, no knowledge of the face of the earth; no account of time, no arts, no letters, no society, and which is worst of all, continual fear and danger of violent death.[13]

Hobbes memorably summarizes such a situation as one in which life would be "solitary, poor, nasty, brutish, and short."[14]

One might here question whether Hobbes's picture of human nature is too pessimistic and cynical. Hobbes anticipates such criticism, however, and answers by pointing to how humans actually behave.

---

[12]Hobbes, *Leviathan*, 1.14.4, p. 80.
[13]Hobbes, *Leviathan*, 1.13.9, p. 76.
[14]Hobbes, *Leviathan*, 1.13.9, p. 76.

Even in a society with a government with police to protect people, he says a person going on a journey will carry a weapon, people lock the doors to their houses, and even within their homes lock up their valuables in a safe.[15]

Our only moral obligations in a state of nature are to follow the dictates of reason. However, the "natural laws" that reason dictates are few in comparison with the natural law found in a thinker such as Aquinas. The first law of nature Hobbes describes is to "seek peace and follow it."[16] Reason tells us that the state of nature is such a bad place that we ought to do whatever we can to leave such a state. In the state of nature we have a right to everything, but reason tells us that we ought to be willing to be content with just that liberty you would be willing to allow others to have against you. This leads to a second law of nature: "that a man be willing, when others are so too . . . to lay down this right to all things, and be contented with so much liberty against other men as he would allow other men against himself."[17] We do not give up our fundamental right to defend our own lives, since for Hobbes that right is "inalienable," but we should be willing to give up other rights on the condition that others do the same.

There are a few other "natural laws" that exist in the state of nature. One is a principle of gratitude in which one acknowledges the debt one owes to benefactors. Yet another is "complaisance," a general principle in which people ought to seek to conform their behavior to that of others so as to achieve stability. Interestingly, Hobbes also says that it is a natural law that one ought to be willing to forgive wrongs done, presumably to prevent unending cycles of revenge and retribution.

However, by far the most significant other natural law is that people should "perform their covenants made."[18] The mutual agreement or contract that people make to end the state of nature is also the beginning

---

[15]Hobbes, *Leviathan*, 1.13.10, p. 77.
[16]Hobbes, *Leviathan*, 1.14.4, p. 80.
[17]Hobbes, *Leviathan*, 1.14.5, p. 80.
[18]Hobbes, *Leviathan*, 1.15.1, p. 89.

of justice and injustice. However, Hobbes believes there can be no abiding covenant or agreement unless there is some mechanism to ensure that the agreement is kept: "The validity of covenants begins . . . with the constitution of a civil power sufficient to compel men to keep them."[19] For Hobbes, this power is the "sovereign" that the people create when they establish the covenant.

Hobbes probably thought that an absolute monarchy was the most effective kind of sovereign, but he is also open to the possibility that the role of the sovereign could be exercised by a legislature. Once a sovereign is established (by whatever means), the sovereign truly is sovereign. The power of the sovereign is irrevocable; Hobbes acknowledges no right of revolution. The sovereign alone decides what the laws are going to be, and thereby decides what is justice and what is injustice. (Thus no law the sovereign establishes can be unjust.) The sovereign must possess a monopoly of deadly force and thus must control the army and militia.

The one limit on the authority of the sovereign follows from this requirement of power. The sovereign who loses effective power to enforce his will loses his sovereignty. This leads to a paradoxical implication. Although there is no "right to revolt," the rebel who is successful in seizing power thereby himself becomes the sovereign.

It is important to recognize that for Hobbes the sovereign is not a party to the covenant. The agreement is not one made between the people and the sovereign, but rather one the people make with each other. The people create the sovereign. This means that the people cannot protest that the sovereign is not keeping the agreement and thus has lost legitimacy, for the sovereign has made no promises. This is one respect in which Hobbes's political philosophy differs fundamentally from that of John Locke, which we will consider later. Locke will develop the idea of a social contract in a very different way that will later influence the American Revolution.

---

[19]Hobbes, *Leviathan*, 1.15.3, p. 89.

There are obvious problems with the idea of a sovereign with such unlimited and unchecked powers. Hobbes understands this, but he would argue that even living in a state with a bad government is better than living in the state of nature. Perhaps those people who today live in areas with "failed states" would agree.

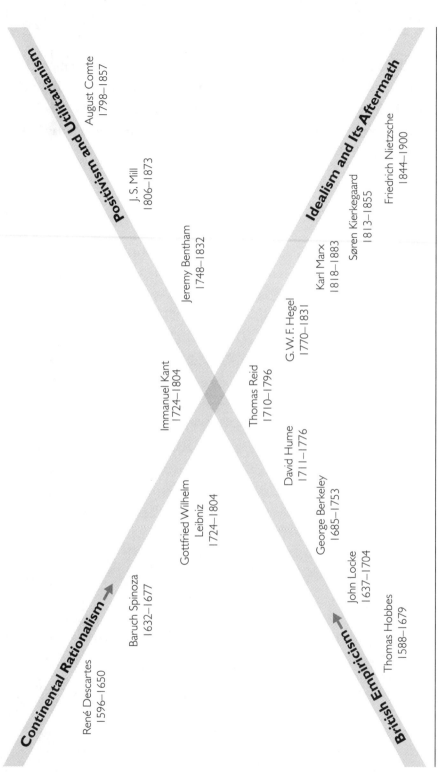

Figure 3. Major figures in modern Western philosophy. *Source:* Adapted from Arthur Holmes

Descartes and the Beginning of Modern Philosophy

FRENCH PHILOSOPHER RENÉ DESCARTES (1596–1650) is universally acknowledged as the father of modern European philosophy. Born in Touraine, he was educated first at a Jesuit school and then at the University of Poitiers. Descartes served as a military officer for the nobleman Maurice of Nassau, but it is likely that his duties were more in line with those of an engineer or educator than actual combat. Descartes moved frequently, living in Paris for a while as well as in the Netherlands. In 1649 he was invited to become part of the court of Queen Christina of Sweden, and he accepted the invitation. Sadly, things did not turn out well. He complained about the cold of the Swedish winter and the queen's requirement that he teach her philosophy beginning at five in the morning. He eventually caught a respiratory infection and died in 1650, only fifty-four years old.

Descartes is best known for his *Meditations on First Philosophy* (1641), usually just called the *Meditations*, and it is mostly this book that I will discuss. However, his major philosophical works include *Discourse on Method* (1637), *Principles of Philosophy* (1644), and *The Passions of the Soul* (1649). Descartes also contributed a pioneering work in mathematics, *Geometry*, in which he shows how it is possible to solve geometrical problems using algebraic equations. To this day, students learning to "graph" algebraic equations in geometrical form or express geometrical forms in algebraic equations use coordinates that are termed "Cartesian" in honor of Descartes's achievement.

Descartes's philosophy is enormously influential in modern Western philosophy, both with respect to what other philosophers took from his views and with respect to the way they responded critically to his views, or views that were taken as his. Because of this importance I shall take a close look at many elements of Descartes's thought, and also provide some critical perspective on his key moves.

DESCARTES'S RATIONALISM

Descartes's work in mathematics was deeply important for his philosophy as well, because he was convinced that mathematics offered a kind of certain knowledge that was the mark of any true science. He did not mean that all sciences are part of mathematics, but rather that the methods followed by mathematicians would lead to success in other fields if emulated by scholars in those fields. The heart of this method is an emphasis on "intuition" and "deduction." The foundations of mathematics lie in basic truths about lines and numbers that are intuitively "seen" (with the "eye" of reason, not the actual eyes by which we gain visual experiences) to be true with certainty. Mathematical knowledge is extended by deducing other truths from these foundational truths, and when this is done correctly those deductions enjoy the same kind of intuitive certainty as the foundational truths. The choice of mathematics as providing a model for knowledge in all fields tilts Descartes toward a "rationalism" that gives empirical knowledge gained by sense experience only a subordinate role in science. This rationalism becomes the dominant strand in European philosophy on the Continent up until the time of Immanuel Kant in the late 1700s.

Contemporary philosophers often refer to Descartes's epistemology as a form of "classical foundationalism." (It is important to recognize that this is a contemporary term, and not one that Descartes or his contemporaries used themselves.) Foundationalism itself is a kind of picture of human knowledge that naturally suggests itself when we think about how a proposition is known; it is a perspective that can already be found in Plato and Aristotle. Clearly, many propositions are known on the basis of other propositions. I know that it is raining right now in Waco, Texas, because I am looking out my window and see raindrops falling. I believe "it is raining right now" is true because I believe that it is true that "I am seeing raindrops falling right now." Or, to use an example that is more fitting for Descartes, I know that "there are more than three prime numbers smaller than 10" because I know that "2, 3, 5, and 7 are prime numbers" and "2, 3, 5, and 7 are smaller than 10." So some knowledge is based on other, more basic knowledge. But what about that more basic knowledge? Could it be based on yet other knowledge? In many cases the answer is clearly yes. However, unless one thinks that a human mind could know an infinite number of truths, or allows for "circular justification" in which propositions that are justified by more basic propositions can in turn justify those same basic propositions, then it is clear that some of the things we know must be absolutely basic or foundational, not derived from anything else we know.

This foundationalist account of knowledge is often metaphorically illuminated by thinking of knowledge as a kind of house or building, and Descartes uses just this picture. Just as is the case with an actual building, it would seem that the "house of knowledge" requires secure foundations if it is to be reliable and stable. (We might here think of Jesus' parable in which he refers to the foolishness of building a house on sand as opposed to solid rock.) Descartes's rationalism was derived from his conviction that the foundational truths for knowledge or science must have the kind of certainty that the foundational truths of mathematics possess. However, knowledge requires not only certain foundations but also secure rules for how the house is built. Thus the same standard of certainty required for the foundational truths is also demanded for what is deduced from those truths. Descartes emphasizes that philosophy can only succeed if it follows the proper rules for achieving these goals. Thus he also places great emphasis on what may be called the search for the proper method of doing philosophy. The philosophers who follow Descartes often disagree about what the proper method is, but at least until the twentieth century they tended to follow his example by assuming that the issue of method is paramount in philosophy. The history of modern Western philosophy is largely a disagreement about the proper method for doing philosophy.

As we shall see, the early modern philosophers who are classified as "empiricists" (such as John Locke and George Berkeley) are also classical foundationalists who demand certainty for the foundations of knowledge. However, for the empiricists the paradigm cases of certainty are not provided by rational intuition, as is the case for mathematics, but by immediate sense experiences, in which some fact is directly observed. Many histories of philosophy emphasize the disagreements between rationalists and empiricists, and those disagreements are certainly real. However, it is important to see similarities as well, and rationalism and empiricism can usefully be described as rival versions of classical foundationalism, sharing the same basic picture of human knowledge and how it is gained.

DESCARTES'S ATTEMPT AT A "RADICAL NEW START" AND HIS UNEXAMINED ASSUMPTIONS

Most of the important characteristics of Descartes's philosophy, including this epistemological foundationalism, can be clearly seen through an examination of the *Meditations on First Philosophy*. "First philosophy" is Aristotle's term for metaphysics, and it is true that the ultimate goal of the *Meditations* is to show how metaphysical knowledge is possible. In particular Descartes wants to prove the existence of God and also the existence of the human soul understood as a nonmaterial entity. Those conclusions are certainly important, but to many readers then and now, Descartes's *method* for reaching those conclusions is of primary importance.

In the First Meditation (of six) Descartes immediately signals one of the most momentous characteristics of his philosophy: the idea of "starting over." Descartes tells us that he had accepted a "large number of falsehoods" as true since he was a child, and that as a result "the whole edifice" of beliefs he had built was "highly doubtful."[1] In contrast to the medieval tendency to begin by considering what past philosophers had said, Descartes heralds the idea of a radical "new beginning": "I realized that it was necessary, once in the course of my life, to demolish everything completely and start again right from the foundations if I wanted to establish anything at all in the sciences that was stable and likely to last."[2] It is this theme of a radical new start that has won Descartes the name of "father of modern philosophy."

To be sure, as we shall see, Descartes's ambitions on this score exceeded his achievements; he did not really start over from a completely fresh slate. There are many points where Descartes continues to draw on concepts and claims embedded in the Western philosophical tradition. Descartes's failure to completely "begin anew" is not duplicity or hypocrisy on his part. The parts of the tradition he continues to accept uncritically were simply parts of his intellectual and cultural inheritance that seemed so obviously true to Descartes that he never thought to question them or even to think about them as things that could be questioned. There is a valuable lesson for all of us here: very often the most important assumptions we make are ones we are not even aware of making. This is one of the reasons why the study of the history of philosophy is valuable. By its study, we can come to see that things that seemed utterly obvious to people in one era seem dubious to those in another era. And we can perhaps sometimes, by comparing our contemporary intellectual world to those past worlds, become aware of assumptions we have that we would otherwise fail to see.

---

[1]René Descartes, *Meditations on First Philosophy* 1, in René Descartes, *"Discourse on Method" and "Meditations on First Philosophy,"* trans. Donald A. Cress, 4th ed. (Indianapolis: Hackett, 1998), 59. Unless otherwise indicated, page numbers following citations of *Meditations on First Philosophy* and *Discourse on Method* are from this edition.

[2]Descartes, *Meditations on First Philosophy* 1, p. 59.

In the very first paragraph of the First Meditation a second momentous characteristic of Descartes's thought that has shaped modern Western philosophy also emerges. Descartes tells us that he is now in a good position to make the new beginning he proposes, because "I have freed my mind from all cares, and I have secured myself some leisurely and carefree time."[3] This will allow him to "withdraw in solitude" and do the intellectual work he needs to do. This sentence expresses a number of assumptions that together form a kind of "package." One assumption is that rational human thought requires a kind of emotional detachment. Since Descartes is untroubled by any "cares" (some translations substitute "worries" or "passions") he is in a good position to make progress toward truth.

It is difficult to decide whether Descartes is here influencing or simply mirroring a deep tendency within the modern Western world. However, it does seem that a great many thinkers in the modern period have echoed Descartes's assumption that rational thought must be objective and detached. The emotions are a kind of distorting filter that must be eliminated if we are to think rationally. The "head" and the "heart" are radically distinct parts of the human person, and the "head" functions best when it is separated from the "heart."

The contemporary scientist Antonio Damasio has published a fascinating book, titled *Descartes' Error: Emotion, Reason, and the Human Brain*, in which he argues that there is strong scientific evidence that the picture of the relation between emotion and reason that Descartes assumes is in fact wrong-headed.[4] Brain scientists today believe that the emotions are strongly linked to a particular area of the brain called the amygdala. Damasio claims that empirical studies of people who have had that part of their brain damaged, and hence are unable to have normal emotions, show that emotions are important, even essential, for good reasoning about real-life problems. People with these kinds of

---

[3]Descartes, *Meditations on First Philosophy* 1, p. 59.
[4]Antonio Damasio, *Descartes' Error: Emotion, Reason, and the Human Brain* (New York: Penguin, 1994).

brain injuries seem in one sense still to be able to reason well, in that they can score as well as others on IQ tests. However, when these people are forced to solve a real-life problem, they turn out to have profound cognitive impairments.

Damasio may not have the last word here, and some philosophers have in fact challenged his work and defended Descartes.[5] But Damasio's challenge at least makes it clear that Descartes has here made an uncritical assumption without any argument. We shall later see that philosophers such as Kierkegaard and Nietzsche, who differ radically from each other, nonetheless agree that our emotions do and should play an important role in our intellectual lives. In addition to assuming that good reasoning must be detached from the emotions, Descartes also seems to take for granted the idea that our best thinking requires a kind of detachment from life and the pressure to act. Once more we have an assumption that, when made explicit, seems at least questionable, and one that will be called into question by thinkers as diverse as William James, Kierkegaard, and Nietzsche. Cool, detached thinking may be best for doing mathematics, but it is not at all obvious that such detachment is advantageous when one is seeking human wisdom.

The last element worth noting in this section is Descartes's notion that good thinking is something that is best done in solitude. This shows a profound bias toward individualism, and it seems solidly linked to the suspicion of tradition that is embedded in Descartes's call for a radical new beginning. The traditions from which Descartes wants to free himself are passed down through communities, and a call to be free from tradition is at the same time a call for individuals to detach themselves from those communities. This kind of critical view of tradition and community will reach a high point roughly 150 years after Descartes, in the Enlightenment philosophy of Immanuel Kant. In his famous essay "What Is Enlightenment?" Kant affirms that the essence

---

[5]For an example see Andrew Gluck, *Damasio's Error and Descartes' Truth* (Scranton, PA: University of Scranton Press, 2007).

of enlightenment is for you, as an individual, to "dare to use your own reason."[6] We may wonder if this individualistic picture of human knowledge does justice to our nature as social beings who depend on each other in almost all facets of existence, including what we know.

THE METHOD OF DOUBT

How does Descartes propose to accomplish his radical new beginning in such a way as to find the kind of certain foundations that will allow him to build a stable house of knowledge? At the heart of Descartes's method lies doubt. He attempts to make a new start by a "general demolition" of his former opinions. This seems paradoxical. (Kierkegaard will argue later that this method is not only paradoxical but also incoherent.) What Descartes wants is truth known with certainty; the path to gaining such truth is a ruthless, universal doubt. Descartes's method here might remind a person of a motto popular among the hippies in the United States who opposed the Vietnam War. "Fighting for peace is like fornicating for chastity." Similarly, doubting would seem to be the opposite of belief and knowledge.

Descartes does not want to be a skeptic, however. His doubt is a method for attaining knowledge, not an end in itself as it was for the ancient Skeptics. Perhaps we should think of this "Cartesian doubt" as a kind of test that our beliefs must undergo. The only way to discover whether there is anything we know with certainty requires that we submit all our beliefs to this test. What passes the test will be something impervious to doubt, something that is indubitable.

We can also think of Descartes's method here as a kind of privileging of doubt over belief. Suppose we find ourselves tempted to believe something but are not completely sure that it is true. Descartes says we should commit ourselves to a policy that could be expressed like this: "When in doubt, doubt." We need only very flimsy reasons to doubt; we

---

[6]Immanuel Kant, *An Answer to the Question: What Is Enlightenment,* in *Practical Philosophy,* ed. Mary J. Gregor (Cambridge: Cambridge University Press, 1996), 17-22.

need extremely good reasons to believe. Descartes assures us that "reason now leads me to think that I should hold back my assent from opinions which are not completely certain and indubitable just as carefully as I do from those which are patently false."[7]

Despite Descartes's assurance that it is "reason" that leads him to think this is the proper attitude to take toward doubt and belief, it seems far from evident that this is the best policy. The American pragmatists will later adopt exactly the opposite policy. On their view, belief is the "normal" state of the human mind, and we should begin "where we are," with all our current beliefs. After all, presumably those beliefs have "worked" for us in some ways and so must have something going for them. We should doubt a belief only when we have good reason to doubt, but that reason to doubt will always rest on some other belief that we are not doubting, at least at that time. On this view it is not even possible to doubt all our beliefs at once, even if it is possible to doubt any of them on occasion. The pragmatists are not alone in making such a point. Thinkers as diverse as David Hume, Thomas Reid, and Søren Kierkegaard agree that universal doubt is in fact impossible, but if someone actually succeeded in doubting everything, such doubt would be incurable.

Descartes provides a number of reasons for doubt. First he notes that most of his beliefs have been acquired through the senses. However, he says that "from time to time I have found that the senses deceive, and it is prudent never to trust completely those who have deceived us even once."[8] Once again we may wonder about the principle Descartes is relying on here. Does the fact that our senses (and other faculties) are fallible really mean that we should never trust them? Descartes apparently thinks so, at least at this stage of his inquiry, and decides not to trust any beliefs gained through sense experience. To see how odd Descartes's policy may seem, consider the situation of a man who is trying

---

[7]Descartes, *Meditations on First Philosophy* 1, p. 59.
[8]Descartes, *Meditations on First Philosophy* 1, p. 60.

to decide whether he can trust that the money in his wallet is genuine currency and not counterfeit money. Suppose the person said, "From time to time I have found that I have been deceived and accepted a counterfeit bill as genuine money. So I should never trust that any of my money is genuine, since it is prudent never to trust completely what has deceived us even once." Not many of us would say this policy is one that "reason" recommends.

Of course to be fair to Descartes we must remember that his doubt is intended as "methodological." Perhaps we should not think of Descartes as actually doubting all his beliefs, but as performing a kind of experiment to see if a person who had put aside all his former beliefs could somehow build up a new and stronger edifice. On such an interpretation, Descartes's doubt is not real doubt at all, but a kind of mental exercise, and on such a reading Descartes's project might look more sensible. However, it counts against such an interpretation that Descartes struggles mightily to find actual reasons to doubt.

For example, in response to someone who might find doubt of all we learn from the senses hyperbolic, Descartes proposes a "dream hypothesis."[9] It is true, he admits, that some of what we learn from sense experience seems quite certain and hard to deny. However, Descartes reminds us, we often have dreams while we are sleeping that are quite vivid and that we accept without question as real at the time. It seems possible that he might be dreaming now. If so, then none of the things he is "experiencing" now exist in an objective manner. Since he has no proof that he is not dreaming, then this seems to cast a very long shadow of doubt over his beliefs.

At this point, it occurs to Descartes that some things even seem true when we are dreaming. Even if the particular things I am experiencing in my dreams do not exist, the "simpler and universal" things that compose the objects in my dreams must be real. Descartes is here thinking primarily of mathematical realities such as numbers and shapes,

---

[9]Descartes, *Meditations on First Philosophy* 1, pp. 60-62.

but he wishes to include "corporeal" things as well insofar as they can be described mathematically. "For whether I am awake or asleep, two and three added together are five, and a square has no more than four sides."[10]

However, Descartes has one last "doubt-hypothesis" in reserve that appears to undermine his claims even to know these certain truths. Descartes has of course long believed in God, an omnipotent being who created him. But what if he were not created by God? "I will suppose therefore that not God, who is supremely good and the source of truth, but rather some malicious demon of the utmost power and cunning has employed all his energies to deceive me."[11] Of course Descartes is not saying he knows he was created by such an "evil demon." However, it seems *possible* that this might be the case, since Descartes has up until now no proof of the contrary. Given that possibility, it looks as if nothing that Descartes believes can be affirmed with certainty.

The problem arises of course because it looks as if any evidence Descartes might have that is contrary to this evil demon hypothesis is fully compatible with the truth of the hypothesis, given the power and cunning of the demon. Contemporary skeptical challenges to knowledge often employ "global" hypotheses of the same nature. How do we know we are not brains in a vat on Alpha Centauri, and that the Alpha Centaurians, with their superior science, are putting in signals to our brains that cause us to have just the experiences we have? Or, how do we know that we are not all living in *The Matrix*?[12]

DOUBT OVERCOME

One might think that this last, global skeptical hypothesis is one that will make it impossible for Descartes to attain any kind of certain truth. What he wants to find is "just one thing; however slight, that is certain and unshakeable."[13] In the Second Meditation he finds certainty in the

---

[10]Descartes, *Meditations on First Philosophy* 1, p. 61.
[11]Descartes, *Meditations on First Philosophy* 1, pp. 62-63.
[12]*The Matrix*, directed by Lana Wachowski and Lilly Wachowski (Burbank, CA: Warner Bros., 1999).
[13]Descartes, *Meditations on First Philosophy* 2, p. 63.

midst of his doubt. Even if he is being deceived by the evil demon, he knows something, namely, that he exists. For even being deceived is a form of consciousness, and Descartes maintains that he cannot doubt his own existence so long as he is conscious. The demon "will never bring it about that I am nothing so long as I think I am something."[14] Or, as Descartes puts it in his *Discourse on Method*, "I think, therefore I am" (In Latin, *cogito, ergo sum*).[15] It is worth noting here that Descartes uses the word *thinking* in a very broad way, to refer to any kind of conscious awareness. "Thinking" in this sense refers to such conscious activities as doubting, believing, denying, understanding, willing, imagining, and even the having of sensory perceptions.[16]

Despite the use of the term *therefore* it would be a mistake to think that Descartes is attempting to *infer* his existence from the fact that he thinks. Rather, he seems to think that the proposition "I exist" is one that he immediately knows to be true whenever he is conscious. This is a truth he knows without any argument or evidence.

If we grant that Descartes has indeed found his "one thing" that he needs to be his basic truth, can he actually build much on such slender foundations? One might think the answer is negative, but Descartes claims he has at least two other things that he knows. First, he knows not only that he exists but also something about his nature. At this point he does not know for sure if he has a body, or if any physical objects exist, but he knows that he exists. However, since he only knows he exists by virtue of the fact that he thinks, it must be the case that he is a "thinking thing."

It is important to note that when Descartes includes sense perception among the types of "thinking" he is not affirming that he actually sees, hears, touches, tastes, and smells physical objects. What he means is that he has experiences that purport to "represent" such objects to him. What he knows for certain is not that such objects exist, but that he

---

[14]Descartes, *Meditations on First Philosophy* 2, p. 64.
[15]Descartes, *Discourse on Method* 4, p. 19.
[16]Descartes, *Meditations on First Philosophy* 3, p. 70.

seems to hear, see, touch, and feel such objects. Descartes here accepts without argument a certain picture of how human sense perception works, a picture often called "representationalism." According to representationalism, the immediate objects of sense experience are not physical objects, but mental representations of physical objects. When I "see" a tree, what I see immediately is not the tree, but some kind of mental representation of the true, a sensation in the mind, one that Descartes will argue (later) is caused to exist in me by the actual tree.

Representationalism is to many philosophers a very plausible view, one that continues to have defenders, and one that has a long and venerable history. However, this seems to be a clear case where Descartes fails to doubt everything but simply assumes something he inherits from the philosophical tradition. Representationalism is not the only possible perspective on perception, and Descartes really offers no argument that this is the right view to take. Thomas Reid will later defend a "direct realist" account of perception, and Reid argues that what I am calling Descartes's representationalism, a view Reid calls "the way of ideas" or "the ideal theory," is the source of many problems in modern philosophy that inevitably lead to skepticism. The seeds of this skepticism are easy to see. If all we ever directly perceive are mental representations, how could we possibly know anything about the causes of such representations, since we have no access to anything but the mental representations? The problems as to how we gain knowledge of the external world and other minds loom large.

Second, in the Third Meditation Descartes claims he knows at least one other thing: he knows what it is to know something. In knowing with certainty that he is a thinking being, he must also "know what is required for my being certain about anything."[17] When Descartes considers how he knows that he exists, the answer is simply that he "clearly and distinctly" perceives this truth. He does not, of course perceive it with his sensory eyes; it is a truth that is simply clear and distinct to his

---

[17]Descartes, *Meditations on First Philosophy* 3, p. 70.

mind or his reason. Descartes therefore claims to know what knowledge is: it is simply a clear and distinct perception of truth, a kind of immediate awareness of truth that rules out any doubt.

Critics have of course challenged both of these claims. Even if it is true that Descartes must exist in order to be conscious, does it follow that he is some kind of "thing," a substantial entity or being that endures over time and does the thinking but is not identical with consciousness itself? As we shall see, philosophers such as David Hume question whether the self Descartes posits really exists as a continuing substance or whether the self might just be a succession of conscious experiences.

As far as the "clear and distinct" criterion of truth, one may wonder how "clear and distinct" this very concept is? Does "clarity" come in degrees? If so, is it clear what degree of clarity is needed for knowledge? Besides this problem, as we have already seen and will see again, there seem to be many truths that are clear and distinct to Descartes that do not appear to be clear and distinct to everyone. In such cases it looks as if the disagreement leads to an impasse. Descartes can offer no argument for the truths that will be the basis for all arguments, and so if a skeptic denies them, there is little he can say.

Having claimed that he knows he exists as a "thinking thing" and that he knows that clear and distinct perception of truth is a guarantee of knowledge, Descartes pauses at the end of the Second Meditation to consider a possible objection. Philosophers of a materialist bent, such as Thomas Hobbes, will claim to have no clear idea as to what a "thinking thing" might be if it is not something identical to a physical object. Furthermore, empiricists (people who believe the foundations of knowledge come through the senses) will argue that an idea or concept cannot be clear unless we can trace it back to the sense experiences that gave rise to it. We might say, for example, that we have a clear idea as to what a physical object such as a piece of wax is, because we can observe the wax. However, we don't have a clear idea as to what a "thinking thing" is.

Descartes responds to such objections by performing an experiment on a piece of wax. The wax is right in front of him. He examines it and notes it has a certain shape, color, size, and scent. He has a concept of the wax as a piece of wax. He then lights a candle and heats the wax. The wax changes color, shape, size, and scent. No sensory properties remain the same. Yet Descartes still understands the wax as a piece of wax. When I think of the wax, it is thus the concept or idea of the wax that is important, not the sensory perceptions. And if I recognize that I understand the wax by thinking, I must recognize that I do in fact know what thinking is. And so I must know myself as a thinking thing. "Even bodies are not strictly perceived by the senses, or the faculty of imagination, but by the intellect alone."[18] Contrary to received opinions and philosophical prejudices, "I know plainly that I can achieve an easier and more evident perception of my own mind than of anything else."[19]

PROVING GOD AS THE GUARANTOR OF KNOWLEDGE

Despite Descartes's claim to know his own existence and to know what knowledge is, the evil demon still looms as a formidable skeptical challenge to knowing much more than this. To show that we know more, Descartes must exorcise the possibility of the evil demon. He turns to this task in the Third Meditation by attempting a proof of the existence of God, understood as a being who has all the perfections. It is especially important for Descartes to dispel the evil demon if he wishes to acquire knowledge that the ideas he has acquired through sense perception in some way refer to objects outside of himself that they "resemble." How does he know that the evil demon is not directly producing these perceptions in his mind, in which case he knows only the representations, not the objects they purport to represent? It is true, Descartes says, that making such judgments based on perception is natural, the result of a "spontaneous impulse."[20] However, that alone

---

[18]Descartes, *Meditations on First Philosophy* 2, p. 69.
[19]Descartes, *Meditations on First Philosophy* 2, p. 69.
[20]Descartes, *Meditations on First Philosophy* 3, p. 72.

does not seem to him to guarantee their truth. He needs some reason or evidence that his natural impulses are trustworthy. Perhaps if he knew he was the creation of a good God (rather than an evil demon) it would be reasonable for him to trust his faculties. So Descartes attempts to prove that God (a being who possesses all perfections) exists and that God is the cause of his existence.

Descartes offers two related arguments for God's existence in the Third Meditation and a third argument in the Fifth Meditation. The first two arguments are both "causal" arguments, ones that start with a claim about the existence of something and then try to show that God is the cause of that something. I will briefly consider each of the three arguments.

Argument one. The first argument starts with the claim that Descartes has an idea of a perfect being (God) and thus at least the idea of God exists. (Descartes says that by "God" he means a being who is "eternal, infinite, [immutable], omniscient, omnipotent and the creator of all things that exist apart from him."[21]) Descartes then affirms that he knows "by the natural light" that a cause must always have at least as much "perfection" or "reality" as its effect. (Descartes also assumes that everything that exists must have a cause.) It follows from this that his idea of God must have a cause and the cause must have at least as much reality or perfection as the idea itself.[22] However, since the idea itself is an idea of perfection, it could not have been created by Descartes himself, who knows he is a very imperfect being. Nor could the idea have been created by any other imperfect being. Only a perfect being could have originated the idea, so only God could have originated the idea of God.

---

[21]Descartes, *Meditations on First Philosophy* 3, p. 73.

[22]I am simplifying Descartes's argument at this point. Descartes distinguishes two senses of "reality," what he calls "formal" and "objective" reality, and the principle that a cause must have all the perfections of its effect only applies to "formal" reality. It is very hard for a contemporary student to understand the distinction Descartes makes here; the terms he employs do not mean today what they meant for him. I think one can understand the thrust of the argument even if one ignores this distinction. Anyone who wants to understand this Cartesian distinction could consult Margaret Wilson, *Descartes* (London: Routledge and Kegan Paul, 1978), particularly chap. 3.

This argument bristles with difficulties for contemporary thinkers. To begin, it does not seem obvious that a cause must always have at least as much reality as its effect, for it often seems that trivial and inconsequential events have tremendous effects. More fundamentally, many philosophers today would question whether it even makes sense to speak of "degrees of reality." Rather, it seems that reality is "binary"; objects are either real or unreal, with no degrees of reality. What such an objection shows is how profoundly Descartes is still shaped by the Western philosophical tradition he claims to have demolished. A deep strand in that tradition going back to Plato's "divided line" is the idea of the "great chain of being." This is a picture of reality in which God is the highest and most perfect being, with angels or other spiritual beings occupying the next rank, and human beings perhaps the rank after that. Below humans are physical objects and below that things like shadows and illusions, things that have very little reality. On this picture one's place in the great hierarchy of being is determined by the degree of reality a thing possesses. For Descartes this view is still a living perspective, and it continues to be to this day for Platonists. However, for many contemporary thinkers, there is no such thing as a "degree of reality." Kierkegaard, for example, says that to speak of perfection is to speak of essence, not existence. If something exists, its degree of perfection is determined by the kind of thing it is, but existence itself does not come in degrees; Kierkegaard quips that reality is subject to the dialectic of Hamlet: "to be or not to be."[23]

Even if we waive those problems, it is hard to tell how much reality the idea of God must have. God himself may possess all perfections and be supremely real, but does this mean the idea of God must be supremely real?

In the end, I believe the force of the argument follows from the intuition that God himself must have placed in us an idea of himself. Perhaps

---

[23]Søren Kierkegaard, *Philosophical Fragments*, trans. and ed. by Howard V. Hong and Edna H. Hong (Princeton, NJ: Princeton University Press, 1985), 41-42n.

one cannot prove that this is the case; certainly many thinkers deny it. One might think, for example, that we produce the idea of God simply by taking our idea of a person, who has a finite degree of power and intelligence and perfection, and by using our imaginations remove the limitations and thus conceive of a person who has all those qualities to an infinite degree. Descartes does consider this objection, however, and he argues that it fails. How is it that we recognize that human persons are imperfect? Descartes argues that to do that we must already have a sense of perfection. (This is an idea that goes back to Plato, who argued that we can recognize imperfections only because we have an innate idea of the perfect Forms.) If Descartes is right, then perhaps humans do have a kind of innate potential for conceiving God, in that we have within us an idea of perfection that cannot have been acquired through experience since no such perfection can be empirically observed.

Argument two. The second argument given in the Third Meditation is also a causal argument, one that holds that God must exist, not merely as the cause of the idea of God that Descartes has, but the cause of the existence of Descartes himself, understood as a "thinking thing." As in the first argument, Descartes holds that whatever exists must have a cause, and he asks what the cause of himself might be. He argues that because he has many imperfections he could not have caused himself to exist. If he had the power to bring himself into existence out of nothing, he would surely have had the power to give himself the perfections he lacks. Descartes argues that he needs a cause of his existence even if he has always existed, since the fact that he existed at some past time does not explain why he continues to exist. So it seems he must be caused to exist by some other being than himself.

Perhaps, however, this other being is some being less perfect than God, such as Descartes's parents. Descartes here argues that this is also unsatisfactory, appealing to the same principle employed in the first argument, that there must be at least as much perfection in the cause as in the effect.[24] It might seem possible for Descartes himself to be caused

---

[24]Descartes, *Meditations on First Philosophy* 3, p. 79.

by something less than God, but such a being cannot ultimately be responsible for the infinite idea of God Descartes possesses. (Here it looks like the second argument is not fully independent of the first one.) If Descartes is caused by some less-than-perfect being, then that being must be caused by something else that can account for the idea of God. If that other being is also less than perfect it will similarly be inadequate. An infinite regress of such causes is impossible, so eventually one must posit a perfect God.

Descartes's second argument actually looks remarkably like a version of the cosmological argument, similar to those found in Aquinas's arguments, with one important exception.[25] Most cosmological arguments begin with the existence of the cosmos, and Descartes begins with his own existence. However, on reflection, this difference hides a similarity, in that at this point the only part of the cosmos that Descartes knows exists is his own self. One might say that, for all Descartes knows at the moment, he is the whole of the cosmos. The other elements of the argument, including the idea that there cannot be an infinite regress of causes, and that only an infinite, perfect being could stop such a regress appear the same. Once one recognizes that this is really a disguised cosmological argument, the argument seems to have the same appeal and be subject to the same objections as other versions of the cosmological argument.

Argument three. The argument given in the Fifth Meditation is the simplest and clearest of the three. It is a recognizable version of what is usually called the "ontological argument" attributed to Anselm.[26] The starting point is the idea of God Descartes claims to have, as a being who has all perfections. Descartes claims that existence is itself a perfection; a God who did not exist would clearly be less perfect than a God who did exist. However, if God is a being who must possess all perfections, and existence is a perfection, then God must exist.

---

[25]See chap. 9 for a discussion of Aquinas's "Five Ways."
[26]See chap. 8 for Anselm's argument in the *Proslogion*.

Descartes offers an analogous argument: a triangle can be defined as a polygon with three angles, but if one considers the idea of such a thing one can clearly and distinctly see that a triangle must necessarily possess three sides. So also, he claims, it is clearly the case that God, understood as a being who must possess all perfections, must possess existence.

The debate about the ontological argument continues to this day, and clearly Descartes does not settle it. As we shall see, Spinoza and Leibniz will defend the argument in some form, while Kant subjects the argument to a memorable critique, holding that existence cannot be a "perfection" of any kind since it is not a property that a thing might have or fail to have. Things that do not exist cannot have any properties at all. Defenders of the argument either claim that existence is a special kind of property, or that, even if existence is not a property, "necessary existence," which is the kind of existence God has, is a property. While the majority of philosophers reject the ontological argument, it continues to have vigorous defenders.

THE PROBLEM OF THE VICIOUS CIRCLE

It is now time to raise a problem for Descartes's project that was posed almost immediately by his contemporaries, the problem of the "vicious circle." Recall that the need to prove God's existence seemed to stem from the possibility that Descartes was created by an evil demon, a possibility that threatened to bring about an almost complete skepticism. To get rid of the possibility of the evil demon, Descartes must prove that he is created by a good and perfect God, who would not have given him inherently defective faculties or maliciously deceived him by giving him a natural tendency to believe what is false. However, if one really takes seriously the evil demon possibility, it looks like no proof of God's existence is possible. Surely, one of the things the evil demon could do is create in someone (like Descartes) an irresistible tendency to believe what is false by giving the individual an inherently defective faculty of reason. It looks like Descartes must prove the existence of God to show that reason is reliable. However, it is obvious that to prove God's existence one must use reason. If reason cannot be relied on, then any proof of God's existence that depends on reason is not reliable. So it looks like Descartes can only prove that reason is reliable (by proving God's existence) by assuming that reason is reliable so he can prove God's existence. Descartes's proof looks like it is viciously circular in that it requires him to assume the truth of what is supposed to be proved.

Descartes circulated his *Meditations* to some of the best minds in Europe and published the objections they raised along with his replies.[27] Since this objection was among those raised by several thinkers (Antoine Arnauld, for example), we know exactly how Descartes responded to the problem. Descartes tries to avoid the circularity problem by making a distinction between what is "rationally clear and distinct" and what humans know by other faculties, such as memory and perception. He claims that what is clearly and distinctly perceived as true by reason is known with certainty, and there is no need of God to guarantee such knowledge. Hence, if Descartes's proofs of God measure up to this "clear and distinct" standard then there is no circularity, at least at the moment a person is contemplating the proof. However, even if one has proved God's existence, a person could not trust his or her memory to this effect, without knowing that memory is a trustworthy faculty, and for this we need to know that God exists. In a similar way, God's existence gives us reason to trust our sensory faculties, which give us reason to believe in the external objects we perceive, even if those reasons do not measure up to the "clear and distinct" standard.

I believe that Descartes's reply does eliminate the problem of circularity, though it raises other difficulties. Among these difficulties, there is one that strikes me as most important. Essentially, Descartes has made a distinction between reason and the other human cognitive faculties, such as memory and perception, and claimed that we can trust

---

[27]René Descartes, *Meditations on First Philosophy, with Selections from the Objections and Replies,* trans. John Cottingham, Cambridge Texts in the History of Philosophy (Cambridge: Cambridge University Press, 1986), 63-115.

reason without proof, but we need a rational guarantee of the reliability of the other faculties. However, it is not obvious why Descartes is justified in accepting one human faculty (reason) on trust without proof, while demanding proof of the others. One might think, as Thomas Reid will later argue, that all of our basic human cognitive faculties "came out of the same shop," and that if one is justified in accepting one as reliable on trust, one is justified in accepting the others on trust as well.[28]

MEDITATIONS FOUR AND FIVE

I will treat Meditations Four and Five very briefly. Having proved God's existence in Meditation Three, and thereby attempted to show that we are the creatures of a perfect God, Descartes is faced with what we might call an epistemic problem of evil. If we are the creation of such a perfect God, why is it that we are such fallible creatures, prone to mistakes?

Descartes answers this question in Meditation Four by providing a kind of "free will theodicy." The reason we make mistakes and have false beliefs is that God has given us a finite intellect combined with free will. Neither a finite intellect nor free will is inherently bad. Any creature God makes will necessarily be less than God and thus finite in some way. Since our intellects are finite, there are limits to what we can know. However, our free will has a kind of infinity in that a creature who has free will necessarily can exercise it with respect to any choice that creature makes. Because this is so we can misuse our free will by deciding to form beliefs about matters that we do not really know about. But God cannot be faulted, either for giving us finite intellects or free will. To be moral and rational beings we must have free will, but if we misuse our free will that is something we ourselves are responsible for.

In Meditation Five, in addition to providing the third proof of God's existence discussed above, Descartes provides an account of the "essence" of material objects. This may seem odd, since at this point Descartes still does not know for sure whether there are any material

---

[28]See chap. 16 for a discussion of Reid's views on this point.

objects. All he knows at this point is that he exists and that God exists. God is not a material object, and in Meditation Six Descartes will argue that he, as a thinking thing, is also not a material object. In that final meditation Descartes offers an argument for the existence of his body and other material objects, but before that he is careful not to assert the existence of any material objects.

Even if he does not know whether material objects exist, Descartes can still describe what a material object would be if it did exist. He can describe the "ideas" of such objects as they appear to him, regardless of whether such ideas represent anything that is real. Descartes claims that when he thinks about material objects the only clear ideas he has of such things are ideas of a mathematical nature. When he thinks of a material object he thinks of something that is "extended" in space and has such properties as "length, breadth, and depth," and he says that the material objects he conceives have "various sizes, shapes, positions, and local motions," with the motions in turn having various "durations."[29] Note that all those properties are ones that can be measured. Thus Descartes's picture of the material world is a picture of a mathematicized world. There is no room in such a world for such properties as colors and sounds and tastes except as subjective sensations in minds that are caused by the "real" objects with their mathematicized properties. Here we can see the influence of the emerging modern scientific view. Descartes's picture of the physical world is a picture of the world as a kind of machine composed of "matter in motion." As we will see, the great exception to this machine-like material world is ourselves.

MEDITATION SIX: MIND AND BODY AS DISTINCT AND THE EXISTENCE OF MATERIAL THINGS

The climax of the *Meditations* comes in the Sixth Meditation, in which Descartes argues that it is reasonable to believe that there are material objects, but that he himself, as a thinking thing, is distinct from any such

---

[29]Descartes, *Meditations on First Philosophy* 5, p. 87.

material object, even though he has a material body that he is tightly linked to. After a review of his former opinions on the subject, he begins with an argument for his own existence as a nonmaterial being.

Descartes's arguments for soul-body (or mind-body) dualism. Descartes begins by claiming that "everything which I clearly and distinctly understand is capable of being created by God so as to correspond exactly with my understanding of it."[30] If this is so then the mere fact that he can clearly and distinctly conceive one thing existing without some other thing is enough to show that those two things are distinct objects. If, for example, an object A exists at time t_1 but not at t_2, while some object B exists at t_2 but not at t_1, then it is clear that A and B are distinct objects and are not identical. To establish that two things are distinct, it is not necessary that they actually exist separately; it is enough that it is *possible* for them to exist separately. Since God can do whatever is logically possible, Descartes is claiming that if it is logically possible for two things to exist separately they must be two distinct objects. What is important is that the objects are separable, not that they are separate.

From here Descartes argues that he does indeed have a clear and distinct idea of himself as a thinking thing, and that he can clearly and distinctly conceive of himself as existing even if no material objects exist. (Recall that at this point Descartes does not know whether there are any material objects, but he does know that he exists.) It is therefore possible for Descartes to exist even if his body does not, indeed even if no material object exists. It follows from this that Descartes, as a thinking thing, must be distinct from any material object, even his own body. He will shortly argue that he does indeed have a body, one that is "closely joined" to himself. However, he is not identical to that body. He is essentially a mind or soul that is immaterial.

It is worth noting what this argument implies and what it does not imply. First of all, it does not actually imply that the soul is separate

[30]Descartes, *Meditations on First Philosophy* 6, p. 96.

from the body; as far as the argument goes it could be that Descartes's mind depends on the body and would perish if his body perishes. As a distinct thing from the body, the soul *could* exist separately from the body, at least if God willed this to be the case. However, Descartes is not here committed to the idea that the soul has a kind of "natural immortality." The argument does not show that the soul necessarily survives death, but only that this is possible if God willed it to be the case.

Because of this the argument does not imply anything about how the soul and the body might be related. As far as the argument goes, the soul and body might be intimately united. For example, it might be the case that, short of a divine miracle, the soul could not function at all without the body. This is important because some philosophers assert that Descartes's "dualism" has been refuted by contemporary neuroscience, which shows that the mind is deeply dependent on the body. However, this is a mistake. When Descartes claims that the soul is distinct from the body because it is separable, this does not entail that the soul is *separate* from the body and can act independently of it, and thus "Cartesian dualism" would seem completely compatible with any degree of dependence the soul might have with respect to the body.

Descartes himself seems to assume that the soul is not only separable from the body but at least has a degree of separation from it. We can see this from the fact that Descartes describes the soul and the body as causally interacting. The body affects the mind through the brain, or perhaps some small part of the brain, and the mind, by virtue of the will, can also cause the body to change states. Thus Descartes holds a stronger form of dualism, a view often called "interactionism," than his argument by itself would justify. This interactionism appeared problematic to many of Descartes's successors, as we shall see. However, Descartes does recognize that the separation of the soul and body is not complete, for he says, "Nature teaches me not merely that I am present to my body in the way a sailor is present in a ship, but that I am most tightly joined and, so to speak, commingled with it, so much so that I and my body constitute one single thing."[31]

Descartes gives one additional argument for his dualistic view that the soul is distinct from the body. This argument takes as its starting point the very different natures of mind and body. We have already seen (in Meditation Five) that the essence of matter is to be extended, and an extended object, however small, is one that can be divided, at least in thought. Descartes claims that the mind is not like this: "For when I consider the mind, or myself insofar as I am merely a thinking thing, I am unable to distinguish any parts within myself."[32] The mind and the body cannot be identical if they have incompatible properties. Since the body has the property of being extended and therefore divisible, and the mind is indivisible, they must be distinct.

Descartes thinks that since the mind is indivisible it must not be extended or occupy space at all. This is one reason that Descartes's interactionism seemed problematic to his successors. It seemed to them that mind and body as Descartes understands them are so different that it is hard to see how one could possibly affect the other. At one point Descartes famously speculated that the interaction might take place in the pineal gland, which seems doubly wrong-headed. First of all, we now know that the more likely region of the body for the interaction to take place is the brain (which Descartes himself affirms in the *Meditations*). However, what is really wrong with this idea is that the problem is not *where* the interaction might take place but *how*.

Probably what Descartes should have said (and what contemporary dualists sometimes say) is that the interaction between mind and body is causally basic. Whenever we reach causally basic relations in nature, nothing more can be said about how they take place. They just do. For example, if we assume that gravity is one of the basic causal forces of nature, no answer can be given to the question as to how one piece of

---

[31]I have taken this particular quotation from a different edition of Descartes, *Meditations on First Philosophy*, trans. Donald Cress, 3rd ed. (Indianapolis: Hackett, 1993), 53.

[32]Descartes, *Meditations on First Philosophy* 6, p. 101.

matter exerts gravitational attraction on another. The law of gravity simply states that this is what happens. In the same way, an interactionist dualist may simply affirm that matter, when configured in a certain way, has the power to affect a mind that is connected to that matter, and vice versa. The relation between mind and body on this view will share some of the mysteriousness that is present whenever we encounter the fundamental laws and structures of nature.

Descartes's argument for the existence of the body and other material objects. Descartes's argument for the existence of the body begins with the fact that he possesses certain "faculties" (abilities) that appear to require a body. For example, it appears that he can change position relative to other objects, and it also appears that he has a "passive" faculty of sense perception, whereby he receives "ideas of sensible objects." These faculties appear not to be part of Descartes as a "thinking thing," insofar as they "presuppose no intellectual act" on the part of Descartes. In fact, Descartes says that "the ideas in question are produced without my cooperation and often even against my will." So if these ideas do not come from Descartes, where do they originate? One might think that God might produce them directly or indirectly, but Descartes claims that if God did this, God would be a deceiver: "I do not see how God could be understood to be anything but a deceiver if the ideas were transmitted from a source other than corporeal things."[33]

In a similar way, Descartes argues for the existence of the material objects we perceive. These objects certainly appear real and independent of us, and our perceptions strongly suggest to us that they are real. Descartes again concludes that it is reasonable to believe in the existence of material objects, since, because God is no deceiver, "everything that I am taught by nature contains some truth."[34] However, though we may affirm the existence of such objects, Descartes cautiously affirms that material objects may be somewhat different in themselves from the way

---

[33]Descartes, *Meditations on First Philosophy* 6, p. 97.
[34]Descartes, *Meditations on First Philosophy* 6, p. 97.

they appear to us. We may be able to discover the true nature of bodies through scientific discovery, but we cannot assume that the true nature of the physical world is immediately obvious or apparent.

DESCARTES'S LEGACY

Descartes's philosophical thought has been enormously influential. Perhaps the most obvious point is that Descartes made epistemology central to modern Western philosophy. One can see this by comparing the starting points of philosophy in the ancient Greek world with modern Western philosophy. For Aristotle and the Greeks, philosophy begins with wonder, and the primary philosophical questions concern the nature of reality and what it means for humans to live wisely. For Descartes, philosophy begins with doubt, and questions about what we can know and what we can rationally believe are central to philosophy. Above all, Descartes initiates a concern with method, a quest for some way to reach truth that will lead to certainty. Descartes's successors have very diverse views of what the proper method for gaining truth is, but virtually all of them are centrally concerned with these questions.

Descartes's legacy for Christians is somewhat mixed. On the one hand, Descartes's arguments that human persons are not identical to their bodies support a conclusion that Christians will find congenial. Although Christians affirm the resurrection of the body as the final state of the person after death, and reject the Platonic view of a disembodied afterlife, Christian eschatology does not fit well with the idea that a person is identical to his or her body. The traditional view that there is an "interim" or "intermediate state" between death and the resurrection, during which the saved exist with Christ, certainly implies some kind of dualism. Even Christians who believe that human persons are essentially embodied and thus that there can be no such intermediate state will affirm some kind of dualism, if they believe that the human person is at death immediately resurrected in a body that is not identical to the one lying in the grave.

It is sometimes thought that "Cartesian dualism" puts a low view on the body, since it identifies the person with the soul or mind. Those who think this may find it more appealing to think of the human person as a compound of soul and body. However, there are ways of conceiving dualism that allow for a more intimate view of the relation of soul and body. Rather than thinking of the soul and body as two "parts" of the person, perhaps we should think of human persons as bodily souls. On such a view, Descartes is right to say that we do not *have* souls. We *are* souls, self-conscious persons or selves. However, we are the kinds of souls who exist in and through a body. We might say the mode of existence of the human soul, at least during this life, is physical or bodily in nature.

However, although some form of mind-body dualism may still seem plausible, especially to Christians, the specific way Descartes worked out his dualism does not. It does appear that Descartes's metaphysic posits too wide a gap between the human mind and the rest of nature. This can be seen from both sides, so to speak. Nature is seen as a vast machine, while the human soul seems to have no links to that machine except causal links. This is problematic from both sides. The medievals, following Aristotle, had thought of all animals (and even plants) as having souls. Humans differed from other animals not by having souls but by virtue of the kind of souls they possessed. Descartes thought that other animals, like the rest of nature, might possibly be just machines, devoid of consciousness. (Notoriously, some of Descartes's followers, though not Descartes himself, were reputed to mistreat animals on the ground that animals could not feel pain!) This picture of the human mind as an immaterial exception somehow placed in a vast machine seemed very implausible to Descartes's successors, who labored hard to find a more unified picture of the natural world. (In the twentieth century, philosopher Gilbert Ryle memorably caricatured this Cartesian picture by describing it as the "ghost in the machine" view.)[35]

---

[35]See Gilbert Ryle, *The Concept of Mind* (New York: Routledge, 2009). This is a sixty-year anniversary edition of the book, originally published in 1949.

Descartes thus bequeathed to his successors an urgent need to find an epistemological method that would make philosophy a genuine "science," as well as a need to find a way to recognize the unique qualities of the human person without disconnecting humans from the natural world.

Continental Rationalism

Spinoza and Leibniz

THE HISTORY OF EARLY MODERN Western philosophy can be told in various ways, but one traditional way of organizing the narrative is in terms of the contrast between continental rationalism and British empiricism. The two traditions were certainly in contact with each other, and there were mutual influences. Nevertheless, there are distinctive ways in which most of the great philosophers in Europe followed Descartes's rationalism, while most of the important thinkers in the British Isles were strongly influenced by the empiricism we have already seen in Hobbes, and will examine more closely in the next chapter, which will focus on John Locke. In order to highlight these distinctive lines of influence, I shall deviate from a strictly chronological order and look first at the development of rationalism on the Continent following Descartes, before circling back to examine the thinking of the British empiricists going on at roughly the same time. Of these continental rationalists, the most influential and important thinkers are Baruch Spinoza and Gottfried Wilhelm Leibniz, and they will be the main focus of this chapter.

SPINOZA

Baruch Spinoza (1632–1677) was a Jewish thinker who lived in the Netherlands. ("Baruch" was his Hebrew name, sometimes changed to the Latin "Benedictus" or even "Benedict" in English.) His family were

Portuguese Jews who had been expelled from that country and sought refuge in the Netherlands. Spinoza was brought up in a traditional Jewish home and received a conventional Jewish education, mostly religious in character. However, his original and unconventional thinking eventually led to his expulsion from the synagogue in Amsterdam, and exclusion from the Jewish community, and he later settled in The Hague. At one point Spinoza was offered a chair in philosophy at the University of Heidelberg, but he declined the offer, fearful that such a position would limit his freedom to pursue the truth as he saw it. He made a modest living grinding lenses, but his fame and reputation spread throughout Europe. His greatest philosophical work is his *Ethics*, a somewhat misleading title in that the book certainly culminates in Spinoza's ethics but also includes a distinctive metaphysical system that undergirds that ethic. Most of what Spinoza wrote, including the *Ethics*, was published posthumously. Besides the *Ethics*, the writings include important treatments of politics, in which Spinoza defends democracy, and also biblical criticism. Spinoza pioneered the critical examination of sacred writings and criticized giving political power to religious authorities.

Spinoza's method. In some ways Spinoza is deeply indebted to Descartes. Like Descartes, Spinoza sees mathematics as an ideal form of scientific knowledge and aspires to reconstruct philosophy using a mathematical method. However, Spinoza carried out this project quite differently than Descartes himself, at least stylistically, and reached conclusions very different from Descartes. Although Descartes endorses the idea of basing philosophy on intuitively clear definitions and propositions that are self-evident to reason, he actually writes his *Meditations* as meditations, offering a personal narrative told from a first-person point of view. Spinoza, however, aspires actually to follow the procedure of someone developing a geometrical system. In his *Ethics* he begins with a series of numbered definitions of key terms, along with a numbered set of axioms, which are supposed to be self-evident propositions.

With these definitions and axioms as his foundation, Spinoza proceeds to prove a large number of propositions, also numbered. Each step of the proof is done in proper logical form. That is, Spinoza justifies each step in the proof by appeal to the definitions and axioms, along with appeals to those propositions already proved. The whole thing reads then like a work of mathematics, not philosophical prose.

Part one of the *Ethics* includes eight definitions and seven axioms. Among the most important of the definitions are those given for "God" and "substance":

> 3. By substance I mean that which is in itself and is conceived through itself; that is, that the conception of which does not require the conception of another thing from which it has to be formed.

> 6. By God I mean an absolutely infinite being, that is, substance consisting of infinite attributes, each of which expresses eternal and infinite essence.[1]

As we shall see, these definitions will turn out to have pervasive and somewhat unexpected implications. After proving a number of key propositions, Spinoza arrives at proposition eleven: "*God, or substance consisting of infinite attributes, each which expresses eternal and infinite substance, necessarily exists.*"[2] A short time later Spinoza follows this with proposition fourteen: "*There can be, or be conceived, no other substance but God.*"[3] We have clearly moved here from method to substance: Spinoza is committed to philosophical monism, the claim that one and only one substance exists.

Spinoza's conclusions, no matter how rigorous his logical arguments, will be no better than his axioms and definitions. If one thinks of definitions as more or less arbitrary decisions as to how a word should be used, then it is hard to see how momentous metaphysical conclusions can be grounded in them. (This is essentially the criticism Hobbes makes of

---

[1]Baruch Spinoza, *The Ethics* 1d3, d6, in Baruch Spinoza, *"The Ethics" and Selected Letters*, trans. Samuel Shirley (Indianapolis: Hackett, 1982), 31.
[2]Spinoza, *Ethics* 1p11, in Shirley, 37-38.
[3]Spinoza, *Ethics* 1p13, in Shirley, 38.

Spinoza.) However, Spinoza is a Cartesian. He believes that his definitions are not arbitrary but reflect a clear and distinct understanding of
ideas. Like Descartes he offers a foundationalist epistemology in which
the basic grounds of knowledge must be self-evident to reason, and he
believes human reason is up to the task of offering us such grounds.

Spinoza's metaphysics. As we have seen already, Spinoza is committed to a metaphysical monism; only one substance exists, and that
substance is God. Everything that exists is in some sense God or "in
God," part of God. The crucial move in developing this view is, I believe,
Spinoza's definition of substance. The concept of substance of course
was originally developed by ancient Greek philosophers. Aristotle, for
example, distinguished substances from attributes.[4] Substances are
those realities that can be conceived as existing independently, on their
own, so to speak. Attributes, on the other hand, cannot be conceived as
existing in isolation. Such properties as "being intelligent" or "being
snub-nosed" cannot exist as free-floating entities. They must be properties *of* something, and that something must be a substance.

Spinoza takes this concept of a substance as that which can be conceived to exist "on its own" and thinks through the implications rigorously. Descartes's metaphysical system was one in which there were
three types of substances. God is the infinite substance that is the cause
of the existence of finite substances. Those finite substances come in
two radically different kinds: material substances that are "extended,"
and nonmaterial substances that are nonextended "thinking things."
Spinoza thinks that this Cartesian picture is incoherent. How can finite
substances, whether mental or material, be *substances* existing independently if they depend on God? It looks like we cannot in fact conceive
of such finite substances existing on their own. If Spinoza is correct in
defining a substance as something "the conception of which does not
require the conception of another thing from which it has to be formed,"
then there are no finite, created substances. God and only God exists.

---

[4]See the discussion of Aristotle's view of substance in chap. 5.

Spinoza's metaphysic thus seems to be a form of pantheism. To be sure, some have denied this, but the arguments against describing Spinoza as a pantheist usually derive from semantic quarrels about what "pantheism" amounts to. However, Spinoza certainly affirms the existence of God, and he certainly affirms that God is not a being distinct from the material world. Indeed, Spinoza goes so far as to say that the one substance that exists can be called "God or nature." This has led to wildly diverse interpretations of Spinoza. Some philosophers, both traditional theists and atheists, have affirmed that Spinoza's view is really just a form of naturalism in disguise; nothing exists except nature. Other philosophers have read Spinoza very differently, calling him a "God-intoxicated" thinker. As we shall see, Spinoza's view of God is certainly radically different from the view found in the traditional theistic religions: Christianity, Judaism, and Islam. However, it seems wrong to think of Spinoza simply as a naturalist. A thinker who affirms that God and only God exists can hardly be an atheist.

The actual proof Spinoza offers for his view has several steps. He argues that when two substances have nothing in common, one cannot be the cause of the other, for causality requires an intelligible connection between cause and effect, but no connection between two things that have nothing in common can be conceived. (Here we see how Spinoza was influenced by the problem of mind-body interaction raised by Descartes.) He also argues that there cannot be two substances with the same nature or attribute, so if there were two substances they would have nothing in common. It follows from these two claims that no substance can be caused to exist by another.

He then argues for the existence of God as an absolutely infinite substance, employing an argument similar to the ontological argument offered by Descartes in his Fifth Meditation. According to this argument, God's essence involves existence since God's essence includes all perfections and existence is a perfection. From all of this it follows that no other substance than God exists. Any other substance would have to be distinguished in some way from God, but since God already has all infinite attributes, there is no attribute any other substance could have that would differentiate it from God.

When Spinoza says that God is a being with "infinite attributes," he means this in a double sense. On the one hand, God has an infinite number of attributes. On the other hand, each of those attributes is possessed by God in an infinite manner. Although God in himself has an infinite number of attributes, Spinoza says that we only are aware of two: thought and extension. When we think of God as a mind we conceive God as God; when we think of God as extension, we picture God as nature. Mind and extension do not refer to distinct substances, as in Descartes, but rather two properties or attributes of one substance. However, Spinoza's intent is neither to reduce matter to thought (as idealism does) or thought to matter (as materialism does). He is a "neutral monist," someone who holds that what is ultimately real has both mental and physical attributes, without being reducible to either of these attributes.

Spinoza thinks that this solves the problem of mind-body interaction, which gave Descartes such difficulties. For two things to interact causally they must be two distinct things. Descartes struggled to explain how two substances that are radically different and have nothing in common could affect each other. However, for Spinoza, mind and body are like two faces of the same coin; two ways the same reality presents itself to us. For him there are no causal links between different substances, because there are no different substances. Corresponding to every physical configuration (including the universe as a whole) there is a parallel mental "idea." The physical and mental are parallel and are "synchronized," so to speak, but there is no causal interaction.

Although God has a mind, Spinoza does not think one should think of God as conceiving various possibilities and then choosing one of them to actualize. Nor does God deliberate about the best means to achieve his ends, for God necessarily does what is best. If one thinks of freedom as the freedom to choose between alternative possibilities, then God is not free. That is not how Spinoza thinks of freedom, however. God is perfectly rational, and all of God's actions are necessary. However, God is still free in the sense that he is unconstrained by anything outside of himself. Nothing can prevent God from acting as he must, and so he is perfectly free in the sense that he is always able to be himself and is completely independent.

Since God is not a being who is distinct from nature, it is also a mistake to think of God as an "efficient cause" that brings nature into being. God is the cause of everything that happens, but God's causality is an "immanent" causality, not the product of a being who is distinct from the world. Spinoza's God seems rather similar to the God of the ancient Stoics.[5] Everything that happens does so because of God, but God is not a person distinct from the world, but more like an immanent principle that pervades the world. Perhaps it would be better to describe Spinoza as a "panentheist" than a pantheist, however. (Panentheism is the view that the natural world is part of God but that God is not reducible to the world.) God's mind means that God is not simply identical to the physical world, even if that world is part of God.

Spinoza thinks that the natural world may legitimately be conceived in two ways. Nature is both *natura naturans* and also *natura naturata*. *Natura naturans* is "nature naturing." When we conceive of nature in this way, we think of nature as active and productive; it is nature "doing its thing." When we conceive of nature as *natura naturata* (nature natured), we think of nature as the result or product of the process. (Some commentators think that it is only the former that could be called God and thus that Spinoza does make a kind of distinction between God and nature, insofar as nature in one sense is conceived as a passive product of divine activity.)

Spinoza also thinks that the whole of the universe expresses what he terms *conatus*, or will. He does not mean by "will" a reflective or

---

[5]See chap. 6 for a discussion of Stoicism.

deliberative process of choice, but rather that each object in the universe in some way wants to be what it is. In animals this expresses itself in what we call the will to live or survive, but even inanimate objects in some way strive to continue to be what they are. The introduction of *conatus* does not introduce teleology into Spinoza's metaphysic. There is no final goal or end that the universe is seeking. Rather, the "will" we see in the universe is simply the way in which each thing (and the whole) is striving to be what it is.

How does Spinoza think about the finite objects that Descartes called substances? Spinoza describes such things as "modes" of God, the particular ways in which God manifests himself. Spinoza does distinguish between what he calls finite modes of God and infinite modes. The infinite modes of God are things like the principles of mathematics and the laws of physics. They exist always and are an immediate, direct expression of God's nature. Finite modes, such as human beings, are also expressions of God's nature, but they are "modifications" of the divine attributes, and as such they have a different status. Finite modes come and go and thus have a kind of contingency.

With the exception of God, however, there is no freedom in Spinoza's universe. Everything is ultimately determined by God's nature, directly or indirectly, and everything that happens is necessary. Humans believe in free will only because of our ignorance of the true causes of what we do. It is ultimately a world in which regret makes no sense. Everything that happens must happen, and so, like the Stoics, Spinoza believes that a wise person should accept events without regret.

Spinoza's ethics. The key to Spinoza's ethical views lies in his view that humans are simply modes of God, as is the whole of nature. As noted above, humans believe that they have free will, but this belief is grounded in ignorance of the causes of human behavior. If all human behavior is caused by past causes, which necessarily produce their effects, then regrets and desires that things could have been different are irrational. Of course Spinoza knows that we humans think that some states of affairs are good and some are bad. However, we make such judgments simply on the basis of what fulfills or frustrates our desires or appetites, whatever they may be. These judgments on our part do not reflect some objective or absolute truth but simply a relation to our desires and appetites.

The wise person seeks to free himself or herself from such emotions as regret by understanding the order of nature. As we come to see that all that happens is necessary, we will free ourselves from what we might call reactive emotion. We cannot change the course of nature, but we can change our attitude toward what happens. (Here again Spinoza clearly mimics the Stoics.)

For Spinoza unhappiness stems from our partial perspective on reality. We are unduly attached to some particular outcome or thing, and feel sadness and even despair when we lose it, although the truth is that such losses are outside our control. Spinoza says we should strive to see the world as God sees it: *sub specie aeternitatis* (under the aspect of eternity). To see the world this way requires us to appreciate the beauty and grandeur of the whole system of reality, none of which could be different than it is. To live in this way constitutes "the intellectual love of God." For Spinoza love for God is not love for a person who might return this love. It is rather more like the awe and wonder one might feel for a beautiful mathematical proof or some deep law of physics.

One may well question whether Spinoza's determinism is really consistent with his recommendation that we seek to change our view of the world and see things from God's point of view. If everything that happens is necessary, then one would think that our regrets and partial points of view are necessary as well. If I regret the death of a child, isn't that regret as necessary as the child's death? If we really have no free will, of what use is it to advise us to change our attitude from one of regret to acceptance? In any case it seems a tall order to expect that most humans will take such a disinterested view of life. If my child or spouse dies, it seems cold comfort to be told that this event is necessary, and that from God's point of view it is part of the necessary structure of the whole of nature.

To some degree Spinoza himself acknowledges the force of these criticisms. He recognizes that his ethical stance is one that is very difficult for most people. He also admits that humans, as part of nature, cannot totally free themselves from their partial perspectives. Spinoza is an "egoist" who holds that each individual seeks his or her own happiness, and he affirms that it is right to do so. However, the best way of achieving true happiness is to reduce the influence of the "passions" on us by seeking to gain more knowledge, especially the kind of knowledge that constitutes the intellectual love of God, whereby we come to understand the necessity of all things. It is this kind of understanding that constitutes true virtue for Spinoza, and this virtue is for him the key to blessedness and even to what he is prepared to call salvation.

LEIBNIZ

The German philosopher Gottfried Wilhelm Leibniz (1646–1716) was an intellectual prodigy, whose brilliance was quickly recognized. He began his university studies at Leipzig, his hometown, focusing on philosophy, but he went on to Jena to study mathematics, and Altdorf to study law. Leibniz developed the infinitesimal calculus at about the same time as Newton. (This great intellectual achievement led to an ugly dispute between Leibniz and Newton, as each claimed to be the first inventor and viewed the other as having stolen the idea; scholars today believe that each man made the discovery independently at about the same time. Newton may have made the discovery slightly earlier, though Leibniz published his results first and had a superior notation.) Leibniz lived an active life as a diplomat and adviser to nobility and royalty. Some of his (never-realized) dreams included a kind of union of European nations, preceding the European Union by centuries, and a plan to reconcile Protestants and Catholics. Leibniz also made important innovations in logic, some of which have been very significant for modern symbolic logic. He published on many philosophical topics, his most important works including *Essays in Theodicy*, *Discourse on Metaphysics*, *The New System of Nature and the Interaction of Substances*, and the *Monadology*. Leibniz was the first president of what eventually became the Prussian Academy of Sciences. Sadly, however, his influence and fame waned in his old age, and by the time he died he was a neglected figure.

Monads, space, and time. Leibniz's most famous idea, one that lies at the heart of his metaphysics, is the idea of a monad. To understand this concept, we must begin by considering objects that are aggregates or compounds. It is obvious that there are such objects, but what about the parts of such compounds? Are they compounds as well? In many cases the answer is surely yes. However, Leibniz was convinced that, metaphysically, there could not be an infinite succession of compounds composed of other compounds, which in turn are composed of yet more compounds. If such an infinite succession is to be avoided, there must be simple substances, things that have no parts.

This is of course exactly the reasoning that led some of the ancient Greeks to the philosophy of atomism, the view that the world is composed of indivisible physical particles.[6] Atomism was being revived at the time of Leibniz. Leibniz, however, was dissatisfied with the notion of a physical atom. If one thinks of an atom as a particle having extension in space, then it is difficult to see why an atom is really indivisible. For no matter how small an atom may be, as long as it occupies some finite amount of space, one can at least conceive of the atom being divided. (In a way, that is what happened in the twentieth century, when scientists learned to "split" atoms and developed nuclear chain reactions.) This led Leibniz to rethink the whole notion of what the smallest substances must be like.

Descartes and Spinoza had both thought that the concept of extension was fundamental to the natural world. One might say that they

---

[6]See the discussion on Democritus in chap. 2.

conceived space as a kind of objective receptacle, something like a giant container, with physical objects occupying various positions in space. Leibniz believed that this conception of space was incoherent in that space was treated as a kind of substance, an objective reality, but a substance with no properties and thus one that could not be distinguished from nothing. Leibniz had the originality to propose that the concept of space and "extended stuff" is not really primitive. Instead he argued that what is really basic or brute in the natural world is something like "energy" or "force," concepts that have application both in human minds and in nature. He proposed that the basic substances were *monads*, which can be described as something like "spiritual atoms." Monads have a location or position (relative to other monads), but they are not extended. They are like points of energy or force. What we call space is not metaphysically basic or primitive, but rather is grounded in monads and their relations to each other. In some ways, then, Leibniz anticipated the modern theory of relativity, in which time and space are not objective entities in which objects reside, but relational realities that are grounded in the packets of energy or force that are the basic constituents of the natural world. Space and time as experienced are part of the phenomenal world. They are not metaphysically basic, but they are grounded in and explained by what is metaphysically basic: the monads. At times Leibniz describes space and time as "well-grounded illusions."

One might try to imagine Leibniz's notions of space and time by thinking of a computer that provides us with a "virtual reality," a space that is a projection of the computer's programming. When we look at the screen we see objects that have spatial (and temporal) relations to each other, but those objects are simply projections of mathematical representations in the computer.

For Leibniz all of reality is composed of monads, from bare material objects to complicated plants and animals. Human persons are also monads, ones that image God, who is the supreme Monad and the source of all other monads. (I will discuss Leibniz's view of God below.) Some monads are richer and more complicated than others, but there is no sharp dividing line between different kinds of monads, as was the case for Descartes, with his two radically different kinds of finite substances. Rather, there is a continuum of monads with no sharp line between the mental and the physical, as was the case with Descartes. Leibniz believes that the universe is a plenitude with a rich diversity of realities, in which every possible niche is occupied.

Monads have a remarkable set of features. Beings with parts can cease to be by decomposition. I can, for example, destroy my watch by taking it apart. However, monads, since they have no parts, can only come into being or cease to be by direct divine action. Monads are also self-sufficient. Each monad is created by God with its entire history, past and future, so to speak, as part of its internal program. Every monad has traces of its entire past and also anticipations of its entire future. In Leibniz's words, a monad is laden with its past and "pregnant with the future."[7] With its program or script, monads cannot be affected by any other monads (except God). Every monad is "windowless," to use Leibniz's powerful metaphor.[8]

Of course the objects that we experience phenomenally in our world appear to have causal relations to each other. On Leibniz's view, this is due to the fact that all the monads conform perfectly to their "scripts." There is a "preestablished harmony" between all the monads, and we can, speaking loosely at the phenomenal level, speak of one event as the cause of another. To draw on a much-used metaphor, the monads are like synchronized clocks, keeping perfect time with each other, but the clocks are not connected. Metaphysically, monads are completely self-sufficient and go their own way.

---

[7]G. W. Leibniz, *Monadology* 22, in Nicholas Rescher, *G. W. Leibniz's Monadology: An Edition for Students* (Pittsburgh: University of Pittsburgh Press, 1991), 19-20. Rescher's student edition includes valuable commentary and fragments of Leibniz's other writings for reference. All citations of the *Monadology* are from this edition.

[8]Leibniz, *Monadology* 7, p. 17.

This all requires that each monad have a kind of internal representation of every other monad. Every monad in some way mirrors the
entire universe.[9] What we would ordinarily call the spatial and temporal
relations between events are made possible by the way these internal
representations are precisely synchronized. When monad A moves
closer to monad B, monad B must also become closer to monad A.

This view of the universe as composed of monads commits Leibniz
to something like panpsychism, the view that mind is not just present
in animals and humans but is pervasive in nature. Something like this
view is also present in Spinoza, with his claim that mind and extension
are the two knowable attributes of God or nature. The two features we
normally associate with minds are thought and will. Leibniz thinks that
all monads have analogues of these two features. Each one contains a
kind of inner representation of the whole of the universe. There is a
sense in which every monad is "aware" of every other. Leibniz calls this
"perception," and he says that the perceptions of inanimate monads
must be distinguished from the "apperceptions" of humans.[10] Apper-
ception is a kind of self-conscious perception, in which we are aware
that we are perceiving, conscious of our representations. (Interestingly,
Leibniz also holds that humans have "little perceptions," which are
something like unconscious perceptions, and so we are not conscious
of all that we perceive.) Monads also have a kind of "will" or "*conatus*"
(as in Spinoza), but again we must distinguish the kind of "will to be
itself" found in the monads of inanimate objects from the self-conscious will found in humans. Despite the distinction between higher
and lower monads, it is clear that for Leibniz there is no sharp dividing
line between what we call the mental and the physical.

Like Spinoza, though in a different way, Leibniz also solves the
problem of mind-body interaction that had so troubled Descartes.
Since there is no interaction between monads, there simply is nothing

---

[9]Leibniz, *Monadology* 56, p. 24.
[10]Leibniz, *Monadology* 13-14, p. 18.

to explain. Human minds are themselves monads, and human bodies are ensembles of monads. The identity of an organic body over time does not require the exact same collection of monads, however. The monads of what we call a physical body may come and go. Rather, in a view that is strikingly like those of medieval Aristotelians, each body has an "intelligible form" that gives it its structure, and as long as this form is preserved the object is preserved. The appearance of interaction between mind and body is explained by the monads with their preestablished harmony.

God and possible worlds. God obviously plays a crucial role in Leibniz's metaphysics as the Creator of the monads. Leibniz believes that God's existence can be proved in a number of ways, but Leibniz is perhaps best known for his version of the cosmological argument. He defends as a fundamental principle what he calls "the principle of sufficient reason."[11] Leibniz formulates this principle in a number of different ways. At times he speaks of truths and says that there must be a reason for every truth. At other times he speaks of events and says that there must be a reason or cause for every event. This principle is the basis of a number of Leibniz's important metaphysical claims. For example, he employs it as part of his argument for the relational quality of time and space, and also to defend what he calls the principle of the identity of indiscernibles, which claims that any two entities that have exactly the same properties must be identical. He also employs the principle to prove God's existence. (Something like the principle of sufficient reason is also clearly present in Spinoza's demand that all of reality be intelligible, although Spinoza does not employ the phrase "principle of sufficient reason.")

Many if not all of the events that occur as part of the course of nature are contingent, which means that propositions that deny the existence of these events are not self-contradictory. Necessary truths for Leibniz are precisely those whose denial is self-contradictory; their truth is thus

---

[11]Leibniz, *Monadology* 32, p. 21.

grounded in another fundamental rational principle, the principle of noncontradiction, which affirms that "p and not-p cannot both be true." Contingent events cannot be their own reason for existing, since their nonoccurrence is logically possible. Hence they need a cause or reason outside themselves. It might seem possible that the cause or reason for one contingent event is some other contingent event or events. However, even if this is true, and every contingent event has as its explanation some other contingent event, there would still be something un-explained, namely, the whole series of contingent events. We might say that we would still have no explanation for why anything exists at all if everything that exists is contingent. This argument makes no reference to time and, if sound, would still be sound even if the universe had ex-isted forever. The principle of sufficient reason requires that there be a reason why the universe exists, and the only adequate reason would be a necessary being, and Leibniz holds that a necessary being who is re-sponsible for the existence of everything contingent would be God.

Does God have a sufficient reason to create the world that he does? Leibniz holds that God does indeed have such a reason. To explain this, Leibniz employs the notion of a possible world. A possible world is simply a maximally large set of events that God could actualize. Not even God can do what is logically impossible, so God could not create a world in which there were only blue objects and in which there also were green objects. But if we imagine a maximally large set of events that logically can be instantiated together we have a possible world. The actual world is a possible world, but there are many others. God, being omniscient and omnipotent, is aware of all the possible worlds and has the power to actualize any of them. Why should he actualize one rather than some other? Leibniz thinks the obvious answer is that God would actualize one world rather than another because it is better. The actual world must then be the best of all possible worlds.

The claim that the actual world is the best of all possible worlds was memorably satirized by Voltaire in *Candide,* and it certainly seems implausible to many. Leibniz, however, claims that this is a rationally defensible view, and embarks on the task of theodicy, a justification of God's ways. He admits that the actual world appears to contain quite a bit of evil. However, Leibniz holds that it must be the best possible world because it is the one God has chosen to actualize.

Our belief that the world could be better is not well-founded. First, we only experience a tiny fraction of the events that make up the world, especially if we consider the fact that there is an eternal future. So it is rash for us to make conclusions about the whole of the universe on the basis of our limited experience. He compares our situation to that of someone who examines a tiny corner of a great painting. If one only sees the tiny corner, the colors and lines may appear to be pointless, but when seen in the context of the whole painting, we can see the purposes they serve. Furthermore, God can bring good out of evil, and so in the long run will be able to bring about more good by allowing evil. Leibniz also employs the Augustinian view that evil is in any case not a positive substance, but merely a lack or defect in God's creation.

Leibniz's notion of a possible world has become important in providing a semantic interpretation of modal terms (terms such as *possible* and *necessary*) in contemporary metaphysics. A logically possible truth, for example, can be defined as one that is true in at least one possible world, while a logically necessary truth is one that is true in every possible world.

There has also been continued debate over Leibniz's claim that God must create the best of all possible worlds. Some have argued that there simply is no best possible world, and so God cannot create the best possible world. Others have argued that God, as a gracious being, is not obligated to create the best possible world, but only a good one.[12] Others have argued that if God decides to create beings with free will, then there may be worlds that are logically possible that God cannot actualize because of the free choices of his creatures.

---

[12]See Robert Adams, "Must God Create the Best?," *Philosophical Review* 81, no. 3 (1972): 317-32.

Human freedom. Leibniz's metaphysical system, like Spinoza's, seems to be deterministic. Each monad necessarily follows the script it has been given, and thus can never act differently than it does. However, unlike Spinoza, who resolutely denies that humans possess freedom, Leibniz defends a "compatibilist" view in which determinism and free will are consistent. Humans are sometimes free, despite the fact that their programs are set, so to speak.

The first element in Leibniz's defense of compatibilism is to distinguish between absolute necessity and hypothetical necessity. What is absolutely necessary cannot be different, for if anything else happened it would imply a contradiction. What is hypothetically necessary is not necessary in itself, but only necessary given some condition. Leibniz equates such hypothetical necessities with what is contingent. An event that is contingent is not absolutely necessary; if some other condition had held, then some other event would have occurred.

In the case of human actions, although they necessarily follow from the nature of the monad that God has created, they are not absolutely necessary because God could have created the monad differently by actualizing a different possible world. Thus there is a sense in which humans could act differently than they do. If a person had different desires, for example, they would act differently. Philosophers who are libertarians find this conditional or hypothetical freedom unsatisfactory, since, given the actual natures God has given to the monads, it seems that everything that actually happens must happen. This is especially the case given that it is not clear that God can really do otherwise than he does, given Leibniz's view that God must actualize the best possible world. (Leibniz claims God's creation is free, but it is not clear this is completely consistent with his overall view.)

Ultimately, Leibniz's compatibilism depends on the intuition that genuine freedom is simply a matter of being determined by one's own self; freedom is freedom from external control. In this sense, every monad, including humans, may be said to have the kind of freedom

Spinoza attributed to God, the freedom of being oneself, since each "windowless" monad is entirely independent of all the others. Leibniz does want to hold that humans have a unique kind of freedom that lower monads do not have, because they have minds. In having minds, humans not only have a kind of representation of the world, as do all monads, but a representation of God, which allows them to be part of a society or kingdom of which God is the monarch. Acts that stem spontaneously from the ideas of a being with a mind are free in that they are truly spontaneous and self-directed.

Leibniz's epistemology. A good place to begin a discussion of Leibniz's epistemology is with his account of truth. He claims that a true proposition is simply one in which the predicate is contained in the subject. This makes good sense for what are often called "analytic" truths that are made true by the meaning of the terms. For example, "a brother is a male sibling" is true because the concept of a brother includes the concept of being male and having a sibling. Such truths are necessarily true. However, Leibniz's view seems very implausible as a general account of truth, for it seems that many truths are contingent and therefore not necessary.

To make his view plausible Leibniz has to make sense of the distinction between what is necessary and what is contingent, and to this end he makes use of the distinction between absolute and hypothetical or conditional necessity just discussed in connection with free will. Contingent truths are just those that are only true given God's decision to actualize the actual world with its particular set of monads and their courses. Given that monads are the only substances, then it turns out to be the case that all the predicates that can belong to a given substance are in fact included in that substance. Every monad contains its whole past and future.

Nevertheless, we can distinguish between those predicates that can clearly be seen to belong to a subject necessarily and those where it is not clear or obvious (to humans) what predicates belong to a subject. God, who knows all truths, can always see that every true proposition is one in which the subject contains the predicate, but this is often not the case with human minds. Thus many contingent truths must be discovered.

Given Leibniz's view that all monads are windowless, it is clear that there is a sense in which all ideas are innate, and this seems a very strong form of rationalism. However, although it is true that all ideas are innate, Leibniz holds that many of our innate ideas are not present to the mind or are present in a confused manner. It appears to us that some ideas are learned from experiencing the world or from other people. Metaphysically this is not so, since all monads are self-sufficient. However, the preestablished harmony makes it appear that monads interact, and thus it also appears that we gain information from others.

Therefore, though Leibniz believes that many of the most important truths can be known through reason alone, particularly by relying on such self-evident principles as the principle of noncontradiction, the principle of sufficient reason, and the principle of the identity of indiscernibles, Leibniz recognizes a role for sense perception as well. Just as space and time are not objectively or metaphysically basic, so all of our ideas are ultimately innate. We can distinguish, however, between those ideas that are transparent to reason and those that are grounded in the appearances of space and time, with their apparently interacting bodies.

CONCLUSIONS TO RATIONALISM IN
EARLY MODERN PHILOSOPHY

Descartes, Spinoza, and Leibniz share a common faith in the power of human reason to reach truth through clear reasoning modeled on mathematics. They all are committed to innate ideas and that there are some truths that are self-evident to human reason. Even the knowledge that may be gained by sense experience needs a rational foundation in order for it to be worthy of acceptance.

Besides these general similarities, Spinoza and Leibniz share some other important similarities. They both hold to panpsychism, or something similar, by holding that mind is a pervasive aspect of the whole of the universe. Both accept determinism as true, although Spinoza concludes from this that humans lack freedom, while Leibniz affirms a compatibilist view that attempts to show that freedom and determinism can both be true. Both Spinoza and Leibniz reject the fundamental dualism of mind and matter found in Descartes, and both reject the idea that different substances can interact. In some way both affirm that the actual world should be embraced. Spinoza does not say, as Leibniz does, that the actual world is the best possible world, and indeed perhaps did not think any other world was possible. However, both affirm that when we see the world from God's point of view it can and should be affirmed as good.

Of course there are obvious differences in their metaphysical stances. Spinoza is an absolute monist who holds that there is only one substance, and that substance is identical to God. Leibniz holds a kind of qualitative monism in that he affirms that all of reality consists of monads. However, Leibniz is a pluralist; there are an indefinite number of monads, and each one is different from every other one in some way. Both reject the dualistic metaphysics of Descartes and repudiate the idea of mind-body interaction. However, it is not clear that the mystery of the mind and its relation to the body is really clarified by this denial of interaction. In some ways, Descartes's view seems closer to common sense and everyday experience, in which it certainly seems that events that happen in the body make a difference to our conscious thoughts and feelings, while our thoughts and desires make a great difference to the body as well.

It has been said that the mind-body problem is the "world-knot" that is linked to almost every issue in philosophy. It has also been claimed, perhaps rightly, that the problem is so hard that virtually every view of mind and body has been held by some philosopher, no matter how absurd. For example, Descartes's successor Malebranche defended "occasionalism," the view that there is no true mind-body interaction but that the appearance of such interaction is due to God's action. For example, when I drop a brick on my toe, the pain I feel is due not to the damage the brick has done to my toe; rather, on the occasion when the brick hits my toe, God himself produces the pain I feel. Despite the great confidence the rationalists have in human reason, it is clear that they did not succeed in solving the great problems of philosophy once and for all.

British Empiricism

Locke and Berkeley

IT IS TIME TO RETURN FROM the Continent to the British Isles for a look at British empiricism. The tendency toward an empiricist epistemology had already been shaped in Britain by Francis Bacon and Thomas Hobbes. The immensely influential philosophy of John Locke, who had studied Descartes carefully but was deeply critical of key elements in Cartesian thought, cemented this tradition and cast a long shadow over all later English-language philosophers.

JOHN LOCKE

John Locke (1632–1704) was born in Somerset, England, from a Puritan family. He was educated at Oxford and held a position there for many years. However, Locke was also involved in practical affairs, as a physician and as an advisor to the Earl of Shaftesbury, a leading political figure. Locke's most important works are *An Essay Concerning Human Understanding* and *Two Treatises on Civil Government*. However, two works dealing with religion are also influential: *The Reasonableness of Christianity* and *An Essay on Toleration*.

We see some of the same focus on epistemology in Locke that we saw in Descartes, and for some of the same reasons. In England arguments concerning religion had been at the forefront of the national consciousness ever since Henry VIII created the Church of England and thereby brought the Reformation to England. After Henry's death, future monarchs alternated between Catholicism and Protestantism, with much blood shed on both sides. Elizabeth I temporarily achieved a kind of middle ground acceptable to much of the country. However, in the seventeenth century, England was convulsed by civil war. Although religion was far from the only issue, the war was fought between Parliament, led by Puritans and other Protestants, and the king, who favored a "higher," more "Catholic" type of church. Locke lived through this time of turmoil as a young man, and his family's Puritan beliefs certainly gave him an appreciation for Nonconformism, and a desire to find a way rationally to settle disputed religious and political questions.

We can see this in his "Epistle to the Reader," which he attaches to the beginning of the *Essay Concerning Human Understanding*. Locke tells us that the origins of the book lay in an argument that Locke had with his friends in his apartment.

> Were it fit to trouble thee with the history of this Essay, I should tell thee, that five or six friends meeting at my chamber, and discoursing on a subject very remote from this, found themselves quickly at a stand, by the difficulties that rose on every side. After we had awhile puzzled ourselves, without coming any nearer a resolution of those doubts which perplexed us, it came into my thoughts that we took a wrong course; and that before we set ourselves upon inquiries of that nature, it was necessary to examine our own abilities, and see what objects our understandings were, or were not, fitted to deal with.[1]

Scholars have determined that Locke and his friends were arguing about religious questions. It is clear that Locke decided that before such questions could be answered, he must first deal with the fundamental questions of epistemology: What can humans know? How do humans know? When are beliefs that are less than knowledge justified? Locke

---

[1]John Locke, *An Essay Concerning Human Understanding*, ed. Peter H. Nidditch (Oxford: Oxford University Press, 1975), 7. Page numbers following citations of *An Essay Concerning Human Understanding* are from this edition.

therefore shares with Descartes a sense that the foundational questions that philosophy must settle are epistemological. He is, like Descartes, seeking a method that will allow him to resolve disputed questions, once and for all.

This faith that epistemology is somehow the foundational part of philosophy is understandable, given the cultural anxiety occasioned by the intellectual tumult accompanying the Protestant Reformation and the scientific revolution, which overturned accepted ideas. We can understand why Locke and his friends (and lots of other early modern thinkers) should think that they must first settle questions about knowledge before deciding what metaphysical and ethical beliefs can be known. The hope was that if only the right method could be found, the important questions could be settled once and for all.

In retrospect, however, this faith in epistemology can be seen to be misplaced, for at least two reasons. For one thing, it turns out to be no easier to reach agreement on epistemological questions than to reach agreement on metaphysical and ethical questions. The dispute about the proper method for philosophy is as intractable as those in other fields. A second reason is that it is easy to see in retrospect that epistemological positions presuppose metaphysical and even ethical views. We can hardly theorize about how humans know things without assuming some things about human nature: what powers we have and which ones are reliable. It may be true that metaphysical and ethical claims presuppose some epistemological views, but it is equally true that epistemology presupposes claims from other parts of philosophy. The dependence relation is reciprocal, and no branch of philosophy turns out to be the foundation for all the others.

Locke's epistemology. I shall discuss Locke's epistemology in four sections. First, I shall look at Locke's celebrated attack on innate ideas, his most basic point of contention with rationalism. Then, I shall examine Locke's empiricist theory of meaning, followed by his accounts of knowledge and rational belief.

The attack on innate ideas. Locke uses the term *idea* as a general term for those mental realities of which we are directly aware. For him an "idea" stands for "whatsoever is meant by *phantasm, notion, species, or whatever it is which the mind can be employed about in thinking*."[2] It is evident that Locke is using the term imprecisely, and he offers no real analysis of what an idea is. He just assumes that we all will know what he is talking about because everyone is directly conscious of these ideas.

However, even if we are all directly aware of the contents of consciousness, it does not follow that we are all clear about the nature of the contents of consciousness. There are several aspects of Locke's use of *idea* that are troublesome. First, Locke does not clearly distinguish the act of thinking from the object of thought. At times he seems to think of an idea as the act by which we think of something, but at other times ideas seem to be what we are thinking of. Second, Locke assumes, as did Descartes, a representational account of the relation between consciousness and the external world. For Locke the primary objects of awareness turn out to be mental. When we perceive the objects in the world or remember events, what we directly perceive or remember are not objects or events, but ideas that serve as representatives of objects and events. As Berkeley will make clear, this creates problems for Locke. Finally, as will become clear, by *idea* Locke sometimes means simply a concept, but at other times an assertion, claim, or proposition.

Assuming we know what an idea is, Locke asks how ideas "come into the mind."[3] Locke argues vigorously that this is the right way to think about ideas; there are no "innate" ideas or principles. The human mind is at first nothing but a *tabula rasa*, a blank tablet or a piece of white paper. We have no ideas until they are imprinted on the mind by experience.

Locke gives several arguments against the view that there are innate ideas. He seems to assume that the burden of proof is on the proponent of innate ideas, so that if he can explain how we become aware of ideas

---

[2]Locke, *An Essay Concerning Human Understanding,* 1.1.8, p. 47 (emphasis original).
[3]Locke, *An Essay Concerning Human Understanding,* 1.1.8, p. 48.

without supposing them innate, then it is most reasonable to suppose that they are not innate. It would, for example, "be impertinent to suppose the ideas of colours innate in a creature to whom God hath given sight."[4] Even if there are some ideas that were universally held by humans, this would not show them to be innate, provided we can give a plausible alternative account of why every person has such ideas.

In fact, however, Locke holds that there are no ideas (or principles) that are universally held. He takes as his test cases such "speculative" principles as "whatever is, is" and "it is impossible for the same Thing to be and not to be." (We can see here that in this case by *idea* Locke is thinking of propositions.) These principles, which Locke says have the best claim of any to be innate, are far from being universally received. For no one can be said to believe or accept a principle that they have never considered, and Locke says the greater part of humankind has never even thought about such propositions. In particular, Locke says such principles are not accepted by "children, idiots, etc.," since such creatures "have not the least apprehension or thought of them."[5]

Of course the rationalist has a ready reply to this, claiming that the doctrine of innate ideas is not a claim that these innate truths are actually known by everyone, but rather that all people have a capacity or ability to recognize their truth once they are brought to their attention. Locke replies that if the doctrine of innate ideas is simply a claim that humans have a capability to recognize ideas (presumably as a result of conscious experience), then all ideas could be said to be innate.

Locke goes on to argue that there are no innate moral principles either. Perhaps the most plausible candidates would be principles of justice and fidelity, which state that humans should keep their contracts and promises. Locke claims that "outlaws and villains" do not accept such principles. Or, if they do accept them, they do so only as "rules of convenience," not as innate laws of nature.[6]

---

[4]Locke, *An Essay Concerning Human Understanding*, 1.2.1, p. 48.
[5]Locke, *An Essay Concerning Human Understanding*, 1.2.5, p. 49.
[6]Locke, *An Essay Concerning Human Understanding*, 1.2.2, p. 49.

Contrary to Descartes, Locke argues that the idea of God is not innate either. Locke says that recent global discoveries have uncovered "whole cultures" who have no notion of God. (Here Locke's empirical knowledge seems faulty.) In any case, even if all humans had an idea of God, this would not show the idea to be innate, since Locke argues the idea of God is grounded in "the visible marks of extraordinary wisdom and power" that appear "plainly in all the work of the creation."[7]

It is easy to see why these arguments seem less than decisive to rationalists. Certainly, Locke does not seem charitable in foisting on the rationalist the claim that innate ideas or truths must be ones that are consciously held by all humans, including children. The rationalist will argue that what Locke cannot explain is why the "speculative principles" he considers are not only known as self-evident by people of normal mental powers when they are considered, but also recognized as *necessarily true*. Experience may tell us how things are, but it is difficult to see how experience can give us knowledge of how things must be. Nevertheless, Locke's view that humans are "white paper" or "blank tablets" has been highly influential, giving rise to the view that humans and human nature are highly malleable, the product of experience and circumstances.

Locke's empiricist account of meaning. Locke, having disposed (to his satisfaction) of the view that humans have innate ideas, must now give an account of how we come to have the ideas we have. His general answer is simple; having supposed that the human mind is originally "white paper, void of all characters," it gains all its materials "from EXPERIENCE."[8] There are, however, two different kinds of experiences, and they are distinct sources for our ideas.

Many of our ideas come from "the objects of sensations." Locke is a "realist" who accepts the view that through our senses we come into contact with real objects through sense perception. Those objects

---

[7]Locke, *An Essay Concerning Human Understanding*, 1.3.9, p. 70.
[8]Locke, *An Essay Concerning Human Understanding*, 2.1.2, p. 104. Capitalization is Locke's.

"affect us" and when they do we gain such ideas as *"yellow, white, heat, cold, soft, hard, bitter, sweet,* and all those which we call sensible qualities."[9] The source of a great many of our ideas is thus "SENSATION."[10]

However, our sensations that give us contact with the external world are not the only source of ideas. We also have a kind of experiential awareness of the "operations of our own mind within us." It is this kind of experience that gives rise to such ideas as *"perception, thinking, doubting, believing, reasoning, knowing, willing,* and all the different actings of our own minds."[11] Locke calls these kinds of ideas "ideas of reflection," and he concludes that all our ideas must either be ideas of sensation or reflection.

There is, however, another important way that our ideas can be classified. Some of our ideas are "simple," basic and unanalyzable, while others are complex, compounds composed of simple ideas. Clearly, for example, our idea of a dog is not derived from a single sensation, since we can distinguish (at least in thought) between the dog's smell, shape, size, color, and so on. Locke does not argue that we do in fact experience simple ideas in isolation, but he argues that they must be distinct because we can clearly conceive one of them being different without altering the others.

Locke proceeds to give an account of how many of our ideas are connected to our sensations, but I will not describe most of the details of the story. Some ideas come by way of one sense, while some come by several senses at once. Still others come by way of both sensation and reflection, and a few, such as existence and unity, are involved in all sensations and reflections since "they are suggested to the understanding by every object without, and every idea within."[12] Such important ideas as solidity come about through the sensation of touch, as do the ideas of "impulse, resistance, and protrusion," which presuppose solidity.

---

[9]Locke, *An Essay Concerning Human Understanding,* 2.1.3, p. 105.
[10]Locke, *An Essay Concerning Human Understanding,* 2.1.3, p. 105.
[11]Locke, *An Essay Concerning Human Understanding,* 2.1.4, p. 105 (emphasis original).
[12]Locke, *An Essay Concerning Human Understanding,* 2.7.7, p. 131.

Locke also makes an important distinction between two kinds of ideas. As already noted, Locke is a "realist" who holds that many of our ideas represent objects to us that exist independently and objectively. Locke describes the features of the object by which it is able to produce the idea in us as a "quality." In general, then, qualities are in objects while ideas are in us. Some of our ideas are ideas of "primary qualities," which Locke defines as those that are "utterly inseparable from the body, in what estate soever it be."[13] Locke argues that if you take a particle of matter it will have such qualities as "solidity, extension, figure, and mobility." If one divides the particle, it will still possess all of these qualities, which are the "primary or original" qualities of bodies. Locke thinks that the primary qualities in bodies produce ideas in us, such as those of "solidity, extension, figure, motion or rest, and number," that directly correspond to those qualities.

The ideas of secondary qualities are different. Secondary qualities are such qualities as color and warmth, and Locke thinks that these qualities "in truth, are nothing in the objects themselves, but powers to produce various sensations in us by their primary qualities."[14] There is something in the objects that produces in us the ideas of secondary qualities, but that something is nothing like the ideas that are produced. The primary qualities are thus in some ways more real and do all the work in furnishing us with our ideas of both kinds. Locke thus presents us with a physical world remarkably like the one Descartes describes in his Fifth Meditation, a world of material objects that can be mathematically described, but that is devoid of colors, sounds, and warmth. Our ideas of primary qualities resemble the qualities themselves, but this is not the case with secondary qualities.

Locke's account of our universal and abstract ideas is somewhat unclear. He does not deny that we possess such ideas, but their status is uncertain. It is obvious that we do not experience universals or

---

[13]Locke, *An Essay Concerning Human Understanding*, 2.8.9, p. 134.
[14]Locke, *An Essay Concerning Human Understanding*, 2.8.10, p. 135.

abstractions. Since the official theory of meaning is that all ideas come from experience, one might expect Locke to be a nominalist, who denies that we have ideas of universals at all, and some do read Locke as a nominalist.[15] However, his view seems to be, not that we have no such ideas, but that they are "creatures of the understanding and belong not to the real existence of anything."[16] The story Locke tells about how the understanding creates these concepts goes something like this: To develop a general or universal concept such as the concept of a "dog," we begin with an idea of a particular dog, with all of its particular qualities, such as size, color, smell, and so on. In order to have a concept that will allow us to refer to dogs more generally, we take this particular idea and simply make it vague. We imagine a dog but a dog that has no particular size or shape or color or smell, so that the idea can represent all dogs to the mind.

The view that abstract concepts are created by the mind is sometimes called "conceptualism," and is supposed to be a kind of compromise between realism and nominalism. Unlike nominalists, the conceptualist accepts that there are abstract ideas but, unlike realists, denies that there are universals in nature. Whether Locke is a conceptualist, and if he is, whether such a view is consistent with his empiricist view of concept formation, are open questions. I shall postpone a consideration of what Locke says about some other important ideas, such as substance, necessity, personal identity, and spirit, until I examine Locke's metaphysics.

Locke's account of knowledge. Although many historians see the relation between Locke and Descartes primarily as one of contrast, given the differences between Descartes's rationalism and Locke's empiricism, there are some important similarities in their accounts of knowledge. One is that both are, to use contemporary terminology, classical foundationalists, who assume that knowledge must have foundations and also that the foundations of knowledge must be highly certain. As we will see, Locke's standards for knowledge are (nearly) as high as Descartes's.

---

[15]See the discussion of nominalism in chap. 10.
[16]Locke, *An Essay Concerning Human Understanding*, 3.3.11, p. 414.

It is because of Locke's commitment to a high degree of certainty that he begins his discussion of knowledge with a surprising claim: we really only know our ideas. Since the mind "hath no other immediate object but its own ideas," it cannot know anything other than ideas. This seems startling. Can't we know anything about the world? If there is anything like knowledge of the external world for Locke, it must be made possible by a knowledge of ideas. This claim on Locke's part stems from two other views he holds. One is that knowledge, since it requires certainty, requires a kind of immediate awareness or "seeing," reminiscent in fact of Descartes's "clear and distinct" intuition. Locke seems to think that we only have this kind of awareness for what is directly or immediately present to the mind. Given his representationalism, it follows that we can only know our ideas. Those who know Berkeley's thought (discussed later in this chapter), will see how close Locke is to Berkeley from the beginning.

What then is knowledge? Locke answers that it is the "*perception of the agreement or disagreement of two ideas.*"[17] When we are considering two ideas we can, in some cases, immediately perceive how they are related or connected, and it is this kind of "seeing" that constitutes knowledge. We can see, and therefore know, that a whole cannot be smaller than one of its parts, or that the number 3 is smaller than the number 5.

Locke says that there are four types of knowledge in his sense. First, there is knowledge that two ideas are identical or that they are not identical. Second, there is knowledge of abstract relations between ideas, other than identity and difference. Locke does not spell out what he means here, but perhaps it is something like this. There is a relation we might term "better than," and the state of affairs "being happy" is better than "being miserable." Similarly, there is a relation between "being a quadrilateral" and "being a square," and we can see intuitively that a square is a kind of quadrilateral.

---

[17]Locke, *An Essay Concerning Human Understanding*, 4.1.2, p. 525.

Third, Locke says that there is knowledge of "necessary coexistence in substances." He gives as an example our knowledge that gold always remains gold, even if put in a fire. (Locke gives no real account of how we can know such necessary facts, and given the account of substance he gives later, this part of his view seems problematic.) Last, Locke says that there is knowledge of "real existence agreeing to any idea." Locke here assimilates the claim to know that something exists to the claim that the idea of that thing "agrees" with the idea of existence.

In addition to distinguishing these four types of knowledge, Locke also distinguishes three grades or degrees of knowledge, corresponding to the degree of certainty each possesses. The highest grade is "intuitive knowledge," which is a kind of clear grasp of ideas that the mind is directly aware of. The second level of knowledge is "demonstrative knowledge," in which knowledge is based on a chain of reasoning, each step of which is supposed to have the same kind of certainty as intuitive knowledge. The second kind of knowledge can be just as certain as intuitive knowledge, but it is harder to obtain due to the need for a chain of reasoning, which introduces new possibilities for mistakes and the need to keep different elements in memory. Locke says that demonstrative knowledge is "not so clear as intuitive knowledge" and thus it has a kind of inferior status in relation to intuitive knowledge.

Strictly speaking, these two forms of knowledge are the only kinds of knowledge: "These two, viz., intuition and demonstration, are the degrees of our *knowledge*; whatever comes short of one of these, with what assurance soever embraced, is but *faith* or *opinion*, but not knowledge, at least in all general truths."[18] However, having just made this pronouncement, Locke immediately adds a qualification: "There is, indeed, another perception of the mind employed about the *particular existence of finite beings without us*, which, going beyond bare probability, and yet not reaching perfectly to either of the foregoing degrees of certainty, passes under the name of knowledge."[19]

---

[18]Locke, *An Essay Concerning Human Understanding*, 4.2.14, pp. 536-37.
[19]Locke, *An Essay Concerning Human Understanding*, 4.2.14, p. 537.

Locke is loath to admit that we do not know of the existence of objects in the external world, and yet he sees that our beliefs about such objects do not measure up to the strict standard for knowledge he has accepted. His solution is, in effect, to say, "close enough." Strictly speaking, we don't have knowledge about objects in the external world, but our certainty of the existence of particular things is great enough that we can say that this is "good enough" to count as knowledge. Even if it is not strictly knowledge, it is close enough that it "passes" for knowledge.

We have here an instance of a quality in Locke that I find endearing, but some might believe to be a philosophical defect. When Locke finds that one of his philosophical principles pushes him toward denying something that one might think is just part of common sense, he does not hesitate to go with common sense. One might think that, given Locke's view that we can only know our ideas, he should deny that we know the existence of physical objects, but he does not do that. As we will see, Berkeley shows more philosophical consistency than Locke does, but one might argue that Locke's commitment to common sense is also a philosophical virtue, reminiscent of Aristotle's attempt to "save the appearances" by incorporating as much of common belief as he can.

What do we actually know? Locke says that we know three kinds of things. We know our own existence by intuition (here he echoes Descartes). We know God's existence by demonstration (again, agreeing with Descartes). We have "sensitive knowledge" of the existence of other things through sensation, although this latter kind of knowledge is limited to knowledge of particulars and is limited to the "existence of things actually present to our senses." Actual knowledge is thus quite limited. Even the existence of other minds or "finite spirits" is not something we can really know, but rests on faith or a type of belief.[20] Locke thus admits that many of our most important beliefs are not absolutely certain. From his point of view, this is acceptable. The certainty we have "is as great as our condition needs."[21]

---

[20]Locke, *An Essay Concerning Human Understanding*, 4.11.12, p. 637.
[21]Locke, *An Essay Concerning Human Understanding*, 4.11.8, p. 634.

Belief, faith, and opinion. It is clear that human knowledge for Locke is quite limited, certainly in comparison with what the rationalists claim we can know. Because of the limits of our knowledge, Locke puts a great deal of emphasis on belief. The foundations of all that we believe must be provided by knowledge, but there is a great deal that we can rationally believe even if these beliefs do not attain to knowledge in the strictest sense. Beliefs that are less than certain for Locke can still be more or less probable, and it is probability that should guide belief. (Locke sometimes uses the word *opinion* for beliefs that are not highly probable.)

Locke is an "evidentialist" with respect to belief. That is, he holds that beliefs should always be based on sufficient evidence. "He that believes without having any Reason for believing, may be in love with his own Fancies; but neither seeks Truth as he ought, nor pays the Obedience due to his Maker, who would have him use those discerning Faculties he has given him, to keep him out of Mistake and Errour."[22] Furthermore, belief comes in degrees, and the degree or strength of a belief should be proportioned to the evidence that a person has. The probability of a belief is proportionate to the evidence a person has for its truth, and the strength of the belief should be similarly calibrated.

Not surprisingly, Locke recognizes that some of our beliefs are not based on evidence that we personally have but on the testimony of others, who either have knowledge or rational belief in such matters. So beliefs based on testimony must, like all beliefs, ultimately be based on other beliefs or on knowledge. Besides the evidence or knowledge the witness has, we also need evidence that the witness is trustworthy. We can and do have evidence for the general trustworthiness of testimony, and can have more specific evidence about how trustworthy a particular witness is.

Locke uses the term *faith* to describe the type of belief that is based on testimony, and he sometimes uses it in a special way to designate the particular kinds of beliefs based on a religious revelation, which is a form of testimony. As already noted, Locke believes the existence of

---

[22]Locke, *An Essay Concerning Human Understanding*, 4.17.24, pp. 687-88.

God can be demonstrated, and he therefore thought that belief in God could reasonably be required by the state of citizens. However, most significant religious beliefs, including Christian beliefs, cannot be demonstrated by reason but are based on a revelation, understood as testimony that ultimately stems from God himself. Locke defines faith in this special sense as "assent to any proposition, not thus made out by the deductions of reason, but upon the credit of the proposer, as coming from God in some extraordinary way of communication."[23] Religion is thus largely a matter of faith in this special sense.

Because most religious beliefs can only be believed and cannot be known to be true, Locke mounts a defense of tolerance in matters of religious belief, at least for those who believe in God. This defense of tolerance does not mean, however, that he abandons his evidentialism when it comes to religious beliefs. Locke is sharply critical of those who do not seek to govern their religious beliefs by reason, and he is particularly hard on those who allow their beliefs to be governed by their passionate "enthusiasm."

Locke gives a clear account of what the relation between reason and religious faith should be. First, he says that revelation cannot give us any new simple ideas, and thus is limited to ideas we have got through experience. Second, it is possible for a revelation to convey to us truths that can also be known by reason. However, when this occurs, those who come to know these truths through revelation do not have the same degree of certainty that those who know them through reason do. Third, we cannot and should not believe anything on the basis of revelation that is contrary to the clear evidence of reason. A follower of Locke then must hold that some scientific truth that is known by reason should not be rejected because it is thought to be contradicted by revelation.

Although we cannot believe what we know by reason to be false, there are truths that are "above reason," however, and those can be believed on the basis of a revelation. Locke goes so far as to say that if we

---

[23]Locke, *An Essay Concerning Human Understanding*, 4.28.2, p. 689.

have a well-grounded revelation, then its teachings should be accepted even if they seem to go against the "probable conjectures" of reason. It is important, however, that we have evidence that a revelation is a genuine revelation coming from God. Locke thinks that we have evidence that the Christian revelation is genuine, the evidence taking such forms as miracles and fulfilled prophecies.

Locke's metaphysics. I have already mentioned Locke's view that the existence of God can be demonstrated. In this section I will discuss Locke's views on a variety of other metaphysical issues. These will include the nature of substance, both material and spiritual, the basis of personal identity, and what kind of free will a human possesses.

Substance. Given Locke's empiricist account of meaning, the concept of substance should be troublesome, since it is not clear what sensation gives rise to the idea of substance. And Locke does indeed find the concept troubling. However—and this is another instance of what I call Locke's commitment to common sense—he does not completely reject the concept.

Locke says that when we try to understand the notion of "pure substance in general," we are pretty much at a loss. The idea of substance is simply the idea of something that "supports" or provides the basis of the properties or qualities that a thing has, but what substance is in itself we really do not know. Amusingly, Locke compares the situation to an Indian who said that the world was supported by a great elephant. When asked what supported the elephant, the Indian answered that it was supported by a great tortoise. When asked what supported the tortoise, the Indian's reply was *"something, he knew not what."*[24] Similarly, Locke says that when we try to conceive of substance all we can say is that it is "something" that somehow provides the support for the other properties of an object, even though we really do not know what it is. Locke does not give up the concept entirely, but in comparison to rationalists such as Spinoza, who found the concept of substance to be

---

[24]Locke, *An Essay Concerning Human Understanding*, 2.23.2, p. 296.

the richest and most important concept humans have, the concept of substance is empty and obscure.

Locke follows Descartes in holding that there are both material and spiritual substances. A spiritual substance is what supports the "operations of the mind" such as thinking, reasoning, and fearing. We don't think that these can happen all on their own, and so we posit a mind to do the thinking, fearing, and so on. However, the notion of a spiritual substance is no clearer (but also no more obscure) than the idea of a material substance. We have ideas of material things as having "solid coherent parts" and "impulse," just as we have ideas of minds as substances as having the powers to think and to act. However, in neither case do we really know what the substances are that possess these qualities.

We do have clearer ideas of particular kinds of substances. We believe, for example, that there are horses and humans and oak trees. The ideas we have about these particular kinds of substances consist mainly of our ideas of the "active and passive powers" that they possess. We know, for example, that horses can run but oak trees cannot, and that a horse can be cut with a knife but a diamond cannot be. The notion we have of "active power" is largely formed from our own active power as spirits.[25]

Identity. Locke holds that we form the general conception of identity (and difference) simply by comparing a thing at one time to that same thing at another time. (This seems dubious, since it seems likely that the concept of the "same thing at another time" already presupposes a concept of identity.)

Locke nonetheless gives different accounts of identity for different kinds of entities. The identity of a finite substance is grounded in its beginning in a particular time and place. This leads Locke to affirm that an entity cannot go out of existence and begin anew, for the new entity would be a different entity by virtue of its new beginning. The concept of substance, however, plays little role for Locke in establishing the identity of concrete entities.

---

[25]Locke, *An Essay Concerning Human Understanding*, 2.21.4, p. 235.

A lump of matter gains its identity simply from its location in space as well as its observable qualities. A plant, such as an oak tree, gains its identity from the way the parts of the tree function together to enable the oak tree to survive, by taking in nourishment, distributing the nourishment to the parts of the tree, and so on. Vegetables can thus lose and gain parts without compromising their identity. Animals are similar except that the continuing life that the animal lives is more complex than the life of a plant.

Locke says a man (a "human being" in contemporary nonsexist language) gets identity in a similar way. A human being is a kind of animal and maintains its identity by virtue of "participation in the same continued life, by constantly fleeting particles of matter, in succession vitally united to the same organized body."[26] The identity of a man, considered in this way, is thus not grounded in the soul. Locke says that if humans have souls (and he believes they do), then one could imagine that souls could inhabit more than one body, as in reincarnation. If having the same soul made for the same man, then Socrates and Pilate could possibly be the same humans, if Pilate possessed the soul of Socrates. But Locke finds this absurd. In effect, Locke argues that even if reincarnation of a soul is possible, the two people who had the same soul would not be the same human beings. The identity of a particular human being is thus grounded in the career of a particular body, born at a particular time and enjoying a unique history.

For Locke, however, a "man" (human being) is not the same thing as a person. Locke's view of what it means to be "the same person" is quite different from the accounts of what it means to be the same human. Rather, the basis of the identity of a person is consciousness. "Consciousness, as far as ever it can be extended—should it be to ages past—unites existences and actions very remote in time into the same *person*, as well as it does the existences and actions of the immediately preceding moment, so that whatever has the consciousness of present and

---

[26]Locke, *An Essay Concerning Human Understanding*, 2.27.6, pp. 331-32.

past actions, is the same person to whom they belong."[27] So for Locke whatever I am conscious of doing or thinking was actually done by me.

Superficially, Locke's view sounds like Descartes's. Locke even says that a "self is that conscious thinking thing," echoing Descartes's language. However, in reality Locke's view is very different from Descartes's. For Descartes the self is an immaterial substance. Locke gives what we might call a functional definition of the self or person. He says that the self is simply identical with whatever is conscious, whether that thing be spiritual or material, simple or complex.[28] For Locke consciousness does inhere in a substance, and he is prepared to say the substance is in fact immaterial, but substance is not essential to personal identity. If my consciousness be annexed to some different substance than the one it currently is connected to, I (as a person or self) go with my consciousness, not the substance. It is the person, identified in this functional way, that is the bearer of moral responsibility, the proper object of rewards and punishments.[29]

Locke's view has many interesting consequences. Imagine a criminal who develops amnesia and has no memory of his crimes. On Locke's view, if the person has "absolute oblivion" then that person no longer exists, even if the human being who committed the crimes still exists. On the other hand, if a person is conscious of some act X that some other human being has done, that person is identical to the person who performed X. Thus, if I remember being Socrates and taking the hemlock, I am in fact Socrates.

Locke's psychological account of personal identity, suitably refined, continues to have defenders today. (Many opponents defend "animalism," which would roughly identify the person with what Locke calls the "man.") However, at least as Locke develops the view, it seems open to a devastating objection, which goes like this: It is surely possible to have false memories, to have an apparent consciousness of

---

[27]Locke, *An Essay Concerning Human Understanding,* 2.27.16, p. 340.
[28]Locke, *An Essay Concerning Human Understanding,* 2.27.17, p. 341.
[29]Locke, *An Essay Concerning Human Understanding,* 2.27.18, pp. 341-42.

having done something that one did not in fact do. It does not seem plausible that mere apparent memories could establish personal identity. What is the difference between a convincing apparent memory that happens to be false and a true memory? The most plausible answer is that what makes an apparent memory a true memory is that the person who has the true memory is in fact the person who had the experience remembered. If this is correct, then memory and psychological identity are not the basis of personal identity. Rather, we must presuppose personal identity to make sense of the notion of true memories and consciousness. It is only if it is true that I am identical to the person who did or thought something that my memory of doing or thinking something can be a true memory. Memory is of course evidence for personal identity, but it does not establish personal identity.

Human freedom and responsibility. Locke treats the question as to whether human persons have "free will" by arguing that this is an improper question. On his view, liberty is not a property that a will can possess, "liberty being as little applicable to the will, as swiftness of motion is to sleep, or squareness is to virtue."[30] Liberty or freedom, according to Locke, does not belong to the will but to the person considered as an "agent." Freedom just means the ability to act or refrain from acting as a person wills. Freedom is a power and thus must belong to an agent. The will is another power of the agent. When the agent is able to act as the agent wills, then the agent is free.

Locke denies that a person can be free to will or not to will an act, but only (sometimes, when he is free) to act as he wills. The will is determined by the mind, as it considers the benefits and disadvantages of various ends and the courses of action that might achieve those ends. This account, like that of Leibniz, is a "compatibilist" view of freedom, in that it makes it possible to argue that even human acts that are causally determined are free. If freedom is the ability to act as I will to act, then if I want to eat an ice cream, and I am able to eat an ice cream, then I am

---

[30]Locke, *An Essay Concerning Human Understanding*, 2.21.14, p. 240.

free, even if my wanting to eat an ice cream is something that I cannot change or control.

Locke supports his view with a famous thought experiment of the "locked room." Imagine a person is in a room and has no desire to leave the room. Unbeknownst to the person in the room, someone has locked the room from the outside and the person could not leave the room if the person desired to do so. As long as the person is able to do what the person wills, Locke claims the person is free.[31]

Locke's political philosophy. Locke's political philosophy, developed in his *Two Treatises on Civil Government,* is just as influential as his epistemology and metaphysics. Locke's *Two Treatises,* published in 1690, are often read as justifying the "Glorious Revolution" of 1688, in which James II was deposed and William of Orange and his wife Mary were installed as monarchs. This revolution was a bloodless one. James had lost virtually all support, and when William came from the Netherlands with an army, virtually everyone went over to his side, forcing James to flee to France. A parliament then met, declared that James had abdicated, and made William and Mary king and queen. This result permanently squashed the idea that the monarch in England was an absolute monarch with no checks on his power. Instead, the government was ultimately controlled by the Parliament, the people's representatives. Locke's views not only justified this change but also in many ways inspired the documents of the American Revolution. Locke is in fact sometimes called the "father" or "grandfather" of the American Revolution, due to the influence of his ideas on such founding fathers as Thomas Jefferson and John Adams.

Locke's account of civil government can usefully be compared with that of Thomas Hobbes.[32] Like Hobbes, Locke holds that the basis of government is a social contract. Also, like Hobbes, he holds that the reason for forming such a social contract is to leave (or avoid) a "state

---

[31]Locke, *An Essay Concerning Human Understanding,* 2.21.10, p. 238.
[32]See chap. 11 for a discussion of Thomas Hobbes.

of nature" in which there is no effective government. Locke agrees with Hobbes that a state of nature is a disagreeable one and that rational humans in such a situation would form a government to protect themselves and their rights.

However, the differences with Hobbes are significant as well. One important difference concerns the natural laws and natural rights that hold within the state of nature. Hobbes had held that in the state of nature humans have a natural right to whatever they can effectively obtain and control, and this is, as Hobbes recognized, a recipe for a desperate struggle, a "war of all against all." There are natural laws in this state, but they are quite minimal until an agreement is made and a commonwealth is formed. Locke, on the contrary, holds that even in the state of nature humans have rights, given to them by God. We are all God's property, and thus it is wrong for someone to take the life, health, liberty, or possessions of another.

Hobbes had also said we have a right to life in the state of nature, but Locke significantly expands on this right by arguing that in the state of nature some people own property and thereby have rights to use and dispose of that property. (For Hobbes there is no property or rights to property without a state.) The protection of property is the major purpose of government: "The reason why men enter into society is the preservation of their property."[33]

There are still similarities with Hobbes, though. Locke agrees that without a government our rights to property are insecure, because each individual has "executive power" to enforce the natural law, and of course individuals are usually biased in their own favor. However, even though property rights may be insecure in the state of nature, they still exist.

How do people acquire rights to property in the state of nature? Locke says God has given humans the natural world in common, and there is no private property originally. To explain how private property

---

[33]John Locke, *The Second Treatise of Government* 7.94, 9.124, in John Locke, *Two Treatises of Government*, ed. Peter Laslett (Cambridge: Cambridge University Press, 1988), 329, 350-51. Page numbers following citations of this work are from this edition.

arises, Locke first argues that each person in the state of nature already has a natural right to their own bodies and the activity they carry on through their bodies. Private property begins when a person finds something unowned in nature and improves what is found by "mixing his labor" with it.[34] Imagine I am wandering around in an unowned forest and find a tree has fallen. Suppose I drag the tree back to my house, turn it into lumber, and then, using the lumber, build a desk. Locke would argue that in this situation you own the desk, because you have "mixed your labor" with it.

Locke does make one important proviso in this account. He says that a person can only do this to some natural material that is unowned if there is an abundance of material in nature so that, after the person has appropriated something, "there is enough, and as good, left in common for others."[35] Needless to say, in a world with limited resources it is difficult to argue that this condition could often have been met. Locke's account, however, has been hugely influential. As we shall see, in a strange irony, Karl Marx will later use something like Locke's account of private property to support the "labor theory of value," which Marx uses to argue that private property (at least for the means of production) should be abolished.[36]

In addition to Locke's view of private property in the state of nature, there is another very important difference between Locke and Hobbes, which concerns the nature of the contract that forms the state. For Hobbes the contract is one that the people make among themselves; the "sovereign" who is created to enforce the contract is not a party to the contract. Since the sovereign is not a party to the contract, this person (or group, if the sovereign is a legislature) cannot be said to violate it. Thus for Hobbes the sovereign has absolute power, and there is no right to revolt against the sovereign. Locke, however, claims that the contract is one made between the people and the government. The

---

[34]Locke, *The Second Treatise of Government* 5.27, pp. 287-88.
[35]Locke, *The Second Treatise of Government* 5.27, p. 288.
[36]See chap. 20 for a discussion of Karl Marx.

people agree to give up their "executive power" that they exercise as individuals in exchange for protection of their rights and for the advancement of the common good. Locke does not doubt that this is a good exchange if the government that is formed is a "civil" government that in fact seeks to protect the lives and property of the citizens. However, a government that does not seek these ends is not a legitimate government at all; it has violated the contract and thus undermined the obligation that citizens have to obey its orders.

For Locke this means that the power of the state must be limited. The only legitimate form of government is limited government, and thus absolute monarchy turns out to be "no form of civil government at all."[37] The reason this is so is that the very purpose of forming a civil society is to end the state of nature, with all its bad features. An absolute monarch, however, who has no checks on his or her power, is still in the state of nature, and in fact is even more dangerous than ordinary individuals in the state of nature would be. Locke holds that no reasonable person would consent to such an absolute monarchy, when it manifestly goes against self-interest:

> As if when men, quitting the state of Nature, entered into society, they agreed that all of them but one should be under the restraint of laws, but that he [that one] should still retain all the liberty of the state of Nature, increased with power, and made licentious by impunity. This is to think that men are so foolish that they take to avoid what mischiefs may be done to them by polecats or foxes, but are content, nay, think it safety, to be devoured by lions.[38]

Monarchs who recognize no limits on their power and do not understand that even a monarch must be subject to the law forfeit their legitimacy. Locke's view of the state then requires that the executive power must not be absolute, but must be checked by an independent judiciary and a legislature that makes the laws. It is easy to see the

---

[37]Locke, *The Second Treatise of Government* 7.90, p. 326.
[38]Locke, *The Second Treatise of Government* 7.93, p. 328.

influence of Locke on the American Declaration of Independence as well as the Constitution.

GEORGE BERKELEY

George Berkeley (1685–1753) was born and educated in Ireland. He studied at Trinity College in Dublin, and there acquired knowledge of emerging modern science as well as such modern thinkers as Hobbes, Descartes, Locke, and Malebranche. Shortly after his university education Berkeley became a fellow of Trinity College and was also ordained as an Anglican clergyman. His career as a clergyman was a success; he served as the dean of Derry and in 1734 was made bishop of Cloyne. In between the two appointments Berkeley actually lived for three years in Rhode Island, making him the only one of the early modern philosophers to spend time in America. His goal while in Rhode Island was to establish a new college in Bermuda, but he never received the needed funding and support, so he returned to Britain in 1731.

Berkeley is best known for two philosophical works: *A Treatise Concerning the Principles of Human Knowledge* (1710) and *Three Dialogues Between Hylas and Philonous* (1713). However, Berkeley also published *An Essay Towards a New Theory of Vision* in 1709, and a book on the foundations of mechanics called *De Motu*. While in America Berkeley wrote a book of Christian apologetics called *Alciphron*, which is philosophically significant as well.

As one might well infer from Berkeley's life as a clergyman, a major motivation for his philosophy was a defense of Christian faith. Berkeley is best known as an idealist, someone who denied the existence of matter. For Berkeley, a belief in the existence of matter was dangerous, leading logically to skepticism and atheism, by way of mechanism. He believed that a material world was one congenial to deists and atheists, since such a world seemed to be one that could run without God. However, although much of Berkeley's motivation for idealism may be grounded in his faith, most of his arguments for his views are independent of any religious commitments. They are often admired by philosophers with no religious commitments, and are regarded as dazzling pieces of philosophy even by those (almost everyone) who are not convinced by them.

Berkeley's idealism. Berkeley's starting point is basically the empiricism of Locke. He accepts the Lockean claim that there are no innate ideas and that the ideas we have come to us either through the senses or by attending to the mind itself. (Locke calls these ideas of sensation and reflection.) Berkeley also agrees with Locke that our original ideas are simple and that complex ideas are compounds formed from simple ideas.

Since Locke is a realist and accepts the existence of mind-independent material objects, and Berkeley is an idealist who denies that any such objects exist, it is common to describe Berkeley as a critic of Locke. It is probably just as correct, however, to see Berkeley as a more consistent version of Locke, a disciple who faithfully follows Locke's premises to conclusions that Locke himself refused to accept. Berkeley's major argument follows directly from Locke's empiricism. Locke, it will be recalled, claims that we only know ideas, since knowledge is "the agreement of two ideas." Berkeley reasons that if we only know ideas, then we do not know of the existence of anything but ideas.

What does Berkeley mean by "idealism"? The view is memorably summarized by Berkeley in the slogan *"esse est percipi"* (to be is to be perceived). Nothing (except minds or spirits) exists except insofar as it is thought or conceived or felt by a mind. He begins by claiming that everyone admits that our "thoughts, passions, and ideas" cannot exist without the mind.[39] The next step is to insist that the sensations imprinted on our senses "likewise cannot exist otherwise than in a mind perceiving them." Then Berkeley goes further and argues that we can make no sense of the claim that there are objects we perceive that exist independently of our perception. "The table I write on I say exists, that

---

[39]George Berkeley, *A Treatise Concerning the Principles of Human Knowledge* 3, in George Berkeley, *A Treatise Concerning the Principles of Human Knowledge*, ed. Johnathan Dancy (Oxford: Oxford University Press, 1998), 103. Page numbers following citations of this work are to this edition.

is, I see and feel it, and if I were out of my study I should say it existed—meaning thereby that if I was in my study I might perceive it, or that some other spirit actually does perceive it."[40] The claim that what I perceive exists completely unperceived is one that Berkeley finds unintelligible. I shall now examine a number of distinct arguments that Berkeley gives for this view.

Berkeley's arguments against matter. 1. The first argument I shall consider is rooted in Berkeley's nominalism. One of the conclusions that Berkeley draws from Lockean premises concerns the existence of abstract ideas or universals. Locke, as we saw above, accepted the existence of abstract or general ideas. We create such ideas by taking particular ideas and divesting them of their particularity, making them vague. Berkeley argues that we simply don't have any such abstract ideas. It is not possible, for example, to think of a dog that has no particular qualities. When I think of a dog I necessarily think of the dog as having a particular size, shape, and smell, even if I do not explicitly attend to those qualities. For Berkeley what we call abstract ideas are just names for groups of particulars that resemble each other enough that we find it useful to group them together. Berkeley thus embraces the nominalism that he believes follows from a strict empiricist account of the origin of our ideas.

It is important to recognize that by "materialism" Berkeley does not mean a view such as Hobbes, who held that only matter exists. Rather, a "materialist" is someone who holds that there are *any* material objects. Thus, on this usage, Locke and Descartes, who are dualists, are also materialists. Berkeley's nominalism, or rejection of abstract ideas, immediately provides him with one argument against materialism. For it is clear that the idea of matter is an abstract idea par excellence. If we have no abstract ideas, we have no idea of matter and no idea what matter is. However, if we have no concept of matter, it is hard to see how one could defend the existence of matter, since one would not even have an

---

[40]Berkeley, *Treatise* 3, p. 104.

idea as to what one was defending. Thus Berkeley claims not only that we have no evidence for the existence of matter but also that the hypothesis that there are material objects has no meaningful content.

One might think the claim that we don't even have a concept of a material object is quite implausible. Surely, one might say, we know about the existence of lots of material objects: houses, trees, dogs, rocks, and tons of others. The claim that these are material objects is just the claim that such things exist and that they continue to do so even when they are not perceived by a mind. Berkeley would claim that this objection misses the mark entirely. In claiming that matter does not exist, Berkeley by no means wants to say that there are no such things as houses, trees, and dogs. Berkeley is even willing to admit that these "things" are substances in the "vulgar sense," meaning that they are perceived combinations of sensible qualities (extension, solidity, weight, etc.) that come to us in a package or combination.[41] All he denies is that there a thing called "matter" or "substance" that is the unexperienced "support" for these qualities. This is pretty much Locke's view of "substance" as "something I know not what" that somehow supports or underlies the observable qualities of things. In this sense Berkeley claims his view is in accord with common sense. He accepts the reality of all the objects we encounter in everyday life; he simply gives a different account of the nature of these things. The concept of matter he rejects is one used by philosophers like Locke, not ordinary people, or at least so Berkeley claims.[42]

2. A number of the arguments Berkeley employs revolve around the representationalism held by both Locke and Descartes. A proponent of matter may, like Locke, admit that it is only ideas that we know directly or immediately, but argue that we can know the existence of material objects indirectly because the ideas we know represent those objects to us. Locke, it will be recalled, holds that some of our ideas, those of

---

[41]Berkeley, *Treatise* 37, p. 115.
[42]Berkeley, *Treatise* 35, pp. 114-15.

primary qualities, enable us to know (in a loose sense of knowledge) the existence of particular objects that exist independently of us.

Suppose we grant, for the sake of argument, that it is possible that there are unperceived bodies that exist independently of us in this way, and that such a view is meaningful. Even if this is so, Berkeley asks how we could possibly know that the claim that there are such things is true. Whatever we know must be known by sense or by reason. By hypothesis in this case we do not sense material objects and thus they cannot be known in this way. On an empiricist view of knowledge, even our knowledge that we gain by reason or inference must be rooted in experience. We know, for example, by experience that fire gives rise to smoke and can therefore reason that there is fire when we see smoke. In the case of unperceived matter, however, we have no experience to draw on. If we never sense material objects, how can we possibly know anything about their relation to our ideas such that we could come to know them through some kind of inference? It looks as if they cannot be known by reason either. It follows that they cannot be known at all.

3. A third argument takes as its target representationalism by criticizing Locke's claim that our ideas of some qualities resemble the (unperceived) qualities that they are alleged to refer to. Berkeley argues that this is impossible because an idea can only resemble an idea. In a way Locke has already conceded the point when he says that knowledge consists in the agreement of one idea with another idea. Berkeley says a color can only resemble another color, and a figure can only resemble another figure. The colors and figures in these cases are, on both sides of the resemblance, things we experience or conceive. This is not so in the case of ideas and the physical qualities they are alleged to resemble. It makes no sense to say that "a color is like something which is invisible."[43] Nor does it make sense to say that something that is hard or soft resembles something that cannot be touched.

---

[43]Berkeley, *Treatise* 8, p. 105.

4. At this point the Lockean may retreat to the distinction between primary and secondary qualities. Locke already concedes that secondary qualities such as color exist only in the mind, except as "powers" in the object that can produce the sensations. However, Locke insists that the ideas of primary qualities do resemble their objects, and thus primary qualities exist objectively and independently. Berkeley argues that this distinction between secondary and primary qualities cannot be maintained. Locke holds that secondary qualities are subjective because they are relative to the observer. What appears red to me (a color-blind person) may not appear red to someone else. The redness I see is thus mental and does not exist independently of me. Berkeley argues that if observer-relativity makes an observed object mind-dependent, then primary qualities are equally subjective. Take for example a coin. When observed from the side it appears as a disk. When observed from front or back it appears to be an oval. An objective, mind-independent object cannot have such contradictory qualities. Thus Locke's argument for the mind-dependence of secondary qualities works just as well for primary qualities.

Berkeley also argues that primary qualities cannot be separated from secondary qualities. If the latter are mind-dependent, so are the former. We cannot experience or even imagine any object's having primary qualities without secondary qualities. It is not possible for an object to be extended but have no color, or to have a physical shape but no texture if touched. The claim that objects exist with primary qualities but no secondary qualities is thus inconceivable according to Berkeley.

Berkeley's positive metaphysics. If Berkeley's arguments against matter work, then the world we experience does not exist independently of minds. This of course seems very implausible, leading to the hoary claim that a tree that falls in a forest would not make a sound if there were no one there to hear it. In fact, if there is no one there to see it the tree would not even exist. The implausibility is nicely captured in a famous limerick by Ronald Knox:

There once was a man who said "God
Must think it exceedingly odd
If he finds that this tree
Continues to be
When there's no one about in the Quad."

The Berkeleyan response is captured perfectly in the following limerick, whose author is unknown:

Dear Sir,
Your astonishment's odd.
I am always about in the Quad.
And that's why the tree
Will continue to be
Since observed by
Yours faithfully,
God

It does seem appropriate to criticize and defend Berkeley in the form of the limerick, a form of poetry named for a town in Ireland!

The serious point in the second limerick is that for Berkeley God is absolutely essential to make sense of the world. Since matter does not exist, the stability, order, and regularity we discover in the natural world are all due to God's activity. We can see why Berkeley sees his philosophy as a bulwark against the idea that the natural universe is a machine capable of running without any Creator God.

Berkeley's world is one in which there are perceptions, things perceived, and perceivers (spirits or minds). God is an infinite mind or spirit, but there are also finite spirits whom God has created. But what exactly is a mind or spirit? Berkeley answers that a "a spirit is one simple, undivided, active being—as it perceives ideas it is called the *understanding*, and as it produces or otherwise operates about them it is called the *will*."[44]

---

[44]Berkeley, *Treatise* 27, p. 112.

Berkeley admits, however, that the mind cannot itself be experienced: "Such is the nature of *spirit*, or that which acts, that it cannot be of itself perceived, but only by the effects which it produceth."[45] Given Berkeley's empiricist account of ideas, this means that we really have no idea of what a mind or spirit is, and he admits that this is the case.[46] This is not really surprising if we recall Locke's claim that the notions of material and immaterial substances are equally obscure. Berkeley realizes that if he defines the mind as a "substance" that supports or upholds the qualities of the mind, then mind starts to look suspiciously like the matter that Berkeley rejects.

However, since so much of Berkeley's philosophy depends on the reality of minds or spirits, he cannot readily give up the concept. He claims, therefore, that even though we no *idea* of mind or spirit, we do have a *notion* of what a mind or spirit is, and this is sufficient to give us an understanding of the meaning of the words. It is not, however, clear exactly what a "notion" is. Is it just a vague or mysterious idea? Perhaps Berkeley believes we have a kind of awareness of our reality as minds even if we cannot step back and experience our minds. It is clear that Berkeley is vulnerable at this point, and we shall see that his successor David Hume exploits this weakness to criticize the whole idea that we are substantial selves.

How does Berkeley make sense of the distinction between what is real and what is merely "mental," as occurs in dreams or imagination? For him the distinction must be made out in terms of experience. What we dream or imagine are ideas, and so are the "real objects" we deal with in everyday life. The difference is that what we call reality *feels* different, and also has a kind of regular structure and order which an imaginary world lacks. Berkeley admits that "real fire" is very different from "imaginary fire," but it is also true that "real pain" is very different from "imagined pain."[47] Yet it is clear that "real pain" is something experienced,

---

[45]Berkeley, *Treatise* 27, p. 112.
[46]Berkeley, *Treatise* 27, p. 112.
[47]Berkeley, *Treatise* 41, p. 116.

and he argues the same is true for real fire. Real objects are distinguished from imaginary objects by the quality of the experiences.

Berkeley also considers the objection that on his view nothing we perceive is actually "at a distance" from us, since all our perceptions exist in our minds. Surely, the critic may urge, some of the things we perceive are distant from us, some further away from others? Berkeley responds to this by arguing that in dreams we have no trouble picturing things as having various spatial relations to each other and to us, even though all the dream is going on in our own minds. On his view, space turns out to be a kind of construction of the mind. Since there are no material objects, there is no need for a "receptacle" or "bucket" for such objects to exist in. Actually, in his first published work, *An Essays Towards a New Theory of Vision*, Berkeley had already defended this view of how vision works. Berkeley's view here is in the ballpark of Leibniz's view of space, in which space is not an objective entity but a product of how each monad "perceives" every other monad. As we will see, Berkeley's view that space is a creation of the subject rather than an objective feature of nature will receive a powerful champion later in Immanuel Kant.

Berkeley must also give an account of natural causation. Since there are no material objects, it is not possible for one physical object to be the cause of the motion of another. Rather, the true cause of every event is God. Strictly speaking, then, when a rock hits a glass pane, it is not the rock that causes the pane to shatter. Rather, God structures the world so that one set of ideas we experience (the rock about to hit the glass) is followed by another set of ideas (the glass breaking). Berkeley admits that it would sound very odd to deny "that fire heats or water cools." However, he says that we simply should distinguish ordinary language from what is strictly true, metaphysically speaking. Just as we say the "sun rises" and "sun sets" even though we know this is actually due to the earth's rotation, so we can, with respect to natural causation, "think with the learned and speak with the vulgar."[48]

---

[48]Berkeley, *Treatise* 51, p. 120.

Berkeley denies that we need to posit material beings in order to account for the order and regularity of the natural world. What we call the "laws of nature" simply represent the orderly processes that God employs in creating and sustaining the world (except in the very rare case of a miracle). In order for us humans to be rational and responsible agents, we must be able to anticipate the consequences of our actions. That requires an orderly system of nature, and God is responsible for that system by giving us regular patterns and structures in the ideas we receive.

The laws of nature (and scientific laws in general) for Berkeley are not explanatory but predictive. Because of this knowledge we often know what will happen. If we throw an apple over a cliff, we know that it will fall and we say it is because of gravity. But "gravity" is not a name for a mysterious force that explains why the apple falls. Rather "gravity" just summarizes how the things we perceive in the world actually behave. The "law of gravity" is a summary of how we experience the world and therefore how we expect the world to behave. For Berkeley that world is fundamentally a world of ideas and spirits.

Few people find Berkeley's arguments convincing. Nevertheless, it is very difficult to see just what is wrong with the arguments. As we shall see, Berkeley's successors, Thomas Reid and David Hume, each argue that there is much to learn from Berkeley even if we do not accept his conclusions.

The Scottish Enlightenment (I)

David Hume

IN THIS CHAPTER AND THE NEXT I shall discuss David Hume and Thomas Reid, two of the greatest British philosophers. Hume and Reid were Scottish contemporaries who were dominant philosophical figures in the eighteenth century and have remained significant, although the relative status of the two thinkers has changed over time. In the late eighteenth and nineteenth centuries, particularly in America, Reid was considered the greater philosopher. Reid's "commonsense" philosophy, sometimes just called "the Scottish philosophy" or "Scottish realism" during that time, dominated American higher education until the early twentieth century. Hume, while recognized as an important figure, was regarded as a skeptic who undermined religious faith, and his thought was less influential. However, as American higher education secularized in the twentieth century, with the development of the great land-grant state universities, Hume's star ascended and Reid began to appear as a lesser figure. Hume continues to be immensely influential in Anglo-American philosophy today; many regard him as the greatest philosopher who has ever written in English. However, beginning in the late twentieth century there has also been a resurgence of interest in Reid. Many philosophers today find Reid's epistemology, especially his account of perceptual knowledge, attractive.

Reid and Hume of course knew each other, and each regarded the other's philosophy as the antithesis of his own. Reid respected Hume as a subtle thinker who had courageously drawn out the consequences of the major assumptions made by Locke and Descartes. However, Reid thought those conclusions were disastrous and thus saw Hume as giving a kind of *reductio ad absurdum* of those philosophical assumptions. Reid is thus usually read as a fierce critic of Hume. Hume seems to have had less respect for Reid, although we know that he read and commented on some of Reid's works prior to publication. In a letter to a mutual friend, Hume complained that "I wish that the Parsons [Reid had been a minister before being appointed to a university chair] would confine themselves to their old occupation of worrying one another, and leave Philosophers to argue with temper, moderation, and good manners."[1] The irritation Hume shows here may indicate that Reid's criticisms stung Hume more than he wished to reveal publicly.

Despite the large differences between Hume and Reid, I shall try to show that there are also some similarities. The two thinkers are more alike than either realized or would have been willing to admit. These similarities are particularly evident if one interprets Hume as a more "constructive" thinker, as is frequently the case today, and less as a skeptic, as was generally the case in the past. As we shall see, whether Hume is a skeptic—and if so, what kind of skeptic he is—are key questions raised by his philosophy.

DAVID HUME'S LIFE AND WORKS

Hume was born to a middle-class Scottish family from Berwickshire, a border province of Scotland south of Edinburgh. His father died when he was quite young, and he was sent to the University of Edinburgh with his brother at the young age of eleven. Hume's family was seriously religious, and as a young person he attended a Presbyterian church

---

[1] The letter is still extant and is reprinted in the following article: P. B. Wood, "David Hume on Thomas Reid's *An Inquiry into the Human Mind, On the Principles of Common Sense*: A New Letter to Hugh Blair from July 1762," *Mind* 95, no. 380 (1986): 411-16.

pastored by his uncle. He left the university at age fifteen, first considering a career in law, but eventually deciding he was interested in more literary pursuits, especially philosophy. Sometime in his early twenties he seems to have lost his religious faith, but it is clear from notes he made from the period that he remained absorbed by religious questions.

In 1739 and 1740 he published *A Treatise of Human Nature* in three volumes. Much of the work was written in France, where he lived quietly (and cheaply) for several years engaged in private study. Hume was very disappointed by the lack of response to this book and complained that it had fallen "deadborn from the press." In 1741 and 1742 he published *Essays Moral and Political*, which was a more successful book. In 1748 Hume rewrote some of the ideas from the first part of his *Treatise* as *An Enquiry Concerning Human Understanding*. This book was both shorter than the *Treatise* and was written in a more popular style. It also contained a controversial attack on the reasonableness of belief in miracles, which certainly attracted attention. As a result, the book finally achieved for Hume the literary reputation he had always wanted.

Twice during his lifetime Hume sought university positions in philosophy, once in Edinburgh and once at Glasgow. Both times he was unsuccessful, despite the efforts of his good friend Adam Smith. The failures were largely due to Hume's reputation as an atheist, or at least as a critic of religion, which stirred up opposition among the clergy as well as some faculty. Hume was able to obtain a library position in Edinburgh, and he also spent some time serving as a personal secretary to two individuals, including an enjoyable sojourn in Paris.

Later in life Hume published a six-volume *History of England*. This book was a huge success and gave Hume not only increased fame but also financial security. In fact, in the later part of Hume's life he was more widely known as a historian than as a philosopher. He succumbed to an intestinal disorder, most likely some form of cancer, in 1776, and was reported by his friends to have died peacefully and with no change in his religious outlook. After his death, his *Dialogues Concerning*

Natural Religion was published, along with a *Natural History of Religion*. Hume's friends had persuaded him to suppress these during his lifetime so as not to increase his notoriety as an antireligious thinker.

HUME'S EPISTEMOLOGY (I): IMPRESSIONS AND IDEAS

Hume follows in the empiricist tradition of Locke and Berkeley, but pushes empiricist principles further than his predecessors. He also introduces some new terminology and makes some distinctions Locke and Berkeley had not made. Hume believed strongly that many ongoing philosophical disputes were due to a lack of clarity in our ideas, and that taking seriously the empirical origin of our ideas would help to resolve those disputes. He shares with other modern philosophers a conviction that the key to resolving philosophical disputes is to follow the proper method, though his understanding of that method differs sharply from such thinkers as Spinoza and Leibniz.

Although Hume accepts an empiricist account of concept formation that is basically similar to Locke's, he introduces a new and more precise terminology that is itself empirically grounded to express the view. Locke had used the word *idea* as a general term for mental events of all kinds, and then distinguished "original" ideas that come from sensation or reflection from later ideas that could be compounds of these originals. Hume distinguishes "ideas" from what he terms "impressions." All of our mental "perceptions" belong to one of these two categories, with ideas forming the "less forceful and lively" of our perceptions. By the term *impressions* Hume says he means to refer to "all our more lively perceptions, when we hear, or see, or feel, or love, or hate, or desire, or will."[2] Impressions then are what we immediately experience, either through the senses or by attending to our own minds. The difference between impressions and ideas can be easily understood if we think of

---

[2]David Hume, *An Enquiry Concerning Human Understanding* 2, in David Hume, *"An Enquiry Concerning Human Understanding"* and *"A Letter from a Gentleman to His Friend in Edinburgh,"* ed. Eric Steinberg (Indianapolis: Hackett, 1977), 10. Page numbers following citations of *Enquiry* are from this edition.

the difference between feeling a pain as a result of sticking one's hand in a fire (an impression) and later on remembering the pain (an idea).

Hume argues that impressions are the source of all of our ideas. Though it seems that in our imaginations we can develop ideas of many things we have not experienced, Hume says that this imaginative power "amounts to no more than the faculty of compounding, transposing, augmenting, or diminishing the materials afforded us by the senses and experience."[3] The relation between impressions and ideas is thus one in which impressions are the original source of all our concepts. What Hume calls ideas are the fainter, less lively "copies" of the vivid originals.

Hume believes that the relation between impressions and ideas provides the key to resolving philosophical disputes. He affirms that careful attention to this principle that ideas are derived from impressions, "if a proper use were made of it, might render every dispute equally intelligible."[4] Here we see the same faith in the value of method that dominates early modern philosophy. Since impressions are vivid, while ideas are less clear, the key to clarifying our concepts is to trace ideas back to the original impressions that gave rise to them. Such a method will banish unprofitable arguments by getting rid of unclear or even meaningless ideas.

> When we entertain, therefore, any suspicion that a philosophical term is employed without any meaning or idea (as is but too frequent), we need but enquire, *from what impressions is that supposed idea derived?* And if it be impossible to assign any, this will serve to confirm our suspicion. By bringing ideas into so clear a light we may reasonably hope to remove all dispute, which may arise, concerning their nature and reality.[5]

Having made the distinction between impressions and ideas, Hume also attempts to give an account of how ideas are formed. He sees himself as developing the first scientific account of how the mind works,

---

[3] Hume, *An Enquiry Concerning Human Understanding* 2, p. 11.
[4] Hume, *An Enquiry Concerning Human Understanding* 2, p. 13.
[5] Hume, *An Enquiry Concerning Human Understanding* 2, p. 13.

a psychological counterpart to the new physics of Newton. Hume argues that there are three principles that govern how different ideas come to be combined or "associated." The principles are something like "brute laws." That is, Hume makes no attempt to explain them; they are just the way our minds work, just as gravity describes how matter works.

These three principles are *"Resemblance, Contiguity* in time or place, and *Cause and Effect."*[6] For example, we see resemblances between certain animals, such as dogs, and we associate those ideas with a common term, *dog*. The similarities between dogs leads us to associate the ideas we have of various dogs. In looking at a particular dog, we see the dog's shape, color, smell, and so on, as all coming from the same place at the same time, and we therefore associate the ideas that come from those contiguous impressions and think of a dog as a single animal. Through cause and effect, we are able to infer things that we do not directly observe. I get an email from a friend and I infer that it was written by my friend even though I am not experiencing my friend. I see smoke on the horizon and infer that there is a fire, even though I do not see the fire. As we shall see, it is cause and effect that is most interesting and important, according to Hume, and he devotes most of his attention to this principle.

HUME'S EPISTEMOLOGY (2): "HUME'S FORK"

Hume's account of knowledge rests on a famous distinction he makes between two kinds of knowledge: "relations of ideas" and "matters of fact." Hume claims that everything we know or believe falls into just one of these two categories. He says that propositions of the first type "are discoverable by the mere operation of thought, without dependence on what is anywhere existent in the universe."[7] Mathematical propositions fall into this category. It is clear that the first two types of knowledge according to Locke's classification (knowledge that is intuitively or

---

[6]Hume, *An Enquiry Concerning Human Understanding* 3, p. 14.
[7]Hume, *An Enquiry Concerning Human Understanding* 4.1, p. 15.

demonstratively certain) make up this category according to Hume. Since relations of ideas do not affirm anything about what actually exists, we can determine their truth purely through reflection. We must, of course, understand the ideas, and since all ideas come from impressions, there is a sense in which we need experience to know relations of ideas. However, once we understand the ideas, relations of ideas can be known without any investigation of the real world. Even if there were no circles or triangles in nature, Hume says, the truths of geometry would still be certain.

Matters of fact are entirely different. Hume says that they are "not ascertained in the same manner" as relations of ideas, "nor is our evidence of their truth however great, of a like nature with the foregoing."[8] How can we tell whether a proposition is a relation of ideas or a matter of fact? The decisive test is this: if a proposition is a matter of fact, then both the proposition and its contrary will be possible. The proposition "the sun will rise tomorrow" is thus a matter of fact, because its denial ("the sun will not rise tomorrow") is not a contradiction, even though we believe (or at least hope) that the denial is false. This also gives us a test for relations of ideas: the denial of a true relation of ideas must either be a contradiction or else entail a contradiction. The important implication that Hume draws from his distinction is that no matter of fact can be proved or demonstrated. Since both the proposition and its denial are possible, we cannot show that the proposition (or its denial) is necessarily true. The only way to know a matter of fact is by appeal to experience, which tells us what the facts are.

Hume appears to take for granted that matters of fact that we are immediately experiencing or remembering can be known, or at least that we sometimes have beliefs about such things that we are sure are true. What he is interested in are matters of fact that we are not immediately experiencing or remembering: "What is the nature of our evidence which assures us of any real existence and matter of fact, beyond the

---

[8]Hume, *An Enquiry Concerning Human Understanding* 4.1, p. 15.

present testimony of our senses, or the records of our memories."[9] Obviously the greater part of what we think we know falls into this category. Virtually all of our scientific beliefs, for example, are of this type, as are many everyday beliefs we rely on all the time. When I ate my lunch today, for example, I believed that the bread on my sandwich would nourish me and not poison me, but those are not facts that I immediately observe when I perceive the loaves of bread.

Hume makes two claims about this "matter of fact" knowledge that goes beyond immediate experience and memory. The first is that all such knowledge is based on one of the three principles of association he has mentioned: the principle of cause and effect. "By means of that relation alone we can go beyond the evidence of our memory and senses."[10] The second claim is that causal knowledge is never a priori, but is always gained through experience. Without experience we would have no knowledge whatsoever of what causes what or what is the effect of what. We know from experience that bread nourishes us but that dirt does not. We know by experience that cotton can burn but that diamonds cannot.

Hume supports this claim by a thought experiment. If a person were suddenly created without any past experience, that person would have no causal knowledge at all. We might think that such a person could observe a billiard ball about to strike another one and infer that the second ball would move as a result. However, this is an illusion based on our past knowledge of billiard balls and other objects. In reality such a person would have no way to know what would happen. Perhaps the second billiard ball would catch on fire, or turn into dust, or just vanish. Any belief we might form in such a situation would be entirely arbitrary. We only learn such things by experience.

Hume's view that all of our knowledge of cause and effect is gained from experience is a strong challenge to the philosophical systems of

---

[9]Hume, *An Enquiry Concerning Human Understanding* 4.1, p. 16.
[10]Hume, *An Enquiry Concerning Human Understanding* 4.1, p. 16.

the rationalists, all of whom rely on some principle of causality that is known a priori and with certainty. For Hume, "every effect is a distinct event from its cause" and therefore can never be known simply by reflecting on the nature of the cause. It is the nature of our causal knowledge that prevents us from knowing the "ultimate cause of any natural operation."[11] Scientists can observe nature and discover how nature behaves, but no ultimate explanation of why nature behaves as it does is possible. We can discover such principles as "gravity, cohesion of parts, communication of motion by impulse," but we cannot really explain why these principles hold. They just do. Bringing mathematics to bear on nature does not really remedy the situation, since the predictions we make with the help of mathematics are no better than the empirical laws we rely on to make the predictions.

HUME'S TREATMENT OF CAUSALITY AND
THE PROBLEM OF INDUCTION

Since all of our knowledge of matters of fact beyond immediate experience and memory depends on causality, it is obviously crucial to Hume to give an account of causality. He has already told us that we learn about cause and effect through experience. But how do we learn such things from experience? *"What is the foundation of all conclusions from experience?"*[12] Hume recognizes that that when we see one object having some causal effect, we normally assume that this is due to "secret powers" that the object possesses. But we do not know of any connection between the qualities we observe and those "secret powers."

Rather, when we make a causal inference, our thinking process seems to go like this, Hume says: *"I have found that such an object has always been attended with such an effect, and I foresee, that other objects, which are, in appearance, similar, will be attended with similar effects."*[13] Hume affirms that the second proposition is generally inferred from the first,

---

[11]Hume, *An Enquiry Concerning Human Understanding* 4.1, p. 19.
[12]Hume, *An Enquiry Concerning Human Understanding* 4.2, p. 20.
[13]Hume, *An Enquiry Concerning Human Understanding* 4.2, p. 22.

and he even is willing to "allow" that the inference is justified.[14] (As we shall see, the question of whether Hume is a skeptic depends on how we understand this claim.) However, Hume asserts that the connection between "this object has in the past been followed by certain effects" and "I believe similar objects in the future will be followed by similar effects" is "not intuitive" and not "made by a chain of reasoning."

We can see this by returning to "Hume's fork." All of our reasoning, according to Hume, is either demonstrative, dealing with relations of ideas, or else deals with matters of fact. It is obvious that we cannot demonstrate that our past experience will be a reliable guide to what will happen in the future. To demonstrate this proposition, its denial would have to be or imply a contradiction. However, Hume says we can clearly conceive of situations in which our past experience would fail to help us anticipate what will happen in the future. Trees might "flourish in December and January, and decay in May and June," and something might fall from the sky that looks like snow but "has yet the taste of salt or feeling of fire."[15] There is no contradiction then in imagining that our future experience will be different from our past experience, and thus we cannot prove that our past experience will always be reliable as a guide to the future.

We generally describe this practice of reasoning from past experience to the future, or reasoning from what we have experienced even in the present to what we have not experienced, as inductive reasoning. So we could say that Hume is claiming that we have no demonstrative proof that inductive reasoning is reliable.

What about the "second fork"? Can't we appeal to experiential evidence to show that induction is reliable, and belief in induction is justified? Someone might reason as follows: "What is now past was once part of the future. In the past when I used induction to make inferences about the future, the principle turned out to be reliable. Since induction

---

[14]Hume, *An Enquiry Concerning Human Understanding* 4.2, p. 22.
[15]Hume, *An Enquiry Concerning Human Understanding* 4.2, p. 22.

has been reliable in the past, we have good reason to think it will be reliable in the future." The problem with this imagined argument is that it is circular. It "begs the question" by assuming the principle in question is true. If we infer that the future will be similar to the past because in the past the past has been a reliable guide to the future, we are *using* induction. If the future in fact turned out to be different from the past, then the fact that the past was a reliable guide to the future in the past would be of no help. If we appeal to induction as providing evidence for induction we are simply assuming what we are trying to show is true.

Now Hume does *not* say we should stop relying on induction. In fact he says that "none but a fool or a madman will ever pretend to dispute the authority of experience."[16] However, he insists that the "inference" (if that is the right term) is not something that can be justified either by rational argument or appeal to experience. It cannot be the former, because there is no contradiction involved in supposing that the laws of nature could change drastically and the future be radically different from the past. It cannot be the latter because any appeal to experience must presuppose and appeal to the very principle we are seeking a justification for.

One might object here that there must be some rational principle that justifies us in using inductive reasoning. After all, everyone does learn from experience. Hume admits this is so: "It is certain that the most ignorant and stupid peasants—nay infants, nay, even brute beasts—improve by experience, and learn the qualities of natural objects, by observing the effects which result from them."[17] However, Hume thinks this fact actually supports his view. If the conclusions we come to on the basis of experience were based on some process of reasoning then small children and animals would not be able to learn as they do. It looks as if inductive reasoning, which is the basis of our causal knowledge, which is in turn the basis of most of our knowledge of matters of fact, is not grounded in any process of reasoning at all.

---

[16]Hume, *An Enquiry Concerning Human Understanding* 4.2, p. 23.
[17]Hume, *An Enquiry Concerning Human Understanding* 4.2, p. 25.

HUME ON THE IMPORTANCE OF CUSTOM OR HABIT

If we ask why we continue to rely on induction, Hume says the answer has nothing to do with reason or evidence. Rather, when we form a belief about what will happen in the future, we are guided by what he calls "custom or habit." In effect Hume turns to empirical psychology to explain why we form the beliefs we do. Custom is for him "a principle of human nature, which is universally acknowledged, and which is well known by its effects."[18] An appeal to custom is an appeal to a principle about how humans in fact behave. It is like an appeal to gravity in physics. Physics describes how matter behaves; psychology describes how people do and must behave. "All inferences from experience, therefore, are effects of custom, not of reasoning."[19] Some see in Hume's appeal to custom the ancestor of cognitive psychology. Hume sees humans as animals, similar to other animals, and he seeks a natural explanation of what we call experimental reasoning.

Hume thinks the fact that custom is a natural principle that governs human behavior is what accounts for the fact that skeptical worries about induction do not change our behavior. We do not need to "fear that this philosophy, while it endeavours to limit our enquiries to common life, should ever undermine the reasonings of common life, and carry its doubts so far as to destroy all action, as well as speculation. Nature will always maintain her rights, and prevail in the end over any abstract reasoning whatsoever."[20] Hume does not think his "skeptical doubts" will have any effect on how people live their lives.

HUME AND SKEPTICISM

It looks as if Hume has arrived at a skeptical position. All of our knowledge of matters of fact beyond our immediate experience and memory is based on causal knowledge. Causal knowledge is all based on induction. Induction itself turns out to be baseless. Students

---

[18]Hume, *An Enquiry Concerning Human Understanding* 5.1, p. 28.
[19]Hume, *An Enquiry Concerning Human Understanding* 5.1, p. 28.
[20]Hume, *An Enquiry Concerning Human Understanding* 5.1, p. 27.

sometimes underestimate the force of Hume's argument here. They think that he is merely saying that we cannot prove or demonstrate that the future will be like the past, so we cannot be 100 percent sure that the sun will come up tomorrow, even though we have good evidence that it will. However, Hume's claim is not simply that we lack proof for inductive reasoning; it is that we have no evidence at all for induction. The "evidence" we want to give turns out to be question-begging.

Most of Hume's contemporaries (including Thomas Reid, as we shall see) took him to be a skeptic, someone who denies that we know anything based on induction. If we assume the kind of epistemology found in Descartes and Locke, Hume does appear to be a skeptic. The "classical foundationalism" found in those thinkers, it will be recalled, held that genuine knowledge must be based on foundations that were highly certain. To be justified, our beliefs must either be self-evident or evident in some other way, or else they must be grounded in such evident beliefs. Hume claims to have shown that this standard cannot be met for most of our important beliefs. From a classical foundationalist viewpoint, Hume has shown that we know very little, perhaps nothing beyond our immediate experience.

However, one might also interpret Hume as calling into question the kind of epistemology found in Descartes and Locke. Many of our beliefs turn out not to be based on evidence but on something like an instinct, a principle of human nature that we follow but cannot justify. Some contemporary philosophers interpret Hume in something like this way.[21] They affirm that in addition to his "skeptical doubts" he offers us a "skeptical solution." Hume, they say, offers us a "naturalized epistemology," in which our knowing is understood as a natural process, akin to the way other animals come to know things. On this reading Hume is not so much a skeptic as someone who is breaking with the epistemology of classical foundationalism. He certainly is repudiating

[21]For a good example of this see William Edward Morris and Charlotte R. Brown, "David Hume," in *The Stanford Encyclopedia of Philosophy*, spring 2016 ed., ed. Edward N. Zalta, http://plato.stanford.edu/entries/hume/.

Spinoza's claim that we can see the world from God's point of view. For Hume we are not gods or modes of God, but animals, whose beliefs are mostly the product of a nonrational instinct.

Part of Hume's motivation in urging this skeptical-sounding view is to recognize the limits of human reason. The kinds of metaphysical systems found in Descartes, Spinoza, and Leibniz go far beyond the competence of what we can rationally justify. Hume certainly thinks that recognizing the limits of reason in this way will also block any kind of natural or philosophical theology, and we shall see this when we examine his philosophy of religion.

One can cite in support of the "constructive" or "nonskeptical" reading of Hume the fact that Hume clearly states that humans cannot stop relying on induction and should not do so. However, it is not hard to see why so many have read Hume as a skeptic. After all, in the end it looks like most of what we believe is not based on any kind of evidence and has no rational justification. What "justifies" our beliefs is something like a nonrational instinct. However, even if this were successful as empirical psychology, it is hard to see how this fact would count as a justification of those beliefs. At the very least Hume perhaps owes us some account of why we ought to rely on this particular instinct, why it is reasonable to do so. It also seems odd, perhaps even ironic, that Hume, having told us that we don't know a priori that everything has a causal explanation, is so confident that there must be some cause as to why we believe in induction, as well as causality. It shows how necessary it is to think this way. Perhaps Hume would say this just proves his point. We believe in causality because we cannot help doing so.

What does causality amount to, then, on Hume's view? The answer is simply this: To know that some event A is the cause of event B is simply to know that events of type A regularly precede events of type B. Empirically, there is nothing more to cause and effect than "constant conjunction." Hume specifically rejects Locke's view that we gain our awareness of causality from our own ability to act by willing. Hume denies that we are aware of any special power by which we move various parts of our bodies. It is in fact again by experience that we learn that we have the power to move certain parts of our bodies, such as our arms and legs, but do not have the power to move other parts, such as our livers or kidneys. Even the mind's power over itself is limited and is something we come to know through experience. It is true that we are aware of volitions, acts of will, but we do not really know why some volitions are effective and others are not. We simply learn by experience that some are and some are not.

Hume recognizes that his account of causality seems to leave out something important. When we say that one event causes another, we think we are saying more than just that events of the first type are regularly followed by events of the second type. We think of a cause as somehow "producing" its effect, even that there is a necessary connection between cause and effect. If we believe that causes and effects are necessarily connected, we must at least have the idea of "necessary connection." Given Hume's doctrine that all ideas come from impressions, where do we even get such an idea?

Hume's answer is that when we experience the repeated sequences that we call cause and effect, a process of conditioning is set up in our own minds. When there is a constant conjunction of events of type A and type B, the two types of events become associated or linked in our minds. The result is that when we experience an event of type A, we expect that an event of type B will occur. We feel it necessary to think of the second event when we experience the first. This feeling is again the result of custom or habit, and it is subjective, not objective, in us and not the world.[22] However, the mind naturally projects this feeling that the second event is linked to the first, which is true subjectively, onto the world. We think that because the experiences are psychologically linked, the events are linked as well. The idea of "necessary connection" does not stem from any impression of something in the world, but is a

---

[22]Hume, *An Enquiry Concerning Human Understanding* 7.2, pp. 50-51.

subjective feeling that reflects psychological conditioning. Empirically, causality is simply constant conjunction.

HUME ON MATERIAL AND SPIRITUAL SUBSTANCES

Hume's view of material substance is really close to Berkeley's, but he manages to state the view in a way that makes it seem less counter-intuitive than Berkeley. Berkeley of course argued that his idealism was compatible with ordinary beliefs and common sense, but even Berkeley recognized that his view was at odds with the way "the vulgar" normally talk. Hume agrees with Berkeley that we have no real idea of matter or some underlying material substance. Rather, as was the case for causality, our belief in matter is a kind of projection onto the world of a psychological tendency or process.

> When we gradually follow an object in its successive changes, the smooth progress of the thought makes us ascribe an identity to the succession. . . . When we compare its situation after a considerable change the progress of the thought is broken; and consequently we are presented with the idea of diversity: In order to reconcile which contradictions, the imagination is apt to feign something unknown and invisible, which it supposes to continue the same under all these variations; and this unintelligible something it calls a *substance, or original and first matter*.[23]

To believe in "matter" as some kind of mysterious underlying substance is thus to believe something that is unintelligible. As Berkeley argues, we have no concept of what matter in this sense is. However, if by "material object" we simply mean to refer to a complex set of impressions that is contiguous in space and time (or the ideas that stem from those impressions), then Hume has no objection to belief in material objects.

In fact, Hume thinks that in some sense we cannot help believing in material objects. Once again he claims an important set of our beliefs is

---

[23]David Hume, *A Treatise of Human Nature* 1.4.3, in David Hume, *A Treatise of Human Nature*, vol. 1, *Texts*, ed. David Fate Norton and Mary J. Norton (Oxford: Oxford University Press, 2000), pp. 145-46. All page numbers following citations of this work are from this edition.

grounded not in reason but in a psychological process that we have no control over. It is this element that distinguishes Hume's account from Berkeley's. Berkeley's arguments are actually irrefutable, according to Hume: *"They admit of no answer and produce no conviction."*[24] So Hume claims we cannot and do not accept Berkeley's view. However, in the end, when Hume affirms a belief in material objects, it turns out that they are pretty much what Berkeley says they are: collections of experiences.

What about spiritual substances? Here Hume rejects Berkeley decisively. Berkeley had rejected material substance, but he affirmed the necessity of minds, or spiritual substances, because he believed it was unintelligible to believe that there could be ideas that did not inhere in a mind. Hence Berkeley accepted both a divine mind and finite minds, as spiritual substances. Hume rejects the idea of spiritual substance, in much the same way Berkeley had rejected the notion of material substance. Berkeley had already conceded that we have no "idea" of the self, but only a "notion." Using his empiricist theory of meaning, Hume argues that we indeed have no idea of the self. "For my part, when I enter most intimately into what I call *myself*, I always stumble on some particular perception or other, of heat or cold, light or shade, love or hatred, pain or pleasure. I never can catch *myself* at any time without a perception, and never can observe anything but the perception."[25] If we do not have an idea of the self, then we cannot believe in its reality, just as Berkeley had argued we cannot believe in matter because we do not have any idea of matter.

The self for Hume is really just a "bundle of perceptions." We are just a stream of psychological events following each other rapidly. The unity of the self is psychological. We posit a "continuing self" in the same way we posit continuing material objects, to account for the similarity things have from moment to moment. Beyond our immediate experience, Locke was correct to see memory as the basis of personal identity, for it

---

[24]Hume, *An Enquiry Concerning Human Understanding* 12.1, p. 107.
[25]Hume, *A Treatise of Human Nature* 1.4.6.3, p. 165.

is memory that connects later perceptions with earlier ones. The idea of a substantial self, or a soul, is again a kind of psychological construction, whereby we posit a mysterious (and unintelligible) substance that somehow unifies or collects the various perceptions. We have come a long way from Descartes's claim that he is directly aware of himself as "thinking thing" and has certain knowledge of his existence.

Although Hume puts forward this skeptical view of the self, he does confess to doubts about it, and it is not hard to see why. In an appendix to the *Treatise* he expresses these doubts forthrightly, though he is not completely clear as to the source of the doubts: "But all my hopes vanish, when I come to explain the principles that unite our successive perceptions in our thought or consciousness. I cannot discover any theory, which gives me satisfaction on this head."[26] Although Hume does not explain clearly the source of his dissatisfaction, the problems likely lie in one of two major problems that beset such a "bundle" theory. The first is that it is difficult to explain what makes one bundle the perceptions of one individual and another bundle the perceptions of another. If I am not a self, but just a succession of experiences, why are my experiences mine and yours yours? If there is no self to "own" experiences it is difficult to answer this question. The second major problem is that throughout his work Hume constantly speaks as if the mind is an enduring object. The mind, for example, constructs the idea of "necessary connection" and "material objects." But what is it that does the construction if there is no mind as an enduring reality? Perhaps Hume should here affirm about the self something like what he affirms of material objects, that we naturally believe in them even though we have no real rational basis for doing so, because we cannot help doing so.

HUME'S PHILOSOPHY OF RELIGION

Hume's philosophy of religion is today regarded by many naturalists as providing a decisive refutation of the natural or philosophical theology

---

[26]Hume, *A Treatise of Human Nature* 3, appendix, p. 400.

found in the medieval philosophers as well as the modern philosophers who are Hume's predecessors. There is no point at which Hume's views are more at variance with those of Locke, Berkeley, Descartes, and Leibniz than in his account of religious belief. All of those philosophers claimed that one could demonstrate God's existence with certainty. Even Spinoza, who clearly rejects the God of theism, offers a rational theology in which the reality of God is of the first importance.

Hume's most influential writings on the philosophy of religion are found in his *Dialogues Concerning Natural Religion*, which was published posthumously. As the title implies, the book is in dialogue form, with three characters: Demea, Cleanthes, and Philo. Demea is a pious figure who relies on what he calls a priori arguments for God's reality. However, the arguments give us no clear conception of what God is like, a conclusion Demea welcomes, since he affirms that God is beyond human understanding. Demea gets relatively little space in the book, and this is understandable, since his rationalistic approach to theology has little appeal to an empiricist such as Hume. Each of the other characters appeals to Demea at times, but he seems mostly intended to exhibit the weakness of nonempirical arguments for God.

Most of the book thus consists of an extended argument between Philo and Cleanthes. Cleanthes bases rational belief in God on a kind of argument from design, in which God must exist as the designer of the natural universe, which shows clear evidence of purposive intelligence. His argument at least has empirical foundations and thus engages Hume's attention. Cleanthes puts his design argument in the form of an argument from analogy. We observe many things, such as machines of various types, which show the purposive adaptation of means to ends. We know that such things are the result of intelligence. If the universe is analogous to these designed objects, then its cause must be analogous to the causes of those designed objects. Thus the cause of the universe must be a powerful intelligent being. It is important that Cleanthes's version of the argument rests on an analogy between the universe as a whole and human-made artificial objects. Other versions of the argument from design, such as Aquinas's Fifth Way, reason directly from the existence of particular objects in nature that show evidence of purposiveness.[27]

Although Philo claims to be a truly religious person, he is skeptical about Cleanthes's argument for a number of reasons. The roots of his skepticism are clearly grounded in something like Hume's own view of causation. Furthermore, Philo seems to get the better of the argument throughout most of the book. Many commentators have therefore viewed Philo as representing Hume's own views, at least throughout much of the book. Although not everyone agrees with this identification of Hume and Philo, when people speak of "Hume's" criticisms of the theistic arguments, they usually have in mind the arguments of Philo.

We can see why a priori arguments or proofs would be suspicious on Hume's view, since such arguments can only be rightly given for "relations of ideas." However, the existence of God, like any existence claim, will be a "matter of fact" for Hume and thus must be known by experience. A priori arguments will thus be of little value, which explains why much of the book focuses on Cleanthes's more empirical argument.

Many of the criticisms of this argument rest on Hume's view of causality, which affirms that causal knowledge must be grounded in experience. Since we have no experience of universe-making or creating, it is clear that claims about the cause of the existence of the universe will be shaky. Cleanthes, as noted above, tries to avoid this problem by appeal to an analogy between the universe and human-made objects, but Philo sees this move as problematic as well.

First of all, Philo claims that the analogy is weak. The universe is vastly larger and more complex than a watch or a pump, and it is difficult to know how similar the universe is to such objects.[28] Second, there are

[27]See chap. 9 for a discussion of Aquinas's argument.
[28]David Hume, *Dialogues Concerning Natural Religion* 2, in David Hume, *Dialogues Concerning Natural Religion*, ed. Richard H. Popkin (Indianapolis: Hackett, 1998), 16-17. All page numbers following citations of this work are from this edition.

many alternative analogies that would imply a different kind of cause.[29] If we think of the universe as similar to a pump, then the cause might be intelligent, but if we think of the universe as similar to a vegetable or animal, then it might come from a seed or hatch from an egg.[30] (Philo recognizes how absurd the latter seems, but he argues that we have no real way of ruling out even views that seem absurd.) Third, Philo claims that for all we know, the material universe itself might contain some kind of causal principles sufficient to produce the universe we see.[31] Hume is writing before Darwin, but he here seems to hope that eventually we would find a natural explanation for the apparent design we see in the world.

Finally, even if we concede that the cause of the universe is probably intelligent, Philo claims the conclusion is religiously inadequate. We have no reason to believe the intelligent cause would be the God that Christians and Jews believe in. We would have no reason to believe the designer was infinite in either power or goodness.[32] Perhaps the universe was made by a junior deity still learning how to make good universes, or by an older deity whose faculties are in decline. In fact, there would be no reason to believe in just one being as the creator. The empirical facts are consistent with a committee of gods being the designer. Philo, by the way, as we will see below, himself does not see these objections as completely eliminating the force of the argument from design.

Besides attacking Cleanthes's version of the argument from design, Philo goes on the offensive by raising the problem of evil, affirming that "Epicurus's old questions are yet unanswered. Is he [God] willing to prevent evil, but not able? Then he is impotent. Is he able, but not willing? Then he is malevolent. Is he both able and willing? Whence

---

[29]Hume, *Dialogues Concerning Natural Religion* 2, pp. 16-18.
[30]Hume, *Dialogues Concerning Natural Religion* 7, pp. 44-45.
[31]Hume, *Dialogues Concerning Natural Religion* 7, pp. 46-47.
[32]Hume, *Dialogues Concerning Natural Religion* 5, pp. 35-36.

then is evil?"[33] Philo is scrupulous in how he raises the problem, however. He does not argue that evil provides a proof of God's nonexistence. It is possible that a good God might have reasons to allow evil, even if we do not know what they are. However, the existence of evil at least poses a severe problem for natural theology, since it shows that the conception of God we would form if we based that conception solely on what we observe in the world would not be a conception of a God who is both completely good and all-powerful.

The theist who is a Christian might well concede Philo's point here. If all we knew about God was formed from observing the natural world, we might lack grounds for affirming with any confidence that God is completely good. For example, if we look at primal or tribal religions, many of them have posited gods who were morally ambiguous, beings that humans are rightly afraid of and seek to placate. Even if it were reasonable to hold that there must be a transcendent being who is the cause of the universe, Christians might insist that we can only know the nature of that God through God's own self-revelation.

Interestingly, in the *Dialogue* this seems close to the position that Philo himself ultimately takes. In the end Philo concedes to Cleanthes that there is at least some weak probability that the world was created by intelligence, but he denies that this conclusion has much if any religious significance. Philo concedes that the most plausible view of the world is *"that the cause or causes of order in the universe probably bear some remote analogy to human intelligence."*[34] That is a conclusion that seems religiously inadequate of course. Philo says that we will likely feel some "astonishment" at the greatness of the object, but also some "melancholy" from its obscurity, along with "contempt" for human reason's inadequacy to tell us more. However, Philo says that "the most natural sentiment, which a well-disposed mind will feel . . . is a longing desire and expectation, that Heaven would be pleased to dissipate, at least

---

[33]Hume, *Dialogues Concerning Natural Religion* 10, p. 63.
[34]Hume, *Dialogues Concerning Natural Religion* 12, p. 88.

alleviate, this profound ignorance, by affording some more particular revelation to mankind."[35] Some commentators have argued that this conclusion is not likely to be sincere but reflects Hume's fear of the consequences of his supposed atheism. However, whether Philo (or Hume) believes this or not, it seems plausible from a Christian point of view. Perhaps natural theology cannot give us adequate knowledge of God, even if it can give us reasons to believe there is a God.[36]

HUME'S ARGUMENT AGAINST BELIEF IN MIRACLES

Besides the discussion of natural theology in his *Dialogues*, Hume is also famous for an argument contained in the *Enquiry Concerning Human Understanding* against belief in miracles. Hume actually gives two different types of arguments in this essay. First, he gives a general argument that even the best evidence we could imagine would not be sufficient to make belief in miracles reasonable. In the last part of the essay he tries to show that the actual evidence we have for miracles is weak and comes nowhere near the standard that would be necessary. The arguments he gives in the second part are more historical than philosophical. For example, he claims that the testimony comes from "ignorant and barbarous tribes" and always from far-off times and places. These arguments are really historical and not philosophical, and they are hardly decisive. They not only assume an arrogant and condescending view of ancient peoples; they also fail to recognize that there are plenty of people in the contemporary world who testify that miracles have occurred.[37]

In both cases it should be obvious that Hume's arguments are epistemological, not metaphysical. Given his skepticism about metaphysics, it is easy to see why he takes this tack, since if we lack metaphysical knowledge it is hard to see how one could show that miracles cannot happen.

---

[35]Hume, *Dialogues Concerning Natural Religion* 12, p. 89.
[36]For a developed version of this view, which sees natural theological arguments as supporting "anti-naturalism," rather than providing adequate knowledge of God, see my *Why Christian Faith Still Makes Sense: A Response to Contemporary Objections* (Grand Rapids: Baker Academic, 2015), 13-27.
[37]See Craig Keener, *Miracles: The Credibility of the New Testament Accounts* (Grand Rapids: Baker Academic, 2011), esp. part 3.

Hume generally assumes that belief in miracles is based on testimonial evidence, and also that testimonial evidence itself requires support. Both of these assumptions can be challenged. Many people claim to have directly observed a miracle or the outcome of a miracle. Furthermore, as we shall see in the next chapter, Reid argues that testimony is a source of basic evidence and does not always require further evidence in order for it to justify belief.

Hume says that when we receive testimonial evidence, one of the ways we evaluate that evidence is by looking at the probability of the content of the evidence. If one of my students tells me that there are cars driving on the streets of Waco, Texas, I will have little reason to doubt this, since the story is highly probable. However, if one of my students tells me that Martians are walking around the Baylor University campus, the story is so improbable that I am unlikely to believe it without strong supporting evidence. So how probable are the accounts given by witnesses who claim that a miracle has occurred?

Hume says that the probability of a type of event is a function of the frequency with which events of that type have occurred in our past experience. He then defines a miracle as a "violation of a law of nature" that is caused by God or some other invisible agent.[38] Since the laws of nature simply describe what we have always observed to happen, if a miracle occurred it would be, by definition, an extremely rare event, an exception to our general experience. It follows from this that the probability of a miracle occurring is maximally low, and so it looks as if it would always be more probable that the witness who affirms a miracle has occurred is either mistaken or lying than that the miracle has actually occurred. To make belief in a miracle reasonable, the falsity of the testimony in favor of the miracle would itself have to be miraculous.[39] Obviously, this is a very high bar to meet.

---

[38]Hume, *An Enquiry Concerning Human Understanding* 10.1, p. 76.
[39]Hume, *An Enquiry Concerning Human Understanding* 10.1, p. 77.

Some critics of Hume have fastened on Hume's definition of a miracle as a "violation" of a law of nature. Laws of nature describe what normally happens, but the laws have the form of "If x, then y." If something different from x occurs, then there is no violation of the law if y does not occur. Since God's actions in bringing about a miracle represent an additional factor not normally present, it can be plausibly argued that the law of nature is not violated. The law of nature simply states what would normally happen in the course of nature if God did not act in an unusual way. However, I do not think this objection is a serious problem for Hume. He could easily restate his argument by dropping the language of "violation" and simply talking about an exception to what we normally observe in nature. There is surely something exceptional about miracles in the sense that Hume means to discuss them. People do not normally rise from the dead, and humans cannot normally walk on water. Recognizing the exceptional character of miracles does not mean that some kind of deistic view of God is being assumed, either. The person who affirms that a miracle has occurred does not have to say that God is active in nature when he normally is not active, but simply that when God acts miraculously in nature, he is acting in a special way, different from his activity in holding nature in being.

Other critics have claimed that Hume begs the question by saying that the experience that supports laws of nature is "inviolable." They say that Hume assumes that miracles never happen (or cannot ever happen) and then concludes that miracles should not be believed. However, though Hume states his argument in a mistaken way at this point, it again looks like the error is one that is easily remedied. Instead of saying that the laws of nature are "inviolable" and describe what always happens, he should have said that the laws of nature describe what generally happens except when miracles occur, and miracles are rare events at best. His argument could still go through on this basis if it were sound otherwise.

However, I do not believe the argument is sound. As I have already mentioned, it does not seem correct that belief in miracles is based solely on testimony. There is also physical evidence and direct experience for some people to support such beliefs. With respect to testimonial evidence it seems to me that Hume's big mistake is to assume that we estimate the probability of a type of event solely on the basis of the frequency with which events of that type occur. Suppose that a giant meteor has hit the Earth only once in all the billions of years of its history. On Hume's view this would imply that it is extremely unlikely that a meteor will ever hit the Earth again. If scientists claim that a meteor is coming our way, according to this account of probability, it would be more reasonable to believe that they are mistaken, since the event they predict is so improbable. However, it would be foolish to take such a view of the scientists' claims.

What has gone wrong in the meteor case? The mistake is to estimate probability solely on the basis of the frequency with which a type of event occurs. In reality we base our judgments on how probable a type of event is on everything we know that might bear on the question. In the case of the meteor we would look at how many meteors there are, and more particularly on the observations that scientists have made about the one they believe will hit the Earth, including its position and direction and velocity.

In a similar way, the probability of a miracle should not be estimated solely on the basis of the frequency with which miracles occur. (In fact, Hume may be wrong in claiming that miracles are extremely rare; many people claim to have personal experience of miracles.) How likely it is that a miracle may occur will depend on many things: Is there a God? If there is a God, would God be likely to have reasons to perform miracles? The answers to these questions might well show that, even if a miracle at any given moment may be improbable, the likelihood of a miracle's occurring sometime might be much higher. Furthermore, in certain circumstances, in which it seems that a miracle would further

God's purposes in some essential way, a miracle might not be so improbable that a credible witness could not reasonably produce belief.

HUME'S ETHICS

The longest section of the *Treatise* deals with ethical questions, and it is
likely Hume thought that his contributions to ethics were among his
most important achievements; he affirms that "morality is a subject that
interests us above all others."[40] Historically, Hume's ethical thought
deeply influenced utilitarianism, through Jeremy Bentham. In the contemporary period Hume is recognized as the ancestor of "antirealist"
metaethical views.

A realist account of ethics is one that sees ethical judgments as objectively true or false, independently of what humans think or feel. "Murder
is morally wrong" is a true proposition, one that states a moral fact, one
that would be true even if humans became so morally depraved as to
value murder and view it as good. Antirealism in metaethics rejects the
idea that moral judgments are true or false independently of human
beliefs, attitude, and emotions. Although the term *antirealism* is a contemporary one that Hume does not use, he clearly holds such a view.
Besides Hume's influence on contemporary antirealism, he also has
inspired a contemporary revival of what is sometimes called "sentimen-
talism," which can be understood in a more realist manner.

Even if Hume is an antirealist, he is far from being a moral nihilist.
He does not want to deny that we can justifiably make moral judgments,
and he even affirms that some of them are true and some of them are
false. However, he wants to claim that these judgments are not stating
matters of fact that are true independently of us. Rather, ethical or moral
truths are expressions of our attitudes or feelings. In this respect they
resemble beauty. When geometers describe the qualities of a circle they
do not include beauty among them. The reason is that "beauty is not a
quality of the circle" but "is only the effect which that figure produces

---

[40]Hume, *A Treatise of Human Nature* 3.1.1, in Norton and Norton, 293.

upon the mind."[41] Moral judgments then reflect the emotional responses we have to facts; they do not express facts that hold independently of those responses.

Morality then, according to Hume, does not consist of "matters of fact" that can be discovered by reason or the understanding. One argument he gives in favor of this view is that if moral judgments were simply objective judgments made by reason, then there would be no inherent connection between a moral judgment and motivation. In Hume's psychology, a person is never moved by reason alone to do anything. Rather, "reason is and ought to be the slave of the passions."[42] Therefore, if moral judgments are linked to our behavior, so that a moral judgment is linked to some tendency to behave in a certain way, this shows that these judgments are not about "matters of fact" discovered by reason, but rather are grounded in the passions. If there is a "matter of fact" that grounds moral judgments, it lies in the facts about our responses to actions. Some actions (and states of character) we approve of and call moral. Others we disapprove of and call immoral. But actions do not possess the character of being moral or immoral independently of ourselves.

Despite this subjective basis for ethics, Hume believes that the substantive ethical judgments that are part of common sense are justified and have a kind of objectivity. The basis for this objectivity lies in human nature. The passions and sentiments of humans are similar enough that we can reach a wide measure of agreement about what is good and bad, what is a virtue and what is a vice. The moral sentiments are basically common to humans, and thus we admire moral qualities, such as generosity and bravery, even when they are found in our enemies, and we disapprove of immoral qualities, such as greediness and ingratitude, even when found among our friends and family. Morality is not founded simply in self-interest, but in sympathetic feelings we have toward

---

[41]David Hume, "Concerning Moral Sentiment," appendix 1 in *Essays Moral, Political, and Literary* (London: Ward, Lock, 1875), 482.
[42]Hume, *A Treatise Concerning Human Nature* 2.3.3, p. 266.

others, feelings that induce us to approve of actions that are "helpful or useful" to the person acting or to others.

Many of our moral judgments are then not really claims about moral facts as they appear to be but expressions of how we feel about various moral situations. Hume does recognize that some of our moral rules are founded on agreements or conventions we make with each other, the basis of the agreements being the "utility" those moral rules have for us. This part of Hume's ethic was later influential on Jeremy Bentham, the founder of utilitarianism.

Hume may be quite right to insist that moral truths are recognized through the emotions. It may be that the anger I feel when I see an act of injustice or the revulsion I feel when I see an act of cruelty are the means whereby I come to recognize that injustice is wrong and cruelty is evil. However, it does not follow from this that these emotions are what grounds the truth of our moral judgments. Rather, if we are indeed moral beings and morality is part of our nature, then our emotions may be capacities for grasping moral truths. Hume's own epistemology cannot allow for this, since we can only come to know facts for him through sense experiences. However, emotions may also be a kind of experience, and like sense experiences, emotional experiences may provide us with information about the world. The problem with Hume's subjectivism is that it implies that good and evil would change if our emotional reactions changed. However, even if we humans became so morally depraved that we approved of rape and murder, it would not follow that rape and murder would be right, but that we humans had lost our capacity to grasp and be motivated by moral truths.

Hume is clearly trying to develop an account of morality that is independent of God and any kind of transcendent order. However, many philosophers worry that human emotions are too frail a foundation for ethical truths, even if they are one of the means whereby we come to grasp those truths.

The Scottish Enlightenment (II)

Thomas Reid

DAVID HUME WAS NOT THE ONLY great Scottish philosopher of the eighteenth century; Hume was a contemporary of Thomas Reid. Reid was born in 1710 in Kincardineshire, a former Scottish county south of Aberdeen on the northeastern side of Scotland. Interestingly, Reid's birthday was the same as Hume's, April 25, though Reid was one year older. Reid attended the university at Aberdeen, studied theology, and became a pastor for seventeen years in Aberdeenshire. During this time, he married and had nine children. He also read Hume's writings during this time and began to develop his own response to the challenges Hume posed.

In 1751 Reid left the parish ministry and became a lecturer in philosophy at the University of Aberdeen. In 1764 Reid published his *Inquiry into the Human Mind on the Principles of Common Sense*. That same year he also accepted a chair of moral philosophy at the University of Glasgow, and he began to acquire followers who would influence generations of students both in Scotland and in America. After retiring in 1780, Reid published two more important books, based on his lecture notes: *Essays on the Intellectual Powers of Man* and *Essays on the Active Powers of Man*. He died in 1796, outliving his wife and eight of his nine children. As noted in the introduction to the previous chapter, Reid's fame and acclaim outshone Hume's throughout the nineteenth century. In the middle part of the twentieth century, interest in Reid ebbed (though it never died out), partly due to the development of logical positivism, a form of empiricism strongly influenced by Hume. However, at the end of the twentieth century and in the beginning of the twenty-first century, interest in Reid has rebounded strongly.

REID'S ATTACK ON REPRESENTATIONALISM

Although Reid is most famous for his philosophy of "common sense," it is easy to misunderstand what he means by this term. *Common sense* is a technical term in Reid's thought. It does not mean the kind of folk wisdom a person might remember a grandmother as having, or simply having the practical ability to make good life decisions. Although to fully grasp Reid's view of philosophy it is important to understand his view of common sense, I think it is best to begin by looking at how Reid actually does philosophy before zeroing in on his views about philosophical method. I shall therefore begin my discussion of Reid by looking at his attack on what I termed "representationalism" in discussing Descartes and Locke. Reid himself calls this view the "way of ideas" or the "theory of ideas." By looking at this attack on representationalism we shall get a clear idea of how radical Reid's philosophy is and how much he differs from virtually all of his modern predecessors. I shall look first at Reid's criticisms of representationalism and then examine his own positive account of perception.

Representationalism is the view that we never directly experience real objects but only representations of those objects. Things themselves do not appear to us, but only "ideas" or "impressions" that represent real objects. On Reid's view this doctrine is the source of many of the problems of modern philosophy. He believes that the doctrines of Berkeley and Hume follow logically from this "philosophy of ideas," and so to avoid skepticism about both material bodies and minds, one must reject this root assumption.

The first point that Reid makes about the theory of ideas is "that it is directly contrary to the universal sense of men who have not been instructed in philosophy."[1] Of course this does not mean that the theory of ideas is false, and Reid does not think it does imply this, but it surely does mean that it is a view for which we need evidence or good arguments. "When we see the sun or moon, we have no doubt that the very objects which we immediately see are very far distant from us, and from one another."[2] Anyone who claims this is *not* the case surely ought to provide good reasons for believing it.

However, when we look to the philosophers who hold this theory of ideas, arguments in favor of the view are hard to find. It rather looks more like an assumption that has been made uncritically. Reid notes that Locke, for example, says the following: "I presume it will be easily granted me that there are such *ideas* in men's minds; everyone is conscious of them in himself; and men's words and actions will satisfy him that they are in others."[3] Reid responds that he is "indeed conscious of perceiving, remembering, imagining; but that the objects of these operations are images in my mind, I am not conscious."[4] Reid notes that Hume admits that the theory of ideas is strongly at variance with the way ordinary humans think about the world: "But this universal and primary opinion of all men is soon destroyed by the slightest philosophy, which teaches us that nothing can ever be present to the mind but an image or perception."[5]

Reid claims that this passage from Hume hardly counts as an argument. The claim that nothing can be present to the mind but an image is what is in dispute. Reid does note that Hume also says that "the

---

[1] Thomas Reid, *Essays on the Intellectual Powers of Man* 2.14, in Thomas Reid, *Essays on the Intellectual Powers of Man: A Critical Edition*, ed. Derek R. Brookes (University Park: Pennsylvania State University Press, 2002), 172. All page numbers following citations of this source are from this edition.
[2] Reid, *Essays on the Intellectual Powers of Man* 2.14, p. 172.
[3] Reid, *Essays on the Intellectual Powers of Man* 2.14, p. 174.
[4] Reid, *Essays on the Intellectual Powers of Man* 2.14, p. 174.
[5] Reid, *Essays on the Intellectual Powers of Man* 2.14, p. 178.

senses are only the inlets, through which those images are received."[6] However, this claim can hardly be taken seriously, since Hume also says that the images that are the objects of perception "have no existence when they are not perceived," but to be "received through the senses" the images would have to exist prior to being perceived.

Probably the only serious argument offered for the theory of ideas is based on the idea that we cannot directly perceive objects because to do that we would have to interact causally with the objects. However, nothing can act or be acted on where it is not present, and the objects we perceive by the mind are not directly present in the mind. Reid responds to this argument by agreeing that nothing can act or be acted on where it is not present. However, he denies that when we perceive objects that this requires such causal interaction. Certainly, when we perceive an object, the object does not act. When I see an orange on the table, the orange is not doing anything at all, and suffers no change by being seen. Reid thinks we have just as little reason to think that when we perceive an object we are acting on the object. Just as I don't do anything to the orange by thinking about it, it is by no means clear that I do anything to the orange by perceiving it.

In reality Reid says we know very little about how we perceive the world, just as we do not really know much about how we imagine things or remember things. "We are at a loss to know how we perceive distant objects; how we remember things past; how we imagine things that have no existence."[7] (I will say more about this ignorance below.) Those who posit ideas as the objects of human mental activity have thought that the theory would somehow explain or help us understand how the mind works. However, Reid maintains that positing ideas does not help us understand or explain how the mind works at all. Such theories "are conjectures, and, if they were true, would solve no difficulty but raise many new ones."[8]

---

[6]Reid, *Essays on the Intellectual Powers of Man* 2.14, p. 179.
[7]Reid, *Essays on the Intellectual Powers of Man* 2.14, p. 185.
[8]Reid, *Essays on the Intellectual Powers of Man* 2.15, p. 193.

So what does Reid propose instead of representationalism? He defends the view that we directly perceive real objects, just as we remember real events. It is not the task of philosophy to justify perceptual beliefs through reasoning. "Every man feels that perception gives him an invincible belief of the existence of that which he perceives, and that this belief is not the effect of reasoning, but the immediate consequence of perception."[9] The philosopher may not want to hear this, but such beliefs "put the philosopher and the peasant upon a level, and neither of them can give any other reason for believing his senses than that he finds it impossible for him to do otherwise."[10]

It is worth pausing to notice that Reid's view at this point is more like Hume's than either of them realized. Hume argued that many of our most important beliefs are not based on any rational argument or evidence but on human nature, which simply cannot help relying on induction and believing in the existence of real objects. Reid also says that the bottom line for such beliefs is the fact that human nature is such that we simply have no choice in the matter. There *is* a difference, however. Hume calls this aspect of human nature "custom," a kind of instinct that seems completely nonrational in character. Reid, however, describes "perception, consciousness, memory, and imagination" as "original and simple powers of the mind and parts of its constitution." This may sound like Hume, but Reid thinks of these "powers" not simply as nonrational instincts but as *gifts*. As a theist, Reid believes that our cognitive faculties are given to us to make it possible for us to know the kind of things we need to know and that are good for us to know. As we shall see, this means that we do have reasons for trusting our faculties.

DIRECT REALISM AND NATURAL SIGNS

Reid's own account of perception is thus a form of direct realism, in the sense that when I walk out of my house and see a tree, it is the tree that

---

[9]Reid, *Essays on the Intellectual Powers of Man* 2.15, p. 193.
[10]Reid, *Essays on the Intellectual Powers of Man* 2.15, p. 193.

I see, not an image of the tree or an idea of the tree. A critic might object at this point by claiming that I surely have certain sensations when I see a tree, just as I have sensations when I feel the heat from a fire or touch a cube of ice. Surely, the critic might say, it is by way of those sensations that perception occurs.

Reid agrees that sensations play an important role in perception. It is indeed the case (perhaps with a few very rare exceptions) that we perceive the world by means of sensations. However, in affirming that we perceive the world by means of sensations, Reid denies that what we directly perceive are sensations. Of course sometimes sensations are the direct objects of mental awareness. If I go to the optometrist to have my eyes checked, he may ask me if the image I am seeing is blurry. In this case I concentrate my attention on my sensation. However, normally I do not focus on my sensations but I perceive other objects through sensations.

Here is how Reid's point could be put. Certainly when we visually perceive objects there is some kind of physical process that occurs, and it is equally certain that sensations are involved. We may not know much about the details of the process (unless we are scientists studying the subject), but we know that light rays come from an object and impinge on our retinas. Then some kind of electrical signal gets sent to the brain, and out of this (in ways that even neuroscientists do not fully understand) a conscious visual sensation arises. However, that visual sensation is no more the object of visual perception than is the retina or the signal sent to the brain. If I am seeing an oak tree, it is the oak tree I see. To think otherwise is to confuse the causal process that makes perception possible with perception itself. Perception is a mental or psychological process, and we must not confuse our understanding of that process with the causal events that make the process possible.

So Reid recognizes that sensations play an important role in perception, but he thinks that defenders of the theory of ideas are mistaken about what this role is. For Reid sensations function as "natural signs" for the extramental realities we can become aware of. Here is how Reid describes the difference between perception and sensation:

> The external senses have a double province; to make us feel and to make us perceive. They furnish us with a variety of sensations, some pleasant, others painful, and others indifferent; at the same time they give us a conception, and an invincible belief of the existence of external objects. ... This conception and belief which nature produces by means of the senses, we call *perception*. The feeling which goes along with the perception we call *sensation*.[11]

By "conception" Reid means our ability to become aware of an object and thereby to be able to think about it as well as have other mental attitudes toward it.

So here is what happens in a case of perception. I shall take the sense of touch as my example, since it is one of Reid's favorite examples also. Suppose I take my finger and touch the table in front of me. I am aware of the table, and I form the belief that the table is hard. We say that the table "feels hard," but the sensation or feeling is not itself hard. The sensation does not resemble the quality; nor is the sensation a "copy" of the quality. Rather, I simply have the sensation and immediately and spontaneously form the belief that the table is hard. The sensation is not what I perceive, but the means whereby I become aware of the table and its hardness. The sensation is a natural sign that "suggests" (Reid's term) to me the quality of the table that I am perceiving by way of the sensation.

There is no logical necessity that I perceive the world by way of sensations, or by way of the particular sensations I have. Bats, for example, probably have quite different sensations than humans for perceiving the world. For all we know, angels might perceive the qualities of the world directly without any sensations at all. Human nature is such, however, that in fact we generally perceive the world through sensations and we perceive particular qualities through particular sensations. Reid may

---

[11]Reid, *Essays on the Intellectual Powers of Man* 2.17, p. 210.

have thought that in a few cases we do not need sensations for perception, but if this is so those cases are rare exceptions.

The role of sensations in perception is not that of providing premises for inferences of some kind. We do not see the greenness of grass and then infer that there is grass in front of us because we are experiencing green sensations. We just see the grass when we have the sensations. The process is psychologically direct, even though the causal process that makes it possible is complicated.

In order for a sensation to be a natural sign, two things must be true. First, the sign must be reliably linked to the thing that the sign signifies. We could say that the sign must be caused by the thing it signifies, and this would be true for Reid in a "popular and loose sense" of cause. (The reason for this qualification is that Reid believes that only agent causality is real causality. We speak popularly of events as causing other events, and Reid accepts this usage, but the real cause is God who upholds the natural order and makes each event follow others in law-like ways.) In addition to the link between the natural sign and the thing it signifies, there must also be a link between the sign and the conception and belief that the sign suggests in us.

Reid makes a distinction between natural signs, such as sensations, and artificial signs, such as highway signs and words in a human language. Artificial signs also signify, but the connections between artificial signs and what they signify is conventional. There are two different types of natural signs. Some natural signs are "original" in the sense that they do not have to be learned and that the sign leads to the conception and belief irresistibly in normal cases. To use the example of touch again, even very small children recognize that when they touch a wall they cannot pass through it. Many natural signs are not original, however, but acquired or learned. A good example would be the lemony smell when one cuts a lemon. After doing this several times we learn that the smell is associated with a lemon and after that simply recognize the lemon through the smell. We must learn to recognize the smell as that of a lemon, but once we do the smell functions as a natural sign. Learned natural signs are subject to being modified by more learning, and they do not operate in the nearly irresistible way found in many original natural signs. But they are still natural signs, means whereby we gain knowledge of the external world.

Reid believes there are other natural signs in addition to sensations. We gain knowledge of other people's thoughts and emotions by facial expressions and bodily gestures. The facial expressions and gestures are also natural signs, because the two conditions for being a natural sign are met. Such facial expressions and gestures are causally linked to the inner events they signify, and they also naturally produce in us awareness of those inner events and beliefs about them. It is not the case that we see someone crying and then go through a process of reasoning and *infer* that the person is sad. Rather, we simply perceive the person as sad by means of the crying.

Someone might object to Reid's view here by pointing out that what Reid calls natural signs sometimes lead us to incorrect perceptual judgments, particularly with respect to learned natural signs. When I walked down a rural road in Michigan last summer, I thought I smelled a skunk. It turned out, however, that one of my neighbors was growing medical marijuana. (I did not know that marijuana in the field has a skunky smell!) And of course we know that a person can simulate facial expressions in order to deceive us about their true mental states. Reid does not think the fact that we sometimes make mistakes by relying on natural signs is really an objection. Unlike Descartes he cheerfully embraces the fallibility of our faculties. Our faculties do not have to operate perfectly to be reliable, and natural signs do not have to be infallible to be important sources of information for us.

REID'S BREAK WITH CLASSICAL FOUNDATIONALISM

This "fallibilism" is I think a second way (besides rejecting representationalism) that Reid differs profoundly from many of the early modern philosophers. Like Descartes and Locke, Reid is a foundationalist in his epistemology, but he rejects what has come to be known as "classical foundationalism."[12] That is, he thinks, as do all foundationalists, that some of our beliefs are based on other beliefs, but that the chain of beliefs cannot be infinite. To stop the chain some beliefs must be basic. Where Reid differs from Descartes and Locke is that he does not insist that the foundational beliefs be ones that are known infallibly. To be sure, Reid does think that there are many things we know with certainty. However, for Reid certainty is a psychological attitude; it is does not require that we rule out the possibility that we are being deceived by an evil demon or that we are not just brains in a vat. (The latter example of course is not Reid's but a contemporary one.) We can be reasonably certain about many things even though there is a possibility that we could be wrong about some of them.

Modern Western philosophy was born out of epistemological anxiety, as we saw in looking at Descartes and Locke, fueled by religious disagreements as well as the scientific revolution. Descartes and Locke wanted to find a method that would make philosophy a genuine science, and nail down the foundational truths we know. This attitude was shared by most of their successors. Locke and Berkeley had a very different conception of the proper method to follow, and a different set of foundational truths, but there is a sense in which they shared these aspirations for objective certainty with Spinoza and Leibniz. Hume and Reid are the first to break with this "classical foundationalist" epistemology. From Reid's perspective, Hume's resort to custom was unsatisfactory because it exchanged the aspiration for infallible knowledge for a skeptical conclusion that gave up on rational justification for important knowledge claims. (Like most of Hume's contemporaries, Reid sees Hume as a skeptic, not as the "constructive thinker" many contemporary naturalists find in Hume.) For Reid our human faculties do not

---

[12]For a good discussion of classical foundationalism, see Alvin Plantinga, "Reason and Belief in God," in *Faith and Rationality: Reason and Belief in God* (Notre Dame, IN: University of Notre Dame Press, 1983), 16-93.

have to be infallible to provide us with reliable foundations for knowledge. It is reasonable to trust them even if they do not always work perfectly.

Reid is a great admirer of Newton, and actually read and taught Newton's writings. He takes from Newton several lessons. One is a commitment to empiricism and particularly to experimental investigations to settle disputes. For Reid this epistemological attitude is made necessary by our fallibility. Another is a commitment to the use of mathematics in physics; it is Newton's use of mathematics that makes his physics superior to that of the Cartesians. Reid also agrees with Newton that the basic explanatory concept in natural science is not that of causation but that of laws. (As noted above, in a strict sense Reid does not believe in "event causation." All causation for him is agent causation.) Scientists do not explain by telling us the causes of events but by discovering the laws that allow us to predict events and explain them after they have occurred.

There is, I believe, a connection between Reid's fallibilistic rejection of classical foundationalism and his rejection of representationalism. Philosophers who demand absolute certainty for their foundational beliefs will be strongly tempted to find those certain beliefs within their own minds, for judgments made about the external world seem riskier. If I claim that the classroom I teach in is hot, I could be mistaken. Perhaps I have a fever and the room feels hot because I am warm. Someone may produce a thermometer and show me that I am mistaken. However, if I retreat to the claim that "the room feels hot to me" it appears I have reached solid ground. I cannot in this case be refuted by a thermometer, for I myself am the best judge of how the room feels to me. We can thus see why a craving for certain foundations would lead to an attempt to ground knowledge in subjective "ideas" or "impressions." Reid's acceptance of our fallibility allows him to reject this demand to make the interior life the foundation of our philosophizing as well.

COMMON SENSE

It is now time to turn our attention to what Reid calls "common sense."
As noted above, it is easy to misunderstand this aspect of Reid's thought.
First, common sense is actually not a "sense" at all, in the way vision or
hearing are senses. It is not even a special kind of rational intuition in
the sense in which mathematicians sometimes speak about intuition.
In speaking of common sense Reid does not posit a mysterious faculty
that "senses" truths. Rather, he means to speak of the ability that all
adult humans who are sane have to grasp certain truths that are "first
principles." All humans beyond childhood with normally functioning
minds know such things as the following: (1) The things we perceive
by the senses really exist and "are what we perceive them to be."
(2) "There is life and intelligence in our fellow men with whom we
converse." (3) Things that I distinctly remember really happened. (4)
"In the phenomena of nature, what is to be, will probably be like to what
has been in particular circumstances." Other principles include beliefs
about having the power to act, "having a certain regard" for human
testimony in matters of fact, and a belief in our own existence and continued personal identity.[13]

Reid does not claim that all of the principles of common sense are
necessarily true; nor are they self-evident in the sense that their falsity
cannot be conceived. Nor is his defense of common sense rooted in the
view that what everyone believes must be true. He is even open to the
possibility that one or more of the principles (though not all of them
simultaneously) could be challenged by a philosopher. In such a case,
however, the challenger bears the burden of proof, and whatever argument the philosopher gives in such a case will inevitably appeal to
some other "first principles" that are being taken for granted. All arguments must have premises, and thus philosophical arguments must

---

[13]These examples are taken from a list of twelve "contingent truths" of common sense that Reid gives
in *Essays on the Intellectual Powers of Man* 6.5, pp. 467-90. I have reworded some of these. Reid ex-
pressly denies that the list he gives is exhaustive. He also says that there are principles of common
sense that are necessary.

start somewhere. Reid believes that they must start with the first principles of common sense. Because of Reid's fallibilism, the principles must not be understood as claims that our faculties never make mistakes. Thus the first principle above is not a claim that we never wrongly perceive an object, but that our perceptual experience is generally reliable in producing true beliefs about objects.

Reid rejects the idea that philosophers should make it their aim to vindicate or justify the principles of common sense. I noted above in discussing perception that for Reid a philosopher and a peasant are basically on the same level, but the same kind of leveling is true for all of the principles of common sense. Philosophy depends on common sense; common sense does not depend on philosophy. Philosophy "has no other root but the principles of common sense; it grows out of them, and draws its nourishment from them: severed from this root, its honours wither, its sap is dried up, it dies and rots."[14] The principles of common sense cannot be justified by the philosopher, not because they are necessarily true or self-evidently true, but because we have nothing more certain that could be the basis for justifying them (or for doubting them).

Reid describes the principles of common sense in a number of different ways. As we have seen, they are principles that are universally accepted by sane adults across cultures and languages and historical epochs. One might object here that in fact skeptical philosophers have doubted many of them, but Reid thinks that is not the case. The doubt that philosophers claim to have about such principles is a kind of faux doubt. Reid distinguishes between a kind of pretended doubt of such things found among philosophers and actual doubt. He does not think any philosopher actually doubts such things, as can be seen by the fact that in "all the history of philosophy, we never read of any skeptic that

---

[14]Thomas Reid, *An Inquiry into the Human Mind on the Principles of Common Sense* 1.4, in Thomas Reid, *An Inquiry into the Human Mind on the Principles of Common Sense*, ed. Derek R. Brookes (University Park: Pennsylvania State University Press, 2000), 19. All page numbers following citations of this source are from this edition.

ever stepped into fire or water because he did not believe his senses."[15] This pretend doubt should be met not with argument but "gentle ridicule," for the denials of the principles of common sense are not just false but absurd. Anyone who *really* doubts such principles does not need arguments or evidence but treatment. He distinguishes Descartes's "phony doubt" from the doubt of a madman. "A man that disbelieves his own existence, is surely as unfit to be reasoned with, as a man that believes he is made of glass. There may be disorders in the human frame that may produce such extravagances, but they will never be cured by reasoning."[16] Those who deny common sense merit either ridicule or treatment; they cannot be helped by arguments designed to justify the principles.

Attempts to justify the principles of common sense frequently appear (and are) circular, since we have to use these principles in order to justify them. Take perception, for example. Someone might argue that we can rely on perception because most of the beliefs we gain through perception turn out to be true. But how do we know this? It is only by the use of perception that we discover that perception is generally reliable.

So the principles of common sense are universally believed by sane adults. Reid also describes them as beliefs that are rooted in human nature, or, as he likes to say, they are grounded in our "constitution." One reason we should accept them is that we really can't help doing so. Even though we can imagine them to be false, we can't really believe that they are false. Denying them would also be practically disastrous. Life either as individuals or in society would be impossible.

Despite the importance of common sense in his philosophy, Reid is not always clear or consistent in his discussion of what it really amounts to. Many times he speaks of common sense as general principles we believe, as I have explained the concept. At other times he seems to think of common sense, not as consisting of explicit beliefs, but more

---

[15]Reid, *Essays on the Intellectual Powers of Man* 2.5, p. 90.
[16]Reid, *An Inquiry into the Human Mind* 1.3, p. 16.

implicit beliefs, judgments that we presuppose or take for granted in the way we live our lives.[17] Reid also sometimes talks about common sense as expressing itself in particular judgments, such as "I see an oak tree on the front lawn," rather than abstract principles or "axioms" about the reliability of perception generally. If common sense consists of such particular judgments, then perhaps the more general principles can be seen either as generalizations of these, or as principles implicit in them or presupposed by them.

In the end the principles of common sense are not known by being self-evident or provable, and thus the standards of classical foundationalism cannot be met. Reid says that the principles are accepted on trust. One might say, then, that for Reid philosophy begins with trust, not doubt. It is a reasonable trust, but trust nonetheless.

TRUSTING OUR FACULTIES AND RESPONDING TO THE SKEPTIC

Like Hume, Reid thinks that to do philosophy well, we must pay attention to psychology. However, his psychology is quite different from Hume's. We might take as an example Hume's distinction between impressions and ideas, and Hume's claim that our ideas are "copies" of impressions. Reid thinks that this claim is simply false and can be recognized as false introspectively. My idea or concept of fire is not a copy of a fire, just as my concept of pain does not resemble pain. Many of our ideas or concepts are in no way "copies" of sensations, even if sensations play a role in our acquiring them.

Reid's psychology makes a general distinction between our intellectual powers and our "active powers." This is, however, not a simple or

---

[17]Nicholas Wolterstorff argues that this characterization of common sense in terms of principles that are taken for granted or presupposed is superior, and I believe he is correct. It does not seem plausible to say that all sane adults actually believe the principles Reid lists, since many never even consider or think about such principles. However, it is plausible to say that people live in such a manner that they presuppose or take for granted such principles, even if they never consciously consider them. See Wolterstorff, "Reid on Common Sense," in *The Cambridge Companion to Thomas Reid*, ed. Terence Cuneo and Rene Van Woudenberg (Cambridge: Cambridge University Press, 2004), 77-100.

absolute distinction. For one thing, we cannot act apart from our knowledge and beliefs, and intellectual activities such as believing and remembering are themselves actions. Nevertheless, we can still distinguish between those powers we have that are mainly cognitive in nature, whereby we gain knowledge of the world, and those powers we have to effectuate changes in the world.

With respect to the intellectual powers, Reid employs a "faculty psychology," distinguishing between various cognitive powers that function in different ways, having different inputs and outputs. Among these powers he includes sensation, perception, conception, reason, memory, induction, and testimony. All of these faculties are rooted in our constitution. We do not necessarily understand how they operate, and we do not need to know how they operate in order to trust them. Each of them is in fact linked to a "first principle" or "axiom" of common sense, and therefore, like other principles of common sense, cannot be justified in a noncircular manner.

Reid sees skepticism as doubting one or more of these faculties, or rather, doubting the output of these faculties. However, he argues that the skeptic is in the end inconsistent and always ends up trusting at least one of these faculties without any argument or justification. Take, for example, a philosopher such as Descartes, who tries to prove that perception is reliable and that there is an external world we know through perception. To prove this Descartes must rely on reason, which is another human faculty. If Descartes tries to prove reason is reliable by proving God's existence, then Descartes is still relying on reason and therefore gives a circular argument.[18] Descartes, and such empiricists as Locke and Hume, similarly rely on sensation; they have no doubt about the reality of the sensations they undergo. However, it looks arbitrary to accept one or more of our human faculties on trust and demand that others be certified or justified:

---

[18]See the discussion of Descartes's "vicious circle" in chap. 12.

The skeptic asks me, Why do you believe the existence of the external object which you perceive? This belief, sir, is none of my manufacture; it came from the mint of nature; it bears her image and superscription; and, if it is not right, the fault is not mine: I even took it upon trust, and without suspicion. Reason, says the skeptic, is the only judge of truth, and you ought to throw off every opinion and every belief that is not grounded on reason. Why, sir, should I believe the faculty of reason more than that of perception; they came both out of the same shop, and were made by the same artist; and if he puts one piece of false ware into my hand, what should hinder him from putting another?[19]

Reid says that he would have nothing to say to a "consistent skeptic" who truly doubts everything, although he clearly does not think it is really possible to do this.[20] However, he argues that the "semi-skeptic," who doubts some of our faculties and accepts others on trust, is inconsistent and arbitrary. Descartes trusted reason because he could not help doing so. Reid argues that the same is true for our other basic human faculties.

This aspect of Reid's thought makes him a pioneer of what is today called "epistemological externalism." The internalist in epistemology holds that the justification for our beliefs must be something internal to consciousness, evidence we are aware of or have access to. The externalist holds that for some of our beliefs what justifies the beliefs are facts about the world. I am justified in relying on the deliverances of perception and memory because they are faculties that are reliable and work reasonably well. Those are facts about our faculties; these are faculties that enable us to "track" truths about the world. However, we cannot prove they are reliable without using them and trusting them, and thus we do not have a noncircular internal justification for them.

The internalist will protest that the mere fact that our faculties are reliable cannot justify our beliefs unless we know they are reliable.

---

[19]Reid, *An Inquiry into the Human Mind* 6.20, pp. 168-69.
[20]Reid, *An Inquiry into the Human Mind* 5.7, p. 71.

Internalism says that we should examine our beliefs and only accept those that pass an epistemological test. The externalist says that to do this we would have to be godlike beings. The externalist says we are finite animals, dependent in the end on our faculties being reliable, if we are to have knowledge, even if we have no proof that this is the case. What should we do, according to the externalist, if we are being deceived by an evil demon? The answer is that there is nothing we could do in that situation. However, we have no good reason to believe in such an evil demon or even take the possibility seriously enough to worry about it. Our default position should be one of trust in our faculties, and that is precisely Reid's view.

An interesting test case for Reid is our use of human testimony in forming our beliefs. Everyone acknowledges that the great majority of what any person knows is learned from others. None of us can possibly check out for ourselves all the scientific and historical knowledge we have. So what justifies us in relying on the testimony of others? The answer of Hume and many others is that testimony is only justified because we have evidence that it is reliable. We are justified in believing what others say (most of the time) because most of the time testimony has turned out to be reliable. (The degree of trust we ascribe to testimony will vary depending on the evidence we have for the trustworthiness of a witness and the probability of the content of the testimony; see Hume's argument against miracles.) However, Reid argues that this justification of testimony is circular.[21] We cannot possibly know that testimony is generally reliable except by relying on others' testimony that they have found it generally reliable. In that case the supposed justification is circular, just like other attempted justifications of our faculties.

Reid recognizes that testimony can be false, and he says that we do adjust our degree of trust in testimony in light of our experience. We are suspicious of people who have lied to us in the past, for example. But we could not gain much knowledge at all, and could not make any

---

[21]For a good discussion, see C. A. J. Coady, *Testimony: A Philosophical Study* (Oxford: Clarendon, 2002).

progress toward discerning when testimony is to be doubted without a basic "default" stance of trusting what others tell us. So if I ask a stranger for directions, I am not necessarily irrational to believe what the stranger says, even if I have no evidence that the stranger is truthful. Children begin life by believing what is told them. It is true that not everything children are told is true, and as a person grows, the person gradually learns when to be more trusting and when to be less trusting. However, without the default stance of trust, one cannot even learn to make such calibrated, critical judgments.

REID ON THE SELF AND FREE WILL

Reid is a strong critic of the Humean view that the self is merely a "bundle" of perceptions, just as he rejects the Berkeleyan view that physical objects are just collections of sensations. In both cases common sense produces in us a belief in a substance that is not identical to a set of perceptions. Against Hume, Reid argues that if my consciousness is a succession of perceptions and thus a "bundle," there must nonetheless be something that does the bundling, since each person has a distinct set of perceptions. Joe and Mary may both have mental lives characterized by a constant stream of different psychological events, but there must be something that makes Joe's experiences belong to Joe and not Mary. Reid argues that what does the bundling cannot itself be an experience or transient psychological state. He agrees with Hume that these are always changing and therefore not numerically identical over time. What makes them all to be the experiences of one self must be that they belong to a self that is distinct from those changing psychological events. Reid regards the belief that I am a self that owns the psychological events that make up my life without being identical to those events as one of the principles of common sense. We cannot argue for this judgment because we could never find premises for such an argument that are more certain than the belief supposedly being defended by argument.

Reid delivers a devastating critique of the Lockean claim that the personal identity of the self is constituted by consciousness or memory. There are clearly things that I did that I do not remember, but my lack of memory does not mean that I did not do them. As a counterexample to the Lockean view, Reid tells the story of young boy who stole some fruit and was punished. Later, the boy grows up to become an officer and acts heroically in a battle. Still later, the officer becomes a famous general. Reid asks us to suppose that the officer remembered being the boy who stole the fruit, and the general remembers being the officer who acted heroically. However, by the time the man becomes a general, he has forgotten about the embarrassing episode of fruit stealing. By Locke's principles, the young boy is identical to the officer, and the officer is identical to the general. However, the young boy is not identical to the general. However, if A = B, and B = C, then A = C. So the young boy is both identical to the general and also nonidentical. Clearly something has gone wrong.

Reid also asserts a dualism between the self and the body. One powerful argument for this stems from personal identity itself. We sometimes talk about identity in a loose way. I have an old boat, and the seats and motor have been replaced. Thus, if someone asks, "Is that the same boat I saw on this lake thirty years ago?" I might say yes, or I might say "more or less the same," because some of the parts of the boat are different. It would make sense to say that it is mostly or partly the same boat. The identity of a person is not like this, according to Reid; it is an all-or-nothing affair. Suppose someone has jumped into a lake to rescue a swimmer in trouble. Someone who has heard about this asks me, "Was it you who saved the swimmer?" If the question is about the identity of the person (as opposed to the achievement), then the answer must be yes or no. It might be true to say that the person who saved the swimmer was helped by someone else, and so the achievement is not completely due to the rescuer. But it would make no sense to say, "The person who did the rescue was mostly or partly me."

The reason for the difference between the boat and the person is that the boat has parts but persons do not. Persons are "simples" that have no parts, and thus there is always an answer to the question as to whether some individual is or is not me. However, bodies obviously do have parts, and so if a person were identical to a body, a person would have parts as well. Persons are therefore distinct from their bodies. Nor is a person simply a succession of psychological states, as Hume suggests. The person or self is the possessor of a series of psychological states but is not identical to any of those states.

Reid also defends a "libertarian" view of the free will of human persons. Locke had defended a "compatibilist" account of freedom, in which people have the kind of freedom required for moral responsibility if they are able to act in accordance with their wills, even if those wills are causally determined. Reid thinks that this is inadequate. For him genuine moral freedom requires that the agent have power to determine the will. Suppose, for example, I am causally determined by some genetically based condition in my brain to will to eat only vegetables. On Reid's view, if this is true, then I am not morally responsible for willing to eat only vegetables. I deserve neither praise nor blame for such actions, because I have no control over them.

Reid does not think that humans always act freely. Sometimes we are so driven by passions that we have no control over our wills. Sometimes our wills are influenced by passions but not determined, and sometimes we have little in the way of passion that moves us, and our actions simply reflect a "cool" judgment about what is good and best. It is only when we have the power to will or not to will an action that we are morally responsible for that action. Strictly speaking, all we have power to do is will an action. Whether we can carry out the action may depend on many things outside our control, including processes in our own body. (I might become paralyzed immediately after willing to perform some action.) I am morally responsible for an act if I will to perform it, even if in fact I find myself unable to perform the act.

How do we know we possess free will? This is again one of the deliverances of common sense, according to Reid. He claims that each of us is immediately aware at certain times of a power to will or not to will an action. Perhaps this awareness is a delusion, but we have no good reason to think that it is. Our belief in free will is in fact a presupposition of our practical lives. We deliberate about whether to perform an act or not to perform an act, assuming we have a real choice. We make promises to other people about what we will do in the future, assuming we have the power to keep those promises. If we did not have free will in the sense of having the power to determine the will, those practices would make no sense. If we have no free will, instead of deliberating about what we should do, we should try to predict what we will do. Instead of promising another person we will do something, we should again try to predict what we will do.

REID'S MORAL PHILOSOPHY

Reid defends the objectivity of morality against two rival accounts that were popular in the eighteenth century. One rival view was the "sentimentalist" view found in Francis Hutcheson and Adam Smith. The sentimentalist saw morality as founded in our human subjective responses. On this account, an evil act is evil because it produces revulsion or disgust in us; a good act is good because it produces feelings of approval. On this view moral judgments are cognitive but grounded in natural facts about humans. The other rival view was the kind of "contract" view associated with Hobbes, in which morality was a kind of agreement made by individuals to further the self-interest of each.

David Hume actually draws on both streams of thought. Like Hutcheson he sees basic moral qualities as grounded in our subjective responses. However, for Hume moral judgments are not genuinely cognitive; they do not state facts. They are not so much *about* our subjective responses as they are *expressions* of those responses. Hume is thus the ancestor of contemporary forms of moral "antirealism" such as expressivism and emotivism. Our moral language, in which we seem to say that moral qualities are objective, results from our human tendency to project our subjective impressions onto the world. Hume sees some of our moral rules, those having to do with justice, in terms of a social contract, one we enter because the agreement is useful or beneficial to all. Hume here speaks of "utility," and this part of his thought had a great influence later on Jeremy Bentham, the founder of utilitarianism.

Against these views, Reid agrees with rationalists such as Richard Price that moral judgments are objective and cognitive. He further agrees with the rationalists that universal moral judgments, such as "lying is morally wrong" are necessarily true, and are known by reason, which is the faculty whereby we understand the relations between ideas. However, particular moral judgments, such as "It was wrong for John to take that tool home and not return it," are contingently true. Such truths follow from a combination of general or universal truths (stealing is wrong) along with particular judgments, such as "this is an instance of stealing." Both kinds of moral judgments are true or false independently of our human subjective responses or any social agreement. Reid is open to the idea that our emotional responses are part of the way we gain knowledge of morality, but he opposes the view that those re-sponses are what make moral actions moral. Rape and murder would not become morally good if human nature became so depraved that we humans found those actions pleasing. Reid's actual normative moral account is unremarkable and unsystematic. He recognizes duties to God, to self, and to others, and mostly of the conventional sort. However, this fits his account that moral knowledge is part of our common human legacy, something that all normal humans have access to.

Reid provides a strong argument for the view that morality is objective and cognitive.[22] The foundation of his argument is an attempt to show that human experience of morality, human action, and human social

---

[22]For a clear account of Reid's views here, see Terence Cuneo, "Reidian Metaethics, Part I and Part II," *Philosophy Compass* 6, no. 5 (2011): 333-49.

interaction all presuppose and depend on the objective reality of morality. A belief in moral objectivity is the best way of accounting for all of these phenomena. For example, Reid points out how we perceive other people as manifesting moral qualities. We recognize some people as kind and generous and others as mean and stingy, just as we recognize some people as clever and witty and others as intellectually slow and oblivious to humor. The perception of moral qualities is no harder than other kinds, and it is hard to see how we could interact with other humans without making such judgments. Reid says that such perceptions are made in the same way as other perceptions, through "natural signs."

Most of these natural signs are learned or acquired signs, and so education and culture play a large role in our acquisition of moral knowledge. However, Reid sees no problem admitting this to be the case, making a comparison with mathematical knowledge. It is clear that education and training are necessary to acquire mathematical knowledge, but no one doubts the objectivity and validity of such knowledge.

Another type of argument is rooted in Reid's view of promise-making and other "speech acts" by which we commit ourselves and place ourselves under obligation. If there was no such thing as objective moral obligation, it would be impossible for us to create moral obligations by making promises. We can hardly put ourselves in a state of obligation if there is no such thing as an obligation.

Reid argues against subjectivist views by pointing out that there is a big difference between moral properties and those properties we attribute to others because of our subjective responses. Everyone recognizes that qualities such as "being popular" or "being well-liked" depend on other people's attitudes. If a politician's poll ratings slump, the politician is no longer popular. However, moral qualities are not like that. If a community becomes racist and approves of cruelty to a minority, that would not change the fact that such behavior is morally wrong.

Reid does not claim that our moral judgments are infallible, and he does not claim that his arguments in favor of moral objectivity constitute a kind of absolute proof. Rather, he places moral knowledge as another of the deliverances of "common sense." This is a kind of knowledge that is present in all normal humans, and thus the default stance should be trust and acceptance. We have the same reason to trust our moral perceptions and intuitions as we have to trust other types of perceptions and intuitions.

REID'S LEGACY

As noted above, Reid's immediate legacy was powerful, especially in America. In the nineteenth century, many liberal arts colleges required a senior-level course, frequently taught by the president, in "moral philosophy," and many of these courses were grounded in commonsense realism inspired by Reid. Much of American theology was shaped by Scottish realism as well, particularly the influential theologians at Princeton Seminary. As American universities began to imitate the German research university rather than the British colleges, this tradition waned. In the twentieth century, the great land-grant state universities became increasingly drawn to this German model, and also increasingly secularized, and the influence of Reid declined.

However, Reid's influence never dropped out entirely. In Scotland views like Reid's continued to be defended by philosophers such as C. A. Campbell. In England G. E. Moore defended a kind of commonsense realism that owed much to Reid, and later "ordinary language philosophers," such as J. L. Austin, continued Reid's careful analysis of linguistic usage as an aid to philosophical insight. In the last fifty years Reid's philosophy of perception has become influential to secular thinkers who are attracted to epistemological externalism. Such thinkers are attracted to Reid because of his stress on finitude, which fits a naturalistic account that stresses continuities between humans and animals. Reid himself was a theist and not a naturalist. His stress on finitude came from an understanding that we are creatures, but creatures of a loving God, whose handiwork can be trusted.

Enlightenment Deism, Jean-Jacques Rousseau, and Mary Wollstonecraft

IN THE NEXT CHAPTER I SHALL CONSIDER the work of Immanuel Kant, perhaps the greatest and most influential of Enlightenment philosophers. However, before moving to Kant, I shall pause to consider some other significant thinkers, some of whom preceded the Enlightenment. These thinkers clearly reflect themes that shaped Kant's thinking.

ENGLISH DEISM

The term *deism* has various senses. Some have used it to designate a view of God as the one who created the universe but who does not actively intervene in the natural world. In this usage deism is contrasted with theism, the view that God not only began the universe but also actively maintains it and is involved with it through his providential guidance. A second sense of deism contrasts it not so much with theism but with "revealed religion." On this view, a deist is someone who defends "natural religion," the idea that the important truths of religion can be known by natural reason, and thus no special revelation is needed. It is this second sense of the term that is mainly relevant to those thinkers called "English deists."

The originator of deism was the seventeenth-century thinker Edward Herbert of Cherbury (1583–1648). Herbert was an aristocrat who wrote *On Truth* and *A Dialogue Between a Tutor and His Pupil*. In these works he defended the claim that true religion is a natural religion that all humans can know through reason. There are five principles of this natural religion, which basically teach that there is a God who should be worshiped, and that true worship of God consists of good moral conduct, which will be the basis for a judgment of humans by God after death. Herbert argues that there is no divinely inspired special revelation, and that Christianity is not superior to other religions such as Islam. Religions that go beyond his five principles are human constructions and are motivated by religious leaders who want to control others and benefit from that control.

Several other English thinkers followed Herbert's lead, including Charles Blount, John Toland and Anthony Collins. Matthew Tindal, whose birth year is uncertain but who died in 1733, published (anonymously) what came to be called "the deists' Bible," *Christianity as Old as Creation, or the Gospel a Republication of the Religion of Nature*, in 1730. This work expresses many characteristic deist themes, purporting to be an attempt to restore an original and pure form of Christianity, while in reality attacking many distinctive Christian doctrines. We find in the deists a curious alternation between attacks on Christianity and attempts to present deism as the true and pure form of Christianity.

Some have tried to enlist Thomas Hobbes, Benedict Spinoza, and even John Locke in the deist camp. Locke, while a rationalist who wanted to check forms of religious "enthusiasm" and tamp down religious violence, certainly was not a deist. Hobbes's own personal religious views are unclear, but his published writings really do not support deism either. Spinoza's writings may have influenced some deists, but his pantheism differs from the views of most of the deists.

Deism as a movement died out in England in the middle of the eighteenth century. However, the ideas of the deists became influential in Germany, in France, and in the United States. Among the founding fathers of the United States, Thomas Paine, Benjamin Franklin, Thomas

Jefferson, and John Adams all seemed clearly seemed sympathetic to deism. The idea that true religion is centered on morality is, as we shall see, one that Immanuel Kant took to heart, and the idea that the doctrines of religion can be supported by reason without appeal to an authoritative revelation also influenced Kant. Although nineteenth-century liberal Protestants in Germany generally avoided the term *deism*, there is certainly similarity to deist themes. Something like deism remains popular among Unitarian Universalist churches in America, and can sometimes be found among those who think of themselves as "spiritual but not religious."

THE FRENCH PHILOSOPHES

Many of the ideas of the English deists were taken up by a group of French thinkers in the eighteenth century who are collectively called the philosophes. These thinkers challenged existing authorities in government, religion, and morality in the name of reason. Their most notable achievement is probably the *Encyclopédie*, edited by Denis Diderot and Jean Le Rond d'Alembert. This epic work ran to thirty-five volumes and was published between 1751 and 1780. The *Encyclopédie* prided itself on its intellectual daring and its willingness to examine established views critically. One of the most important contributors was Voltaire (1694–1778), who explicitly defended what he called deism against both atheism and traditional religious beliefs. Voltaire is probably most famous for *Candide*, in which he satirized Leibniz's view that this is the best of all possible worlds.

The most radical wing of the philosophes went beyond deism to an explicit embrace of mechanistic materialism and atheism. The most well-known of this group was Baron d'Holbach (1722–1789), who denied the existence of God, nonphysical human souls, and even human free will. On d'Holbach's view, since humans are simply physical entities, we are completely controlled by the laws of nature, which dictate how material beings must act at every moment.

The philosophes are often credited or blamed for the convulsion that France underwent beginning in 1789 that we call the French Revolution. Although it is likely that these thinkers would have been horrified by some of the excesses of the revolution, as well as the authoritarianism of Napoleon, it certainly seems true that their critical spirit helped make such an event possible. The triumph of French armies through most of Europe in the years that followed in turn made it possible for these radical French ideas to spread throughout the continent.

JEAN-JACQUES ROUSSEAU

Rousseau was born in Geneva, Switzerland, in 1712, to a middle-class family. His mother died when he was an infant, and his father was exiled from the city when Rousseau was ten, leaving him to be raised by a pastor. His education was haphazard, and he left the city at sixteen. He was helped by a noblewoman, the Baronne de Warens, who arranged for him to travel to Italy, where Rousseau converted to Catholicism. (He later went back to the Calvinism of his native city.) Rousseau considered becoming a priest and for a time made a living as a music copyist. Again with the help of the Baronness, he moved to France, spending time in Lyons and also Paris. Rousseau actually composed some serious music, including a much-performed opera, *Le Devin du Village* (*The Village Soothsayer*). While in France, Rousseau met many of the philosophes, and at first was on friendly terms, but eventually fell out with them. The source of the disagreement is not hard to understand, since the French Enlightenment philosophers were enthusiastic advocates of science and culture, while Rousseau from the beginning saw "civilized" societies as corrupting of individual character.

In terms of family life, Rousseau met an uneducated laundry maid in 1745, Thérèse Levasseur, who became his lover, and whom he eventually married. The woman bore him five children, but all of them were abandoned at a foundling hospital. This very likely meant that the children died, and opponents later cited this failure to take care of his children as evidence of low character.

In 1749 Rousseau found out about an essay contest sponsored by the Academy of Dijon, on the question as to whether the development of the arts and sciences had improved morality or made things worse. According to Rousseau himself, he had an idea for this essay in a flash and submitted an entry arguing that humans are born good but that society is corrupting. This is a sentiment that Rousseau consistently defended throughout his life, memorably expressed in his maxim that "man is born free but is everywhere in chains." His essay won first prize and made Rousseau famous overnight.

Rousseau wrote a second discourse, *Discourse on the Origins of Inequality*, for a different prize. Though he did not win this time, he began to develop his account of human psychology and society. His mature works, for which he is most famous, include a novel, *Julie, or the New Heloise,* and his most important work in political philosophy, *The Social Contract.* Rousseau's thoughts on education are memorably expressed in *Emile.*

The last portion of Rousseau's life was troubled. He was banished from both Paris and Geneva for unorthodox views. He was invited to Scotland by David Hume, and spent some time there. However, the relation with Hume degenerated into a nasty quarrel, and Rousseau by this time seems to have developed paranoid delusions that others were plotting against him. He was also troubled by a quarrel with Voltaire. Rousseau died in 1778, but his remains were put in the Pantheon in Paris after the French Revolution, a tribute to the influence his ideas had on French radicals. Rousseau's posthumously published *Confessions* is a very frank autobiography that by no means always presents Rousseau favorably.

Rousseau's psychology. Rousseau claims that the most basic human instinct is "self-love" (*l'amour de soi*), a drive for preservation, that expresses itself initially as a tendency to attend to basic physiological needs such as food and shelter. He does not see this self-love as bad or evil; in fact originally humans have a capacity to satisfy these basic needs. They are endowed by a good God with what they need. Humans are not completely selfish either, but also have a tendency to feel compassion for others and care about their well-being. In this early "state of nature," humans are free in the sense that they are not slaves of their appetites, and they have the potential to develop into rational and self-conscious beings, as society becomes more complex and social relationships develop. However, these characteristics bring with them in turn very undesirable conditions, including deception, oppression, and domination. Originally, then, humans have a kind of innocence, and the development of society is a kind of "fall." Rousseau thus clearly rejects the Christian idea of original sin in favor of a more Pelagian view that evil is the result of the corrupting effects of society.

In more complex societies humans develop a different form of self-love (*l'amour propre*), which depends on the opinions of others. *L'amour propre*, sometimes translated as "pride" or "vanity," is a much more ambiguous quality, since it leads to endless competition and a struggle for recognition from others, which is connected to attempts to control and dominate others. Although this drive takes very toxic forms in contemporary societies, Rousseau nonetheless attempts to sketch ways to organize society. Rousseau does believe in the potential of reason to discern how humans can live together, but he pessimistically thinks that reason is more often put at the service of dominating and oppressing others. When reason is put to good use, it becomes conscience, a moral quality that goes beyond instinct.

Political philosophy. Rousseau is best known for his political philosophy, which is a form of social contract theory that can usefully be compared with those of Hobbes and Locke. In *The Social Contract* Rousseau tries to describe an ideal society where the oppression and domination prevalent in human societies could be eliminated or at least minimized. Like Locke, Rousseau believes that the legitimacy of the state when it exercises coercive power over the people flows from the citizens of that state.

A key concept in his account is the notion of the "general will." The general will refers to a kind of ideal, a will in which the will of all citizens is included or reflected. Thus, when the state expresses the general will, it does not really limit a person's freedom, even when the person is forced to act in a particular way. Sometimes Rousseau describes this general will in procedural terms as the product of negotiation among the citizens, and sometimes he describes it as a nonexistent ideal, what the citizens *would* will if they truly understood their own best interests. The exercise of power by the sovereign is justified when the sovereign expresses the general will. Paradoxically, the sovereign can "force people to be free" by compelling them to act in accord with their own best interests. (Here some see a totalitarian undertone in Rousseau.)

One thing that is puzzling about Rousseau is that he does not endorse representative government, as does Locke. Rather, he seems to favor a kind of direct democracy in which the citizens as a whole make up the sovereign. Perhaps he was influenced here by his early experiences in the relatively small city of Geneva, since such direct democracy seems unsuited for a large state. Rousseau is fearful of the effects of partisan groups, and he distinguishes the general will from the "will of all," which is something like a sum of the actual wills of everyone. The general will and "will of all" can coincide if people understand their own good and will it, but the two wills can diverge and frequently do.

One troubling issue for Rousseau arises from the combination of two of his beliefs. Rousseau believes that the state cannot work unless the citizens have a degree of virtue. However, in the current corrupt state it does not appear that this is the case. He tries to solve the problem by positing a benevolent legislator who, taking advantage of the plasticity of human nature that Rousseau holds to, will help people become better through good laws. However, it is not clear where the benevolent legislator will come from, and again there is a troubling undertone in which people are forced to do what is for their own good.

Rousseau and the Enlightenment. In some ways Rousseau is a typical Enlightenment figure. Probably the most important themes in Rousseau that helped shape the Enlightenment are his emphases on freedom and his individualism. Rousseau's status as one of the icons of the Enlightenment is symbolized by the fact that Immanuel Kant, the quintessential Enlightenment philosopher, had a picture of Rousseau in his office. In some ways, Kant's admiration for Rousseau is puzzling, since for Kant morality is grounded in pure reason, while Rousseau gives great importance to feeling. However, it is, I believe, Rousseau's commitment to individual freedom that Kant most admired. As we shall see, the concept of individual autonomy plays a central role in Kant's ethics.

Rousseau's distance from traditional Christian faith is another point where he is a characteristically Enlightenment figure. In *Emile* he recounts a tale of a Savoyard vicar that defends a kind of "natural religion" congenial to deism. (This part of the book led to its being censored and Rousseau himself being exiled.) Rousseau's faith in the basic goodness of human nature and his belief in the plasticity of human nature are also shared with most Enlightenment thinkers.

Rousseau's relation to the Enlightenment is ambiguous, however, as illustrated by his stormy relations with the philosophes as well as Hume. Rousseau's pessimistic view of human society, as well as his idea that science and culture have undermined human goodness, are in some ways the antithesis of Enlightenment thinking. It is not surprising, then, that Rousseau will later influence Romantic thinkers, who emphasized feeling over reason.

One area where Rousseau has continued to be influential is in the area of education. *Emile* advocates a kind of "natural education," which is geared to personal development more than the inculcation of information. Although Rousseau knows that it is not possible to go back to the "state of nature," and even says this would not be desirable, there is in his thought a basic faith in the goodness of human nature if it is allowed to develop in a natural and instinctive way. Paradoxically, this faith in what is "natural" is combined with a faith in the plasticity of human nature and the power of social arrangements to bring out what is "natural."

MARY WOLLSTONECRAFT

One glaringly obvious feature of the history of Western philosophy is that it is an overwhelmingly masculine story. This is not surprising, since for most of Western history women were regarded as inferior to men and not given the opportunity for an education. A history of philosophy must focus on the philosophers that have been influential historically, and in the West, that means focusing largely on the work of men, although contemporary philosophers have been engaged in retrieving some of the work of women who were largely overlooked in their own day. One important woman whose work was recognized even in her own time is Mary Wollstonecraft (1759–1797).

Wollstonecraft was a true Enlightenment figure, a contemporary of Kant. Sadly, she died in childbirth when she was only thirty-eight. She was born of a downwardly mobile family, in which her father had dissipated a sizable inheritance. Remarkably, though she had little formal education, her writings reveal a deep knowledge both of many ancient philosophers and some important modern philosophers, such as Locke and Leibniz. Wollstonecraft lived a tumultuous and somewhat scandalous life. As a woman of modest means, she worked at various times as a ladies' companion and a governess. She founded a school, but it was short-lived and financially unstable. During a sojourn in France, she had an affair with an American, and bore him a child, but was crushed when he rejected her, even attempting suicide. After returning to England, she married William Godwin, an equally radical thinker, but died giving birth to their child Mary, later to become famous as Mary Shelley, the author of *Frankenstein; or, The Modern Prometheus* and the wife of the poet Percy Shelley. After Wollstonecraft's death, Godwin wrote a controversial and very frank account of her life, one that doubtless harmed her reputation during that period, though that was almost certainly not Godwin's intention.

Wollstonecraft is best known for two works: *A Vindication of the Rights of Men, in a Letter to the Right Honourable Edmund Burke*, and *A Vindication of the Rights of Woman with Strictures on Political and Moral Subjects*. The former, as the latter part of the title hints, is largely a critique of Edmund Burke, who had famously written a memorable attack on the French Revolution, in which he had (correctly) predicted that the revolution would devolve into anarchy, which would in turn lead to despotism. Burke saw the French Revolution as a dangerous attempt to reshape society in accordance with abstract rational principles, and he defended the idea that social changes should be gradual and ought to take account of the history and culture of the region. Wollstonecraft responded by arguing that Burke was simply rationalizing a society that was unjust, in which inherited rank and fortune prevented most people from fully realizing their rights. She saw those rights, in a fashion that showed the influence of Locke, as God-given endowments, and she argued that governments ought to be assessed on their ability to protect those rights and advance the common good. Interestingly, in some of her later writings, Wollstonecraft moved somewhat closer to Burke's view, because she came to see that the inequality and oppression created by a free-market system could be even worse than the kind of inequality based on inherited rank and status. She became increasingly critical of what we today would call a "consumerist" society.

A Vindication of the Rights of Woman is certainly Wollstonecraft's most-discussed work. In some ways the book seems somewhat old-fashioned now, in that her argument for women's equality is grounded in the view that the family is the basis of society. Wollstonecraft argues that women could not be good wives and mothers without being given the opportunity to become educated and enjoy the full rights of citizenship. So her argument for the empowerment of women is not based fundamentally on what is best for women but what is best for society, though she also argues that the reforms she calls for would advance the happiness of women. Wollstonecraft argues that the institution of marriage as it existed in her society was fundamentally unjust to women. Marriage ought to be based on friendship and equality, but marriage in her society viewed women as property.

Wollstonecraft's views have received more attention in the late twentieth century than they did in her own time. Her defense of women's rights as beneficial to marriage was undermined in her own era by her own tumultuous life, in which she had a child out of wedlock. However, she is now recognized as a pioneer in defending the full humanity of women, although some contemporary feminists have actually criticized her for defending women in terms of supposedly "male" values. However, she is a perfect exemplar of Enlightenment thinking, measuring her society by rational standards, and she anticipates by several centuries the thinking of what we today call "liberal feminism."

Immanuel Kant

IMMANUEL KANT IS A TOWERING FIGURE in the history of modern Western philosophy. He is in many ways the preeminent figure of the Enlightenment, and is undoubtedly the most important German philosopher. Kant in fact wrote an essay called "What Is Enlightenment" and memorably answered the question by asserting that to be enlightened was "to dare to use your own reason." Kant was himself the product of the European rationalist tradition, a student of a disciple of Christian Wolff, who was himself a disciple of Leibniz. Yet Kant was also deeply influenced by British empiricism, particularly through the writings of David Hume.

Kant was born in 1724 and lived until 1804, and during all of those eighty years resided in what was then the German city of Königsberg in East Prussia. (The city is no longer part of Germany, but is now called Kaliningrad and is part of Russia, though geographically isolated from the rest of Russia.) Kant's family were devout Lutherans of a pietist persuasion, and this upbringing left a permanent mark on Kant, as we shall see. Kant studied at the University of Königsberg, absorbing rationalist metaphysics but was also deeply impressed by Newtonian science. After working as a tutor for a few years, he became a lecturer at the university, and in 1770 he succeeded his old professor Martin Knutzen as professor of philosophy. Kant never married, but had many friends. There is a legend that the people of the city could set their watches by Kant, who took a walk from his house at precisely 4:30 p.m. each day. Whether this story is true or not, it is undoubtedly the case that Kant was a disciplined scholar who worked very hard, as shown by the large number of long, difficult, and influential books he published.

The most famous of these works are his three monumental "critiques." His *Critique of Pure Reason* was published in 1781, with a second, significantly changed edition in 1787. The *Critique of Practical Reason* appeared in 1788, while the *Critique of Judgment* came out in 1790. A shorter attempt to summarize the first *Critique, Prolegomena to Any Future Metaphysics*, was published in 1783. To these works Kant added a number of very influential works in moral philosophy, such as the *Groundwork of the Metaphysics of Morals* (1785) and the *Metaphysics of Morals* (1797), as well as a hugely important work in the philosophy of religion, *Religion Within the Bounds of Mere Reason* (1793). Kant also wrote important books about the philosophy of science and about social and political issues, such as *Perpetual Peace* (1795). Kant's concern with war and peace is shown in an earlier essay in which he proposed a "League of Nations" to bring about an end to war. (Many of these books have been translated several times, and the English titles often vary.)

KANT'S ATTEMPT TO RECONCILE
SCIENCE, MORALITY, AND RELIGION

Before plunging into the details of Kant's often complicated philosophy, it is important to have a sense of Kant's overall aims. As a man of the Enlightenment, Kant was fully committed to science and a scientific picture of the world, and he regarded Newtonian physics as the height of intellectual achievements. Although Kant esteemed Newton highly, he nonetheless thought that Newtonian physics required an adequate philosophical foundation. Without such a foundation, science itself was vulnerable to skeptical challenges, such as the challenge Hume's philosophy of causation posed. So one of Kant's main aims could be summarized as the vindication of Newtonian science. Kant believed that science was dependent on such key concepts as substance and causation, which had been undermined by the philosophy of Berkeley and Hume. He also was convinced that a better philosophical account of the mathematics that was clearly foundational to Newtonian science was necessary.

However, Kant was also fully aware of the threat that Newton's mechanistic physics seemed to pose to morality and religion. Newton himself did not see things this way, but was fully committed to a religious understanding of the universe. However, many thinkers of the eighteenth century had moved, as we saw in the last chapter, to a deistic or even openly materialistic view of the universe, and such a worldview seemed to leave little room for human freedom or God. Kant wanted to find a way to do justice to science that left room for the kind of human freedom he saw as essential to morality. He also wanted to find a justification for religious beliefs that would be independent of the claims of natural science and thus not vulnerable to refutation by science. Although Kant in his mature years did not regularly attend church services, he remained deeply religious and deeply concerned about religious questions.

The solution was to link religion to morality. However, for this to work, morality itself had to be rescued from the threat of mechanism. Kant memorably describes his philosophy as an attempt to "deny *knowledge*, in order to make room for *faith*."[1] His meaning was that the attempt to ground morality and religion in metaphysical claims is a failure, but that this failure is actually a blessing. If we have a clear understanding of the limits of theoretical reason (reason that is employed to understand the world scientifically), we will see that this reason cannot provide a foundation for morality and religion, but also that it cannot be a threat or problem for them.

---

[1]Immanuel Kant, *Critique of Pure Reason*, trans. Norman Kemp Smith, 2nd ed. (London: Macmillan, 2007), B xxx, p. 29. For those unfamiliar with Kant scholarship, scholars denote the different editions of the *Critique* with "A" and "B," for the first and second editions, respectively. All page numbers following text locators in this chapter correspond to the edition of the work first cited.

KANT'S RELATION TO EMPIRICISM AND RATIONALISM

As noted before, Kant began his philosophical career as a rationalist in the tradition of Leibniz, relying on reason to demonstrate the existence of God and other important truths. Kant himself credits the "recollection of David Hume" as the "very thing which many years ago first interrupted my dogmatic slumber" and gave his philosophical thought "a quite new direction."[2] Kant's own conclusions are radically different from Hume's, but he credits Hume as the person who first clearly stated the problems that philosophy must solve. Hume was "the acute man to whom we owe the first spark of light."[3]

It is clear that what first moved Kant here was Hume's critical treatment of the concept of cause and effect, a concept Kant saw as essential for science. Hume had shown that one could not derive an adequate concept of cause and effect from experience. Kant concluded from this that the concept must be one that is a priori, one that is not derived from experience but that "sprang from the pure understanding."[4] Kant then claims that the concept of cause and effect was just one of a number of a priori concepts that the understanding employs to make sense of the world. The key to resolving the problems of metaphysics lay in a careful investigation of these a priori concepts. Through such an investigation Kant proposes to establish whether metaphysics is possible at all, and, if it is, what kind of metaphysics can be rationally justified. As we will see, Kant hopes to show that there is such a thing as a priori knowledge, and that this knowledge provides the necessary foundations for natural science. However, Kant believes that this metaphysical knowledge cannot give us insight

---

[2]Immanuel Kant, *Prolegomena to Any Future Metaphysics*, trans. Paul Carus (Indianapolis: Bobbs-Merrill, 1950), introduction, 260, 8. Most English translations of Kant include in the margins the pagination of the standard German edition of Kant, called the Akademie edition. This allows the English reader to compare English translations easily. When two numbers are given in this chapter, the first number refers to this German edition, while the latter page number refers to the English cited source.

[3]Kant, *Prolegomena*, 260, 8.

[4]Kant, *Prolegomena*, 260, 8.

into reality that goes beyond what humans can experience. Metaphysical knowledge as knowledge of transcendent realities that go beyond any possible experience is impossible.

Kant thus proposes a kind of synthesis of rationalism and empiricism. The rationalist is correct in claiming that there is such a thing as a priori knowledge. However, the empiricist is correct in claiming that our knowledge cannot give us any insight into realities, such as God and an immortal soul, that transcend the limits of experience. The synthesis rests on an understanding that "though all our knowledge begins with experience, it does not follow that it all arises out of experience."[5] Humans do have pure, a priori knowledge that is not derived from experience. However, this knowledge is strictly limited and does not give us the kind of theoretical grasp of transcendent reality that earlier metaphysicians had aspired to.

KANT'S "CRITICAL PHILOSOPHY"

For Kant, like his early modern predecessors, philosophy is in need of a method that will put it on a sure path. Descartes had attempted to give philosophy a sure ground through a method of universal doubt. Spinoza had attempted to do philosophy by rigorously following the method of geometry. Locke had proposed to resolve religious and political controversies by developing an empiricist epistemology that would certify what we really know and what we can rationally believe. Hume believed that philosophical disagreements largely stem from lack of conceptual clarity, and had proposed a method of tracing ideas back to the "impressions" that gave rise to the ideas, thereby clarifying those ideas and providing a way to resolve, and in some cases dissolve, philosophical disputes.

Kant's own view about the proper method of philosophy has two important elements: for him philosophy must be rooted in a "critique" of reason itself, and it must radically change its view of the relation between thought and reality, a change that is usually called Kant's

---

[5]Kant, *Critique of Pure Reason*, B 1, p. 41.

"Copernican revolution." In this section I shall discuss the first idea, and in the next explain the second.

The idea of "critique" is obviously central to Kant, as its appearance in the titles of three of his greatest works makes plain. Kant's philosophy is often called "the critical philosophy." In some ways, Kant is simply following the plan laid out by Locke, who claimed that before resolving first-order disagreements in ethics or religion or metaphysics we must first get clear as to what humans can know and how they know it. Epistemology, and not metaphysics, thus becomes "first philosophy."[6] However, Kant does not think empiricist philosophers like Locke and Hume, with their focus on sense experience, had fully grasped the importance of *reason* in the acquisition of knowledge. Kant thus thinks that what is crucial is a critique of the powers of reason itself, so as to determine what can be known a priori (independently of experience), what can be known a posteriori (on the basis of experience), and what cannot be known at all.

It is easy to see the appeal of this attempt to secure a method that would resolve philosophical disputes once and for all. Kant, like Locke, thinks that in order to resolve the basic questions humans disagree about we must first figure out how we come to know what we know, and thus what it is possible to know. The problem with this idea is that there is no guarantee that agreement will be any easier to achieve in epistemology (about what is the proper method for philosophy to follow) than in any other area of philosophy. It may well be true that metaphysical and ethical claims implicitly depend on epistemological assumptions, but it may equally be true that epistemological claims depend on metaphysical assumptions about human nature. For example, it seems plausible that epistemology must make assumptions about the rational faculties we have and how they work.

Kant's vision of a critique of reason raises a particularly difficult problem that can be posed using the framework of Thomas Reid. From

---

[6]See the discussion of Locke in chap. 14.

what standpoint is the critique of reason to be carried out? What tool or instrument shall we use? It looks like the only possible tool we can use is reason itself. In that case it does not seem reasonable to claim that reason is somehow unreliable until we have given it a critical evaluation. The reason this is so is that if reason is not reliable, there is no reason to think the critique of reason we carry out using reason will be reliable. So even to engage in a critique of reason, some kind of faith in the reliability of reason must be assumed.[7]

This may not be fatal to Kant's project. Kant might agree that we have no choice but to begin with some degree of faith in the power of reason. However, Reid would then raise a question about why we should not extend this same trust to our other human faculties. If we begin with trust in reason, why should we not trust perception, memory, and other human cognitive faculties? As Reid says, "they came out of the same shop."[8] Reid of course thinks that all these cognitive faculties are gifts from God, but even atheists should agree that our faculties are all the products of the same process. If beginning with faith or trust is reasonable for one of our faculties, why not for others?

The issue of Kant's relation to Reid and commonsense philosophy is actually important. Kant himself begins his *Prolegomena* with a slam at Reid. Kant says that Reid and the other opponents of Hume "should have penetrated very deeply into the nature of reason, so far as it is concerned with pure thinking—a task which did not suit them. They found a more convenient method of being defiant without any insight, namely, the appeal to *common sense*. . . . To appeal to common sense when insight and science fail, and no sooner—this is one of the subtle [*sic*] discoveries of modern times, by means of which the most superficial ranter can safely enter the lists with the most thorough thinker and

---

[7]There is a parallel here to the problem of the "vicious circle" in Descartes (see chap. 12). Descartes appears to say that he must prove God's existence in order to show there is no evil demon, and therefore that he can rely on his reason. However, it is obvious that if reason is not reliable, then the proof of God cannot be relied on. So Descartes must assume the viability of reason.

[8]Thomas Reid, *An Inquiry*, in *Thomas Reid's Inquiry and Essays*, ed. Ronald Beanblossom and Keith Lehrer (Indianapolis: Hackett, 1983), 85.

hold his own."[9] This passage actually reveals Kant's failure to understand what Reid meant by "common sense." If Kant himself must begin with a basic trust or faith in our human cognitive faculties, then his own view is actually far closer to Reid's than Kant himself realized.[10] My own suspicion is that the difference between Kant and Reid reflected in this passage shows that Kant, unlike Reid, still aspires to the kind of epistemological certainty that classical foundationalism sought. Reid was, as we have seen, a fallibilist who cheerfully accepted the fact that our human faculties are liable to error, and he does not seek any kind of absolute foundation for knowledge or think that such a foundation is necessary. Kant, as we shall see, still thinks that human knowledge, including scientific knowledge, requires some kind of foundation that is completely certain.

KANT'S "COPERNICAN REVOLUTION"

How are we to obtain this certain knowledge? Kant agrees with Hume that empirical knowledge can never be absolutely certain. Experience provides knowledge of contingent facts, but it cannot tell us what is true universally or what is true necessarily. One can observe an apple falling from a tree, but one cannot through experience come to know that gravity operates as a universal law. Experience can tell us what happens, but it cannot tell us that what happens is something that must happen. Knowledge of what is universal and necessary must therefore be a priori in character.

We have seen that modern philosophers, beginning with Descartes and Locke, have (with the exception of Reid) mostly been representationalists, who have accepted the assumption that we have no direct

---

[9]Kant, *Prolegomena*, 259-60, 6-8.

[10]Interestingly, one of the leading Kant scholars, Karl Ameriks, has argued that Kant is in fact a commonsense philosopher who is close to Reid. Kant begins, like Reid, by *assuming* that humans have knowledge and that our basic faculties are reliable. Kant then goes on to ask how it is possible that we gain this knowledge. Ameriks argues that the critical passage on commonsense philosophy quoted above actually is directed at German followers of Reid, who did not really understand the Scottish thinker. See Karl Ameriks, "A Commonsense Kant?," *Proceedings and Addresses of the American Philosophical Association* 79, no. 2 (2005): 19-45.

experience of external reality, but are directly aware only of "ideas" or "impressions," mental entities that represent that world to us. The problem immediately arises as to how we can ever know that our mental representations accurately give us knowledge of external reality, a difficulty that Berkeley's philosophy makes very clear. Reid, as we have seen, tries to solve the problem by giving up representationalism in favor of a direct realism in which we perceive and remember external realities directly.

Kant's solution is entirely different. He proposes what he calls a "Copernican revolution" in how we view the problem. Instead of assuming that there is an objective, mind-independent reality, and asking how our ideas can accurately represent that reality, Kant proposes that in certain respects reality must conform to the way we represent it. Instead of assuming that our concepts must conform to objects, we should assume that objects must conform to certain of our concepts. Kant believes that the human understanding "has rules which I must presuppose as being in me prior to objects being given to me, and therefore as being *a priori*."[11] Copernicus had revolutionized astronomy by proposing that the Sun is the center of the solar system rather than the Earth. The Earth revolves around the Sun, rather than the Sun revolving around the Earth. Kant's philosophical revolution is equally radical but really could be called an anti-Copernican revolution. Copernicus had decentered the Earth as the home of humans, making it just another planet. Kant, on the other hand, wants to look at external objects as knowable because they must conform to the human understanding. The human mind becomes the center of the intellectual universe.

Kant's view is often illustrated by analogies of various kinds. Suppose that you are wearing rose-colored sunglasses. You can know in a kind of a priori way that whatever you see will have a rose-colored tint, at least until you take off the sunglasses. If one is viewing a black-and-white screen and sees a man wearing a tie, one can know a priori that the tie

---

[11]Kant, *Critique of Pure Reason*, B xvii, p. 23.

will be black, white, or some shade of grey. This will be true regardless of what color the tie is in reality. The black-and-white screen is not capable of representing the tie in any other way. In a similar way, Kant thinks that we can know a priori that the world we experience and know will have certain characteristics, because our minds can only represent that world in certain ways. It is obvious that we cannot "take off" our minds as we might be able to remove a pair of sunglasses, and so we can know some things for certain about the world. That knowledge will be a priori in a stronger sense than is the case for the sunglasses or the black-and-white screen, since we have no alternative to using the cognitive equipment we have.

For Kant, this a priori knowledge gives us the universal and necessary truths that are necessary to provide a proper foundation for science. However, a worry about this solution may occur pretty quickly. It may well be that when we are wearing the rose-colored glasses we can know that the world we see will be rose-colored. But we may still wonder whether the actual world is really like the world we see. Our "a priori" knowledge only tells us how the world will appear to us when we are wearing the glasses, and that appearance may be different from the way the actual world really is. Similarly, on Kant's view, we can know a priori that the world will appear to us in certain ways, because that is the only way our minds can represent that world. But how do we know that the actual world is the way it appears to us?

For reasons that will become clear, Kant does not see this as a problem. He accepts that our scientific knowledge of the world, based on our experience of the world, is only knowledge of how the world appears to us, not necessarily how it is in reality. To use Kant's own language, science only gives us knowledge of the "phenomenal world," the world as it appears to us, but does not give us knowledge of the "noumenal world," the world as it is in itself. So if Kant's account of a priori knowledge is successful, the knowledge made possible will only be a knowledge of appearances. Some would say this is a heavy price to pay, and in fact is itself a form of skepticism. However, Kant thinks that this limitation to our knowledge is actually good.

KANT'S TECHNICAL TERMINOLOGY

Up until the eighteenth century, the great modern philosophers in the West had not been university professors, but made their livings as diplomats or lens grinders or lawyers or physicians. The exception is Thomas Reid, who taught philosophy at two universities. However, even Reid had been a pastor for many years before becoming a professor. With Kant philosophy becomes a profession. Like all professions, this comes with both benefits and costs. The benefits include the rigor that Kant develops in his arguments and views. The costs include a technical terminology, something that just about every profession requires. To be sure, earlier philosophers also had a specialized language and defined certain terms in technical ways. However, the linguistic machinery Kant employs is much more complicated and wide-ranging than that of his predecessors. To understand the details of Kant's philosophy, then, we have no choice but to explain some of that technical terminology.

The first important distinction is between what Kant calls "the transcendent" and the "transcendental." Kant uses the term *transcendent* to refer to entities that cannot be experienced; they go beyond any possible human experience. He has in mind here such traditional metaphysical entities as God and the soul, and he tries to show we cannot have knowledge of such things. The "transcendental," in contrast, does not refer to some entity that transcends experience but a condition or state of some entity that is *presupposed* by all of experience. We *can* describe and gain knowledge of what is transcendental. As an example, to be discussed in the next section, space and time are transcendental, because they are presupposed by experience and necessary for experience.

Next, I shall explain how Kant describes the powers or faculties of the human mind. Human reason can be used both theoretically, so as to gain knowledge, and practically, as a source of action. (We shall later discuss practical reason when looking at Kant's ethics.) When we seek knowledge, and thus use reason theoretically, there are three powers the mind possesses. The first is "intuition," which is the power to receive sensory representations of the world, as when we see or hear or touch things. The part of Kant's philosophy that deals with intuition is termed the "transcendental aesthetic." It is transcendental in that Kant seeks what is universal and necessary for experience, and it is aesthetic in the sense that it involves sensations. (The Greek root of the word *aesthetic* has as its root meaning something like "sensation.")

The second important power the mind possesses is "understanding," which is the power to form judgments about the world by applying concepts to the sensations we receive. The part of Kant's philosophy devoted to describing what is universal and necessary when we form judgments is called the "transcendental analytic." The third and final important faculty is "reason," in a narrow sense. (Kant also sometimes uses reason in a broader sense to refer to all the powers of the human mind.) In the narrow sense, reason is the power to make inferences, to see how judgments are logically related. It is by reason that we see that some judgments logically imply other judgments, and that some judgments are logically presupposed by others. The part of Kant's philosophy that looks at reason in this narrow sense is called the "transcendental dialectic."

Another important distinction Kant makes is one I have already been employing, the distinction between what is known a priori, not on the basis of experience, and what is known a posteriori, on the basis of experience. Literally the Latin terms mean "prior to" and "posterior to," but this meaning is somewhat misleading. We actually do not know anything prior to experience, but nonetheless, some of what we know is not known on the basis of experience. As already said, the marks of a priori knowledge are universality and necessity, since these are characteristics that cannot be derived from experience.

In order to distinguish Kant's view from Hume's one more distinction must be made, and that is the distinction between a judgment or proposition that is "analytic" and one that is "synthetic." An analytic proposition is one whose truth or falsity is purely a function of the meaning of its terms. As Kant puts it, in an analytic proposition the predicate is in some way already "contained" in the subject, and the proposition makes this clear by providing an analysis of the subject. Standard examples would be "a brother is a male sibling" and "a vixen is a female fox." Kant himself gives "all bodies are extended" as a standard example of an analytic proposition, since the notion of extension is already implicitly contained in the concept of a body.[12] However, the proposition that "all bodies are heavy" is synthetic, even if it should turn out to be universally and necessarily true, since the concept of weight is not part of the concept of a body.

KANT AND HUME

We can now compare Kant's classification of the kinds of human knowledge with that of Hume. Hume, it will be recalled, had said that all propositions are either "matters of fact" or "relations of ideas." All claims about reality, including scientific claims, are matters of fact for Hume. A matter of fact can be recognized from the fact that its denial is always logically possible. "The sun will rise tomorrow" is a matter of fact, since there is no contradiction involved in conceiving the possibility that "the sun will not rise tomorrow." Relations of ideas for Hume are demonstrable or provable, but that is because they make no claims about reality; their truth or falsity simply reflects the meanings of our terms. The negation of a true relation of ideas will always be self-contradictory or will imply a self-contradiction. Importantly, Hume thinks that mathematical truths are examples of "relations of ideas."

For Kant, Hume's classification of propositions that can be known into matters of fact and relations of ideas is too simple. Some of the propositions Hume calls relations of ideas, such as "a brother is a male sibling," Kant describes as analytic propositions. With respect to such

---

[12]Kant, *Critique of Pure Reason*, A 7 / B 11, p. 48.

analytic propositions, Hume and Kant agree that they are a priori in character. There is also agreement about many of the propositions Hume calls matters of fact, propositions such as "men are on average taller than women." Kant describes such propositions as synthetic and a posteriori. Both Hume and Kant agree that such propositions cannot be known simply by understanding the meanings of the terms; they must be known on the basis of experience. So, using Kant's language, Hume and Kant agree that there are analytic propositions that are a priori and synthetic propositions that are a posteriori.

The disagreement between Hume and Kant revolves around the question as to whether there are any knowable propositions that are both synthetic and a priori. Such propositions would not be knowable simply on the basis of knowing the meanings of the terms, since the predicate is not derivable simply from the subject. However, unlike what Hume says about relations of ideas, synthetic, a priori propositions would tell us meaningful truths about reality, truths that hold necessarily and with universality. The key to understanding Kant's critical philosophy then is to see how synthetic, a priori knowledge is possible.

We can summarize Kant's view using table 1.

Table 1. Kant's and Hume's classification of human knowledge

	Synthetic Propositions	Analytic Propositions
a posteriori	YES (both Hume and Kant)	NO (both Hume and Kant)
a priori	NO (Hume) YES (Kant)	YES (both Hume and Kant)

The disagreement between Hume and Kant concerns the lower left-hand box. Both agree that there are a priori analytic propositions, and both agree that there are no analytic propositions that are a posteriori. They also agree that there are synthetic propositions that are a posteriori. Hume rejects the claim that there is such a thing as synthetic a priori knowledge, while Kant believes such knowledge is actual and provides the foundations for mathematics and natural science.

THE TRANSCENDENTAL ANALYTIC:
KANT'S VIEW OF MATHEMATICS, SPACE, AND TIME

Kant thinks Hume went wrong in his account of mathematical knowledge. Hume claims that mathematical truths are simply "relations of ideas," propositions whose truth depends solely on the meanings of their terms. In Kant's language, Hume saw mathematical propositions as analytic and not synthetic. However, Kant argues that this is a mistake. The basic truths of arithmetic and geometry are not analytic but synthetic. It is true that the propositions of mathematics are a priori. This can be seen from the fact that "they carry with them necessity, which cannot be obtained from experience."[13] However, Kant argues that Hume mistakenly thought that mathematical propositions were analytic because of this a priori character. It might seem that $7 + 5 = 12$ is analytic and can be derived simply from the law of noncontradiction. However, Kant says that this is false. "The concept of the sum of $7 + 5$ contains merely their union in a single number, without its being at all thought what the particular number is that unites them."[14] The proposition is thus synthetic. Similarly, Kant claims that the principles of geometry are synthetic as well. Mathematical propositions give us new information; they do not merely unpack the meanings of words, as Hume thought. Kant says that the concepts of mathematics must be "constructed," and that what makes it possible for the mind to construct these concepts is a special kind of intuition.

Kant's method here is "transcendental." That is, he is not trying to justify mathematical knowledge. Rather, he assumes we have such knowledge, and asks how it is possible. What kind of intuition underlies mathematical knowledge? How is "pure mathematics" possible?

It is clear, and Kant has already asserted this, that mathematics cannot be based on ordinary, empirical intuitions, or sense experiences. The proposition that "$7 + 5 = 12$" is not an empirical generalization. It

---

[13]Kant, *Prolegomena*, preamble, §2, p. 268, pp. 15-16.
[14]Kant, *Prolegomena*, preamble, §2, p. 268, p. 16.

would not be falsified if someone tried to count 7 things and then 5 things and counted them as 13. Rather, we know a priori that if someone did this, that person would have miscounted. Similarly, we know a priori that all triangles have three sides. Since mathematical propositions are a priori what makes them possible must be a kind of pure, a priori intuition. But how are such intuitions possible?

Kant explains this by a bold claim about the foundations of geometry and arithmetic. I shall start with geometry. What makes geometry possible is that we have an a priori intuition of the character of space. We can know without any empirical investigation that the straightest distance between two points will always be a straight line because we have a pure intuition into the character of space. We have this intuition because space is not an objective feature of the world we experience. Rather, space is "nothing but the form of all appearances of outer sense."[15] We can know a priori what the character of space is because space is just the way our minds organize the representations we receive from the "outer world." We can know a priori that all the representations we receive from the world will be organized spatially, as well as something about the nature of those representations, because space is not something that "exists of itself," but is simply the way our minds necessarily receive the representations we get from the external world.

Here it is helpful to remember the analogy of the rose-colored sunglasses. If you have such sunglasses on, you can know in advance that everything you see will have a rose-colored tint. Similarly, if you have a human mind, you will necessarily organize all experiences of the outer world spatially. Since the mind itself is the source of space, the mind can know a priori both the nature of space and that anything we come to know outside of our own minds will have a spatial character.

Kant gives a similar account of our knowledge of arithmetic. Just as geometry is made possible by an a priori intuition of the character

[15]Kant, *Critique of Pure Reason*, A 26 / B 42, p. 71.

of space, so arithmetic is made possible by an a priori intuition of the character of time. As space is the "form of outer sense" so time is the "form of inner sense."[16] The key concept in arithmetic, on Kant's view, is the concept of succession, and so our grasp of time is what enables us to have a knowledge of the necessary truths of arithmetic. Everything we experience that comes from "outer sense" is organized spatially, but temporality is a necessary feature both of outer sense and of our awareness of our own mental happenings. It follows from this that humans can only experience what is temporally organized; time is a necessary condition of *all* human experience. Everything we experience that is external to the mind is both temporally and spatially organized.

These are certainly bold and surprising claims. Newton and his followers had conceived of space as a kind of container in which all physical objects exist, and time as an objective feature of nature. Both Leibniz and Berkeley had challenged such a view, seeing space and time as fundamentally relational in character rather than as objective realities. Kant saw space and time not as fundamental features of a reality that exists independently of human knowledge, but as the forms of intuition that the mind provides to organize its experiences. It follows that the spatio-temporal world we come to know through experience is not the world as it is in itself; it is the world as it appears to us. A person who is wearing sunglasses can remove them, but we have no way to "take off" the fundamental forms of intuition by which we organize our experience. We have no knowledge of "noumenal reality," reality as it really is independently of us, but only knowledge of phenomenal reality, reality as it appears to us. For Kant this outcome is not skepticism, for the phenomenal world is in one way objective. It is the same for all of us, since we all have the same a priori intuitions and the "forms" of experience are universal.

---

[16]Kant, *Critique of Pure Reason*, A 33 / B 49, p. 76.

THE TRANSCENDENTAL ANALYTIC:
THE A PRIORI FOUNDATIONS OF PHYSICS

We have already noted that it was Hume's treatment of cause and effect that woke Kant from his "dogmatic slumber." Kant thought that if Newtonian physics was genuine science (and that was indeed his view), then it required a foundation of truths that were universal and necessary. Such truths must therefore, like the propositions of mathematics, be synthetic but also a priori. Such truths would provide a "pure science of nature" that would give physics a secure foundation. (It is clear from this that Kant still aspires to the kind of classical foundationalist epistemology seen in Descartes and Locke, in which the foundations of knowledge are certain.) For Kant, this synthetic a priori knowledge requires synthetic, a priori concepts.

Of course many of the concepts that we employ to characterize the natural world are empirical concepts, derived from experience, as Hume thought. We know what it means to say that sugar is sweet because we have tasted the sweetness of sugar. However, concepts such as "sweet" and "warm" seem subjective in nature. The room may feel warm to me but not to others. The sugar will not taste sweet if my taste buds are in an abnormal state. Such judgments are mere "judgments of perception," subjectively valid only. In order for a perception to become experience, such empirical concepts must be "subsumed" under a pure, a priori concept of the understanding. Such concepts as that of cause and effect and substance, which the empiricists had such difficulty making sense of, are precisely the pure concepts that are required.

The concept of sugar as a substance is also empirical, but it is not purely empirical, as is the case for sweetness. In order to perceive a lump of sugar as "sugar," an enduring physical object, not only must we think of the sugar as a collection of subjective sensations, but we must rather think of all those qualities as inhering in a "substance." Such a substance is an objective part of nature. The concept of sugar thus presupposes an a priori concept, that of substance. Empiricists such as Locke were mistaken to think that the concept of substance can be derived from a sensation. It is rather a pure, a priori concept.

The concept of "cause and effect" is also an a priori concept. What Kant saw as Hume's skeptical treatment of causality stemmed from a failure to realize that not all concepts are empirical in origin. Kant thinks that such a priori concepts are in some way implicit in or presupposed by many of our empirical concepts, and they make it possible for us to conceive of nature as an objective system.

Where do we get these a priori concepts? Kant says that, like space and time (the forms of intuition), these concepts are derived from the mind itself. In this case it is the understanding, that human faculty whereby we make judgments about the world, that does the work. Kant calls these pure concepts the "categories of the understanding." We can know a priori that whatever we experience will be temporally organized because that is the only way our minds can organize our experiences. In a similar way, we can know a priori that certain concepts, the categories of the understanding, apply to all of nature, because our minds have a determinate structure. There are only a finite number of types of possible judgments that humans can make; corresponding to each of the types of possible judgments there is an a priori concept.

Kant affirms that there are exactly twelve types of logical judgments that we can make, with those twelve logical types grouped into four groups of three.[17] He basically takes this list of types of logical judgments from traditional, Aristotelian logic. For example, one of the groups of three concerns "relations." We can make a "categorical judgment," as when we affirm that "x is y." But we can also make a hypothetical judgment: "If x then y." Finally, we can make a disjunctive judgment: "Either x or y." Corresponding to the first of these (categorical judgments) is the concept of substance; if we say "x is y" we are saying that there is some underlying stuff that connects x and y. Corresponding to the second, or hypothetical form of judgment, is the

---

[17]Kant, *Prolegomena*, chap. 2, §21, pp. 302-3, pp. 50-51.

concept of causality. It is our ability to judge that "if x happens, then y will happen" that gives rise to the concept of cause and effect. The third type of judgment in this group (disjunction) gives rise to the category of community.

Kant claims there are twelve of these synthetic, a priori concepts, with each corresponding to one of the forms of logical judgment. Kant thereby claims to have solved the problem of how synthetic, a priori knowledge of nature is possible, and to have shown just what such knowledge consists of. It must be confessed, however, that it is not always easy to understand just how Kant derives these categories from the logical table of judgments. There are also doubts about whether we can know that the list of types of logical judgments Kant gives is really exhaustive. Is it not possible, for example, that different cultures employing different languages might categorize the world in different ways? Kant simply assumes that human reason in all times and places is the same.

When we make judgments what we are doing is "uniting representations in one consciousness."[18] For this uniting to produce representations that are more than "subjective or accidental," we need rules or principles that govern the uniting. The logical principles of judgments are what make it possible to go beyond a merely subjective uniting. The categories derived from these possible ways of thinking about the world give us a kind of understanding of how the world must be. They give us the pure, foundational knowledge that physics requires and allow us to make judgments that are "objectively valid."[19] They provide us with "universal laws of nature, which can be known *a priori*."[20] This provides, Kant thinks, a solution to the problem of induction that vexed Hume. We can know a priori that whatever happens will be connected to other events as causes and effects, and that whatever qualities we observe will be qualities that are owned by substances, enduring objects. In addition

---

[18]Kant, *Prolegomena*, chap. 2, §22, p. 304, p. 52.
[19]Kant, *Prolegomena*, chap. 2, §23, p. 306, p. 53.
[20]Kant, *Prolegomena*, chap. 2, §23, p. 306, p. 53.

to the concepts of substance and cause, Kant includes in the list of the categories such concepts as quantity and quality.

We could summarize Kant's view here in the following way: Knowledge of the external world is not made possible simply by receiving sensations. Rather, knowledge requires the active contributions of the mind. Knowledge of the world requires that I possess a concept of an objective world that is independent of me, and thus is distinct from me. Paradoxically, that objective world is partly made possible by the activity of the mind itself, which distinguishes what is objective and universal from what is subjective by a priori principles.

Is Kant's view a form of idealism? It might seem so since it looks like the world as we know it is at least partly the result of the mind's activity. As we shall see in the next chapter, some of Kant's successors thought that his views did indeed logically lead to idealism. Kant himself claims that he is a "transcendental idealist" but an "empirical realist." From the point of view of experience, the world is objective and independent of us. Kant claims his view is quite different from Berkeley's. The world is, we might say, empirically real. Kant himself stresses that there is such a thing as "noumenal reality," reality that exists independently of us, and that this reality is the source of the representations that come to us from outside ourselves. However, although we can know that this noumenal reality exists, we can never know it except as it appears to us and as it is categorized by our minds. Thus the world that we know is also "transcendentally ideal."

Just as was the case with the forms of intuition, the "objective knowledge" made possible by the categories of the understanding does not seem so objective to critics. We can know a priori, says Kant, that all experiences will conform to certain laws. But that does not mean that those laws actually apply to objects as they really are in themselves. Kant cheerfully admits this: "I do not say that things *in themselves* possess a magnitude; that their reality possesses a degree; their existence a connection of accidents in a substance."[21] The world as we

---

[21]Kant, *Prolegomena*, chap. 2, §26, p. 308, p. 56.

experience it will always appear to us in these ways, and has to be known in these ways, but the world in itself could be quite different.

As we shall see later, for Kant this is a fortunate outcome. If the knowledge we gain through science was truly metaphysical knowledge of reality as it is in itself, then there would be no room for human free will. All of reality would be governed by inexorable chains of causation, and the possibility of free actions would vanish. Along with freedom would go morality as well as religion, which Kant derives from morality.

SOME CRITICAL THOUGHTS ON KANT'S "CRITICAL PHILOSOPHY"

Some of the difficulties in the major conclusions of Kant's philosophy will become clear when we look at his successors. However, I want to pause briefly at this point to note that many of Kant's claims are far from obvious. Kant criticizes his rationalist predecessors as "dogmatists" and tries to put forward a "critical philosophy" that will avoid unfounded assumptions. However, Kant himself makes many assumptions that others reject, and thus it is not clear that he himself is as free from "dogmatism" as he thinks.

I will mention just a few of the many points in Kant's philosophy that could be questioned. To begin, his accounts of space and time seem problematic to many. Kant tries to explain how we have knowledge of mathematics by seeing this knowledge as rooted in a pure intuition of space and time, understood not as objective realities but as part of the mind's own structure. Kant thinks his view provides the best explanation of how mathematical knowledge is possible. However, Kant's own account of mathematics, while it still has defenders, is quite controversial. Kantian "constructivism" (as it is called) in the philosophy of mathematics is contested both by "formalists," who follow Hume in thinking that mathematics is a kind of formal game played by rules we invent, as well as by mathematical realists or Platonists, who hold that mathematical knowledge is grounded in a pure intuition of objective realities (things like numbers and geometrical forms) that exist objectively though not in space and time. Neither of those rival views of mathematics requires the bold and speculative view that space and time are fundamentally the result of the activity of the mind. The fact that contemporary mathematicians have invented non-Euclidean forms of geometry casts at least some doubt on the claim that the truths of geometry are somehow known as a priori truths.

Kant's claim that physics requires a foundation of synthetic, a priori truths also seems dubious to many. The physicist may need to *assume* such principles as causality and induction, but perhaps assumptions are all that is required. It may be that Kant's claim that physics requires a "pure" and absolutely certain basis is a reflection of a classical foundationalist epistemology that has itself been accepted uncritically. On some interpretations, contemporary physics not only does not require such principles as the ones Kant puts forward as necessary truths; it has even rejected some of them. According to one important interpretation of quantum physics, there is genuine indeterminacy in nature; and thus the principle of causality, understood as a universal law, far from being a synthetic, a priori truth, may be false.

THE TRANSCENDENTAL DIALECTIC: KANT ON METAPHYSICS

Besides intuition and understanding, the third faculty or power of the human mind according to Kant is reason. Intuition receives representations, and understanding makes judgments about those representations. Reason is the power to make inferences, to see what propositions logically are implied by other propositions. Intuition gives rise to a priori concepts by virtue of our pure intuitions of space and time. The understanding gives rise to a priori categories that are grounded in the logically possible types of judgments we can make. In a similar way, reason gives rise to a priori concepts that reflect what Kant sees (relying again on Aristotle's logic) as the logically possible types of syllogistic

inferences. Kant calls these concepts the ideas of reason. The understanding gives rise to the categories we use to understand our experience, but reason "contains in itself" ideas that are "necessary concepts
whose object *cannot* be given in any experience."[22] Reason is thus the
source of our ideas of what is transcendent, the objects of traditional
metaphysics. It turns out there are three such ideas, the idea of the self
as the soul, the idea of the world-as-a-whole, and the idea of God, corresponding to the three types of syllogisms: categorical, hypothetical,
and disjunctive. As we shall see, Kant's account of traditional metaphysics is both positive and negative. Positively, he argues that we necessarily can (and indeed must) *conceive* of the soul, the world-as-a-
whole, and God. Negatively, however, he argues that we cannot have
genuine knowledge of these transcendent realities.

Each type of syllogism seeks to explain something by way of a condition, but that condition that provides the initial explanation also
needs an explanation through some further condition, and so on indefinitely. Kant does not think that an infinite, uncompleted series of
conditions is satisfactory, but the only way to complete such a series
would be to conceive of an "unconditioned condition," a final explanation that requires no further explanation.

The categorical syllogism (A is B, B is C, therefore A is C) gives rise
to the idea of an absolute subject, which is presupposed by every predicate, but to which no predicate applies. Kant thinks this is the source
of the idea of the soul as a "thinking substance," which is "the ultimate
subject of thinking which cannot be further represented as the predicate of another thing."[23] Although we can and must form the concept
of such a self, Kant claims that its existence as a permanent substance
that can survive death cannot be proved.

The hypothetical syllogism (If p then q, p, therefore q) gives rise to
the idea of the world as a whole. If we explain q by p, it seems equally

---

[22]Kant, *Prolegomena*, chap. 3, §40, p. 327, p. 75.
[23]Kant, *Prolegomena*, chap. 3, §47, p. 334, pp. 82-83.

legitimate to try to explain p. However, whatever condition we use to explain p would in turn seem to cry out for explanation in turn. An infinite, incomplete series of explanations seems unsatisfactory, yet the only way to have a complete explanation would be to have some condition that requires no explanation, an "unconditioned condition." This concept is essentially the idea of the world as a completed whole, which would explain everything but require no further explanation.

The third type of syllogism is the disjunctive syllogism: "Either p or q, not p, therefore q." If one imagines the "sum total of all possibilities,"[24] it would seem that one is imagining "the supreme and complete material condition of the possibility of all that exists,"[25] and that would seem to be God, the ultimate ground for the existence of everything. As Leibniz had already affirmed, it seems there are many alternative possible universes or worlds, and it makes sense to ask why the actual universe exists rather than any alternative. The idea of God would be the idea of some ground or principle that is the "unconditioned condition" for the existence of the world.

So reason can and must form ideas of these transcendent, metaphysical objects. However, it is impossible to gain any knowledge of their reality or nature. Kant's view of metaphysics and his view of reason is thus unusual: he thinks that theoretical reason necessarily raises certain questions that it itself can never answer: "Human reason has this peculiar fate that in one species of its knowledge it is burdened by questions which, as prescribed by the very nature of reason itself, it is not able to ignore, but which, as transcending all its powers, it is also not able to answer."[26] Reason is unable to gain knowledge of the objects of the ideas of reason because our knowledge is limited to what we can experience. The forms of intuition and categories of the understanding provide the basis for knowledge. We know a priori that these apply to the world as it appears to us, but we do not know that they apply to the

---

[24]Kant, *Critique of Pure Reason*, A 572 / B 600, p. 488.
[25]Kant, *Critique of Pure Reason*, A 576 / B 604, p. 491.
[26]Kant, *Critique of Pure Reason*, A vii, p. 7.

noumenal world, the world as it is in itself. The ideas of reason however, transcend any possible experience. They are noumenal realities, not part of the phenomenal world. We cannot experience the absolute self, the world as a whole, or God as the ground of existence. But what we cannot experience we cannot know.

It is true that we cannot help but *think* of these metaphysical realities. But this, according to Kant, is just a subjective need of reason, and cannot establish the objective reality of what we need to conceive. The illusion of metaphysical knowledge of these realities arises when we confuse this subjective need with an objective rational necessity.

The ideas of reason do have a valuable role as what Kant calls "regulative ideals." These transcendent ideas prevent us from taking any finite condition or explanation as ultimate or final. They provide a kind of ultimate goal, a holy grail of theoretical reason that ensures we do not take some finite explanation as absolute, final, or complete. Additionally, as we shall see later in this chapter, when reason is practically exercised Kant says that belief or faith in these metaphysical realities is justified, even if they are not objects of theoretical knowledge. However, we could not *believe* in such realities if we had no concept of them, so the fact that reason necessarily forms these ideas is itself valuable. However, although the ideas of reason have this valid "regulative" or pragmatic value, Kant affirms that they cannot be used "constitutively" to give us metaphysical knowledge of the supersensible.

THE ILLUSIONS OF METAPHYSICS

Besides his general argument that we have no knowledge of that which goes beyond experience, Kant subjects the traditional metaphysical arguments about these ideas to specific criticisms, giving concreteness to his claim that metaphysical knowledge is an illusion grounded in the confusion between the subjective needs of reason and what is objectively rationally necessary. The idea of the soul as an absolute self arises out of our need always to think of an "I" as the subject of every experience. Kant admits that whatever I experience must be conceived as "my experience." As he puts it, there is an "I think" that must accompany all our experiences. But the fact that we must think of our experiences in this way does not show that we have an actual intuition of any kind of absolute self. The illusion that our need to think about our experience this way gives us knowledge of the self is called the "paralogism" of pure reason.[27]

With respect to the idea of the world-as-a-whole, Kant says that when we try to use this idea theoretically, reason falls into contradictions, or "antimonies," thus giving us the "Antimony of Pure Reason."[28] We can, for example, offer proofs that seem compelling that the world is both unlimited in space and time and that it is limited. It seems we can prove both that the world consists of absolutely simple elements (atoms), but also that there are no simple elements. Similarly, we can offer apparently convincing proofs that there are no free causes in the world, but also that there are genuinely free causes. We seem to be able to prove that there is a necessary being but also that everything that exists is contingent.

For Kant these antimonies are a clue or sign that reason has exceeded its proper limits or boundaries. The only way to resolve the apparent contradictions is to recognize that our theoretical knowledge is limited to the phenomenal world and does not extend to the noumenal. When we distinguish between the phenomenal and the noumenal, we can resolve the apparent contradictions. In the case of the first two antimonies, dealing with the finite and infinite qualities of space, time, and matter, both of the two contradictory propositions (both the thesis and the antithesis) turn out to be false. The reason this is so is that they employ a "false concept" of time and space, conceiving of space and time as objective realities rather than as forms of intuition. With respect to the second two antimonies, Kant thinks that both the thesis and antithesis may possibly be true, but one is true of the world as known phenomenally, while the other

---

[27]Kant, *Critique of Pure Reason*, A 341-405 / B 399-432, pp. 411-69.
[28]Kant, *Prolegomena*, appendix, p. 381, p. 131.

is possibly true of the world understood noumenally. The phenomenal world is a world in which there is no freedom, since the category of causality can be known a priori to apply to it. Furthermore, the phenomenal world is a world of contingency, where nothing is absolute or unconditioned. However, Kant holds that this may not be the case for the noumenal world. In fact, he will argue that practical reason give us grounds rationally to believe in both God and free will.

Kant also subjects three of the traditional arguments for God's existence to criticism. The three arguments he considers are the ontological argument, the cosmological argument, and the argument from design, which he terms the "physico-theological" proof. The ontological argument, as we have seen, was developed by Anselm, and championed by Descartes, Spinoza, and Leibniz. The argument holds that God as an all-perfect being must possess all perfections. Since existence is itself a perfection, God must exist.

Kant criticizes the argument by claiming that for existence to be a perfection, it must be a "predicate" or property that a thing can possess or fail to possess. However, Kant argues that "existence" does not refer to a quality or property in this way. A man can have hair or lose his hair and become bald, and still be the same man. However, existence is not a property like "being bald." A real tiger and an imaginary tiger may possess all the same properties. If existence is not a property, then it cannot be a perfection either and the argument fails.

The cosmological argument is criticized on the grounds that it covertly rests on the ontological argument, and so if the ontological arguments fails, the cosmological argument fails also. The cosmological argument claims that the universe consists of contingent objects, which require an ultimate cause. However, any cause that was itself contingent would still require a causal explanation. Hence the only adequate explanation would be a being that exists necessarily. Kant argues that his critique of the ontological argument shows that we cannot really form a concept of a being that exists necessarily. To think of such a being is illicitly to think of existence as a property of something, and Kant claims existence is not a property at all.

The third argument that Kant criticizes is the argument from design. We observe lots of things in nature that appear to be the result of intelligence, and so we infer that nature itself is the work of an intelligent designer. Kant actually praises this argument as one that has a good deal of plausibility:

> It would therefore not be uncomforting but utterly vain to attempt to diminish in any way the authority of this argument. Reason, constantly upheld by this ever-increasing evidence, which, though empirical, is yet so powerful, cannot be so depressed through doubts suggested by subtle and abstruse speculation, that it is not at once aroused from the indecision of all melancholy reflection, as from a dream, by one glance at the wonders of nature and the majesty of the universe.[29]

So in one sense Kant endorses this argument as a kind of natural inference that makes belief in God plausible. However, he still maintains that this is only *belief*, not knowledge. The reason this is so is that the argument is not "apodictic." That is, it is not absolutely impervious to doubt or unchallengeable. In fact, the argument covertly depends on the cosmological argument, for even if it is sound, all it would prove is that the world had a designer, not that there is an all-powerful being who created the world from nothing. The designer could have been less than perfect and might have used preexisting materials.

Kant's criticisms of these three theistic arguments have been hugely influential historically. However, it is not clear that his criticisms are as devastating as many believe. To begin, Kant sets the standard very high. He still holds to a classical foundationalist conception of philosophy as providing conclusions that are absolutely certain. If this is the standard, then arguments that are not absolutely convincing to everyone are simply failures. However, it seems likely that no philosophical

---

[29]Kant, *Critique of Pure Reason*, A 624 / B 652, p. 520.

arguments will pass such a test. Arguments might well make their conclusions plausible or probable to some people without being convincing
to everyone. If an argument is logically valid and has premises that seem
more plausible than their denial, the argument would seem to provide
at least some support for its conclusion, even if it is not a "proof" that
settles the issue once and for all. Furthermore, a theistic argument
might be valuable even if it does not directly support all the traditional
attributes of God. For example, it may be correct that the argument
from design does not prove that the universe was created from nothing
by an all-powerful being. But it would still be significant if the argument
from design established that it was reasonable to believe that there was
some intelligent being beyond the natural order that was responsible
for that order, even if the argument left open the character of that being,
and did not settle the question as to whether the being used preexistent
material or created the universe from nothing.

Second, the specific criticisms Kant makes seem less powerful than
he claims. For example, some have rejected the claim that existence is
not a perfection. However, even if Kant is right about existence not
being a property, it may be true that "existing necessarily" is a property.
After all, it seems obvious that it is impossible for things like round
squares to exist. However, if we can form a concept of something that
cannot possibly exist, it looks like we could form a concept of something that cannot possibly fail to exist. And that is exactly the concept
the ontological argument needs.

In any case it is certainly not obvious that the cosmological argument
requires one to accept the soundness and convincingness of the ontological argument. It may be true that the cosmological argument requires the *concept* of a being that exists necessarily. However, that does
not mean that the cosmological argument requires that the existence of
such a being can be established on purely conceptual grounds.

Kant's general picture of the limits of human knowledge also can be
questioned. Kant may be right in thinking that human experience is

always temporal in character. However, he seems to think this entails that a nontemporal God cannot be experienced. However, this claim seems to rest on a "representationalist" view of how experience works, which requires some kind of likeness between our representation of a reality and the reality. However, as Reid pointed out, what we experience may be vastly different from the experience itself. We experience objects as hard through touching, but the sensation of "hardness" is not itself hard. Similarly, it is not obvious that God, even if God is nontemporal, could not reveal himself through a temporal experience.

KANT'S MORAL PHILOSOPHY

Kant himself did not see his claims about the limits of reason and the impossibility of metaphysics as threatening to morality and religion, but rather the reverse. It is true that we cannot prove the existence of God and the soul. However, theoretical reason does at least provide us with these ideas, and the limits of reason mean that it is equally impossible to show the nonexistence of God or the soul, and thus atheism is no more theoretically secure than theism. For Kant, the limits of theoretical reason are actually a benefit to morality and religion. As noted before, human reason is employed not only theoretically to gain knowledge, but also practically, to decide on actions. It is through practical reason that we gain a justified belief in God and a soul that can survive death, as well as a belief in our own freedom. To make sense of these claims we must turn now to Kant's ethics, which has been just as historically influential as his epistemological account of knowledge.

Kant's most-read work in his ethics is his *Foundations of the Metaphysic of Morals*.[30] In the first section he starts with what he calls the "common sense conception" of morals, obviously assuming that ordinary people do have some kind of awareness of what is moral. He begins the work with the sweeping claim that "nothing in the world— indeed nothing even beyond the world—can possibly be conceived

---

[30]Sometimes translated as *Groundwork of the Metaphysic of Morals.*

which could be called good without qualification except a *good will*."[31] Kant recognizes that there are many goods, such as intelligence and courage, but argues that these goods can actually be "bad and harmful" if not accompanied by a morally good will. An evil criminal who is intelligent and courageous can do more harm than a criminal who lacks these virtues. So he concludes that the only absolute and unqualified good is a good will, and he means by that what we might call a virtuous will or a morally good will.

However, what is it for the will to be morally good? For Kant, what makes the will good is a connection to duty. It is obvious, he thinks, that a will that goes contrary to moral duty is not good. However, Kant does not think that it is sufficient that we will *in accordance* with our duty. People sometimes do what is morally right but not for moral reasons. A shopkeeper may treat his customers honestly because he fears that if he does not, he will get a reputation for being dishonest and will lose profits. There are also people "so sympathetically constituted" that they find "inner satisfaction" in helping others.[32] Kant claims that if we only do what is morally right because of such reasons, our actions do not have true moral worth. Genuine moral goodness requires that we not only do what is morally right but also do it for the right kind of reasons. We must not merely act in accord with duty, but for the sake of duty. We should do our duty because it is our duty.

But what is duty? Kant answers that "duty is the necessity of an action executed from respect for law."[33] The morally good person does not simply act on impulse or to achieve some goal or end that is desired, but rather seeks to follow a principle. What makes an action morally right is not the results or consequences connected to the act, but the principle on which the act is based. However, what law or principle can determine our wills if we remove any concern for results

---

[31]Immanuel Kant, *Foundations of the Metaphysics of Morals*, trans. Lewis White Beck (Indianapolis: Bobbs-Merrill, 1959), 393, 9.
[32]Kant, *Foundations*, 398, 14.
[33]Kant, *Foundations*, 400, 16.

or consequences? Kant's answer is that "nothing remains to serve as a principle of the will except universal conformity of its action to law as such."[34] To act on the basis of law is to act consistently, on the basis of a principle. The very concept of a law therefore provides the content of the foundational principle of morality. A law is a principle that must be consistently followed, and for Kant, this is the key to morality: "I should never act in such a way that I could not also will that my maxim should be a universal law."[35] Kant eventually terms this principle the "categorical imperative," although, as we shall see, he formulates the principle in various ways.

By a "maxim" Kant means a subjective principle of action, a principle that could actually determine my action. When we are considering what to do in some specific situation, there are always many maxims I could choose to follow. Suppose I need money to pay for some important bill, and I might be able to borrow what I need from a friend. To get my friend to loan me the money, I must promise to repay it. However, I know that I won't have the funds to do that. Should I promise to repay the money anyway? In that case I would be following the maxim, "When I am in need I will make promises that I know I cannot keep." Kant thinks that if we reflect on this maxim we will see that it is not one that could be willed as a universal law. Promising to do what one knows one cannot do is rationally incoherent. The person who does this cannot possibly will that it should be a universal law that people should promise to do things they do not intend to do. Rather, such a person is following a maxim that cannot be universalized, making his own case an exception. Even ordinary people have this kind of moral knowledge: "Inexperienced in the course of the world, incapable of being prepared for all its contingencies, I ask myself only: Can I will that my maxim become a universal law? If not, it must be rejected."[36]

---

[34]Kant, *Foundations*, 402, 18.
[35]Kant, *Foundations*, 402, 18.
[36]Kant, *Foundations*, 403, 19.

Kant holds that our knowledge of morality comes from reason itself. It is a priori knowledge and not based on experience. Only reason could be the basis of laws that hold necessarily and universally. We do not gain our knowledge of morality from examples. Rather, we must already have knowledge of morality to judge that some example is worthy to be emulated.[37] Even our understanding of God as morally good presupposes that we already have a moral ideal of perfection and see God as exemplifying this ideal.[38] Reason is not given to humans to help us to become happy or achieve our desires; instincts and experiential shrewdness are of more use for such ends.[39] Hence, "it is clear that all moral concepts have their seat and origin entirely *a priori* in reason."[40]

Kant describes statements about what we ought to do as "imperatives" or commands. Most imperatives are *hypothetical* in nature.[41] Their validity depends on a condition, an "if" that may or may not hold. First-year college students are told that "if you want to become a physician, you ought to take organic chemistry." If I do not want to become a physician, then this imperative will not apply to me. There are some imperatives that are valid for everyone because they are rooted in desires or goals that everyone has, such as happiness. However, even these imperatives do not hold unconditionally or categorically, but are rooted in the contingent fact of human psychology that all humans want to be happy. The supreme principle of morality is one that must be categorical or unconditional.

Kant affirms that there is just one categorical imperative, though he does think that there are alternative ways to formulate what amounts to the same principle. Here he echoes the commonsense morality he began with and claims that the categorical imperative's content can be derived simply from its form: "For since the imperative contains

[37]Kant, *Foundations*, 408, 25.
[38]Kant, *Foundations*, 408-9, 25.
[39]Kant, *Foundations*, 395, 11-12.
[40]Kant, *Foundations*, 411, 28.
[41]Kant, *Foundations*, 414-15, 31-32.

besides the law only the necessity that the maxim should accord with the law, ... there is nothing remaining in it except the universality of law as such to which the maxim of the action should conform."[42]

Kant tries to illustrate what this formula means by giving several specific examples. One example concerns a man who is in despair because of a series of evils and who is tempted to take his own life. Kant argues that this would be contrary to reason since it could not be right to see the "principle whose special office is the improvement of life" as one that could universally justify taking life. The second example is the one dealing with a promise to return borrowed money discussed above. A third example deals with self-improvement, the rational duty to cultivate one's own faculties. Kant thinks one could not rationally will as a universal law that humans should never seek to improve themselves by developing their faculties. The final example he gives is of a man who fails to have any sense he ought to help other humans who are struggling. Kant thinks it is irrational to will such self-centeredness as a universal law since the person who fails to help others will surely need assistance himself at some point.

Kant says that it follows from this that there is only one categorical imperative, which is: "Act only according to that maxim by which you can at the same time will it should become a universal law."[43] This version of the categorical imperative is often called the "universal law of nature" formula. However, Kant formulates the principle in several other ways. One of the most influential is what is called the "humanity" or "end-in-itself" formula: "Act so that you treat humanity, whether in your own person or in that of another, always as an end and never as a means only."[44] Kant bases this version on the idea that a rational being, as the possessor of a rational will, must value himself or herself as something that has unconditional worth, and consistency requires that all other rational beings be valued in a similar way. Note that Kant does not

---

[42]Kant, *Foundations*, 420-21, 38-39.
[43]Kant, *Foundations*, 421, 39.
[44]Kant, *Foundations*, 429, 47.

rule out using others as a means to our ends; he realizes that all humans do that. What he affirms is that we must not think of humans *solely* as means. The person who delivers my mail serves my ends, but I must remember this person is also someone who has intrinsic worth or value.

A third version of the categorical imperative is usually called the "autonomy" formula. Kant says that a person who follows morality is obeying a law that comes from their own reason. Such a person is therefore free and autonomous. If I do what is morally right out of a desire for pleasure or fear of punishment, then I am not free since my actions stems from "inclinations" or emotions. Kant says such motivation is "heteronomous," and not autonomous. However, if I do what is morally right simply because it is morally right, then I am determined by my own will as a rational being. I am the author of the law I must obey. This means that the categorical imperative can also be stated as "the Idea of the will of every rational being as a *will that legislates universal law.*"[45]

The fourth version of the categorical imperative is the "kingdom of ends" formula. Kant likens being a moral agent to being a citizen of a "kingdom of ends" that is a "systematic union" of beings "under common laws."[46] A rational being belongs to such a kingdom when "he gives universal laws in it while also himself subject to these laws." The categorical imperative can then be characterized as the necessity of only acting on those maxims that could be legislated for such a kingdom.[47]

Interestingly, although Kant affirms that every moral being is a citizen of this kingdom, he makes a distinction between those who are merely members of the kingdom and the one who is "sovereign." The sovereign also legislates the moral laws, but the sovereign has no duties, which pertain only to the members. The reason for this is that the sovereign has a "holy will," and therefore is never tempted to do anything other than reason demands. Human beings, on the other hand, have a divided

---

[45]Kant, *Foundations*, 432, 50.
[46]Kant, *Foundations*, 433, 51-52.
[47]Kant, *Foundations*, 433-34, 51-52.

will, and so require duties. Only God can be the sovereign, since the sovereign must be a "completely independent being without need and with power adequate to his will."[48]

Thus Kant says that the kingdom has a "Head" or ruler and that God is this "Head."[49] Despite his emphasis on autonomy, and view of each citizen as a legislator, Kant also affirms that it is correct to view all moral laws as divine commands.[50] In the next section, in discussing the relation between morality and religion, I shall say more about what this might mean, as well as explaining why Kant thinks it is rational to believe in God.

Kant affirms that all of these various formulations of the categorical imperative are equivalent. However, it is not clear in what way they are supposed to be equivalent. They certainly do not appear to have the same meaning. It is often argued, for example, that the end-in-itself formula has more content than the universal-law formula. The universal-law formula seems problematic in several ways. One is that there seem to be many possible maxims a person could will to be universalized that do not look like moral laws. Suppose I willed it to be a universal law that people should try not to step on cracks in the sidewalks. Such a maxim might appear pointless and difficult to observe, but it does not seem to lead to any rational contradictions. A second problem is that it is often unclear exactly what maxim underlies a possible action. Actions can be described in many different ways. Lying to a Nazi who is seeking a Jew who is hiding in your house could be described as deceiving another person but also as saving an innocent life.

The end-in-itself formula seems to offer more content, since it posits that humans have an intrinsic dignity or worth that must always be respected. In some ways it is philosophically close to the biblical principle that one ought to love one's neighbor as oneself, assuming that the "neighbor" includes all humans. It is probably not an accident that Kant,

---

[48]Kant, *Foundations*, 434, 52.
[49]Kant, *Foundations*, 434, 52.
[50]Kant, *Foundations*, 439, 57.

raised in a Lutheran, Christian home, should find such a view plausible. There is certainly nothing like it in Aristotle. Aristotle was surely a rational being, but it never occurred to him that slaves and women were "ends in themselves," beings with an equal dignity or worth.

FREEDOM, GOD, AND IMMORTALITY

As we saw above, Kant rejected theoretical arguments that attempt to prove the existence of God or the existence of an immortal soul in humans. However, Kant argues that as rational, moral beings, humans ought to *believe* in God and in immortality. Along with a belief in freedom, these ideas are what he calls the "postulates" of practical reason, beliefs that are justified because they are necessary if we are to live rational moral lives. This is what Kant meant when he said that he had to limit knowledge to make room for faith.

Let's begin with a belief in freedom, which Kant says "must be presupposed as the property of the will of all rational beings."[51] Freedom is theoretically problematic because causality is one of the "categories of the understanding" (explained earlier in this chapter). These categories necessarily are applied by theoretical reason in all scientific knowing, and thus, from the viewpoint of theoretical knowledge, everything in the world, including humans, appears to be causally determined. However, when we act morally we must see ourselves as autonomous, not determined by anything but our own reason, and thus we cannot believe our actions are simply a product of nonrational causes. The solution to this apparent contradiction is to recognize that theoretical reason does not give us knowledge of noumenal reality, reality as it is in itself, but only of phenomenal reality, reality as it appears. When we look at ourselves as objects of knowledge, we appear determined, but it is possible to believe that in reality we are rational beings who transcend the mechanistic causal order. Not only is this possible; it is necessary, since rational action would be impossible without this

---

[51]Kant, *Foundations*, 447, 66.

belief. This belief in freedom is not theoretical knowledge, but it is fully justified. Not only is it the case that theoretical reason only gives us knowledge of how things appear; it is also the case that in principle theoretical reason could not give us good reasons to reject what is necessary for practical reason. The reason for this is that even theoretical reasoning is in the end something we *do*. One cannot deny practical reason on the basis of theoretical reason, because this would undermine theoretical reason as well.

Kant argues that morality also provides a basis for belief in God. As we saw in the previous section, moral actions must be done for the sake of duty, not to attain happiness or any other end. Nevertheless, Kant affirms that all humans desire happiness, and aim at happiness in their actions. This is perfectly legitimate so long as we do not seek happiness by violating the moral law. What we necessarily seek is what Kant calls "the highest Good," which is a world in which people are both perfectly virtuous and happy.

We are not allowed to seek happiness, for ourselves or others, by doing what is immoral, and so we must always limit our seeking of happiness to following morality. There is a problem here, however. It does not appear that following morality necessarily or even generally leads to happiness. Empirically, it seems that those who violate morality often are the "winners," and those who follow morality lose out. We can only hope that moral actions will lead to happiness (eventually and in the long run) if we have some reason to believe that the universe in which we live is in fact a moral universe, one in which moral actions can be effective and lead to happiness. But to believe the universe is a moral universe in which moral actions and happiness are connected, we must believe that the universe is created and controlled by a moral power. Only if there is a God can we hope that the highest good can be achieved through moral action. If God does not exist, then we would be in the absurd situation of necessarily seeking to achieve an end that we believed it to be impossible to achieve.

Although we cannot theoretically prove that God exists, we are entitled to believe that there is a moral ground to the universe, and that can only be God.

Kant justifies a belief in life after death in a similar way. We are required by reason to become morally perfect, but Kant (perhaps reflecting his Lutheran upbringing) holds that no human can achieve that goal in a finite lifetime. The best we can do is make progress toward that ideal. Since Kant holds that "ought implies can," it follows from this that we must have the opportunity to continue our moral improvement after death. Once more, although we cannot theoretically prove the existence of a soul that can survive death, Kant holds that since even our knowledge of ourselves is knowledge of how we appear, it is possible to believe that each of us is a unified self that transcends the spacetime world of knowledge.

RELIGIOUS BELIEF AND PRACTICE

Kant does not see the religious life merely as belief in God. In a late work, *Religion Within the Limits of Reason Alone*, he tries to give a fuller picture of what a rational religion would look like. Strictly speaking, Kant does not claim that religion must be limited to what can be known by reason. Rather, he describes his book as a kind of experiment, in which he attempts to see how much of the religious truth known through revelation can be preserved within a framework that limits itself to what can be known by reason.

Interestingly, Kant begins with a consideration of what he calls "radical evil," and there admits that humans have a propensity for evil so strong that it appears that we cannot change ourselves merely by an act of will. The problem is complex, since it appears we need some solution to the problem of our past failures and the resulting guilt, as well as help in becoming a new person (grace). Kant recognizes that this seems to imply that humans need help to become morally good, and that religions (such as Christianity) offer such help through such things as "works of grace, miracles, mysteries, and means of grace."[52] Kant's view is that reason does not deny the possibility of such things, but that since such supernatural things cannot be known, then reason "cannot adopt them into her maxims of thought and action." Perhaps we do need God's help to become what we should be, but it is not necessary for us to know what God must do. Rather, "it is essential to know *what man himself must do* in order to become worthy of this assistance."[53] We must strive to do all we can, and then we can properly hope that God will do what is necessary to complete our transformation.

Kant does not deny the possibility that God has acted in history to make salvation possible, but he denies that salvation depends on knowledge of what God has done. It is possible, for example, that God has revealed true religion, which is the religion of morality, in history. The reason for this is that even though it would be possible for humans to arrive at this truth through reason, it might take them a long time. By giving a special revelation, God could speed up the process. However, once we have such a revelation Kant believes that we can discern the correctness of its essential teachings through reason. Thus, even if God has revealed the truth to us, we do not have to believe such truth simply because it has been revealed. Kant then proceeds to give a kind of rational reconstruction of the core doctrines of Christianity. For example, the "Son of God" is an ideal of moral perfection, and we can believe in such an ideal whether or not it has been historically exemplified. In a similar way Kant reinterprets or redescribes the doctrines of the atonement, the Spirit, and the church. With regard to the latter a distinction is made between an actual ecclesiastical body and the "true Church." Historical churches of various "faiths" can play a valid role as long as they approximate and serve the latter, which is a pure moral community. The triumph of such a community would amount to the "coming of the kingdom of God."

---

[52]Immanuel Kant, *Religion Within the Limits of Reason Alone*, trans. Theodore M. Greene and Hoyt H. Hudson (New York: Harper & Row, 1960), bk. 1, "General Observation," 47.

[53]Kant, *Religion*, bk. 1, "General Observation," 47.

Kant thus defends a kind of Christianity that is reduced to moral action, telling us that a "moral religion" does not consist in "dogmas and rites," bur rather in "the heart's disposition to fulfil all human duties as divine commands."[54] In the end Kant's version of Christianity is one in which humans must merit salvation through their own efforts: *"Whatever, over and above good life-conduct, man fancies that he can do to become well-pleasing to God is mere religious illusion and pseudo-service of God."*[55] Kant's account of religious faith is historically influential, one of the leading influences on the "liberal" versions of Christianity that developed in Protestantism in the nineteenth century. Liberal Christianity is sometimes summarized in the slogan "the fatherhood of God and the brotherhood of man." This captures true religion from a Kantian perspective pretty well. Kant gives us a God who is a moral judge and whom we relate to by living morally with our fellow humans.

THE *CRITIQUE OF JUDGMENT* AND
KANT'S AESTHETIC PHILOSOPHY

This chapter is already a long one, but that perhaps befits the enormous importance of Kant's philosophy. Kant worked in every field of philosophy, and his influence has been significant on many of them. I cannot possibly in one chapter do justice to all of these areas, such as Kant's political philosophy or his philosophical anthropology. (The latter is, unfortunately, marred by racist assumptions common to the era, despite its being the age of "Enlightenment.") However, I do not wish to totally ignore the importance of Kant's third "Critique," the *Critique of Judgment*.

This book attempts to deal with a problem that seems to have occupied Kant relatively late in his career, the problem of how to obtain a unified view of the world, and also to have a unified philosophy. The *Critique of Pure Reason* seems to teach us that the world as we know it scientifically is a deterministic world, subject to laws. The *Critique of*

---

[54]Kant, *Religion*, bk. 2, "General Observation," 79.
[55]Kant, *Religion*, bk. 4.2.2, 158.

Practical Reason seems to show that we must think of ourselves as free rational agents, not as the product of some mechanism. Yet we are part of that world, and must act freely as part of that world.

As we have already seen, Kant attempts to show that there is no contradiction between these two viewpoints by arguing that the world that science knows is only the phenomenal world, the world as it appears to us, which leaves us free to believe that in reality we have the freedom that practical reason demands. Still, although there is no contradiction between the two viewpoints of theoretical and practical reason, it seems that the two parts of Kant's philosophy lack unity. We do not know how to relate one to the other, even if they are compatible.

In Kant's philosophy, the faculty of judgment is the power that enables us to develop and apply concepts to the world. It provides a kind of mediation between the world as we know it through the senses on the one side to ourselves as the possessor of reason on the other side. *The Critique of Judgment* examines this power to see if a kind of unity can be found, a viewpoint that connects the nature we know to ourselves, and provides unity both to our view of nature and to our thinking.

One clue that this unity might be achievable is that we experience nature aesthetically, not just as an object of scientific knowledge. We often see objects and events in nature as either beautiful or sublime, for example. For Kant, beauty is linked to purposiveness. If we can legitimately see nature as teleological, and not simply as a vast mechanism, then it perhaps will not be so alien to our lives as moral beings. It is for this reason that Kant spends a great deal of this book developing a theory of aesthetics, both in relation to nature and to human artistic achievements.

The actual account of art that Kant develops is very complex, and an adequate treatment would probably require another chapter as least as long as this one.[56] However, the main elements that have been most

---

[56]For a clear and scholarly account of what is going on in the *Critique of Judgment*, see Douglas Burnham, *An Introduction to Kant's "Critique of Judgment"* (Edinburgh: Edinburgh University Press, 2000). Burnham also has a clear and relatively short account in his article, "Immanuel Kant: Aesthetics," in the *Internet Encyclopedia of Philosophy*, https://www.iep.utm.edu/kantaest.

influential can at least be briefly summarized. Kant's account is somewhat paradoxical in that he wants to argue that our aesthetic judgements have their origins in our sensibilities; they are "judgments of taste." However, he rejects the view that they are therefore purely subjective. On the contrary, when we make aesthetic judgments about what is beautiful or sublime, we claim that others ought to agree with us. Our judgments purport to have a kind of universal validity and necessity. In order to make such judgments, Kant says we must take a "disinterested" view of what we are judging.[57] Kant also says that we must see what we judge as "purposive without a purpose." When we view a work of art, we recognize it as the work of purposive intelligence, but we do not regard it simply as an object that has some external purpose. One might say that it has its teleology within itself.

Kant's view here is widely influential and gives rise to the later slogan "art for art's sake." Something like this view is found in the very plausible view that great art transcends narrow utilitarian purposes. However, questions can be raised about whether Kant's view is universally true or merely reflects the new role that art was coming to play in Western culture. In previous cultures, both in the classical and Christian worlds, much of the greatest art clearly had mundane purposes. The Greeks adorned their drinking goblets with exquisite carvings. The great stained-glass windows in cathedrals were meant to enhance worship and educate people. The culture of "high art," which divorces art from other uses, may reflect particular stresses in modern Western culture, a culture in which art was increasingly called on to do what religion had done previously: give to human life meaning.[58]

---

[57]This claim that art should be disinterested was something of a commonplace at this period, a view held by people such as Shaftesbury, for example, and by Schopenhauer later. As we shall see in chap. 23, Nietzsche thinks this view of art is fundamentally mistaken.

[58]For a vigorous argument that art is not just for aesthetic contemplation but should be integrated into our daily lives, see Nicholas Wolterstorff, *Art in Action: Toward a Christian Aesthetic* (Grand Rapids: Eerdmans, 1987). Wolterstorff recognizes the value of museums and concert halls, but argues that it is mistaken to view art as something intended for disinterested contemplation.

The two aesthetic qualities Kant concentrates on are beauty and the sublime. Beauty is chiefly a matter of a harmony of matter and form, and is recognized through a kind of aesthetic sensibility or taste. The sublime, found in such things as thunderstorms and vast mountains, is experienced in what overwhelms us either through size or force. Sublime objects lack harmonious form. Nonetheless, we are attracted to the sublime because it provides a kind of expressive intimation of the infinite and unlimited quality of our own minds. Kant also gives a very influential account of artistic genius, something that has no counterpart in science. The genius is a kind of force of nature. The genius must have artistic training and skill, but training and skill alone cannot account for genius, which is what provides art with "soul."

In the end Kant attempts to argue that the beauty and sublimity we see in nature provide a kind of analogy between nature and the artistic achievements of humans. The world we live in is enough like the objects we create to allow us to see that world as not totally alien to ourselves. Since we humans are fundamentally moral creatures, the beauty we see in nature becomes a kind of symbol of morality, providing a unifying connection between nature and ourselves.

German Idealism
and Hegel

KANT THOUGHT OF HIS PHILOSOPHY as the "critical philosophy," and believed that he had undermined traditional metaphysical claims to have knowledge of what is transcendent. For him there is no *knowledge* of God, the soul as a transcendent object, or the world as a whole. One of the ironies of the history of modern Western philosophy is that Kant's philosophy led directly to what may be the most exuberantly metaphysical program of the modern period, a movement variously called Absolute Idealism or German Idealism. There are, as we shall see, a variety of views describable under that label, but all of them see reality as in some way grounded in an "Absolute," variously described as "Mind" or "Spirit." The term *Spirit* may be less misleading, since *Mind* suggests a kind of personal metaphysical agent, and at least some of the figures described as German Idealists do not believe in such a personal agent, even though they sometimes use traditional religious language that might suggest that they do.

We have, of course, already encountered idealism in the philosophy of Berkeley. However, Berkeley's idealism is rooted in Lockean empiricism, and is memorably summarized in Berkeley's slogan: "To be is to be perceived." On this view the only things that exist are perceptions and the minds in which perceptions subsist. If one were to try to summarize German Idealism with a similar slogan, it might be something like this: "To be is to be *conceived*." The starting place is not Lockean empiricism but Kant's critical epistemology. Reality does not consist of subjective sensations, but the view can be described as idealism since it regards what is real as in some way inconceivable independently of the intellect.

In a sense, for the German Idealists, reality has a more objective character than it does for Berkeley. There is an objective world, and that world does not consist solely of subjective sensations. The German Idealists do not really deny the reality of matter, or a natural world composed of physical objects. However, they maintain that when we fully understand the nature of that objective world, including its material character, we discover that we cannot make sense of it as something existing independently of mind. In a sense this is true for Berkeley as well, since Berkeley is a theist who holds that God is the Creator of everything that exists other than himself. However, for German Idealism there is a tendency toward pantheism rather than theism. The relation between the world and the Absolute that conceives that world is more intimate than theists typically allow. Thus German Idealism also has similarities to Spinoza's absolute monism.

The resemblance to Spinoza extends to differences in how Idealism is interpreted. Spinoza clearly says that the only substance is God, but he also says that God and nature are the same thing. Is this just a form of naturalism in religious language? Or does Spinoza think that God as Mind involves some kind of self-consciousness that is not reducible to nature? Commentators do not agree, although in the contemporary world, in which naturalistic views are overwhelmingly popular among philosophers, opinions tend toward seeing Spinoza as a naturalist who simply thinks that traditional religious attitudes can be shifted to the universe itself. As we shall see, there is a similar ambiguity in German Idealism, particularly in the philosophy of Hegel.

German Idealism reached the height of its popularity in Germany in the early to middle part of the nineteenth century. However, even after the movement declined in Germany it made a surprising advance in the late nineteenth century and early twentieth century in Great Britain and, to a lesser extent, in America. Though Idealism is no longer a popular philosophy, its historical influence has been immense. Part of that influence has consisted of inspiring critical reactions, as we shall see in Marx and Kierkegaard. However, German Idealism has had a powerful influence on theology and even on such movements as American pragmatism.

In this chapter I shall discuss the philosophies of J. G. Fichte and Friedrich Schelling very briefly, and the thought of G. W. F. Hegel at greater length. However, before looking at these specific philosophies, I shall give a general sketch of how one might move from a Kantian position to one of Absolute Idealism. This sketch is not intended as a historical description of the thought of any particular idealist, but more as a kind of logical account of the kind of thinking that made Idealism seem appealing to Kant's successors.

FROM KANT TO ABSOLUTE IDEALISM

Kant himself insisted that he was not a metaphysical idealist, but a "transcendental idealist." That is, he argued that the world as we know it is indeed partly structured by mind, which supplies the forms of intuition (space and time) as well as the categories of the understanding, including such concepts as substance and causality. The world as we know it is thus the phenomenal world, the world as it appears to humans. Kant insisted, however, that there is such a thing as the noumenal world, the world as it really is in itself, thus distinguishing his view from Berkeleyan idealism. Interestingly, Kant frequently describes the noumenal world as the world as God sees it, thus distinguishing our human knowledge from God's point of view. It is possible that one motivation for the rejection of this Kantian distinction is that we humans do not like to acknowledge our creaturely limitations. We want to see our own knowledge as godlike in character.

German Idealists all saw this Kantian affirmation of the reality of the noumenal world as problematic, and it is easy to see that it is philosophically difficult. Kant affirms the reality of a world that he also affirms is un-knowable. But how we can *know* the existence of what is unknowable? Unless we can conceptualize the noumenal world using the categories of human understanding, it would seem to be not only unknowable but also unthinkable. Kant claims, for example, that mathematics is grounded in our intuition of space and time, the a priori forms we supply for the impressions we receive from the noumenal world. However, how can we conceive of a world that cannot be described spatially and temporally, and that we cannot even apply mathematical concepts to? Can we even say that the noumenal world is *one* world? "One" is after all a number. Are there objects in the noumenal world? Presumably, if there are enduring objects, they would have to be substances, but Kant argues that the concept of "substance" is one that cannot be legitimately employed beyond the phenomenal world. And why should we believe in the reality of such a noumenal world anyway? Obviously, we cannot say that such a world *causes* the appearances, since for Kant the concept of causality can also only legitimately be applied within the world of appearances.

Worries like these led such thinkers as Fichte and Schelling to argue that the idea of a noumenal world forever beyond the reach of human knowledge is incoherent. Instead we should affirm that the world as we know it (what Kant called the phenomenal world) simply is the real world. The first step in the movement to Idealism is thus to identify the Kantian phenomenal world with noumenal reality. What we humans know is the Real.

The second step follows quickly once this move is made. The Idealists accepted Kant's "Copernican revolution." That is, they thought that Kant had successfully shown that the world as we know it is not "mind-independent," but one that is structured by mind: the forms of intuition and the categories of the understanding. In some sense there would be no world without a mind to think that world.

But what mind is it that does this work? This question leads to the third crucial step. It seems obvious that the world exists independently of any finite mind or ego. All such minds or egos are themselves objects in the world, knowable as are other parts of the world. I do not bring the world into existence by my thinking, and the same is surely true of every finite mind. The mind that structures reality must then be an Absolute "I," an infinite mind or spirit that can be identified with God.

Does this Absolute have an existence that is in any way independent of the world? Or is the world that is known identifiable, in a Spinozist fashion, with the Absolute? These are the questions that have led to different strands of interpretation for Idealism.

JOHANN GOTTLIEB FICHTE

J. G. Fichte (1762–1814) was the child of poor parents in Saxony, but he received an education through the patronage of a local noble who recognized Fichte's intellectual gifts. After working as a private tutor, Fichte was a professor at the University of Jena, and later, in Berlin, after that university was founded. In his early period Fichte was known for somewhat radical political and religious views, including support for the French Revolution and an argument that a religious revelation must conform to Kant's moral philosophy. Kant himself helped Fichte get one of his early works published, and this work created a sensation in Germany. Fichte's critical views on religion later led to attacks on him as an atheist and even a nihilist, which required him to resign from his professorship at Jena.

Although Fichte saw himself as a follower of Kant, he quickly rejected the Kantian distinction between the phenomenal and noumenal worlds, and set out to develop a unified system that would preserve what he saw as Kant's valid insights. Fichte described this system as a *Wissenschaftslehre*, meaning a "theory of science" or "doctrine of science." "Science" here does not refer to the natural sciences, as the word usually does in contemporary thought, but to the project of a unified account of the whole of knowledge. Fichte believed that such a unified system could only be made possible by a unified starting point. He believed that one of the central problems in Kant's philosophy was the tension between Kant's theoretical philosophy and practical philosophy. The latter was one in which the freedom of the self was foundational, but the former described the "phenomenal world" as determined and mechanistic.

Fichte believed that the only possible way to achieve such a unified system was to start with practical reason, beginning with an "I" that is conscious of its own freedom. There are really only two possibilities: to start with the free self or to start with a mechanistic account of "things." Neither starting point can be proved or demonstrated. However, if one starts with objects, it is impossible to give an account of the self or the "I" that does justice to its nature. However, if one starts with the "I" or the self, Fichte thinks that it is possible to explain or make sense of the world of objects, following a Kantian line of argument. He tries to argue that the free self in some way requires the world of objects as its field of action. In this way he thinks his unified system justifies a metaphysical idealism as philosophically true, but he argues that this idealism is consistent with a kind of commonsense realism, thus avoiding the problems of Berkeley. For Fichte the starting point in the self is in some sense morally required, for without this starting point I cannot understand my moral vocation. He thus affirms what he calls the "primacy of practical reason." The Absolute must then be conceived in moral terms.

FRIEDRICH WILHELM JOSEPH VON SCHELLING

As a young person, Friedrich Schelling (1775–1854) attended a Protestant seminary in Tübingen, where he became friends with Hegel and also the poet Friedrich Hölderlin. Over a long life, Schelling changed his philosophical position numerous times, ending his career holding Hegel's old chair of philosophy at the University of Berlin, while developing a position that critiqued Hegel. In his early writing, however, Schelling follows Fichte in developing a form of Idealism. It is not surprising that Schelling develops a view that is similar to Fichte since he was wrestling with the same problem that faced Fichte: how to reconcile the freedom and spontaneity of the self that knows nature with a nature that appears deterministic. Kant had tried to solve the problem by removing the self that is free from the phenomenal world to the noumenal world. However, in his late *Critique of Judgment* Kant explores the idea that nature itself contains more than mechanism. This book explores our sense of beauty and the sublime, and it suggests connections between the beauty perceived in nature and the freedom embodied in human artistic works.

We saw that Fichte was deeply influenced by Kant's moral and practical philosophy, but Schelling is more shaped by Kant's aesthetics. Schelling agrees with Fichte that we cannot simply see nature as a mechanistic play of objective forces. However, we cannot simply see it as something that is the product of a self either, because the self can only be a self in relation to what is an "other." Thus the "I" and the natural world must in some way form a unity. The natural world is part of a "subject," but a subject that is at an elemental level unconscious. How is it possible for thought to know a reality that is in some way opaque to thought? The answer lies in aesthetic experience. The artist is conscious of his or her intentions as a producer of art, but the work of art itself as a product always transcends those intentions. Aesthetic experience of nature, in a similar way, helps us grasp a world that cannot be reduced to the explanations of science. The natural world is indeed the product of mind, but mind that is not fully transparent to itself. Schelling's writings are often obscure, and it is unclear exactly what is the status of this Absolute that is "subject-object." Is the natural world a manifestation of some kind of transcendent Subject, or is Schelling simply redescribing the natural world in terms that make it sound more personal and less mechanistic? The answers are far from obvious.

GEORG WILHELM FRIEDRICH HEGEL

G. W. F. Hegel (1770–1831) was born into a Protestant family in south Germany (Stuttgart), but was not especially pious. As noted above, he attended the theological seminary in Tübingen, where he became friends with Schelling and Friedrich Hölderlin. However, the theology taught there seemed scholastic and arid to Hegel and his friends, who spent much time discussing Kant's philosophy and the exciting developments associated with the French Revolution. Hegel moved away from Christian orthodoxy, though he continued to affirm, particularly in his mature thought, that his philosophy was in fundamental harmony with the Christian religion. (Whether this is true is dubious, however.) Hegel's first philosophical work was a comparison of Fichte's and Schelling's metaphysics, in which he was quite critical of Fichte and seems to side with Schelling. However, he eventually moves away from Schelling's position as well, though with Schelling's help he accepted a professorship at Jena, where Schelling was already teaching.

Hegel's first important philosophical work, and perhaps even today his most influential book, is his *Phenomenology of Spirit*. Older translations render this as *Phenomenology of Mind*. The German word is *Geist*. Dictionary definitions render this term as both "mind" and "spirit," and many Hegelians in the late nineteenth century translated it into English as "mind." However, contemporary scholars, for reasons to be explained, think that "mind" is misleading and that "spirit" is much closer to what Hegel intends.

Hegel claims, somewhat romantically, that he completed the book at Jena as the guns began to fire for the important battle that occurred there during the Napoleonic wars. As the result of the battle, the university closed, and Hegel had to move, publishing *The Science of Logic* and later, *Encyclopedia of the Philosophical Sciences in Outline*. These books helped him secure the chair in philosophy at the University of Berlin, where he died of cholera in 1831. During his time in Berlin he published an influential work in political philosophy, the *Philosophy of Right*. After his death many of his lecture series given at Berlin were published, including ones on *Philosophy of History*, *History of Philosophy*, *Aesthetics*, and *Philosophy of Religion*.

The **Phenomenology of Spirit.** Hegel's *Phenomenology of Spirit* is a difficult book in many ways. In part it reads like a kind of strange history of Western culture, including accounts of art, religion, and philosophy, drawn from periods and areas as diverse as ancient Egypt and Greece, and modern France and Germany. The book also includes social and political descriptions of human social arrangements of various kinds, and excursions into various scientific matters. To make matters more complicated, the "history" is only loosely chronological, as Hegel jumps back and forth between the ancient, medieval, and modern periods. To make sense of this, one must recognize that the book is not intended to be straightforward history; rather, it is a kind of "self-help" manual, in which Hegel promises to help his reader ascend from the standpoint of ordinary, commonsense perspectives on the world and arrive at the standpoint of "Reason," which eventually makes possible "absolute knowledge." The assumption is that this intellectual journey is one that the human race has already made. The long and arduous historical process described is one that a contemporary individual can under-stand and recapitulate in his or her own consciousness, with Hegel's help. I try to give some account of what Hegel does in the work below.

Hegel's critique of epistemology as foundational philosophy. One of Hegel's most interesting contentions can be seen in a criticism he makes against Kant. Hegel says that a "main line of argument" in Kant's "critical philosophy" is that, prior to inquiring about God or essences or any-thing else, we must first examine the "faculty of cognition," to see if it is up to the task.[1] Hegel is surely right here in his view of Kant. Kant's major emphasis is that philosophy must begin with a "critique" of the powers of reason, one that will help us see what it is possible to know and what cannot be known. However, this idea that an inquiry into the powers of human cognitive faculties is somehow foundational to all philosophy is not unique to Kant. Something very similar is present in

---

[1] G. W. F. Hegel, *Logic* 1.10, in G. W. F. Hegel, *Hegel's Logic*, trans. William Wallace (Oxford: Claren-don, 1975), 14.

many of the modern philosophers, beginning with Descartes and Locke. We might call this view the "primacy of epistemology."

Hegel thinks that the idea that before we can decide what we know we must first develop a correct theory of knowledge and how knowledge is gained is absurd. If we want to examine the "faculty of cognition," the "instrument" by which we know things, what instrument can we use except the one we want to investigate? If we don't know anything, how could we possibly develop an account of what knowledge is, or know how we gain knowledge? Even to examine the limits of reason we have to use reason. Hegel holds that philosophical understanding of a subject must *follow* the achievement of knowledge; it is not a precondition for knowledge. This is just as true for epistemology as it is for any other subject area. In a memorable line from the *Philosophy of Right*, Hegel tells us that "the owl of Minerva" (symbolizing philosophy) only takes flight "when the shades of night are gathering."[2] Thus to make epistemology some kind of foundational discipline that precedes knowing is impossible. "To seek to know before we know is as absurd as the wise resolution of the scholastic, not to venture into the water until he had learned to swim."[3] On this view the process whereby one gains knowledge is also the process by which one shows how knowledge is possible, and how it is justified.

The starting point and method of philosophy: Hegel's **Phenomenology of Spirit.** Hegel's rejection of the primacy of epistemology goes hand in hand with his own account of how philosophy should be done. One important question concerns the starting point of philosophy. Kant had criticized his rationalist predecessors as "dogmatists" who thought that philosophy was grounded in a priori metaphysical claims, known by pure reason. Some of Kant's successors thought that the only alternative to such dogmatism was to begin with some assumptions or presuppositions that were affirmed on faith. Hegel rejects both of these

---

[2]G. W. F. Hegel, *Philosophy of Right*, trans. T. M. Knox (Oxford: Oxford University Press, 1967), preface, p. 13.
[3]Hegel, *Logic* 1.10, p. 14.

alternatives. He says the philosopher must start with "immediacy" or with "ordinary consciousness." This is not a return to Reid's philosophy of common sense, because Hegel is not affirming that the views of the ordinary person are truths that must be accepted. Rather, this standpoint provides a starting point for rational reflection, which Hegel claims must be "dialectical" in nature, a concept we will shortly examine.

In effect, Hegel says, "start where you are." However, "where you are" is just that: a starting point. It does not provide some kind of certain foundation on which the house of knowledge can be built. Hegel thus rejects the "foundationalism" present in both empiricism and rationalism in modern Western philosophy. What we must do is begin with the claims and assumptions that are present in ordinary consciousness and common sense, but subject those claims to critical scrutiny. That scrutiny, however, cannot be made from some kind of external standpoint. It does no good to criticize one point of view from some other dogmatic point of view. Rather, for Hegel, *all legitimate philosophical criticism is internal in nature.* The proper method for philosophy is to begin with some standpoint and think through the internal tensions and "contradictions" it will reveal when it is rigorously examined. Such critical examination must justify itself by showing that whatever "new" view arrived at is superior to the starting point, even when judged by the aims of that initial view itself. Thus what is "true" in the old view is not abandoned but preserved in a kind of higher truth.

The *Phenomenology of Spirit*, like almost everything in Hegel's philosophy, has a tripartite structure. The first part, titled "Consciousness," begins with our ordinary consciousness of objects that seem independent of us, and tries to show how such a consciousness eventually comes to see that the knowledge it has of objects is shaped by the contributions of the mind. (This section basically recapitulates a Kant-type account of knowledge of the world.)

The second part, "Self-Consciousness," moves from a focus on knowledge of the world to knowledge of the self that makes possible such knowledge. One of Hegel's distinctive views is that self-knowledge depends on others; I do not really know myself until I encounter the self-consciousness of others. Hence the section on self-consciousness follows the journey of the individual who is seeking an identity in relation to other selves. This intersubjective encounter initially takes the form of competition. In a famous section, titled "Lordship and Bondage" (sometimes translated "Master and Slave"), Hegel argues that when one consciousness encounters another, each seeks to dominate or control the other, seeking an identity by extracting recognition from the other. A life-or-death struggle ensues, in which the stronger individual wins, and the weaker submits to the stronger to save his life. It appears that the master is the true self, since the slave is property controlled by the master, and the master seems to have the recognition that was sought from the other. However, Hegel argues that the relationship undergoes a kind of reversal. The master is just a consumer and depends on the slave to supply the master's needs. The slave, however, through being forced to work, acquires skills and a consciousness of his own power, and it gradually becomes clear that it is the master who is dependent on the slave's abilities.

The relationship is ultimately not satisfactory for either master or slave, and Hegel extends the narrative through forms of self-consciousness he calls "Skepticism" and "the Unhappy Consciousness." In the former there is a retreat to an inner life to compensate for the unsatisfactory character of the actual community. In the latter, the self becomes aware of an ideal self that could be realized, but thinks of this ideal as a transcendent reality (such as God) that cannot be experienced or made concrete. (Hegel is probably here giving his own characterization of medieval Christian spirituality, always going on pilgrimages and seeking a relationship with a God perceived as transcendent.) What the self is seeking is a true community, "an I that is a we." Such a community would provide the individual with an identity, but would still allow the individual self to be a true individual.

Hegel thinks ancient city-states, such as Athens, provided an identity of sorts by providing a community. Ultimately, however, these communities were particular and provincial; they could not withstand rational criticism that seeks what is universal. Such communities are experienced as external to the self and therefore limit freedom. The breakup of the city-state led to the birth of an individual consciousness, but such a consciousness is alienated from itself because of its failure to be rooted in a community. There is an antithesis between a community that stifles individual identity, and an individualism that promises freedom but cannot provide an identity. As we will see, the modern liberal state is supposed to reconcile this struggle between the individual and society, providing a society in which there is freedom, equality, and mutual recognition.

After describing self-consciousness, the *Phenomenology* moves on to describe the standpoint in the next section, titled "Reason." Hegel here describes the developing self-consciousness that is made possible in this new type of society. The individual becomes aware that the divine is not a transcendent reality existing separately from world. Rather, the divine manifests itself in that world, supremely in the human spirit itself. Hegel looks at this manifestation of Spirit in such human activities as art, religion, and philosophy itself. Thus the concluding chapters of the *Phenomenology* fall under the titles "Spirit," "Religion," and "Absolute Knowing," the standpoint from which a genuine understanding of the whole is possible. We now begin to see why the translation of *Geist* as "Mind" is misleading, since "Spirit" is fully actual in human communities of a certain kind and the activities that such communities make possible.

Hegel's philosophy summarized (and why it is impossible to summarize). A concise and clear summary of Hegel's philosophy is a daunting, perhaps impossible task. I shall attempt to lay out its main character by explaining six propositions. If I am successful, the reader will understand why this summary in one sense is all wrong: Hegel's philosophy resists being reduced to a set of propositions. One might think of this summary as a ladder that one must climb up, but that must be kicked away once one has ascended. I will nonetheless attempt a summary by giving six accounts of Hegel's view of "the True." The term *the True* is chosen rather than *Truth* because Hegel's account is both ontological and epistemological. He is giving an account both of what is real and of our knowledge of the real.

Proposition 1: The True is the whole. One reason Hegel's philosophy cannot be summarized is that he views his philosophy as in some way giving the ultimate truth about the whole of reality. Hegel sees the history of philosophy as a series of attempts to describe reality, but those attempts are always to some degree one-sided and partial. To get at the truth, one must try to see the truth in each of those views and put them together. Any single propositional claim is inevitably one-sided and partial. The True can only be provided by the story as a whole.

Reality is for Hegel, as it was for Spinoza, an interconnected whole. Though he does not want to deny differences, as did Parmenides, he is ultimately a monist who affirms that all of reality is one. His goal is to help us see the unity while continuing to recognize the differences.

For this reason, it is difficult to criticize Hegel. If one presents an objection, Hegel's response is to accept the objection—as another one-sided and partial account that needs to be incorporated into Hegel's own view. Hegel's critics thus face a difficult challenge: How does one avoid having one's thought appropriated by Hegel as one more partial expression of the truth? As we will see, Kierkegaard, one of Hegel's greatest critics, worries about this issue and fears that he will become a "paragraph" in Hegel's system. Kierkegaard's response to the problem is not to attack Hegel directly but to use humor to point out the problems in Hegel's thought.

Proposition 2: The True is the rational. Kant had argued that the human mind necessarily conceives the world in a certain way, but that we cannot know that reality in itself (the noumenal world) is as we must conceive it. Hegel fundamentally disagrees, holding that what is real is rational, and what is rational must ultimately be real. The idea that there is an unsurpassable gulf between the way human reason conceives the world and the way the world actually is must be rejected. In the end, if we have good reason to think reality is a certain way, then we must affirm that it is that way. This lies at the heart of Hegel's Idealism. The claim that reality is fundamentally "Spirit" is essentially a claim that reality is rational.

Proposition 3: The True is a process. As already noted, Hegel is, like Spinoza, a monist who affirms that the whole of reality is one interconnected whole. Spinoza had affirmed this claim by arguing that all of reality is one *substance,* which can be variously described as God or nature. One of the key claims of Hegel's *Phenomenology* is that "everything turns on grasping and expressing the True, not only as *substance* but equally as *subject.*"[4]

What does it mean to say that reality is a subject and not just a substance? For Hegel, a subject is a being that *becomes* what it ultimately is. The problem with the concept of substance is that it is too static. Since reality is Mind or Spirit, it must be conceived as a dynamic process, so that only at the end does it become clear what it was all along. To understand reality we must see it not only as what it is at some particular standpoint but also as what it is becoming, and what it will finally be.

Proposition 4: The True is dialectical. The process that characterizes reality for Hegel is *dialectical.* This key term is difficult to understand because it is both ontological and epistemological for Hegel. That is, "dialectic" describes both the character of the process by which reality becomes itself, and also the character of the thinking that allows us to understand that process. This makes sense for Hegel, of course, since "what is rational is actual and what is actual is rational."[5]

---

[4]G. W. F. Hegel, *The Phenomenology of Spirit,* trans. A. V. Miller (Oxford: Oxford University Press, 1977), 9-10.

[5]G. W. F. Hegel, *Encyclopaedia,* in *Philosophy Classics,* vol. 4, *Nineteenth-Century Philosophy,* ed. Forrest E. Baird and Walter Kaufmann (Upper Saddle River, NJ: Prentice-Hall, 1997), 44.

Let us begin with dialectic as a description of the process by which what is real becomes what it truly is. Basically, the process is one in which something, in order to become itself in a deeper, truer way, must negate itself. Paradoxically, something must become what it is not in order to become what it is.

To understand this, we might begin by thinking of the process by which a human person becomes a mature adult, which provides an illustration of dialectical progress most people can understand. A young child has a sense of self, an identity, but this identity is acquired from the parents. The child internalizes the values and beliefs it gains from caregivers. However, in order for the child to become a genuine adult, this identity must be critically tested. It is common for the adolescent to reject or rebel against those parental values. In Hegel's language the adolescent negates its established identity. (For Hegel, negativity is the moving force of history and progress; nothing can become anything without negating what it has been.) However, pure negativity is unstable and unsatisfactory. Eventually the child must affirm a positive identity, and this may well include a modified version of what was inherited from the parents. However, this identity now belongs to the person in a deeper way; it is not just something inherited, but something freely chosen.

A distinctive feature of Hegel's dialectic is its tripartite character. Typically, there is movement from an initial positive state to a second state, which is a negation of the first. Out of that conflict, a third phase results, a new and higher form of positivity, one that preserves what is true and valuable in the first two elements. However, this new positive element has its own one-sidedness and limitations, leading to a new negation, and the dialectic thus continues. Textbooks sometimes describe the three moments of the dialectic as "thesis, antithesis, and synthesis," but Hegel himself rarely uses this language. The first moment of the dialectic describes something "in-itself," and thus gives an account of being. The second, negative moment typically involves self-consciousness, described as being "for-itself," since self-consciousness is characterized by the ability to step back or negate what one is. The third moment incorporates and transcends the first two. It is "in-itself and for itself," subjective and objective in character.

The tripartite character of Hegel's thought is very evident if one merely looks at the table of contents of his major works. In the "System" that Hegel provides, there are three major elements: Logic, Philosophy of Nature, and Philosophy of Spirit. Logic describes Spirit "in-itself." Hegel also describes the Logic using the language of religion. He says that Logic provides a description of God "in-itself," an account of God prior to creation of the world. (As we shall see, this language is likely pictorial or metaphorical and is not to be taken literally.) Philosophy of Nature describes Spirit as matter, Spirit that has objectified itself and become what it is not. Matter is Spirit, but it is "slumbering spirit," spirit that has negated itself and does not appear immediately as spirit. The Philosophy of Spirit describes Spirit as "in-itself and for-itself," giving an account of the natural world's overcoming of its negativity and discovery of itself as Spirit. This happens primarily in human persons and communities, that part of the natural world that has gained an understanding of its own spiritual character. Subjective Spirit manifests itself in individual consciousness, and Objective Spirit in social communities and institutions. Absolute Spirit (art, religion, philosophy) are the activities carried on by individuals in such communities, having both a subjective and objective reality.

Proposition 5: The True is the concrete. For Hegel the dialectical process moves from the abstract to the concrete. Hegel is critical of all ideals that are posited as unattainable ideals. He believes that reality itself is a process that moves from an abstract form of being to one that is concrete. However, Hegel's conception of what is "concrete" is not what one might think. In contemporary culture, intellectual thought is regarded as "abstract," and raw experience tends to be seen as concrete. However, Hegel sees raw experience as abstract because it resists a rich and differentiated description. In the end, raw experience is something we can only gesture at, or describe as "this," something we are experiencing "here and now." For Hegel what is concrete is richly differentiated, and thus describable in concepts, though dialectically, and not simply through static propositions. Thus, for Hegel, ideals such as God or the norms of ethics must move from abstraction to concrete reality. This means they must be realized in concrete material fashion, chiefly through human communities and the spiritual activities that such communities make possible. Even if ideals are not fully realized, they must be seen as realities that are in process of coming into existence. The gap between what is and what ought to be is merely provisional for Hegel.

This means that human history is deeply meaningful. It is literally the theater in which the divine is becoming itself fully. Hegel actually uses the Christian doctrines of the incarnation and the coming of the Holy Spirit to describe this. God is for him not an abstract entity existing in some realm distinct from space and time. The incarnation is seen as a story or myth that reveals the unity of the divine and the human, and the indwelling of the Spirit means that God is not to be thought of as a remote being in heaven, but something that is manifest in human life. Thus Hegel's account of Spirit leads directly to a philosophy of history that we will consider below.

Proposition 6: The True is a system. Hegel insists that since reality is Spirit, and what is real is rational, ultimately all of reality must be understandable as a manifestation of Spirit. As we saw above, views that might seem to be objections to Hegel's view are regarded as partial, one-sided versions of the truth. Hegel is convinced that his account of reality provides an account that in principle enables an understanding of everything. By claiming reality is a system Hegel does not mean that one can deductively arrive at particular facts. Rather, he means that in retrospect those facts can be understood in relation to other truths, and the account as a whole provides the ultimate meaning of being. The rationality of being is in effect the intelligibility of being.

Hegel's philosophy of history, ethics, and political philosophy. As we have seen, for Hegel God is not a particular personal being, like the God of classical theism, who is distinct from the natural world. Rather, in some sense all of reality is Spirit. The natural world is Spirit, but it is Spirit that is not fully aware of itself as Spirit. It is in human communities that Spirit comes to full self-consciousness. This means that for Hegel human history has a profound meaning. History is the place where God or Spirit comes to be what it is and fully realizes itself.

Hegel claims that Reason is the ultimate ruler of history. To use traditional religious language (as Hegel himself does), it is God who governs the world.[6] This claim is spelled out in what would be called (in the twentieth century) a grand "metanarrative." Since history is governed by Reason, the meaning of history is fundamentally the story of the spread of freedom, since freedom is only realized through Reason, which secures autonomy. The account Hegel provides is decidedly "Eurocentric," as he thinks that the end or goal of history has been realized in the modern European states. As Hegel sees human history, there is a progression from "Asian despotism," in which only the ruler is free, to the Greek city-state (such as Athens), in which some are free, though the state still depends on slavery. Finally, in the modern European state, slavery is abolished and all are citizens. Society provides a community of equality in which everyone is recognized by everyone, and all are equal. The dialectic of competition, epitomized in the lordship and bondage story, is finally overcome. Thus for Hegel the modern state is in a true sense the "end of history," the realization of the goal that history has been seeking all along. We might even go so far as to say that Hegel here provides a kind of "realized eschatology," in which the modern state is seen as the fulfillment of the kingdom of God.

This account sounds extremely optimistic, even triumphalist, but Hegel's account of the process by which history has proceeded is

---

[6]G. W. F. Hegel, *Reason in History: A General Introduction to the Philosophy of History*, trans. Robert S. Hartman (New York: Liberal Arts Press, 1953), 47.

anything but optimistic. As Hegel sees things, it is only through negativity that all progress is possible, and thus it is not surprising that the
"progress" of history has depended on death and destruction. Hegel
again appeals to religious imagery, invoking the Christian view that
Christ's death has overcome evil, by describing human history as a
"Golgotha" that has made Spirit's triumph possible.

When Hegel says that history is the triumph of Reason, and that it
manifests itself in the achievement of universal freedom, he does not
mean that this is what historical agents were seeking. Rather, Hegel says
that it is the "cunning of Reason" that Spirit uses the selfish motives of
historical agents for its own goals. Thus Napoleon may have aimed at
personal glory and not the fulfillment of human freedom, but he was
nonetheless the agent of Spirit in achieving its goals. Napoleon undermined the ancient medieval state and made the modern state possible.
He thus became what Hegel described as one of the "world-historical
individuals," the people who play a decisive role in history, even though
their own personal goals may be entirely distinct from the ends they
make possible.

Hegel's suspicion of abstract ideals that remain merely abstract
shapes his ethical thinking as well. As we saw in the last chapter, Kant
had developed a rational ethic grounded in the categorical imperative,
a principle of reason that can be used to test the various "maxims" that
humans consider as principles for action. Hegel calls this kind of individual ethic *Moralität*, and criticizes it for being too abstract and formal.
It cannot give an actual individual guidance for life. For reason to guide
actual human life it must become embedded in the laws and customs
of a "people" or a "folk." The modern nation-state is the embodiment of
such a "people." Since Hegel sees the modern state as realizing the demands of reason, it is logical that the requirements of the state take
precedence over the requirements of individual conscience and even
over social institutions such as the family and "civil society." Hegel,
unlike Hobbes and Locke, does not see the state as an institution

created by individuals through a contract that aims at the fulfillment of their individual ends. Rather, in some sense the state is what makes it possible for individuals to have an identity, to be who they are. Society is constitutive of the individual, not just a tool created by individuals for their own ends.

Hegel, like Kant, wants ethics to be universal, but he demands what he calls a "concrete universal," a universal that has been actualized in history. Unlike Kant and Hume, Hegel does not believe in a sharp distinction between "facts" and "values," or between what is and what ought to be. We must recall that the "real is the rational and the rational is the real." So what is universal must be realized in history.

Absolute Spirit and philosophy of religion. The modern Western state provides the community for the self-realization of Spirit. However, within those communities Spirit comes to full self-realization through those activities that constitute what Hegel calls "Absolute Spirit." These activities are art, religion, and philosophy. All three of these make possible an awareness of God or Spirit. Their object is thus the same. However, they differ in the manner in which Spirit is apprehended. In art, Spirit is grasped immediately through the senses. Religion involves more conceptual content, as religion grasps God through what Hegel calls "picture-thinking." We might translate this into the language of narrative or even "myth." Philosophy is the activity in which Spirit is grasped purely as Spirit, and thus in some sense philosophy provides a fuller and clearer account of the "Truth," which art and religion both grasp in their own way. Hegel thus does not hesitate to view philosophy as the arbiter of theological truth, even though it does not state those truths in theological language.

Of course within each of these three spheres of activity there are lower and higher forms. Hegel argues that Christianity is the "Absolute Religion" and is thus truer than other religions, because its trinitarian view of God allows for a God who is not sharply distinct from the human community, but has become incarnate as a human, and who dwells as Spirit within the community of those who worship "in spirit and in truth." Thus Hegel claims that his philosophy can be seen a defense of Christianity against the skepticism of the Enlightenment, and the critical attacks of Kant and Hume. On Hegel's view, this philosophical vindication of Christianity also gives Christianity immunity from the attacks based on historical-critical study of the Bible. The "picture-thinking" that religion employs cannot be undermined by scientific study of history. Religious truth is embedded in history, but it cannot be deduced from historical facts.

In a later chapter I will examine Kierkegaard's critique of these claims. Here I will merely summarize Kierkegaard's reaction: he thinks that Hegel's "defense" of Christianity is really a betrayal, because it makes Christianity into something essentially different from what it is.

The aftermath of Hegel's philosophy: Left-wing versus right-wing Hegelianism. Even before Hegel died his followers had divided into what were called "right-wing" and "left-wing" Hegelians. They divided over what most humans disagree about: religion and politics. The right-wing Hegelians took seriously Hegel's language about logic as an account of God independent of creation. They thus tried to interpret Hegel's philosophy in a way that was more or less consistent with Christian orthodoxy. God was for them a reality not reducible to what was manifest in the natural world. It is probably best to interpret such a view as a form of panentheism. God is not wholly separate from creation, but he is not reducible to creation either. God is manifest in creation but has a degree of transcendence.

The right-wing Hegelians also interpreted Hegel in a politically conservative manner. They emphasized the way his philosophy offered a justification of the modern liberal state as the "end of history," and thus rejected any radical alternatives to the status quo.

The left-wing Hegelians had a very different take. They emphasized Hegel's claim that the divine only exists insofar as it becomes concrete in history. On this view Hegel does not really believe in a God who transcends the natural order and exists independently of that order. Rather, they interpreted Hegel's religious language as an attempt to make sense of religious values in a world with no extra-empirical realities. Hegel uses the language of religion to describe what is divine and absolute in immanent human experience.

Politically the left-wing Hegelians emphasized the idea that dialectical progress always requires a negation of the status quo. Thus for them Hegel's philosophy justified a rigorous and ruthless critique of the status quo in Prussian Germany.

The argument between right-wing and left-wing Hegelianism continues to the present day. A few of Hegel's contemporary defenders view him as providing an account of the world in relation to God, in which God is seen as an "Absolute Mind" becoming manifest in the world. Such a view gives Hegel affinities with Plotinus and other pantheistic thinkers. However, the dominant strands in contemporary Hegel interpretation see him as rejecting any kind of God who is a conscious agent distinct from the world. Rather, Hegel uses traditional religious language, as did Spinoza, to describe what is divine about the world, particularly the human world insofar as it transcends what is merely natural and animal-like. This kind of interpretation is perhaps close to the left-wing Hegelianism that followed Hegel. On this view the metaphysical religious language Hegel employs must be regarded as symbolic or mythical. Hegel recognizes the "divinity" and "universality" of contemporary Western culture, but does not accept any robust realities that transcend our world.

Neo-Hegelianism. Surprisingly, after Hegel's influence in Germany began to wane, in the mid- to late nineteenth century, his philosophy developed a dominant position in the United Kingdom and even became significant in the United States. The prominent figures in the United Kingdom were Bernard Bosanquet, F. H. Bradley, and J. M. E. McTaggert, and in America Josiah Royce. This view is often called "neo-Hegelianism." Although its proponents thought they were defending

Hegel's view, many philosophers would argue that there were significant differences. British neo-Hegelianism was an exuberantly metaphysical view, in which all of reality is grounded in being conceived or thought by an absolute mind. The most striking feature of this metaphysical view was that the Absolute was regarded as timeless. Thus ultimate reality is beyond time, and temporality itself cannot be ascribed to what is ultimately real. There is a passage in Hegel's *Phenomenology of Spirit* that can be interpreted as implying this timelessness of the absolute, but in general there is a marked difference between the thinking of the British neo-Hegelians and Hegel himself.

This version of Absolute Idealism dominated British philosophy in the late nineteenth and early twentieth centuries. It was in fact these views that provoked the "revolt" by such thinkers as G. E. Moore and Bertrand Russell that eventually became known as "analytic philosophy," a style of philosophy that remains dominant in Great Britain and North America.

Karl Marx

KARL MARX WAS BORN IN GERMANY in 1818, though he lived the greater part of his life in England and died there in 1883. Though Marx's family was Jewish, the father had converted to Christianity so that he could practice law. (Jews were prohibited from many professions during this period in many European countries.) Despite the family conversion, it is not likely that Karl Marx was ever a committed Christian believer. Marx is of course best known as a revolutionary, political theorist, and economist. He was the inspiration of the worldwide communist movement that led to the creation of the Soviet Union after the Bolshevik revolution in Russia in 1917. However, he also inspired the creators of what is now known as democratic socialism, which has been and continues to be an important political force, particularly in Western Europe.

Marx began his intellectual career as a philosopher, completing a doctoral dissertation on the difference between the philosophies of nature of Epicurus and Democritus. It is probably not accidental that both of these thinkers gave little attention to the gods, so Marx had a secular bent from early on. In addition to this dissertation, Marx wrote a number of early articles and books of a philosophical nature. Some of these, such as the *Economic and Philosophical Manuscripts* and the "Theses on Feuerbach," were unpublished during his lifetime, and others, such as "On the Jewish Question," and "Contribution to a Critique of Hegel's Philosophy of Right," were published in a short-lived and obscure journal, the *German-French Yearbook*. These writings were therefore largely unknown in Marx's later period, when he became famous as the author of *Capital*, and the man who, along with his co-worker Friedrich Engels, inspired the creation of revolutionary political parties all over Europe. The rediscovery of these early philosophical writings has led to a renewed interest in Marx as a philosopher.

What is the relation of these early philosophical writings to Marx's more mature work? Orthodox communists devoted to Leninism generally regard the early work as unimportant, "juvenile" work, not essential to the "scientific socialism" attributed to the later Marx. Oddly, some conservative anti-Marxists are equally dismissive of this early work. This reaction by conservatives may not be so odd after all, since the early writings of Marx contain many ideas that could be described as humanistic in the sense that they are shaped by a vision of human flourishing that is attractive. Those who want to dismiss Marx as having nothing of value to say therefore have reasons to ignore these early writings.

Scholars who study Marx are increasingly drawn to the view that there is a connection between Marx's early philosophical writings and his more mature work, a connection that sheds light in both directions. There certainly are changes as Marx turns his attention more directly to politics and economics. However, a good case can be made that some of the changes are largely changes in the language Marx uses; some of the core ideas of the early works remain in his mature work, though expressed differently. I shall argue that there are critical weaknesses in Marx's early writings that endure throughout his career; in other words, some of the problems in Marx appear early. However, there are also attractive elements in the early writings that remain in the later work as well. These must be recognized if we are to understand why so many millions of people were inspired by Marx's vision, and why some continue to find his work helpful.

MARX'S RELATION TO THE YOUNG HEGELIANS AND FEUERBACH

Marx's early writings show his involvement with the movement variously called the young Hegelians or the left-wing Hegelians. As noted in chapter nineteen the younger or left-wing Hegelians disagreed with their establishment "right-wing" Hegelian counterparts on religion and politics. The right-wing Hegelians interpreted Hegel as affirming the existence of a transcendent God who nonetheless manifests himself within the natural order. For them Hegel is, if not a traditional theist, at least someone who is attempting to preserve belief in a God who is real. The "young Hegelians" took Hegel's religious language as an attempt to appropriate traditional religious language for a view that sees the divine as something wholly immanent. There is no God other than nature and the historical process. God is a symbol of ideals that are embedded in this process, and which can be called divine in the sense that they are worthy of our devotion.

Politically, the establishment Hegelians saw Hegel as offering a vindication of the status quo, providing an argument that the modern state (particularly Prussia!) was the "end of history," the culmination of the historical process. The left-wing Hegelians disagreed, seeing Hegel's dialectic, which privileges negativity and sees progress as always stemming from the destruction of the status quo, as offering a radical critique of modern Western societies. Their goal was a radical criticism of the existing order.

One of the most influential of the young Hegelians was Ludwig Feuerbach, author of *The Essence of Christianity*. Feuerbach's thought breaks with German Idealism decisively, endorsing a form of materialism in which *der Mann ist was der isst* (a man is what he eats). *The Essence of Christianity* is most important for its development of what is often called the "projection theory of religion." The basic idea, which is hardly new, is that instead of God creating humans in his own image, humans have created God in their image. Feuerbach develops this idea specifically with respect to the Christian claim that God is essentially love. Humans are ideally social beings who should live together in a loving community, an idea Feuerbach expresses by saying that humans are "species beings." But in reality, humans fail to live this way, competing with each other and oppressing each other. However, we have a longing for our true nature, and in compensation for our failure to be our true selves, we "project" an image of an ideal human self, understood as a fully complete, loving, and powerful being. The being is of course God.

God is an illusory being for Feuerbach, one who reflects in a distorted fashion our own deepest needs. However, though God does not exist, our creation of God does have real consequences. Feuerbach thinks that humans devote their time and energy to pleasing this imaginary being at the expense of our relationships to each other. Feuerbach wants us to abandon any concern for an imaginary God and devote ourselves to healing our fractured social relationships.

Feuerbach's work was immensely important for Marx. In fact, making a pun on the meaning of Feuerbach's name in German, Marx goes so far as to say that "there is no other road . . . to *truth* and *freedom* except that leading *through* the stream of fire [the Feuer-bach]."[1] Marx enthusiastically adopted Feuerbach's view of human nature as essentially social, as well as his rejection of idealism and acceptance of materialism. However, the embrace of Feuerbach was not uncritical, as can be seen in Marx's "Theses on Feuerbach." These eleven theses were written by Marx in 1845, but not published until 1886, in a form slightly edited by Engels.

The very first thesis claims the "chief defect of all hitherto existing materialism—that of Feuerbach included—is that the thing, reality, sensuousness, is conceived only in the form of the *object of contemplation*, but not as *sensuous human activity, practice*."[2] This passage is quite reminiscent of Hegel's famous claim that it is essential to conceive Spirit as "subject" and not just as "substance." In fact, Marx goes on to say that because materialism neglected the subjective, active side of

---

[1]Karl Marx, "Luther as Arbiter Between Strauss and Feuerbach," in *Writings of the Young Marx on Philosophy and Society*, ed. and trans. Loyd D. Easton and Kurt H. Guddat (Indianapolis: Hackett, 1997), 95.

[2]Karl Marx, "Theses on Feuerbach," in *Karl Marx and Frederick Engels: Collected Works*, vol. 5, ed. Jack Cohen et al. (New York: International Publishers, 1976), 6. Page numbers following citations of this work are from this edition

reality that it was left to Idealism to develop this, though Idealism did so only "abstractly." We can see therefore that in embracing Feuerbach, Marx has not totally abandoned Hegel. We will see below how Marx attempted to combine a form of materialism with Hegel's dialectic, thus arriving at "dialectical materialism."

In thesis three Marx makes another very significant criticism of previous forms of materialism: Here Marx discusses what he calls the materialist doctrine that human beings are the product of circumstances and upbringing, and that the key to changing human nature is to change those circumstances. The problem with this materialist view is that it sees human beings merely as objects to be re-engineered; it "forgets that it is men who change circumstances and that the educator must himself be educated."[3] The social engineers who are supposed to change the circumstances inevitably become an elite class, and thus such a view "is bound to divide society into two parts, one of which is superior to society."[4] This shows a commendable concern for human equality and a recognition of the dangers of an elite class who wants to transform society in a way that does not involve the active consent and participation of the whole of society. The warning is ironic, however, since in reality the communist systems inspired by Marx, established in the Soviet Union and still existing in China, North Korea, Vietnam, and Cuba, all involve just this kind of division of society into two parts. All of them are based on the model of a "vanguard party" that tolerates no threats to its power.

In several of the other theses, Marx criticizes Feuerbach's account of religion as well. Marx agrees with Feuerbach that God is a human invention, and thus that the "religious world" has its foundation in a "secular basis."[5] However, Feuerbach fails to see that religion is not the main problem, and that abolishing religion will not really solve the human problem. Religion is created by particular social conditions, and

---

[3]Marx, "Theses on Feuerbach," 7.
[4]Marx, "Theses on Feuerbach," 7.
[5]Theses 4, 6, and 7 are particularly important on this point.

thus can only be overcome by changing society in ways that will make religion unnecessary. As Marx himself says in a different essay, religion is "the opium of the people, the soul of soulless conditions, the heart of a heartless world."[6] Merely getting rid of religion will not help much, if the world is still heartless and people still need some kind of consolation. Hence Marx concludes, in thesis eleven: "The philosophers have only *interpreted* the world in various ways; the point, however, is to *change* it."[7] Marx's own philosophical reflection has led him to embrace an activist, revolutionary agenda, for "man must prove the truth ... of his thinking in practice" (thesis 2).[8]

MARX ON HUMAN ALIENATION

The background for the "Theses on Feuerbach" can be found in the *Economic and Philosophical Manuscripts*, written slightly earlier in 1844, though not published until 1932, long after Marx died. In this unpublished and unfinished work, Marx in some ways sounds like a twentieth-century existentialist, in that he focuses on what I will call the problem of alienation. Alienation is a condition in which human persons are in some way separated from or distant from their true selves. Hegel had already focused on this problem in his *Phenomenology of Spirit*. For Hegel humans derive their identity from the community that defines them. The ancient city-state, such as Athens, provided such a community, but this community was provincial and one-sided and did not do full justice to the individual. It did not fulfill the demands of reason. The history of Western civilization is the history of the attempt to build a genuine community that offers individuals the equality and freedom demanded by reason. At one point in the *Phenomenology*, Hegel describes a form of Spirit he calls the "Unhappy Consciousness." The Unhappy Consciousness has a conception of the ideal self, but thinks of

---

[6]Karl Marx, *A Contribution to the Critique of Hegel's "Philosophy of Right,"* in Cohen et al., *Collected Works*, 3:175.

[7]Marx, "Theses on Feuerbach," 8.

[8]Marx, "Theses on Feuerbach," 6.

this true self as a separate, metaphysical reality, like the traditional God of theism. What Hegel really provides here is something like a projection theory of the divine; it is no accident that Feuerbach, who had been a Hegelian, should develop his own version of the projection theory of God.

The projection account of Feuerbach, like Hegel's "Unhappy Consciousness," is thus really an account of human alienation. It is because we humans have failed to become the true social beings that would make us flourish that we invent an imaginary being, God, who is simply ourselves presented as an alien, separate being. For Feuerbach, the key to overcoming alienation thus lies in overcoming religion, focusing our energies on building a human society rather than on the kingdom of God. Marx agrees with Feuerbach that religion is a form of alienation, but he does not see overcoming religion as the key to overcoming alienation. Religious alienation for Marx is a symptom of an underlying form of alienation that is more basic.

We saw in the last chapter that for Hegel the key social institution for overcoming alienation is the state. It is the modern liberal state that has created genuine community. Marx disagrees profoundly with Hegel on this point. He sees the modern state as an instrument of oppression. It provides an illusory form of community. Just as religion offers an illusory "kingdom of God," in which all are equal, the state offers a "political equality" that is illusory. All citizens are equal before the law, but Marx sees this equality as a fraud that allows one group of people to dominate and control the rest. The idea that the state was an instrument of domination and control was by no means unusual in Marx's day. This was an era in which "anarchism," a view that holds that the state must be abolished in order for a genuine human society to be formed, flourished. Marx agrees with the anarchists that the state is an instrument of oppression and a form of alienation. The state is, like God, a kind of "alien power" that reflects what genuine human life should be like, but rather than creating such life, it is controlled by the powerful for their own interests. However, just as was the case for religious alienation, Marx does not see political alienation as the fundamental form of alienation.

The problem with attempts to abolish religion or the state is that they do not recognize that these forms of alienation are grounded in something deeper. Religion is something our oppressive world makes necessary. In a similar way, in an individualistic, dog-eat-dog society the state is a necessary means of preventing a "war of all against all," the "state of nature" that Hobbes describes. In order to abolish religion and the state, one must abolish the conditions that make religion and the state necessary. For Marx, these conditions are economic. The most basic form of alienation is the alienation of humans from their work.

Marx begins his account in the *Economic and Philosophic Manuscripts* with what he claims is an actual economic fact: "The worker becomes all the poorer the more wealth he produces, the more his production increases in power and size."[9] This premise may seem controversial today, as we associate the development of industry with the growth of the middle class and greater prosperity. However, in the early stages of the Industrial Revolution Marx's claim seemed very plausible, as wages seem to have fallen as industry took hold. Wages were so low that even with child labor and the employment of whole families, workers often struggled to survive. For Marx, this was a paradox. Why should the lives of workers become worse just when human society is becoming more productive? The answer lies in understanding that the "wage-labor" that is the basis of capitalist industry is a form of alienation. Marx describes four dimensions to this alienation.

The most basic form of the worker's alienation is simply the alienation of the worker from the object he produces. "The worker is related to the *product of labor* as to an *alien* object."[10] John Locke, in his account of private property, had already argued that an object becomes my own

---

[9]Karl Marx, *Economic and Philosophic Manuscripts of 1844* 22, in Cohen et al., *Collected Works*, 3:271-72. Page numbers following citations of this work are from this edition.

[10]Marx, *Economic and Philosophic Manuscripts of 1844* 22, p. 272.

when I have "mixed my labor with it."[11] However, although under capitalism the worker does pour himself into the object he makes, when that object is finished it does not belong to the worker but to the factory owner. We can understand why it is that if the worker is more productive, he is not the one who will benefit. Under capitalism the satisfaction that the artisan gets from the object he makes is also lost because the worker cannot see what is made as really his own.

The second dimension of alienation is the way in which the worker becomes estranged from his own activity as a worker. Rather than being fulfilled by meaningful work, the activity of the worker is repetitive and meaningless, only a source of income. Marx believes that it is in work that humans should find their true identity, but under capitalism work becomes something to be endured, something that has no intrinsic meaning or value. "As a result, therefore, man (the worker) only feels himself freely active in his animal functions—eating, drinking, procreating, or at most in his dwelling and in dressing-up, etc.; and in his human functions he no longer feels himself to be anything but an animal. What is animal becomes human and what is human becomes animal."[12]

The third dimension of alienation is the estrangement of the worker from his life as a "species-being."[13] Marx means by this, as we have seen, that humans are essentially social creatures, and this is reflected in work that is cooperative or social. However, under capitalism each worker is competing with each other. If one worker asks for better working conditions or wages, he risks being replaced by another who will do the job for less. Any sense of solidarity or community among the workers is destroyed.

Finally, the workers are directly estranged from other humans. Since the worker is essentially a "wage-slave" who must sell his living labor to another, that other who owns that work is alien and hostile. It is at this point that Marx describes what becomes the key to his account of

---

[11]See the discussion on Locke in chap. 14.
[12]Marx, *Economic and Philosophic Manuscripts of 1844* 23, pp. 274-75.
[13]Marx, *Economic and Philosophic Manuscripts of 1844* 24, p. 275.

human history: the class struggle. However, Marx remembers the dialectic of "master and slave" in Hegel, in which the oppressed worker eventually gains power through work.[14] We shall see that Marx can claim that this is in fact the destiny of the worker under capitalism.

STANDING HEGEL ON HIS FEET: MARX'S DIALECTICAL ACCOUNT OF HISTORY

Marx seems to have gone far beyond Hegel at this point, and indeed he has. Indeed, Marx comes to see Hegel and philosophy as something like religion: a reflection in the realm of ideas of realities that are material. Hegel's philosophy of Spirit can actually be seen as a secularized version of the religious alienation Feuerbach describes. Surprisingly, however, Marx believes that there is still something to be learned from Hegel. If Hegel's account of the development of Spirit is a reflection in thought of a more basic material process, then it still may contain truth, in just the way that a reflection in a mirror contains a likeness to what it reflects. All that has to be done is recognize that in the mirror things are reversed.

Marx changes the metaphor slightly to describe his relation to Hegel. What must be done to Hegel is not to reverse the image from right to left, but turn it upside down. He says that he found "Hegel standing on his head," and therefore had to turn him so that he could stand on his feet.[15] This means the dialectical account of history that Hegel provides, properly deciphered, contains truth if it is "flipped." Marx therefore offers his own "dialectical materialism," in which humans are not simply understood as clumps of matter but as active beings who are engaged in actualizing themselves, much as Hegel thought Spirit was actualizing itself in human history. Hegel's dialectical account of history is married to Feuerbach's materialism.

---

[14]Marx, *Economic and Philosophic Manuscripts of 1844* 25-26, pp. 279-81.

[15]This famous statement of Marx about his relation to Hegel can be found in the afterword to the second German edition of *Das Kapital* (*Capital*). The various prefaces and afterwords that Marx (as well as Engels) wrote for this work can be found in most English editions. This afterword can be found online at the Marxists Internet Archive, "Afterword to the Second German Edition," https://www.marxists.org/archive/marx/works/1867-c1/p3.htm.

Since human history is the history of class struggles, the dialectical forces that clash for Marx are not primarily ideas but social classes. The dialectical account of Hegel is just the reflection in thought of these material forces. Nonetheless, Marx offers, as did Hegel, a grand story of human history in which it has a kind of telos or end. The foundation of the story is the doctrine of historical materialism, which sees the dominant forces of human history to be economic in nature. The world of human work is the economic "base"; what happens in religion and politics and philosophy is all part of the "superstructure," and is ultimately determined by the base.

The grand story begins for Marx with "primitive communism," found in tribal or communal societies where private property in the modern sense is unknown. This communism is far from being a lost paradise. There is a kind of equality and lack of exploitation, but also a brutal struggle to survive. It is undermined by the development of "division of labor," specialized work that leads to the existence of private property and social classes.

Early societies of this kind are built on agriculture, and the major classes are the aristocratic, warrior class, which owns the land and the slaves that till it, though of course there are traders and artisans as well. The state is largely the possession of the emperor or supreme ruler, just as was true in Hegel's account of history.

Feudal societies in the Middle Ages were also largely agricultural in nature, though oppressed serfs who escaped from the landed estates to which they were bound found refuge in cities and towns, developing guilds that led to a small middle class of merchants and artisans. Gradually the towns gained more power as guilds and artisan craftsmen led to the development of early, small forms of manufacturing, and the increasing importance of the middle class, the "burghers" or "bourgeoisie."

The Industrial Revolution transformed early manufacturing, leading to "big industry." The small artisans and independent farmers were increasingly forced to become day laborers in factories. This class made up of propertyless workers, which Marx calls the proletariat, has become increasingly important in the industrial age. Small businesses are swamped by the efficiency of the great factories, with the larger and more successful enterprises continually driving smaller competitors out of business, leading to monopolies. The cobbler making shoes cannot compete with the shoe factory; even farming becomes big business.

In each phase of this history, the dominating political class is the class that controls the key instruments of production. Thus political power in the medieval period is concentrated in the aristocracy, who own the land, but in the early modern period the middle class begins to contest the supremacy of the landed nobility. Marx sees a kind of "cultural lag" that operates through these changes. The newer economic system grows up within the political and ideological womb of the older economic system. The dominant class oppresses the lower classes, but through this oppression the ruling class creates its own antithesis, reminiscent of the Hegelian dialectic of master and slave. Finally, the newer classes, supported by their new economic power, are so strong that they are able to take political control. Since those with power do not voluntarily relinquish it, this normally requires a revolution. The French Revolution is seen as the model for this. It is a "middle-class revolution," in which those with new economic power wrest political power from the king and the nobility.

In the industrial period, the class structure is becoming greatly simplified. Increasingly, the class of capitalists, the owners of big business, becomes smaller, as monopoly forces drive smaller firms out of business. Conversely, as the class of capitalists becomes smaller, the class of the proletariat becomes larger, and formerly middle-class people are thrown into this class by inexorable economic forces. The capitalist depends on the proletariat, but in creating the proletariat it is bringing into existence its own dialectical nemesis.

There is, Marx thinks, an economic contradiction at the heart of capitalism, the crisis of "overproduction." Economic laws decree that the wage of the workers will on average just be enough for bare subsistence. Yet the capitalist cannot make a profit without selling the goods that are made. If workers are paid a mere subsistence wage, they will not have the spending power to buy the enormous quantity of goods the factory produces. If the output cannot be sold, then workers must be laid off. However, this simply further compounds the problem of over-production, since there are now even fewer workers being paid. The result is a spiral of unemployment, and throughout the nineteenth and twentieth centuries, there were recessions and depressions that seemed to happen exactly as Marx predicted.

Marx believed that eventually the system must collapse. The worker, just in order to survive, will have to seek a revolution and take control of the means of production, which will be socially owned. However, the revolt of the proletariat will be different from any previous revolution in human history. All previous revolutions resulted in one class toppling another class, while still oppressing other classes. Marx thinks that with the great simplification of class structure in capitalism this oppression will no longer be the case. In an industrial society, the proletariat forms the vast majority of the population, and there is no lower class to exploit. The proletariat will therefore take power not as a class to oppress other classes, but as a class that will create a classless society. We will finally be at the "end of history," a society of plenty, with no need for exploitation of any kind. We will have a society in which each will contribute according to his or her ability and take according to his or her needs. With the end of exploitation, the state as an instrument of exploitation will "wither away." Religion will also gradually go away as the masses will no longer need the "opium of the people."

Marx claims to have developed a "scientific socialism," which he distinguishes from the "utopian socialists" of his day. However, there is a decidedly utopian character to Marx's account of life after the proletarian revolution establishes a "classless society." A "new humanity" will come into existence that will not be selfish and acquisitive. The abundance of good and services made possible by modern industry means that the competitiveness created by scarcity will no longer exist.

CAPITAL: MARX'S TURN TO ECONOMICS

Marx spent a great part of the last part of his life writing *Das Kapital* (*Capital*). In this work he tries to show that the ideas he had arrived at via Hegel and Feuerbach could be "scientifically" or empirically established though study of economics and actual historical events. Marx thinks that his form of socialism is not rooted simply in ethical ideals but in facts. I have already noted how he distinguished his own "scientific socialism" from what he calls "utopian socialism," which takes its foundation in some ideal. Interestingly, however, this attempt to claim the mantle of "science" is actually Hegelian in character, as Hegel had described his own system as "science." Furthermore, the rejection of ideals that are transcendent is characteristic of Hegel. Unlike Kant, who began ethics from an a priori ideal, Hegel always tries to see the ideal as something emerging in actuality, a "concrete universal." Ironically, therefore, even when Marx turns away from philosophy to what he sees as empirical science, he is nonetheless following in Hegel's footsteps.

In *Capital* Marx aims to do several things. One is to explain how profit is possible under capitalism. One might not think this is a problem; after all, no one would invest in a factory if there were no prospect of a return on the investment. Yet Marx thinks there is something puzzling about profit, if one assumes, as classical economists did, that humans are to be conceived as rational economic agents. By and large, when such agents make an exchange, unless one party is deceived or cheated or simply uninformed, equal values are exchanged for equal values. People do not willingly pay more than the fair market value for an item. An automobile customer will not pay $50,000 for a car that could be purchased for $25,000 down the street. So it would seem that when an item is purchased, the price paid should approximately average the value of the item. However, presumably the seller would have to pay an amount equal to this value to create or obtain what is sold. How then is profit possible?

Marx's answer to this requires a distinction between two kinds of value: exchange-value and use-value. The two are very different. Use-value is just what the term implies: the value something has for us when we use it. The air we breathe has a great use-value; without it humans cannot survive. However, except in very unusual circumstances the air we breathe has no exchange-value; no one (as of yet) bottles and sells ordinary air to breathe. Commodities that are bought and sold have a use-value; otherwise no one would want them. However, the exchange-value of a commodity does not necessarily reflect its use-value.

The exchange-value of an item is what it is worth relative to other commodities that are bought and sold. Obviously, the price of a barrel of oil or a bushel of wheat varies all the time in accordance with the laws of supply and demand. Nevertheless, Marx thinks that the fluctuation in exchange-values nevertheless revolves around what one might call its true exchange-value, which is the cost of production of a commodity. When oil can be produced for $50 a barrel, and oil is selling for $80, more people will produce oil and the supply increases. Of course, as the supply increases the price will fall in accordance with economic laws. However, if the price falls below $50, the assumed cost of production, oil companies will stop producing oil, since they would otherwise lose money. In this case supplies will shrink, and prices will go back up.

This means, according to Marx, that the exchange-value of a commodity will in the long run center on its average cost of production. However, when the commodity is sold the capitalist hopes to make a profit. How is this possible if equal values are being exchanged for equal values? Where does the extra or "surplus value" come from?

The answer for Marx lies in the peculiar nature of human "labor-power." Under capitalism, labor is a commodity like any other, daily bought and sold on the labor markets. Like any other commodity, labor-power has both a use-value and an exchange-value. The exchange-value of a laborer's work will be, on average, the cost of producing it, that is, the cost of keeping the worker alive. Marxists call this view the "subsistence theory of wages." If it were correct, then in the long run the average wage of an unskilled worker could not far exceed the cost of providing the minimum amount of food, housing, and clothing to keep a worker (and perhaps his family, so he can reproduce) alive.

Suppose one is calculating the exchange-value of some textile, such as a shirt. The shirt is made of cotton. Some value is provided by the raw material itself; this reflects labor since the cotton must be planted and harvested. Then the cotton must be processed, and eventually the shirt manufactured, both of which require labor. Suppose the shirt sells for $10. Some of this exchange-value is due to the raw material, and some can be attributed to the machinery that the capitalist has invested in. Of course, the worker's labor adds value as well. How much of the value comes from each element will of course vary.

However, for Marx, all of the exchange-value of the shirt is ultimately due to labor. This is called the "labor theory of value," and it provides the key to understanding how profit is possible. The value of the cotton reflects the work to plant and harvest it; the added value of the processing reflects labor. Even the value added by the machinery reflects labor, since the machines had to be produced by work as well. All of these add value but, assuming equal values are exchanged for equal values, no "surplus value" is created.

The secret of surplus value is explained by the special character of labor. Although labor is a commodity under capitalism, it has a use-value, as does every other commodity. The use-value of oil is that it can be burned for fuel; wheat can be eaten for food. *The use-value of labor power is that it produces exchange-value.* Surplus value is made possible by the fact that there is a difference between the value of what a worker produces and the worker's own value as a commodity. The factory worker who is making shirts may produce exchange-value worth $20 an hour. In ten hours of work he can therefore produce $200 of exchange-value.

However, this value may exceed the worker's own exchange-value. Remember that the worker's wage will approximate the cost of keeping the worker alive (subsistence theory of wages). Perhaps $100 per day will suffice to keep the worker alive, yet the capitalist, when purchasing the laborer's work, gets the whole value of the output. The difference between the value of the worker's labor, valued as a commodity, and the value of what the worker can produce explains how profit is possible. All profit ultimately comes from the worker. The capitalist buys the worker as a commodity, but gets the "use" of the worker, which is to create value. If the worker can create more value than it takes for his own subsistence, then profit is possible.

In *Capital* Marx does not use the language of alienation found in his early work. However, there is a concept that seems very similar. As just noted, Marx holds to a labor theory of value, in which the exchange-value of a commodity is a product of labor. However, Marx argues that this is hidden in standard economic theories. People think of the "value" of an object as if it were an independent quality vested in the object, rather than being the expression of work. Marx says this belief in the objective value of commodities is a kind of superstition, in which objects are endowed with occult qualities, and he calls it "the fetishism of commodities." What is really going on, he thinks, is the product of human labor is not recognized as what it is, but is seen as a mysterious object. Most economists today reject the whole premise of Marx's argument, seeing "value" not as an objective feature of commodities but as a function of subjective desires. "Value" is just what someone wants and is willing to pay for.

Marx believes this central claim from *Capital* helps explain the widespread misery found in the working classes in Marx's day. Marx documents this misery by relying on the reports of the factory inspectors of the British government itself. It also explains why the solution to the problem is not simply to raise the workers' wages. In the long run wages cannot be raised more than their market value, because a capitalist who wants to be generous and pay more will be undercut by a competitor. (Something like this may underlie the problems caused by "outsourcing" and "globalization" in the contemporary economy in Western countries; jobs are lost to places where wages are lower.)

Surprisingly, Marx does not say that the capitalist is cheating the worker. He claims he is not giving a moral critique, because under capitalism the worker normally gets a fair market price for his labor. So the problem is not that the capitalists are evil people who cheat their workers. Given the system, they may be paying a fair wage. The problem lies in the system itself, which does not allow the worker to receive what is necessary to live a humane life.

Marx also thinks that in *Capital* he gives a compelling explanation of the "overproduction" that is endemic to capitalism and that leads to periodic depressions and recessions. The "contradiction" at the heart of capitalism is that it is the most productive economic system in history, producing an amazing output of goods and services, while paying the worker too little to be able to buy those products.

SUBSEQUENT HISTORY OF MARXISM

Marx and Engels predicted that socialism would inevitably be achieved in the advanced industrial countries of the world, such as Great Britain and Germany. The reason for this is that on their view true socialism is only possible when its material preconditions have been provided, and this requires the productivity of an industrial society. (One of Marx's errors may have been that he *overestimated* the power of capitalism, thinking that its productivity will suffice to transform human nature.) However, things did not turn out as Marx and his followers predicted.

It is in fact true that in the major Western countries, large socialist movements formed by the end of the nineteenth century. The growing power of labor unions and millions of voters gave socialists a large stake in countries such as France and Germany. However, as soon as socialist parties began to participate in democracy, the urgency of revolution began to recede. Through the ballot box, workers achieved such things as minimum-wage laws, worker protections, and universal health insurance. When socialists began actually to participate in government, then calls for revolution began to look problematic. One can hardly expect a government minister to support a revolution to overthrow himself! These movements eventually led to what was termed "revisionism." Perhaps Marx and Engels had been wrong to think that the goals of socialism would require a revolution; the goals of socialism could be achieved through democratic, peaceful processes. Gradually, the socialist parties of Europe became committed to what we today term "social democracy."

Marx had predicted that the workers of each country would ally with their fellow workers in other countries against the capitalists. However, when push came to shove, in World War I, this turned out not to be the case. Nationalistic and patriotic sentiments were far stronger among workers than Marx had thought would be the case. The various socialist parties of Europe each supported their own governments as France and Great Britain went to war with Germany and Austria-Hungary.

There was one exception, however. During World War I, Russia incurred one military disaster after another. The czar became so unpopular that he was overthrown by a revolution. The revolution was initially a democratic revolution, not a Marxist one. However, the revolutionary government continued the war and also became unpopular. Eventually a small group of radical Marxists called Bolsheviks staged a second revolution and seized control of the government, eventually leading to the creation of the Soviet Union of Socialist Republics, the world's first officially communist state.

The achievement of socialism in Russia should not have been possible on Marx's own theory. Since Russia was one of the least industrialized states in Europe it lacked the "material preconditions" that Marx claimed was the necessary basis for socialism. The population was not dominated by a proletariat who would easily abolish social classes but by peasants. The Bolsheviks, led by Vladimir Lenin, believed that a small group of workers, led by a "vanguard party" that understood the direction of history, could seize control of the state and bring about socialism in Russia through iron discipline. Thus, despite the claims of the Bolsheviks to be Marxists, a good case can be made that Leninism was a Marxist heresy. The heart of Marxism is the claim that the moving force of history is economic; Lenin substituted the political will of the party and its military arm for this economic process.

It is not too surprising then that Leninism quickly moved toward totalitarianism. As some of Lenin's old party comrades themselves predicted would happen, first the party began to rule in the name of the workers on behalf of the workers. However, there were no real democratic checks that allowed the workers (much less the peasants and other parts of the population) to control the party. Rather, the party attempted to control every part of life and tolerated no other centers of power. Eventually, the central committee of the party became the real power. In 1924, after Lenin's death, Josef Stalin took control and quickly became a dictator, controlling the central committee. Stalin killed millions of his own people, many through starvation and many others through executions and prison camps. Life in the Soviet Union became a grim mockery of the "new humanity" that Marx thought socialism would bring about.

Of course, the Soviet Union eventually collapsed; the verdict of history on its economic policies seems clear. Communist regimes (of a sort) still exist in China, Vietnam, Cuba, and North Korea, although it seems increasingly the case that these regimes are Marxist in name only. The main legacy of communism they continue to exhibit is one-party rule and a tendency to infringe on human rights. Perhaps Marx himself would not be surprised, since he consistently argued that the attempt to create socialism in a nonindustrial country would fail. However, my own judgment is that while Marx would probably have been horrified by the monstrous injustices of Stalinism and Maoism, he nonetheless prepared the way for those terrible events. Specifically, Marx placed little value on the freedoms and rights cherished by liberal democracies. Marx thought that such "political" freedoms were relatively unimportant in comparison with economic injustice. History has shown, however, that a disregard for human rights and political freedoms makes possible societies that are both economically unjust and willing to use the power of the state against individual citizens. Certainly, the democratic socialist parties of Europe seem much more attractive, since many of these countries, such as those of Scandinavia, while certainly having problems, seem to have combined a generous social safety net with democratic freedoms and the rule of law.

A CRITICAL EVALUATION

Some of the worst features of communist societies may reflect deviations from Marx's teachings. There is something appealing about Marx's concern for humane working conditions, and his desire for a society characterized by cooperation rather than exploitation. Students who read Marx's *Capital*, and learn about working conditions in nineteenth-century factories, are often appalled, especially when they realize that Marx is drawing on the reports of the British government's own factory inspectors. Some of the problems Marx addresses are clearly still with us. Those who work or have worked in fast-food restaurants or in "big box" retailers for low wages and little or no benefits can appreciate Marx's account of work as alienating. The replacement of workers by automation, and the outsourcing of jobs to low-wage areas are issues Marx focused on, and they are clearly still with us. Marx's analysis of the impact of economic forces on history has revolutionized such academic disciplines as history and political science. Despite the demise of communism, Marx remains an important and relevant thinker.

However, there are also deep problems in Marx's thought that must not be forgotten. Perhaps the most important is Marx's view of ethics. As already noted, Marx insists that his critique of capitalism is not an ethical critique. In fact, Marx seems to reject any kind of objective ethical framework, seeing all ethical views as culturally relative expressions of underlying economic forces. Ethical systems are just "ideologies" that mask and justify oppression. Lenin later appeals to this view of ethics and justifies violence as the price that has to be paid to bring about socialism, and this kind of "whatever means is necessary" ethic has been all too common among revolutionaries.

Marx's refusal to make an ethical condemnation of capitalism is consistent with his philosophy. However, this rejection of ethics seems contradicted by the ethical passion Marx burned with as a human being. He is clearly outraged by the way workers were used up and tossed aside; he is offended by a lack of concern for human suffering. This seems blatantly inconsistent. However, I do not think such inconsistency is unusual among people who reject an objective ethical framework and espouse some kind of cultural relativism. On my view morality is hardwired into human nature, and only sociopaths are free from moral judgments and emotions. It is not too surprising that as a human being Marx continues to think and feel in moral terms, even if his official theory is that morality is just a product of a bourgeois society.

Speaking as a Christian, I believe another deep problem with Marx's views is that he does not take sin seriously. Marx does not believe in original sin, and he therefore thinks that we can transform human nature simply by transforming the environment in which humans live. If Marx had taken human sinfulness seriously, he might have realized that even in a highly productive society where there is relative abundance, humans can still be selfish and greedy. He might also have realized that power put into the hands of social engineers can easily be used for the benefit of the engineers rather than the people. This is exactly what happened in the Soviet Union. Party and government officials became a "new class," which allocated goods and services for their own benefit, just as had older dominant economic classes.

In addition to his failure to take morality and sin seriously, there are also deep problems in Marx's economic theory. Marx claims that labor is the sole source of profit. If this were true then the most labor-intensive industries should be the most profitable. However, just the opposite seems to be the case. Industries become more profitable by becoming more efficient and replacing workers. The subsistence theory of wages also seems dubious. At least in democratic countries with strong labor movements, wages have increased dramatically through minimum-wage laws, collective bargaining, and even enlightened capitalists, who realize that only well-paid workers can buy the output of industry. Despite these problems, Marx's ideas will continue to be debated in a world that is increasingly globalized. It is also worth pointing out that some of Marx's ideas have now been widely accepted by people who do not identify as socialists. The *Communist Manifesto* called for free public education, universal suffrage, and a graduated income tax. All are present in most Western democracies today.

Søren Kierkegaard

SØREN KIERKEGAARD WAS BORN in 1813 and died in 1855 when he was only forty-two. The cause of his death is mysterious, though some have speculated he had spinal tuberculosis, because there was paralysis of the lower body. Except for a couple of relatively short visits to Germany, he lived his whole life in and around Copenhagen, Denmark. In this short life, he wrote a vast amount of work. During his lifetime he published around twenty books. (The exact number is difficult to determine since some writings originally published separately were later published as one volume, while parts of books he published together have also been published separately.) He wrote another nine books that were published after his death, some complete but others unfinished. He also left copious journals and notebooks, published in seven large volumes in the latest edition, not to mention many volumes of letters. What is amazing, however, is not the quantity but the sheer genius displayed in this vast literature. It is safe to say that any one of Kierkegaard's ten most important books would have sufficed to make him an important and enduring figure in the history of Western philosophy.

In my view Kierkegaard is the greatest Christian philosopher since the medieval period. In a way that is comparable to such thinkers as Augustine and Aquinas, Kierkegaard is as much theologian as philosopher. He has had an enormous influence on contemporary theology, much of it through such thinkers as Karl Barth, Emil Brunner, Rudolf Bultmann, and Paul Tillich. However, his impact on secular philosophers has been equally important, as can be seen in such twentieth-century thinkers as Albert Camus, Martin Heidegger, and Jean-Paul Sartre. Even Ludwig Wittgenstein paid tribute to Kierkegaard, saying that although Kierkegaard was "too deep for me," Kierkegaard was "the most profound philosopher of the 19th century."[1] Nor is Kierkegaard's influence limited to theology and philosophy. He has had a deep impact on fields as diverse as literary theory and communications.

KIERKEGAARD'S LIFE

Kierkegaard was the youngest of seven children born to Michael Pedersen Kierkegaard, a wealthy Danish merchant, and his second wife. The father had been born in a very poor family on the west side of Jutland. One miserable, cold night as he tended sheep, the father had climbed a hill and cursed God because of his terrible life. Strangely, very soon after this, the father's life was transformed. He was invited to Copenhagen to work for a childless relative. He inherited the relative's business and proved to be a superb businessman himself, becoming very rich. However, he struggled his whole life with feelings of guilt and what was then termed "melancholy" but would doubtless today be called depression. Those emotions were passed on to the youngest son, perhaps biologically, but certainly through the way the son was raised as well. In addition to the early episode of cursing God, which the father never forgot, there is one other possible source of the older man's guilt. After the first wife died, Michael Pedersen Kierkegaard quickly married a woman who was a servant in the house, who was already pregnant with their first child.

Little Søren was given a strict upbringing, and in fact complains that he never really was allowed to be a child. From his earliest days he was introduced to such "strict" Christian concepts as sin and atonement. As good Danes, the family of course belonged to the state Lutheran church. However, the father also attended a Moravian meeting, and Kierkegaard's

---

[1]Norman Malcolm, *Ludwig Wittgenstein: A Memoir*, 2nd ed. (New York: Oxford University Press, 1984), 106.

childhood therefore also included a strong dose of pietism and what would today be called an "evangelical view" that stressed the importance of religious faith as something that required passionate personal appropriation. During his university years, Søren rebelled against his father's strict Christianity. We do not know exactly what his wildness involved, but it is clear that Kierkegaard felt enormous guilt, and he consistently described himself later as a "penitent." Søren was reconciled both to his father and to the faith before the father's death.

The most momentous events in Kierkegaard's life revolved around a beautiful young Danish woman named Regine Olsen. Kierkegaard had met Regine in 1837, when he was twenty-four and she was only fifteen. In 1840, after a relatively brief but emotionally intense courtship, they were engaged. However, Søren realized almost immediately he had made a huge mistake. He did not believe it would be right to marry her unless Regine fully understood him. However, that would require him to explain his depression and guilt to her, and that would in turn require Kierkegaard to disclose his relation to his father, which he felt he could not do. Kierkegaard decided that he must break the engagement. To make things easier for Regine, he pretended to be a cad, thinking that if she hated him she would be glad the marriage had been called off. Regine, however, was not fooled. She and her family fought hard to get Kierkegaard to go through with the marriage, but he was sure his path was right and stuck to his guns. He broke the engagement and fled the city's gossip by going to Berlin for a period. (While in Berlin, Kierkegaard attended Schelling's lectures, amazingly in the same lecture hall as Friedrich Engels!)

There is no doubt that Kierkegaard loved Regine deeply. He thought about her every day, wrote about her constantly in his journals throughout his life, prayed for her regularly, and even left her all his possessions in his will. (It did not amount to much; Kierkegaard had gone through the money he inherited from his father. What little he did have was refused by Regine, who had married someone else, except for a few very personal letters and books.) However, despite the love Kierkegaard had for her, he believed he could not be a good husband for her, and he was very likely right about this. At the time Kierkegaard gave all these events a religious interpretation, seeing himself as someone who had been called by God to renounce the joys of ordinary domestic life, as an "exception." His willingness to renounce Regine seemed to him a test of his devotion to God, similar to God's testing of Abraham by asking him to sacrifice Isaac, a biblical story that Kierkegaard writes powerfully about in *Fear and Trembling*. (Later, he wavers about whether he was right to break the engagement, at times thinking that if he really had had faith, he would have married Regine.)

Whether Kierkegaard's conduct was right or wrong, there is no doubt that this experience made him an author. Part of his motivation in beginning to write was to communicate with Regine, since after breaking the engagement, real communication was impossible, especially after Regine married Fritz Schlegel, a government official who later became governor of the Danish West Indies. So Kierkegaard dedicates his early works to "that individual," unnamed but "who will someday be named." He was determined that if he could not live with Regine in time that she would be linked to him in eternity, famous as the muse who inspired a great author.[2] Of course Kierkegaard's works were not simply personal communication to Regine. It is also clear that he was motivated by a deep Christian faith and a sense of calling from the very beginning. It is now time to examine this authorship.

KIERKEGAARD'S AUTHORSHIP

Kierkegaard's writings are not only extensive but also very puzzling to the uninitiated reader. The most striking and immediately obvious feature is that there are two streams of works. There are a large number of books that seem to have an "aesthetic" character. The authorship of

---

[2]For a great exploration of this, see Joakim Garff, *Kierkegaard's Muse: The Mystery of Regine Olsen* (Princeton, NJ: Princeton University Press, 2017).

these books is attributed, not to Kierkegaard himself, but to various pseudonyms Kierkegaard created. A striking example is Kierkegaard's first major work, *Either/Or*, which made his name in Denmark. This is a two-volume work supposedly edited by one Victor Eremita (Victor the Hermit). Victor claims to have found the writings in a secret drawer of a used desk he purchased. The first volume purports to be the papers of an aesthete, who is just called "A" by Victor, though the volume culminates in a famous "Diary of a Seducer," written by a man named Johannes, who may or may not be "A." In this first volume, "A" extols what he calls the aesthetic life, which is a life lived for the moment, in which a person seeks to satisfy desire and defeat boredom. Volume two of the book consists of a series of letters to "A" from Judge William, an older married man, who defends the ethical life and tries to get "A" to see the problems with living as an aesthete and to commit to such ethical ideals as marriage and vocation.

Either/Or is followed quickly by a string of other pseudonymous works: *Fear and Trembling* by Johannes de silentio (Silent John), *Prefaces* by Nicolaus Notabene, *Repetition* by Constantine Constantius, *Philosophical Fragments* by Johannes Climacus, *The Concept of Anxiety* by Vigilius Haufniensis (Latin for the "Watchman of Copenhagen"), and *Concluding Unscientific Postscript to the Philosophical Fragments*, also by Johannes Climacus. I shall discuss below the purpose of this pseudonymous authorship, but it is important to recognize that Kierkegaard was not trying to write anonymously. There were abundant signs that he was the author of these books, including putting "S. Kierkegaard" on the title page of some of them as "editor," and virtually everyone in the intellectual elite knew that Kierkegaard was the author.

At the same time that Kierkegaard was publishing these pseudonymous works he also was publishing a string of works called *Upbuilding Discourses* (*Edifying Discourses* in an older translation) under his own name. There are eighteen of these in the first period of his authorship, published in collections of two, three, or four of these short "talks."

These "discourses" are sermon-like in character, though Kierkegaard did not call them sermons because he was not ordained to preach. (Kierkegaard prepared for a career as a pastor by doing the "pastoral seminary" training after he finished his PhD, but he never became a priest.)

Kierkegaard himself discusses this "duplicity" in the authorship in a short book *On My Work as an Author* as well as in his posthumous *The Point of View for My Work as an Author*. Both of these works maintain that there is actually a unity in the authorship. He claims that his "authorship, regarded as a *totality*, is religious from first to last."[3] Kierkegaard's concerns are not generically religious either, since "the whole of my authorship relates itself to Christianity."[4] Kierkegaard himself admits that an author's testimony about such things is not always reliable, and so he urges his readers to verify his claim by going to the works themselves. He says that his concern with Christianity is something "anyone can see, if he wants to see, must also be able to see."[5] If Kierkegaard's religious writings had all come late, with the aesthetic writings early, then it might be plausible to think that Kierkegaard had changed over the course of his work, perhaps through a religious conversion. However, the fact the *Upbuilding Discourses* were published contemporaneously with the aesthetic writings is evidence that this is not the case.

Kierkegaard actually describes himself as a kind of Christian missionary. Of course he did not mean that he was called to leave Christendom to introduce the gospel into an area that had no knowledge of Christianity. Danish society of the time assumed that virtually everyone in Denmark was a Christian, with the exception of those who were Jewish. Everyone was baptized at birth and later confirmed as a member of the state church. Being a good Danish citizen and being a Christian were simply indistinguishable. Kierkegaard was convinced

---

[3]Søren Kierkegaard, *The Point of View*, trans. and ed. Howard Hong and Edna Hong (Princeton, NJ: Princeton University Press, 1998), 6 (emphasis original).

[4]Kierkegaard, *Point of View*, 23.

[5]Kierkegaard, *Point of View*, 6.

that this was an enormous error, an "illusion." Genuine Christianity requires a person to be "born again," to acquire a new nature. Genuine Christianity can never be identified with any human culture that one absorbs simply by growing up in a particular society. Thus, so far from thinking that everyone was a Christian, Kierkegaard fears that Christianity is in danger of vanishing. For almost all of his life he remained a loyal and active part of the church, regularly taking Communion and occasionally even preaching. However, at the end of his life he actually attacked the church by claiming that "New Testament Christianity" has simply ceased to exist.[6]

Kierkegaard therefore says that his missionary calling is to "Christendom," and that his task is to "reintroduce" Christianity into a supposedly Christian country. This is, he thinks, harder than being a missionary to a pagan land, since before presenting Christian faith he must first dispel the illusion that everyone is already a Christian. Dispelling an illusion is a difficult task, and it calls for creative forms of communication. Simply confronting the illusion head-on by telling people their error is likely to make them defensive and thus achieve nothing. Kierkegaard thus decided that his communication must be "indirect" and not "direct."

KIERKEGAARD ON HUMAN EXISTENCE AND COMMUNICATION

One might well wonder why Kierkegaard wrote philosophy if he saw his calling as that of a missionary. The answer to this puzzle lies in Kierkegaard's diagnosis of the causes of Christendom's failure. Kierkegaard thought that his day was one that greatly prized intellectualism and knowledge. The highest human achievements require an objective detachment, in which personal questions and life problems are put aside. In a way one can see the beginnings of this attitude in Descartes, the

---

[6]Søren Kierkegaard, "A Thesis—Just One Single One," in *"The Moment" and Late Writings*, ed. and trans. Howard Hong and Edna Hong (Princeton, NJ: Princeton University Press, 1998), 39.

father of modern Western philosophy, when he claims, at the beginning of the *Meditations*, that he was now in a position to achieve certain knowledge because he had no practical issues to deal with and was "troubled by no passions."[7] When this kind of intellectualism is applied to the religious life, the result is that the Christian life is confused with objective knowledge of the truths of Christianity. However, Christianity is not merely knowing a set of propositions, or even believing propositions in a purely intellectual way. The biblical concept of faith or belief (*pistis*) is not mere intellectual assent, but includes trust and a willingness to commit one's whole life to the truth of what is believed.

Kierkegaard sees Christianity as a way of life, a way of existing. To fail to see that genuine Christian faith shapes a person's life as a whole is to fail to understand Christianity. Christianity is at bottom an answer to what we should call the problem of human existence. Kierkegaard thinks his contemporaries do not understand Christianity because they have forgotten what it means to *exist* as a human being. Christianity provides the answer to the problem of human existence, but if one does not understand the problem, one will not understand the solution.

Kierkegaard uses a Danish verb meaning "to exist" in a special way to refer to the distinctive mode of being of a human person. The task of a human person is to become a self; in fact selfhood itself is a task. In one sense every human is a self, of course. Each person exists as a conscious subject. However, Kierkegaard believes that God has given every human person the task of becoming the self he or she was created to be. We are created as unfinished creatures, and are given the privilege of participating in our own development. This happens every day through the choices we make; each of us is constantly defining the self. Though everyone is a "self of a sort," most of us are pretty mediocre. Imagine, Kierkegaard says, a wagon driven by a drunken peasant who falls asleep and lets the horses go whichever way they choose. Such a person is a "driver" only in a comical sense. In a similar way, many humans are more

---

[7]See chap. 12 for a discussion of Descartes.

or less "asleep," and allow their "choices" to be made by their environment or their impulses. They "exist" and "have selves" in pretty much the same way that the peasant "drives" the wagon. Their selves lack enduring character and thus have no real identity.

Now it is possible to be intellectually developed in the sense of "objective knowledge" without really developing as a self. Meaningful choices require commitment, but commitment is "subjectivity" and not detached objectivity. Kierkegaard thinks that intellectual thought alone never makes a choice. It is true that before choosing I may reflect on the choice, and often this is right and important to do. However, reflection is not the same thing as choice. Finally to choose I must end the process of reflection, and Kierkegaard thinks that this requires a kind of emotional attachment, a form of caring. The caring involved can be of various kinds, but generically Kierkegaard describes them all as forms of "subjectivity" or "inwardness." It is not enough to *know* that some action is best; I must *want* to do what is best. To choose to act, a person must stop the process of reflection, so that action is possible.

Kierkegaard's contemporaries do not understand Christianity because they have "forgotten what it means to exist."[8] Kierkegaard therefore begins his missionary activity by attempting to give his contemporaries a renewed understanding of human existence, a properly philosophical task. We can now understand why Kierkegaard engages in philosophy, and why even some secular philosophers who reject his Christianity are nonetheless attracted to his account of human existence.

Since the root of the problem lies in an overvaluing of objective knowledge, one can see that Kierkegaard's task is a difficult one. If Kierkegaard were simply to produce a "system," by giving his contemporaries a set of true propositions about the nature of human existence, he might well make matters worse by contributing to this overvaluation of objective knowledge. Kierkegaard therefore decided that his

---

[8]Søren Kierkegaard, *Concluding Unscientific Postscript to Philosophical Fragments*, trans. Howard V. Hong and Edna H. Hong (Princeton, NJ: Princeton University Press, 1992), 249.

communication must be subtle and indirect. He must try to catch his readers with their guard down if he wants to communicate what we might term existential knowledge.

Objective knowledge can, Kierkegaard thinks, be communicated directly. I can utter the proposition "Abraham Lincoln was president of the United States during the Civil War." This proposition is true, and the person who hears me and believes what I say can come to know a new fact. No personal appropriation or subjective attitude is required. However, if what I want to communicate is what Kierkegaard calls subjective truth (truth about existence, truth that must be lived), then something more is required of the hearer. Simply to grasp the meaning of a proposition is not enough. Rather, the hearer must seek to think through what it would mean to live in accordance with this truth. Kierkegaard says that such communication requires a "double reflection." The hearer must think not only about the meaning of what is communicated but also about the meaning of the communication in relation to his or her own life. This second reflection is something the hearer must do for himself or herself, and thus successful communication must be "indirect." Kierkegaard's pseudonymous authorship is an attempt to communicate in this indirect way.

THE PSEUDONYMS AND THE THREE SPHERES OF EXISTENCE

It is now time to address the purpose of Kierkegaard's use of pseudonyms. As already noted, the pseudonyms were not an attempt to hide or disguise Kierkegaard's authorship of the works. Rather, each of the pseudonyms is best thought of as a fictional character whom Kierkegaard created. The pseudonymous authorship as a whole can be viewed as a vast novel in which each of the pseudonyms is a character. Kierkegaard's purpose in creating the pseudonyms is similar to that of a novelist who populates a fictional world with characters who do not exist in real life.

Think for example of Dostoevsky's *The Brothers Karamazov*. Much of the novel is a kind of running argument between two brothers, Ivan and Alyosha Karamazov. (I will here ignore the other two brothers in the novel.) Ivan is a freethinking atheist, while Alyosha is a devout Christian. Of course, neither character is identical to Dostoevsky, though since Dostoevsky was himself a believer he surely is closer to Alyosha than to Ivan. Nevertheless, Dostoevsky's Ivan is a compelling character, and many readers even think that Ivan gets the best of Alyosha. What Dostoevsky seems to have wanted to do is create a realistic, living argument between the two figures, neither of whom is a caricature. They do not just tell us about their worldviews but embody them. One can see why such an existential dialogue between the two would indeed help foster the kind of subjective reflection on the part of Dostoevsky's readers that Kierkegaard wanted to foster in his own readers. Kierkegaard would doubtless say that the novel is a great example of indirect communication.

If one thinks about different views of human existence, including its purpose and how it should be lived, one might think that there are countless different views, and in one sense that is correct. However, Kierkegaard believed that all these different views of human existence can usefully be understood as variations on a few basic answers. There are basically three views of human existence: the aesthetic view, in which a person lives for momentary satisfaction; the ethical view, in which a person is committed to the realization of ideals; and the religious view. Kierkegaard calls these the "three stages on life's way" and also sometimes the "three spheres of existence." (I shall explain below how they can be both stages and spheres.) This account of the alternative ways of living a human life provides a kind of "common currency" that acts as a backdrop to Kierkegaard's pseudonymous authorship. Kierkegaard himself describes this account of the stages of existence as a kind of map in which a person can locate himself or herself in relation to others. All of the pseudonymous characters seem to assume something like this view, although each has his own distinctive place within the map.

Thus Johannes the seducer, who writes the concluding section of volume one of *Either/Or*, sees life as a quest for enjoyable moments and the defeat of boredom. Judge William, the author of volume two, believes that a genuine human self is grounded in faithful commitments such as marriage and commitment to one's vocational calling. Other pseudonyms, such as Johannes de silentio, seem to be religious, or at least to inhabit the border of a religious view. Kierkegaard's pseudonyms do not just tell us about their views of life; they embody them, just as Dostoevsky's characters do. By creating them Kierkegaard hopes to engage in indirect communication. He wants his readers to think seriously about human existence and their own lives. Perhaps in confronting characters such as Johannes the seducer or Judge William, the readers will see something of themselves and gain a clearer understanding of who they are and perhaps who they want to become. Kierkegaard ultimately thinks that a religious view of life, and more specifically a Christian view, is the best and most adequate view. However, he wants his readers to come to see this for themselves. He wants them to become "subjective thinkers" who recognize what an enormous task it is to become a self.

I shall now try to give a brief summary of Kierkegaard's account of the "stages of existence." I shall have to simplify; Kierkegaard's account is far more complicated than a book of this length can accommodate, and Kierkegaard gives different versions of the view in different parts of his authorship, when he is concerned with different problems. I shall begin with an account of the view understood as "stages" and then explain how they can also be viewed as "spheres." The "stages view" obviously includes a kind of developmental picture of human psychology.

The aesthetic life. The aesthetic life is devoted to satisfying one's desires. One might think that this is simply a version of the ancient Greek philosophy of hedonism, which defines the good life in terms of pleasure, but Kierkegaard recognizes that human desire is too multifarious to be captured by a single term like pleasure. The aesthete does not simply desire some identifiable quality called pleasure. Whatever the aesthete wants he (or she) wants. Kierkegaard's character "A" illustrates this point beautifully in *Either/Or*: "If I had in my service a submissive jinni who, when I asked for a glass of water, would bring me the world's most expensive wines, deliciously blended, in a goblet, I would dismiss him until he learned that enjoyment consists not in what I enjoy but in getting my own way."[9]

Kierkegaard characterizes the whole of the aesthetic life as one that is lived for the satisfaction of desire. Of course desires vary enormously, but Kierkegaard describes desires as ranging on a continuum between two extremes. On one extreme is the person who lives to satisfy elemental sensuous urges. The mythical figure of Don Juan, who supposedly seduced 1,004 women in Spain alone, perfectly symbolizes this pole of the aesthetic life. Don Juan himself is a mythical ideal, the "incarnation of sensuousness." This first type of aesthete is described as the "immediate aesthete" in that he or she simply bases life on biologically given sensuous urges (although there is a sense in which all aesthetes are "immediate" in that they refuse to take on selfhood as a *task* in which one *ought* to become a certain type of person).

However, the aesthetic life can also take on a refined, intellectual character. Here one might imagine the aesthete who does not care to get drunk or have one-night stands, but who lives for fine art and music. This second type of aesthete, the "reflective aesthete," can be very intellectually and culturally developed, and thus would not seem to be "immediate" in the same way that the first type is. Nevertheless, the refined aesthete still lives for the moment. He or she literally wants to make life into a series of satisfying moments.

The aesthetic life is the first stage of human existence in the sense that all children are natural aesthetes. What the child wants is always wanted now, and the ability to defer gratification is a difficult

---

[9]Kierkegaard, "Diapsalmata," in *Either/Or I*, ed. and trans. Howard Hong and Edna Hong (Princeton, NJ: Princeton University Press, 1987), 31.

achievement for all of us. There is nothing wrong with a child's being a child. However, the process of growing up and becoming an adult involves recognizing that not all desires can be or should be satisfied. The healthy adult is someone who has an identity. This person knows who he or she is, and decides what desires should and should not be satisfied based on those ideals.

Thus there is in the natural course of things a movement from the aesthetic stage of life to the ethical stage discussed below. However, since human beings are spiritual beings endowed with the freedom to decide whom they will become, this movement does not happen automatically. One does not automatically acquire an ethical self by going through puberty or reaching a certain age. A person can, like Peter Pan, refuse to grow up, and the aesthetic life can become a self-conscious choice. We can now understand how it is that the aesthetic life can be a "sphere of existence," and not just a stage one grows out of. That is precisely the situation of Kierkegaard's character "A," who refuses marriage, work, and indeed any kind of commitment that would restrict his freedom to seek enjoyment.

It is not hard to see that the aesthetic life in all its forms faces challenges. There are challenges posed by external realities. It is hard to live a life of enjoyment if one is poor or stricken by illness. In that sense the aesthete is a hostage of fortune or luck. But even the fortunate aesthete faces challenges. The person who gets drunk and has multiple sexual affairs may get liver disease or sexually transmitted diseases, not to mention facing the wrath of disappointed partners. Perhaps the most serious challenge for the fortunate aesthete is simply boredom, a problem "A" addresses memorably in "The Rotation of Crops" in *Either/ Or I.* The advantage of the more reflective aesthete over the more immediate form would seem to be the ability to vary one's enjoyments so as to combat boredom. However, even the reflective aesthete may come to feel, with the writer of Ecclesiastes, that "all is vanity," even after having sampled every form of human desire. Even the most skilled aesthete may become bored and depressed. The ethical individual sees this as showing the emptiness of the aesthetic life.

The ethical life. The ethical life, just like the aesthetic life, comes in many forms, and Kierkegaard's different pseudonyms give somewhat different accounts of ethical existence. All of these accounts, however, agree that the ethical life is an attempt to achieve a unified self, to gain a coherent identity. All agree that the ethical life sees the human self as a task. The self is something a person must seek to become.

In volume two of *Either/Or,* Judge William writes two very long letters to the younger aesthete "A" to help him see the problems with aesthetic existence and move him to the ethical. The first letter deals with the aesthetic validity of marriage. Some critics have argued that Kierkegaard sees the choice between the various spheres of existence as a "radical choice" for which no reasons can be given, since it is a matter of choosing what reasons to accept as good reasons.[10] However, Judge William does not see things this way at all. He argues for the superiority of the ethical life over the aesthetic life, not just on ethical grounds, but on aesthetic grounds. His essay on marriage begins by assuming the value of romantic love, something the aesthete prizes. The aesthete believes that marriage, which involves commitment and obligation, cannot coexist with romantic love, but Judge William argues this is not so. It is the lovers themselves who want their love to be permanent, and want to make promises to each other. Rather than destroying romantic love, marriage enables romantic love to endure, to gain a history, offering a satisfaction that casual love affairs cannot match.

Judge William's second letter, "Equilibrium Between the Aesthetic and Ethical," is an extended account of what it means to be a self. It contains a more general version of the argument in the first letter: a person who chooses the aesthetic ultimately will be disappointed. However, a person who chooses the ethical gets the aesthetic is well;

---

[10]See Alasdair MacIntyre, "The Predecessor Culture and the Enlightenment Project of Justifying Morality," in *After Virtue,* 3rd ed. (Notre Dame, IN: Notre Dame University Press, 2007).

what is beautiful and satisfying is enhanced by ethical commitment. The most important choice, according to Judge William, is the choice to take choices seriously. He claims, somewhat naively perhaps, that the person who takes on the task of becoming a self by choosing responsibly will surely choose correctly. Such a person will recognize the importance of such things as marriage, work, and friendship in building a meaningful life. Judge William's version of the ethical life thus defines the ethical in terms of human social relationships and institutions.

The judge is a religious man, but he sees complete continuity between the religious life and the ethical life. One pleases God by becoming a respected ethical self, and the judge is optimistic that a person can do this by making the right choices. The judge certainly recognizes that humans make mistakes, and he even affirms the necessity of repentance in the ethical life. However, his general stance is optimistic. Still, at the very end of volume two there is a strong hint that there are problems in the ethical life that even the judge has an awareness of. The judge finishes the volume by including a sermon sent to him by a priest from Jutland. The theme of the sermons is "the edification to be found in the thought that over against God we are always in the wrong."[11]

The religious life. The limits of the ethical life come into view when a person confronts two things that are part of every human life: suffering and guilt. Neither the aesthete nor the ethical person has any real account of what meaning these may have in human existence. Johannes de silentio, the pseudonymous author of *Fear and Trembling*, gives a clear statement of the problem sin poses for the ethical life: "An ethics that ignores sin is an altogether futile discipline, but if it asserts sin, then it is for that very reason beyond itself."[12]

Fear and Trembling provides a dramatic and powerful account of the relation between the ethical and the religious that contradicts Judge

---

[11]Kierkegaard, *Either/Or II*, ed. and trans. Howard Hong and Edna Hong (Princeton, NJ: Princeton University Press, 1987), 339-54.

[12]Søren Kierkegaard, *Fear and Trembling*, ed. C. Stephen Evans and Sylvia Walsh, trans. Sylvia Walsh, Cambridge Texts in the History of Philosophy (Cambridge: Cambridge University Press, 2010), 86.

William's optimistic view of them as continuous. The book centers on the biblical story of the binding of Isaac from Genesis 22. In this story God tests Abraham by asking him to take his son Isaac, the "child of promise," and sacrifice him. Abraham obeys, but at the last minute God sends an angel who commands Abraham not to harm the child, but to sacrifice a ram instead.

Abraham, who is described by Johannes as a completely ethical man, is recognized as a model of religious faith, not only by Jews, but by Christians and Muslims as well. However, in this biblical story, that faith does not show itself by Abraham's fulfillment of his familial duties, as Judge William might have assumed should have been the case, but by Abraham's willingness to trust God and obey God, even when God commands Abraham to do something that seems ethically wrong. Silentio argues that this means that *if* there is no telos or goal for human life higher than ethics, then Abraham is not a hero to be admired, but a murderer. He does not settle the issue for his reader but simply presents a dilemma: *either* there are such things as a "teleological suspension of the ethical" (an end higher than the ethical, which takes precedence over it) and an "absolute duty to God" *or* else Abraham is lost.

It is not merely Judge William who had assumed that the religious life was basically reducible to the ethical life. Immanuel Kant had already argued that "whatever, over and above good moral life-conduct, a man fancies he can do to become well-pleasing to God is mere religious illusion and pseudo-service of God."[13] Consistent with this judgment, Kant had pronounced that a man in Abraham's situation would be absolutely wrong to act as Abraham had done.[14] The general tendency of the "liberal theology" developed in the early nineteenth century was to identify true religion with "the fatherhood of God and the brotherhood of man." To be a good religious person is simply to be

---

[13]Immanuel Kant, *Religion Within the Limits of Reason Alone*, trans. Theodore M. Greene and Hoyt H. Hudson (New York: Harper & Row, 1960), 158.

[14]Immanuel Kant, *The Conflict of the Faculties*, trans. Mary J. Gregor (Lincoln: University of Nebraska Press), 115.

a good person. Silentio's account of Abraham is a direct challenge to this type of theology and this view of the religious life.

Silentio describes himself as a person who does not himself have faith, but who admires Abraham and wishes he were like Abraham. But what is the attraction? Why would anyone want to be in Abraham's shoes? Silentio hints at the answer by describing a variety of characters who are unable to fulfill Judge William's injunction to become a self through making the right choices. These characters include Sarah from the book of Tobit from the biblical Apocrypha, Shakespeare's Gloucester from *Richard III*, and the character of the Merman from the Danish legend of Agnes and the Merman. What these characters all have in common is that they are flawed creatures, unable to "accomplish the universal" by fulfilling the ethical roles society demands they occupy. Such persons may be interested in Abraham's story, for it seems to offer hope that there is another path to becoming an authentic self than simply ethical willing.

Early in the book Johannes imagines Abraham as an ethical hero who commits suicide rather than obey God's fearsome command. Johannes says that such an Abraham would be admired, and "his name would not be forgotten, but it is one thing to be admired, another to become a guiding star that rescues the anguished."[15] Who are the anguished ones, and how can Abraham be a guiding star for them?

Johannes only gives a few hints in *Fear and Trembling*, by describing the flawed characters mentioned above. However, suppose Judge William's optimism about the human condition is misplaced? What if the flawed characters such as Shakespeare's Gloucester and the Merman are not just strange tragic figures, but characters who tell us something that is true of all of us? From the point of view of Christianity, this is indeed the case, since all human beings are seen as sinful. Johannes himself strongly suggests that the meaning of his book requires some attention to sin: "As soon as sin is introduced, ethics runs aground precisely upon

---

[15]Kierkegaard, *Fear and Trembling*, 17-18.

repentance, for repentance is the highest ethical expression but precisely as such the deepest ethical self-contradiction."[16]

In a later pseudonymous work, *Concluding Unscientific Postscript*, the author Johannes Climacus expands on this insight. Climacus has a deeper conception of the ethical than Judge William. He sees the ethical life as the foundation of the religious life. The truly ethical person does not just conform to the ethical norms of his or her society, but has an absolute commitment to the absolute and a relative commitment to the relative.[17] The difficulty is that we humans generally live for what is relative. We care about such worldly goods as money, fame, and success. The genuinely ethical person understands that this means "resignation" is necessary, and resignation is a willingness to give up all such relative ends for the sake of what is infinite. That turns out to be difficult; it requires suffering or dying to self, and that in turn leads to the discovery of guilt. What began as an ethical life has taken on a religious coloring, and Climacus says that resignation, suffering, and guilt-consciousness are, respectively, the "initial, essential, and decisive" expressions of a kind of natural religious life that he terms "Religiousness A."

Individuals who are living in the sphere of Religiousness A have developed the kind of "inwardness" or "subjectivity" that prepares them to hear the good news of Christianity, which Climacus calls "Religiousness B." An earlier work under the same pseudonym, *Philosophical Fragments*, had already tried to make it clear that Christianity is grounded in a divine revelation that takes the form of God himself becoming incarnate. Christ is not merely an ethical teacher or someone who has a new philosophical doctrine to propose. God's presence as a human is itself the teaching, and salvation is only possible through faith in the "God-man" who has really appeared in history. Religiousness B is thus a religion of "transcendence," not grounded in teachings that human reason could have come up with on its own.

---

[16]Kierkegaard, *Fear and Trembling*, 86n.
[17]Kierkegaard, *Concluding Unscientific Postscript*, 387.

Climacus (who is close to Kierkegaard on this point) maintains that faith in the incarnate God cannot be based on philosophical argument or even historical evidence. Although he says that the God-man will obviously offer "signs" to reveal who he is, the idea that God could become a human being is not something that human reason could ever make probable. It is "the absolute Paradox," and faith in the God-man is something that God himself must give to the disciple. Faith is only possible by an encounter with Christ, which must be "first-hand," whether the disciple be a historical contemporary eyewitness or someone from a later generation who learns about God's work through testimony. Since those who come later also receive faith directly from Christ, they too are "contemporaries" even if they are not historical contemporaries. They are people who seek to follow Christ.

Religiousness A involves the discovery of guilt, but it has no real solution to the problem. Christianity first reveals that our guilt is sin, meaning that the problem is not one that we can solve on our own. After revealing to us how serious the problem is, Christianity then offers a solution to the most important existential problem humans face. The Christ who is the object of faith is also the one who atones for sin, and faith therefore includes a belief that sins are forgiven. Thus for Kierkegaard a person only becomes a Christian through the "consciousness of sin."

TRUTH AS SUBJECTIVITY

The task of moving through the stages on life's way is thus a journey in which a person's "subjectivity" is reshaped and reformed. To become a true self is to acquire the right kind of subjectivity, have the right desires, fear, and hopes. Kierkegaard's pseudonym Johannes Climacus thus claims, in a famous passage in *Concluding Unscientific Postscript*, that "truth is subjectivity." This claim has often been misunderstood as the claim that truth is subjective, the view that what is true for one person may be false for another. However, a careful look at what Kierkegaard says makes it clear that he is not a subjectivist or relativist about truth.

The question he wants to consider is not primarily about the nature of propositional truth, but rather how it is possible for an individual to be "in the truth." He compares two views about this question. On the "objective" view, there is no consideration given to how the individual is related to the truth, but all the attention is paid to the question of whether what the individual believes is objectively true. On this view, the individual is assumed to be "in the truth" if what the individual believes is objectively true.

On the "subjective" view, the focus is on the relation between the individual and what the individual believes. Climacus says that on this view "if only the how of this relation is in truth, the individual is in truth, even if he in this way were to relate himself to untruth."[18] Note that this does not mean that what the individual believes somehow becomes true if one is related to it in the right way. What is objectively true and untrue is not changed. What is changed is whether the individual's life is "in the truth." Climacus illustrates what he means by proposing a comparison between two individuals. Consider someone who lives in the midst of Christianity and goes into God's house, the house of the true God, with the knowledge of a true conception of God, and now prays, but prays in untruth. Now consider someone who lives in an idolatrous land but prays with all the passion of infinity, even though his or her eyes rest on the image of an idol. Where is there more truth? The one prays in truth to God though he worships an idol; the other prays in untruth to the true God and therefore in truth worships an idol.[19]

Note that this does not mean that the pagan's propositional beliefs are correct, nor that the beliefs of the "Christian" are false. Rather, it means that merely having intellectual, propositional truth does not suffice to make a life true. To live "truly," a person's beliefs must be embodied in that person's subjectivity if they are to shape the person's life. This example does not mean the situation of the pagan is

---

[18]Kierkegaard, *Concluding Unscientific Postscript*, 199. In the original this passage is italicized for emphasis.
[19]Kierkegaard, *Concluding Unscientific Postscript*, 201. (This paragraph is just a paraphrase of Kierkegaard's text.)

exemplary, or that he would not be better off if he understood the truth about God. The pagan's life may have more truth than that of the hypocritical Christian, but that does not mean it could not contain even more truth. Climacus himself makes it clear that objective truth matters also: "Just as important as the truth, and of the two the even more important one, is the mode in which the truth is accepted."[20] So the claim that truth is subjectivity does not mean that objective propositional truth has no importance.

Climacus goes on to say that the claim that "truth is subjectivity" is a kind of "Socratic claim," and not really a distinctively Christian one. He says that the Christian begins talk about truth and subjectivity by insisting that "subjectivity is untruth."[21] Because of our sinfulness the Christian says we can only acquire the kind of truth we need in our lives through faith in Christ. Thus it is indeed important to know the truth about Christ, but even this truth must be believed by becoming a disciple, a follower of Christ. It is only Christ himself who can say that his life is itself truth: "I am the way and the truth and the life" (Jn 14:6).

KIERKEGAARD'S CRITIQUE OF HEGELIANISM

In Kierkegaard's day, Hegel's philosophy was deeply influential in both Germany and Denmark. Therefore, though it is clear that Kierkegaard learned much from Hegel, his philosophy is in many ways a sustained critique of Hegelianism. What offended Kierkegaard most deeply in Hegel was Hegel's claim that the truth of Christianity could be expressed more clearly in the language of philosophy. Kierkegaard thought that Hegel saw the Christian gospel of the incarnation as a story that symbolized the fact that the divine had become incarnate in human society. On this view God is to be identified with the values and customs of modern Western culture, rather than in the historical figure of Jesus of Nazareth. Thus Hegel's philosophy provides a kind of justification of

---

[20]Kierkegaard, *Concluding Unscientific Postscript*, 247.
[21]Kierkegaard, *Concluding Unscientific Postscript*, 207.

modern society as offering us the ultimate truth about what it means to be human. Those fortunate enough to be living at the "end of history" can now understand the true meaning of those religious stories offered by Christianity. One might say that Hegelianism is an esoteric form of Christendom, while Christendom is an exoteric form of Hegelianism.

Hegel's philosophy can thus be seen as a justification of "Christendom," which assumes that "we are all Christians," and identifies the "superior" Christian as the one who has an intellectual perspective on the story of human history. Hegel claims to offer a "scientific system" that provides "absolute knowledge." Perhaps religious faith is something necessary for the unintellectual masses, but the intellectual who understands world history has gone beyond faith. Kierkegaard rejects this view of faith and human knowledge. Faith is for him a passion that God himself creates in a person when that person encounters the Jesus of the Gospels and is willing to receive the gift that God offers in Christ. Faith is not a human achievement, and no human being, whether intellectually gifted or not, can go "further" than faith. Christian faith is the highest passion a person can possess.

Kierkegaard realizes that to challenge this Hegelian view, he must do more than merely disagree with its conclusions. He must attack the method that Hegel claims will lead to absolute knowledge. As we saw in chapter nineteen, Hegel claimed that his method was presuppositionless. Rather than begin with some kind of faith commitment, Hegel claims to begin with ordinary consciousness and show dialectically how such a view necessarily leads to Hegel's own view. Kierkegaard attacks this Hegelian method at a number of different points.

The primary problem concerns the issue of who is supposed to think in this presuppositionless way. Hegel claims, like Spinoza, that his method allows a person to think in a purely objective, dispassionate way. The Hegelian philosopher does not merely think abstractly, as all philosophers must, but eventually reaches the perspective of "pure thought." Kierkegaard tries to show that such a perspective is a chimera; no existing human being can actually think this way. We are all finite, historically situated beings, and we cannot see the world from God's point of view. Thus Kierkegaard's pseudonym Johannes Climacus affirms that "a logical system is possible . . . but a system of existence is not possible" for an existing human person.[22] Rather, "existence itself is a system—for God," who as an eternal being stands outside history.[23] However, reality as we experience it is always changing, and is in flux, and so are human knowers. It follows that no human being can achieve a system of knowledge. There is a final, absolute truth: for God reality is a "system." However, no human being can achieve a systematic understanding of reality that is both comprehensive and final. Because there is a final truth, we humans can see our attempts to know reality as approximations of that truth, but they can never be final and unrevisable.

However, the Hegelian method not only fails to achieve a final result. Kierkegaard also claims that it fails at the beginning as well. How does the systematic thinker get started? Kierkegaard claims that it is through a decision, and that no actual thinker can start without assumptions. (Here he takes Fichte's side over against Hegel.[24]) We come to philosophy as actual persons with our beliefs, desires, hopes, and fears, and it is not possible for us to shed these and begin with "pure thought."

In the end Kierkegaard claims that Hegel's philosophy is actually comic. For Kierkegaard comedy always involves a kind of incongruity or "contradiction." In the case of Hegel there is an obvious contradiction between the pretensions to be "pure thought" and the obvious, all-too-human character of the philosophy produced. Kierkegaard also claims that the Hegelian system, which seems to make the final end of human life to be a kind of knowledge of human history, "contains no ethic." In one sense Kierkegaard is wrong, in that Hegel does discuss ethics. The point Kierkegaard is trying to make is that even in ethics, Hegel's philosophy aims at intellectual understanding rather than action.

---

[22]Kierkegaard, *Concluding Unscientific Postscript*, 109 (translation modified).
[23]Kierkegaard, *Concluding Unscientific Postscript*, 118.
[24]See the discussion of Fichte in chap. 19.

Kierkegaard thus compares the Hegelian system to a magnificent mansion that stands empty; the owner does not live there but in a dog kennel on the property.

Kierkegaard also sees Hegel's philosophy of history as one that empties human life of its meaning. Suppose Hegel is right that we have now reached the end of history, and that we can now understand what Spirit has been trying to achieve all along. What meaning could that have for all the millions of people who have toiled and suffered over the millennia to make the actualization of Spirit possible? Hegel's view is a kind of "slaughter-bench" theory of history, in which most human lives have been meaningless. Kierkegaard would certainly make the same criticism of a Marxist view of history, which similarly says that the meaning of human life is that it leads to a kind of perfect society at the end of history.

For Kierkegaard the meaning of human life is found in the thought that each of us has been created by God and given the task of becoming selves. In one sense the task is the same for everyone. In another the task is different for everyone. God creates individuals as individuals and places us in our own unique historical situations. Everyone has the opportunity and privilege of carrying out this task, living before God and accountable to God. No human life is wasted or meaningless by virtue of when a person happens to live.

The task of becoming a human self is harder in the modern world, according to Kierkegaard. The development of mass media, such as newspapers and magazines, leads to a kind of anonymous authority called the "public." We all live in fear of having a view that goes against what "they say," that will go against public opinion or what "we" all know. Kierkegaard believes that small, concrete forms of community have been undermined by modernity, leaving all of us as "naked individuals" subject to the impersonal authority of the public. For him the solution lies in faith. If each of us turns to God in faith and becomes the self God wills us to be, perhaps as authentic selves we can find genuine forms of community as well. Sadly, Kierkegaard seems not to have experienced such genuine community himself. He did not see the church as part of the solution. Rather, he increasingly comes to see the Danish church as simply part of "Christendom," making people believe they are Christians while in fact allowing people to live in essentially pagan ways.

This leads Kierkegaard to increasingly harsh and bitter criticisms of the church. In the last few months of his life, he openly attacked the state church, and the system in which pastors were official servants of the state, claiming that "the Christianity of the New Testament has ceased to exist." Although Kierkegaard himself refused any alliance with the "free churches" who wanted a Christianity distinct from the state church, his late newspaper and magazine writings had a significant influence on the growth of such "free churches" all over Scandinavia.

KIERKEGAARD'S CHRISTIAN ETHICS

Prior to this late attack on the church, Kierkegaard left a rich legacy of explicitly Christian writings. These books are either nonpseudonymous, such as *Works of Love* and *Christian Discourses*, or are attributed to a special Christian pseudonym, Anti-Climacus. (The Anti-Climacus writings include *The Sickness unto Death* and *Practice in Christianity*.) These writings explore the Christian life in a deep way, emphasizing the idea that the true Christian must be a follower of Christ, who is willing to accept suffering and even persecution for the sake of the Savior. *The Sickness unto Death* provides a kind of Christian psychology, seeing the human self as the task of synthesizing seemingly contrasting qualities. As creatures we must accept part of ourselves as necessary things we did not choose and cannot change. But we nevertheless are given possibility by God, who is the one for whom all things are possible. We are temporal creatures with an eternal destiny, given the task of acquiring eternal life in time.

Works of Love has a particular importance in this late or "second authorship." In this work Kierkegaard goes beyond the ethical understood as a stage on life's way or sphere of existence to develop an explicitly Christian ethic. This ethic centers on the two great biblical commands: we must love God above all else, and also love our neighbors as ourselves. Because we should love God above all else, we must obey God's command to love the neighbor. This love of the neighbor cannot be identified with any natural human love, such as friendship, romantic love, or even family love. Neighbor love is the love we are commanded to have for every human being, who is made in God's image, and has the "inner glory" that can only be seen with the help of the light of eternity. Thus we must love not just our friends and family, but also strangers and even our enemies. Friends and spouses must be loved as neighbors as well. Without having neighbor love as the foundation of our natural loves, they are easily corrupted and can become idols. Love for God and love for neighbor are thus indissoluble for Kierkegaard. No human account of ethical obligation can substitute for God's authority, though Kierkegaard says that modern Western philosophy is a kind of "mutiny" in which we try to free ourselves from that authority. The result of the mutiny is not freedom, but a world in which there is "doubt" and a "vortex," a world of lawlessness and anarchy.

KIERKEGAARD'S RECEPTION

Since Kierkegaard wrote in Danish, he was not much known outside of Scandinavia at his death for several decades to come. However, in the late 1800s Kierkegaard began to be translated into German, and Germany was at the center of intellectual culture in Europe at the time. A famous critic named Georg Brandes began to give lectures on Kierkegaard throughout Europe, and soon Kierkegaard was read by philosophers and theologians throughout the Continent and in England and Scotland as well. In Spain, a philosopher and novelist named Miguel de Unamuno began to write about Kierkegaard. Shortly after the shattering experiences of World War I, the German-Swiss theologian Karl Barth used Kierkegaard's writings as part of his attack on theological liberalism in his *Commentary on Romans.* Kierkegaard began to be read by Catholic as well as Protestant thinkers, and eventually (in the 1930s and 1940s) was translated into English, mostly by David Swenson of the University of Minnesota and by Walter Lowrie, an Anglican theologian. (Interestingly, Kierkegaard was translated into Japanese before English, by Japanese scholars who encountered him in Germany.)

Although Kierkegaard's philosophy was late arriving on the Western intellectual scene, when his writings did appear they seemed prophetic to many. Kierkegaard had rejected the optimism of the nineteenth century and foreseen the dangers of mass society. He had given a penetrating analysis of human existence in which we are all facing a new crisis of meaninglessness. Eventually Kierkegaard influenced those twentieth century philosophers we today term "existentialists," such as Martin Heidegger, Jean-Paul Sartre, and Albert Camus. Since most of these thinkers were atheists, Kierkegaard's fame as the "father of existentialism" came at some cost to our understanding of his own concerns as a Christian thinker. To understand his work, one must read him as "the individual" to whom Kierkegaard himself directed his work, seeing him in terms of his own concerns. While Kierkegaard certainly had a great influence on existentialism, it is important not to anachronistically read back into his own work the concerns of these later thinkers.

John Stuart Mill and Nineteenth-Century Positivism

HAVING SPENT SEVERAL CHAPTERS ON the continent of Europe looking at Immanuel Kant and his successors, it is now time to travel back across the English Channel and pick up the story in the United Kingdom. Prior to looking at Kant, we had examined two great philosophers of the Scottish Enlightenment: David Hume and Thomas Reid. In the short run, both in the United Kingdom and even more in the United States, Reid's "commonsense realism" seemed dominant over Hume's philosophy. However, Hume's blend of empiricism and skeptical attitude toward the supernatural was far from dead, and eventually it reemerged to become very influential. Indeed, many English-speaking philosophers would now describe Hume as the greatest philosopher of the modern West. In this chapter I shall briefly discuss the work of the French philosopher Auguste Comte and of Jeremy Bentham, before giving a more in-depth treatment of John Stuart Mill.

AUGUSTE COMTE

Some of the ideas of Auguste Comte (1798–1857) overlap with those of Bentham and Mill, and indeed for a time Comte and Mill were allies. In his day Comte was famous and influential as the founder of positivism, which became a worldwide movement in the nineteenth century. Nineteenth-century positivism should be distinguished from the twentieth-century movement known as neopositivism or logical positivism, which arose in Vienna after World War I and became the dominant form of philosophy until the 1950s. The two movements share a commitment to empiricism in their epistemology, and both give a high place to science understood as an empirical endeavor. Nineteenth-century positivism combined this faith in science with progressive political reform programs. The logical positivists were more apolitical, marrying their empiricism to the new symbolic logic that had been developed by such thinkers as Bertrand Russell and Ludwig Wittgenstein. The logical positivists were committed to an austere theory of meaning that held that all meaningful statements must be empirically verifiable. On this view, statements about God and even normative ethics had no cognitive meaning at all. They were not even false taken as factual assertions. Nineteenth-century positivists were also antagonistic to traditional religious belief, but they did not go so far as to claim that religious language was meaningless.

The nineteenth-century positivists did not accept such an austere theory of meaning, and they lacked the logical tools of the later positivists. However, they were, if anything, even more optimistic about the promise of science to transform the world for the better. Comte himself had begun his career as a private secretary for Saint Simon, a radical French political thinker, and he remained a defender of progressive movements all his life.

Comte is regarded as the father of sociology as a scientific discipline, and he is one of the first thinkers to develop a philosophy of science that attempted to distinguish the natural sciences from other kinds of disciplines. Comte developed a classification of the "six fundamental sciences" (mathematics, astronomy, physics, chemistry, biology, and sociology) as well as an account of what makes a genuine science. As part of this account Comte offered the "law of three stages" as an account of how a science develops. Humanity's intellectual development begins with the "theological stage," in which explanations of natural events are given in terms of the actions of gods. For example, at this stage thunder might be explained as the result of Thor throwing his hammer. The theological stage is succeeded by a "metaphysical stage" in which supernatural agents are replaced by abstract principles. At this stage a god like Thor is replaced with something like a "sonic principle" that inheres in the clouds. The final stage is the stage of "positive science" (from which positivism derives its name), in which humans seek explanations in terms of empirically discoverable generalizations or laws. These laws are not absolutes but are best seen as provisional in nature as science gets closer and closer to the truth.

Comte's account of science as essentially superseding theology has been enormously influential among a certain class of intellectuals, and provides a popular explanation of why religious belief seemed to be declining in Europe as science progressed. Ironically, however, it seems more of an a priori assumption on Comte's part than a historical claim that can be backed up with empirical evidence. It seems more plausible to view magic as the forerunner of science, since science and magic share a goal of controlling and mastering the physical world. Comte seems not to have noticed that many of the greatest scientists, such as Isaac Newton, were deeply religious people, and that science often seems to foster the sense of awe that engenders religious faith, rather than replacing that faith.

Comte himself recognized the need for something like religion. He realized that humans need something to believe in that would provide their lives with meaning and purpose. He therefore founded and spent the last part of his life attempting to promote what he called "humanism," understood as the religion of humanity. This attempt on the part of Comte lost him much of his support. Early in his career his positivism enjoyed the support of thinkers such as John Stuart Mill, whom I discuss below. Mill, however, along with many other followers, broke with Comte over the idea of a "religion of humanity."

JEREMY BENTHAM

Jeremy Bentham, who lived from 1748 to 1832, was an Englishman trained as a lawyer, but who devoted his life to writing about morality and political and social reforms. He is renowned as the inventor of utilitarianism, the moral philosophy that grounds all of morality in the principle that the rightness of an action is a function of its tendency to lead to happiness. In a long and active life, Bentham was involved in many practical disputes over public policy issues, with some success and many disappointments. This in turn led to active advocacy of political reform and greater democratization in England. Interestingly, Bentham's ideas became well-known internationally and were published in many languages well before he became famous in his native country. Oddly, and somewhat gruesomely, Bentham asked that his own head and body be mummified and placed on display at University College, London, because he believed that the public display of dead bodies would be useful for public instruction, and this was actually done.

Bentham spent much of his life working on very practical issues of reform. A good example, and one very close to Bentham's heart, was the idea of a "Panopticon," which was a type of building design for an institution, such as a prison, in which humans require constant supervision. Bentham had the idea that a circular building, with windows on the inside of the circle, and a room in the middle of the circle where those in authority could view each room, would be ideal for public correction, since he believed "the more strictly we are watched, the better we behave."[1] Perhaps Bentham, who seems to have rejected belief in God, still found it necessary for humans to have someone who constantly watches them! Though the Panopticon was never built in England, versions of it were built in the United States.

Rather than examining all of Bentham's popular plans, I shall focus on his moral philosophy, which provided the theoretical basis for all his

---

[1]Jeremy Bentham, "Farming Defended," in *Writings on the Poor Laws*, ed. Michael Quinn (Oxford: Clarendon, 2001), 1:277.

proposed reforms. The heart of Bentham's moral theory is found in the principle that morality should aim at "the greatest happiness for the greatest number." Happiness is in turn defined in hedonistic terms, as the presence of pleasure and the absence of pain. Bentham memorably underlines the importance of pain and pleasure at the very beginning of his *Introduction to the Principles of Morals and Legislation:* "Nature has placed mankind under the governance of two sovereign masters, *pain* and *pleasure.* It is for them alone to point out what we ought to do, as well as to determine what we shall do."[2]

Bentham arrived at this attempt to ground morality in pleasure and pain through the influence of empiricism. One of his formative experiences had been hearing the great jurist William Blackstone lecture on law at Oxford. Bentham recoiled from Blackstone's defense of English common law, as well as the philosophical commitment to natural law that Blackstone had, memorably claiming that the notion of "natural rights" was "nonsense upon stilts."[3] (For this reason Bentham was sharply critical of the United States Declaration of Independence, since it begins with a claim about God-given natural rights that are inalienable.) In his search for a reasonable and secular grounding for morality, Bentham was drawn to David Hume's use of the idea of "utility," and he was determined to find a basis for morality in experience rather than in religion, tradition, or some theory of human nature. The sensations of pain and pleasure seemed perfectly suited for the job.

Bentham was both a psychological hedonist and an ethical or normative hedonist. That is, he believed that as a matter of fact human actions are always motivated by a desire to achieve pleasure and avoid pain (psychological hedonism), but he also believed that humans ought to seek happiness understood in this hedonistic way. There is a tension,

---

[2]Jeremy Bentham, *Introduction to the Principles of Morals and Education* (London: T. Payne and Son, 1780), 1.1, p. 7.
[3]This essay can be found under the title "Nonsense upon Stilts," in Jeremy Bentham, *Rights, Representation, and Reform: Nonsense upon Stilts and Other Writings on the French Revolution,* ed. Philip Schofield, Catherine Pease-Watkin, and Cyprian Blamires (Oxford: Oxford University Press, 2002), 317-401.

however, between Bentham's psychological hedonism, which is egoistic, and his moral hedonism. The psychological hedonist claims that each person seeks their own happiness, but Bentham's moral theory claims that each of us ought to seek the greatest happiness for all, and do so in an impartial manner. How can the egoism of Bentham's psychology be made consistent with the impartiality of his morality?

Bentham answers this question by appealing to what he calls "sanctions," which tie our personal happiness to the happiness of others. Sanctions are of different types, but they all link to pleasure and pain as rewards and punishments. Some sanctions are simply rooted in the natural, physical world, as when a person suffers because of imprudent actions. A person may act to gain an immediate pleasure at the cost of greater pains down the road, perhaps by drinking to excess that leads to a hangover. Other sanctions are rooted in the power of the state, which sometimes punishes those who seek their own happiness at the expense of others. Some are rooted in social opinion, since people commonly get pleasure from the approval of others and pain from their disapproval. Bentham realizes that sanctions do not work perfectly, and part of his program is to seek to reform society in ways that bring personal and communal happiness together by providing the right kinds of rewards and punishments. Bentham is committed to a kind of experimental method, in which policies and programs should be evaluated by their consequences. He is in fact one of the sources of the idea of "cost-benefit analysis," ubiquitous in contemporary economics, government, and business.

How will the evaluations be done? Bentham was optimistic that happiness could be quantified, and thus that we could obtain objective results that would show what policies and actions are conducive to happiness. He even developed a kind of mathematical formula, called the "felicific calculus," which could be used to compare alternative actions and policies. This formula took into account various aspects of pleasure and pain, but only those aspects that could be quantified. These included such things as how long the pleasure or pain endured, the intensity of the pleasure or pain, how many people experience the pleasure and pain, and the "purity" of the experiences, since Bentham recognized that some pleasures and pains are connected and one does not get one without the other. As we shall see in our discussion of Mill, this quantitative hedonism seems problematic for a number of reasons, and Mill disagrees with Bentham on this point.

JOHN STUART MILL

John Stuart Mill is in the eyes of many the greatest of the nineteenth-century philosophers committed to empiricism. He was born in 1806 and died in 1873. Mill's father James Mill was a close friend and follower of Bentham, so John Stuart Mill absorbed utilitarian principles at an early age. He was given an intense education by his father, learning the classics, languages, and history beginning when he was only three. At the age of twenty he had a kind of nervous breakdown, which he attributed partly to the intensity and one-sidedness of his formation, and he recovered partly by learning the importance of the emotions and "feelings" for life.

Mill is many ways the epitome of empiricism, attempting to ground all of human knowledge in sense experience. He is, like Comte, an advocate of "positive science." He was in fact a friend and ally of Comte early on. Mill's empiricism is in some ways more complete and consistent than Hume's. Even Hume, it will be recalled, did not see mathematics as an empirical discipline, but rather classes mathematical truths among what he called "relations of ideas," propositions that can be known a priori. Mill, however, tried to give an account of mathematics and logic that rooted them in our psychological experiences of counting and reasoning. Mathematical truths are simply empirical generalizations that are massively and uniformly verified by our experience. Few philosophers, even those who are empiricists, have followed Mill in this view, often called "psychologism," since it seems obvious that mathematics and logic do not simply report how things happen to be, but rather include necessary truths. However, it is completely unclear how the experiences of how people actually think and count could give us insight into what is necessarily true. Experience can tell us how things are but not how they must be. Mill did, however, develop a set of practical methods for arriving at empirical, inductive conclusions, methods that are employed by scientists even today.

Mill's moral philosophy is most clearly described in *Utilitarianism*, where he attempts to explain and defend a view that is clearly inspired by Bentham but departs from him at some crucial points. Like Bentham, Mill holds that the "foundation of morals" is "Utility," or "the Greatest Happiness Principle," which asserts that "actions are right in proportion as they tend to promote happiness, wrong as they tend to produce the reverse of happiness."[4] Also, like Bentham, Mill says that happiness and unhappiness are to be defined in terms of pleasure and pain. Thus "pleasure, and freedom from pain, are the only things desirable as ends; and that all desirable things . . . are desirable either for the pleasure inherent in themselves, or as means to the promotion of pleasure and the prevention of pain."[5]

Qualitative versus quantitative hedonism. However, this apparent agreement with Bentham about hedonism hides a substantial disagreement. As we saw, Bentham was a quantitative hedonist, who said that pleasures, aside from differences in such dimensions as duration and intensity, are all the same. Assuming that the quantity is the same, there is no basis for saying that the pleasure one gets from reading great poetry or a great novel is any better than the pleasure one might get from watching a rerun of a mindless television sitcom, or, for that matter, looking at pornography. Mill disagrees with this: "It would be absurd that while, in estimating all other things, quality is supposed to be considered as well as quantity, the estimation of pleasure is supposed to depend on

---

[4]John Stuart Mill, *Utilitarianism*, ed. Roger Crisp (Oxford: Oxford University Press, 1998), 55.
[5]Mill, *Utilitarianism*, 55.

quantity alone."[6] Thus Mill holds that a life with qualitatively higher pleasures, such as those that are connected to our "higher" mental faculties, may be more desirable than a life solely devoted to crasser physical pleasure, even if the latter includes more pleasure and the former includes more pains of various kinds (as is often the case with highly reflective people). Mill thus claims that "it is better to be a human being dissatisfied than a pig satisfied; better to be Socrates dissatisfied than a fool satisfied."[7] If the pig or the fool think differently it is only because they do not understand what it would be like to live on a higher plane.

In many ways Mill's view seems far more plausible than Bentham's, but it does introduce problems that Bentham does not face. One difficulty is that if one admits that pleasures differ in quality, it becomes much more difficult, perhaps impossible, to comparatively evaluate the consequences of actions. Qualitatively different goods seem incommensurable, and so the kind of mathematical calculation that Bentham wanted will be impossible. However, the whole appeal of utilitarianism is that it is supposed to provide an objective way to settle on what is morally right. If consequences cannot be objectively compared, this advantage is undercut. Mill admits this in a way, appealing simply to what individuals would prefer rather than to some kind of mathematical result, but this introduces a strong element of subjectivity to the evaluation, since different people notoriously prefer radically different things.

A second problem is that it is not clear that Mill is really a hedonist anymore, despite his claim to be one. If pleasures that involve the development of "higher" human faculties are superior to other kinds of pleasure, why is this the case? It cannot be that they simply are more pleasant, for that is Bentham's view. If pleasures that include the development of our higher human faculties are qualitatively superior to those that do not, it seems that developing those faculties is intrinsically good, and thus pleasure is not the only good worth seeking.

---

[6]Mill, *Utilitarianism*, 56.
[7]Mill, *Utilitarianism*, 57.

Mill seems to equivocate on the objective value of some other things as well, such as moral virtue. It is a truism of morality that a morally good person will sometimes sacrifice his or her happiness to do what is morally right. At one point Mill says that sacrificing one's own happiness is never good as an end, but only as a means: "A sacrifice which does not increase or tend to increase, the sum total of happiness, it considers as wasted."[8] Later, however, Mill claims that utilitarianism affirms that moral virtue (which certainly sometimes requires the sacrifice of happiness) is something intrinsically good: "It [utilitarian doctrine] maintains not only that virtue is to be desired, but that it is to be desired disinterestedly."[9] This seems like a contradiction, and Mill tries to resolve the problem by saying that virtue, though not originally part of happiness, is something that people can be conditioned to desire as *part* of happiness. However, if I only desire virtue when it is part of my own happiness, it does not seem that I value virtue for its own sake. Mill wants to remain a hedonist, but his own moral intuitions keep pushing him away from this Benthamite doctrine. It may be true that everyone (or almost everyone) desires happiness, but it is not true that happiness is the only thing people value intrinsically. Nor is it true that human happiness can be identified with the presence or absence of identifiable sensations of pleasure and the absence of pain.

Like Bentham, Mill tries to connect personal happiness with the utilitarian end of the happiness of all through sanctions. Although Mill clearly does not think God is necessary as a sanction for morality, he is happy to say that if there is a God, and God wills us to seek the happiness of others, then God could provide sanctions for morality, at least for those who believe in God. The legal system provides other external sanctions, and social approval and disapproval yet another. However, the most important sanction that brings together personal happiness and morality is the internal feeling of conscience, or devotion to duty.

---

[8]Mill, *Utilitarianism*, 64.
[9]Mill, *Utilitarianism*, 82.

Mill believes this sense of duty is acquired and not innate, and he hopes that education and parenting practices will be such as to develop and strengthen it.

Mill's arguments for utilitarianism. Mill says that questions about ultimate ends "do not admit of proof" in the logical sense of that term. As a good empiricist, he therefore makes appeal to "our senses, and our internal consciousness."[10] He thus tries to make an experiential argument for happiness as the ultimate end of morality: "The only proof capable of being given that an object is visible, is that people actually see it. . . . In like manner, . . . the sole evidence it is possible to produce that anything is desirable, is that people do actually desire it."[11] This argument has been famously criticized as an instance of what twentieth-century philosopher G. E. Moore later called "the naturalistic fallacy" in ethics. From the fact that someone desires something, it may follow that it is the kind of thing it is possible to desire. However, it certainly does not follow from the fact that someone desires something that what is desired is something that *ought* to be desired, something that it is good to desire.

Even if we could infer that something is desirable from the fact that it is desired, it would by no means follow that happiness is the sole intrinsic good. Empirically, it seems evident that people value many things for their own sake besides happiness. Mill, however, believes that "each person, so far as he believes it to be attainable, desires his own happiness."[12] That being so, he concludes that "happiness is a good; that each person's happiness is a good to that person, and the general happiness, therefore, a good to the aggregate of all persons."[13] This hardly follows. Even if it were true that each person considers his or her own happiness to be a good, it would not follow that the happiness of anyone else (much less everyone else) would be a good for that person.

[10]Mill, *Utilitarianism*, 81.
[11]Mill, *Utilitarianism*, 81.
[12]Mill, *Utilitarianism*, 81.
[13]Mill, *Utilitarianism*, 81.

Individuals might well see happiness as a zero-sum game, in which individual happiness can only be acquired at the expense of others' happiness. Even if one admits that happiness as Mill understands it is a
good, it would not follow that it is the sole intrinsic good, and that it can
therefore be the foundation of all of morality.

Rule utilitarianism versus act utilitarianism. Bentham seemed to
think that utilitarianism could and should be applied to each and every
distinct act. The right thing to do in every situation is to choose the act
that seems most likely to lead to the greatest happiness for the greatest
number. However, critics objected to this on a number of grounds.
People rarely have time to make complex calculations before acting, and
in any case it seems certain that our knowledge of the consequences of
our actions is highly incomplete and fallible. Mill responds to these
objections by admitting that in the great majority of cases the utilitarian
will, like more traditional moral theories, rely on established moral
maxims or rules, such as to tell the truth, and not to kill or harm others.
Most of the time we rely on "intermediate" or "secondary" principles,
rather than the principle of utility itself.[14] These subordinate principles
are themselves justified by the principle of utility. People do not have
to begin from scratch when deciding what to do, since during the whole
of time "mankind have been learning from experience the tendencies
of actions."[15]

Mill here seems to be moving toward making a distinction later philosophers will develop, between what we now call act utilitarianism and
rule utilitarianism. The act utilitarian holds that for each individual
action we should simply try to follow the principle of utility and perform
the act that is likely to lead to the greatest happiness for all concerned.
The rule utilitarian says that this is not possible or perhaps not even
desirable. Rather, when we make moral decisions we ought to follow
moral rules or principles. However, if one asks how those moral rules

---

[14]Mill, *Utilitarianism*, 70.
[15]Mill, *Utilitarianism*, 70.

or principles are justified, the answer is that it is by following these rules that we have the best chance of achieving the greatest happiness for all.

Since this is a distinction made by later utilitarians, it is not surprising that it is not completely clear where Mill stands on this issue. Perhaps his view is something like this: most of the time we should follow the moral principles that past experience has shown to be generally conducive to the general happiness. However, in exceptional circumstances, in which it is clear that following the rule will not be in accord with the principle of utility, then an exception should be made. If that is correct, then Mill is really an act utilitarian, albeit one who thinks that most of the time we have to rely on general rules. The problem with rule utilitarianism is that if the ultimate aim of action is to achieve the happiness of all affected, it is hard to see why we should rely on a rule in a case where doing so will evidently not be conducive to the general happiness.

Utilitarianism and the problem of justice. In contemporary philosophy, Mill's utilitarianism is often called "classical utilitarianism," and is now regarded as one species of a broader category of moral theory, called consequentialism. A consequentialist is simply someone who, like Mill, believes that the morality of an action is a function of the consequences of the action. One can easily see that there are forms of consequentialism different from Mill's. For example, one might reject hedonism altogether and explicitly state that the good consequences that morality requires us to seek include more than just pleasure and the avoidance of pain.

One grave problem that faces every form of consequentialism, including Mill's utilitarianism, is whether it can give an adequate account of justice. Intuitively, it seems quite possible to act in a way that leads to the greatest happiness for all but that still involves treating some individuals unjustly. Consider, for instance, the case of a racist society. Suppose that 95 percent of a society is composed of one ethnic group, with the other 5 percent a different group. It is possible that if the majority group is racist, then their happiness will be furthered by racist laws and institutions. Now it is true that this will be at the expense of the minority, but it might still be the case, since the great majority of people are racists, that there will be more happiness overall in the racist society than in a society that rejects racism. This may be so even if one considers the issue from an impartial point of view, that is, counting the pleasures and pains of every individual equally. Surely, however, a racist society that discriminated against a minority in this way would be unjust. So it appears that one could seek to follow the principle of utility, advancing the greatest happiness of the greatest number, in a way that goes against what justice demands.

Mill had a greater appreciation for this problem than did Bentham. Bentham was a strong proponent of democracy and had great faith that democratic rule would eliminate oppression and injustice. However, Mill recognized that sometimes pleasing the majority of people could be accomplished at the expense of a minority, or perhaps some individuals. Hence he attempted to give an account of the special importance that justice has, while still sticking to utilitarian principles.

Mill's account of justice links it to the notion of rights. Strictly speaking, Mill agrees with Bentham that there are no "natural rights," but rights are grounded in society. "To have a right . . . is to have something which society ought to defend me in the possession of."[16] However, rights are especially important, because they are linked to the "most vital of all interests," which is our personal security.[17] Mill thinks that if we lack security, no other goods are of much value, since we could at any moment lose all those other goods. Thus he thinks that our need to be safe leads us to think that society has a special obligation to protect this interest. The claim that we ought to be secure in this way "assumes that character of absoluteness, that apparent infinity, and incommensurability with all other considerations" that we associate with matters of justice, and indeed of moral right and wrong generally.[18]

---

[16]Mill, *Utilitarianism*, 98.
[17]Mill, *Utilitarianism*, 98.
[18]Mill, *Utilitarianism*, 98.

The bottom line however is that justice in the end depends on utility. Mill can think of no reason why society should extend to individuals such rights except "general utility." In the end we should value justice and extend rights to individuals because it will advance the general happiness. Perhaps Mill thinks that if society persecutes or discriminates against a minority, then all of us will feel less secure, and therefore will be less happy, since we will realize that the same thing could be done to us.

The problem with this answer is that it just does not appear to be empirically correct. If one examines the culture of the American South in the days in which lynchings of black people were common, there is little evidence that the majority of people were worried about this injustice. Indeed, lynchings often seemed like public festivals, in which the whole town would turn out to enjoy the spectacle. People who are racists do not worry about the mistreatment of the victims of the race they despise. Even if Mill were right on the empirical question, and it were true that injustice generally leads to less general happiness, this would not mean that justice is grounded in utility. To see whether this is so one must consider a case where the two might conflict. Such cases are certainly possible, even if it were true (which sadly is not the case) that they are very rare. Many philosophers therefore think that all forms of consequentialism, including utilitarianism, fail to give a complete account of morality because they do not adequately account for justice.

Other problems with utilitarianism. There are a number of other problems with utilitarianism and its consequentialist cousins. One might be called the problem of special relationships. Mill stresses that utilitarianism requires a strict impartiality in which one seeks the greatest good for the greatest number, taking into account all who might be affected by an action. However, it is hard to see how such impartiality is compatible with the special relationships that are central to a flourishing human life. Suppose, for example, that I have $200 budgeted to spend on Christmas presents for my children. It seems very likely that if I spent that sum buying presents for some impoverished children who are strangers to me that the total amount of happiness I would achieve would be much greater. However, most people would think it is permissible to spend extra funds on one's own children even if this does not in fact create more happiness than some alternative. Some utilitarians might here be willing to "bite the bullet" and say that I ought to spend the money on strangers in this case, but a general stance of this sort would make special relations very difficult or even impossible to maintain.

Another special relation might be the relation a person has to himself or herself. Suppose I am considering engaging in what might seem to be a harmless pleasure, spending $10 to go to a movie this weekend. There are, however, starving children in places in the world, and it is quite possible that if I were to donate that $10 to a charity that is seeking to feed these children I could save a life. One might think that my duty according to utilitarianism would be to donate the money and forego the movie. This is far from a hypothetical case; some prominent utilitarians have argued that this is exactly what I should do.[19] The same kind of dilemma would arise for almost any expenditure I might make that is not aimed at saving my own life. The irony is that a philosophy devoted to personal happiness appears to require everyone to renounce personal happiness almost completely.

Another difficult problem for the utilitarian concerns what are sometimes called "elimination arguments." If my moral duty is simply to seek to produce the greatest possible balance of happiness over unhappiness in the world, one way to do that would be to seek to eliminate very unhappy people. There are almost certainly some people whose lives contain a great deal more pain than pleasure. If one simply euthanized such people one would eliminate a great deal of pain while losing only a modest amount of pleasure. One might object that this would cause distress to the friends or family of the people eliminated, but one could

---

[19]See Peter Singer, "Rich or Poor," in *Practical Ethics*, 2nd ed. (Cambridge: Cambridge University Press, 1993).

easily propose to limit the eliminations to people who are hated by others, and whose demise would only create still more happiness. Such an idea might seem far-fetched, but proposals to legalize euthanasia often are based on a similar idea: that a person whose life promises more pain than pleasure should be able to choose to end that life. It has also become commonplace in some countries to abort fetuses with handicaps, presumably because the lives of handicapped people do not score high on utilitarian grounds.

There is certainly something right about utilitarian and consequentialist principles. In general it makes sense to take into account the consequences of our actions and prefer better outcomes to worse ones. Such a principle is particularly plausible to those with nonreligious worldviews, since it grounds morality only in familiar experiences that anyone can share. However, even if it right to pursue good consequences, it does not seem right to hold that this is the only thing that matters ethically. Most moral thinkers have held that some actions have moral character in themselves. Even if one could achieve equally good results by lying or telling the truth, it would surely be better to tell the truth. Some kinds of acts are not just wrong because they generally lead to bad results; they seem wrong in themselves, even if sometimes we think that they must be done as "lesser evils."

Christians at least believe that we humans are not placed in the world solely to be producers of good consequences. We are on a journey where we are seeking to become people who have certain characteristics. Character matters as well as results.

Mill on liberty. In addition to Mill's defense of utilitarian moral theory, he is well known for his defense of freedom and limited government in his book *On Liberty*. In this book Mill explores in some depth the worry that a democratic government might oppress minorities or individuals. He argues that government should not try to do what individuals or private organizations can do better. Mill's worry about the oppressive potential of the state puts a check on any idea

that the power of the state should be used to coerce people into practices that will make them happier. People should even have the right
to act in ways that are harmful to themselves. It is only when our
conduct threatens to harm others that the state has a right to intervene.
Mill's vision is sometimes called "classical liberalism," but it is closer
to the contemporary view called libertarianism than what is often
called liberalism today.

This is a very individualistic vision of society, one that is the antithesis
of the Hegelian communitarian view that the identity of the self requires a social community. Mill seems to reject the idea that there is
some kind of common good that the state should promote. If humans
are deeply social, it is not clear that we can distinguish between allowing
individuals to harm themselves and harming society. For example, take
such risky behavior as smoking and riding motorcycles without helmets.
One might think that such people harm only themselves. However,
their risky behavior may overburden our common medical system, as
well as cheating friends and family, and society at large, of the contribution they might have made to the common good.

Despite the problems, this individualism has been deeply influential
in Western societies, and especially in America. We can see in Mill's
thinking here the origins of the idea that humans have a right to suicide
as well as women having a right to abortions, for "over himself, over his
own body and mind, the individual is sovereign."[20]

---

[20]John Stuart Mill, *On Liberty*, ed. David Spitz, Norton Critical Editions (New York: W.W. Norton,
1975), 11.

Friedrich Nietzsche

THE LAST OF THE WESTERN PHILOSOPHERS I shall examine in this history is the German thinker Friedrich Nietzsche. This is not the last chapter of the book, however. I will append a concluding chapter with some lessons I have learned from the study of Western philosophy. And of course Western philosophy does not stop with Nietzsche, but continues through the twentieth century and into the twenty-first. However, I believe the last 125 years is too fresh to have the proper perspective on this history. We do not really know which philosophers from the twentieth century will still be read two hundred years from now. As a result, a history of twentieth-century philosophy would have to include so much that it would require at least a separate volume of its own. There are so many philosophers who currently seem important that I could easily write a book just on the last century that would be as long as the one I have written on the roughly 2,400 years preceding it. I will try in the concluding chapter to give a brief sketch of the major trends in philosophy after Nietzsche, but a full treatment would make this unmanageably large.

Of course there is something arbitrary about stopping with Nietzsche, as there would be with any other stopping place. I considered adding a chapter on American pragmatism to this book, since Charles Sanders Peirce and William James did much of their work in the last part of the nineteenth century. However, the most famous pragmatist, John Dewey, is definitely a twentieth-century figure, and it seemed wrong to treat two of the pragmatists without the third. Given the length of the book, it seemed better to me to have one less chapter than one more.

A strong case can be made for ending with Nietzsche. As we will see, in many respects Nietzsche challenges and undermines almost of the philosophers who came before him. He therefore helps us raise important questions about the whole story of Western philosophy. (The same could be said for Dewey and several other twentieth-century thinkers.) Nietzsche embodies many of the themes and emphases that will dominate the twentieth century. He also raises in an acute way questions about the place Christianity has occupied in Western culture, questions about Christianity's future, as well as questions about the future of what we might call Western morality, which Nietzsche sees as linked to religion. Nietzsche himself insists that Western culture now faces the problem of nihilism, and his philosophy will help us see why this is so, and consider possible responses to nihilism.

NIETZSCHE'S LIFE

Friedrich Nietzsche was born in Saxony in 1844. His father and grandfather were Lutheran ministers, but the father died when Nietzsche was only four years old. The young Friedrich was raised by a household of women: his mother, grandmother, sister, and two unmarried aunts. Despite this upbringing (or maybe because of it) Nietzsche was later to put a great emphasis on strength, virility, health, and masculinity. Ironically, he himself suffered from chronic ill health as an adult.

Nietzsche studied philology at the University of Leipzig, but his reading ranged deeply over Greek philosophy. His brilliance was quickly realized, and he was given the chair of philosophy at the University of Basel when he was only twenty-four years old and had not yet completed his doctorate. Nietzsche stayed there ten years and wrote several important works, including *The Birth of Tragedy from the Spirit of Music*, which I will discuss below. In 1879, however, he resigned his professorship because of his chronic bad health, and spent most of the rest of his life traveling around Italy, hoping the climate would boost his health, and supporting himself by his writings. In 1889, when he had just completed a number of his most important works, Nietzsche collapsed on the street in Turin, Italy. He saw a man beating a horse and broke down in tears as he put his arms around the horse's neck. Although he survived ten more years, passing away in 1900, he was never sane again. He was first taken to a clinic and then to an asylum, but was taken care of by his sister for the final years of his life. (I will say more on this relationship later.)

SCHOPENHAUER'S INFLUENCE ON NIETZSCHE

As a young thinker Nietzsche initially fell under the sway of Arthur Schopenhauer (1788–1860), whose philosophy was a kind of strange version of Idealism. Schopenhauer followed Kant in distinguishing between reality as it appears and reality as it really is. He also follows Kant in arguing that the world as it appears is a construction of the intellect. So far Schopenhauer would seem to be an Idealist like Fichte, Schelling, and Hegel. However, he argues that reality as it is in itself is not the work of a rational Mind. It is basically a kind of mindless will, a nonrational instinctive form of desire. All of this is explained in his most important work, *The World as Will and Representation*.

Most Western philosophers, going back to Plato and Aristotle, have thought of the will as a kind of rational appetite. Our will is shaped by our understanding of the good, and particular acts of will are generally preceded by reflective deliberation. Schopenhauer's understanding of the will is vastly different. The will is a kind of blind instinctive force, a gnawing emptiness that is incapable of being filled. All of reality consists of this blind force, but our intellect masks this by representing the world as a kind of rational structure. We construct a world of "representations," but what we represent to ourselves through the intellect is something that we grasp through our own self-consciousness.

Schopenhauer's philosophy seems to lead to a pessimistic view of human existence, and indeed he is known as "the great pessimist" of

German philosophy. The world is not a rational place; it is not the creation of a good, personal God, and it has no final meaning or purpose. Schopenhauer was interested in Asian thought, and his philosophy has some affinities with Buddhism. The will as this gnawing instinct that cannot be satisfied leads to misery and suffering. The best that we can do to mitigate this suffering is to attempt to moderate our desires through ascetic practices, and to cultivate selfless compassion for others. Schopenhauer also believes that art offers some consolation for humans, because when we contemplate or experience works of art we are, at least temporarily, taken away from a fixation on our own desires and captivated by a kind of disinterested love for that work of art.

The young Nietzsche fell under Schopenhauer's sway, and Schopenhauer left a permanent mark on his thought. Eventually, Nietzsche broke with Schopenhauer (as he tended to do with figures who were important to him), particularly with respect to the value of compassion. The mature Nietzsche comes to see Schopenhauer as a reflection of what Nietzsche calls "European decadence," which has lost touch with its vital forces. However, some things from Schopenhauer endure: Nietzsche adopts an atheistic stance that rejects any cosmic purpose or meaning for the universe or human life. He also takes from Schopenhauer a conviction that reality is fundamentally shaped by the will, understood as a blind, instinctive force. Finally, Nietzsche, especially in his early work, gives art a central place in human life.

NIETZSCHE ON THE BIRTH OF TRAGEDY

Nietzsche's first important book was *The Birth of Tragedy from the Spirit of Music*. The book moves seamlessly between Nietzsche's work as a philologist, his interests as a philosopher, his fascination with ancient Greek culture, and his attempt to understand his own times. The book is an attempt to answer the question as to why and how the ancient Greeks invented tragedy. Today, we take theater for granted, but it was invented by the ancient Greeks, and Nietzsche tries to discover its origins.

The book describes Greek culture as a synthesis of two contrasting forces, which Nietzsche describes as the Apollonian and Dionysiac, named of course for the two gods Apollo and Dionysus. Apollo, the sun god, stands for the forces of order and form. Dionysus, the god of wine, represents the vital instinctual forces in Greek culture, which come to expression in ecstasy and excess. Apollo expresses the individuated, which can be understood. Dionysus comes to expression in madness and in the communal revelry in which the individual becomes part of a larger reality. One can easily see the influence of Schopenhauer in this tension between the two forces. The worshipers of Dionysus periodically engaged in communal revelry, characterized by drunkenness and music, which is seen as the most elemental and Dionysiac of all the arts.

Nietzsche's hypothesis is that this Dionysiac revelry provides the origins of tragedy. A distinctive feature of Greek tragedy is the chorus, which plays a key role in making clear the underlying issues and advancing the plot. Nietzsche believes it is the chorus that provides the beginnings of Greek tragedy, which evolves into its recognizable form by the imposition of Apollonian form on the wild, instinctive elements of tragedy. Thus the Greek art of tragedy is the result of the interplay between these contrasting and yet necessary aspects of human existence.

Tragedy is important for Nietzsche because Greek theater was able to communicate to the audience a tragic understanding of human existence. The world as seen by tragic poets such as Aeschylus is not a moralistic world in which the good is rewarded and the evil punished. "Whoever approaches the Olympians with a different religion in his heart, seeking moral elevation, sanctity, spirituality, loving-kindness, will presently be disappointed . . . we are confronted by luxuriant, triumphant *existence*, which deifies the good and the bad indifferently."[1] The world of Greek tragedy is a world that is irrational, a world dominated by instinctive desires. The Apollonian form

---

[1]Friedrich Nietzsche, *"Birth of Tragedy"* and *"The Genealogy of Morals,"* trans. Francis Golffing (Garden City, NY: Doubleday, 1956), 29.

imposed by the play provided the aesthetic frame that allows the audience to face the harsh reality of a world that has no final meaning, but is driven by wild passions. One might say that tragedy provides some of the functions of a religion for the Greeks, giving humans the strength to embrace their fate and reconciling them with a reality that does not care about them.

On Nietzsche's view, Greek tragedy was destroyed by Greek philosophy, and in particular by Socrates. It was Socrates who had the nerve to insist that reality make sense, particularly moral sense. However, the world of tragedy is not a world where the demands of reason and morality are satisfied. Socrates's demand for moral clarity helped prepare the West for the triumph of Christian morality. As I will explain in some detail below, Christian morality according to Nietzsche is a morality of weakness, a slave morality that tames and undermines the vital instinctual forces. Nietzsche sees the history of the West, not as a story of triumphal progress, as did Hegel, but a history of the development of weakness and decadence.

At the time Nietzsche wrote *The Birth of Tragedy*, he had developed a close friendship with Richard Wagner, the famous composer of operas based on pre-Christian Nordic mythology. Nietzsche saw in Wagnerian opera the possibility of an art form that could do for the modern world what ancient tragedy had done for the Greeks. Wagner's operas pointed toward a new rekindling of the Dionysiac spirit, which had become anemic. Nietzsche actually dedicated the book to Wagner.

Soon thereafter, however, Nietzsche became disillusioned with Wagner, just as he had turned on Schopenhauer. Rather than seeing Wagner as a kind of artistic messiah who could rejuvenate European culture, he decided Wagner was himself just another product of European decadence. Part of the reason for the break can be found in Wagner's anti-Semitism. Wagner was part of a group of extreme anti-Semites, the kind of person that would late gravitate to Hitler and the Nazis. Although Nietzsche himself frequently writes things that have an anti-Jewish character, he detested the kind of anti-Semitism Wagner and his friends displayed. The final straw for Nietzsche came when Wagner wrote a Christian opera, *Parsifal*, which appeared to Nietzsche to be a kind of betrayal.

GOOD-AND-BAD VERSUS GOOD-AND-EVIL

Perhaps Nietzsche's most original and influential thinking centers on his view of morality, which is linked to his view of the history of morality, developed in most detail in his *Genealogy of Morals*. First, it is important to see that for Nietzsche morality is a completely human creation. He does not believe in moral laws or a moral truth that somehow transcends human history. There are various forms of morality, and all of them are, as Nietzsche said about another topic, "human, all too human."

When Nietzsche looks for the history of Western morality, he sees a contest between two radically different and opposing moral viewpoints. The original morality, seen in the Homeric epic the *Iliad*, as well as in Nordic mythology, was a morality of "good-and-bad." This form of morality, also called master morality or the morality of the aristocracy, is a morality invented by the strong, dominant conquerors, the warriors who established control over the masses. As Nietzsche tells the story, the original system of values was grounded in the self-confidence and self-assertiveness of the masters. They saw themselves (and the qualities they possessed) as "good," while the masses were seen as bad. Part of the evidence Nietzsche cites is the etymology of the words *good* and *bad*. Originally, he argues, in many languages the words for "good" are virtually synonymous with "noble," while the words for "bad" typically just mean what is common or base or low. The values of the masters are those qualities that enable them to be victorious: strength, courage, and a sense of honor. The "bad" qualities of the masses are those that make them weak; they are sickly, cowardly, dishonorable.

Master morality places little value on such virtues as pity or compassion. It is a morality in which the strong do what they want and what they can. The weak masses are contemptible, and toward them the nobles behave as they wish. I will be discussing Nietzsche's metaphysics later, but it is already apparent that Nietzsche's view of human nature stresses the importance of power. We see here the influence of Schopenhauer's view of reality as fundamentally "will."

The "slave revolt" in morality begins with the resentment of the masses at their ill-treatment on the part of the masters. (Nietzsche uses the French term *ressentiment* to designate this reaction.) Naturally, the weak do not relish being treated badly by the nobles. "The beginning of the slaves' revolt in morality occurs when *ressentiment* itself turns creative and gives birth to values."[2] The value system created by the slave mentality is fundamentally different from that of master morality. Master morality is positive in character; the master says yes to himself and what is like himself. However, slave morality is reactive. This kind of morality, "denied the proper response of action, compensates for it only with imaginary revenge."[3] The master defines himself by what he is; there is a kind of honesty and spontaneity in his view of things. The slave defines himself by what he is not. Slave morality is fundamentally negative. The slave also wants power, but the slave is too weak actually to oppose the master, so he takes revenge in thought.

From the slave perspective, the oppressive master is evil, as are the qualities of the master: cruelty and aggression are the qualities of those who will one day (perhaps after death) pay a terrible price for their wanton ways. The good are the people who are like the slave: the weak, the poor, the meek. To use the language of Jesus in the Sermon on the Mount, these people are blessed. They are the people who will inherit

---

[2]Friedrich Nietzsche, *On the Genealogy of Morality*, ed. Keith Ansell-Pearson, trans. Carol Diethe, Cambridge Texts in the History of Political Thought (Cambridge: Cambridge University Press, 1994), 20.

[3]Nietzsche, *Genealogy*, trans. Diethe, 20.

the kingdom of God. Mary's song (from the first chapter of Luke) expresses the sentiments perfectly: God has

> scattered those who are proud in their inmost thoughts.
> He has brought down rulers from their thrones
>> but has lifted up the humble.
> He has filled the hungry with good things
>> but has sent the rich away empty. (Lk 1:51-53)

Nietzsche does not actually quote from the Sermon on the Mount or the Magnificat, but he could have, for these passages perfectly illustrate what he has in mind. It is perfectly clear that it is biblical morality he has in mind. *"The slaves' revolt in morality* begins with the Jews: a revolt which has two thousand years of history behind it and which has only been lost sight of because—it was victorious."[4] Nietzsche has harsh words for the ancient Israelites: "It was the Jews who, rejecting the aristocratic value equation (good = noble = powerful = beautiful = happy = blessed) ventured, with awe-inspiring consistency, to bring about a reversal and held it in the teeth of their unfathomable hatred (the hatred of the powerless), saying, 'Only those who suffer are good, only the poor, the powerless, are good.'"[5]

In a later section I will discuss the issue of Nietzsche and anti-Semitism, but it is important to recognize that Nietzsche's anger at Judaism is really fueled by his anger at Christianity. In Nietzsche's eyes, the worse sin of Judaism was to give us Christianity, since it is Jesus of Nazareth who is the embodiment of all these Jewish values. Nietzsche even interprets Christian anti-Semitism as a byproduct of a diabolical strategy by which Judaism could foist its values onto the world. "Is it not part of a secret black art of truly *great* politics of revenge, a far-sighted subterranean revenge, . . . that Israel had to denounce her actual instrument of revenge before all the world as a mortal enemy and nail him to the cross so that 'all the world,' namely all Israel's enemies, could

---

[4]Nietzsche, *Genealogy,* trans. Diethe, 18.
[5]Nietzsche, *Genealogy,* trans. Diethe, 18.

safely nibble at this bait."[6] Nietzsche's real target is not Judaism, but Christianity, a Christianity that has "triumphed repeatedly over all other ideals, all *nobler* ideals."[7]

GUILT AND THE PRIESTLY CLASS

To complete the story Nietzsche adds an account of the origin of guilt, which is closely linked to the morality of good and evil. The origins of guilt, according to Nietzsche, are bound up with the notion of debt. In more primitive human societies, if a debtor was unable to pay back what was owed, the lender would take satisfaction by punishing the unfortunate debtor. Nietzsche is not completely sure how things went, since the origins of guilt lie far back in human history, but he conjectures that making another person suffer was a way of balancing a debt: "To the extent that to *make* suffer was in the highest degree pleasurable, to the extent that the injured party exchanged for the loss he had sustained . . . an extraordinary counterbalancing pleasure: that of *making* suffer."[8] Nietzsche thinks this helps us see why from the beginning guilt and suffering were intertwined. It is also clear that the origins of guilt are connected closely to cruelty, a trait that Nietzsche believes to be a fundamental element of human nature. (He casually mentions that even in "good old Kant" it is true that the "categorical imperative smells of cruelty.")[9]

The concept of guilt attached to Western morality does not seem purely social, however, as people often feel guilt about having done morally bad things even if their acts are unknown to others. To explain this development, Nietzsche bring in the class of the priest. In ancient caste societies, the priestly caste is of course, like the masters, an elite caste. However, despite the fact that the nobles and priests are both

---

[6]Nietzsche, *Genealogy,* trans. Diethe, 18.
[7]Nietzsche, *Genealogy,* trans. Diethe, 19.
[8]Friedrich Nietzsche, *On the Genealogy of Morals,* trans. Walter Kaufmann and R. J. Hollingdale (New York: Vintage, 1969), 65.
[9]Nietzsche, *Genealogy,* trans. Kaufmann and Hollingdale, 65.

elites, there is a competition for dominance between the two groups. The priest cannot compete with the warrior on the basis of physical strength, and so must substitute cunning and shrewdness. Religion for Nietzsche is partly a symbolic expression of what a society reveres, and so the priest, as the guardian of religion, is the representative of something higher than the individual. The individual always owes a debt to society and, since the gods represent what is highest for society, the individual owes that debt to the gods. The priest teaches the people to feel this debt, and thus the priest gains power as well. We might say the priest is the custodian of the debt.

Guilt as debt owed thus becomes internalized, something felt by the individual even when there is no debt to any specific person. How is the debt to be paid? The people are taught to turn their cruel instincts on themselves, to inflict punishment on themselves rather than others. This has the added benefit of giving a meaning to other sufferings. Besides inflicting suffering by teaching guilt, the priest also interprets the ordinary suffering of humans as guilt. The priest thereby teaches people that it is their own fault that they suffer. The suffering they cannot avoid is a punishment. When that punishment is not sufficient the priest teaches the people to punish themselves. The priest makes all suffering bearable because he gives to suffering a meaning. "What really arouses indignation against suffering is not suffering as such but the senselessness of suffering."[10]

On Nietzsche's view the priestly caste plays a key role, not just in the invention of guilt, but in the whole development of the morality of good and evil. The priest shrewdly uses the *ressentiment* of the masses against the masters to gain power for the priest. Nietzsche goes so far as to characterize the ancient Jews as a whole as a "priestly nation of *ressentiment par excellence*," far exceeding the talents of the "Chinese or the German," who have "similar talents" but are just "fifth-rate" in comparison with the

---

[10]Nietzsche, *Genealogy*, trans. Kaufmann and Hollingdale, 68.

Jews.[11] Though the contest between master morality and slave morality is still in some ways ongoing, Nietzsche claims that because of the church, the values of Judaism have generally triumphed over those of a noble race such as the Romans. At the time of the Renaissance there was a brief renewal of the older morality, but the Reformation destroyed this brief revival. The French Revolution, though apparently secular and even atheistic, was in fact another manifestation of this "Christian morality," with its talk of equality and fraternity, and with its victory, the "*ressentiment*-instincts of the rabble" triumphed over the last genuine nobility left in Europe, that of France.[12] The development of guilt leads to the development of conscience and the "bad conscience," the person who lives with a sense that he or she deserves to suffer, deserves punishment.

NIETZSCHE'S AMBIVALENCE ABOUT CHRISTIANITY AND CHRISTIAN MORALITY

So far it seems that Nietzsche is a fan of master morality and despises the Christian morality of good and evil. It is undeniable that Nietzsche finds much to detest in Christianity and Christian morality. He even attacks the growth of democracy and the emergence of socialism as noxious products of Christian morality. Many nonreligious people and even antireligious people who totally reject Christian faith are still, Nietzsche thinks, in the thrall of Christian morality. "Who amongst us would be a freethinker if it were not for the Church? We loathe the church, *not* its poison."[13] So Nietzsche is clear about his view that Christian morality is far from good. It contradicts our nature, and is not what it seems to be on the surface. The religion that claims to be about love is really all about vengeance and resentment.

However, Nietzsche is too subtle and complex a thinker to simply dismiss Christian morality as totally bad. His message is not to go *back* to a master morality of good and bad. Instead he calls us to go forward:

---

[11]Nietzsche, *Genealogy*, trans. Kaufmann and Hollingdale, 53.
[12]Nietzsche, *Genealogy*, trans. Diethe, 33.
[13]Nietzsche, *Genealogy*, trans. Diethe, 19.

as summarized by the title of one of his most important books, we must go *"beyond* good and evil." Despite his antipathy to Christianity, he recognizes that much that is good and valuable was made possible by the Christian moral revolution.

We can see this by examining the character Nietzsche calls "the blonde beast," the kind of pure "Aryan" from previous ages who embodies the older morality. Nietzsche describes this figure not as someone we should aspire to become, but as a "beast." There are times when he longs for this figure, who is certainly more in touch with his instinctual, animal nature than contemporary humans; but Nietzsche knows that such people no longer are really possible. And that is not altogether a bad thing. The problem with the "blonde beast" is that he is basically stupid. Nietzsche says that it is the slave revolt in morality that has made humans more intelligent, and he acknowledges that without the slave revolt in morality, the human race would have been less intellectual than it has been.

So it is not too surprising that Nietzsche regards the bad conscience, and the morality of good and evil that gave rise to it, as something inextricably connected to civilization. "I regard the bad conscience as the serious illness that man was bound to contract under the stress of the most fundamental change he ever experienced—that change which occurred when he found himself finally enclosed within the walls of society and of peace."[14] In this situation, the aggressive instincts humans possess, such as "hostility, cruelty, joy in persecuting, in attacking" could not be expressed in their natural way, externally.[15] For Nietzsche "all instincts that do not discharge themselves outwardly *turn inward*."[16] Civilization requires that these instinctive drives must be sublimated, and Nietzsche sees much of civilization as something made possible by this self-denial. Self-denial, or what Nietzsche calls the "ascetic ideal," makes possible great art, science, and even philosophy, all of which are

---

[14]Nietzsche, *Genealogy*, trans. Kaufmann and Hollingdale, 84.
[15]Nietzsche, *Genealogy*, trans. Kaufmann and Hollingdale, 85.
[16]Nietzsche, *Genealogy*, trans. Kaufmann and Hollingdale, 84.

discussed in the third essay in the *Genealogy of Morals*. Nietzsche does not simply want to return humans to a primitive "state of nature" devoid of all the things that self-denial makes possible. Rather, he wants humans to recognize that their lofty ideals are grounded in very primitive instincts that are still part of us though we often pretend they do not exist. Nietzsche wants us to see the "dark side" of our virtues. "The *delight* that the selfless man, the self-denier, the self-sacrificer feels from this first: this delight is tied to cruelty."[17]

In the end, even though Nietzsche detests much about Christian morality, he recognizes that it has made humans beings "more interesting," and given them powers that they would otherwise have lacked. Thus "the bad conscience is an illness, there is no doubt about that, but an illness as pregnancy is an illness."[18] In *Thus Spake Zarathustra* Nietzsche describes the figure of the "Overman," who will go beyond what humans have achieved thus far. The Overman is not pictured as a blond beast, but as a creative and powerful figure who exercises this power of self-denial for the sake of ends that are more healthy, honest, and natural. Nietzsche is certainly critical of Christian morality, but he nonetheless values what it has made possible.

WAS NIETZSCHE A RACIST?

As we saw above, Nietzsche often uses anti-Semitic language and employs anti-Semitic stereotypes. His use of racial stereotyping is not restricted to Jews. He frequently uses racially charged language about groups and seems to rank nations in terms of their racial makeup. To cite one example out of many, Nietzsche connects the origin of the Latin term for "bad" (*malus*) with "the common man as the dark-colored, above all as the dark-haired man . . . as the pre-Aryan occupant of the soil of Italy who was distinguished obviously from the blond, that is, Aryan, conqueror race by his color."[19] These elements in his

---

[17]Nietzsche, *Genealogy*, trans. Kaufmann and Hollingdale, 88.
[18]Nietzsche, *Genealogy*, trans. Kaufmann and Hollingdale, 88.
[19]Nietzsche, *Genealogy*, trans. Kaufmann and Hollingdale, 30.

writings raise the question as to whether Nietzsche's thought is deeply stained by racism.

The question is also raised by the history of Nietzsche's reception. Nietzsche's sister, who took care of him after he went insane, was an anti-Semite. Although Nietzsche himself did not approve of his sister's anti-Semitism, this sister was Nietzsche's literary custodian and edited a collection of Nietzsche's unpublished writings that highlighted Nietzsche's own anti-Semitic passages. This had a great impact on how Nietzsche's thought was received in the first half of the twentieth century. Long after Nietzsche's death, his sister publicly supported Hitler, and Nietzsche was embraced by the Nazis and even came to be seen as the semi-official philosopher of the Nazi movement. Even today, it is not uncommon for neo-Nazis and other members of the extreme right to embrace Nietzsche.[20] So it is understandable that people who regard racism as repugnant often recoil from Nietzsche's thought, both in the past and today.

Many Nietzsche scholars argue today that this is both unfortunate and deeply unfair to Nietzsche. One argument they employ is that, despite his own use of anti-Semitic language (which defenders often argue is anti-Judaism rather than anti-Jewish), Nietzsche was strongly critical of the anti-Semites of his day. This argument has weight. Nietzsche does frequently criticize anti-Semites, including his own sister, and Nietzsche's dislike of anti-Semitism was part of the antagonism that developed between Nietzsche and Wagner, who was a notorious anti-Semite. Here is an example of his contempt for the anti-Semites: "I also do not like these latest speculators in idealism, the anti-Semites, who today roll their eyes in a Christian-Aryan-bourgeois manner and exhaust one's patience by trying to rouse up all the horned beast elements

---

[20]A good example is provided by Richard Spencer, a white supremacist who was in 2016 one of the more prominent supporters of Donald Trump. Spencer invented the term *alt-right* and founded the periodical *Radix Journal*. He was one of the featured speakers at the white nationalist rally in Charlottesville, Virginia on May 13, 2017, at which a counter-demonstrator was killed.

in the people."[21] In addition to criticizing anti-Semites, Nietzsche is also no fan of German nationalism and does not believe in German superiority. When he talks about contemporary European peoples, he frequently mocks Germans and Germany.

The arguments Nietzsche's defenders give do convince me that Nietzsche was not a kind of proto-Nazi, and I agree with them that if Nietzsche had survived (as did his sister) to see the coming of Hitler, he would have disliked the Nazis. Seeing Nietzsche as the philosopher of Nazism is unfair to him and blocks us from recognizing what is valuable in his thought. However, though it seems right that Nietzsche was not really anti-Semitic, and that he would have disliked Nazism if he had lived to see it, this does not mean that Nietzsche's thought is not in some ways conducive to racist and fascist ways of thinking. Nietzsche may or may not personally have been a racist (though he certainly says racist things), and he was not a German nationalist.[22] However, Nietzsche's moral philosophy can and has been used to justify racist and nationalist views. I do not mean by this merely that some of Nietzsche's followers have been racists and nationalists. That is true, but the same could be said of Christianity. What I mean is that there are elements in Nietzsche's thought that provide some support for such views. At least it must be said that in rejecting traditional Western morality, Nietzsche undermines many of the objections that can be raised against racist views.

To begin, Nietzsche's view of morality as a purely human creation means that one cannot claim that it is objectively true that mistreating fellow human beings is wrong. On Nietzsche's view there is no such thing as objective moral truth. Consistent with this view, Nietzsche also rejects the ideal of human equality and rejects the idea of human or natural rights, since he sees it as a product of Christian or slave morality. Someone who shares Nietzsche's view

---

[21] Nietzsche, *Genealogy*, trans. Kaufmann and Hollingdale, 158.
[22] One might of course think that someone who says racist things is certainly a racist. Perhaps this is true, but Nietzsche sometimes says as a provocation things he may not really have believed.

cannot really object to the enslaving or killing of people because of their race on the grounds that this violates human rights or is an affront to human dignity, because Nietzsche does not believe in such things. Nietzsche is an antirealist about morality, which means there simply is no such thing as moral truth. Nietzsche may not have liked anti-Semitism, but he has no basis for saying that anti-Semites have mistaken moral views.

Not only is it the case that Nietzsche is an antirealist about morality. He also scorns many of the values and virtues of traditional morality. In particular, he has little use for the virtues of compassion and pity, and often seems to justify the idea that those who are strong have no obligation to help those who are weak, sickly, or suffering. Nietzsche does not denounce hatred and cruelty; instead he goes out of his way to insist that these are in some ways normal and fundamental parts of human nature, and even that they are disguised elements in conventional virtues. Thus Kant's ethic of duty is said to be an ethic of cruelty, and Christian love is at bottom fueled by envy and resentment. One might say that Nietzsche "normalizes" the base elements of human nature (which are certainly present, but not often praised). If one follows such a view it is difficult to see on what basis one could object to cruelty against those who are weak, or argue against stirring up hatred between the races. Perhaps it is not surprising then that one of the most famous of twentieth-century philosophers, Martin Heidegger, who was deeply influenced by Nietzsche, joined the Nazi party and was deeply anti-Semitic.[23] Heidegger seemed completely unfazed by the persecution of Jews and others, and indeed never apologized or admitted he was wrong in becoming a Nazi. Heidegger had, one might say, a tin ear for compassion, and it is not too surprising that someone deeply influenced by Nietzsche would have this malady.

---

[23]The evidence for this is now overwhelming. See the publication of Heidegger's diaries, *Ponderings: Black Notebooks*, trans. Richard Rojcewicz, 3 vols. (Bloomington: Indiana University Press, 2016–2017).

THE MANY VERSIONS OF NIETZSCHE:
NIETZSCHE'S PERSPECTIVISM

Nietzsche's writing style is unique. In one sense his books are beautifully written, full of humor and sarcasm and never dull. However, most of his books are written in numbered sections, and they often appear to wander from topic to topic. There is almost never anything like a careful argument and nothing that resembles a "system." Nietzsche seems more devoted to provoking his readers than giving them a settled view they should believe. Perhaps this is why Nietzsche often appears to contradict himself, or at the very least, allows tensions to appear in his writings that he makes no effort to resolve.

There are, one might say, many different Nietzsches, and there are therefore wildly divergent interpretations of what Nietzsche's philosophy is really all about. Nietzsche had a profound influence on twentieth-century philosophy, but the influence has been very different for different streams of philosophy. There is, for example, what we might call the "existentialist Nietzsche," profoundly influential on such thinkers as Heidegger, Sartre, and Camus. This Nietzsche emphasizes, as did Kierkegaard, that the self is more a project than a substance. He tells us that the task of the individual is to "become what you are." (The big difference from Kierkegaard is that Nietzsche's self is created simply out of nature, while for Kierkegaard selfhood is a task assigned to us by God.)

A second Nietzsche is what we might call the "naturalistic Nietzsche." This is the Nietzsche who calls our attention to the fact that we humans are basically animals governed by nonrational instincts. Our philosophies, our ethical theories, our religions, are all products of this nature. The naturalistic Nietzsche criticizes Christian morality because it is rooted in a false view of human nature, and he demands a kind of ruthless honesty in facing up to the truth about that nature. It is not that Nietzsche ever offers anything like arguments in favor of naturalism, any more than he offers arguments on behalf of his atheism, which will be discussed below. Rather, Nietzsche assumes this is the true account of ourselves and our world, and he marshals all his rhetorical skills to help us see that truth. The naturalistic Nietzsche also roots his ethical imperatives in this naturalism, constantly telling us, in the words of Nietzsche's character Zarathustra, that we must be "faithful to the earth," live our lives as bodily beings in touch with nature and our own instincts.

A third Nietzsche is what we might call the "proto-postmodernist Nietzsche." In the latter half of the twentieth century, a number of thinkers, especially Michel Foucault, begin to be suspicious of truth claims of all kinds. Marx had already developed a kind of suspicion of philosophy, religion, and other "ideologies," seeing them as having as their real purpose the support of economic oppression, bolstering the position of the ruling classes. Foucault, under the influence of Nietzsche, extends this kind of suspicion to all kinds of claims and groups, teaching his followers to see various truth claims as disguised expressions of power and domination.

Nietzsche lays the groundwork for this kind of view of human thinking, because he stresses the way that even philosophies are shaped, not by rational thought, but by the instinctive desires of the philosopher: "Gradually I have come to realize what every great philosophy up to now has been: the personal confession of its originator, a type of involuntary and unaware memoirs."[24] This view of Nietzsche cuts in different directions. On the one hand, it seems to provide a kind of undercutter that makes us suspicious of the claims of philosophers, who are not telling us how the world really is but rather expressing their own deepest desires. On the other hand, Nietzsche insists that "falseness" may not be a bad thing: "The falseness of a given judgment does not constitute an objection against it, so far as we are concerned. . . . The real question is how far a judgment furthers and maintains life. . . . We are, in fact, fundamentally inclined to maintain that the falsest judgments . . . are the most indispensable to us, that man cannot live without accepting the logical fictions as valid."[25]

---

[24]Friedrich Nietzsche, *Beyond Good and Evil*, trans. Marianne Cowan (Chicago: Henry Regnery, 1969), sec. 6, p. 6.
[25]Nietzsche, *Beyond Good and Evil*, sec. 4, p. 4.

This pattern of thinking culminates in what has come to be called Nietzsche's "perspectivism." Nietzsche becomes suspicious of the whole idea of "facts" and "objective truth." To the empiricist who believes we can ascertain facts he responds: "I would say, no, facts is precisely what there is not, only interpretations. We cannot establish any fact 'in itself': perhaps it is folly to want to do such a thing."[26] Even physics is "only an interpretation of the universe, an arrangement of it (to suit us, if I may be so bold), rather than a clarification."[27] There is no such thing as "seeing the world as it really is." Rather, "there is *only* a perspective seeing, *only* a perspective 'knowing,'" and all our perspectives shaped by the will.[28] Nietzsche does not shrink from applying this perspectivism to his own thought, agreeing that even the claim that everything is an interpretation is an interpretation.

The tension between the naturalistic Nietzsche and the perspectivist, postmodernist Nietzsche is evident. The naturalistic Nietzsche is convinced that atheism is *true*, famously announcing that "God is dead."[29] He does not mean, of course, that God once existed but ceased to do so. Rather, God has never existed; what has died is our belief in God and what that belief sustained. Nietzsche accuses slave morality of being dishonest, of disguising its envy as goodness, its hatred as love. However, the whole notion of dishonesty presupposes that there is a way things really are, and thus seems parasitic on the notion of objective truth. It cannot be true that God does not exist, if there is no such thing as objective truth. Why should we believe Nietzsche if his claim that God is dead is simply an expression of his own desire that God not exist? Nietzsche actually suggests something like this in *Thus Spake Zarathustra*, where he has his "prophet" Zarathustra give a kind of "argument" for atheism: "But to reveal my heart entirely to you, friends: *if* there were

---

[26]Friedrich Nietzsche, *The Will to Power*, trans. Walter Kaufmann (New York: Vintage, 1968), 267.

[27]Nietzsche, *Beyond Good and Evil*, sec. 14, p. 15.

[28]Nietzsche, *Genealogy*, trans. Kaufmann and Hollingdale, 119.

[29]From Friedrich Nietzsche, "Madman," in *The Gay Science*, trans. Walter Kaufmann (New York: Vintage, 1974), sec. 125, p. 181.

gods, how could I endure not to be a god! *Therefore* there are no gods."[30] (Some have suggested that Nietzsche's own antipathy to Christianity might be unconscious anger at his pastor father who in a way deserted Nietzsche by dying when Nietzsche was only four.)

A dilemma faces Nietzsche at this point. If his atheism and naturalism are only an "interpretation" fueled by his own will, then why should we believe that this is the way things are? However, if atheism and naturalism are the truth about reality, how can perspectivism be adequate? At one point Nietzsche even suggests that a belief in truth is linked to a belief in God, and that those who truly believe that God is dead must give up belief in truth as well, suggesting that the "free spirits" who are skeptical about God are not genuinely free because *"they still have faith in truth."*[31] Nietzsche may well be right to connect belief in God with truth. I shall attempt to show in my concluding chapter how an honest admission of our epistemic limitations may coexist with a commitment to truth.

NIETZSCHE ON THE DEATH OF GOD AND THE THREAT OF NIHILISM

I have already noted Nietzsche's famous claim that "God is dead." This theme recurs repeatedly in *Thus Spake Zarathustra*, but it is most memorably expressed in a parable titled "The Madman" in *The Gay Science*, sometimes translated as *Joyful Wisdom*: "Have you heard of the Madman who on a bright morning lighted a lantern and ran to the market-place calling out unceasingly: 'I seek God! I seek God.'"[32] The Madman provokes some satire and sarcasm, as the people around don't believe in God, and they ask the Madman if God has lost his way or emigrated. The insane man "transfixes" these bystanders with his gaze and responds pointedly:

[30]Friedrich Nietzsche, *Thus Spoke Zarathustra*, trans. R. J. Hollingdale (Baltimore: Penguin, 1969), 110.
[31]Nietzsche, *Genealogy*, trans. Kaufmann and Hollingdale, 150. Nietzsche himself draws here on his own discussion of truth as based on "metaphysical faith" in *Gay Science*, sec. 344.
[32]Nietzsche, *Gay Science*, sec. 125., p. 182 (emphasis original).

"Whither is God?" he cried. "I will tell you! *We have killed him*—you and
I! All of us are his murderers! But how did we do this? How could we
drink up the sea? Who gave us the sponge to wipe away the entire horizon? What were we doing when we unchained this earth from its sun?
Whither is it moving now? Whither are we moving? . . . Backward,
sideward, forward, in all directions? Is there still any up or down? Are
we not straying as through an infinite nothing?"[33]

The Madman continues to emphasize the enormity of the event of
God's death, and the consequences it will bring. However, he recognizes that those consequences may not as yet be recognized: "I have
come too early, . . . my time is not yet. This tremendous event is still on
its way, still wandering,—it has not yet reached the ears of men. . . . This
deed is still more distant from them than the most distant stars,—*and
yet they have done it themselves.*"[34]

The parable of the Madman dramatically portrays one of Nietzsche's
most important themes: the possibility of nihilism that the death of God
brings with it. Many of the antireligious thinkers of the nineteenth
century (Comte would be an excellent example) had assumed a complacent attitude toward the loss of religious belief. According to these
thinkers, we can dispense with religious belief without this undermining
our moral beliefs and practices. Nietzsche thinks this is deeply mistaken;
he thinks that secular thinkers do not recognize how deeply their morality is grounded in Judeo-Christian beliefs. Once the consequences of
abandoning those beliefs is fully realized, Nietzsche thinks the results
will be profound, and they could be devastating. The destruction of the
value system Western culture is built on brings with it the threat of nihilism, a state of affairs where "nothing is true, everything is permitted."[35]

However, nihilism for Nietzsche is only a threat and a possibility; it
is not inevitable. He hopes that the death of God will lead to the

---

[33]Nietzsche, *Gay Science*, sec. 125, p. 182.
[34]Nietzsche, *Gay Science*, sec. 125, p. 182.
[35]Nietzsche, *Genealogy*, trans. Kaufmann and Hollingdale, 150. This motto, which Nietzsche attributes
to a Middle Eastern order called the Assassins, is echoed by Zarathustra in *Thus Spoke Zarathustra*.

creation of a new and higher form of morality, a morality that goes "beyond good and evil." The Madman echoes this hope: "Is not the greatness of this deed too great for us? Must we ourselves not become gods, simply to appear worthy of it? There has never been a greater deed; and whoever is born after us—for the sake of this deed he will belong to a higher history than all history hitherto."[36]

THE *ÜBERMENSCH* AND THE DOCTRINE
OF ETERNAL RECURRENCE

The confidence and hope expressed by the Madman is captured in Nietzsche's concept of the *Übermensch*. This term was originally translated as "Superman," but with the advent of a certain comic book character that translation no longer works. It is sometimes translated quite literally as the "Overman," meaning an individual who is higher than or goes beyond what is human.[37] The concept is elaborated most fully in Nietzsche's work *Thus Spake Zarathustra*. In this work, which Nietzsche himself considered his most important and profound book, Nietzsche creates a prophetic figure, Zarathustra, who provides wisdom to his disciples.

Zarathustra expresses the basic idea of the Overman in this way: "Man is a rope, fastened between animal and Overman—a rope over an abyss."[38] In other places Nietzsche describes human beings as a bridge. Humans are not "ends in themselves," as Kant thought, but we are great because we have the possibility of becoming something great.

Nietzsche does not provide many specific characterizations of the Overman. The reason for this is that the Overman will be something fundamentally new, and we cannot at present fully imagine what this new type of person will be like. What we do know is that the Overman will be a creator of values, and that those values will in some way be healthier and more honest than those of Christian morality. Zarathustra

---

[36]Nietzsche, *Gay Science*, sec. 125, p. 181.
[37]The Nazis tried to appropriate the notion of the "Superman," by interpreting this figure as literally someone to be created through racial breeding and eugenics, but this is a caricature of Nietzsche's view.
[38]Nietzsche, *Thus Spoke Zarathustra*, 43 (translation modified).

puts the Overman at the center of his message: "Behold, I teach you the Overman. The Overman is the meaning of the earth. Let your will say: The Overman *shall be* the meaning of the earth."[39]

Those who aspire to become the Overman must be people who "remain true to the earth."[40] They will not be "despisers of life," which is the inevitable result of Christian morality, and they will reject any kind of supernatural hope or belief in life after death. The Overman will be someone who lives life passionately, and will not be afraid to say that "my happiness should justify existence itself." Zarathustra goes so far as to say that "it is not your sin, but your moderation that cries to heaven, your very meanness in sinning cries to heaven."[41] Nevertheless, Nietzsche does not picture the Overman as a kind of "wanton" who simply does whatever he feels like doing and is incapable of sacrifice and self-discipline. Rather, the Overman has inherited the ability to discipline himself, but puts that power to use for the "earth" rather than heaven.[42]

One of the great temptations that the Overman must overcome is the temptation to feel contempt for human life. It is easy to see that Nietzsche himself often expresses contempt for contemporary humans, who in his view have a paltry, mediocre grasp of human existence, and live in a way that is full of falsehood and hypocrisy. Anyone with Nietzsche's views who looks closely at contemporary society will therefore be tempted to a kind of despair, a nausea occasioned by the miserable quality of most human lives. Despite his rejection of the morality of good and evil that most people live by, the Overman must somehow still affirm the basic goodness of life. It is not clear, however, exactly how this is to be done. Perhaps it simply requires a heroic act of will.

The great test for the Overman can be found in an idea that Nietzsche considered to be of great importance, but which he only wrote about a

---

[39]Nietzsche, *Thus Spoke Zarathustra*, 42.
[40]Nietzsche, *Thus Spoke Zarathustra*, 42.
[41]Nietzsche, *Thus Spoke Zarathustra*, 42-43.
[42]Nietzsche, *Thus Spoke Zarathustra*, 44.

few times.[43] Nietzsche was intrigued by an idea found in ancient India and also among the Pythagoreans and Stoics in ancient Western philosophy: the idea of the eternal recurrence or eternal return. The idea is sometimes defended as grounded in the nature of the physical world. Suppose that the particles of matter in the universe are finite. If that is so, then there will also be a finite number of combinations of those particles. If one assumes that each combination is equally probable, and also that the universe is temporally infinite in both directions, then it might seem that every combination of particles would occur at some point. However, if we really accept that time is infinite, then we might think that every combination has already occurred, and will occur again. If that is so, then everything that happens has happened before, and will happen again, for an infinite number of times.

Some think that Nietzsche really believed in the truth of the eternal return as a sober metaphysical doctrine. Viewed in this way, the doctrine of the eternal return might seem to provide a kind of naturalistic eschatology to replace the Christian view of the end times. It is true that such a view does not seem consistent with Nietzsche's perspectivism and general skepticism about metaphysical doctrines. It is also true that as physics the doctrine seems unjustified, since the Big Bang seems to imply the universe is not infinite in time. Even if the physical universe were infinite in time, it is unclear why every configuration of matter would be equally probable and have to occur even once, much less an infinite number of times. However, consistency and rational justification do not seem to be things Nietzsche cared much about.

However, even if Nietzsche did not believe in eternal recurrence as literal, metaphysical truth, we might see it as something like an eschatological myth, a story that has real value to the "higher human being" Nietzsche wants to make possible. For the Overman, or the person who aspires to become the Overman, the doctrine of the eternal return

---

[43]For example, in Nietzsche, *Gay Science*, 285 and 341, and in *Thus Spoke Zarathustra* ("On the Vision and the Riddle," 178-79).

offers a profound test. If one really loves life, one must be able to say yes to all that happens. One must be able to say, even in the face of death, "Was *that* life? Well, then! Once more!" One must not just accept everything that happens, through a kind of resignation, but must actively will that whatever happens will happen again, over and over. That may not be hard for moments when we experience great joy and exhilaration, but it will not be easy for all that is boring, all that involves suffering, and all that is found in the lives of those things that Nietzsche himself detests, such as Christian morality. Paradoxically, being "true to the earth" requires the Overman to say yes even to all that seems untrue to the earth. The Overman must embrace *amor fati*, the love of fate: "My formula for greatness in a human being is *amor fati*: that one wants nothing to be different, not forward, not backward, not in all eternity. Not merely bear what is necessary, still less conceal it—all idealism is mendaciousness in the face of what is necessary—but *love* it."[44]

Interestingly, Nietzsche's ideas of the Overman and the eternal return play important roles in Stanley Kubrick's famous film *2001: A Space Odyssey*, as well as the novel by Arthur Clarke on which the film is based. (The soundtrack for the film even begins with Richard Strauss's tone poem *Also Sprach Zarathustra*, which was inspired by Nietzsche's book.) Though the film seems ambiguous and hard to grasp at many points, it does appear to tell a grand narrative of the ascent of human beings from being primitive creatures to something higher, though contemporary humans seem overly intellectual and out of touch with what we might call their Dionysiac nature. At the conclusion of the film, the astronaut ages and appears to die, but somehow reappears as a child, perhaps suggesting a kind of "return" or at least a "redoing" of life. This may not be exactly what Nietzsche had in mind, but it does show the power of his ideas in contemporary culture.

---

[44]Friedrich Nietzsche, *Ecce Homo*, trans. Walter Kaufmann (New York: Vintage, 1969), 258.

24

Conclusions

Some Lessons from the History of Western Philosophy

In this final chapter I shall try to do several things. First, I shall give a brief sketch of some of the main movements of philosophy in the twentieth century. I shall try to give descriptions of some of the movements that a sequel to this volume would cover if I ever have the time and inclination to write such a volume. The reason for this is to give some indications of the ways the influence of the history of Western philosophy are still being felt. Second, I shall try to describe some of the lessons I have drawn from the history of Western philosophy over the many years I have taught the subject. In conclusion I shall offer some convictions about the way forward in philosophy, particularly for Christians.

PHILOSOPHY AT THE BEGINNING OF THE TWENTIETH CENTURY

At the end of the nineteenth century, philosophy was dominated by two movements that drew on earlier traditions, and a movement that challenged those traditions and some aspects of the entire Western tradition. One of the movements that drew on an older tradition was Idealism in the form of neo-Hegelianism, discussed briefly in chapter nineteen, which dominated philosophy in the United Kingdom in the later nineteenth century and early twentieth century. The other movement that was a continuation of an older tradition was positivism, discussed in chapter twenty-two, which clearly was a continuation of Humean empiricism.

The third, most original movement that developed late in the nineteenth century was pragmatism, most prominently found in the thought of a trio of American thinkers: Charles Sanders Peirce, William James, and John Dewey. As the name implies, each pragmatist philosopher was interested in testing philosophical views by looking at their practical implications. Each made important contributions, and each one was quite different from the others. Peirce is best known for original and powerful ideas about logic, philosophy of science, and epistemology. James, who contributed to psychology as well as philosophy, developed a kind of empiricism that differed markedly from that of the British empiricists, one that emphasized experience as fluid and dynamic. Instead of seeing experience as consisting of static "ideas" derived from "impressions," James saw experience as the product of continual interaction between the self and the world. James also gave a well-known defense of the rationality of religious belief in a famous essay, "The Will to Believe."

Dewey drew on his pragmatist predecessors and worked in every field of philosophy, arguing that Western philosophy has been harmed by a "quest for certainty" (the title of one of his books) and also by a depreciation of practical activity in comparison with contemplation. Dewey probably had his greatest influence in the fields of political philosophy and philosophy of education, defending the value of liberal democracy and arguing that education ought to be focused on interaction with the environment and not a passive reception of ideas. Although the pragmatists were for a time eclipsed by other philosophical movements that developed in the early to mid-twentieth century, their reputation and influence currently seem to be growing.

The pragmatists collectively challenged many of the elements of the "classical foundationalism" that we have seen has been dominant in the epistemology of modern Western thought. Peirce, for example, challenged the Cartesian tendency to give primacy to doubt over belief. Instead, Peirce argued that it is reasonable to begin with the beliefs that we have, since they have shown some pragmatic value or they would not have survived. We ought to be open to doubting any of our beliefs, but we should only doubt when we have reason to doubt. The pragmatists all developed what we now call a "coherentist" view of human belief, seeing our beliefs as less like a "house" that requires absolutely certain foundations, and more like a net or web in which everything is connected to everything else and beliefs are mutually supporting. Our beliefs stand the test of reason and experience as a package and not simply as isolated propositions. The pragmatist emphasis on philosophy as something that connects to real experience and life is helpful. However, James and Dewey sometimes go beyond looking for pragmatist criteria for truth and actually define truth as what "works." This claim continues to resonate in the contemporary world, but to some it seems to lead to a loss of faith in objective truth. As we shall see, there are similar pragmatist themes in later twentieth-century philosophers.

ANALYTIC AND CONTINENTAL PHILOSOPHY

Since the early twentieth century, modern Western philosophy has been divided into two large camps, often called analytic philosophy and continental philosophy. This is really an oversimplification. Each of these camps is full of very diverse groups of philosophers who may disagree with those in their own "camp" on almost everything, and may actually (sometimes without realizing it) be closer on some issues to some people in the other camp. The two camps are not definable by commitments to any particular doctrines or views, but more by styles of philosophizing and particular historical influences. They tend to read different texts and use different vocabularies. In what follows I will try to sketch each of these two camps, but an adequate treatment would require a lengthy book of its own.

Analytic philosophy. Analytic philosophy is the movement (or, to be more accurate, the set of movements) that has dominated English-speaking countries since the 1920s. It had its origins in two independent developments that soon interacted. The first was the "realist revolt" against Absolute Idealism that was carried out in England, the biggest influences being Bertrand Russell and G. E. Moore. Although Russell and Moore were very different from each other, they both rejected the arguments for Absolute Idealism that began with Kantian accounts of knowledge as shaped by mind. Instead they defended forms of "realism" that viewed human knowledge as knowledge of an objective world that exists independently of the knower. Moore in particular showed the influence of Thomas Reid's older commonsense philosophy. In one memorable presentation, Moore attempted to show the existence of mind-independent objects by simply holding up his two hands and showing them to the audience. Moore was also extremely influential in his work in ethics.

Russell was deeply influenced by earlier British empiricism, but he also brought to philosophy a deep commitment to new logical tools that allowed philosophers to give sophisticated analyses of propositions. (This is partly the origin of the term *analytic philosophy*.) Russell was himself one of the developers of "quantified logic," an advance over traditional Aristotelian logic. In modern symbolic logic, a proposition can have a "quantifier," such as the "existential quantifier," used when one wishes to say that some entity satisfying some particular description actually exists, and the "universal quantifier," when one makes claims about all entities of a certain type, whether or not any entities of that type actually exist. Some philosophers had thought that a meaningful proposition about a nonexistent object requires that the nonexistent object must have some kind of reality in order for us to meaningfully refer to it. On Russell's analysis this was not true. He argued that a proposition like "The present king of France is bald" does not require that there be some kind of real but nonexistent present king of France. Rather, the proposition can be analyzed in something like the following way: "There exists some entity X, such that X is the king of France right now and X is bald." All we need in order to meaningfully deny the existence of such a king is to refer to a "variable" such as "some entity." This example may sound trivial, but the use of variables and quantifiers allowed Russell and other analytic philosophers to give accounts of many troublesome propositions.

The second development that had a profound influence on twentieth-century analytic philosophy was the reemergence of positivism in the form of logical positivism. Logical positivism was initially a product of a group of German philosophers in Vienna who formed the Vienna circle. These philosophers were in some ways the German counterparts to Russell, as they were excited over the potential of the new symbolic logic to transform philosophy. Like nineteenth-century positivists, they aspired to give a precise account of the nature of science, showing how science is rooted in empirical claims about experience. However, as I explained in chapter twenty-two, they rooted their view in the "verifiability theory of meaning," which claimed that all meaningful propositions, except those that are "analytic" and therefore true because of the definitions of the terms, must be empirically verified. In some ways this was a contemporary version of the distinction Hume had made between "relations of ideas" and "matters of fact."

Although logical positivism was initially a German movement, it was popularized in the English-speaking world by an English philosopher, A. J. Ayer, who explained its leading tenets in his book *Language, Truth, and Logic*.[1] Many of the members of the Vienna circle were Jewish, and as the Nazis came to power in Germany, and later Austria, most of them took refuge in England and America, taking university positions and thus spreading the views of the positivists throughout the English-speaking world.

A key figure who links the logical positivists to the British realists, while not really belonging to either group, is the philosopher Ludwig

---

[1] I cannot resist at this point passing on a joke from one of my own graduate professors, the Polish logician Casimir Lewy, who said in class that he found the title of Ayer's book very puzzling. It is true, he said, that the book says a little about language, but "there is almost nothing about logic and not a word of truth."

Wittgenstein. Wittgenstein was also from Vienna, and had gone to England prior to World War I. Initially he went to Manchester to study engineering, but later spent time in Cambridge, having intense discussions with both Russell and Moore. He returned to Austria in 1913 and fought in the Austrian army in World War I, being taken prisoner in 1918. During the war Wittgenstein wrote the first draft of his *Tractatus Logico-Philosophicus*, in which he claimed (somewhat immodestly) to have solved all the problems of philosophy! The book develops a "picture theory of meaning," which views propositions as representations or models of the facts of the world. The world consists of "atomic facts," each of which can hold or fail to hold independently of every other fact. This is mirrored in the atomic propositions that mirror the facts, and which can be combined using logical operators (such as "and," "or," and negation) to form compound propositions, whose truth is determined by their atomic components. Wittgenstein thought that propositions and facts shared a common structure or logical form, and that this is what made it possible for language to picture reality. However, that logical form cannot itself be described in language; it can be *shown* in language but cannot be said. Quite consistently, Wittgenstein says that the propositions of his own book about logical structure are attempts to express what cannot be said. Thus the person who understands the book will see it as a kind of ladder that one kicks away after having climbed up it: "My propositions serve as elucidations in the following way: anyone who understands me eventually recognizes them as nonsensical."[2]

The *Tractatus* had a profound impact on the Vienna circle positivists, and Wittgenstein did have some discussions with this group. It also influenced Russell, who developed his version of "logical atomism." The positivists interpreted the "atomic propositions" as those that are empirically verifiable, and thus thought that all of science could be based in experience, in accordance with their verifiability theory of meaning.

---

[2]Ludwig Wittgenstein, *Tractatus Logico-Philosophicus* 6.54, in Ludwig Wittgenstein, *Tractatus Logico-Philosophicus*, trans. D. F. Pears and B. F. McGuinness (London: Routledge and Kegan Paul, 1961), 151.

Wittgenstein himself was not a positivist, and the *Tractatus* really does not give us examples of the atomic facts or the propositions that mirror them. In fact, the conclusion of the book moves toward a mystical stance. So far from seeing science as the solution for all human problems, Wittgenstein says that "when *all possible* scientific questions have been answered, the problems of life remain completely untouched." Although only "facts" can be put into words, the most important things for Wittgenstein cannot be said: "There are, indeed, things that cannot be put into words. They *make themselves manifest.* They are what is mystical."[3]

Since Wittgenstein thought he had solved all the problems of philosophy, it makes sense that after writing the *Tractatus*, he gave up philosophy and tried his hand at various jobs, including being an elementary teacher and a gardener. However, he began to have second thoughts about his own earlier work and returned to Cambridge in 1929, resuming his work as a philosopher. In this "later" period, Wittgenstein developed a new approach to philosophy and language, rooted in the insight that language is not merely a tool for expressing facts, but is used for all kinds of life purposes. From this new perspective, "to imagine a language is to imagine a form of life."[4] In his later period, Wittgenstein focuses on the way language is actually used in ordinary life, rather than looking at language simply as a means of expressing scientific facts. For many purposes, the meaning of a word is understood by looking at how it is used. This later work of Wittgenstein spawned a kind of "ordinary language analysis" that was significant in the 1950s and 1960s.

Analytic philosophy since that period has become too diverse and pluralistic to describe in any simple way. The diversity was made possible partly by the demise of logical positivism, which was almost universally regarded as dead by the latter part of the twentieth century. The death blow was that the positivist view of language, which attempted to

---

[3]Wittgenstein, *Tractatus* 6.522, in Pears and McGuinness, p. 151.
[4]Ludwig Wittgenstein, *Philosophical Investigations*, trans. G. E. M. Anscombe, 3rd ed. (New York: Macmillan, 1968), 8e.

rule out metaphysics and theology by requiring verification by sense experience, turned out to be incompatible with science as well. If "unobservable entities" cannot be meaningfully talked about, then it is hard to see how scientists can theorize about black holes and quarks. The demise of positivism led to all kinds of new developments, including a revival of metaphysics. Even Christian philosophy has become part of the story. Christian philosophers such as William Alston, Alvin Plantinga, and Nicholas Wolterstorff from the United States helped found the Society of Christian Philosophers, currently one of the largest societies meeting in connection with the American Philosophical Association. In the United Kingdom Richard Swinburne also gave Christian philosophy a prominence that seemed unimaginable in the 1960s.

Continental philosophy. There are two major influences on the development of what is loosely called continental philosophy. One is Edmund Husserl, a German philosopher who was the founder of the philosophical movement known as phenomenology. (The major society for continental philosophy is SPEP, the Society for Phenomenology and Existential Philosophy.) Like many of the modern philosophers we have examined in previous chapters, Husserl strongly believed that philosophy needed to develop a method that would allow it to become genuinely scientific. Philosophy's task was to provide a foundation for all the special sciences, and Husserl thought that phenomenology was what was needed. Phenomenology is best described as an attempt to describe experience as we experience it. If all knowledge is based on experience, then an account of experience and how it provides evidence for our beliefs and theories provides a foundation for all the sciences. Husserl thus shares two of the characteristic aims of modern Western philosophy: a preoccupation with method and a desire to show how philosophy provides a foundation for knowledge.

Husserl believed that our "natural attitude" is to focus on the world rather than our experience. We naturally focus on the things we experience rather than the experiences themselves. Phenomenology requires a suspension or "bracketing" of this natural attitude, so that we can try to describe experience itself. When we do this, we notice that one of the fundamental features of many forms of human consciousness is that they possess "intentionality." Our mental acts are usually directed *at* something, or they are *about* something, and hence intentionality could be called "aboutness" or "directedness." An examination of intentionality allows us to distinguish two poles of our experience, an object pole called the "noema" and a subject pole called the "noesis." The noesis refers to the act of consciousness, while the noema refers to the object of consciousness.

These can vary independently. For example, dreaming, believing, and hoping are all distinct conscious acts, but acts of each type could have the same noematic content. I could dream of being married, believe that I am married, or hope that I will be married. Of course the same type of noetic act can obviously have very different contents. I can believe or hope many different things.

Husserl thought that when we use the phenomenological method and focus on experience as it is lived, the picture is very different from that provided by the British empiricists. We do not find static "ideas" but a dynamic reality in which self and world are always in relation. Experience has a "focus and fringe" structure, in which an experienced object is always perceived against a "horizon of possibilities" that provides a background to the experience. This horizon of meaning is thus fundamental to experience. We experience an object not just as what it is, but as what it could possibly be. Husserl hoped that phenomenological analysis would allow the philosopher to clarify "essences" that would provide the understanding that could provide a foundation for the sciences.

Although Husserl hoped that his phenomenological method would allow philosophy to become a "rigorous science," his legacy has been very different from that which he wished or expected. Part of the reason for this is the second big influence on continental philosophy, the movement called existentialism. Existentialism is a twentieth-century movement, but it was inspired by the work of Kierkegaard and Nietzsche, discussed in chapters twenty-one and twenty-three. Both of these thinkers had a profound influence on the German thinker Martin Heidegger, a student of Husserl who is usually credited with the development of existential phenomenology. In his most important work, *Being and Time*, Heidegger transformed Husserl's concept of intentionality into an existential concept. Human existence, or *Dasein*, is "being-in-the-world," understood not merely as a cognitive or mental intentionality, but as a practical engagement with the world. We come to grasp the world primordially not from a theoretical stance, but as an agent who uses tools and understands the world as a theater for action. Heidegger goes on to describe *Dasein* in terms that capture its fundamental features, such as "thrownness." We are fundamentally temporal beings who find ourselves in a world not of our own making. Our lives are shaped by a socially defined network of meanings, rooted in what "they" (others) say, but Heidegger holds that as we confront our own deaths, the possibility of an individually authentic existence opens up. (Heidegger here exercised significant influence on German theologian Rudolf Bultmann.) Heidegger hoped that his existential description of *Dasein* would lead to a deeper philosophical understanding of "the meaning of being," since *Dasein* can be seen as the place where being "shows itself."

Unfortunately, Heidegger joined the Nazi party and seems to have been an enthusiastic supporter of Hitler, as well as an anti-Semite, something briefly discussed in chapter twenty-three. His later work is difficult to characterize, but he continued to seek for the "meaning of being," looking more to poetry and art than to phenomenology to give us the clues we need.

Heidegger's early existential phenomenology in turn inspired a group of French philosophers, including Jean-Paul Sartre and Maurice Merleau-Ponty, who attempted to give phenomenological descriptions of human existence. All of these existential phenomenologies incorporated the existential emphasis on the self as an achievement rather than simply as a substance. Sartre in particular seemed to capture the mood of Europe before and after World War II, emphasizing individual human existence as a free creation. Sartre's existentialism differed from both Nietzsche and Kierkegaard. Unlike Nietzsche, he rejected the idea that humans can be defined by some natural category such as the will to power, stressing that "existence precedes essence," and thus that it is up to the individual to decide who he or she is. Unlike Kierkegaard, Sartre held that God does not exist, and thus the human person who must create a self is alone and forlorn in the world. Sartre notably claimed that since God does not exist, it is up to the individual self to create moral values.

Just as was the case with analytic philosophy, it is impossible to give a simple or concise description of continental philosophy over the last half of the twentieth century. One dominant theme is a rejection of the classical foundationalism so characteristic of modern Western philosophy. The continental tradition embraces the finitude and historicity of the human condition. This epistemological modesty sometimes is described as "postmodernism," since it seems to challenge the views of many modern philosophers shaped by the Enlightenment. In some cases this postmodernism appears to take the form of a rejection of realism. Reality is not independent of the human mind but is "constructed" by humans. Jacques Derrida raises questions about the ability of language to refer to a stable reality independent of ourselves. Michel Foucault, following Nietzsche, sees human thinking as shaped by attempts to dominate and control our fellow human beings. Claims to truth are seen as disguised expressions of a will to power. The issues raised by this are complex, and an adequate treatment is beyond the scope of this chapter. Nevertheless, I will later in this chapter offer some convictions about what is right and what is wrong with such postmodern ways of thinking.

PHILOSOPHY AND THE RELIGIOUS
CHARACTER OF THE HUMAN SELF

One important lesson to be drawn from the history of Western philosophy concerns the relationship between philosophy and religion. It is not uncommon to find thinkers, mostly secular but including some religious people, who draw a sharp line between philosophy and the kind of thinking about religion generally called theology. There are many examples of this kind of "boundary-policing." For example, in contemporary philosophy of religion, philosophers who defend religious views, particularly Christian views, are sometimes criticized as "not really being philosophers." Real philosophers must be objective and neutral in their approach to religious questions, and genuine religious commitments, if they exist, ought to be bracketed or put aside.[5]

Another example can be found in the way the history of ancient philosophy is often portrayed in textbooks. The story often is told like this: philosophy begins when thinkers begin to recognize the problems with religious views (such as those found in Homer's descriptions of the gods), and look for natural, scientific explanations for natural phenomena. On this account, philosophy is a kind of replacement for religion; philosophy paves the way for a scientific worldview that displaces a religious worldview.

I think the true story of ancient philosophy, as developed in chapters two through six, is very different. It is correct that most ancient philosophers subject the Homeric deities to critical scrutiny and find them rationally deficient. And it is also true that many ancient philosophers are the recognizable ancestors of what we today describe as natural

---

[5]J. L. Schellenberg's influential work is a good example of this attitude. Schellenberg himself combines a type of skepticism with atheism, and often suggests that philosophers of religion who are committed to a particular faith are in some way less "objective" than people such as himself. This perspective can be clearly seen in the very title of one of his articles, "Is Plantinga-Style Philosophy of Religion Really Philosophy?" This article is available on his personal website (www.jlschellenberg .com). According to the website, it is to be published in J. Aaron Simmons, ed., *Christian Philosophy: Conceptions, Continuations, and Challenges* (Oxford: Oxford University Press, forthcoming).

science. But to claim that such a concern for natural explanation somehow displaces religious views and concerns is just mistaken. Although Socrates was executed partly for his critique of Athenian religion, it is clear that Socrates himself was deeply religious, and even that he saw his philosophical work as a divine calling (see chap. 3). Plato and Aristotle, while critical of Homeric views of the gods, see thinking about what is divine as essential to their philosophy, and their conceptions of the divine remain deeply influential on the theologies of Christianity, Judaism, and Islam (see chaps. 4 and 5). Even the Epicureans, with their mechanistic view of nature, continued to believe in the gods. In fact, it is plausible that their claim that the gods do not intervene in human affairs and do not care about human beings was itself religiously motivated. Much of the ancient world was gripped by fear of the gods, a fear that was reasonable given the Homeric depictions of the gods. What Epicurus offered to his followers was deliverance from the anxiety caused by bad theology, but the rejection of bad theology can still be seen as a kind of theology. Indeed, the great scholar Pierre Hadot has argued that the ancient schools of philosophy were themselves very much religious communities, whose members not only practiced logical thinking but also functioned much like groups of monks, with practical exercises, liturgies, and ceremonies.[6]

The attempt to divorce philosophy from religion also has a baneful effect on how medieval philosophy is viewed. Since medieval philosophy is so obviously shaped by religious concerns and views, many prestigious departments of philosophy more or less ignore this period, or give it minimal attention. Courses in ancient philosophy and modern philosophy may be offered or even required, but courses in medieval philosophy are much less central to the curriculum. The medieval period is often caricatured as "the Dark Ages" when in fact it was a period of great intellectual advance and creativity.

---

[6]See Pierre Hadot, *Philosophy as a Way of Life*, trans. Michael Chase (Oxford: Blackwell, 1995), and also Hadot, *What Is Ancient Philosophy*, trans. Michael Chase (Cambridge, MA: Belknap Press of Harvard University Press, 2002).

One can also see the bad effects of the divorce of religion from philosophy in the way the history of modern philosophy is often presented. The religious concerns and views of philosophers are frequently ignored or minimized. I have, for example, seen serious scholars who claimed that John Locke was a deist, even though Locke wrote a book titled *The Reasonableness of Christianity*, in which he appeals to miracles and fulfilled prophecies. Spinoza is frequently described as a naturalist or even an atheist, although no concept seems more central to Spinoza than the concept of God. True, Spinoza rejects the personal God of Judaism and Christianity, but it hardly seems reasonable to deny that he was in many ways a profoundly religious man, one who was devoted to the "intellectual love of God," as he understood it. The religious views of thinkers such as Descartes are frequently not taken seriously. Kant is often celebrated for having demolished the traditional arguments for God's existence, but many Kant scholars fail to take Kant's own moral argument for faith in God very seriously. Kant's moral philosophy is correctly seen as one that stresses human autonomy, but Kant's claims that we should see all of our moral duties as divine commands and that God is himself the sovereign of the "kingdom of ends" are often ignored entirely.

As I see things—and this is one of the positive lessons to be drawn from postmodernism—philosophy is done by actual human beings, who are shaped by their hopes and fears and desires, and not just their beliefs. Nietzsche and Kierkegaard are right to point out that none of us is the embodiment of "pure reason." It is natural that the religious convictions of those who are believers will shape their approach to philosophy. However, the same is true for unbelievers. Their thinking is also shaped by their antireligious views. It is, I think, significant that David Hume seems to have lost his childhood faith, and I believe his unbelief shapes his thinking, just as Thomas Reid is shaped by his Christian faith. What makes the work of both thinkers "philosophy" is not a fictitious stance of "neutrality" or "objectivity," but a willingness to look at arguments for and against their own views and an honest attempt to arrive at what seems to them to be the truth.

The reason religion cannot be completely divorced from philosophy is that philosophy is done by human beings, and human beings are incorrigibly religious. It is natural for humans to wonder whether the natural world is all there is, and to ponder what happens to humans after death. Contemporary cognitive psychologists actually confirm this, and claim that there is abundant evidence that humans are "hardwired" by evolution to believe in God or gods.[7] Most of the psychologists who affirm this are themselves atheists, and think that this natural tendency is a kind of trick played on us by evolution. However, if there is a God, and if God created humans to have a relation with himself, then there is no reason to think that the human tendency to believe in God is an illusion, even if it is the result of an evolutionary process by which God created humans. If Christianity is true, then humans were made in God's image, and their intended destiny is to have a relation with God. If humans are deeply religious by nature, it is hard to see how philosophy can be sharply segregated from religion, or why it should be.

MODERN PHILOSOPHY AND THE QUEST FOR CERTAINTY AND A "METHOD"

We have seen that modern philosophy, from Descartes and Locke onward, is dominated by anxiety over the security of our knowledge and belief claims. John Dewey might not be right in characterizing the *whole* of Western philosophy as dominated by the "quest for certainty," since the ancient and medieval worlds did not evidence a preoccupation with epistemological questions as the foundation of philosophy. Modern philosophy may begin with doubt, but ancient philosophy clearly began with wonder. The primacy of epistemology seems to be a distinctively modern development, and so Dewey's judgment seems

---

[7]See Scott Atran, *In Gods We Trust: The Evolutionary Landscape of Religion*, Evolution and Cognition (Oxford: Oxford University Press, 2002), and Deborah Kelemen, "Are Children 'Intuitive Theists'? Reasoning About Purpose and Design in Nature," *Psychological Science* 15 (2004): 295-301.

correct for the modern period. This desire for objective certainty leads to another characteristic of modern philosophy: a great concern for *method*. Just about every modern philosopher is distressed by the lack of assured results in philosophy, and just about every one of them tries to remedy the situation by committing to a method that will allow philosophers to obtain assured results. Even Dewey, though a fallibilist, has great faith in his own method, the method of empirical science.

For Descartes it is the method of universal doubt, grounded in a commitment to the power of reason. Spinoza is similarly committed to the power of reason, and believes that the method of mathematics will make it possible to reach assured results. Locke, Berkeley, and Hume are committed to a very different method, one that grounds all ideas and beliefs in sense experience. Kant puts his faith in what might be called the "critical method," in which reason turns its attention on its own powers to determine what can be known and what cannot be known. Hegel rejects Kant's method and puts his faith in the method of dialectical reason to make it possible for philosophy to become a rigorous science that will gain "absolute knowledge." Even in the twentieth century the dream of certainty through a method had not died. The logical positivists believed that symbolic logic and a devotion to natural science could provide a scientific philosophy, while Husserl's phenomenology is explicitly claimed to be a method that will allow philosophy to become scientific, and provide a foundation for all the other sciences.

My own judgment is that this hope for a method that will produce certainty and settle the big questions of philosophy once and for all has turned out to be a vain one. The idea that epistemology could be a kind of "foundational science" for the rest of philosophy is attractive; one can see why Descartes and Locke went down this road. If we cannot resolve metaphysical and ethical disputes, why not seek to first determine how the disputes should be resolved? However, my judgment is that the disagreements in metaphysics and ethics that prompted philosophers to turn to epistemology reoccur in epistemology itself, and are just as intractable there as in other fields.

On reflection this makes sense. It may be true that metaphysical claims presuppose epistemological views of how those claims can be known. But it is equally true that epistemological claims presuppose substantive metaphysical commitments about human beings and their nature as knowers. Think for example of the difference between the ancient tradition, which holds that human beings are essentially rational beings, and Nietzsche's view that reason is simply an expression of an instinctive will to power. It seems to me that epistemology, metaphysics, and ethics are equally primordial, interconnected, and mutually dependent, but it is not possible to make one part of philosophy the absolute foundation for the others.

It is clear from the list of methods that modern philosophers have endorsed that philosophers disagree about the proper method for philosophy as much as they disagree about anything else. At least this is so if we think of a "method" as what I would call an "algorithmic method," a method that if properly followed would guarantee truth. There are of course methods that virtually all philosophers use: logical arguments, dialectical consideration of pros and cons, imaginative posing of thought experiments. But these philosophical methods, while they help us make progress in certain ways, do not lead to the kind of objective certainty that early modern philosophers aspired to.

Why is it the case that philosophical disagreements are never finally resolved? Why is it that the history of philosophy reads like a never-ending argument between enduring worldviews? From the ancient world to the contemporary world we find disputes between materialists and idealists, empiricists and rationalists, theists and atheists. I think at least part of the answer lies in the fact that the answers provided to the questions of philosophy ultimately lead, as the Greeks saw so clearly, to different ways life must be lived. One reason people disagree about philosophical questions is that they want to live their lives in different ways. A commitment to a philosophical view (at least on the deepest questions) is not merely assenting to a set of propositions, but a decision as to who I am and who I want to become.

From my perspective, the lesson to draw from this is that we must give up the quest for an absolute, objective certainty that would eliminate philosophical disagreement. As a Christian, I believe that humans are finite creatures, and as such are fallible. My secular friends who do not believe in God may express the thought differently, but they generally agree we are fallible creatures and incapable of seeing the world as God sees it (or would see it if God existed). Spinoza thought philosophers should aspire to such a viewpoint, but it is difficult to see how human beings could ever see the world from God's point of view. We are always somewhere and therefore never occupy "the view from nowhere." Not only are we fallible animals. We are historically situated, products of our own times and cultures and places. If Christianity is true, we are also sinful creatures, and our sinfulness is another factor that shapes and impairs our cognitive faculties. This means that we must give up the hope for an algorithmic method that will settle the arguments of philosophers once and for all. We humans would like a guarantee that we cannot be mistaken. On my view no such guarantee is possible for creatures like ourselves. The big question is, what does this acceptance of finitude and fallibility mean? In my concluding section I shall try to provide some answers.

NIETZSCHE, KIERKEGAARD, AND THE FUTURE OF WESTERN PHILOSOPHY

Nietzsche in many ways represents a fundamental departure for Western philosophy. His naturalism and materialism are not totally new, but can be found prefigured in Epicurus and Lucretius. His "love of fate" can be found in Spinoza. However, even ancient figures such as Epicurus and Lucretius, and certainly modern figures such as Spinoza, valued reason over instinct and demanded moderation and self-denial in their ethic.

Nietzsche seems to embody something new: a determined attempt to think through the implications of seeing humans as animals dominated by instinctive desires, especially the desire for power. Perhaps the only philosopher who anticipates some of Nietzsche's attempt to see humans simply as nonrational animals is David Hume, with his strong emphasis on "custom" understood as a nonrational instinct.

Nietzsche thus represents what I have called the acceptance of finitude with a vengeance. Nietzsche's influence on what is called postmodernism is profound. Kant's philosophy may embody a kind of "antirealism," in which the world we know is partly constructed by the mind. However, for Kant the mind that does the constructing is a rational, universal mind. Also, Kant does not identify reality as we humans know it with reality in itself, and so there is still an ultimate, objective truth about a reality that is independent of the human mind, even if we humans cannot grasp that truth through science. Those antirealists who follow Nietzsche are different. The world that they see us humans constructing is not an objective, universal world. There are multiple "worlds" shaped by the differences between cultures and even individuals. And there is no longer a basis for belief that there is an ultimate, objective truth independent of human thinking, since there is no God who knows such truth.

The influence of Nietzsche is partly salutary. It is true, as I argued in the previous section, that we do philosophy as whole persons, not purely objective embodiments of an impersonal reason. Our thinking is shaped by whether we are male or female, religious or antireligious, committed to morality or devoted to absolute individual freedom, and by our social and cultural locations. To the degree that postmodernism deflates the myth of an objective reason that claims to deliver a final truth that is independent of our human identities, it is something to be welcomed. Postmodernism can be viewed as a useful corrective to what some would call the hubris of the Enlightenment, which purported to offer a final truth that is independent of any faith commitments or traditions.

The Enlightenment ideal can be pictured in the following way: At the entrance to the temple of learning, all who enter are required to divest themselves of their particularities. It should make no difference if one is black or white, male or female, rich or poor. In reality, however, the Enlightenment pose of disinterested objectivity prevents actual knowers from recognizing their biases, and can allow some groups to put forward views that very much reflect their own particularities as if they were purely objective. It also fails to recognize that sometimes our particularities are not filters that block us from unvarnished truth, but instruments that help us see things we would otherwise miss. The reality of oppression is often not clearly seen without hearing the voice of the oppressed. However, the danger is that this postmodernist critique of reason will degenerate into a relativistic despair of objective truth altogether.

It is useful to compare Nietzsche here with Kierkegaard. Kierkegaard, like Nietzsche, recognizes the importance of the emotions in human life. The motto of his first book, *Either/Or*, is striking: "Is reason alone baptized? Are the passions pagans?" Kierkegaard, responding to Hegel's claim to deliver absolute knowledge, agrees with Nietzsche that we are not purely rational creatures, and that we can never obtain a godlike point of view. His pseudonym Johannes Climacus make this plain: "A logical system is possible, but a system of existence is impossible for anyone but God."[8] We humans can certainly construct logical systems, but they never perfectly capture the whole truth about existence. Our systems can never be totally complete or final in the sense that they are unrevisable. However, it is important that Kierkegaard does not think this means that there is no objective truth that we can seek. Reality is a system for God, and objective truth is simply the truth as God knows it. Furthermore, since we are created in God's image, there is reason to hope that our search for truth will not be completely in vain. We remain

[8]Søren Kierkegaard, *Concluding Unscientific Postscript to Philosophical Fragments*, trans. Howard V. Hong and Edna H. Hong (Princeton, NJ: Princeton University Press, 1992), 109. This quotation is my own translation.

finite, fallible, and sinful creatures, but if we are God's creatures we have reason to hope that we can at least approximate the truth we need to have as human beings. It is something like this faith in our cognitive powers that underlies Reid's philosophy of common sense as well.

There is one important difference between Reid and Kierkegaard. Although both are fallibilists who do not exhibit the kind of anxiety over our finitude that shapes so much of modern philosophy, Kierkegaard has a much greater sensitivity to the ways in which human sinfulness shapes our intellectual lives. Despite the fact that Reid was a Presbyterian minister, as a child of the Enlightenment he tended to underestimate the effects of sin on our cognitive lives. However, both of them show that belief in God can provide an important protection against intellectual despair and skepticism. At the same time faith in God can also provide a check on intellectual arrogance and pride, for it means we cannot forget that we humans are fallible creatures. We may be made in the image of God, but we are also made from the dust of the earth.

It is easy to see that the postmodern critique of reason can easily become self-refuting if universalized. If all human thinking is just a disguised expression of a desire to dominate others, then someone who asserts that this is true is also attempting to dominate others. However, if that is the case, why should we think that this claim (or any other) is *true*? If someone in the grip of the postmodern critique of the Enlightenment abandons the notion of truth altogether, then there is no reason to believe that what such a person says is true.

Richard Rorty, for example, was trained as an analytic philosopher, but eventually came to the view that the kind of pragmatism he found in Dewey, Heidegger, and the later Wittgenstein leaves no room for the idea that there is an objective truth to be sought. Philosophy can no longer see its goal as giving a true representation of reality; it cannot be "the mirror of nature." Rorty is widely reputed to have quipped that "truth is what your colleagues will let you get away with saying." Perhaps this was not meant seriously, but Rorty did seriously defend the claim that it is false that human persons have rights because they possess some moral quality, a unique dignity or value. Instead, Rorty says that humans have rights because we as a community decide to extend rights to them.[9]

Rorty complacently assumes that views such as his will have no adverse consequences, and that society is inexorably moving toward greater freedom and equality. This is progress, not because we are moving toward objective moral truth, but because Rorty approves of the direction of history. We *say* it is "true" that people have rights, not because they truly possess an intrinsic dignity, but because people such as Rorty and his friends like the fact that society has moved in this direction. We do not say people have human rights because it is true, but rather it is true because we say it. That may be fine for morally well-brought-up people like Rorty, who was the grandson of Walter Rauschenbusch, a well-known Protestant theologian. However, what if one's friends are neo-Nazis and racists? What "truths" will they let each other get away with saying?

In reality the postmodernist who despairs of objective truth and the modern philosophers who aspired to a method that would give us objective certainty about that truth are much closer to each other than is immediately obvious. Both of them accept the following hypothetical proposition: "*If* there is objective truth, then there must be a method that will guarantee that we have access to that truth." The great modern philosophers who were classical foundationalists believed in the antecedent clause: they believed in objective truth. Logically, they concluded that there must be a method that would give us access to that truth, and set about finding that method. Thinkers such as Rorty accept the same hypothetical proposition, but draw a very different conclusion. They think that is clear that there is no such method that will do the job, and they (just as logically) conclude that there is no such thing as objective truth.

---

[9]See Richard Rorty, *Philosophy and the Mirror of Nature* (Princeton, NJ: Princeton University Press, 1979), 177-78.

Suppose, however, that this hypothetical proposition is false, as fallibilists such as Reid and Kierkegaard affirm. Suppose that there is indeed objective truth, but there is no algorithmic method that guarantees us access to that truth. Christian philosophers can, I believe, embrace this possibility without despair. They can hold both that there is a truth to seek, and reasonably hope we can achieve an approximation of that truth if we seek honestly and with passion. Those who know they are made in the image of God will have reason to trust that their human capacities are trustworthy, the gifts of a gracious and loving God. Thus there are resources in the Christian faith that may help protect philosophy itself from the despair that threatens those who aspire to the kind of knowledge Spinoza thought possible, but who realize that it is not humanly achievable.

Of course this confidence in reason does not mean that human reason is unlimited, and it does not mean that humans can learn everything they need to know simply by using their own powers. Christianity teaches that the ultimate truth about God and human beings is found in a historical revelation, one that began with the people of Israel and culminated in Jesus of Nazareth. If this is so, then one of the things a sound philosophy must grasp will be the limits of philosophy itself. Such a recognition is in no way a repudiation of reason. If we are finite, fallible creatures, then what would truly be unreasonable would be the claim that there are no limits to reason. A Christian philosophy, even one shaped by biblical faith, will always recognize that there are truths that must be believed because God has revealed them. Those truths may be the ground of a Christian philosophy, but they are not truths that could be achieved simply through human thinking.

General Index

Scripture Index

Finding the Textbook You Need

The IVP Academic Textbook Selector
is an online tool for instantly finding the IVP books
suitable for over 250 courses across 24 disciplines.

---

ivpacademic.com